The United Nations and the European Union:
An Ever Stronger Partnership

The United Nations and the European Union: An Ever Stronger Partnership

Edited by

Jan Wouters
Frank Hoffmeister
Tom Ruys

T·M·C·ASSER PRESS
The Hague

Published by T.M.C.ASSER PRESS
P.O.Box 16163, 2500 BD The Hague, The Netherlands

<www.asserpress.nl>

T.M.C.ASSER PRESS' English language books are distributed exclusively by:

Cambridge University Press, The Edinburgh Building, Shaftesbury Road,
Cambridge CB2 2RU, UK,
or
for customers in the USA, Canada and Mexico:
Cambridge University Press, 100 Brook Hill Drive, New York, NY 10994-2133, USA

<www.cambridge.org>

ISBN 90-6704-231-5
ISBN 978-90-6704-231-4

PREFACE

In a fast-changing world, effective multilateralism is indispensable. Globalisation is not a synonym for chaos. It needs a rule-based framework to function properly.

The United Nations, with its universal mandate and legitimacy, is the pivot of the multilateral system. It is uniquely placed to serve as a platform for developing global solutions. In times of growing common challenges, from new security risks to managing the world economy, from state-building to combating climate change, this is all the more important.

The European Union is the UN's natural partner. Our commitment to effective multilateralism is not a rhetorical profession of faith. It is a defining principle of our foreign policy. We have a clear self-interest in advancing the global agenda, given our exposure to international opportunities and challenges. In addition, the EU, with its broad toolbox of foreign policy instruments, is particularly well-equipped to create synergies with the UN. Relations between the EU and the United Nations have thus developed over time into a rich network of interaction, spanning the entire range of EU external relations.

This book astutely analyses these various forms of cooperation: from crisis management to promoting long-term peace and security, from defending human rights to protecting the global commons, from fighting disease to fostering development and reducing poverty. In so doing it also reflects the growing role of the European Union as a responsible global actor.

Having served in both the UN and the EU, advancing smart multilateralism and the EU-UN partnership is a *leitmotif* of my work as Europe's External Relations Commissioner. We must build on the accomplishments of the UN Reform Summit in September 2005, such as the creation of the Human Rights Council and the Peace-Building Commission, and continue honing the tools of global governance. All countries stand to gain from these reforms and from a well-managed UN.

This also means that the EU must play an even more proactive role in the global arena. We must live up to our increasing international responsibility and become more effective, coherent and visible in our external relations, not least in the UN context. In a complex world, 'fortress Europe' is not the answer.

Effective multilateralism is not about building a 'world government'. It is about making sure we have the instruments to manage globalisation. This timely book provides food for thought on how to achieve that, for both academics and practitioners of foreign policy.

Dr. Benita FERRERO-WALDNER
EU Commissioner for External Relations
and European Neighbourhood Policy

SUMMARY OF CONTENTS

PART FIVE
Outlook

LIST OF ABBREVIATIONS

ACABQ	Advisory Committee on Administrative and Budgetary Questions
ACP	Africa, Caribbean and Pacific countries
ADI	Acceptable daily intake
AFDI	Annuaire français de droit international
AJIL	American Journal of International Law
AMIS	African Union Mission in Sudan
AMM	Aceh Monitoring Mission
APR	Annual Progress Report
ASEAN	Association of Southeast Asian Nations
ASEM	Asia-Europe Meeting
ASP	Africa Stockpiles Programme
ATM	Autonomous trade measures
AU	African Union
BTWC	Biological and Toxin Weapons Convention
BWI	Bretton Woods Institutions
CAC	Codex Alimentarius Commission
CANZ	Canada, Australia, New Zealand
CARDS	Community Assistance for Reconstruction, Development and Stabilizaton
CARICOM	Caribbean Community
CCEURO	Codex Coordinating Committee for Europe
CCGP	Codex Committee on General Principles
CFA	Committee on the Freedom of Association
CFSP	Common Foreign and Security Policy
CFSAM	Crop and Food Supply Assessment Mission
CHR	Commission on Human Rights
CIA	Central Intellligence Agency
CIS	Commonwealth of Independent States
CITES	Convention on International Trade in Endangered Species
CLCPRO	Commission for Controlling the Desert Locust in the Western Region
CMLRev.	Common Market Law Review
CND	Commission on Narcotic Drugs
CODEV	Council Working Group on Development
CoE	Council of Europe
COHOM	Council Working Party on Human Rights
COJUR	Council Working Group on Public International Law
COMAR	Council Working Group on Maritime Law
COMECON	Council of Mutual Economical Aid

CONUN	Council Working Group for the United Nations
COREPER	Committee of Permanent Representatives in the Council of the European Union
COTER	Council Working Group on Terrorism
CSCE	Conference on Security and Co-operation in Europe
CSD	Commission on Sustainable Development
CSO	Civil Society Organization
CSTO	Collective Security Trade Organization
CTBC	Comprehensive Test Ban Treaty
CTC	Counterterrorism Committee
CTED	Counterterrorism Executive Directorate
CTF	Consultative Task Force
CWC	Chemical Weapons Convention
DC	Development Committee
DDA	Doha Development Agenda
DDR	Disarmament, Demobilisation and Reintegration
DPA	Department of Political Affairs
DPKO	Department of Peacekeeping Operations
DLCC	Desert Locust Control Committee
DRC	Democratic Republic of Congo
EBRD	European Bank for Reconstruction and Development
EC	European Community
ECB	European Central Bank
ECCAS	Economic Community of Central African States
ECE	Economic Commission for Europe
ECHO	European Commission Humanitarian Aid Office
ECJ	Court of Justice of the European Communities
ECLO	Emergency Centre for Locust Operations
ECOFIN	Council for Economic and Financial Affairs
ECOSOC	UN Economic and Social Council
ECOWAS	Economic Community of West African States
ECR	European Court Reports
ECSC	European Coal and Steel Community
ED	Executive Director
EDF	European Development Fund
EEA	European Environment Agency
EEAS	European External Action Service
EEG	Eastern Europe Group
EESC	European Economic and Social Committee
EFC	Economic and Financial Committee
EFSA	European Food Security Agency
EFTA	European Free Trade Area
EIB	European Investment Bank
EIDHR	European Initiative for Democracy and Human Rights
EJIL	European Journal of International Law
EMOP	Emergency Operation

EMU	European Monetary Union
ENP	European Neighbourhood Policy
EoL	Exchange of Letters
EP	European Parliament
EPC	European Political Cooperation
EPSCO	Employment, Social policy, Health and Consumer Affairs Council
ESCG	Global Information and Early Warming Service
ESDC	European Security and Defence College
ESDP	European Security and Defence Policy
ESS	European Security Strategy
ETA	Euskadi Ta Askatasuna, Bask Separatist Movement
ETUC	European Trade Union Confederation
EU	European Union
EUEI	EU Energy Initiative
EUISS	European Union Institute for Security Studies
EUMC	European Union Military Committee
EUPAT	European Union Police Advisory Team
EUPM	European Union Police Mission
EURATOM	European Atomic Energy Community
EUROSTAT	Statistical Office of the European Communities
EUSR	European Union Special Representative
EUWI	EU Water Initiative
FAFA	Financial and Administrative Framework Agreement
FAO	Food and Agricultural Organisation
FAO-OIE	World Organization for Animal Health
FATF	Financial Action Task Force
FCTC	Framework Convention on Tobacco Control
FFS	Farmer Field School Programmes
FIVIMS	Food Insecurity and Vulnerability Information and Mapping Systems
FLEGT	EU Action Plan on Forest Law Enforcement, Governance and Trade
FMD	Foot-and-mouth disease
FRY	Federal Republic of Yugoslavia
FSAU	Food Security Analysis Unit
FTA	Free Trade Agreement
FYROM	Former Yugoslav Republic of Macedonia
GA	General Assembly
GATT	General Agreement on Tariffs and Trade
GB	Governing Body
GCC	Gulf Cooperation Council
GDPRD	Global Donor Platform for Rural Development
GEF	Global Environment Facility
GFCM	General Fisheries Commission for the Mediterranean
GIEWS	Global Information and Early Warning System

GIS	Geographic Information System
GMEF	Global Ministerial Environment Forum
GNP	Gross National Product
GPGs	Global public goods
GRULAC	Groups of Latin American and Caribbean Countries
GSP	Generalised System of Preferences
HCOC	Hague Code of Conduct against the Proliferation of Ballistic Missiles
HIPC	Highly Indebted Poor Countries
HLP	High-Level Panel on Threats, Challenges and Change
HPAI	Highly Pathogenic Avian Influenza
HQ	Headquarters
HRC	Human Rights Council
IAEA	International Atomic Energy Agency
IBRD	International Bank for Reconstruction and Development
ICAO	International Civil Aviation Organization
ICC	International Criminal Court
ICCPR	International Covenant on Civil and Political Rights
ICJ	International Court of Justice
ICFTU	International Confederation of Free Trade Union
ICM	International Civilian Mission
ICSID	International Centre for the Settlement of Investment Disputes
IDA	International Development Association
IFA	International Financial Agreement
IFAD	International Fund for Agricultural Development
IFC	International Finance Corporation
IFF	Intergovernmental Forum on Forests
IFI	International Financial Institutions
IGAD	Intergovernmental Authority on Development (for East Africa)
IHR	International Health Regulations
IISD	International Institute for Sustainable Development
ILC	International Labour Conference
ILC	International Law Commission
ILM	International Legal Materials
ILO	International Labour Organization
IMEC	Industrialized Market Economy Countries
IMF	International Monetary Fund
IMFC	International Monetary and Financial Committee
IMO	International Maritime Organization
IPTF	International Police Task Force
IOE	International Organization of Employers
IPEC	International Programme on the Elimination of Child Labour
IPM	Integrated Pest Management
IPPC	International Plant Protection Convention
IPTF	International Police Task Force
IRA	Irish Republican Army

ISAF	International Security Assistance Force
ISPM	International Standards for Phytosanitary Measures
ITLOS	International Law of the Sea Tribunal
ITU	International Telecommunications Union
JRC	Joint Research Centre
KSIP	Kosovo Standards Implementation Plan
KTA	Kosovo Trust Agency
LEAD	Livestock, Environment and Development
LON	League of Nations
MARPOL	International Convention for the Prevention of Pollution from Ships
MDB	Multilateral Development Bank
MDGs	Millennium Development Goals
MDTF	Multi-donor Trust Fund
MEA	Multilateral Environment Agreement
MEDA	Euro-Mediterranean Partnership
MIGA	Multilateral Investment Guarantee Agency
MONUC	UN Mission in the Democratic Republic of Congo
MoU	Memorandum of Understanding
MS	Member State
NATO	North-Atlantic Treaty Organisation
NAC	North Atlantic Council
NGO	Non-governmental organisation
NPT	Non-Proliferation Treaty
NSS	National Security Strategy
nyr	Not yet reported
OAS	Organization of American States
OAU	Organization of African Unity
OCHCHR	Office of the High Commissioner for Human Rights
ODA	Official Development Assistance
ODA	Official Development Aid
OECD	Organization for Economic Co-operation and Development
OHCHR	Office of the High Commissioner for Human Rights
OHS	Occupational Health and Safety
OIC	Organization of Islamic Conference
OJ	Official Journal of the European Union
OSCE	Organization for Security and Cooperation in Europe
PBC	Peacebuilding Commission
PEFA	Public Expenditure and Financial Accountability
PIF	Pacific Islands Forum
PISG	Provisional Institutions of Self-Government

PRSC	Poverty Reduction Support Credit
PRSG	Poverty Reduction Support Grant
PRSP	Poverty Reduction Strategy Paper
PSC	Policy and Security Committee
RDL	Rapid Deployment Level
REIO	Regional Economic Integration Organization
RIO	Regional Integration Organization
RRF	Rapid Reaction Force
SAA	Stabilization and Association Agreement
SADC	Southern Africa Development Community
SAP	Stabilization and Association Process
SBAS	Standby Arrangement System
SCIMF	Subcommittee on International Monetary and Financial Issues
SC	Security Council
SCO	Shanghai Cooperation Organization
SD	Sustainable Development
SFOR	NATO Stabilization Force
SIA	Sustainable Impact Assessments
SIS	Schengen Information System
SOEs	Socially-owned enterprises
SP	Strategic Partnership
SPCRP	Sudan Productive Capacity Recovery Programme
SRSG	Special Representative of the UN Secretary-General
SSR	Security Sector Reform
STM	SAP Tracking Mechanism
TAIEX	Technical Assistance and Information Exchange Instrument
TCC	Troop-contributing country
TCE	Treaty establishing a Constitution for Europe
TCP	Technical Cooperation Programme
TEC	Treaty establishing the European Community
TEU	Treaty on European Union
TOC	Transnational Organized Crime
TRIPs	Trade-Related Aspects of Intellectual Property Rights
UN	United Nations
UN AFP	United Nations agencies, funds and programmes
UNCBD	United Nations Convention on Biological Diversity
UNCCD	United Nations Convention for Combating Desertification
UNCED	United Nations Conference on Environment and Development
UNCLOS	United Nations Convention on the Law of the Sea
UNCTAD	United Nations Conference on Trade and Development
UNDP	United Nations Development Programme
UNECE	United Nations Economic Commission for Europe
UNEO	United Nations Environmental Organization
UNEP	United Nations Environmental Programme

UNESCO	United Nations Educational, Scientific and Cultural Organization
UNFCCC	United Nations Framework Convention on Climate Change
UNFF	United Nations Forum on Forests
UNFPA	United Nations Population Fund
UNGA	United Nations General Assembly
UN-HABITAT	United Nations Human Settlements Programme
UNHCR	United Nations High Commissioner for Refugees
UNICE	Union of Industrial and Employers' Confederations of Europe
UNICEF	United Nations (International) Children's (Emergency) Fund
UNICPOLOS	United Nations Informal Consultative Process on Oceans and the Law of the Sea
UNICRI	United Nations Interregional Crime and Justice Research Institute
UNIDO	United Nations Industrial Development Organization
UNMIK	United Nations Mission for Kosovo
UNOCHA	United Nations Office for Coordination of Humanitarian Affairs
UNODC	United Nations Office on Drugs and Crime
UNRWA	United Nations Relief and Works Agency
UNSCR	United Nations Security Council Resolution
UNSG	United Nations Secretary-General
UNSR	United Nations Special Rapporteurs
UNSTAT	Statistical Division of the United Nations Secretariat
UNTS	United Nations Treaty Series
UPU	Universal Postal Union
WB	World Bank
WCL	World Confederation of Labour
WCT	WIPO Copyright Treaty
WCSDG	World Commission on the Social Dimension of Globalisation
WEOG	Western Europe and Others Group
WEU	Western European Union
WFP	World Food Programme
WHA	World Health Assembly
WHO	World Health Organization
WIPO	World Intellectual Property Organization
WMD	Weapons of mass destruction
WMO	World Meteorological Organization
WPPT	WIPO Performances and Phonograms Treaty
WPSDG	Working Party on the Social Dimension of Globalisation
WSSD	World Summit on Sustainable Development
WTO	World Trade Organization
WWF	World Wildlife Fund
ZaöRV	Zeitschrift für ausländisches öffentliches Recht und Völkerrecht
ZeuS	Zeitschrift für europarechtliche Studien

INTRODUCTION

by Jan Wouters, Frank Hoffmeister and Tom Ruys

1. Background of the Book

For several years, representatives from the European Union have been saying that the EU and the UN are 'natural partners' in multilateralism.[1] Numerous factors feed this opinion, which is largely shared by European citizens, who often – justly or unjustly – view themselves as the 'better peoples of the United Nations'.[2] Both organizations find their origins in the same desire to eliminate 'the scourge of war'. A comparison of the principles and purposes moreover affirms the fundamental like-mindedness of the two institutions. *De lege lata,* Article 11, paragraph 1 of the Treaty on European Union ('TEU') explicitly refers to conformity with the principles of the United Nations Charter[3] whereas, *de lege ferenda,* under the Treaty establishing a Constitution for Europe ('EU Constitution'), 'respect for the principles of the United Nations Charter' constitutes one of the objectives of the Union's external actions[4] and the EU is committed to 'promote multilateral solutions to common problems, in particular in the framework of the United Nations'.[5] Last but not least, the European Union has presented itself as a reliable and vital partner for the workings of the United Nations. Some of the figures are well-known: together the 25 EU Member States contribute no less than 38% of the UN's regular budget (compared to some 22% by the United States and some 20% by Japan), more than two-fifths of the UN peacekeeping budget and around half of all UN Member States'

[1] See, e.g., Commissioner Ferrero-Waldner's notes on UN Summit press conference, 12 September 2005, available at <http://www.europa-eu-un.org/articles/en/article_5011_en.htm>.

[2] B. Fassbender, 'The better peoples of the United Nations? Europe's practice and the United Nations', 15 *EJIL* (2004) pp. 857-884, at p. 857.

[3] Article 11(1), first and third indent, Treaty on European Union, Consolidated version of the Treaty on European Union, OJ (24 December 2002) C-325/5.

[4] Article I-4(4) Treaty establishing a Constitution for Europe, OJ (16 December 2004) C-310/1. See also Article I-41(1) and (7) as well as III-292(1), first para., and (2)(c) EU Constitution. Specifically as far as development cooperation is concerned, see Article III-316(2) EU Constitution; as far as humanitarian aid is concerned, see III-321(5) EU Constitution.

[5] Article III-292(1), second para., EU Constitution.

J. Wouters et al., eds., The United Nations and the European Union

contributions to UN funds and programmes.[6] The EU (EC and Member States combined) is also the largest provider of official development assistance (ODA), accounting for some 54%.[7]

At the start of the 21st century, EU-UN cooperation has gained new impetus as common ground between the two organizations has expanded – notably through the rapid development of the EU's Common Foreign and Security Policy (CFSP) – to cover matters concerning not only trade and development, humanitarian aid and protection of the environment, but also the promotion of human rights, the fight against terrorism, crisis management, etc. In this context, the EU has adopted a new credo of 'effective multilateralism', firmly enshrined in the European Security Strategy of December 2003, which declares that 'strengthening the United Nations, equipping it to fulfil its responsibilities and to act effectively, is a European priority'.[8] The United Nations has generally responded positively to this *rapprochement*. Indeed, given the present workload of the world organization, it could well use an able and willing partner for example to alleviate its financial and logistical burdens, to provide political/diplomatic support for the implementation of the Millennium Development Goals or the environmental agenda, or to assist in crisis management (at present, some 75.000 blue helmets are deployed worldwide). This is also evident from the 2005 September Summit Outcome Document, in which heads of State suggested the expansion of consultation and cooperation between the United Nations and regional and sub-regional organizations through formalized agreements.[9]

The strengthened emphasis from the EU side on supporting the UN stems not only from an altruistic desire to further UN goals, but also from the EU Member States' joint ambition to establish the European Union as a 'global actor' in the international sphere. Both aims, however, require that EU Member States coordinate their actions so as to speak with one unified European voice, regardless of the entity or person that ultimately presents this position. So far, the EU's influence on the world stage has fallen short of its economic and combined political weight. For this reason, the European Commission submitted a series of practical proposals to the Council in September 2003 on how the EU could be more effective in its contribution to shaping policy within the UN,[10] which have in the meantime fuelled closer *intra*-EU and *inter* EU-UN coordination.

---

[6] See 'The enlarging European Union at the United Nations: making multilateralism matter', January 2004, available at <http://ec.europa.eu/comm/external_relations/un/docs/brochure0104.pdf>, at p. 6.

[7] Ibid., at p. 4.

[8] 'A Secure Europe in a Better World' – a European Security Strategy, adopted by the European Council on 12 December 2003, available at <http://ue.eu.int/uedocs/cmsUpload/78367.pdf>.

[9] 2005 World Summit Outcome, UNGA Res. 60/1, 16 September 2005, para. 170.

[10] European Commission, Communication on 'The European Union and the United Nations: the Choice of Multilateralism', 10 September 2003, COM (2003) 526.

2. Focus and Objectives of the Book

Against this background of invigorated EU-UN relations the present volume seeks to answer two core questions throughout the various chapters. Firstly, to what extent does the EU enjoy a formal status at the various UN bodies, manage to speak with one voice and influence UN decision-making? Secondly, to what extent does the growing EU-UN partnership further the aims and activities of the United Nations?

As regards the first aspect, the daily business of EU activity within the UN seems to be invisible, but tangible. For the innocent bystander, strolling Manhattan's 41st Street between 2nd and 3rd Avenue, it is almost impossible to know that here lies the very nerve centre of EU/EC activity at the United Nations. Contrary to dozens of national delegations to the UN, no flag, seal or emblem gives away its whereabouts. Only the coming and going of officials and diplomats, wearing either a blue badge (for delegates from the European Commission or from the EU Council) or a red badge (for delegates from national representations), travelling to the consultations rooms at the 20th floor every morning, reveals something of the intense diplomatic activity taking place behind these glass walls. Likewise, the obligatory photo-shoot in front of the now 192 flags lined up before the UN's Headquarters arguably reveals as little about EU visibility at the United Nations as our short walk through 41st Street. Yet, once we enter UN grounds and attend some of the meetings that take place in the main bodies or in the consultation rooms in the basement, we soon discover that EU/EC presence at the United Nations is an established reality. The indicators are manifold: e.g., the presence of the European Commission in the General Assembly, be it in the blue observer seats; the presentation of common statements by the EU Presidency in open debates in the Security Council, etc. Coordination among EU Member States on UN matters and EU/EC-UN interaction has indeed become a matter of day-to-day reality and increasingly shapes the work of EU officials, diplomats of EU Member States as well as UN staff. Thus, to assess the EU impact within the United Nations, one should analyze the institutional framework under which the Union's main actors (the European Commission, the Council and EU Presidency, the High Representative for the CFSP, and, at various instances, the Member States themselves) engage in UN decision-making, as well as the extent to which EU Member States act in a unified manner. The present volume will hence take a closer look into the 'who', 'how' and 'why' of these complex processes and try to critically assess them.

The second question turns to the actual results of the growing EU-UN partnership. Here we must ask ourselves whether the EU's profession to 'effective multilateralism' has proven credible, or, in other words, whether the EU has put its money and efforts where its mouth is. In this respect, it is important to have a look at the substance of EU positions and action in different policy fields. We have asked authors to assess the EU's performance in several areas of human development, such as refugee, human rights, development and environmental policy. Furthermore, a critical analysis of EU output in the security area is measured against cooperation with the United Nations in sub-areas like crisis management, the fight against terrorism and specific UN-EU cooperation on the ground.

3. Structure of the Book

In order to match with its focus and objectives, the book contains five main parts. The *first part* addresses the legal status of the EU/EC at the UN as well as EU coordination with regard to the main UN bodies. Frank Hoffmeister and Pieter-Jan Kuijper examine the legal framework for EU statuses in the UN and go on to discuss actual EU/EC participation in the main UN organs and their subsidiary bodies, specialized agencies, related organs, and UN Conferences. Esa Paasivirta and Dominic Porter give an assessment from the field on EU coordination at the General Assembly and ECOSOC, describing the interaction between the activities at the Council Liaison Office in New York and in Brussels. Ambassador Johan Verbeke evaluates how EU Member States that are permanent or elected Security Council members exercise their coordination and consultation obligations under Article 19 TEU, while making suggestions on how to improve these processes in the absence of a single EU seat in the Council.

As the book aims at providing a comprehensive overview of the various facets of cooperation between the European Union and the United Nations in the broad sense, it does not only cover the UN's principal organs, but also funds, programmes and specialized agencies. Thus, *part two* contains examples on EU/EC participation in a number of specialized agencies. The first contribution, by Joergen Maersk Pedersen, deals with the unique position of the EC as full-fledged member of the Food and Agriculture Organization, examining EC participation in several FAO projects and initiatives, and the Codex Alimentarius Commission. Rudi Delarue examines EU coordination at the International Labour Organization and the role of the EC in the development of the 'decent work for all' agenda. Carole Garnier, Daniel Daco and Francesca di Mauro scrutinize EC representation at the IMF and in the World Bank Group and examine how this representation can be strengthened. The chapter by Lucia Cavicchioli addresses the role of the EC at UNESCO, in particular in light of the decision to grant the European Community enhanced observer status during the negotiations of the Convention on Cultural Diversity. Lastly, Barbara Eggers and Frank Hoffmeister assess the role of the EC in the main organs of the World Health Organization, as well as in the negotiation of Framework Convention on Tobacco Control and the WHO's International Health Regulations.

The *third part* contains a number of substantive contributions in the broad sphere of human development. Thus, Judith Kumin addresses cooperation on refugees, *inter alia*, discussing the strategic partnership between the EU and UNHCR and

UNHCR's position *vis-à-vis* the EU's asylum policy. Hadewych Hazelzet identifies the actors involved in EU human rights policy and their role in UN fora such as the General Assembly's Third Committee on social, humanitarian and cultural matters, the (now abolished) Commission on Human Rights and the newly established Human Rights Council. Jochen Jesinghaus' chapter deals with UN-EU cooperation with regard to sustainable development and the implementation of the Millennium Development Goals, including through the work of the Commission on Sustainable Development. Finally, Aurore Maillet focuses on EU support for UN environmental policy, for example regarding the Kyoto Protocol, and addresses the EU-backed proposal to transform UNEP into a specialized UN agency.

Part four is devoted to UN-EU cooperation on security issues. Jan Wouters and Tom Ruys first give an assessment of cooperation in crisis management, both on the structural and operational level, while Jim Cloos sets out a number of concrete lines of action for future cooperation. Sven Biscop and Edith Drieskens address the EU's commitment to effective multilateralism from a more fundamental perspective, examining the importance of the European Security Strategy for UN-EU relations. Kennedy Graham examines how the present cooperation in crisis management and other security-related matters can be transformed into a balanced division of tasks, which may serve as a model for cooperation between the UN and other regional and sub-regional organizations. Gijs de Vries' chapter addresses EU support for UN counterterrorism standard-setting and for the implementation of Security Council Resolutions 1267, 1373 and 1540, as well as the role of human rights in the fight against terrorism. Finally, Michael Karnitschnig undertakes a case-study of the successes and shortcomings of UN-EU cooperation throughout the United Nations Mission for Kosovo (UNMIK), to serve as lessons-learned for future cooperation in the field of nation-building.

The *fifth part* of the book offers an outlook on future developments and thereby reconsiders the two contextual factors mentioned above, i.e., UN reform and EU enlargement. Thus, Ambassador Roman Kirn examines the impact on UN decision-making of the fact that EU Member States, after the 2004 enlargement, belong to different regional groupings at the United Nations. In their respective contributions Danièle Smadja and Jo Leinen focus mainly on UN reform. The former evaluates the extent to which the European Union has thus far acted as a key player in the various aspects of UN reform. The latter assesses the World Summit Outcome from the perspective of the European Parliament, stressing the need for democratization of the United Nations through the establishment of a United Nations Parliamentary Assembly. We conclude the book with an epilogue presenting and assessing the main findings of the volume.

This systematic *tour d'horizon* with both horizontal and thematic chapters is designed to complement existing literature, which generally focuses on security-related aspects, such as terrorism or conflict prevention, or on the political aspects of EU-UN cooperation.[11] This, however, is not to say that the book may offer an exhaustive overview of EU-UN cooperation. Indeed, given inevitable constraints in time and space, some UN programmes (e.g., UNCTAD or UNFPA) or specialized agencies (e.g., ICAO and WIPO), as well as some thematic issues, such as humanitarian aid and development assistance, are only discussed in the margin. Still, we hope that the breadth and depth of the contributions make it a fairly comprehensive overview, offering new insights on sometimes neglected but important institutional, legal and policy issues as well as painting a broader picture of UN-EU cooperation at large.

[11] See, *inter alia*, M. Ortega (ed.), *The European Union and the United Nations: partners in effective multilateralism*, (EU-ISS Chaillot Paper No. 78, June 2005), available at <http://www.iss-eu.org/chaillot/chai78.pdf>, 105 p.; K.V. Laatikainen and K.E. Smith, *The European Union at the United Nations: intersecting multilateralisms* (Basingstroke, Palgrave 2006), 256 p.; V. Kronenberger and J. Wouters (eds.), *The European Union and conflict prevention: policy and legal aspects* (The Hague, TMC Asser Press 2004), 614 p.; V. Kronenberger (ed.), *The European Union and the international legal order: discord or harmony?* (The Hague, TMC Asser Press 2001), 640 p.

Part One

EU Status and Coordination at the Principal UN Bodies

Chapter 1
THE STATUS OF THE EUROPEAN UNION AT THE UNITED NATIONS: INSTITUTIONAL AMBIGUITIES AND POLITICAL REALITIES

by Frank Hoffmeister* and Pieter-Jan Kuijper**

1. Introduction

Let us begin with a little anecdote: It is the last week of October 2005. Imagine you are the legal adviser to Brazil in the 6th Committee of the UN General Assembly and you take part in the discussion concerning the annual report of the International Law Commission (ILC) on the subject 'responsibility of international organizations', which is in the process of being codified. The following scene plays out before your eyes and ears: the chair gives the floor to the United Kingdom, whose representative says: 'Mr. Chairman, I have the honour to speak on behalf of the EU and the acceding countries Bulgaria and Romania'.

The person welcomes the progress made by the ILC, and then he announces a change behind the name plate. He states: 'With your consent, I would like the remainder of the Statement to be delivered by the representative of the European Commission, (…). He will express the view of the European Community on those points which are directly relevant to the Community'.

You see someone descending from the row of observers above the British delegation's place. He takes the place of the UK delegate and continues to speak. You suddenly realize there's a change in the accent and it is probably no longer an Englishman speaking, but you concentrate on the substance and you provisionally conclude for yourself that the speaker must be European. Later on, you look at the distributed printout of the statement, which is entitled: 'Responsibility of international organizations – Statement on behalf of the European Union and the European Community', indicating the names of the UK and Commission Legal Advisers who spoke.[1]

---

* Prof. Dr. F. Hoffmeister (Free University of Brussels), Member of the Legal Service of the European Commission.

** Prof. Dr. P.-J. Kuijper (University of Amsterdam), Principal Legal Advisor in the European Commission.

[1] Responsibility of International Organizations; Statement on behalf of the European Union and the European Community – Sir Michael Wood, The Legal Adviser, Foreign and Commonwealth Of-

J. Wouters et al., eds., The United Nations and the European Union

This practical example shows two things: First, the representation of the European Union is difficult to understand for others. Second, representation is not just decided internally by the European Union (EU[2]), but must follow the relevant UN rules. It is, as the UK speaker said to the chair, 'with the consent' of the other UN members, that the EU is active there.

We will first address the institutional ambiguities of the possible different legal statuses of the EU in the UN system. Can the European Union and/or the European Community be a full participant in the UN system, or at least an observer? Then we will discuss the political realities by giving an overview over the current situation. We will finally briefly review other forms of EU-UN cooperation and conclude.

2. Legal Framework for EU Statuses in the UN

The legal framework for the EU's statuses within the UN has two dimensions: one of an international law character, and one involving the application and interpretation of European law. They must be distinguished from one another. From a European perspective, the correct organizational level must be identified. From a UN perspective, the relevant rules on the different available statuses within the organization need to be applied.

2.1 European law

2.1.1 *EC rules*

Under the Treaty establishing the European Community, the Community is endowed with international legal personality (Article 281 EC). In order to achieve a status for the European Community within a UN body, the European Commission may formulate the relevant requests with the political backing of the Council under Article 302 EC.[3] Based on that provision, the Commission may enter into procedural agreements with the body in question on behalf of the Community; as a matter of law, such agreements may include the granting of an observer status for the Community.[4] However, if a particular Community status can only be brought about by

fice, United Kingdom and Pieter Jan Kuijper, Principal Legal Advisor, European Commission, Sixth Committee, 60th Session of the General Assembly, 25 October 2005.

[2] In this article 'European Union (EU)' is used to encompass the European Community (first pillar) supplemented by the common foreign and security policy (second pillar). When only second pillar action is meant, we speak of the 'second-pillar EU'. On the legal background for this differentiation see below Section 2.1.

[3] Under Part A, Fifth paragraph of the Luxembourg compromise of 1966 the Commission agreed to consult the Council on the opportunity, the modalities and nature of the relations it intends to establish on the basis of Article 302 EC (EC Bull. 3-1966).

[4] J-P. Jacqué, 'La participation de la Communauté économique européenne aux organisations internationales universelles', *AFDI* (1975), at p. 924. The European Court of Justice observed that

modifying the UN body's constitution the Council must grant a negotiation mandate to the Commission under Article 300(1) EC and conclude the modification agreement itself under Article 300(2) EC.

Having been admitted to a UN body, the Community is represented by the European Commission, as long as the Treaty does not provide otherwise.[5] Historically, the most important example of such exceptions could be found in former Article 116 EC, according to which Member States were required to conduct a common policy in international economic organizations. Under the 'Rome-formula' of 1974[6] the role of the Community spokesman should be fulfilled by the representative of the country holding the office of President and the Commission representative, the division of duties being decided at the same time as the Community position is defined. Accordingly, Community delegations in UN bodies in the 1970s and 1980s consisted of Commission and Council representatives alike. The Commission acted normally as Community spokesman on matters concerned with common policies, but Community interventions could also be delivered by the Council representative, if a practical need to do so arose. With the entry into force of the Maastricht Treaty in 1993, former Article 116 EC was abrogated (and transposed into the second pillar – see below). Since then Community delegations for a UN conference or meeting of a UN body are led by the Commission with participation from the Council secretariat where appropriate. Under Section 21 of the Framework Agreement on relations between the European Parliament and the Commission of 26 May 2005, they may also include a certain number of parliamentarians with consultative function upon their request.[7]

Community admission to a UN body has different consequences for the Member States, depending on the nature of Community competences. In areas of exclusive EC competence Member States are not entitled to negotiate or to undertake, individually or collectively, international obligations unless authorized to do so by the Community;[8] this includes decisions taken in and by international organizations.[9] In areas of shared competence, such a situation may arise once the Community has legislated so as to cover the field in question[10] – otherwise, the Community

---

the exchange of letters between the European Commission and the ILO of 1989 led to the observer status of the European Community at the ILO, ECJ, Opinion 2/91, [1993] *ECR* I-1959, at 1066.

[5] This principle is not explicitly laid down in the EC Treaty, but may be deduced from a variety of provisions like Article 300(1) and Article 282 2nd sentence EC. The Commission's function as external representative is now codified in Article I-26(1) 6th sentence of the Treaty establishing a Constitution for Europe: 'With the exception of the common foreign and security policy, and other cases provided for in the Constitution, it [the Commission] shall ensure the Union's external representation'.

[6] COREPER decision of 12 September 1974 (I/119/74).

[7] On the practice of the European Parliament to ask for participation in Community delegations see R. Corbett, F. Jacobs and M. Shackleton, *The European Parliament*, (London, Harper 2003, 5th edn.) at p. 203.

[8] ECJ, Case 22-70 *ERTA*, [1971] *ECR* 263, 274, para. 16.

[9] ECJ, Opinion 1/78, [1979] *ECR* 2871, 2915 et seq.

[10] ECJ, Opinion 2/91, [1993] *ECR* I-1959, 1077-1080.

and the Member States are entitled to put forward their views while ensuring the unity of external representation. In areas of parallel competence such as development policy Community and Member State action do not exclude each other.[11] In remaining areas, Member States may be under an obligation not to frustrate the external action of the Community.

2.1.2 *EU rules*

With the entry into force of the Treaty establishing the European Union in 1992, the system became more complex. Member States were careful not to create another international legal personality. Rather, they conceived that the 'Union shall be founded on the European Communities, supplemented by the policies and forms of cooperation established by this Treaty' (Article 1(3) EU). One policy and form of cooperation concerned the common foreign and security policy (CFSP), including a European security and defence policy (ESDP). Both CFSP and ESDP are regulated by Title V EU. In these areas, the European Union is represented by the Presidency (Article 18(1) EU), assisted by the Secretary-General of the Council exercising the function of High Representative for the common and security policy (Article 18(3) EU). The Commission is fully associated (Article 18(4) EU). Furthermore, Member States shall bring forward EU positions in international organizations in which they are a member (Article 19(1) EU). Union action under CFSP rules would not affect Member States' ability to act individually in the same field. The latter are, however, obliged to support the Union's external and security policy actively and unreservedly in a spirit of loyalty and mutual solidarity (Article 11(2) EU).

The original conception of a Union 'founded on the Community' and 'supplemented' by CFSP action (the 'cross-pillar-EU'), underwent significant changes in practice. Especially after the revision of the CFSP Chapter with the Treaty of Amsterdam in 1997, the European Union developed more and more into an autonomous organization, which would have to be separated from the European Community. Importantly, agreements under Article 24 EU, were now concluded by the Council of the European 'on behalf of the EU',[12] implicitly suggesting the existence of a Union with separate legal personality.[13] Such European Union does not

[11] ECJ, Case C-181/91 and C-248/91 *Parliament/Council and Commission*, [1993] *ECR* I-3685, para. 16; ECJ, Case C-316/91 *Parliament/Council*, [1994] *ECR* I-625, para. 26.

[12] See Council Decision No. 2001/352/CFSP of 9 April 2001, OJ (5 May 2001) L-125/1. (Agreement between the EU and Yugoslavia on the EU monitoring mission in Yugoslavia); Council Decision No. 2001/682/CSPF of 30 August 2001, OJ (11 September 2001), L-241/1 (Agreement between the EU and the Former Yugoslav Republic of Macedonia on the EU monitoring mission in FyROM).

[13] A. Dashwood, 'The European Union – A New international actor' (Editorial comment), *CMLRev* (2001), at p. 825; C. Trüe, 'Rechtspersönlichkeit der Europäischen Union nach den Vertragsänderungen von Amsterdam: Wer handelt in GASP und PJZ?', *ZeuS* (2000), at p. 127; R.A. Wessel, 'The Inside Looking out: Consistency and Delimitation in EU External Relations', *CMLRev.* (2000), at p. 1135 et seq ; Marquardt, 'La capacité de conclure des accords internationaux dans le

coincide with the definition in Article 1(3) EU (comprising three pillars), but could rather be referred to as 'the 2nd pillar Union', meaning the European organizational framework entrusted with conducting CFSP and ESDP matters only. Against that background, two legal interpretations are possible when the Member State holding the Presidency of the Council takes the floor in the UN 'on behalf of the European Union'. A traditional view regards these Presidency statements as the common positions of the 25 Member States (only[14]) under Article 19(1) EU,[15] whereas another view cites them as examples where the 'second-pillar-EU' is represented in the UN under Article 18(1) EU.[16] Which view non-EU Member States adhere to, when confronted with statements of the Presidency on behalf of the EU is not clear.

2.1.3 *EU/EC rules*

To complicate things further, certain cross-pillar subject-matters may sometimes call for a common intervention of the different European actors. Article 3(2) 2nd sentence EU expressly tasks the Council and the Commission to ensure consistency in the external activities of the Union as whole and to cooperate to this end. In such a situation, different legal options are available for the European institutions. A first option is that the Commission expresses a Community position, covering also certain aspects of Member States' competence, including CFSP. That solution is common in bilateral relations between the EU/EC with third States, where the Commission usually speaks on a broad range of matters. The Commission may even negotiate on the basis of a broad Council mandate so-called mixed agreements, which will later be concluded on behalf of the Community and all its Member States, on the one part, and the third State, on the other part. The reversed option is that the Presidency expresses an EU position on CFSP/ESDP matters, but also covering certain aspects of (non-exclusive) Community competence. That solution is traditionally practiced in international organizations, where the Community is not a member on its own. A third option may be to organize alternate interventions of the Presidency or the Commission, speaking respectively for the '2nd pillar-EU' and the Community, and to organize such interventions from the bench of a *de facto* single EU/EC delegation.

---

domaine de la coopération policière et judiciaire en matière pénale', in G. de Kerchove and A. Weyembergh, *Sécurité et justice : enjeu de la politique extérieure de l'Union européenne*, (Bruxelles, Editions de l'ULB 2003), at p. 179.

[14] I. Winkelmann, 'Europäische und mitgliedstaatliche Interessenvertretung in den Vereinten Nationen', *ZaöRV* (2000), at p. 413.

[15] Article 19(1) EU reads: 'Member States shall coordinate their action in international organizations. (…) *They* shall uphold the common positions in such forums' [emphasis added].

[16] K. Lenaerts and E. De Smijter, 'The United Nations and the European Union, Living Apart Together', in K. Wellens (ed.), *International Law: Theory and Practice, Liber amicorum Eric Suy*, (The Hague, Kluwer Law International 1998), at p. 439.

2.2 UN law

2.2.1 *Membership*

As a classical international organization, the United Nations is composed of States only. Article 3 of the UN-Charter refers to the original founders, and under Article 4 of the Charter, accession is only open to 'other peace-loving *states*'. Accordingly, the EU/EC cannot become a member of the UN, unless that provision is modified. However, under Article 108 of the Charter, a two-thirds majority of the members in the General Assembly, and ratification by two-thirds of the UN members including all the permanent members of the Security Council is required. In specialized UN organizations and agencies with a legal personality separate from the one of the main organization, the legal situation is not much different. Their constitutions are generally not open for membership of other international organizations, and amendments require very large qualified majorities.

UN rules may be more conducive to EC membership, if an international organization under UN auspices may be founded anew. That situation arises, in particular, if the General Assembly or another UN body convenes a conference for the negotiating of a new multilateral UN convention. Such conventions may well establish treaty bodies that, sometimes, turn out to be the organs of a newly founded international organization. If and insofar as the EC manages to be part of the negotiating process, it may also be able to convince its partners that the Convention should be open for membership of the EC itself. In such a situation, a clause enabling a 'regional economic integration organization' to sign and ratify the Convention would make the Community – as a Contracting Party to the Convention – also a founding member of the new organization.[17]

2.2.2 *Observer status*

Although not regulated in the UN Charter, observer status has been granted to many entities in UN practice.[18] Each UN organ may decide whether it will do so or not; subsidiary bodies normally follow the practice of the main body, but sometimes they may even go beyond. Accordingly, the precise content of that regime varies according to the UN body's decision in question. The presence of an observer may be limited to formal meetings. Formal interventions are usually only possible at the end of all the interventions of the parties or official participants, thereby often carrying less political weight. Moreover, observers may not propose amendments, pre-

---

[17] For practical examples of such 'REIO clauses' see below Section 3.4.

[18] See the UN Secretariat guidelines on observer status, *United Nations Juridical Yearbook* 1975, p. 167, para. 21; a discussion of the relevant practice can be found in N.S. Knol, 'Non-State Actors in International Organizations: an attempt at classification', available at <http://www.uu.nl/content/03Sybesma.pdf>.

side over meetings or serve as *rapporteur*. Obviously, observers have no right to vote.

2.2.3 *Full participation*

Full participation is another non-regulated status, which may also be described as 'enhanced observer' status. In the basic capacity as observer, a full participant may be invited to all meetings, including the informal ones. He may have the right to make proposals and amendments. He may not face restrictions as regards timing or length of his interventions. He may also serve as *rapporteur* or preside over meetings. Falling short of membership, the only restriction he faces is that he will not have a right to vote, nor to block consensus. The status of full participation may follow from a liberal reading of the rights of observers, or may necessitate additional procedural decisions of the UN body in question, normally adopted by simple majority.

2.3 **Interaction of UN rules and EU/EC rules**

It goes without saying that the institutional ambiguities created by the EC and EU Treaty on external representation of Europe are not conducive to achieving a generally satisfactory European status in the UN system. UN partners may well be ignorant of the European architecture, and they are not obliged to follow the legal details thereof. Therefore, the question whether the EU or the EC, or both should represent a European position in the UN is mostly left to the European institutions themselves. What counts for UN partners is that Europe's choices cannot be imposed on them. Rather, UN members will insist that they decide which status to grant to the EU/EC – whoever applies to be represented. In this respect, they may be reluctant to grant membership status, and they have a considerable procedural leverage in this respect. In return, the presence of the EU/EC may be more acceptable as observer or full participant. That allows at least for some European visibility within the UN, albeit combined with certain practical handicaps. Sometimes, UN partners may, however, be unwilling to grant any access to a specific UN body to the EU/EC as such. In such cases, the general obligation of loyalty under the both the EC and the EU Treaty should stimulate Member States to act broadly in the interest of the Community and of the EU. That might trigger the option of combined 'cross pillar EU' representation to the outside world. The Member State holding the EU presidency may represent all the Member States in common foreign and security policy matters, and additionally address Community matters. It goes without saying that this option does not really enable the EU/EC to bring it its own institutional expertise, political, financial or other contributions into the UN system.

3. EU Practice in the UN System

3.1 EU coordination on UN matters

EU coordination on UN matters has increased dramatically over time. Historically, such coordination occurred in the framework of the old Article 116 EEC, which required the Commission to propose common positions for the Member States voting in UN bodies on economic issues. The most famous example concerns the GA resolution on the economic rights and duties of States of late 1974[19] where the Commission had proposed to Member States to vote in the negative.[20] Furthermore, political coordination on UN matters occurred occasionally within the framework of the European Political Cooperation.[21] Since 1992, several CFSP working groups cover a much broader area. Next to specific thematic working groups like the ones on counter-terrorism ('COTER'), on human rights ('COHOM') a horizontal working group on UN matters ('CONUN') is meeting on a monthly basis. In 1995, it issued guidelines on 'EU-coordination in the United Nations'[22] and agreed upon the main lines for EU positions on cross-cutting issues. Hence, CONUN prepares, for example, EU opening statements in the General Assembly or Council declarations on UN reform at large.

With that input from Brussels, the permanent representations of Member States and the Commission delegation in New York and Geneva have the task to finalise and/or adapt Community and EU positions on the ground. In addition, the Council secretariat has posted (modest) liaison offices in both New York and Geneva to assist Member States during coordination. For diplomatic purposes the Council officials are, however, integrated into the Commission delegation for the purpose of the relations with the host country.

3.2 Principal UN organs and their subsidiary bodies

3.2.1 *Security Council*

In the Security Council, EU Member States are the primary actors. Under Article 19(2) EU, it is the duty of each EU Member State sitting in the Council to uphold EU positions. A considerable practice of general EU coordination and concertation between the permanent members and the other Member States has developed over

[19] UNGA Resolution 3281 (XXIX) of 12 December 1974.

[20] See J-P. Jacqué, loc. cit., *supra* n. 4, at pp. 944-946 with further details. At the time five Member States followed the Commission proposal and voted against the resolution, whereas four Member States abstained.

[21] On EU coordination on UN matters in the 1980s see P. Brückner, 'The EC and the UN', 1 *EJIL* (1990) p. 174 et seq.

[22] Council of the European Union, Doc SN 2435/01 of 10 April 1995, discussed in I. Winkelmann, loc. cit., *supra* n. 14, at pp. 417-420.

time in New York. Against that background, EU members of the Security Council increasingly co-sponsor draft resolutions.[23] In contrast, the participation of the EU/EC as such, necessitates *ad hoc* decisions of the Security Council. Under Article 37 of its Rules of Procedure, the Council may invite any UN Member State which is not a member of the Council, to participate in the discussions of any question. This allows an EU Member State holding the EU Presidency, but not being a member of the Council, taking the floor in the Security Council on behalf of the EU, provided that there is an EU position. Otherwise, another EU Member State currently being a member of the Council (either on a permanent or an elected basis) may exercise this function. The Presidency may also mandate the EU High Representative to make an EU intervention from the nameplate of the Presidency. In return, the Commission may only be invited to meetings of the Security Council on the basis of Rule 39, which refers to 'other persons, whom it (the Security Council) considers competent for the purpose, to supply it with information or to give other assistance in examining matters within its competence'.

EU Presidency statements have indeed occurred in the Security Council since the Irish Presidency in the second half of 1996.[24] Interestingly, both EU High Representative Solana (on 29 January 2002 on Africa, having been given the floor by the then Spanish Presidency) and Vice-Secretary-General Feith of the Council Secretariat (on 21 July 2004 on regional organizations) also addressed the forum. Another *novum* occurred on 27 January 2006, when the Tanzanian Chair of the Security Council gave the floor within a single speaking slot to the Austrian Presidency (on ambassador level) and the European Commission (Commissioner Michel for Development) to contribute to the discussions about the situation in the Great Lakes' Region, each speaker sitting behind their respective nameplates. From an UN point of view, this constituted a combined application of Security Council Rules 37 and 39. From an EU point of view it was a single 'cross-pillar-EU' intervention under Article 3(2) EU.

Another fascinating case for 'cross-pillar EU' participation is the newly founded Peacebuilding Commission, established as a common subsidiary body of the Security Council and the General Assembly.[25] Although it is too early to assess the practical functioning of this body, it may well turn out that the European Community will be invited to all its meetings as an 'institutional donor' next to the World Bank

---

[23] See, e.g., Security Council Resolution 1696 (2006) demanding Iran to suspend uranium enrichment by 31 August 2006, which was co-sponsored by the United Kingdom, France and Germany. § 4 of the resolution endorses the common proposals of 'China, France, Germany, the Russian Federation, the United Kingdom and the United States, with the support of the European Union's High Representative'.

[24] J. Wouters, 'The European Union as an Actor within the United Nations General Assembly', in V. Kronenberger (ed.), *The European Union and the International Legal Order: Discord or Harmony?*, (The Hague, TMC Asser Press 2001), at p. 375.

[25] UNGA Resolution 60/180 of 20 December 2005; UNSC Resolution 1645 (2005) of 20 December 2005.

and the IMF.[26] In addition, the EU may be admitted to country-specific meetings as a relevant regional organization involved in relief efforts and/or political dialogue.[27] In any case, a single European delegation with representatives from the Commission (for the EC) and the Presidency, assisted by the Council secretariat (for the EU) will have to ensure the unity of external representation and speak with one voice in the Peacebuilding Commission.

3.2.2 *General Assembly*

In 1974, the General Assembly invited the European Economic Community to participate in the sessions and work of the General Assembly in the capacity of observer.[28] This observer status applies to the plenary as well as to all committees and sub-committees of the Assembly.

In practice, EU and Community statements are delivered more and more frequently.[29] Matters discussed in the first (disarmament and international security), fourth (decolonization) and fifth (budget) main Committee do regularly touch upon Member States or '2nd pillar-EU' competence. Although EU coordination has increased dramatically in the first committee, split votes between EU Member States remain to be seen mainly as regards nuclear disarmament issues.[30] Similarly, the fourth committee still witnesses some EU split votes on non self-governing territories.[31] On the other hand, the fifth committee does not give rise to political frictions among EU Member States, given that even budgetary priorities are nowadays discussed in advance in CONUN.

The second (economic and financial), third (social, humanitarian and cultural) and sixth (legal) Committee are of interest for an active EU/EC participation. As general rule of thumb, one may identify Community statements, expressed by the Commission from the observer bench, on trade and agricultural/fisheries issues in the 2nd Committee, whereas EU positions are put forward with almost 100% cohesion on other economic matters by the Presidency. Interventions in the 3rd Committee on human rights issues are mainly EU statements, delivered by the Member State exercising the Presidency of the Council. Traditionally, there were no EU positions for the sixth committee. However, following more intense coordination of international law issues in the relevant Brussels Council working group (COJUR),

---

[26] See para. 9 of the two previously cited resolutions.

[27] See para. 7(b) of the two previously cited resolutions.

[28] UNGA Resolution 3208 (XXIX), 11 October 1974: 'The General Assembly, wishing to promote cooperation between the United Nations and the European Economic Community, requests the Secretary-General to invite the European Economic Community to participate in the sessions and work of the General Assembly in the capacity of observer'.

[29] For a succinct empirical overview of EU coordination between 1995-1999 in the General Assembly see J. Wouters, loc. cit., *supra* n. 24, at p. 375.

[30] J. Wouters, loc. cit., *supra* n. 24, at p. 389.

[31] I. Winkelmann, loc. cit., *supra* n. 14, at p. 421.

some EU positions have been recently elaborated in particular with regard to the International Criminal Court.[32] Moreover, certain topics of the yearly report of the International Law Commission are nowadays subject to EU coordination so that 'three-pillar EU' statements can be presented jointly by the Presidency and the Commission, as described in the introduction.

EC participation is also possible in a range of subsidiary Assembly bodies. The Community may receive invitations from the governing bodies of the environment programme (UNEP),[33] the children's fund (UNICEF),[34] the development programme (UNDP),[35] the population fund (UNFPA),[36] the world food programme (WFP),[37] the relief and works agency for Palestine refugees (UNRWA) and the settlements programme (UN-HABITAT).[38] Actual coordination of EU or Community positions in these funds and programmes remains, however, still limited[39] given individual Member State's tendency to use their election to a restricted governing body to foster foremost national policy goals. A special case is the executive board of the High Commissioner for Refugees (UNHCR). From a European perspective the present observer status at the formal meetings[40] is deemed to be inadequate because the Community is excluded from important preparatory informal discussions, though it is one of the major donors of the UNHCR and EC competence in the field grew considerably with the Treaty of Amsterdam. However, a March 2000 request for full participation is still pending due to US resistance.

3.2.3 *Economic and Social Council*

Due to the invitation from the General Assembly, the Community also enjoys observer status in the ECOSOC under Article 71 of the UN-Charter. The relevant invitation dates back to 1979 and was confirmed in 1992.[41] Practically, similar ar-

---

32 J. Wouters, loc. cit., *supra* n. 24, at p. 399.

33 Rule 68 of the Rules of Procedures of the UNEP Governing Council of 28.7.2004, available at <http://www.unep.org/resources/gov/Rules.asp>.

34 Rule 50(2) and 51 of the UNICEF Executive Board Rules of Procedure of 20.5.1994; E/ICEF/177/Rev. 6.

35 Rule 16(3) of the UNEP and UNFPA Executive Board Rules of Procedure of May 1997, DP/1997/32.

36 Ibid.

37 Article XV of the WFP Executive Board Rules of procedure (undated), reprinted in a WFP document of 2004 called 'General Rules, Financial Regulations, Rules of procedure of the Executive Board', available at <http://www.wfp.org/aboutwfp/how_run/general_regulations.asp?section=1&sub_section=3#>, at p. 55.

38 Rule 63 of the UN-Habitat Governing Council Rules of procedure (not published on the UN-HABITAT Webpage).

39 S. Biscop, 'Security and development: a positive agenda for a global EU-UN partnership', in S. Biscop, F. Francioni, K. Graham, T. Felício, J. Laurenti and T. Tardy (eds.), *The European Union and the United Nations* (Chaillot Paper, No. 78, June 2005), at p. 17.

40 Rule 38 of the UNCHR Executive Committee's Rules of procedure, A/AC.96/187/Rev. 5.

41 Rule 79 of the ECOSOC Procedures: ECOSOC Resolution 1949 (LVIII) E/5715/Rev. 2: 'Representatives of intergovernmental organizations accorded permanent observer status by the General

rangements as the ones regarding the Assembly apply. The Community intervenes in the plenary mostly as observer in areas of exclusive EC competence, whereas other matters of shared or parallel competence are either covered by a 'three-pillar' EU statement from the Presidency or left to Member States individually if no common position can be reached.

In the functional commissions of ECOSOC the Community may participate generally as an observer. A horizontal ECOSOC decision of 1983 settles this status for the Commissions on Narcotic Drugs (CND), on Crime prevention and Criminal Justice, on Science and Technology for Development, on the Status of Women, on Population and Development, and on Social Development, as well as for the Statistical Commission.[42] In the aftermath of the Rio Summit of 1992 on development and environment, the Community became a full participant in the newly founded Commission on sustainable development. The relevant ECOSOC decision of 1995 provides:[43]

> '(a) The European Community, while not being a member of the Commission on Sustainable Development, shall be entitled to participate fully, within its areas of competence, in the work of the Commission or any subsidiary body thereof, in accordance with the present decision. Such full participation shall include the right to speak and the right of reply, as well as the right to introduce proposals and amendments. Such full participation shall also include the right to raise as a point of order the fact that consultations are continuing among the Community and its member States on a matter on which a final decision is about to be made and for which the Community is the representative on the Commission in accordance with the present decision, provided that the right to raise this point of order shall not include the right to challenge the decision of the Chairman in response to that order.
> The Community shall not have the right to vote but may submit proposals that shall be put to the vote if any member of the Commission so requests. The participation of the representatives of the Community shall in no case entail an increase in the representation to which the member States of the Community would otherwise be entitled (...).'

Against the background of this enhanced status, the profile of the European Community, represented by the European Commission, in the Commission on sustainable development is remarkable. On the other hand, the Community from time to time faces obstacles to contribute to substantial discussions in other functional Commissions. For example, in 2005 an EC contribution reflecting the experience and methodology of EUROSTAT was challenged in the Statistical Commission.

Finally, the Economic Commission for Europe (UN-ECE) has been receptive to active Community participation since 1958. Initial contacts with the Commission

Assembly (...) may participate, without the right to vote, in the deliberations of the Council on questions within the scope of the activities of the organization'.

[42] Rule 74 of the Rules of Procedures of the Functional Commissions of the ECOSOC (1983), E/5975/Rev. 1.

[43] ECOSOC Decision 1995/201 of 8 February 1995.

led to observer status of the Community in 1975.[44] Since then UN-ECE Conventions allow for the formal accession of the European Community as a regional economic integration organization. Nowadays, the Community ratifies as a matter of routine many technical regulations emanating from UN-ECE Conventions, primarily in the sector of motor vehicles.[45]

3.2.4 *International Court of Justice*

Since only States enjoy standing before the International Court of Justice under Article 34(1) of its Statue, the European Community cannot be a party to any dispute brought before the highest judicial organ of the United Nations. Rather, it may be asked by the Court in its capacity as a 'public international organization' to furnish information relevant to the case before it (Article 34(2) Statute and Article 69 of the Court's Rules of Procedures).

However, it is not excluded that the Community may appear before the Court in deliberations on advisory opinions, if so requested by the Court (Article 66(2) of the Statute). In 1971, this opportunity has been granted to the OAU in the Namibia case. In the recent opinion on the legality of the Israeli wall in the occupied territory, participation of the European Community could have been thought of given the practical impact of the question for the implementation of the Association Agreement between the Community and its Member States with Israel and the respective interim agreement with the Palestinian Authority. However, in contrast to the League of Arab States and the Organization of the Islamic Conference[46] the Community did not submit such a request to the Court, and was hence not participating in the proceedings. Rather, Ireland submitted a written submission on its own behalf and – separately – on behalf of the European Union as the then Presidency of the Council.[47] Contrary to its own submission and those of other Member States, that intervention contained merely a descriptive summary of all official EU positions on the Palestine question, but did not elaborate further on the law. Neither any European State, nor the Presidency made an oral statement before the Court.

Another avenue for formal EC participation before the Court is open under Article 43(2) of the Court's Rules of Procedures, as amended in September 2005.

[44] J-P. Jacqué, loc. cit., *supra* n. 4, at p. 928. In 1975, the former Soviet Union ceased opposing observer status for the Community and made sure that the same status was granted to COMECON.

[45] Compare, e.g., Council Decision 97/836/EC of 27 November 1997 with a view to accession by the European Community to the UN-ECE Agreement concerning the adoption of uniform technical prescriptions for wheeled vehicles, equipments and other parts, OJ (17 December 1997), L-346/78. Under that decision the Community may also accede to new UN/ECE Regulations in that area. See COM (2005) final of 7 December 2005, proposing a Council decision on the accession of the Community to the UN-ECE Regulation No. 107 on provisions concerning the approval of category M2 or M3 vehicles with regard to their general construction.

[46] ICJ, Advisory Opinion of 9 July 2004, *Legal Consequences of the Construction of a Wall in the Occupied Palestine Territories*, para. 6.

[47] ICJ, ibid., para. 9.

Under that provision the Court may notify a public international organization of cases where the interpretation of a convention is at stake to which the organization is a party. In view of the fact that the Community is a party to the UN Convention on the Law of the Sea, the Court asked it in October 2005 whether it would like to submit observations in the case of Nicaragua/Honduras. Since the case only concerned maritime delimitation where no EC competence was involved, the EU High Representative and the Commission declined that offer after internal discussion in the Council working group on international law. Nevertheless, in other law of the sea cases the Community may well take up such invitations and participate in the relevant proceedings, just like it already does before the International Law of the Sea Tribunal (ITLOS) or arbitration tribunals established under ITLOS.

3.3 Specialized agencies and related organizations

The present EC status in UN specialized and related agencies varies considerably. It ranges from full membership to a lack of status and includes several intermediate situations that can be broadly equated with full participant or observer status.

3.3.1 *Membership*

In the mid-eighties the Food and Agricultural Organization (FAO) was chosen as a test case for EC membership, as it was a technical, but quite important specialized agency, where the EC had extensive competence (mainly in agriculture and fisheries) and of which the Soviet Union (normally strongly opposed to EC participation in international agreements and organizations) was not a member.[48] EC membership materialized in FAO as of November 1991,[49] enabling the Community and its Member States to exercise membership rights on an alternate basis. As a result, the Community, in matters of its competence, may cast a number of votes equal to the number of its Member States which are entitled to vote.[50] An inter-institutional agreement between the Council and the Commission lists the respective powers of the Community and the Member States and explains whether a Member State or the Community speaks and votes on specific issues. Community coordination has become routine business because, *inter alia*, the European Court of Justice has confirmed that Community discipline is subject to judicial control under Article 10 EC.[51]

---

[48] J. Sack, 'The European Community's membership of international organizations', *CMLR* (1995), at p. 1227.

[49] See in detail R. Frid, 'The European Economic Community: A member of a Specialized Agency of the United Nations', 4 *EJIL* (1993), at p. 239 et seq.

[50] Article II.10 of the FAO Constitution, as amended 1991.

[51] ECJ, Case C-25/94 *FAO*, [1996] *ECR* I 1469, at para. 50.

Against that background, the EC also became a member of the CODEX ALIMENTARIUS in November 2003.[52] The Codex is a subsidiary common body of the FAO and WHO which is entrusted to set international standards on food safety with direct relevance under the WTO Agreement on Sanitary and Phytosanitary Standards.[53] Membership rights of the Community follow the FAO pattern with one noteworthy difference. In the Codex the voting power of the Community depends on the presence of Member State delegates.[54] This is a legally unsatisfactory arrangement for the Community because Member States vested competence in the Community by concluding the EC Treaty: they do not grant *ad hoc* 'empowerments' through their presence.[55] Politically, this requirement gives Member States the possibility under Codex rules to jeopardize Community positions by deliberate absence. Indeed, such situation arose in May 2004. Two Member States, which had opposed the COREPER decision establishing the relevant Community position by qualified majority, left the room in Rome just before the Community delegate voted for an international standard protecting the geographic indication 'Parmesan'. However, under Community law, such behaviour reducing the voting power of the Community from 15 to 13 votes constitutes an infringement of the duty of loyal cooperation. It could, as a matter of last resort, lead to an infringement procedure before the Court of Justice. Fortunately, Member State discipline increased after that incident so that Community positions are nowadays regularly presented with the full backing of all Member States in the Codex Alimentarius.

The EC has also become a member of the WTO, even as original member in 1994.[56] However, this was the continuation of the former practice of Community membership in the GATT,[57] and the WTO is only related to the UN system. As regards the second related organization, the International Atomic Energy Agency (IAEA), it is not excluded that EURATOM will ask for an upgrade of its present observer status[58] to membership in the near future given its vast competences in the area of peaceful research and use of nuclear energy.[59]

---

[52] Council Decision 2003/822/EC, OJ (26 November 2003), L-309/14. Annex II and III of that decision contain the declaration of competence and the relevant intra-Community rules on coordination.

[53] See Article 3(4) of the SPS Agreement.

[54] See Article II.8 of the Rules of Procedure of the Codex Alimentarius Commission, available at <http://ftp.fao.org/codex/Publications/ProcManuals/Manual_15.pdf>.

[55] See the critique of J. Sack, loc. cit., *supra* n. 48, at p. 1241, with respect to similar arrangements in certain commodity agreements.

[56] Article XI(1) of the Marrakesh Agreement establishing the WTO.

[57] See ECJ, Cases 21-24/72 *International Fruit Company*, [1972] *ECR*, at p. 1219, where the Court held that the Community is bound by the substantial GATT-obligations of the Member States as a matter of treaty succession. On that basis, the Community exercised *de facto* membership rights within the GATT system without having formally acceded to the GATT.

[58] See the cooperation agreement between Euratom and IAEA of 23 December 1975, OJ (23 December 1975), L-329/28.

[59] See Communication from the Commission of to the Council of 16 March 2006 on enhancing the status of the European Atomic Energy Community at the International Atomic Energy Community, COM (2006) 121 final.

3.3.2 *Full participant status*

An intermediate situation exists in several specialized agencies where external EC competence is constantly growing over time, either through treaty amendments or through the adoption of internal EC legislation covering a certain policy field. Accordingly, the EC's participation in the relevant UN body is becoming more and more urgent.

A good example is the ICAO. Following an exchange of letters of February 1989, the ICAO Council had invited the Community representative[60] from 1989 onwards on an *ad hoc* basis to certain sessions only. As this cumbersome procedure did not allow the Community to exercise an active role in all the fields where the Community had legislated in the meantime, the Commission asked the Council for an authorization to negotiate Community accession to ICAO in April 2002.[61] Member States were initially reluctant to go down that road, but came back to the dossier in January 2004 in the follow-up of the open-skies judgments of the European Court of Justice.[62] As an intermediate step, the Irish Council Presidency wrote a letter to the President of the ICAO Council, asking for a means how to ensure a more effective Community participation in the meetings of the ICAO Council.[63] Details of this participant status without a right to vote were then laid down in an exchange of letters between the President of the ICAO/Council and the Commission.[64] Accordingly, the ICAO Council now considers inviting the European Community to participate in all its meetings in which items will be discussed for which the Community has manifested its interest. In the aftermath of this upgrading of Community status in early 2005, Community coordination on ICAO matters is steadily increasing in Brussels, although it has still been difficult to formally adopt internal rules relating to the adoption and presentation of Community positions in the ICAO Council on matters of Community competence.

Similarly, the Community is playing a more and more active role in the WHO and the UNESCO. In both organizations it is admitted as an observer on the basis of an Article 302 EC exchange of letters[65] and allowed to participate in the relevant

---

[60] The ICAO Council referred to participation of the European *Commission* in its meetings. The Commission, formally backed by a COREPER decision of 11 November 1988 on the 'request for participation, as observer, of the Community in the International Civil Aviation Organization', made it clear in its accreditation letter to ICAO that it would represent the Community.

[61] SEC (2002) 381 final of 9 April 2002.

[62] ECJ, Case C-476/98, *Commission/Germany*, [2002] *ECR* I-9855, paras. 103-113 with annotation by F. Hoffmeister, 98 *AJIL* (2004), pp. 567-572.

[63] Letter from Seamus Brennan, Minister for Transport of Ireland, in his capacity of President of the Council of the European Union to Dr. Assad Kotaite, President of the ICAO Council of 22 April 2004 (unpublished).

[64] Letter from ICAO President Dr. Assad Kotaite, to Commissioner de Palacio of 27 October 2000 (unpublished); Letter from Commission Vice President Jacques Barrot to ICAO President Dr. Assad Kotaite of 7 February 2005 (unpublished).

[65] Exchange of letters between the European Communities and the World Health Organization (WHO) laying down the procedure for cooperation between the two organizations of 28 April 1982,

meetings of the plenary and executive organs. Having received special invitations from the World Health Assembly the Community negotiated the Framework Convention on Tobacco Control (1999-2003)[66] and the International Health Regulations (2003-2005)[67] in the WHO together with the Member States since large parts of the Convention and the IHR fell under Community competence. In a similar vein, the Community was invited by the UNESCO Executive Board[68] to participate actively and as fully as appropriate[69] in the negotiations of the Convention on cultural diversity in 2005. Finally, the ever-increasing set of internal market legislation in the field of intellectual property rights led to active participation of the Community in the World Intellectual Property Organization (WIPO). Whereas the EC enjoys general observer rights on the basis of an administrative arrangement of 1997 between the Commission and WIPO, it was granted full participant status in some WIPO expert committees in 2001[70] and 2006.[71]

3.3.3 *Other statuses*

The European Community's relationship with the International Labour Organization already started in 1958.[72] Observer status was formally granted in 1989.[73] After

---

OJ (28 October 1982) L-300/20, and of 14 December 2000, OJ (4 January 2001) C-1/7; Exchange of letters of 15 September 1964 between the European Commission and UNESCO.

[66] Decision of the World Health Assembly WHA 52.38 of 24 May 1999, para. 1(3).

[67] Decision of the World Health Assembly WHA 56.28 of 28 May 2003, para. 2.

[68] Decision No. 171 EX/47 of the UNESCO Executive Board, 26 April 2005, para. 3.

[69] After the adoption of that decision, the UK representative (as incoming Presidency sitting on the Board), made the following (unopposed) statement to the Executive Board:
'The Decision refers to active participation as fully as appropriate.
The European Union considers that this active participation shall consist, within the negotiation of the convention, of the ability to speak as other participants. Such active participation shall also consist of the ability to reply, to put forward proposals and amendments on issues for which it has competence at formal meetings. It shall also include the ability to take part in the discussion of procedural issues within the context of the Draft Cultural Diversity Convention and the ability to take part in the committees, working groups, formal or informal meetings set up in the course of the work relating to negotiation of this Convention. The European Community shall have its own nameplate.
The European Community may not chair committees or sub-committees or serve as rapporteur unless there is full consensus. The European Community shall not have the right to vote nor break or block consensus.
Furthermore, European Community participation does not mean an additional voice. Indeed, the European Community decides in internal coordination whether the Commission will speak, in matters of its competence, on behalf of the Community and its Member States. During this process, we have been open to providing further explanations concerning competences of the Community as regards the draft Convention whenever it speaks and we will continue to do so.'

[70] Rules of procedures for standing WIPO committees (WIPO/GRTKF/IC/1/2) of 5 April 2001, point 7.

[71] The EC was admitted as full participant to the WIPO Advisory Committee on Enforcement in April 2006.

[72] Agreement on relations between the International Labour Organization and the European Economic Community of 7 July 1958, OJ (27 April 1959) 027, at p. 521.

the introduction of new social policy powers under the Amsterdam Treaty of 1997, the input of the EC in that organization has been considerably strengthened – however, due to special features of the 1919 constitution,[74] the Community is not yet in a position to become a party to any ILO convention, and is therefore ousted from a whole sector of law despite its undisputed external competence.[75] Hence, such competence has to be exercised through the medium of the Member States acting jointly in the Community's interest.[76] Despite this handicap, Community coordination on ILO matters is slowly gaining ground both in Brussels and in Geneva and the Community raises its profile in ILO discussions on the political level.

The Community has been less successful in the International Maritime Organization (IMO). Notwithstanding considerable Community legislation in the field of maritime transport, the Council did not yet authorise the Commission to negotiate about Community accession with the IMO.[77] Furthermore, the IMO secretariat interprets an exchange of letters of 1974[78] as granting observer status only to the European Commission and not the European Community. On the one hand, this view did not prevent the Commission from submitting formal positions 'on behalf of the Community and its Member States' in the negotiations of the 2002 Protocol on the 1974 Athens Convention relating to the carriage of passengers and luggage by sea, and to obtain a clause permitting the accession of the Community to that Protocol.[79] On the other hand, statements made by the Commission 'on behalf of the European Community' in the four principal IMO committees have been recently challenged with the formalistic argument that such entity was unknown to the organization. Therefore, current EC statements need to take recourse to a rather complicated and unusual formula[80] and must sometimes be read out by the Presidency rather than the Commission. In addition, this environment fuels tendencies of certain Member States to present national positions which are at odds with the agreed Community position. Finally, the IMO Secretariat has even refused to circulate notifications emanating from the Community about Community legislation related to certain IMO conventions, such as MARPOL, to other IMO Member States,

---

[73] Exchange of letters of 21 December 1989 and 22 December 1989 between the European Commission and the International Labour Organization, OJ (1989), C-24/ 8, renewed by an exchange of letters of 14 May 2001, OJ (8 June 2001), C-165/23.

[74] Under Article 19(5) of the ILO Constitution, ILO Conventions can only be ratified by ILO members.

[75] J. Sack, loc. cit., *supra* n. 48, at p. 1239.

[76] ECJ, Opinion 2/91, [1993] *ECR* I-1061, paras. 36-38.

[77] SEC (2002) 381 final of 9 April 2002.

[78] Cooperation Agreement between the IMCO (which later became the IMO) and the European Commission of 28 June 1974.

[79] Article 19 of the 2002 Protocol to the Athens Convention relating to the carriage of Passengers and their luggage at Sea. (IMO Doc. LEG/CONF.13/20 of 19 November 2002).

[80] Community Statements in the IMO are made by 'the Presidency of the Council of the European Community, acting on behalf of the EU Member States [a footnote lists all 25 Member States] and the European Commission'.

thereby severely hampering the correct information of contracting Parties as regards the implementation of these Conventions.

Another unsatisfactory situation exists with regard to the IMF. When the EC became exclusively competent for monetary policy as regards the 12 Euro Member States, the IMF Executive Board granted observer status to the European Central Bank.[81] Accordingly, the ECB is invited for discussions on Article IV consultations,[82] fund surveillance over the policy of individual euro-area members, the role of the Euro in the international monetary system, the world economic outlook, global financial stability reports and world economic and market developments. In other areas, the EC view is presented by the Executive Director of the Member State holding the Euro 12 Presidency, assisted by a representative from the Commission;[83] furthermore, the European Commissioner for Finance may address the bi-annual meetings of the Governing Council. In return, the observer status of the EC in the World Bank Group seems to be more effective, given that the EC is an important donor of development aid. Accordingly, the Commissioner for Development seems to have more influence in the strategic discussions of the World Bank's Governing Council.[84] Nevertheless, the visibility and influence of the Community could be increased if it spoke more often with a single voice.[85]

Finally, the existing Community observer status at the United Nations Industrial Development Organization (UNIDO) is largely dormant. No particular EC status exists in the International Telecommunications Union (ITU), the Universal Postal Union (UPU) and the World Meteorological Organization (WMO).

3.4 UN Conventions

The question of Community participation in international treaty negotiations under UN auspices first arose in the area of commodity agreements. When the former

[81] Decision No. 11875 (99/1) adopted by the IMF Executive Board on 21 December 1998 granting observer status to the European Central Bank, reviewed by IMF Executive Board Decision of 27 December 2002 (Decision No. 12925).

[82] Under Article IV(3) of the IMF Articles of Agreement, the IMF consults on the exchange rate policies of its members.

[83] See Article 113(4) EC and the conclusions of the European Council of December 1998. For a detailed discussion of the specificities of EC external representation in the area of monetary policy see B. Martenczuk, 'Die Außenvertretung der Europäischen Gemeinschaft auf dem Gebiet der Währungspolitik', *ZaöRV* (1999), p. 93 et seq.

[84] Under Article V Section 8 of the IBRD Articles of Agreement (amended 1989) the IBRD shall cooperate with other public international organizations. Section 4(b) of the Rules of Procedure of the Governing Council (as of 1980) allows the invitation of observers to its meetings. Similar arrangements apply in the International Development Agency, the International Finance Corporation and the Multilateral Investment Guarantee Agency.

[85] See the Commission communication 'Accelerating Progress towards Attaining the Millenium Development Goals – financing for development and aid effectiveness', COM (2005), 134 final, 12 April 2005.

USSR resisted formal EC participation in the Rome sugar conference of 1968, the UN Legal Council put forward the following opinion:

> 'The Conference could invite the Community to participate in the Conference without vote, and permit the representative of its Commission to act as spokesman for the Community on matters relating to sugar. (…) This procedure could be employed in a commodity conference without infringing upon the United Nations requirements (…) while at the same time satisfying the Community's institutional arrangements'.[86]

As UN members accepted this 'Rome-formula', the Community has since then regularly participated in international commodity negotiations. Furthermore, it was allowed to become a formal party to these commodities agreements, directly mentioned as the then 'European Economic Community',[87] or, later on as 'the European Community'[88]or even as 'the European Union'.[89] Today, the Community has become a party to virtually all commodity agreements under UN auspices, sometimes to the exclusion of Member States,[90] sometimes in parallel with some or all of them.[91]

When the General Assembly convenes diplomatic conferences to negotiate a multilateral convention under UN auspices in other areas, it has become standard practice to invite the European Community as well. This is especially true if and in so far as it is conceivable that the European Community may become a party to the Convention. Accordingly, under the relevant rules of procedures, the European Community is allowed to take part in the negotiations as a full participant. That development started with respect to the UN Convention on the Law of the Sea (1982/1994) and was continued with a range of multilateral environmental conven-

[86] Opinion prepared for the United Nations Sugar Conference of 24 May 1968, UN Juridical Yearbook 1968, p. 201-202.

[87] This development started with Articles 36 and 38 of the Grain Agreement of 28 November 1967, OJ (23 March 1970), L-66/2, which was the first commodity agreement to which the Community became a party.

[88] See, e.g., Article 5 of the International Tropical Timber Agreement of 1 April 1994, OJ (17 August 1996), L-208/4.

[89] See, e.g., Article 4(1) of the International Cocoa Agreement of 12 December 2002, OJ (17 December 2002), L-342/2.

[90] See, e.g., International Agreement on Olive Oil and Table Olives of 14 November 2005, OJ (19 November 2005), L-302/46; International Grains Agreement of 30 June 1996, OJ (27 January 1996), L-21/49; International Sugar Agreement of 13 November 1992, OJ (23 December 1992), L-379/15; International Cocoa Agreement of 12 December 2002, OJ (17 December 2002), L-342/2; International Jute Study Group, OJ (27 April 2002), L-112/34.

[91] See, e.g., Food Aid Convention of 13 April 1999, OJ (24 August 1999), L-222/41; International Tin Agreement of 21 June 1976, OJ (14 August 1976), L-222/3; International Tropical Timber Agreement of 1 April 1994, OJ (17 August 1996), L-208/4; International Coffee Agreement of 24 September 2001, OJ (11 December 2001), L-326/22; International Lead and Zinc Study Group, OJ (22 March 2001), L-82/21; International Nickel Study Group, OJ (24 October 1991), L-293/23; International Copper Study Group, OJ (10 April 1991), L-89/39; International Rubber Study Group, OJ (10 August 2002), L-215/13.

tions. The most recent examples include the UN Palermo Convention against transnational organized crime (2000)[92] and the ongoing negotiations on a UN convention on the rights of persons with disabilities. In all these cases, the European Commission negotiated on behalf of the European Community with a mandate granted by the Council of Ministers under Article 300(1) EC.

Once the final text of a UN convention is adopted, the Community may well sign and later on conclude it as a 'regional economic integration organization'. 'REIOs' are sometimes defined as organization to which Member States have transferred competence to conclude international agreements in the area of the convention.[93] Accordingly, the clause is not specifically targeted at the European Community but is general in nature. Nevertheless, in practice, only the Community made use of these clauses and has become a party to UN conventions, *inter alia*, in the fields of the law of the sea and conservation of maritime resources,[94] environmental protection,[95] and health.[96] European Community ratification procedures of UN conventions in the fields of cultural diversity (UNESCO Convention) and justice and home affairs (Palermo Conventions on corruption and transnational organized crime) are underway.

In all these cases, the Community has or will become a party next to its Member States. While this entails a division of labour within the treaty bodies along the lines of Community membership in FAO or the Codex Alimentarius, this situation triggers another important consequence for the Member States as regards eventual dispute settlement. As the Court of Justice recently held with respect to UNCLOS,

---

[92] See C. Rijken and V. Kronenberger, 'The United Nations Convention against transnational crime and the European Union', in V. Kronenberger (ed.), op. cit., *supra* n. 24, at p. 481, p. 491 et seq.

[93] For an early definition see Article 1 of Annex IX of the UN Convention on the Law of the Sea, OJ (23 June 1998), L-179/3.

[94] Council Decision 98/392/EC of 23 March 1998, OJ (23 June 1998), L-179/1 (UNCLOS); Council Decision 98/414/EC, Annex B, OJ (3 July 1998), L-189/14 (Straddling Stocks Convention).

[95] Council Decision 81/462/EEC of 11 June 1981 on the conclusion of the Convention on long-range transboundary air pollution, OJ (27 June 1981), L-171/11; Council Decision 88/540/EEC of 14 October 1988 concerning the conclusion of the Vienna Convention for the protection of the ozone layer and the Montreal Protocol on substances that deplete the ozone layer, OJ (31 October 1988), L-297/8; Council Decision 94/69/EC concerning the conclusion of the United Nations Framework Convention on Climate Change, OJ (7 February 1994), L-33/11; Council Decision 2002/358/EC concerning the approval of the Kyoto Protocol to the UN Framework Convention on Climate Change, OJ (15 May 2002), L-130/1; Council Decision 93/98/EEC of 1 February 1993 on the conclusion of the Convention on the control of transboundary movements of hazardous wastes and their disposal (Basel Convention), OJ (16 February 1993), L-39/1; Council Decision 98/216/EC of 9 March 1998 on the conclusion of the UN Convention to combat desertification in countries seriously affected by drought and/or desertification, OJ (19 March 1998), L-83/1; Council Decision 93/626/EC of 25 October 1993 concerning the conclusion of the Convention on Biological Diversity, OJ (13 December 1993), L-309/1; Council Decision 2002/628/EC of 25 June 2002 concerning the conclusion of the Cartagena Protocol on Biosafety, OJ (31 July 2002), L-201/48.

[96] Council Decision 2004/513/EC of 2 June 2004 concerning the conclusion of the WHO Framework Convention on Tobacco Control, OJ (15 June 2004), L-213/8.

Member States are no longer entitled to settle disputes between them by using the dispute settlement system provided under the UN Convention, if and insofar as the substance relates to Community competence. In such a situation, only the Court of Justice is the competent judicial body to settle the dispute according to Article 292 EC.[97]

3.5 UN Conferences

Another important type of UN forum are World Conferences. Again, it is standard practice to include formulations in the procedural rules that allow the European Community to be treated as full participant.[98] On that basis, the Community participated in a whole range of UN World Conferences on development issues since the Rio summit in 1992, namely in Barbados (1994) and Mauritius (2005) on the sustainable development of small island developing stats, in Monterrey (2002) on the financing for development, and in Johannesburg on sustainable development (2002). Examples in other policy fields include the World Conference on Women (Beijing 1995), on Racism (Durban 2001) and on information society (Geneva 2003/Tunis 2005). Only in 2005, at the UN World Conference on Disaster Reduction in Kobe (Japan), did a controversy arise again in this respect. Due to the resistance of the United States, the Preparatory Committee of the World Conference was unable to

---

[97] ECJ, Case C-459/03 *Commission /Ireland*, Judgment of 30 May 2006, nyr.

[98] Full participant status of the Community is usually reflected by certain standard paragraphs in the rules of procedure. A good example can be found in the following provisions for the World Summit on sustainable development of Johannesburg 2002 (A/Conf.199/2 and Corr. 1):
'Rule 1: The delegation of each State participating in the Summit and that of the European Community shall consist of a head of delegation and such other representatives, alternate representatives and advisers as may be required.
Rule 3: (…) the credentials shall be issued by either the Head of the State or Government or by the Minister for Foreign Affairs or, in the case of the European Community, by the President of the European Commission.
Rule 24: (1) Notwithstanding rule 23, the President shall accord the right of reply to a representative of any State participating in the Summit or of the European Community who requests it. Any other representative may be granted the opportunity to make a reply.
(2) The statements made under this rule shall normally be made at the end of the last meeting of the day, or at the conclusion of the consideration of the relevant item if that is sooner.
(3) The representatives of a State or of the European Community may make no more than two statements under this rule at a given meeting on any item. The first shall be limited to five minutes and the second to three minutes; representatives shall in any event attempt to be as brief as possible.
Rule 47: Each State participating in the Summit and the European Community may be represented by one representative in the Main Committee established by the Summit. It may assign to the Committee such alternate representatives and advisers as may be required.
Rule 62: Save where otherwise specifically provided with respect to the European Community in these rules of procedure, representatives designated by other intergovernmental organizations invited to the Summit may participate as observers, without the right to vote, in the deliberations of the Summit, the Main Committee and as appropriate, any other committee or working group on questions within the scope of their activities.'

present agreed procedural rules to the Conference. However, under the elegant formula of a 'provisional application of the provisional rules of procedure'[99] the Community succeeded to be treated as full participant in Kobe. The Commission thus intervened on behalf of the Community both in the plenary and the relevant workshops and re-inforced EU coordination in the drafting committee on the final declaration, where agreed EU positions where usually presented by the then Luxemburg Presidency.

As a full participant, the EC may also take part in the consensus arising at the end of a World Conference. Different formulations have been used to enable to cover the EC as co-author of the political declarations adopted by a World Conference. The Rio-summit 1992 accepted a footnote in Agenda 21, according to which the term 'Governments' will be deemed to include the European Economic Community within its areas of competence.[100] Other World Conferences did not need such an assimilation clause, since the political declarations were made by the 'representatives of the peoples of the world' (Johannesburg 2002) or 'the delegates to the World Conference' (Kobe 2005), which included the Community.

4. UN–EU Cooperation

Whereas the status of the EU/EC in the UN mainly relates to internal functioning of the United Nations, the UN may also come across the EU/EC as a partner in its external activities. The two key documents of 2003 – a Commission communication on the United Nations[101] and the European Security Strategy[102] – both emphasized the political significance that the European Union attaches to the United Nations as the focal point of effective multilateralism. Against that background the EU and the UN have increased their day-to-day cooperation in many fields since early 2000. Summarizing the relevant tools, we can identify the following ongoing areas of intensive cooperation.

---

[99] See the report on the UN World Conference on Disaster Reduction of 16 March 2006, A/CONF.206/6, para. 18: '…the conference considered the provisional rules of procedure. As there was not yet an agreement on the adoption of the text, the Conference agreed to function on the basis of the provisional rules'. The provisional rules of procedure contained the standard participation clauses for the European Community in square brackets, indicating that the text was not agreed in the Preparatory Committee.

[100] UNGA, Report of the United Nations Conference on Environment and Development (Rio de Janeiro 3-14 June 1992), UN Doc A/CONF/151/26/Rev.1.

[101] 'The European Union and the United Nations: the choice of multilateralism', COM (2003) 526 of 10 September 2003, p. 9; welcomed by the Brussels European Council of 12 December 2003, Presidency Conclusions, para. 90. Compare also the conclusions of the General Affairs and External Relations Council of 8 December 2003 on EU-UN relations.

[102] 'A Secure Europe in a Better World – a European Security Strategy', adopted by the European Council of Brussels on 12 December 2003.

4.1 Cooperation on field projects

Firstly, the Community may serve as an implementing agency for UN projects or vice versa. Whereas such cooperation was mainly subject to the *ad hoc* rules, both organizations tried to simplify relevant procedures by concluding a Financial and Administrative Framework Agreement (FAFA) in 2004.[103] Under that agreement, a single set of rules applies for all EU-UN projects. It also covers specialized agencies insofar as they accede to the FAFA. Accordingly, the many projects in the areas of development policy, humanitarian assistance, food safety, refugee policy, environmental protection, etc., should be quickly disbursable for both sides. In addition, following an idea that was announced back in 2001,[104] the European Commission has in the meanwhile concluded with several specialized agencies (legally non-binding) Memoranda of Understanding. Entitled as 'Strategic Partnerships', these memoranda channel an exchange of information and ensure project coordination of the Commission and the UN partner in their respective fields of action.[105]

4.2 Political cooperation

Secondly, another interesting formal aspect of EU-UN cooperation was established by the Göteborg summit in June 2001.[106] It was agreed to hold the EU Ministerial Troika with the UN Secretary-General; the EU High Representative and the European Commission for External Relations should also intensify their contacts with the UNSG and his Deputy. Furthermore, the Council and Commission services should initiate direct contacts with the UN Secretariat. In practice, desk-to-desk exchanges take place between the external relations services of the Commission and their UN counterparts. Particular country or thematic desks twice a year discuss their strategic and tactical policy approaches with a view of complementing each other's action. Sometimes these interactions become very intense, like in the common UN-EU attempt to ensure accession of a unified Cyprus into the EU. One of the interesting features of the discussions was the constant interaction between Commissioner Verheugen and the UN Special Advisor for Cyprus, de Soto, from 1999-2004. Several Commission officials were even seconded to the UN secre-

---

[103] The text and more background information on the FAFA is available at <http://ec.europa.eu/comm/europeaid/tender/gestion/cont_typ/onu/index_en.htm>.

[104] Commission communication to the Council, 'Building an effective partnership with the UN in the field of development and humanitarian affairs', COM (2001) 231 final of 2 May 2001.

[105] Strategic partnerships have so far been concluded with UNDP, WHO, ILO, UNHCR, UNRWA, WFP, UNICEF, FAO and UNOCHA (2005). For a typical example see the text of the Strategic Partnership with UNOCHA in OJ (25 February 2005), L-52/42.

[106] 'EU-UN cooperation in conflict prevention and crisis management'. Annex to the Presidency conclusions, Göteborg European Council, June 2001.

tariat for the final phase of the Cyprus negotiations in March 2004.[107] The idea was to make available to the UN expertise on Community law allowing Annan and his Special Advisor to assess immediately whether certain proposals made by the two parties would be in conformity with the Annan Plan and with the *acquis communautaire;* in his final report Annan called this assistance and support provided by the European Union as a model for EU-UN cooperation.[108] Very close interaction of both organizations also occurred as regards Kosovo, where the EU leads since 1999 the 'Pillar IV' of the UN Interim Mission in Kosovo (UNMIK) on reconstruction and development.[109]

4.3 **Security cooperation**

Thirdly, in the field of CFSP and ESDP, UN-EU cooperation has become significantly closer in the aftermath of the common declaration on crisis management of September 2003.[110] Since then, a Steering Committee of high UN and EU officials reviews on an bi-annual basis progress on the four core areas identified in that declaration (lessons learned, training/exercises, communication, planning). An unpublished Article 24 EU agreement secures the exchange of classified information between the partners. Nowadays, not only EU Member States, but the 'second-pillar-EU' as such is offering active support for UN peace-keeping missions even outside the near neighbourhood like the Balkan countries. For the purposes of this overview it is sufficient to quote the UN mandated[111] Operation Artemis (Congo 2003[112]) and the operation to support ONUMIC for the elections in Congo 2006.

In addition, the EU is heavily involved in the shaping and implementation of UN counter-terrorism policy. In this respect it may be noted that the EU special coordinator on counterterrorism, Mr. de Vries, is heard in the UN Sanctions Committees in New York, and the UN Special Rapporteur on the respect for human rights in counterterrorism, Scheinin, was recently invited to make a presentation to the relevant Council working group in Brussels.

---

[107] See F. Hoffmeister, *Legal Aspects of the Cyprus Problem – Annan Plan and EU Accession* (The Hague, Martinus Nijhoff Publ. 2006), p. 164 et seq.

[108] Report of UN Secretary-General Annan on his good offices mission in Cyprus of 28 May 2004, UN Doc S/2004/437, para. 94.

[109] See UNSC Res. 1244 of 12 June 1999.

[110] Joint Declaration on EU-UN cooperation in crisis management, New York, 24 September 2003, available at <http://europa-eu-un.org/articles/It/article_2768_It.htm>.

[111] UNSC Res. 1484 of 30 May 2003.

[112] Council Joint Action 2003/423/CFSP of 5 June 2003, OJ (11 June 2003), L-143/50. For a discussion of operation Artemis see T. Tardy, 'EU-Un cooperation in peacekeeping: a promising relationship in a constrained environment', in: S. Biscop, F. Francioni, K. Graham, T. Felício, J. Laurenti and T. Tardy (eds.), op. cit., *supra* n. 39, at p. 49.

5. Conclusion

Painting a picture on the status of the European Union at the United Nations may not result in a beautiful Rembrandt with a golden undertone of good old State sovereignty. Rather, an artist would possibly have recourse to some abstract modern techniques, where the colours are constantly changing. Nevertheless, one may find some recurring themes. First, there is a trend to upgrade the observer status of the European Community to that of a full participant throughout the entire UN System, including the specialized agencies and conferences, in order to reflect the increased competences of the Community in a wide range of policy areas. This goes hand and hand with an upgrade for the role of the European Commission as the spokesperson of the Community. Second, there is increased EU coordination in the CFSP and other areas of Member States' competence. Respective EU statements are usually made by the Presidency and add to the political visibility of the respective Member State in charge. Third, a largely unsettled situation exists in 'cross-pillar' situations, where *ad hoc* arrangements need to ensure the unity of external representation of the 'cross-pillar-EU'.

Taking a look in the 'outer life' of UN-EU cooperation, we may note that both organizations are fairly 'conservative' in dealing with each other. As accepted actors on the international scene they use traditional instruments of inter-state cooperation like common declarations, international agreements, exchange of staff and political coordination. Furthermore, the EU is prepared to carry out UN-mandated peacekeeping operations, but reluctant to subject its troops to UN command in UN-led missions.

Put together, we find that the considerable institutional ambiguities both in the UN and EU legal frameworks lead to different political realities in various parts of the UN system. Nevertheless, this 'state of the art' may well become more and more common for the United Nations profiting from the inherent reflex of the European Community in favour of effective multilateralism as an essential tool to foster international cooperation.

Chapter 2
EU COORDINATION AT THE UN GENERAL ASSEMBLY AND ECOSOC: A VIEW FROM BRUSSELS, A VIEW FROM NEW YORK

by Esa Paasivirta* and Dominic Porter**

1. Overview of the UNGA and ECOSOC Work

The EU is today perceived as a unified actor in the near totality of meetings of the UN General Assembly (UNGA) and the Economic and Social Council (ECOSOC). A decade ago this was not the case. The story of the intervening years is certainly one of progressive institutional developments, at least on the side of the EU, but it is as much, if not more, a matter of an evolving physical presence and culture. In many areas one can see two features: rules and reality, or theory and practice, coincide to produce the full picture as to how the EU has become an indispensable player at the UN.

While the EU lacks formal status at the UNGA, and the European Community (EC) remains merely one permanent observer amongst many others,[1] the EU in all its manifestations is undoubtedly a cohesive and transcending force on the UNGA scene. It acts as a political (rather than geographic) group at the UN. In geographic terms, the EU straddles conventional UN regional borders. The majority of the 25 EU Member States belong to the 'Western European and Others' group, some eight of them belong to the Eastern European Group (Estonia, Latvia, Lithuania, Hungary, Poland, Slovakia, Slovenia and the Czech Republic), and one to the Asian group (Cyprus).[2] This dispersal of group membership has permitted the enlarged EU to spread its influence more effectively since 2004. Furthermore, there is a tendency – in fact a regular pattern – for the EU to reach out to states which are not EU members and associate them to its official positions ('alignment procedure').[3]

---

* Legal Adviser, European Commission Delegation to the United Nations (New York), Adjunct Professor, University of Helsinki.

** Human Rights and Social Affairs Adviser, European Commission Delegation to the United Nations (New York).

[1] UNGA Resolution 3208 (XXIX) of 11 October 1974.

[2] On regional groups see Chapter 20.

[3] These states regularly include the EU's acceding and candidate countries, which currently include Bulgaria, Romania, Croatia and Turkey, as well as the potential candidate countries in the

J. Wouters et al., eds., The United Nations and the European Union

In broad terms, the UN's work can be divided into two segments: one involving UNGA and ECOSOC, and the other involving the Security Council. UNGA and ECOSOC work on issues across the board: social and economic matters, human rights and humanitarian issues, the environment, development of international law, and security and disarmament issues. In this context, these principal organs of the UN system typically address 'framework issues': trying to find long-term solutions to persistent global problems, be it in the form of a treaty or convention, UNGA resolution or a UN programme. This is very different from the nature of the work of the UN Security Council, which generally addresses 'spot issues' concerning threats to international peace and security, which are of an immediate nature and require a pointed solution in short-term. These are the hard core security issues which hit political headlines and where the role and importance of the Security Council has been revived in a dramatic way since the early 1990s and the end of the Cold War.

Whilst there is coordination amongst EU Member States on Security Council matters, there is no question that the reflex of seeking and promoting a common position, typically under the leadership of the EU Presidency, is more firmly entrenched in the GA and ECOSOC. And within these organs, the relative preponderance of the 25 Member States is greater in matters relating to peace and security (core areas of CFSP), whilst the role of the European Community, with the Commission as its representative, emerges most in matters pertaining to development and related issues.

The UNGA, the main deliberative organ of the UN, is composed of Member State representatives, each with one vote. It works in many formats and at many different levels. To the outside world, the UNGA ministerial plenary meetings are the most familiar sight, taking place at the beginning of each regular session, in mid September. They are often addressed by heads of state or government or senior ministers, expressing their views on the most important international issues at hand. However, the UNGA continues to meet throughout the year, from September to September, in both formal and informal structures and formats. Understanding the functioning of the UNGA requires an insight into the day-to-day conduct of proceedings, from the formal sessions to the most informal of 'consultations', from the august meetings in the GA Hall, with its complex rules of procedure and six-language interpretation, to the numerous gatherings in basement meeting rooms and the delegates' lounge. The physical location and degree of informality which characterize meetings can play as big a role as the official procedures and terms of participation.

Beneath the UNGA plenary meetings, most issues are addressed in the six main committees, organized according to subject areas: First (Disarmament and Security) Committee; Second (Economic and Financial) Committee, Third (Social, Humanitarian and Cultural) Committee; Fourth (special Political and Decolonization)

Balkans, and quite often, neighbourhood states Moldova and Ukraine, as well as EEA states Norway and Iceland.

Committee; Fifth (Administrative and Budgetary) Committee and Sixth (Legal) Committee. Apart from these main committees, UNGA work is also carried out year around in subsidiary organs including boards, commissions, *ad hoc* committees and working groups, each reporting to the GA on its respective issues.

When in formal session, the main committees and subsidiary organs follow the UNGA Rules of Procedure. However, each committee also has its unique 'established practice' and culture of working. For example the Fifth (Budget) Committee had taken every decision for the last 20 years by consensus until 28 April 2006 when a vote was called on the issue of broad-based management reform proposals. The Second Committee has also traditionally continued its work until consensus is reached, but during the last couple of years, certain annual resolutions – notably on 'trade and development' have ended in deadlock, and been the subject of votes. The Third Committee meanwhile has long had a tradition of voting when no middle ground is found, most typically in the case of so-called country-situation human rights resolutions where the 'principles' of human rights meet the geopolitical 'realities' of the perceived fairness or otherwise of subjecting a given country for special scrutiny. In the Sixth Committee, too, consensus has been the well-entrenched tradition, until 2005, when it resorted to a vote on the issue of human cloning.[4] Whether resolutions are adopted by consensus or by a vote is not insignificant. UN tradition has it that language previously agreed by consensus, for example, can normally be re-used with minimal expectation of re-opening discussions. Meanwhile, recourse to paragraphs which have been disputed in the past will most often mean that they will continue to attract dissent.

What does all of this mean in practice? At everyday level, it means numerous meetings, at all layers of the UN, in the hope of securing a consensus of the international community on all manner of issues of global concern. This same is true for the ECOSOC, within a somewhat more limited range of subjects. Even though ECOSOC has limited (54 state) membership, this is in fact only materially relevant for the relatively few items which come to a vote. In practice, the formal settings, in terms of time spent, amount to a fraction of the total meetings. Most UN business is handled through informal consultations, and this is almost always the case with the preparation of the UNGA Resolutions. These informal consultations are meetings open to all interested states and permanent observers, but normally not open to NGOs or other civil society groups, which take place in the UN building. Often they take place without any secretariat support or interpretation, and are chaired by the state which is the main actor behind an initiative. Other 'informals' – notably on issues of more far-reaching concern – may be served by the Secretariat and chaired by a chosen facilitator. However, strictly speaking, both institutionally and in terms of procedure, they are not UN meetings, even though the great bulk of UN work gets done in this way.

---

[4] This was ultimately adopted by the UNGA by vote as the United Nations Declaration on Human Cloning (Resolution 59/280).

The same applies in the case of ECOSOC and its Functional Commissions – while the main sessions do comprise set-piece 'general debates', where the EU Member States, and the European Community, may intervene in addition to the Presidency, the speech delivered by the Presidency is invariably a fully coordinated statement on behalf of the EU. Outside these formal set-pieces, notably in negotiations to prepare outcome documents (from Ministerial declarations to 'Agreed Conclusions'), the meetings will be informal in nature, with the Presidency typically speaking for the EU, but supported by other Member States and the Commission in the margins, or from the floor.

Thus it is established that the EU acts in the UNGA and ECOSOC as a unified force, projecting its common positions amongst the 192 Member States of the UN. For this to happen there has to be prior 'coordination' amongst the Member States and the Commission. There are three things that have facilitated this unity and made it possible for the EU to act in such a coherent and consistent manner:

- a common institutional framework;
- contextual legal rules requiring coordination and
- the provision of appropriate physical space for the coordination to take place.

Although it is not fully clear what counts more in the end, a room or a rule, the following sections attempt to outline some aspects of EU coordination in practice.

2. A View from Brussels: Coordination as Common Rules and Preparatory Meetings in the Council

As regards the institutional framework, it should be recalled from the outset that there has always been an external dimension in the process of European integration and that this has influenced its development from the very beginning. Today, external relations and foreign policy matters make up a sizable part of the meeting agendas in Brussels. In the regular meetings of foreign ministers of the Member States – the 'General Affairs and External Relations Council' – hardly any aspect of traditional foreign policy remains uncovered. Its layered structures, COREPER, the Political and Security Committee, and the numerous Council Working Groups testify to the same evolution. On the Commission side, altogether four Commissioners and six Directorates-General are exclusively dealing with external relations and foreign policy.

The basic parameters governing the EU's work in the international sphere, both in the sense of the Common Foreign and Security Policy (CFSP) and the external aspects of European Community action, are incorporated in the Treaty on the European Union and the Treaty Establishing the European Community. Both Treaties frame the EU's action in the UN context. They contain both substantive and contextual provisions. 'Coordination', amongst the Member States or between the Member States and the institutions, is a contextual provision which is incorporated in Article 19 of the EU Treaty and stems from several provisions of the EC Treaty.

From the earliest of the Common Provisions of the EU Treaty, the EU sets itself the fundamental objective to 'assert its identity on the international scene'. Detail is then provided in Article 19 of the EU Treaty, applicable in the context of matters that fall within the CFSP, which provides as follows:

> '1. Member States shall coordinate their action in international organizations and at international conferences. They shall uphold the common positions in such forums.
>
> In international organizations and at international conferences where not all the Member States participate, those which do take part shall uphold the common positions.
> 2. Without prejudice to paragraph 1 and Article 14(3), Member States represented in international organizations or international conferences where not all the Member States participate shall keep the latter informed of any matter of common interest ....'.[5]

Related provisions are contained in several articles of the EC Treaty, which are relevant in particular to the coordination and cooperation between the institutions and the Member States. In its most general format, this principle is contained in the 'loyalty' provision in Article 10 of the EC Treaty. The case-law of the Court of Justice has recognized a general 'duty of cooperation' between the institutions and the Member States in areas of shared competences, i.e., competence partly falling within the competence of the Community and partly remaining the national competence of the Member States. The Court stated as follows:

> '[I]t is essential to ensure close cooperation between the Member States and the Community institutions, both in the process of negotiation and conclusion and in the fulfillment of the commitments entered into. That obligation to cooperate flows from the requirement of unity in the international representation of the Community ...'.[6]

The EC Treaty contains several specific provisions related to coordination and cooperation in different areas. For example, Article 180 EC dealing with the area of development cooperation provides that:

> '1. The Community and the Member States shall coordinate their policies on development cooperation and shall consult each other on their aid programmes, including in international organizations and during international conferences. They may undertake joint action. Member States shall contribute if necessary to the implementation of community aid programmes.

---

[5] Article 19 Treaty on European Union, OJ (24 December 2002) C-325/17.
[6] ECJ, Opinion 1/94, pursuant to Article 228(6) of the EC Treaty, [1994] *ECR* I-5267, para. 108.

> 2. The Commission may take any useful initiate to promote the coordination referred to in paragraph 1.'[7]

These are the basic institutional parameters within which the Member States and the Institutions act, and they have by now given rise to a well-established practice in Brussels regarding the preparation of UN issues before each GA as well as during the course of the session. Every year, well ahead of the beginning of a UNGA session, a draft paper is circulated by the Presidency which outlines the basic line to take on various agenda points in the forthcoming UNGA session. It is submitted to EU coordination in the framework of the Council and goes through several revisions before the UN session starts. This triggers a coordination process in the relevant Council Working Groups, but which can take place at different levels in Brussels. That process feeds into the positions which the EU will take on the spot in New York, although as we shall see below, it is not generally responsive or dynamic enough to serve as a means for ensuring 'real time' coordination.

The Council also often issues conclusions ahead of major UN meetings – notably the so-called Summits and Conferences – which serve as basic EU positions, but these are confined to broad guidelines and key principles. This was the case for instance with the UN reform issues ahead of the Summit that took place in September 2005 in New York. Most of the preparation of such Conclusions takes place in the relevant Council Working Groups in Brussels, where experts from EU Member States meet under the leadership of the Presidency, together with the Commission representatives and the Council Secretariat. Such Working Groups include CONUN (dealing with fundamental approaches to UN issues), CODEV (Development issues), COHOM (UNGA Third Committee, Human Rights Council related issues) and COJUR (international law issues). Forthcoming UNGA meetings can also be discussed in other Working Groups dealing with specific sectors like the External Fisheries Working Group or COMAR addressing law of the sea issues. In these preparatory meetings the participants together formulate the general line to take in the forthcoming UN meetings. It is also considered whether diplomatic demarches need to be conducted to promote the EU's position ahead of a major event in different non-EU capitals, either by the EU Presidency or in a 'Troika' format (Presidency, forthcoming Presidency, Commission and often CFSP High Representative).

3. A View from New York: Coordination in Real Time

No amount of advance preparation and subsequent Brussels-based coordination can substitute for lengthy negotiations – and hence multiple EU coordination meetings – 'on the ground'. Indeed, aside from cases where the UNGA produces legally

[7] Article 180 of the Treaty establishing the European Community (EC Treaty), OJ (24 December 2002) C-325/110.

binding Conventions requiring formal ratification from states and/or the European Community, there is rarely time for Ministers in capitals or their delegates in Brussels collectively to endorse the outcome of a negotiation – this too being done by the New York based diplomats. There are exceptions – such as the 2002 Monterrey Conference on Financing for Development, for which the negotiations had been completed (in New York) before the arrival of the delegates in Mexico, hence the EU's formal approval of the text was given in advance by the relevant Council formation in Brussels.

A more typical, and instructive, case was the process leading up to the EU's decision to support the text of an UNGA Resolution to create a new Human Rights Council, a central part of the UN reform package. The EU and other States had very clear ideas of what they wanted to attain from the outset, back in the weeks preceding the UN Summit in September 2005. But as negotiations resumed in New York after the Summit, and indeed threatened to collapse in acrimony at various times, the EU needed to show flexibility in order to achieve a workable and concrete result. At each stage this required intensive coordination and negotiation on the ground, with many EU Ambassadors in New York having to persuade their headquarters to swallow less than ideal permutations of composition and thresholds for membership on the new body in order to maintain a common EU front. The decision on whether or not to support the President of the General Assembly's final compromise text was difficult for several EU states, for various reasons. In this particular case, a provisional, but hard fought agreement amongst Heads of Mission in New York to support the text was temporarily unraveled by discussions at Ministerial level in Brussels, which happened to be scheduled for the next working day. Further hastily convened meetings at the level of New York based EU Heads of Mission were therefore needed to retrieve the common position in support of the proposal.

These brief examples are illustrative of how the EU's internal coordination process rests on a fast-moving network of transatlantic as well as localized consultations. It may start in Brussels, and return there at various intervals, but in most cases the final stages are played out in the meeting rooms of the Council's offices in New York, with EU Member State delegates to the UN liaising directly with their ministries, whether by phone, encrypted fax or blackberry, to secure their final instructions.

In short, whether the EU is engaged in a UNGA plenary discussion on UN reform, or a Committee, or a Functional Commission of ECOSOC, events almost always reach a point where they move too quickly for Brussels-based coordination to remain an effective tool. Statements for delivery by the Presidency, for example, are now very often prepared through the New York Office of the Council Secretariat's system of EU circulars, rather than by the equivalent Brussels-based system. Meetings of the EU convened in the Council's offices, or when time is very short, on the UN premises, enable 'real time' coordination to take place on a constant basis. Such coordination may be needed to fine-tune an EU position in response to consultations with like-minded partners, or in order to react to the positions of less supportive UN Member States in an on-going negotiation process. For example, a draft resolution prepared by capital-based experts (an 'EU Resolution') will often undergo substantial rewriting as New York-based delegates strive to achieve the widest possible support for the initiative. Sometimes this means working to accommodate the concerns of the entire UNGA membership, as when the EU runs a thematic resolution on a broad-based subject such as eliminating religious intolerance, where the search for consensus is in many ways an end in itself. Other times – for instance on a Third Committee 'country human rights situation' resolution – it means achieving sufficient support to have a chance of winning a vote, since it is usually clear in advance that consensus cannot be reached. In the areas of economic and financial matters dealt with by the Second Committee no such clear differences of approach are made, as striving for consensus on issues of development or the environment is the main objective.

It should be stated, however, that the fact that EU coordination in New York happens in real time does not mean that everything is handled by locally based diplomats. Aside from the constant liaison between these diplomats and their headquarters, EU Member States regularly send experts to most substantive sessions, especially when the start and end dates are foreseeable. Sometimes these delegations from EU capitals are extremely large, comprising the full spectrum from the level of a Minister to an array of officials from sectoral as well as foreign ministries. Parliamentarians and representatives of civil society may also form part of a national or European Commission delegation – this being almost systematically true for sessions of the UN's Commission on Sustainable Development, or the Commission on the Status of Women.

In all, there are annually over 1000 EU coordination meetings in New York. These take place in the Council Secretariat's meeting rooms which are located on the 20th floor of an office block near the UN premises. Meetings normally take place in the morning at 9am or earlier, to allow time before 10am when most UN meetings are convened. The formations in which these coordination meetings gather correspond generally to the UNGA Committee structure, for instance First Committee EU experts, Second Committee experts, etc. There is also a hierarchy of levels in New York, with Heads of Mission (Ambassadors) meeting at least weekly to discuss those questions which are either deemed most important, or which have proven difficult to resolve at the working level. The physical set-up of these meetings mirrors that of the Working Groups of the Council in Brussels, including the seating order. The state holding the EU Presidency sits at one end of a long table, flanked by the Council Secretariat, the Commission at the opposite end, and the Member States on the sides, moving places every six months in keeping with the rotating Presidency of the Council of the European Union. As noted above, the missions of the EU Member States and the Commission in New York are connected through a local electronic mailing system (CIREU) which is used to pass messages for convening the different coordination meetings and circulating documents to the relevant experts.

Aside from their primary function of confirming or establishing a common EU position, these regular EU coordination meetings are useful in terms of 'burden sharing'. This can mean permitting the small Member States to give their input to common EU positions which are then reliably carried forward by the Presidency (without the need for that state to follow every step of a negotiation), and it can allow delegates to gather information on UN activities far more broadly than the resources of individual small missions would otherwise allow. On the other hand, working with 25 states can mean that a Presidency, small or large, may seek assistance from another state in representing the EU, where this is difficult for logistical reasons.

The EU coordination process has thus become a central feature of the daily working life of all EU diplomats posted to New York. It may not always be as efficient as possible; there can be a burdensome 'compilation effect' to combining the detailed inputs of several Member States. It may take up what can seem a disproportionate amount of time; sometimes hours are spent fine-tuning a position on a relatively minor issue. It may even expose differences of view which might otherwise remain below the surface. Yet successive Presidencies, with the assistance of their colleagues, have sought steadily to improve and streamline the coordination process. The fact that every Member State will have its semester in the 'hot seat' means that there is a powerful shared interest in making EU coordination a genuinely effective, smooth and helpful process.

What is certain is that the reflex and culture of coordination is now well and truly entrenched in the approaches of all EU Member States at the United Nations. Indeed, the will of the Member States to achieve a common position on issues before the UNGA and ECOSOC almost always prevails over any single national concern. Moreover, contrary to some expectations, the immediate impact of the 2004 enlargement from 15 to 25 Member States was not to make the achievement of common positions more cumbersome. In fact, as many new Members tended initially to side with the prevailing view, there was a tendency for critical masses to 'snowball' behind marginal majority positions, accelerating the process of convergence rather than hindering it. It remains to be seen whether this effect will persist, or whether the new Member States will become more assertive in impressing their own views upon the EU coordination process.

4. Delivery of EU Positions at the UN

Projecting the EU's view can take many forms and happens at different levels. This leads us back to the matter of the physical reality of informal negotiations and the different formats in which they take place. We shall also see how important it can be for the Presidency, once mandated to speak on behalf of the EU, to be given a certain degree of room for maneuvering. It is also worth examining the question of the effectiveness of the EU in more formal negotiations, and raising the issue of whether speaking with 'one voice' should always mean speaking through a single spokesperson.

The delivery of the EU's position, resulting from the coordination processes described above, is normally carried out first and foremost by the Presidency. Other Member States, the Commission and the Council Secretariat can and do assist the Presidency in presenting the EU position outside the confines of the formal meeting. Occasionally, other Member States will speak in formal and informal meetings proper, though this is almost never done without prior agreement or consultation with the Presidency in question. When other EU Member States do intervene they refer to the Presidency statement which has usually been delivered before individual interventions. Indeed, the Presidency may explicitly request EU partners to add their voices in support of the common position, especially in cases where the atmospherics of a meeting might otherwise lead to the Presidency's voice appearing isolated, despite the fact that it represents many countries' views. There is a need for a balance between dogmatism and pragmatism in such cases – the value of having a solid common position, for example, might risk being undermined if it looks (or rather sounds) like the view of one person in a room packed with over a hundred delegates. There is thus a certain case-by-case approach, sometimes planned in advance, sometimes initiated on the spot, depending on the evolution of a debate.

In most situations, however, the Presidency speaks alone, making it clear that it speaks on behalf of the 25 Member States or, as is often the case, also for non-EU States which have associated themselves with the EU position. Frequently the EU Presidency speaks for up to 35 States, and this is both understood and respected by the wider UN membership. Despite the extremely broad scope of EU coordination at the UN, there are however still some isolated instances where the EU Presidency does not present a common position, either as a matter of 'tradition', or exceptionally, following a failure to secure agreement among the 25. An example of the first situation is when an EU Member State runs a resolution in the UNGA in so-called 'national capacity'. If an EU Member State has traditionally tabled a resolution (often dating back to before its membership of the EU), it may continue to do so, after consulting the other EU Member States, and securing their support in principle. In these cases the Presidency does not speak on behalf of the EU, but at the same time it is expected that EU Member States are supportive of the initiative in question.[8]

There are some issues where the EU has not been able to reach a common position or where coordination is not pursued from the outset. The question of Security Council reform is the most obvious and topical example where the differences of

---

[8] For instance, in the Third Committee of the UNGA, Denmark traditionally runs a resolution on the prevention of torture; Finland runs a biennial resolution on summary or arbitrary executions; Austria runs a biennial resolution on human rights in the administration of justice; Italy runs a text on strengthening the UN crime prevention and criminal justice programme, and so on.

views amongst the EU Member States cannot be bridged, resulting in the EU not acting jointly, but individual Member States for themselves. Another recent example, where the positions of the EU Member States were influenced by differences in ethical outlook, religious tradition and history, was the resolution concerning human cloning, with the result that not only was the UNGA split and had to vote, but the EU Member States equally ended up voting in a split manner.[9] Analysis of the voting pattern of EU Member States in the UN perhaps provides us with the most reliable quantified evidence of steadily increasing cohesion over recent years, and several studies have been carried out in this regard.[10] Suffice to say here that in the GA Committees and ECOSOC instances of split voting amongst the EU are very rare, accounting nowadays for somewhere around 3% of resolutions considered.

The formal UN sessions set certain obvious restrictions to the presentation of EU views by the Commission even in cases when the issues concerned would internally fall within the exclusive Community competence. In terms of speaking order, this would normally imply that the Commission would have to speak after all UN members have spoken and it would do so from the EC observer seat. The Commission interventions are therefore more likely to happen in informal sessions where there is no set order of speakers and where the UNGA Rules of Procedure do not apply. For example, it is the practice that the Commission negotiates the annual UNGA resolution on sustainable fisheries on behalf of the 25 Member States, in close cooperation with the Presidency and the interested EU Member States. Likewise, the annual UNGA resolution on trade and development is conducted by the Commission both in terms of coordinating it internally within the EU and negotiating it with other UN Member States. In both cases, the end result of these informal consultations is carried out by the Member States adopting the final resolution at the UNGA, whereby the EU Presidency normally makes a common EU statement.

Exceptionally, the European Commission (strictly speaking, on behalf of the European Community) takes the floor in formal negotiation sessions amongst states, if allowed by the Chair, and not objected to by other states. There must be prior agreement on this within the EU, in view of the Community competences at stake. At working level meetings, this has happened for instance in the framework of the Sixth Committee addressing issues concerning the topic of responsibility of international organizations. The Commission routinely speaks on the EU's behalf on issues of trade or agriculture. Moreover, in a recent meeting of the UN Ad Hoc

[9] In this case, on the one side, Austria, Germany, Hungary, Italy, Ireland, Malta, Poland, Portugal, Slovakia and Slovenia voted in favour of the Resolution, whereas Belgium, Cyprus, Czech Republic, Denmark, Estonia, Finland, France, Latvia, Luxemburg, Lithuania, the Netherlands, Spain, Sweden and the United Kingdom voted against (Greece did not vote).

[10] See, e.g., P. Luif, *EU Cohesion in the UN General Assembly* (Paris, European Union Institute for Security Studies), Occasional papers No. 49/December 2003; K. Smith, 'Reflections on EU Coordination in the UN', Fornet CFSP Forum, available at <www.fornet.info>, Vol. 2, Issue 1, January 2004, pp. 1-3; K. Verlin Laatikainen, 'Assessing the EU as an Actor in the UN', ibid., pp. 4-9.

Working Group on Biodiversity in Areas beyond National Jurisdiction, which took place in February 2006, the seating order of the EC was adjusted, placing it before observers but after all states, following from the wording of the annual UNGA Resolution on Oceans and the Law of the Sea which invited Parties to the Law of the Sea Convention to participate in that meeting, which was conducted under the auspices of UNGA. On the same grounds, this pattern has also been followed in the recent meeting of UNICPOLOS (June 2006), an UNGA subsidiary organ dealing with law of the sea developments, often closely linked to fisheries policy.

Straying beyond the strict confines of the UNGA, there are cases where the EC is granted a form of 'enhanced' observer status – principally at political level 'Summit and Conference' type meetings. Thus, the EC was accorded such status at the Rio and Johannesburg Summits in 1992 and 2002, and maintains it at the annual sessions of the ECOSOC functional Commission on Sustainable Development. In these cases, the specific status accorded to the EC is set out in the GA resolution which sets the 'modalities' for the event or body. On a more *ad hoc* level, it may be noted for example that the Commissioner Michel, in charge of development cooperation in the European Commission, addressed the Security Council in 2006 when it held an open debate on post-conflict situations in the Great Lakes region of Africa. In this case, it was upon invitation by the Chair, and not objected to by other participants. Evidently, such a case implied the Commission speaking as an institution with substantial experience and knowledge of the matter at hand, not as a representative of the EU 25.

In essence, for the Commission to speak at the UN (in its capacity of representing the European Community), two conditions normally have to be met. Firstly, the issue at stake has to fall within the core EC competences, being predominantly a matter for its exclusive competence, or involving issues where the Community is a significant financial contributor. Secondly, the institutional UN context has to be such that effective action is not hindered by rules or formal status and procedure, which most often means informal UN consultations.

It should be recalled that there are, in addition, a certain number of official meetings which take place at the UN, and which are served by the UN Secretariat, but which are not institutionally UN meetings. These include most obviously meetings of Contracting Parties to a particular international treaty, such as the annual meetings of the State Parties to the Law of the Sea Convention and the meetings of the Parties to the UN Fish Stocks Agreement, to which the European Community is a Contracting Party. In such meetings, the seating follows the names of the Parties in alphabetical order, and the Commission speaks on behalf of the European Community.

5. The Culture of Cohesion and Issues of Effectiveness and Principle

The culture of EU cohesion which has been traced throughout this chapter is founded upon intensive common preparation, a unified and strategic external identity, and the ways and means of presenting EU positions with one voice. The culture stems from a combination of a common institutional framework and practical working habits. It was the Maastricht Treaty of 1991 (entry into force 1994) introducing its specific provisions on the Common Foreign and Security Policy and providing for coordinated action at international organizations which triggered this culture of cohesion in the EU's external relations. At all levels of the UN, but especially in the UNGA and ECOSOC, it is manifested in the fact that common EU positions are formed and held in the quasi-totality of cases. The sense of the EU as a single actor has evolved to the extent that it is a familiar sight to all partners at the UN, and is the pattern of behaviour which is now expected of the EU.

But another broad evolution since Maastricht, an inevitable side-effect of the EU's increasingly cohesive behaviour, has also been that achieving common positions with the Union has become as important and time consuming as the projection of that position on the UN stage. Since Maastricht, the Council (whether in its Brussels based formations or *in situ* at the UN), has become the central facilitative forum for foreign policy action. Every national delegate from the EU Member States nowadays spends as much time with his or her EU colleagues, as with other colleagues at the UN.

A couple of issues should be noted here. Firstly, the legal and institutional underpinnings to the EU's common behaviour are certainly for most New York based delegates secondary to the day-to-day reality of 25 Member States spending hours together in common meeting rooms. The ease with which this situation has developed is of course inspired by a foundation of genuine common values and interests, and triggered by the common institutional framework. But it is at least as much facilitated by more mundane facts such as the provision of assigned Council meeting rooms in New York since 1994. As noted above, more than a thousand coordination meetings take place on these premises every year.

A second consideration concerns the practical manifestation of the treaty-based principle of the EU speaking with 'one voice'. In virtually all UNGA meetings, this voice is that of the Presidency. Yet there are arguments to suggest that rigidly confining the delivery of the EU's position to one Member State may not always make for the most effective action in all circumstances, and indeed the EU has begun to develop a practice not merely of burden-sharing, but also occasionally of multiplying interventions through states speaking in support of the Presidency when circumstances so merit. This may be all the more likely when the official EU common statement, having almost inevitably been prepared 'by committee', finishes up lacking the rhetorical and substantive 'hard edge' which can be more easily achieved in a statement delivered by one Member alone. Overall, though, the value of the single voice lies in its creation of order and predictability.

On the ground in New York, the rotating EU Presidency's role and profile provide third countries with a clear answer to the Kissinger question of 'who to call' in the EU. The EU is viewed as being critical to the outcome of all genuine negotiations, a fact reflected in the eagerness of any chairperson or facilitator keen on reaching a successful conclusion to engage the EU spokesperson throughout the process. Similarly, the EU holds numerous 'troika' meetings with all of the key players and groups at the UN throughout the year, and such meetings are viewed as helpful if not indispensable by most interlocutors. There are troika meetings at different levels, from Head of Mission to the working level, and troikas with the President of the General Assembly, the UN Secretary-General and his most senior staff. Nowadays all 25 ambassadors of the EU Member States have informal lunch meetings four times a year with the UN Secretary-General.

6. Concluding Remarks

Coordination is about context and compromise, requiring adjustment of individual positions in order to achieve a common EU line and uniform representation. EU coordination at the UN works remarkably well. It is ingrained in the working habits of the EU diplomats dispatched to New York. It is supported by both common rules and common physical space. In the end, it also depends on a substantive and realistic judgment that more is achieved by the EU's Member States when acting together than any state could manage alone.

The lack of formal status remains an issue, and it often complicates effective participation for instance where matters falling within the European Community (EC) competence are involved. However, current practice and developments demonstrate that the EU at the UN is not hindered by an absence of institutional certainty, either at the level of the EU as the future of the Constitutional Treaty is in the balance, or at the level of the UN where the EU has no formal status. The story of the EU at the UN over the last decade is one of continuity and progress. In the work of the UN General Assembly, as well as ECOSOC and other related bodies, the EU is, and is perceived to be, a highly unified and important force. The role played by the EU is one of constant support for the multilateral system. It is a role which comes very easily to a group which is born of many of the same ideals as the United Nations, and to its Member States which have, over forty years or more, become very familiar with the practice of constructing policies from a standpoint which is not uniquely domestically driven. Ultimately, both the EU and the UN are founded on the same core principle: that international cooperation is an essential prerequisite if common challenges are to be effectively, and equitably, tackled.

Chapter 3
EU COORDINATION ON UN SECURITY COUNCIL MATTERS

by Johan Verbeke*

1. Introduction

It is the explicit ambition of the European Union to affirm its identity on the international scene (Article 2 EU Treaty). One way of contributing to this ambition is to aim at effective action in international organizations. With its 25 Member States, contributing to almost 40% of the UN budget, the European Union should have what political scientists call 'actor capacity', i.e., the capacity to exert decisive influence so as to shape the perceptions and expectations of others in the international system. With a view to exerting effective influence within the United Nations, the EU coordinates its positions to the maximum extent possible. In this paper we will study this EU-coordination as it relates to UN Security Council matters.

2. EU Coordination on UN Security Council Matters – the Legal Framework

Before discussing the politics and current practice of EU-coordination on Security Council matters, it seems appropriate to look at the few legal provisions which bear on the subject. The relevant article of the law as it stands, i.e., the Treaty on European Union, is Article 19 (Annex I). In its first paragraph, this Article states that 'Member States shall coordinate their action in international organizations (…)' and that 'they shall uphold the common positions in such forums'.[1] More relevant for Security Council matters is the second paragraph of this Article which states

* Ambassador, Permanent Representative of Belgium to the United Nations in New York since 2004. The opinions expressed in the current paper reflect the personal views of the author, and not necessarily those of the Belgian government.

[1] By virtue of Article 14, paragraph 3 Treaty on European Union, the same holds true for joint actions and by virtue of Article 37, paragraph 2 for questions relating to police and judicial cooperation in criminal matters. See K. Lenaerts and P. Van Nuffel, *Constitutional Law of the European Union* (London, Sweet and Maxwell 2005) p. 823.

J. Wouters et al., eds., The United Nations and the European Union

that 'Member States which are also members of the UN Security Council will concert and keep the other Member States fully informed'. This paragraph continues with a specific reference to those EU Member States that are permanent members of the Security Council: they 'will, in the execution of their functions, ensure the defence of the positions and the interests of the Union, without prejudice to their responsibilities under the provisions of the UN Charter'.

Let us briefly comment on these Treaty provisions. As regards the general obligation contained in the first paragraph of Article 19, much will depend upon what is to be understood by 'coordination', an extremely elastic concept which is open to both strong and weak interpretations and points less to results to be obtained than to the mode of conduct to be followed. As regards the obligation to 'uphold the common positions', it is clear but important to note that these cannot be upheld unless they exist. Moreover, the use of the definite article 'the' in the sentence 'the common positions' seems to indicate that this obligation refers to common positions formally adopted under the Common Foreign and Security Policy (CFSP) Treaty rules. The conclusion of this reading of the first paragraph of Article 19 seems, therefore, to be fairly straightforward: if the EU wants to have any impact within the UN as an Organization, and more specifically within the Security Council as a main body of the UN, it would be of clear benefit to have common positions relating to matters falling within the competence of the Security Council, i.e., matters essentially related to peace and security.

As regards the second paragraph of Article 19, a distinction must be made between the EU members generally, i.e., both permanent and non-permanent members of the Security Council and the EU permanent members proper.

The former have a double obligation. The first one is the obligation to 'concert' among themselves. The second one is to 'keep (...) fully informed' the other Member States, i.e., those not sitting in the Security Council. The duty to concert among the EU Security Council members is a fairly dynamic obligation as it requires an interactive exchange of ideas and opinions. The duty of information-sharing with the broader EU membership would, *prima facie*, appear to be a more static obligation. As we will see, however, this obligation to keep the other Member States 'fully informed' has evolved into a practice of consultation, going beyond the mere information sharing.

It is somewhat surprising to see that the obligations imposed upon the EU permanent members go further than those set upon the members generally, and hence the non-permanent members specifically. The EU permanent members are indeed obliged to 'ensure the defence of the positions and the interests of the Union'. This is a fairly broad mandate as the positions (and not just 'common positions') and particularly the interests of the Union cover almost anything what the Union stands for. Sure enough, this fairly broad mandate is being narrowed down by a very important qualification: the EU permanent members will ensure the defence of the positions and interests of the Union, 'without prejudice to their responsibilities under the provisions of the UN Charter'. [2]

This latter qualification will require some specific comment. As it is more directly related to the politics of EU-coordination in Security Council matters, we will take it up separately in a later section of this paper.

3. The EU-Presence in the Security Council – One Seat or One Voice

It is quite obvious that the strength and impact of the European Common Foreign and Security Policy (CFSP) as well as of the European Security and Defence Policy (ESDP) on matters before the Security Council is determined, first and foremost, by the mere presence of EU Member States in the Security Council. Although such presence is not a sufficient reason for the CFSP and the ESDP to have an effective impact on the Security Council business, it is a necessary condition for it to be the case. As is well-known, the EU is not, as such, present in the Security Council. It is not even a member of the United Nations.[3] Nor can one say that the EU is 'represented' in the Security Council by or through its Member States sitting in the Council, either as permanent or non-permanent members. Because no such representation exists in law.

[2] One is somewhat puzzled by this broader obligation and concomitant qualification as it applies to the EU permanent members only and not to the EU non-permanent members as well. The EU-Treaty seems indeed to make a distinction between permanent and non-permanent members as regards their Security Council mandate that cannot be traced back to any relevant provision of the substantive (i.e., non procedural) chapter of the UN Charter on the Security Council, entitled 'Functions and Powers' (Articles 24 through 26 of the UN Charter), where no distinction whatsoever is made between both these categories of members. See K. Mahbubani, 'The Permanent and Elected Council Members', in D.M. Malone (ed.), *The UN Security Council, From the Cold War to the 21st Century* (Boulder, Rienner 2004). It is therefore quite significant to note that the word 'permanent' occurring in the last sentence of the second paragraph of Article 19 of the EU Treaty has been dropped in its twin-disposition occurring in the Draft Treaty establishing a Constitution for Europe (Article III-305, see Annex II). Under the Constitution the broader obligation would apply without distinction to both EU permanent and non-permanent members, thus ending what we found to be an anomaly. Irrespective of whether or not the Treaty establishing a Constitution for Europe would one day enter into force, one seems comforted by this development of the minds in considering all EU members of the Security Council as having the same prerogatives and obligations under the CFSP with respect to Security Council matters.

[3] Indeed, as is well-known, and sometimes regretted, the European Union (EU) has no legal status in the United Nations. To start with, the EU has no legal personality. But even if it had, it could not become a member of the UN as it is not a State (Article 4 of the UN Charter). It is true that the European Community (EC) has obtained the 'observer' status in the UN General Assembly in 1974, but that does not help as far as the Common Foreign and Security Policy (CFSP) or European Security and Defence Policy (ESDP) are concerned, as these fall outside the range of EC competences. See S. Keukeleire, *Het buitenlands beleid van de Europese Unie*, (Deventer, Kluwer 1998) p. 160.

Still, these EU-Members, by their mere presence in the Security Council, have the potential to exercise a decisive European influence on Security Council matters. How that influence is being exercised will be discussed later. We now would like to only focus on the mere numerical presence of EU-Members in the Council. As things stand today, the European Union is assured of at least two seats in the Security Council, these being the two permanent member seats reserved for France and the United Kingdom. The maximum number of seats which the EU could theoretically occupy in the Security Council is six.[4] In practice and on average, the EU can count on four Member States in the Council. By way of illustration, these members were, for the last few years, and currently are, in addition to the two permanent members:

2003 : Germany, Spain
2004 : Germany, Spain (+ Romania as candidate member)
2005 : Denmark, Greece (+ Romania as candidate member)
2006 : Denmark, Greece, Slovakia.

The net result is that, numerically, the EU has a rather comfortable position in the Security Council. In 2006, for instance, no less than 1/3rd of the seats are in EU Member States' hands, while the 25 EU-Member States stand for only about 1/8th of the total 192 UN Member States.

But is this comfortable numerical position by itself a guarantee for the EU to exercise decisive influence on Security Council matters? In an interview to Die Welt on 24 March 2003 in the context of the Iraqi crisis, the EU High Representative, Javier Solana, complained about the absence of a single EU representation, and thus an EU seat proper, in the Security Council: 'The EU is not represented by one seat in the UN. (…) What makes it difficult for the EU and me is that the EU has four members in the UN Security Council. (…) Imagine what influence Europe could have had if it had spoken with one voice. The lesson we learnt is that Europe is losing influence when it does not speak with one voice'.[5] Is Solana right? Would one EU seat have made any significant difference?

For the sake of clarity, let us make a few distinctions. First of all the distinction between messenger ('seats') and message ('voice'). What the EU should primarily

---

[4] Indeed, the EU is currently represented in three regional groups (out of five) which each can deliver non-permanent members to the Security Council: the Western European Group delivers two non-permanent members, the Eastern European Group (with Estonia, Latvia, Lithuania, Czech Republic, Slovakia, Hungary, Slovenia and shortly Romania and Bulgaria) delivers one non-permanent member and the Asian Group (with Cyprus as only EU-Member in it) delivers again two non-permanent members to the Security Council. The groups in which the EU is not represented are the African Group and the Latin American Group.

[5] See S. Biscop and E. Drieskens, 'Effective Multilateralism and Collective Security: Empowering the UN', in K. Smith and K. Laatikainen (Eds.), *Intersecting Multilateralisms: The European Union and the United Nations* (Houndmills, Basingstoke, Hampshire: Palgrave Macmillan 2006), pp. 118-119.

care for is that all of its messages be un-equivocal, not necessarily that these be carried by one single messenger. One may have as many EU messengers as one wants, what counts is that they all carry the same message. One could even make the case that the European influence in the Security Council would gain by having multiple spokesmen, provided again they all speak the same language. Solana is right by stating that Europe is losing influence when it does not speak with one voice, but that itself does not necessitate one single EU seat within the Security Council. One should not confuse seats with voices, messengers with messages. What counts is one voice, not one seat.

Secondly, in this debate on a single EU seat in the Security Council, one must be cautious not becoming prey to the fallacy of *petitio principi*, i.e., of begging the question. One single EU seat would not, in itself, have guaranteed a coherent EU Iraq policy. Most probably, in such case, the EU voice would simply have been a lame voice. Again, it can help to state the logics of the matter straight: the strength of the EU voice is dependent on the strength of the EU policy that it is called upon to articulate, not the other way around. That is where we have to start: by elaborating single coherent EU policies (preferably in the form of 'common positions') which can be 'voiced' (through a single EU seat or – perhaps preferably – multiple EU Member States seats) with authority in the Security Council. That is how EU influence can be played out. As one can see, in the process we have shifted ground from New York to Brussels, from the place where the policies must be 'voiced' to the place where they have to be elaborated in the first place: the Policy and Security Committee (PSC), the Committee of Permanent Representatives (COREPER) and the Council of Ministers.

4. The Politics of EU Coordination on UN Security Council Matters

A difficult question to be addressed now concerns the extent to which EU Security Council members are bound by EU policy when acting within the Council. We have seen that the EU Treaty provides an important qualification to the duty to defend EU positions and interests by adding that this should be done 'without prejudice' to the responsibilities of the Security Council members under the provisions of the UN Charter. Two readings can be offered of this qualification: a narrow, fairly legalistic reading and a broader, political reading. The latter, which will be defended here, draws us into the politics of EU coordination on UN Security Council matters away from the legal framework sketched above.

The narrow reading of the Article 19 qualification 'without prejudice' is as follows; Article 103 of the UN Charter provides that the obligations under the Charter shall prevail over the obligations under any other international agreement. One such obligation under the Charter is contained in Article 24: it is the obligation for 'prompt and effective action' in respect of which the 'primary responsibility for the maintenance of international peace and security' is conferred on the Security Council. According to the narrow reading of Article 19 of the EU Treaty, the qualification 'without prejudice' contemplates the contingency of an EU Security Council member having to act promptly and effectively under Article 24 of the UN Charter with regard to matters on which the EU has no (current) common position. In such case he would be allowed to act as he sees fit.[6] This reading is not only narrow and legalistic, but ultimately trivial: when there is no EU common position to defend, the very qualification 'without prejudice' simply becomes moot.

A non-trivial reading of Article 19 would be, quite to the contrary, that the responsibilities of a EU Security Council member under the UN Charter may occasionally conflict with the EU positions and interests which that member is, as a rule, ensured to defend, and that in such cases the responsibilities under the Charter may have to prevail. In this connection the following considerations could be made.

First, in exercising their primary responsibility for the maintenance of international peace and security, the Security Council members act on behalf of the entire UN membership of 192 independent States (Article 24, paragraph 1, UN Charter). While fully entitled to defend its EU common position, a responsible EU Security Council member should nevertheless also take into account the 'positions and interests' of the broader membership. Second, once an EU Security Council member threads the Security Council, he enters into another world with its own rules of procedure, tacit understandings, negotiation culture and political dynamics. While the proper defence of the EU (common) positions and interests should no doubt be the rule, one can easily imagine situations in which such defence may be at odds with the prevailing dynamics, may be tactically counter-productive, may need some partial revision, etc.[7]

An example is the debate in the Security Council, in February 2005, aimed at agreeing on the text of a Presidential Statement on the report of the International Commission of Inquiry on Darfur, recommending the involvement of the International Criminal Court (ICC) as regards the gross violations of human rights and humanitarian law which had occurred in Darfur. As an input to that debate within the Security Council, and fully aware of the reluctance of the United States of such ICC involvement, the European Union (through its Political and Security Commit-

---

[6] 'This would appear to authorize those EU Member States (sitting in the Security Council) to adopt a position independently in respect of matters on which the Union has not yet reached a common position where the Security Council is required to reach an urgent decision'. See K. Lenaerts and P. Van Nuffel, op. cit., n. 1, at p. 823.

[7] This is in no way specific for the United Nations. All international organizations have their own political and institutional culture. For a country such as Belgium, being member of a multiplicity of international organizations (Benelux, EU, NATO, OSCE, UN – to name just a few), it is interesting to see how one and the same national position gets 'translated' into these different multilateral fora. Anyone interested in these 'culture chocks' should, for instance, watch and compare the behaviour of EU Ambassadors working on the basis of identical instructions in such fora as NAC (North Atlantic Council – NATO) and PSC (Policy and Security Committee – EU).

tee) skilfully adopted the following declaration: 'The Commission of Inquiry recommends that those responsible should answer for their acts before the ICC. In this context, the EU reaffirms its constant support for the ICC, and reiterates its common position on the ICC, while noting that it is for the United Nations Security Council to take a rapid decision on this matter'. This EU position is quite remarkable as it – wisely – anticipated upon the specific dynamics within the Security Council on this contentious point.

5. EU Coordination among the EU Members in Practice

So-called 'Article 19 consultations' take place in New York, once a week, at two levels: at the level of the Ambassadors (Permanent Representatives, Heads of Mission) and, more extensively, at the level of the collaborators in charge of Security Council matters. The quality of these consultations has improved over the years. Paradoxically, the Iraqi crisis of 2002-2003 has given these consultations and exchanges of ideas a boost, as a divided EU-membership wanted its respective points of view clearly stated and articulated. Although the enlargement of the EU with ten new members in 2005 (from Estonia to Slovenia) has temporarily somewhat hampered the intensity of consultations, the overall underlying dynamic keeps going in the right direction. Two positive trends should be specifically mentioned:

- firstly, the shift from retrospective briefings on the activities of the Security Council in the recent past, towards a prospective view on the upcoming agenda, allowing participants not just to be 'informed' over what already has been decided, but increasingly to state their views on agenda-items still to be considered by the Security Council;

- secondly, and in connection with the foregoing, there is an increasing openness on behalf of the EU-Members sitting (either permanently or not) in the Security Council, not just to provide information on Security Council business, but also to be receptive to opinions of other Member States on items under consideration by the Security Council.

Overall, then, one could say that the EU consultation process is fairly satisfactory, within limits. And these limits are two-fold. First there is the fact, already mentioned, that one cannot – on the supply side – expect the EU Security Council members to lay all their cards open on the table. However much they would like to be EU-loyal, they have loyalties, and perhaps obligations too, towards the other Security Council members that they must respect for the sake of being and continuing to be trusted fellows within that principal organ of the United Nations. Second – and this time on the demand side – one must dare say that EU non-Security Council members do not always demonstrate a keen interest in Security Council matters.

The claim, on behalf of the non-Security Council members, to be fully informed and perhaps consulted on matters for which they show no particular interest is, indeed, somewhat paradoxical if not self-defeating. For the consultation-mechanism to remain healthy, one will need the right balance between supply and demand, between what both the EU Security Council and non-EU Security Council members can meaningfully contribute to the process as a whole.

6. EU 'Concertation' among the EU Security Council Members

When discussing the issue of the single EU seat in the Security Council as compared to the multiple EU Member States seats within the Council, we have noted that, as things stand today, the EU can expect to be 'represented' in the Council by, on average, four EU Member States. That is quite a critical mass for a European Union that has the ambition indeed to be a credible and responsible player on the world scene, including in matters pertaining to peace and security.

It is therefore fairly obvious that, when discussing EU-coordination on Security Council matters, one should pay no less attention to the coordination among the EU Member States actually sitting in the Security Council than to the overall coordination among the EU Member States generally, as we just did.[8] As we have seen, this is not just an option, but an obligation contained in the second paragraph of Article 19, which obliges the EU Security Council members to 'concert' among themselves.

The prime purpose of this 'concertation' among the EU Security Council members should consist in refining, if not defining, the European positions to be defended in the Security Council debates.

In this connection, one should refer to the informal arrangements which the then four Security Council members France, United Kingdom, Germany and Spain, agreed upon on 21 June, 2002. Specifically, they agreed to meet at Ambassadorial level at the beginning of each month to identify subjects where, working together, they could have most impact.

The importance of this 'concertation' among the sole EU Security Council members also resides in the fact that the overall EU-coordination among all the members of the EU can only benefit from a more coordinated approach, through 'concertation', by those of them that effectively sit on the Security Council. Conversely, this 'concertation' among the EU Security Council members can usefully draw on the overall coordination with the EU-membership at large.

[8] J. De Ruyt, *Un Ministre pour une Politique Etrangère Européenne* (European University Institute, Policy Papers, No. 05/02, 2005) pp. 39-40.

7. Room for Improvement of EU Coordination

Although the EU-coordination on UN Security Council matters can be said to be satisfactory, improvements undoubtedly remain possible.

For a start, we could strive to have more EU (common) positions on matters before the Security Council. It is indeed somewhat odd to expect the EU Security Council members to behave 'europeanly', when no European position exists on the matter at hand.

Furthermore, when elaborating (common) positions it would be useful to have these positions framed in such a way to make them 'user-friendly' with regards to the UN Security Council context in which they may be called to play a role. As noted earlier when discussing the politics of EU-coordination, the logic of the European Union's foreign, security and defence policy (CFSP and ESDP) does not necessarily match, let alone coincide, with the UN logic as enshrined in the Charter and demonstrated by UN practice. Both, the EU and UN, reflect two different 'universes of discourse'.[9] If EU decision-making aims to have an effective impact on UN Security Council decision-making, it must be so calibrated and framed that its' decisions, particularly common positions, are effectively translated into UN-language.

This requires, no doubt, a stronger interaction between Brussels and New York. In Brussels it would seem that the Political and Security Committee (PSC) is best placed to act interactively with New York. But for them to be in a position to effectively do so, they need to be informed, as much as possible in real time, about developments in New York. Reports by the Heads of Missions, or perhaps from the Council Secretariat's Liaison Office in New York, to the PSC Ambassadors in Brussels should feed an informed debate resulting, ideally, in common positions which can smoothly be fed into the UN Security Council machinery.

There is also room for improvement on the more practical level in New York within and among EU delegations. Some suggestions could be:

- to include within the delegations of the EU Security Council members, representatives of the current EU presidency and/or the Council Secretariat;
- to strengthen the role of the EU Council Secretariat Liaison Office in New York in EU coordination with a view to having it become the institutional memory for EU Security Council members (particularly non permanent members) in carrying-out their mandate;
- to more frequently call for *ad hoc* Article 19 consultations at the level of the Security Council collaborators whenever developments so require.

---

[9] As stated by S. Biscop and E. Drieskens, op. cit., n. 5, at p. 124: 'An additional problem is that EU common positions and/or CFSP declarations/statements adopted by the EU on topics discussed in the UN Security Council rarely present the right framework for representing the EU in the UN Security Council'.

8. EU Cooperation in the Implementation of UN-Sanctions

One more specific form of coordination, perhaps cooperation, among EU Members should briefly be mentioned. It is the EU cooperation in the implementation of UN sanctions. As is well-known, it is much easier to take restrictive measures, i.e., sanctions, than to have them effectively implemented, even when the political will to do so is present. One of the main reasons that sanctions are often difficult to implement is due to the fact that they must be transposed into the national legal and administrative systems of the UN Member States.

Given the intricacies and idiosyncrasies of the national legal and administrative systems, such transposition can be quite a technical challenge. That is why the EU Member States decided to reflect on setting-up a coordination-mechanism aiming at ensuring that Security Council dictated sanctions could be as smoothly and as rapidly as possible transposed and incorporated into the legal systems of the European Union and its Member States. The core idea consists in going up-stream, i.e., in contributing to the framing of the sanctions resolutions before they are decided, in such a way that their implementation downstream can be carried out smoothly. In March 2005 the then Luxembourg EU-Presidency organized a seminar on this subject in New York which resulted in non-binding Presidency Conclusions. These conclusions state, *inter alia*, that the sharing of 'sanctions elements' of draft UN Security Council resolutions at an early stage in the Article 19 framework, would greatly facilitate their efficient and rapid implementation by the EU and its Member States.

These conclusions are not legally binding, particularly as regards the EU members of the UN Security Council who are expected to make these 'sanctions elements' of draft resolutions available to the other EU Member States as soon as possible. But they definitely set the stage for an enhanced cooperation among Member States for sanctions questions which, although essentially technical in nature, ensures their effective implementation and thus contributes to the overall effectiveness of the United Nations. That is part and parcel of what effective multilateralism is about.

Annex I

Article 19, Treaty on European Union

(1) Member States shall coordinate their action in international organizations and at international conferences. They shall uphold the common positions in such forums.

In international organizations and at international conferences where not all the Member States participate, those which do take part shall uphold the common positions.

(2) Without prejudice to paragraph 1 and Article 14(3), Member States represented in international organizations or international conferences where not all the Member States participate shall keep the latter informed of any matter of common interest.

Member States which are also members of the United Nations Security Council will concert and keep the other Member States fully informed. Member States which are permanent members of the Security Council will, in the execution of their functions, ensure the defence of the positions and the interests of the Union, without prejudice to their responsibilities under the provisions of the United Nations Charter.

ANNEX II

Article III – 305, Draft Treaty establishing a Constitution for Europe

1. Member States shall coordinate their action in international organizations and at international conferences. They shall uphold the Union's position in such fora. The Union Minister for Foreign Affairs shall organize this coordination.

In international organizations and at international conferences where not all the Member States participate, those which do take part shall uphold the Union's positions.

2. In accordance with Article I-16(2), Member States represented in International organizations or international conferences where not all the Member States participate shall keep the latter, as well as the Union Minister for Foreign Affairs, informed of any matter of common interest.

Member States which are also members of the United Nations Security Council shall concert and keep the other Member States and the Union Minister for Foreign Affairs fully informed. Member States which are members of the Security Council will, in the execution of their functions, defend the positions and the interests of the Union, without prejudice to their responsibilities under the United Nations Charter.

When the Union has defined a position on a subject which is on the United Nations Security Council agenda, those Member States which sit on the Security Council shall request that the Union Minister for Foreign Affairs be asked to present the Union's position.

Part Two

UN-EU Cooperation in Certain UN Specialized Agencies

Chapter 4
FAO-EU COOPERATION: AN EVER STRONGER PARTNERSHIP*

by Jœrgen Mærsk Pedersen**

1. Introduction

The Food and Agriculture Organization of the United Nations (FAO) leads international efforts to defeat hunger. Serving both developed and developing countries, it acts as a neutral forum where all nations meet as equals to negotiate agreements and debate policy. FAO is also a source of knowledge and information. It helps developing countries and countries in transition modernize and improve agriculture, forestry and fisheries practices and ensure good nutrition for all. Since its founding in 1945, it has focused special attention on developing rural areas, home to 70% of the world's poor and hungry people. FAO has 189 member countries and one member organization, the European Community.

FAO's activities cover four main areas:

- Putting information within reach: FAO serves as a knowledge network. It uses the expertise of its staff – agronomists, foresters, fisheries and livestock specialists, nutritionists, social scientists, economists, statisticians and other professionals – to collect, analyse and disseminate data to aid development. A million times a month, someone visits the FAO Internet site to consult a technical document or read about its work with farmers. FAO also publishes hundreds of newsletters, reports and books, distributes several magazines and hosts dozens of electronic fora.
- Sharing policy expertise: FAO lends its years of experience to member countries in devising agricultural policy, supporting planning, drafting effective

** Director, FAO Liaison Office with the European Union and Belgium, Brussels. This chapter is the result of a collective effort by many FAO colleagues. I would especially like to express my thanks to Ms. Anne De Lannoy and Mr. Bart Van Ommen who have been both contributors to and co-editors of this chapter and to the following main contributors: Mr. Richard China, Mr. Joseph Domenech, Mr. Clive Elliott, Ms. Tina Farmer, Mr. Henri Josserand, Mr. Peter Kenmore, Mr. Kazuaki Miyagishima, Mr. Ramesh Sharma, Mr. Mark Smulders, Mr. Henning Steinfeld, Mr. Keith Sumption and, Mr. Benoist Veillerette.

J. Wouters et al., eds., The United Nations and the European Union
© 2006, T·M·C·Asser press, The Hague, The Netherlands

legislation and creating national strategies to achieve rural development and hunger alleviation goals.

- Providing a meeting place for nations: on any given day, dozens of policy-makers and experts from around the globe convene at headquarters to forge agreements on major food and agriculture issues. As a neutral forum, FAO provides the setting where rich and poor nations can come together to build a common understanding.
- Bringing knowledge to the field: FAO's breadth of knowledge is put to the test in thousands of field projects throughout the world. FAO mobilizes and manages millions of dollars provided by industrialized countries, development banks and other sources to make sure the projects achieve their goals. It provides the technical know-how and in a few cases a limited source of funds. In crisis situations, it works side-by-side with the World Food Programme and other humanitarian agencies to protect rural livelihoods and help people rebuild their lives.

This article will first recall the institutional relationship between FAO and the EC and the evolution of their cooperation (Section 2). Section 3 presents some relevant case studies how the strategic partnership works in practice. Section 4 reviews the EC membership in the Codex Alimentarius before concluding (Section 5).

2. FAO and the EU: from Project to Programme Approach

2.1 EC membership in FAO

Initially, relations between the European Community and FAO were governed by an exchange of letters signed in 1962[1] between the President of the European Commission and the Director-General of FAO aiming to facilitate the coordination of the two institutions' activities. European Commission representatives participated as observers in FAO governing bodies meetings as well as in important technical meetings.

The European Community became a member of FAO in 1991,[2] when a modification in the FAO Constitution[3] allowed for membership by regional economic organizations. As a result, it occupies a rather unique position within the UN system. The arrangement provides for the alternate exercise of membership rights by the EU Member States and the EC. This means that the EC is entitled to exercise those rights as a full-fledged member in areas that fall within its competence. However, this alternation in the exercise of rights does not apply to FAO organizational

[1] Exchange of letters of 9 December 1962, OJ (7 June 1962) No. 043, pp. 1356-1359.

[2] Resolution of 22 November 1991, OJ (16 December 1992) C-326, p. 238.

[3] Articles II(4)–(10) FAO Constitution, at <http://www.fao.org/DOCREP/003/X8700E/x8700e01.htm#P8_10.>

questions or budgetary affairs, which are reserved for EU Member States. The EC is therefore not represented on the FAO Programme Committee, Finance Committee, and Constitutional and Legal Committees. As regards the financial arrangements, the EC is not required to contribute to the FAO budget but pays a lump sum determined by the FAO Conference and used to cover administrative and other expenses arising out of its membership.[4]

2.2 FAO-EC cooperation

Since 1991, field cooperation has gradually increased, especially after the conclusion, in January 1993, of a first administrative arrangement concerning the procedures of the technical cooperation. During the period 1993-2005, EC contributions to FAO projects amounted to approximately US $ 175 million (or about US $ 14 millions per year) and the trend is clearly upward (see chart 1).

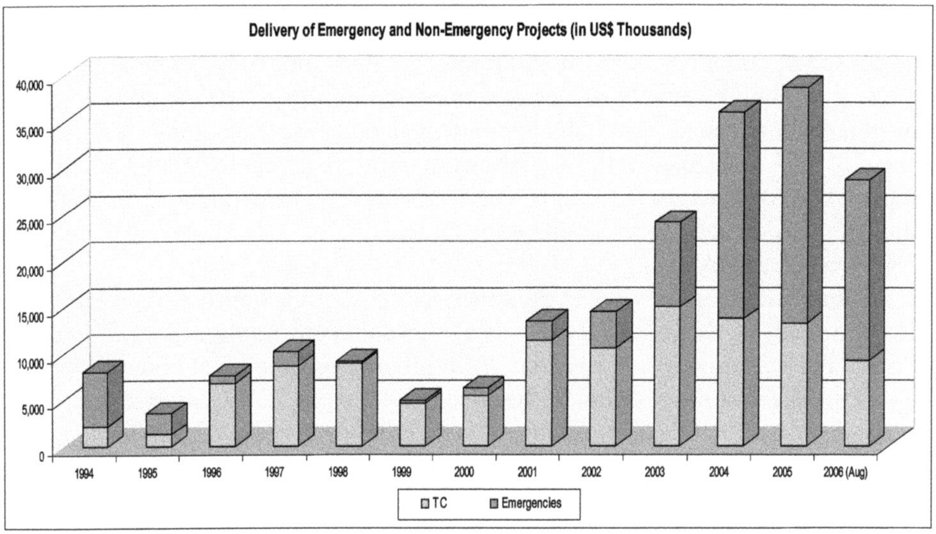

Now that the delivery of EC contributions to the FAO has reached a level of nearly US$ 40 million per year, the EC has become the largest single funding source of the field programme of FAO, representing about 10% of its total expenditures.

Although the volume of cooperation has significantly increased, especially in recent years, the EC's role goes far beyond that of a donor. In fact, over the years, the relationship between the two institutions has developed into a true partnership, aiming at complementarities and synergy between the respective programmes of work and budget. Through this partnership, (i) FAO's strategic capacities in core areas of its

[4] For more details on the practical functioning of EC Membership, see below Section 4 on the experience under the Codex Alimentarius, a subsidiary body of FAO and WHO.

mandate are strengthened, (ii) the involvement of the EC in upstream policy dialogues in fields of mutual interest is enhanced, (iii) convergence of policies and strategies is sought, and (iv) knowledge and information exchange promoted.

Moreover, the Commission's different services are involved from the early stages of project identification, formulation and monitoring. In many cases, proposals for cooperation are identified at field level, between FAO Representatives and EC delegations, while maintaining a continuous dialogue with the Commission headquarters in Brussels for policy issues, in particular through the Brussels-based FAO Liaison Office with the European Union and Belgium.

In the field programme of FAO, a gradual shift away from the project to the programme approach may be noted and this may eventually have an impact on the cooperation with the EC, as well. The shift from the project to the programme approach means that, from a situation in which only self-contained projects are delivered (normally with limited national or regional ownership and therefore often less sustainable from the institutional and public point of view), FAO is increasingly providing various mixes of technical, operational and/or financial services in the context of larger development programmes that are not managed by the Organization itself, but preferably owned and managed by the governments or regional institutions concerned. Since this approach has raised accountability issues (e.g., who will be responsible for the overall result of the programme?), the 32nd Session of the FAO Conference in December 2003 has approved a revision of the financial rules of the organization to facilitate the application of special national execution (NEX) business models.[5]

Another important development concerns decentralization (or 'devolution' in EC terminology). Since May 2000, the Commission has implemented a major reform of the management of its external aid programme, the main objectives being to make radical improvements in the speed and quality of EC external aid, while ensuring robust financial procedures. A key component of the reform is the extensive devolution of aid management tasks and responsibilities to the EC delegations in the countries concerned. As a result of this devolution, EC delegations are now responsible for project preparation, contracting, and financial and technical implementation, and they have received substantial extra staffing and technical resources. This development has obviously had important consequences for the cooperation

[5] Standard agreements are now available for any of three basic situations: (i) The first situation, which is denoted by the term *Model A*, would envisage FAO providing technical support only, with the project being executed by Government agencies. Under this model, funds would be held and managed by the government or other national entity and FAO's responsibility would be limited to the provision of technical support services; (ii) the second situation, denoted by the term *Model B* would envisage FAO providing technical support services together with financial and operational support services specified in the Agreement. Funds would be placed under the management of FAO and released for national implementation subject to the controls and monitoring mechanisms specified in the Agreement; (iii) The third situation, denoted by the term *Model C* would be similar to Model B, except that the funds would be provided to FAO by an external donor, to whom FAO would report on their use.

with the FAO and obviously poses important challenges for the FAO representations in the countries concerned.

The FAO is responding to this challenge by reforming its field structure in light of the outcome of the recent evaluation of decentralization in the FAO and of the decision by the FAO conference in November 2005 on the FAO Director-General's reform proposal for the organization. In terms of geographical distribution, during the period 1993-2005 51% of the FAO/EC projects were executed in Africa, 20% in Asia, 7% in Latin America, 6% in the Near East and 1% in Europe. The remaining 15% was used for actions of an inter-regional or global nature (see chart 2).

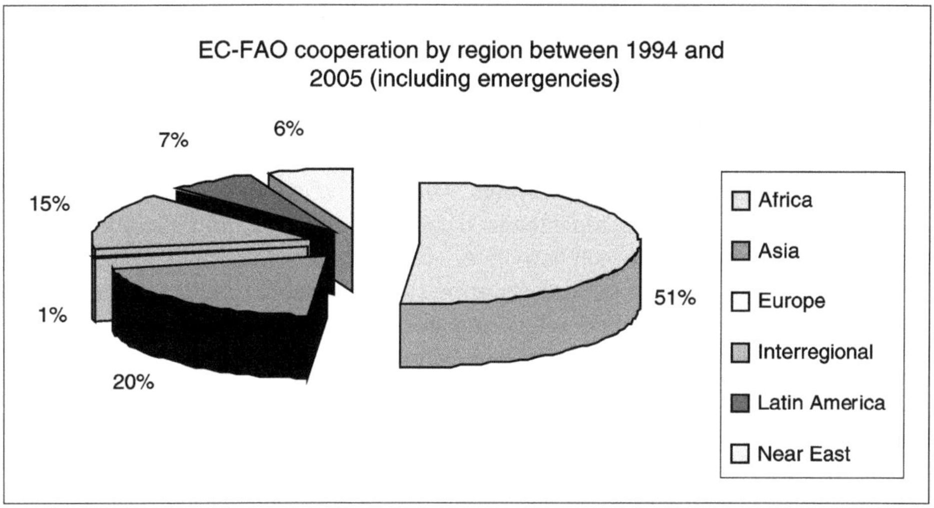

Africa has been of particular importance in FAO-EC cooperation. It was in Africa, in 1993-1994, that the Commission implemented its first emergency interventions in cooperation with FAO. However, from 1996 onwards, development projects received increased attention. In this connection, animal health, early warning systems, plant protection, seeds improvement and production, agricultural statistics, have constituted the bulk of FAO/EC cooperation.

In South and Central America, cooperation has focused on food security and nutrition in Peru and Bolivia. A long-term effort (1991-97) focused on the provision of improved seeds in Haiti, and on the protection of tropical forests in South America, with a special emphasis on the protected areas of the Amazonian watersheds.

In Asia, activities carried out in the region comprise information and analysis for sustainable forest management in South and Southeast Asia, early warning systems in former Soviet states, a major integrated pest management programme for cotton covering five countries, and a programme for seed multiplication and distribution in Afghanistan.

Since 2003 a number of important developments have taken place with regard to FAO-EC cooperation. The first was the updating of the 1991 Framework Cooperation Agreement. On 29 April 2003, a Financial and Administrative Framework Agreement (FAFA) was signed between the UN and the EC.[6] The FAO acceded to the FAFA through an exchange of letters between the FAO Director-General Diouf and Commissioner Nielson on 17 July 2003. The second development was the adoption of the EU's multilateral policy: 'The European Union and the United Nations: the Choice of Multilateralism'[7] in December 2003. This led to intensive negotiations between the EC and some UN agencies, among them FAO, with the objective of establishing strategic partnership agreements. Such a Strategic Partnership (SP) was signed by the Director-General of FAO and the responsible EC Commissioner in September 2004 on the basis of Article 302 of the EC Treaty and the FAO Constitution.

The overall objective of the SP is to work towards the shared Millennium Development Goals by making the greatest possible contribution to alleviating rural poverty and hunger in developing countries. This will be achieved through enhanced policy dialogue at all levels and enhanced cooperation in the field, including financial cooperation on operational activities. The SP covers five main areas of cooperation (and 15 sub-areas): (i) food security; (ii) sustainable rural development and agricultural policies; (iii) food safety and quality; (iv) natural resources management; and (v) statistical cooperation and information exchange.

Finally, the context in which country-level UN agencies, funds and programmes are working has changed. The Millennium Declaration and the Millennium Development Goals (MDGs) provide a framework of outcomes agreed by governments worldwide. Increasingly, national development and poverty reduction strategies (including PRSPs) are geared to the achievement of the MDGs. This greater degree of alignment between national and global goals and strategies, and the expectation of greatly increased resource transfers, is reflected in the growing share of budget support in donor funding, although there remains a place for projects. As set out in the Rome Declaration[8] in 2003 and subsequently in the Paris Declaration on Aid Effectiveness,[9] the international effort to harmonize and align development assistance and technical collaboration around national policies and strategies is moving ahead. Capacity development and responsiveness to needs are the key to enabling

[6] Financial and Administrative Framework Agreement between the European Community and the United Nations, 29 April 2003, at <http://europa.eu.int/comm/europeaid/tender/gestion/cont_typ/onu/index_en.htm>.

[7] Commission of the European Communities, 'The European Union and the United Nations: the choice of multilateralism', 10 September 2003, COM (2003) 526final,welcomed in the Presidency Conclusions, Brussels, 12-13 December 2003, p. 23.

[8] Rome Declaration on Harmonization, 25 February 2003, available at <www1.worldbank.org/harmonization/romehlf/Documents/RomeDeclaration.pdf>.

[9] Paris Declaration on Aid Effectiveness, 2 March 2005, at <http://www.oecd.org/dataoecd/11/41/34428351.pdf>.

partner countries to manage their own development processes. These developments are likely to influence the scope and nature of the partnership between the EC and FAO, whereby the above-mentioned NEX business models developed by FAO may become important instruments for cooperation at country level.

3. The EU/FAO Strategic Partnership at Work

3.1 **Food security**

3.1.1 *Food security information for action – The examples of Mozambique and Somalia*

The partnership between the European Community and FAO in the field of food security started in 1995, when FAO and the EC Food Security Programme (predecessor of DG8/AidCo) developed a framework for collaboration at headquarters, regional and country levels. This led to a joint programme of work in the food security domain in several countries, in particular in Mozambique, Angola, Somalia, Sudan and Palestine, but also in the Southern Africa Development Community (SADC region), the Commonwealth of Independent States (CIS), and globally under the FAO-led initiative on Food Insecurity and Vulnerability Information and Mapping Systems (FIVIMS).

Traditionally, the EC-FAO partnership in the food security domain has focused on strengthening national food security information systems, while also addressing capacity building in food security analysis, food security and nutrition policy formulation, market and trade analysis and policy support, multilateral trade negotiations on agriculture, and other food security-related interventions.

a) *The EC-FAO Food Security Programme – 'Information for Action'*
The ongoing €15 million 'EC-FAO Food Security Programme – Information for Action'[10] aims at enhancing national and local capacity to generate, manage, and use food security information from different sectors for more effective policy and programme formulation and interventions. It places special emphasis on linking short-term and long-term information needs, and aims at strengthening policy-making and programme implementation capacity by making sure information truly meets policy-makers' needs. This multi-disciplinary country-based initiative covers more than 20 countries and draws on FAO's wealth of expertise in early warning and remote sensing, economic and policy analysis, statistics, nutrition, inter-agency coordination, as well as training and capacity building. Country activities under the EC-FAO Food Security Programme take place in 3 different contexts: countries under protracted crisis and conflict; countries in a state of chronic food insecurity

[10] See <http://www.foodsecinfoaction.org/News/index.htm>.

and poverty and countries undergoing structural economic transformation. Special features of the Programme include an EC-FAO Consultancy Fund for additional studies (based on joint EU Delegation and FAO Representation requests from country level), as well as financial and technical support to the Global Donor Platform for Rural Development (GDPRD).

b) *Linkages between information and policy*

Consultations at national and international levels have revealed the FAO's major role as a coordinator and facilitator of policy dialogue among stakeholders and national actors. In this role, the FAO coordinates a series of activities and events aimed at raising awareness on the importance of accessing reliable and comprehensive food security information as the basis for policy formulation.

For example in East Africa, the Horn and Great Lakes regions, the Programme has emphasised strengthening the links between food security analyses, needs assessment and response. A Food Security Council with the participation of High-level Ministries has been established in Sudan and a Food Security Analytical Team to support governmental institutions has been set up in Kenya.

c) *Partnerships at country level: the examples of Mozambique, Somalia and the Commonwealth of Independent States (CIS)*

A particularly noteworthy partnership exists with the Government of *Mozambique* in the following domains: food security information systems development, including for market transparency; early warning and vulnerability analysis, advice on food security and nutrition policies and strategies, including the formulation of a national food security and nutrition strategy; support to the Technical Secretariat for Food Security and Nutrition (SETSAN), and; support to market and trade information and analysis, including the formulation of a national trade policy.

Another important partnership has been established in the context of monitoring and analysing the food security and nutrition situation in *Somalia*, a country under protracted crisis and without a national government for the past 13 years. Since 2000, FAO has provided overall managerial, technical and administrative support to the largely EC-funded Somalia Food Security Analysis Unit (FSAU), which provides evidence-based analysis of Somali food, nutrition and livelihood security to enable both short-term emergency responses and long-term strategic planning to promote food and livelihood security for the Somali people. In addition, the European Commission's technical team in Nairobi meets regularly with the FAO-FSAU team to ensure strong linkages between the generation of information and appropriate interventions. In this context, the EC and FAO Delegations for Somalia work closely on both humanitarian emergency and development issues. This close partnership ensures a more strategic approach to food security programming, as immediate relief efforts are integrated alongside longer-term programming which addresses the underlying causes of food insecurity in Somalia

In the *Commonwealth of Independent States*, the partnership began in the early nineties, when the EC asked the FAO to prepare a brief on the food security situation of the 15 Member States of the former USSR for submission to the G-7 meeting in Tokyo in 1992. Since then, the FAO has monitored the overall food security situation in all the CIS countries with EC assistance and has prepared many alerts and reports in the critical years of the nineties. In 2000, the nature of the partnership changed, with FAO training members of the governments of Armenia, Azerbaijan, Georgia, Kyrgyzstan and Tajikistan to produce their own food security assessments and reports, thereby assisting these countries to fulfill some of the conditions agreed with these governments in the framework of the EC-Food Security Programme mentioned above. Since April 2005, this partnership has been extended to Moldova. The new programme entitled 'Food Security Information for Action' focuses on improving the availability and quality of food security information, reinforcing the capacity of the governments to formulate policies and strategies to reduce food insecurity and poverty as well as raising the awareness of the impact of food insecurity and poverty on development strategies.

3.1.2 *Global Information and Early Warning System on food and agriculture (GIEWS)*

The FAO Global Information and Early Warning System (GIEWS) was established in 1975 to monitor the food supply and demand situation at global, regional and country levels in order to provide early warnings of impending serious food shortages.[11] For countries facing a widespread and serious food emergency, FAO and the World Food Programme (WFP) jointly carry out so-called Crop and Food Supply Assessment Missions (CFSAMs), at the request of national governments. The primary purpose of these missions is to provide accurate, timely and credible information on imminent food security problems in a country or a region so that appropriate actions, including food aid, can be taken by the governments, the international community, and others, to minimize the impact of the food emergency on the affected populations. Emergency Operations (EMOPs) of WFP are jointly approved by WFP and FAO to ensure that agricultural markets are not distorted by excessive food aid.

a) *EC funding to help improve Crop and Food Supply Assessment Missions (CFSAMs)*

Since January 2004, GIEWS has been engaged in a dialogue with the important donors and stakeholders to find ways to strengthen the process and the methodology of Crop and Food Supply Assessment Missions (CFSAMs). Specific improvements so far include regional pre-mission consultation and coordination meetings (especially in southern Africa), preparation of guidelines for the FAO Representa-

[11] See <http://www.fao.org/giews/english/about.htm>.

tives and World Food Programme Country Directors, preparation of CFSAM timeline charts, training of staff and consultants in remote sensing technology. In addition, GIEWS is carrying out several studies to update and strengthen the CFSAM methodology and guidelines: analysis of the role and behavior of markets and prices in emergency situations, estimation of commercial imports in the context of market liberalization and inclusion of non-cereals, particularly roots and tubers such as cassava and sweet potatoes in the national balance sheet. This activity is being carried out with funding of € 500.000 from the EC. The EC/FAO Facility funded several Crop and Food Supply Assessment Missions (CFSAMs) in the past.

b) *GIEWS workstation*

The European Community has also funded the development of a web-based and integrated information system known as 'GIEWS Workstation' to serve as a key tool for food security and vulnerability analysis at global, regional and national levels. The funds are managed through the EC-FAO Food Security Programme under the supervision of the FAO Global Information and Early Warning Service (ESCG). The purpose of the Workstation is to improve the capacity of the international and national communities to manage food security and early warning-related information at different levels of detail, to streamline and standardize food security information and strengthen the links between FAO and the regional and national early warning centres. To do so, the database architecture is open, adaptable to local situations, and manageable at both country and FAO headquarter levels. The GIEWS Workstation can handle many types of information from remote sensing, Geographic Information System (GIS), data on crop and livestock production, population, prices etc...in standard format. In the next 3 years, the GIEWS Workstation programme will be installed in about a dozen pilot countries to promote national analysis for food security monitoring and early warning purposes.

3.1.3 *Productive capacity recovery programme in Sudan*

After the signature of the Comprehensive Peace Agreement of 9 January 2005 in Sudan, the EU requested FAO to build on its on-going relief operations in the country and to draw on its technical expertise and post-conflict experience in order to design the Sudan Productive Capacity Recovery Programme (SPCRP), which will cover ten of the most vulnerable states in northern and southern Sudan for a total of € 80 million. Being responsible for the preparation process, FAO established local preparation task forces, provided them with technical assistance, methodological guidance and on the job-training. It mobilized local knowledge and experience, reviewed the proposals of various stakeholders, investigated local conditions and undertook a thorough technical and social feasibility study of a number of proposed activities.

As a result of this participatory process, the Sudanese-owned recovery programme will start to be implemented in mid 2006. It will include two complementary components: (i) capacity building of public and private stakeholders in the field of agriculture and rural development to re-establish basic services (advice, animal health, marketing) in the rural areas, and; (ii) a series of eight medium size investment projects in the ten states to relatively quickly materialize the SPCRP interventions in areas particularly affected by the conflict or by droughts. Each of these projects will combine institutional strengthening, infrastructure rehabilitation, advisory services (such as Farmer Field Schools for which FAO has extensive experience in neighbouring countries) and revived access to markets to take advantage of peace. Areas of interventions include irrigation rehabilitation, livestock production and marketing, fisheries, crop improvement, feeder road rehabilitation and access to markets.

This experience shows a good complementarity between the EU (contributing financial resources in support of peace building and local capacities) and FAO (bringing its technical expertise and experience in developing local ownership of the programme) in particular in Sudan where local capacities are extremely low as a result of long-lasting conflict. Both organizations are now committed to long-term collaboration in the country. Sudanese counterparts and the EU agreed that FAO should play an important role in the implementation of the SPCRP. FAO, with the support of other UN agencies where required, will manage the overall programme, provide technical know-how, build local capacities and make sure that projects are of the highest technical standards.

3.1.4 *Stopping the desert locust invasion*

The Desert Locust *Schistocerca gregaria* (Forskål, 1775) intermittently threatens food security when unusually widespread and heavy rains fall in their semi-arid breeding habitats, resulting in a dramatic increase in numbers, swarms formation and finally the invasion into agricultural areas. This occurred in the Western Region[12] of the Desert Locust distribution area and to a lesser extent in the Central Region (9 countries around the Red Sea) from October 2003 to September 2005. In August 2004, the FAO re-established the Emergency Centre for Locust Operations (ECLO),[13] to assist the control campaign by the affected countries in their efforts to limit the damage to crops and pastures and prevent the upsurge from developing into a plague which could spread over a larger part of Africa, across the Arabian peninsula, possibly as far as the India/Pakistan border.

---

[12] This region includes Algeria, Chad, Libya, Mali, Mauritania, Morocco, Niger, Senegal and Tunisia.

[13] ECLO compromises technical experts from the Plant Production and Protection Division and operational staff from the Emergency Operations and Rehabilitation Division.

By mid-December 2005, FAO[14] appeals for international assistance had raised cash contributions up to US$74.84 million. The European Community responded to the July 2004 Appeal by approving in early October 2005 over € 25 million for locust control in Chad, Mali, Mauritania, Niger and Senegal.[15] The general objective is to safeguard the food security in the Western Region and particularly in the Sahelian countries through i) the provision of the necessary means (mainly pesticides, protective clothing, flying hours for survey and control) for treating approximately 1 million hectares of locust infestations; ii) the strengthening of the national capacities for efficient emergency and preventive locust control; iii) the implementation of good agricultural practices including the development of alternative, environmentally friendlier control methods, and; iv) a better coordination of the preventive measures at the level of the Commission for Controlling the Desert Locust in the Western Region (CLCPRO) during the 2004 and 2005 locust control campaigns. The final beneficiaries of this programme are the rural populations living in affected areas, through the assistance provided to the National Desert Locust Units, and the Plant Protection, Human Health and Environment Services in the affected countries. Thanks to funding by the EC, the FAO could strengthen the national capacities through the provision of technical, financial and logistical resources required for effective locust control. An Independent Evaluation Mission of the locust campaigns is under way and its operational findings and recommendations will be reported to all partners in order to strengthen plague prevention and the control of future outbreaks and upsurges.

Investing in the preventive approach of Desert Locust management is a much lower cost option than funding emergency control during a major upsurge. Accordingly, the Desert Locust Control Committee (DLCC), comprising 60 countries affected by the Desert Locust, adopted a preventive control strategy advocated by the FAO Emergency Prevention System for Transboundary Animal and Plant Pests and Diseases (EMPRESS): i.e., the Desert Locust component (EMPRES) Programme, which started in 1994.[16] EMPRES aims to assist affected countries to prevent Desert Locust emergency through enhanced national intervention capacities and strengthened regional cooperation. The EC has long shown interest in supporting this approach. An additional way of strengthening the Desert Locust preventive control strategy is the establishment of an emergency fund to initiate locust control operations at the time of early outbreaks and prevent them from growing into major upsurges. Improved techniques for early warning throughout the whole Desert Locust distribution area are another essential component for prevention addressed by EMPRES together with the development of more environmentally friendly products for locust control.

---

[14] FAO launched its first Appeal in February 2004 for an amount of US$9 million The amount gradually increased as the situation worsened until it reached US$ 100 MILLION IN August 2004.

[15] Project agreement (OSRO/RAF/427/EC), 2004.

[16] Programme Document, Emergency Prevention System for Transboundary Animal and Plant Pests and Diseases, Desert Locust Management in the Central Region, 2000.

3.1.5 *Restoring livelihoods in Indonesia and in Sri Lanka after the Tsunami tidal wave*

The tsunami tidal wave of 26 December 2004 in Indonesia severely damaged the provinces of Aceh and North Sumatra and hit the eastern and western coast of Sri Lanka, causing extensive damage to life and property in 12 out of the 14 coastal districts, from Jaffna along the east coast up to Gampaha on the west coast. The FAO immediately responded to assist in the early recovery and reconstruction of the agriculture and fisheries sectors and assist the poorest and most vulnerable farmers and fishers to resume their livelihoods. The European Commission's humanitarian aid office (ECHO) contributed over € 5.6 million in Indonesia and over € 4 million in Sri Lanka to FAO emergency and rehabilitations operations to provide emergency assistance for the restoration of food security and sustainable livelihoods amongst tsunami-affected fishers, farmers, women and other vulnerable groups in Aceh. Because of the positive outcome, in the second year after the tsunami a follow-up of rehabilitation projects is being envisaged.

In Aceh, the FAO and ECHO reached out to support nearly 30.000 beneficiaries in the agriculture sector alone with the provision of basic seeds and tools valued at over US$1 million so families could restart income-generating activities. Technical training was provided to farmers on saline soil crop management and leaching techniques to improve soil structure and leach salts from the roots. Workshops on sustainable aquaculture rehabilitation were conducted in cooperation with the Directorate General of Aquaculture, the Network of Aquaculture Centers in Asia Pacific. FAO is also implementing a small-scale fish processing project to help local coastal villagers earn extra income by selling dried fish. Furthermore, brackish water ponds (tambak) for fish rearing are also being rehabilitated to provide not only protein to villager's diets, but also the opportunity to make alternative income.

In Sri Lanka, and more specifically in the Northeast part of the country, FAO and ECHO are supporting more than 8.000 fishermen through the provision of fishing gear and boat repair to allow the resumption of fish production. About 500 boats are being repaired to high standards and about 15.000 sets of good quality fishing gears with accessories are being distributed. An additional 6.000 families are further benefiting from employment in small-scale workshops for the repair of damaged vessels, marketing and processing activities. Over 2.000 kits for homestead gardening are being delivered to women-headed households that lost their home and were allocated new land. Moreover, the project focuses on improving fishing techniques, post-harvest handling and processing of fish to obtain higher prices and reduce wastage, and is providing training to improve beneficiaries' nutrition and health practices. In order to strengthen coordination, minimize risk of duplication and promote good technical practices FAO is collaborating with several local partner organizations (NGOs, extension services of fisheries and agriculture departments and universities). Re-establishing livelihoods is the over-riding objective and FAO continues to focus on approaches that re-capitalize households and support services and marketing systems to promote local empowerment and community participation in helping tsunami affected coastal villages regain their way of life.

3.2 Food safety and quality – Prevention and Control of Transboundary Animal Diseases

3.2.1 *Food and Mouth Disease Commission*

Foot-and-mouth disease (FMD) is the most contagious livestock disease, and was a yearly feature of livestock agriculture in Europe until the 1970s. The devastating impact of the foot-and-mouth disease European pandemic in 1951-52, which involved almost all countries and directly affected cattle on over 800.000 farms, prompted the establishment in 1954 by European countries of a specific Commission within the framework of FAO to coordinate efforts at regional level (EUFMD Commission). The threat of invasion of exotic virus types of food and mouth disease to which European livestock were not protected resulted in the establishment of a Tripartite (FAO/EC/International Office of Epizootics) decision-making mechanism in the late 1950s. It utilises the FAO/UN capacity, especially through the EUFMD Commission, to rapidly implement projects, including routine and emergency vaccination campaigns in the strategic gateways through which the virus has often entered Europe. This mechanism enabled Europe to largely keep out the various waves of exotic viruses that have been swept through West Asia and the Near East in each of the past 5 decades.

The Tripartite decision-making mechanism has also been used for addressing crisis situations in areas outside of the EU which immediately threaten the health status of livestock in the European region. Examples of such crisis situations include FMD incursions into the Balkans in 1996, in North Africa in 1999, as well as regular and emergency actions to prevent the FMD spread through the 'gateways' - mainly in the southern Balkans (Thrace region), and the Caucasus. The disastrous food-and-mouth disease epidemic in the United Kingdom in 2001, which did not originate close to Europe in the traditional risk areas, but from a much more distant source, and which spread further to three other EU Member States, has shifted political and technical attention to the other sources of infection in around 60 countries in parts of Asia, Africa and South America.

As the EU membership grew, so did the importance of the EC contributions to the multi-donor trust funds (MDTF). In later years a separate fund for EC and EU Member States' contributions was established. The recent 2005-2008 agreement of some € 4.5 million between the EC and the FAO recognizes the need to address the problem of widespread global infection as a potential source of infection for Europe, and, in relation to the expansion of the EU to the east, to extend measures to protect Europe from virus invasions coming in from west Asia.

3.2.2 *Avian influenza: stopping the disease at its source*

Safeguarding animal production and human health are major objectives of both the FAO and the EC and their respective services are working together to reach these common goals. Highly Pathogenic Avian Influenza (HPAI), due to a H5N1 virus, has become a very important issue over the last 2 years for animals as well as being a high risk for humans. The crisis has devastated the poultry sector in several Asian countries, with severe socio-economic impacts on producers, in particular small holder livelihoods, domestic and international trade and food security. The risk for human health is of major concern since the HPAI/H5N1 avian origin virus could mutate or reassert its genes with an AI virus from humans (seasonal influenza) and then become a new virus that is highly contagious and pathogenic for humans. Several international avian influenza pandemics in humans have already occurred in the past, and the new H5N1 virus in Asia could be responsible for a new human pandemic.

The FAO has immediately responded to the crisis in early 2004, and invested $ 5.5 million to implement seven National Technical Cooperation Programmes (TCPs) in infected countries and six Regional or International TCPs to assist countries in developing prevention and control strategies, improving surveillance and diagnostic capacities, protecting farmers and workers from infection and implementing control programmes to fight against the outbreaks. More recently, FAO has added another US $ 4 million to implement 9 regional TCPs in regions newly at risk (the Middle East, Eastern Europe and the Caucasus, West Africa, Eastern and South Africa, North Africa, South and Central America and the Caribbean). Since the beginning of the crisis, the collaboration with the European Commission and the European country members has been active in various ways, such as direct support from certain country members of to FAO activities (France, the Netherlands), contributions of European experts to FAO programmes especially through participation in country missions (UK, the Netherlands, Germany, France, Italy), training and laboratory diagnostics. Several European institutions have been strongly involved in the implementation of the FAO's TCPs.

FAO experts have participated in EC meetings, particularly those organized by the DG Health and Consumer Protection and were also involved in the working group of the European Food Security Agency (EFSA). FAO has also contributed to the preparation of the programmes of the DG Research on various fields related to avian influenza (vaccines, epidemiology, and role of wild birds) through its participation in several meetings and its involvement as a member of the EU Technology Platform for Global Animal Health.

The role of migratory birds in disseminating the virus over a long distance was strongly supported by recent epidemiology evidence in certain parts of China, Mongolia and Russia and FAO alerted the European countries and the rest of the world on the possible expansion of HPAI from Asia to the Middle East, Europe and Africa. Following the contamination of Western Russia, Turkey, Ukraine, Romania and Croatia, the European Union intensified surveillance, particularly on wild birds, prepared itself to combat the disease in case of an outbreak and developed human pandemic preparedness plans. FAO collaborated in the preparation of both these information and awareness campaigns. The FAO-OIE (World Organization for Animal Health) Global Strategy to prevent and control avian influenza was used as a basic document by the EC and European Union country members to support developing countries to eradicate the disease. It was also used for the development of regional and national strategies.

With regard to the international dimension of the crisis, the FAO and the EC have collaborated closely to increase support to contaminated countries or to new countries and regions at risk. At an important meeting held in Geneva (7-9 November, 2005) co-organized by WHO, FAO, OIE and the World Bank, with strong participation by the EC and country members participants agreed on a global action plan to control avian influenza in animals and simultaneously limit the threat of a human influenza pandemic. It was followed by a pledging Conference in Beijing, China in mid January 2006, which paved the way for massive investments from the international community to support the animal health and human health services and all involved stakeholders to prevent and combat avian influenza.

The EC and the European Member States will take part in this international effort and FAO will be one of the international agencies to implement or assist in implementing the programmes at the national, regional and global levels. This HPAI crisis shows time and again that due to globalization and environmental changes, highly contagious diseases are of transboundary nature and that the best way to prevent their introduction to Europe and other non infected countries is to address the disease at source, which is – most of the time – in the developing world. FAO is ready to strengthen its collaboration with the EC in the field of animal health and veterinary public health for the common benefit of European country members and developing countries.

3.3 Sustainable rural development and agriculture policies

3.3.1 *Assistance of developing countries in agricultural negotiations*

The *Plan of Action* of the World Food Summit[17] commits the FAO to assist developing countries on trade issues and, in particular, in preparing for multilateral trade negotiations, including in agriculture, fisheries and forestry, *inter alia*, through studies, analysis and training.

With mounting requests by Members for technical assistance on trade-related issues, the FAO formulated in 1999 an *Umbrella Programme for Training on Uruguay Round and Future Negotiations in Agriculture* The programme entailed de-

[17] Rome Declaration on World Food Security and World Food Summit Plan of Action, 13-17 November 1996.

veloping resource manuals on key Uruguay Round trade agreements relevant to agriculture, and organizing sub-regional workshops covering all developing countries and transition economies. This required substantial financial resources which were raised successfully, co-financed by the FAO and various donor countries, including the EU which contributed to the implementation of six regional workshops for the African, Caribbean and Pacific countries.

A total of 14 successful regional workshops were organized where 846 trade officers from 151 developing countries and countries in transition participated. As trade negotiations and trade policy issues continued to take the centre stage in development and requests for FAO assistance in these areas intensified, the FAO adopted a successor programme – Umbrella II – in 2001, which continues to be implemented.[18]

3.3.2 *Livestock and environment – promoting environmentally sustainable livestock production*

The EU has been instrumental in the conceptualization and implementation of the Livestock, Environment and Development (LEAD) Initiative. The LEAD Initiative is an innovative inter-institutional project to address the complex interactions between livestock, environment and development. LEAD focuses on the protection and enhancement of natural resources as affected by livestock production while alleviating poverty and preserving human health. The EU participates in the multi-donor LEAD steering committee providing guidance for the development of the LEAD programmes. The EU has provided funding for two major LEAD activities, namely a project on industrialisation of the livestock sector in the peri-urban areas of developing countries elaborating policy recommendations and strategies for environmentally and socially more sustainable livestock development, and an electronic decision support tool conceived to convert the analysis of livestock-environment interactions into concepts, terms and tools.

3.3.3 *Integrated Pest Management on Cotton*

More insecticides are used on cotton than on any other crop. From 1999 to 2004, the FAO-EU Integrated Pest Management Programme for Cotton in Asia included six countries (Bangladesh, China, India, Pakistan, Philippines and Vietnam) that produce 45% of the world's cotton. Prior to the impact of the programme, typically 15-20 sprays were applied per season.

Through educating farmers in integrated pest management (IPM), Farmer Field School Programmes (FFS) help farmers so that profits can be increased, health risks reduced and production made more sustainable. Farmers improved their crop

[18] Information on Umbrella I and Umbrella II two programmes, including projects documents, available at <http://www.fao.org/trade/capacity_en.asp>.

incomes by 25% and reduced pesticide use by more than 40%. Over 1,500 IPM Facilitators from governmental and non-governmental organizations learned in season-long courses how to educate men and women farmers. Over 90,000 farmers graduated from Farmer Field Schools and of these, over 900 became qualified Farmer Facilitators able to carry out FFS independently.

The Programme prompted countries to build their own national projects, resulting in greater ownership, initiative and commitment. To enhance institutional sustainability, the Programme promoted impact assessment, farmer research, quality monitoring and greater involvement of NGOs. The Programme emphasised a more equitable role of women and protection of the environment and agrobiodiversity. Given the impact that the Programme has achieved, the EU has become more visible in rural areas, especially in South Asia. New projects with several millions euros of national government funds have been formulated following the success of the FAO-EU IPM Programme for Cotton in Asia.

3.3.4 *The Africa Stockpiles Programme*

Several thousand tonnes of obsolete pesticides have accumulated throughout the African continent over the last four decades. These dangerous chemicals threaten the environment and surrounding communities – often the poorest and most vulnerable – through the contamination of food, water, soil, and air. The objective of the Africa Stockpiles Programme, which is partially supported by the EU, is to clean up and safely dispose of all obsolete pesticide stocks from Africa and establish preventive measures to avoid future accumulation. Bringing together the skills, expertise, and resources of a diverse group of stakeholders, the Africa Stockpiles Programme is a strategic partnership that offers a rapid, sustainable solution to this urgent problem.

An important integral component of each country project within the Africa Stockpiles Programme is a review of legislation, policy and action related to pesticide life-cycle management. Regulation of pesticides from the point at which they are produced or imported into the country, through to their distribution, sale, storage use and to the management of empty containers and waste products is the basis of a country's ability to manage pesticides. Equally important is the ability to enforce the legislation. The review is expected to highlight weaknesses that will be addressed within the scope of the ASP by designing and implementing relevant measures. Such measures may include training, expert advice, information and education programmes and limited investment in infrastructure. The ultimate objective of these activities will be to ensure that each country participating in the ASP will be better able to manage pesticides so as to avoid the accumulation of obsolete stocks in the future.

3.4 Statistical cooperation and information exchange

3.4.1 *Fisheries statistics and information system*

Fisheries are a fundamental source of food and livelihood for people around the world. The FAO's Fisheries Department is committed to supporting responsible fisheries management and the conservation of living aquatic resources for present and future generations. To facilitate and secure the sustainable development of fisheries and aquaculture, the FAO promotes the Code of Conduct for Responsible Fisheries.[19] The European Union supports the Code of Conduct, recognizing that responsible fisheries management is essential to deal with the increasing threats to ecosystem diversity and productivity and to the sustainable contribution of aquatic resources to the nutritional, economic and social well-being of the world's growing population. The EU has proven instrumental in strengthening responsible fisheries: it has consistently underlined the need for effective management throughout the fisheries chain – from catching, to landing, to marketing, to consuming – and has backed many actions bolstering sustainable fisheries. Several programmes, drawing on FAO expertise and experience, have been actively supported by the EU, serving as a means to forge strong partnership initiatives.

In recent years there has been a growing concern for the health of Mediterranean fisheries whose stocks risk being over-fished to the point of depletion. In response, FAO has focused on optimizing the management of fisheries in the Mediterranean. Accurate multidisciplinary knowledge of fisheries and fishery resources is a prerequisite for sound policy-making and responsible fisheries governance. To help acquire such reliable information, FAO partnered with the EU to develop MedFIss (Fishery Statistics and Information System in the Mediterranean).[20] The General Fisheries Commission for the Mediterranean (GFCM) approached the European Commission for assistance in upgrading national fisheries statistics and information systems throughout the area. MedFIss was endorsed for an initial three-year duration beginning in 2004 in order to develop and establish a region-wide integrated statistical fisheries information system for the Mediterranean, which will serve as the basic mechanism for national and international bodies to monitor the state of the Mediterranean fisheries. Such a system would be based on national fishery statistics systems, enhanced and standardized with the assistance of MedFIss to meet both national and international requirements. This regional system is designed to ensure that the information necessary for tracking sustainability indicators and establishing reference points is collected in a reliable and timely manner. The main tenet of MedFIss is to promote and support the process of standardizing

[19] The Code of Conduct for Responsible Fisheries was adopted at the Twenty-eight Session of the FAO Conference on 31 October 1995 as Resolution 4/95.

[20] 'Fishery Statistics and Information System in the Mediterranean' (MedFIsis) GCP/INT/918/EU, signed July 2004.

and regionalizing an essential multidisciplinary information-base, a necessary condition for the responsible management of Mediterranean fisheries. This regional perspective is pursued through concerted and coherent actions implemented at country level.

4. Regulatory Frameworks: Codex Alimentarius and International Plant Protection Convention

4.1 Codex Alimentarius

4.1.1 *International trade and food-safety regulation*

The Codex Alimentarius Commission – CAC or 'Codex' for short – was created as a joint subsidiary body of the FAO and the WHO in 1963.[21] The founders of Codex were first and foremost concerned with protecting the health of consumers and ensuring fair practices in food trade. Through harmonisation, they envisaged fewer barriers to trade and a freer movement among countries, which would benefit populations and would help to reduce hunger and poverty. Over the years Codex has created a voluminous body of international food-safety regulation, comprising several hundred standards in the strict sense, thousands of residue limits, and dozens of guidelines and codes of practice.

Codex standards and related texts have always provided guidance on food safety and quality for use by governments. Their application remains voluntary. Codex standards and related texts acquired a new dimension, however, as a consequence of developments in the multilateral trading system. The 1994 Uruguay Round Agreements not only brought into being the World Trade Organization (WTO), but for the first time also incorporated agriculture and food under operationally effective rules and disciplines. The Agreements on the Application of Sanitary and Phytosanitary Measures (SPS Agreement) and on Technical Barriers to Trade (TBT Agreement) specifically address the problem of reconciling health and other technical regulations with the basic principles of the world trading system (non-discrimination, proportionality of restrictions). Both Agreements acknowledge the importance of harmonising standards internationally in order to address the risk of sanitary, phytosanitary and other technical standards becoming barriers to trade. With regard to food safety strictly speaking, Article 3 of the SPS Agreement explicitly refers to Codex as the provider of relevant international standards. With regard to technical regulations and standards (including packaging, marking and labelling requirements, and analytical procedures for assessing conformity with technical regulations and standards), the TBT Agreement also refers to internationally recognised standards, such as those produced by the Codex Alimentarius Commission.

---

[21] See <http://www.codexalimentarius.net/web/index_en.jsp>.

Under current WTO law, Codex standards have thus become an integral part of the legal framework within which international trade is facilitated through harmonisation. This is significant especially if seen in combination with the WTO's strengthened dispute settlement arrangements. Since Codex standards and related texts are considered as the benchmarks against which national measures and regulations are evaluated, a WTO member whose food-safety measures are based on Codex standards is effectively safe from being accused of illicitly impeding international trade. Conversely, a member whose measures go beyond Codex standards needs to provide scientific justification for the necessity of these measures, or else it risks having them declared illegal in a WTO dispute settlement.

4.1.2 *EC accession to Codex*

a) *Reasons and negotiations*

The European Union as a whole is the world's largest exporter and importer of food, and thus clearly has large stakes in the development of international food standards. Within the EU, most food-safety legislation has been harmonised since the early 1990s at the latest, as a precondition for the functioning of the internal market. And in 2003, after a lengthy process of both internal and external negotiations, the European Community became a Codex member in its own right, alongside EU Member States.

Prior to that, the European Commission was involved in the Codex process of standard-setting, but was only allowed to attend Codex meetings as an observer. In this capacity, the delegates of the European Commission had the right to speak only after all Codex members had spoken and had no right to vote. This situation, in which much of the food legislation in the EU was harmonised, but only EU Member States were members of Codex and therefore entitled to speak and vote, was confusing for third countries. It suggested that food legislation was still a national competence. The situation was all the more confusing as a delegate of the Member State which held the Presidency of the EU (rotating every six months) would speak on matters which were harmonised within the EU, and thus one and the same delegate could be heard speaking as EU President at one point, and as individual Member State at another.

In addition, the European Commission's status of observer also created practical coordination problems internally, since during Codex meetings the Commission delegation was sitting separated from the delegation of the EU Presidency and the Council Secretariat.

It took more than ten years for the EC to become a full Codex member – counting from the beginning of its FAO membership in 1991, which, from a purely legal point of view, would already have entitled it to be member of the CAC too. This was due to negotiations required among both EU Member States and with third countries. The Commission considered that the discrepancy between internal and external allocation of competencies weakened the European position in Codex and therefore advocated EC membership. In contrast, many Member States were satisfied with the existing situation and consequently favoured the then existing status quo. More specifically, Member States stressed potential negative consequences of EC membership for the input of their experts in Codex meetings, arguing that if these experts would no longer be in the position to speak on all matters on the agenda of a Codex meeting, their willingness to attend (and governments' willingness to finance their attendance) would decrease. Consequently, the EU as a whole would have less impact in Codex meetings than before.

These discussions led finally to a compromise between the Community and Member States, allowing delegates from Member States to speak (but not vote) on matters which were harmonized within the EC.

EC membership in Codex necessitated changes in the Codex Rules of Procedure which was debated in the Codex Committee on General Principles (CCGP). This debate concerned the membership of 'regional economic integration organizations' more generally, but it was clear that relevant decisions would exclusively concern the EC for the time being. During the discussions at CCGP, many Codex Member Countries expressed reservations against the proposed changes in the Rules of Procedure. They feared that the EC membership in the Codex would lead to an increase of its power. During the debate, it was agreed that, in case of a vote in a Codex meeting, only the votes of those Member States actually present in the meeting would count.[22] Still several Codex Members were concerned about the right of EU Member States to speak also on matters which were harmonised within the EU. One of those Members tabled a proposal according to which Member States of a regional organization would have been allowed to speak only on matters which belonged to their exclusive competence.

In view of remaining differences in the CCGP, the decision on whether or not to amend the Rules of Procedure of Codex was referred to the Codex Alimentarius Commission itself. Meeting in July 2003 in Rome, the CAC could not reach a consensus either and resorted to a roll-call vote. In the end the amendment which would enable the EC to become Member of Codex was approved by 73 countries and rejected by 12, while 13 countries abstained. With 85 votes cast in total, the amendment thus gained the necessary two-thirds majority. The Council of the European Union formally adopted its decision on accession to the Codex in November 2003[23] and, following the notification of accession made by the Director-General of the FAO, the EC became an official full member several days later.

b) *EC membership: how does it work?*

When considering the proposal for EC membership in Codex, two models were available. The first is the WTO model. As trade policy is the exclusive competence

[22] Rules of Procedure of the Codex Alimentarius Commission, Article II.8, available at <atftp://ftp.fao.org/codex/Publications/ProcManuals/Manual_15e.pdf>.

[23] Council Decision 2003/822/EC of 17 November 2003, OJ (26 November 2003) L-309/14.

of the European Community, the EC speaks with one single voice in WTO meetings. Only the delegate from the European Commission speaks on behalf of the EC, while the delegates of the Member States remain silent. The position of the EC is coordinated before and at the margin of WTO meetings. The second is the FAO model, where competencies are allocated to either the EC or Member States or both ('mixed competence') for each individual item on the agenda. Given that food legislation in the EU is not fully harmonised, the WTO model was considered inappropriate for the purposes of Codex. Therefore, the FAO model was proposed for EC membership in Codex. Hence, the division of competencies between the EC and its Member States is explicitly defined for each point on the agenda of a Codex meeting, and speaking or voting rights are allocated accordingly. More specifically, four cases exist:

- 1) Member States competence and Member States vote; this applies to organizational and procedural matters (elections and adoption of agendas or reports) or when no harmonisation at EU level has taken place;
- 2) EC competence and EC vote; concerning questions which have been completely or to a large extent harmonised at EU level;
- 3 and 4) Mixed competence with the right to vote attributed either to the Member States or to the EC, depending on the level of harmonisation.

Specific Council Working Parties are organized in order to decide on the division of competences and to elaborate common positions where possible. These meetings are preceded and followed by rounds of electronic consultations. Commission working groups with Member States experts are also used to elaborate technical EC position papers. Generally speaking, the technical expertise of the Member States, in addition to that of the Commission services, is crucial for the elaboration of EC positions, and Member States are expected to continue devoting sufficient resources to Codex matters and remain very active in this field.

In all cases, the Member States' delegations retain their right to speak and intervene in Codex meetings, as long as their interventions remain in line with the coordinated position, should one exist. Moreover, both Member State and EC delegations are free to participate in drafting sessions and working groups, where no formal decision is taken. The participating members nevertheless have to inform others of the progress of such informal discussions. Finally, the EC has officially renounced to all 'eligible functions' – concerning, e.g., the chairmanship of Codex committees – and leaves these exclusively to the Member States.

In making these arrangements work, the Codex Contact Point for the EC plays a central role. In accordance with the CAC Procedural Manual, it has been created by the Commission within its Directorate-General for Health and Consumer Protection and acts as the link with the Codex Secretariat. The Contact Point also coordinates all relevant Codex activities at EU level, in particular the establishment of common positions with the Member States, and more generally promotes Codex activities throughout the EU. In addition, the EU is currently re-assessing and re-arranging structures which enable the food industry, consumers, traders and all other stakeholders concerned to express their points of view on Codex matters, so as to ensure that its positions are elaborated with an appropriate balance of policy and technical advice.

4.1.3 *Scientific advice and dispute settlement*

From the very beginning, the work of Codex has been a risk management activity, based on sound science. Experts and specialists in a wide range of disciplines have contributed to ensure that its standards withstand the most rigorous scientific scrutiny. In the elaboration of the standards, Codex takes into account results of risk assessment and other scientific data available. Three scientific structures, although independent from Codex, are very much linked to it: the joint FAO/WHO Expert Meeting on Pesticide Residues (JMPR), the Joint FAO/WHO Meeting on Microbiological Risk Assessment (JEMRA), and most famously the Joint FAO/WHO Expert Committee on Food Additives (JECFA), which was created before the CAC itself and evaluates contaminants and veterinary medicine residues in addition to food additives.

Recent institutional developments in Europe have gone in a direction which is similar to that represented by Codex and the joint FAO/WHO expert bodies. In the EU, the independent European Food Safety Authority (EFSA) is now in charge of providing to the EU institutions the scientific expertise necessary to draft the most science-based legislation practicable. The EFSA was established by Regulation 178/2002,[24] also known as the General Food Law. Its establishment was one of the major actions identified in the Commission's 2000 White Paper on Food Safety,[25] drafted to draw lessons from the feed and food crises of the late nineties (BSE, dioxin, etc.).

The similarity of institutional structures, however, cannot guarantee that substantive scientific opinions always converge. The economic, political and cultural context of particular countries or trading blocs can also be a factor influencing the nature and significance of scientific risk assessment. That is why, sometimes, 'science' can differ from one country to another. Organizations such as Codex can ensure that these differences are reduced to a minimum and that all reasonable efforts are made to promote a high level of convergence in the approach towards the assessment and management of risk. However, they cannot prevent all conflicts over specific regulatory measures and their impact on international trade.

---

[24] EC Regulation 178/2002 of the European Parliament and the Council of 28 January 2002, OJ (1 February 2002) L-31/1.

[25] European Commission, White Paper on Food Safety, 12 January 2000, COM (1999) 719final, available at <http://ec.europa.eu/dgs/health_consumer/library/pub/pub06_en.pdf>.

If Codex standards and related texts are in line with pre-existing EU legislation on the subject, the potential for such conflicts is very small. In other, less common cases, the EU is faced with Codex standards which diverge from its own legislation. Such cases pose an important challenge for EU-UN interaction, especially since there is no particular intra-European procedure for the transposition of Codex standards into EU legislation. The example of benzoates in soft drinks, for which a maximum level of 600 mg/kg was adopted at the last meeting of the CAC in July 2004, can be used as an illustration. In the relevant EU legislation, the maximum level is set at 150 mg/kg, because this level has been shown to be sufficient to obtain the desired preservation effect and an acceptable shelf life for product. Intake estimations performed in the EU Member States have shown that the intake of benzoates by adults and children is very close to exceeding the acceptable daily intake (ADI) of 5 mg/kg bodyweight set for these substances. Taking into account that beverages are often the major contributors to the intake of additives, the EU considers the proposed level of 600 mg/kg too high to ensure that the ADI would not be exceeded. The proposed maximum level for benzoates of 600 mg/kg was finally adopted on an interim basis, with the understanding that a review be conducted within 3 years as regards intake data. The EC delegation expressed its concern about this level given the potential to exceed the ADI and the absence of technological need.[26] The EU objective now will be to submit data supporting its position to secure a review of the maximum level in Codex. However, if such data is not found to be convincing by other Codex members, the EU faces the dilemma of either adopting a Codex standard which it considers to endanger the health of its consumers, or allowing its own maximum level to continuously diverge from the Codex standard and hence run the risk of being challenged before the WTO.

4.1.4 *Wider Europe and Codex*

On 1 May 2004, the EU was enlarged with 10 new Member States, bringing the number of Members from 15 to 25 and expanding the EU population to 450 million consumers, more than the USA and Russia combined. The population of the EU will reach 485 million people very soon after the next enlargement to Bulgaria and Romania. All these new and prospective EU Member States were or are already Codex members. The new Member States are currently establishing an active Codex Contact Point in order to involve and inform all stakeholders: national administrations, industries, consumer associations, etc. In addition, dedication of adequate human resources is necessary to follow and coordinate all the Codex work at national level, participate in Codex meetings and coordination meetings at European level. Moreover, it has to be underlined again that the expertise present in each Member State is necessary for the good progress of work in Codex.

[26] ALINORM 04/27/41 paras. 27-29.

Yet European participation in Codex is not limited to the EU and its members. The importance of non-EU countries in Europe is considerable; there are another 18 countries representing more than 350 million people. In addition to the EC as a Member, Europe as a Codex region thus comprises 44 countries and represents 25% of the total members of Codex. So far, however, the participation of non-EU European countries in Codex has in general been low, with a few exceptions. There is therefore a huge opportunity to develop the real weight of Europe in Codex, and the EU is very much open for putting in place measures in this sense. The Codex Coordinating Committee for Europe (CCEURO) is an excellent forum to improve the coordination and communication among European countries and especially between non-EU and EU members. These have a lot in common, and a lot could be done to facilitate international trade and protect the European consumers by acting jointly in Codex.

4.2 The International Plant Protection Convention

The International Plant Protection Convention (IPPC) is an international treaty concluded within the framework of the FAO.[27] Contracting Parties agree to secure common and effective action to prevent the spread and introduction of pests of plants and plant products, and to promote appropriate measures for their control. The Contracting Parties undertake to adopt the legislative, technical and administrative measures specified in the Convention and in supplementary agreements. As of 1 December 2005 the Convention had 143 Contracting Parties. Secretariat services are provided by the FAO.

Phytosanitary measures are taken to exclude, or reduce the spread of plant pests and, thus, protect plant health. The Convention recognizes the sovereign authority of Contracting Parties to regulate the entry of plants, plant products and other regulated articles to prevent the introduction and spread of pests. However, such measures should be dictated by phytosanitary considerations and be technically justified to minimize interference with international trade. One of the major activities pursued through the IPPC is the harmonisation of phytosanitary measures. For that purpose, the Contracting Parties have established an international standard setting mechanism through which International Standards for Phytosanitary Measures (ISPMs) are adopted. Within the WTO Sanitary and Phytosanitary Agreement, the IPPC is recognized as the international standard setting organization for plant health.

In 1995, the text of the Convention was amended, and one of the changes in the text allowed the European Community to become a Party to the Convention. This reflected the shared responsibility for phytosanitary issues by the European Community and its Member States. After the entry into force of these amendments in

[27] International Plant Protection Convention, adopted Rome, 6 December 1951, revised, available at <https://www.ippc.int/IPP/En/default.jsp>.

2005, the European Community has become a Party to the Convention.[28] It closely works with other Members of FAO in the standard setting procedure and other activities of the IPPC. It has recognized that the participation of developing countries in standard setting is a priority to ensure wide acceptance of international standards, thus enabling trade in agricultural products. The European Community makes regular financial contributions to enable developing countries to participate in all stages of the standard setting process and in information exchange.

5. Conclusion

With regard to the institutional relationship between the EC and the FAO and the evolution of their cooperation (Section 2), the following may be concluded:

- Until the European Community became a member of the FAO in 1991 there was not much cooperation between the two institutions. In the following ten years the cooperation remained at a relatively low level, characterized by the EC simply being a donor to the FAO. More recently, the changes in EU policies towards the United Nations system have opened opportunities for a changed relationship. The Financial and Administrative Framework Agreement (FAFA) from July 2003 and the Strategic Partnership (SP) agreement from September 2004 have laid the foundations for developing a stronger partnership. Consequently, the cooperation between the two institutions has grown significantly, both quantitatively and qualitatively, in recent years, and is also likely to grow further in the future
- Although the financial contribution of the EC to the field programme of FAO is important (i.e., with 10% of the total, the EC is the largest single contributor), the cooperation is characterized as a partnership, rather than donorship.
- In geographical terms, the cooperation is mainly focused on Africa (>50%), while in terms of substance the focus is on the five principals areas of cooperation as identified in the Strategic Partnership agreement: (i) food security, (ii) sustainable rural development agricultural policies , (iii) food safety and quality , (iv) natural resources management and (v) statistical cooperation and information exchange;
- Decentralization (or 'devolution' in EC terminology) and the international trend towards harmonisation and alignment (including sector-wide approaches and budget support) are challenging the scope and nature of the cooperation and, in particular, stimulating a shift from a project to a programme approach.

---

[28] Council Decision of 19 July 2004, OJ (14 August 2004) L-267/37.

With regard to specific case studies on how the partnership works in practice (Section 3), it may be noted that project cooperation:

- tends to develop on politically sensitive issues (e.g., food security information, fish stock information and GIEWS) and where the results of the Organization's normative work may be applied (e.g., studies, guidelines, analytical tools, etc.);
- is normally based on FAO's comparative advantages as a neutral specialized agency of the UN, able to provide independent policy advice and to facilitate dialogue on issues within its mandate among wide varieties of stakeholders, including governments, small farmers, private enterprises, NGOs/CSOs, etc. (e.g., the cases of Mozambique and Somalia;
- strengthens the Organization's global emergency prevention and early reaction functions on specific transboundary issues (e.g., food crises, plant disease and animal health crises, etc);
- takes advantage of the Organization's ability to manage multi-donor trust funds to address global issues (e.g., EMPRES);
- aims to be catalytic (e.g., capacity building of LDC negotiations in world trade negotiations).

Finally, the interactions between the EU and the Codex Alimentarius Commission display the following characteristics (Section 4):

- High economic and political stakes, which result from enormous overall volume of international food trade (valued at around 500 billion euros per year) and the EU's prominent position therein, combined with the salient role of the Codex standards in WTO law;
- a slow but eventually successful process of 'Europeanisation' in the EU external food-safety policy, which created the preconditions (political, legal and institutional) for EC accession to Codex;
- difficult negotiations with non-European Codex Members regarding the conditions of EC membership;
- a history of actual EC membership, which, despite its brevity (little more than two years at the time of writing), has shown the complex internal arrangements to work smoothly;
- a pattern of convergence between EU and UN/Codex institutions for the provision of scientific advice to risk managers, which, however, may not entirely prevent cross- cultural differences in the production and evaluation of scientific evidence, and finally;
- ongoing efforts to better integrate European Codex Members which are not also EU Member States into the existing framework of multi-level food – safety governance.

As an overall conclusion it can be said that the relationship between the EC and the FAO has changed considerably over the years, and has demanded much flexibility and adaptability, especially on the part of the FAO. When problems and shortcomings arose or were identified both institutions sought to improve the situation by means of substantive and political dialogue. When changed policy circumstances opened up for increased cooperation with the United Nations, the FAO endeavoured a closer dialogue with the EC in order to enhance the cooperation. When EC policies changed, e.g., concerning decentralization and aid modalities, the FAO tried to adapt to such new situations. In brief, the experience of the FAO has been that by taking advantage of opportunities a partnership has gradually been established, a partnership which has become ever stronger, especially in recent years. The partnership is based upon the shared goal of alleviating rural poverty and hunger. The main condition for a continuing strengthening of the partnership would be to keep and deepen the confidence existing between the two institutions from a technical to a political level. This demands also that the FAO will be able to deliver the expected output as a partner and that the FAO shows itself able of adapting to an ever faster changing environment. With its continuing reform process the FAO seems to be on the right path.

Chapter 5
ILO-EU COOPERATION ON EMPLOYMENT AND SOCIAL AFFAIRS

by Rudi Delarue*

1. Introduction

The cooperation between the European Union (EU) and the International Labour Organization (ILO) has progressively intensified in recent years. Both organizations are important regulators and actors in the area of employment and social affairs. Against the background of globalisation and the gradual evolution of the EU as a global player, there is also growing political convergence on the basis of shared values.

One important common ILO-EU objective is the fostering of decent work for all in national and regional policies. In 2000 the ILO adopted an integrated agenda on this item. The same goal is reflected in the European social agenda[1] and the revised European Lisbon strategy of promoting hand in hand economic competitiveness, employment and social cohesion. Against that background, international awareness grew that combating poverty and the achievement of the Millennium Development Goals (MDGs) require both a fair globalisation and a stronger contribution of employment, social cohesion and decent work for all. World leaders stated at the UN Summit on the Millennium Declaration of September 2005:

> 'We strongly support fair globalization and resolve to make the goal of full and productive employment and decent work for all, including for women and young people, a central objective of our relevant national and international policies as well as our national development strategies including poverty reduction strategies, as part of our efforts to achieve the Millennium Development Goals. These measures should also encompass the elimination of the worst forms of child labour, as defined in International Labour Organization Convention No.182, and forced labour. We also resolve to ensure full respect for the fundamental principles and rights at work.'[2]

* Administrator at the European Commission, DG Employment, Social Affairs and Equal Opportunities; the views expressed in this contribution do not necessarily reflect the official position of the European Commission.

[1] COM (2005) 33 final.

[2] UN GA Res. 60/1 September 2005, para. 47.

J. Wouters et al., eds., The United Nations and the European Union

The leaders not only stressed the internal dimension of the decent work agenda, but also made it a central objective of international policies. This, again, had previously been emphasized by both the EU and the ILO. On the ILO side, the final report of the World Commission on the Social Dimension of Globalisation (WCSDG) had underlined the importance of the objective of decent work for all and of the social dimension of regional integration, as a stepping stone towards a stronger social dimension of globalisation.[3]

On the EU side, the process of promoting employment and social policy in external relations and external assistance was more cumbersome. Two important initial steps were the Commission communication on the promotion of core labour standards and social governance in the context of globalisation in 2001[4] and the renewed Exchange of Letters between the ILO and the Commission signed on 14 May 2001. This was followed by a 2004 Commission communication on the social dimension of globalisation supporting the recommendations of the WCSDG and tabling initial Commission proposals on the same issue.[5] These two Communications mobilised the other European institutions and the Member States. The European Council embarked on this subject in December 2004 and June 2005. The Council adopted detailed conclusions on the promotion of core labour standards in July 2003 and on the social dimension of globalisation in March 2005. The Council expressly supported the ILO decent work agenda including a more intense cooperation between ILO and EU. The Council also called for a more intense cooperation between ILO, WTO and the International Financial Institutions (IFI's) in order to improve global policy coherence. Finally, the European Parliament adopted similar positions in July 2003 and November 2005.[6] The European social and economic committee and the committee of the regions also expressed support in February and March 2005 for the ILO decent work agenda and for a stronger role of the EU in harnessing globalisation and promoting decent work.

The key EU development and external assistance objectives and implementation did not cover employment, social cohesion and decent work before 2005. The Commission proposed in July 2005 to include these themes in the future objectives and themes of EU development policy and external cooperation.[7] This resulted in a joint declaration (the European consensus) adopted on 20 December 2005 by the three EU institutions recognizing the relevance of employment, social cohesion and decent work for all as defined by the ILO in relation to development and external cooperation.[8] However this declaration will have to be implemented by the

---

[3] WCSDG, final report, February 2004, ILO, Geneva.

[4] COM (2001) 416 final.

[5] COM (2004) 383 final.

[6] Report of the EP, A05/0251/2002 (rapporteur M.H. Gillig) and Report of the EP, A6/0308/2005 (rapporteur M. Brjec).

[7] COM (2005) 311 final.

[8] Joint statement 'The European Consensus', 20 December 2005, OJ (24 February 2006) C-46/1. The European consensus on development has to be seen as a clear indication that the EU is pursuing a different approach than the Washington consensus.

programming of EC and EU Member States development and external cooperation at country, regional and thematic level.

There is also more and more interest in other parts of the world for the EU economic and social experiences and its specific model of social, economic and political integration. The EU has for instance engaged in cooperation with Latin America and the Caribbean on social cohesion and with sub-regions such as the Andean Community and Mercosur. The EU is cooperating with the African Union on employment and social policy and is exploring cooperation with the Asia-Europe Meeting (ASEM) on employment. The EU has also established cooperation with the countries of the Euro-Mediterranean Partnership (MEDA) on social protection issues. The action plans already agreed in 2004-2005 with a number of neighbours in the framework of the EU neighbourhood policy include the ILO core labour standards and other standards and objectives related to employment, social policy, equal opportunities and decent work. The ILO and its tripartite constituents could play an important role in the implementation of the action plans.

The overall cooperation between EU and ILO has to be situated in the context of both the longstanding relations between the ILO and the 25 EU Member States and of the relations between the ILO and the EU institutions. It has also to take into account the role and involvement of national, European and international organizations of employers and workers. Accordingly, this contribution will first recall the ILO's specific ILO institutional structure and then review EU participation in the different fields of the ILO activities. Finally, EU-ILO cooperation at country level will be looked at before concluding.

2. The ILO's Specific Institutional Structure

2.1 **The 1919 constitution**

The ILO was established in 1919. The Declaration of Philadelphia of 1944 updated and extended its objectives and statutes and is part of its Constitution. The ILO signed an agreement with the UN in 1946 recognizing it as the first specialized UN agency.[9]

The functioning of the ILO is different in relation to a number of key aspects from the general UN systems and the other specialized agencies. The mean features are: (1) the tripartite decision-making process; (2) the negotiation, adoption and supervision of labour standards and (3) the adoption of policy orientations.

---

[9] V.Y. Ghebali, 'The ILO, a case study on the evolution of UN specialized agencies', in R. Ago and N. Valticos, *International organisation and the evolution of world society* (Dordrecht, Martinus Nijhof Publishers 1989, Vol. 3).

2.2 Tripartite nature of the ILO decision-making process

The tripartite nature of the ILO means that not only governments but also employers and workers representatives are involved in ILO decisions. This implies that International Labour Conventions and Recommendations, conclusions on the supervision of international labour standards or policy orientations are prepared, discussed and adopted on a tripartite basis.

This tripartite representation applies to all the decision-making bodies such as the International Labour Conference (ILC), the Governing Body (GB) and sector and other technical meetings. The ILC meets once a year in June. As a plenary organ, it is the highest ILO authority and negotiates and adopts international labour conventions, recommendations and other instruments. It is also dealing with the supervision of these standards and decides on ILO policies and priorities. A national delegation at the ILC consists of representatives of workers, employers and governments. A tripartite national delegation at the ILC has 4 votes: 2 for the government, 1 for the workers delegate and 1 for the employer's delegate. Each group can use it votes in an autonomous way. The executive GB and its committees meet twice a year in a full session in March and November and a short one-day session in June and, *inter alia*, prepare sessions of the ILC, ensure the follow-up of ILC decisions and oversee the policy implementation and operations of the ILO.

2.3 Negotiation, adoption and supervision of labour standards

Under Article 19(1) of the ILO Constitution, different options for standard setting are available. The ILO may adopt legally binding conventions. Such conventions need to be ratified by ILO Member States (Article 19(5)(d) of the ILO Constitution). The ILC can also adopt Recommendations. These will be communicated to all Member States for their consideration with a view to effect being given to them by national legislation or otherwise (Article 19(6) of the ILO Constitution).

The Constitution provides for different systems of supervision. Ratified conventions and recommendations are supervised through a regular reporting system (Article 22). This implies that ILO Member States have to send in reports on the application in law and practice of ratified conventions at regular times. In addition, employers and workers can submit observations. The ILO has established a Committee of independent experts on the application of conventions and recommendations (CEACR). The CEACR submits a report to the June ILC.

The ILC establishes at each of its sessions the tripartite committee on the application of conventions and recommendations. This tripartite committee supervises the overall evolution on the application of labour standards and selects a number of cases for discussion at the ILC on the basis of the report of the committee of experts.

In addition the ILO Constitution provides the possibility to lodge representations (Article 24) and complaints (Article 26). Workers or employers organizations can file a representation of non-observance against a Member State in relation to the violation of a ratified convention. An ILO Member State can lodge a complaint against another Member State if it is not satisfied that the other Member is securing the effective observance of any Convention which both have ratified (Article 26(1) of the ILO Constitution). This procedure has not been used in practice. However more important is that one or more workers or employers delegates can lodge at the ILC a complaint against an ILO Member State for violation of a ratified convention (Article 26(4)). In such a situation, the ILO may investigate the matter and can establish a Commission of Enquiry to consider the complaint, to report on its findings and to issue recommendations to address the situation. The ILO can take appropriate action in case of continued non-compliance (Article 33 of the ILO Convention). This can include the request to Member States and international organizations to take measures of a political, legal and even economic nature against the Member State in order to secure the compliance with the ratified convention. The Article 26(4) is procedure has for instance been used in the case of Burma/Myanmar for forced labour (convention 29) and in the case of Belarus for freedom of association (convention 87). In addition the Article 33 procedure is used against Burma/ Myanmar since 2000.

The ILO has also introduced a specific system of complaints in relation to its constitutional principles of freedom of association and collective bargaining. The complaints are dealt with by the tripartite Committee on the Freedom of Association (CFA) and its conclusions and recommendations are submitted to the ILO GB. This system is very important in practice as national, regional or international workers and employers organizations can lodge complaints against any ILO Member State in case of alleged violations of the ILO constitutional principles. This system does not require ratification of the convention 87 on freedom of association or convention 98 on collective bargaining.

The ILO can also adopt other instrument then conventions and recommendations. Examples are the 1998 Declaration on Fundamental Rights and Principles at Work, the 1977 Tripartite Declaration of Principles on Multinational Enterprises, Codes of Practice such as on AIDS/HIV at work and privacy protection and non-binding frameworks such as the 2006 multilateral framework for a rights based approach to migrant workers. A possible supervision of such Declarations, Codes or Frameworks requires a specific follow-up mechanism. This has been introduced for the 1977 and 1998 Declarations.

2.4 Adoption of policy orientations

Beyond the function of standard setting, the ILO increasingly deals with policy-making. The International Labour Conference is empowered to adopt policy orientations and action plans. The ILC adopted for instance action plans on youth employment (2005), migrant workers in the global economy (2004), improving health and safety at work (2003) and on extending social protection to those excluded from current systems (2001). The ILO also engages in international dialogue in employment and social issues with other international actors and agencies such as the UN, WB, regional development banks, WHO (World Health Organization) and IMO (International Maritime Organization). The ILO is also trying to develop cooperation with the WTO (World Trade Organization).

3. EU Participation in the ILO's Activities

The ILO's specific structure has a huge impact on the ability of the European Union to participate within its work programme. This section will review the historical development of the EU's participation in the ILO and then look closer into the fields of standard setting and policy-making in current practice.

3.1 **Historical development**

All 25 EU Member States are members of the ILO and their combined regular and extra-budgetary contributions to the ILO constitute a very significant share in the ILO budget.[10] The European Community as such is not a member of the ILO, but contributes to an increasing number of ILO activities, programmes and projects by extra-budgetary contributions.[11] Furthermore, it has established close cooperation with the ILO since many years.

Given that the European Coal and Steel Treaty of 1952 included important social provisions, a cooperation agreement was signed between the European Coal and Steel Community and the ILO already in 1953. The EEC Treaty of 1957 also contained from the outset a number of social policy provisions that were of immediate relevance for ILO-EC relations such as on free movement of workers, coordination of social security schemes and equal treatment on pay between men and women. Moreover, it established general objectives and principles on the progressive improvement of living and working conditions. Against that background, the EEC Commission and the ILO Office signed in 1958, 1960 and 1961 a series of

---

[10] ILO GB, 294th session, Geneva, November 2005, GB 294/PFA/1: the combined share of the 25 EU Members States in the ILO regular budget is approx. 36.50%. The second contributor is the United States with 22% and Japan third with 19.48%.

[11] The EC extra-budgetary contributions increased very significantly since 2004. According to the ILO report No. VI on technical cooperation, submitted to the June 2006 ILC, the EC was the third most important ILO donor by 2005 with 19 million Euros. These contributions involve a wide range of activities, programmes and EC budget lines covering both internal and external EU policies. 13 EU Member States are part of the top 20 for extra-budgetary contributions (period 2000-2004). The United States is the most important single contributor with 40.60%.

agreements fixing the terms of cooperation. These were complemented and extended by Exchange of Letters of 5 October 1961 and 2 November 1961.

A new phase started with the exchange of letters of 21 December 1989 and 22 December 1989.[12] Represented by the Commission, the European Community obtained observer status in the International Labour Conference and in the Governing Body. The Commission shall ensure that ILO representatives, where appropriate, are invited to attend meetings of bodies depending on the Commission which deal with social and employment issues of interest to the ILO. The two institutions organize annual high level meetings.

In May 1999, the Amsterdam Treaty entered into force. It foresaw the strengthening of the EU social dialogue and contained new EC competences in the area of employment and social policy. The EC negotiation mandate for the WTO Seattle Ministerial Round also included detailed reference to the need for strengthening the ILO and the cooperation between ILO and WTO.[13] The Cotonou agreement between the EU and the ACP (Africa, Caribbean and Pacific) countries also included provisions on the ILO core labour standards.[14] Against this background, the Commission and the ILO Office renewed the exchange of letters on 14 May 2001.[15]

The EoL was signed on behalf of the Commission by the Commissioner responsible for employment and social affairs. Reconfirming the observer status of the Community within ILO, the 2001 Exchange of Letters also established the overall strategic framework for the cooperation as it includes all relevant internal and external EC policies. Furthermore, it recognizes the ILO as a political organization, functioning on the basis of a political mandate defined in its constitution and as a regulator establishing international labour standards. It underlines the relevance of the ILO as an actor present at global, regional and national level through its services and in particular through its tripartite constituents dealing with technical, development and political cooperation aiming at promoting the effective implementation of its strategic objectives such as the decent work agenda. Finally, in July 2004, the Commission and the ILO signed a strategic partnership in the field of development cooperation that will be implemented through the 2001 Exchange of Letters.[16] The European Economic and Social Committee (EESC) also signed in

[12] Exchange of Letters between the EC and the ILO of 21 December 1989 and 22 December 1989, OJ (1 February 1990) C-024/8.

[13] See also the annex of the Communication on promotion core labour standards in the context of globalisation, 18 July 2001, COM (2001), 416 final.

[14] However this part of the Cotonou agreement (Article 50) was not implemented as it could have been. The inclusion of the ILO decent work agenda in the 20.12.2005 European consensus on development should contribute to the effective application of Article 50 of the Cotonou agreement.

[15] Renewed exchange of Letters, 14 May 2001, OJ (8 June 2001) C-165/23. The Commission and the ILO signed on 15 July 2004 also a strategic partnership in the field of development cooperation. This partnership will be implemented through the 2001 EoL as it already includes development cooperation and as it fixes the institutional and administrative arrangements.

[16] The strategic partnership in the field of development cooperation was based on a 2001 Commission Communication on establishing partnerships between the EC and UN Agencies,

2005 a Memorandum of Understanding with the ILO. This MoU illustrates the relevance of the role of organized civil society in EU-ILO relations. However the EESC cannot represent the EC at an external forum as it is a consultative committee established on the basis of national representatives of employers, workers and other groups such as organizations of consumers and farmers. Furthermore the 1999 Amsterdam Treaty recognized the important role of bipartite European social dialogue. Unlike the EESC, the European social dialogue process is not only of a consultative nature but can result in European agreements.

3.2 General EU coordination and presentation of EU positions

3.2.1 *Coordination*

Formal EU coordination meetings in Geneva are announced, at the request of the Presidency, by the Council secretariat to the delegations of the EU Member States and the Commission in Geneva. Commission, Presidency and Council secretariat consult on the schedule and timing of initial EU coordination at the start of the ILC, the GB and other relevant tripartite meetings.

The organization of subsequent meetings depends on contextual factors, such as the complexity or sensitivity of the issues at stake, the progress made in the possible preparation of EU positions, discussions with other groups or governments and regions or countries and the tripartite discussions. Commission, Presidency and Member States also exchange views and information on the proceedings of the EU coordination taking into account the work of other groups and governments. Since the abolition of interpretation by the Council in 2004 for EU coordination meetings at the UN or UN agencies the coordination takes place in the ILO building or in the UN premises during the ILC. This has increased visibility of EU coordination and has facilitated close contacts with other formal or informal groups.

Formal EU coordination in Brussels is announced by the Council secretariat. However, such coordination is not very frequent. An exception is the preparation in 2005 of the ILO 2006 consolidated maritime convention as this text is touching upon an impressive number of EC Directives and Regulations in the field of social and maritime transport policy.

An important practical complication for comprehensive and formal EU preparations of the June ILC is the late arrival of key preparatory ILC reports and docu-

---

Programmes and Funds. However, it has to be highlighted that the ILO functioning, institutional framework and mandate are very different from for UN programmes and other UN agencies. The ILO is combining normative, political, technical and development oriented activities. The EC did not reserve a specific budget for the strategic partnerships in the field of development. The co-funding is therefore based on specific support for programmes and projects in developing countries and regions and it operates according to the same administrative and financial arrangements as the 2001 Exchange of Letters.

ments. The ILC documents are only available in March and even later.[17] In addition, the agenda of the Council social affairs working group is often very busy in the period March- May in view of the preparation of the June EPSCO Council. Therefore, the Commission and the Presidency agreed in 2005 and 2006 to organize informal expert meetings in advance of the ILC in order to prepare and facilitate EU coordination meetings at the 2005 and 2006 ILC June sessions.[18] The Commission services are also preparing Commission services information notes with a view to contribute to EU coordination and to facilitate EU coordination at the ILC.

3.2.2 *Presentation of EU positions*

At the ILC, the Presidency, or another Member State on behalf of the Presidency, presents EU common positions and amendments. In some cases, the Presidency intervenes on behalf of the large majority of EU Member States. The Commission has also the possibility, as observer, to intervene on behalf of the Community at its own initiative or in agreement with the Presidency.[19] The Commission is effectively using this possibility. However, it cannot subscribe to an amendment or a sub-amendment and cannot vote.

At the GB, EU positions are presented by the Presidency or another EU Member State on behalf of the Presidency as not all states are presented therein. Some of the larger EU Member States are permanent GB members while smaller countries are full or substitute member during three years on the basis of a rotation, depending on their affiliation with the Western or Eastern European regional groups. Non-members can attend the ILO GB as observer. The Community can also intervene in its

[17] The ILO has already made important efforts to advance the publication of preparatory ILC reports that constitutes the basis for discussions of new conventions, recommendations, declarations, revision of existing texts, resolutions and for the functioning of the supervisory mechanisms. However the ILO must ensure that comments and observations of national tripartite constituents, the international organizations of workers and employers and other relevant stakeholders are integrated or reflected in the preparatory reports. In addition the ILC cycle is on an annual basis and this practice has shown that this is rather short for ensuring a comprehensive and timely preparation.

[18] In 2005 an informal expert meeting was organized and co-funded in Brussels by the Commission on the draft convention for work in the fishing sector and on the general discussion on youth employment. The Commission also informed EU MS experts on other relevant developments such as the ongoing investigation on the alleged violation by Belarus of ILO Convention No. 87 on freedom of association under the EC GSP Regulation. The draft promotional framework for OHS on the agenda of the 2005 ILC was discussed in the margin of the May session of the preparatory government meeting of the tripartite EU consultative committee on OHS in Luxemburg. The second and final reading of the draft framework for OHS at the June 2006 ILC was discussed at an expert meeting in Brussels on 25 April 2006. Representatives of social partners were invited to attend a part of this meeting in order to exchange views. Another expert meeting will be organized in Geneva the day before the start of the June 2006 ILC on the proposed recommendation on the employment relationship.

[19] Standing Orders of the ILC (Art. 14, 9, Art. 56, 7).

capacity as observer both in the plenary, the committees or in specific steering committees.[20]

The Commission has already used this possibility, for example on the social dimension of globalisation, on employment in the global textile sector after the phasing out of the multi fibre agreement, on migrant workers, on the global employment agenda, on maritime transport, on technical cooperation issues and the annual steering committee of the programme on the elimination of child labour (IPEC).

The fact that EU positions, such as EU agreed amendments and statements, are mainly presented in the ILC and the GB by the Presidency and not by the Commission is ignoring the EC institutional arrangements as enshrined in the EC Treaty. Third countries, social partners and even EU Member States representatives tend to confuse the way the EU is expressing its positions with the nature of the competencies (EC or second pillar competences under the Common Foreign and Security Policy). The main part of EU action in ILO is covered by the first pillar (EC) covering employment, social policy, equal opportunities, development and external assistance, economic and financial affairs, enterprise policy and common policies such as trade, agriculture, fishing, transport and migration. It would be more appropriate to agree between the Presidency and the Commission on which topics EC competence is preponderate with the consequence that on these issues the Community position is presented by the Commission, whereas on other issues the Presidency could present the EU view.

3.2.3 *Recent practice*

Before 2001, EU coordination mainly concentrated on new ILO standard setting activities that affected or could have affected EC legislation such as on occupational health and safety (OHS) and on night work for men and women.[21] In return, the EU seems to have been absent in the ILO debate on globalisation before 2001, as indicated in a recent publication on globalisation and international institutions covering ILO, EU, OECD and WTO.[22]

EC Member States did not accept to organize upstream preparations in Brussels in advance of the ILC, even for complicated issues such as chemical substances or health and safety in mining. All the work had to take place in Geneva directly coinciding with the international negotiations and with discussions with other groups

[20] Standing Orders of the ILO GB, 1.9; the EC as recognized international governmental organization can intervene in all discussions without voting rights. It has therefore more possibilities to intervene then for instance an ILO Member State that is not a member of the ILO GB.

[21] ILO and the EC have developed and adopted, during the last twenty years, important new policies and standards on these issues.

[22] V.A. Leary and D. Warner (eds.), *Social issues, globalisation and international institutions, labour rights and the EU, ILO, OECD and WTO* (International Studies in Human rights, Leiden-Boston, Martinus Nijhoff Publishers 2006, Vol. 84).

such as the workers and employers, the Industrialised Market Economies organized informally in IMEC and with other countries and regions. Within national administrations and even within social partners ILO and EU affairs were in fact almost considered as two different and totally autonomous spheres. All this was very confusing for EU Member States experts arriving at the ILC in Geneva and committed to contribute in concrete terms to the promotion of decent work for all. It was neither conducive for strengthening the relevance of ILO activities and standards in the EU system at a time that the EU entered into a number of successive Treaty revisions affirming the growing interaction between internal and external policies and actions.

In recent years EU Member States have been more and more recognizing the added value of both timely upstream and on-the-spot EU coordination in particular in relation to the ILC. It contributes to a better understanding of EU internal and EU global interests and of the potential synergies between national, EU and international agendas. It also facilitates dialogue with other groups, regions and countries. A good concrete example of the high added value of EU coordination was the February 2006 maritime ILC session that adopted the ILO 2006 consolidated maritime convention. Good EU coordination also contributed to the successful outcome of the ILC 2004 general discussion on migrant workers in the context of globalisation with the adoption of an ILO action plan including the basic principles of a non-binding multilateral framework for a rights-based approach towards migrant workers. At the ILC 2005, the EU supported a very balanced resolution and action plan on youth employment. The EU coordination also facilitated dialogue and coordination with other regions such as Africa, Asia- Pacific and Latin America and Caribbean and with social partners.

The growing importance of ILO work on the social dimension of globalisation since 2000 can now also be felt in the GB.[23] The ILO GB relevant working party on the social dimension of globalisation (WPSDG) deals since 2002 with the preparatory work and establishment of the World Commission on the Social Dimension of Globalisation and the follow-up of its final recommendations of February 2004. The WPSDG also looks at the promotion of policy coherence and decent work in the context of globalisation. Both the Commission and the Presidency –or another EU Member State that is full member of the GB on behalf of the Presidency – intervenes with statements in the WPSDG.

However, EU coordination in the framework of the GB has not yet developed its full potential. A number of EU Member States tend to give priority to preparatory discussions and even statements in informal groups (mainly IMEC), even on sub-

---

[23] The 1999 Council mandate for the WTO Ministerial Seattle also included the creation of a standing forum between ILO and WTO and the strengthening of the ILO. Globalisation affects not only trade policies but also many other EU policies such as employment and social affairs, agriculture, transport, home affairs and justice, development and external cooperation, economic and financial affairs, enterprise policy, education and culture and international governance issues.

stantive issue that are of relevance for the EU such as CSR, employment strategy, social policy, technical cooperation, the selection of future themes for discussion at the ILC, the functioning of the supervisory system and the future functioning of the ILO.

Still, the EU as such is increasingly present and visible in ILO meetings and activities. The complexity, the nature and intensity of the EU-ILO cooperation and relations can vary according to the issues at stake. The institutional context for standard setting activities or for discussions on the future functioning of the ILO is of a different nature than policy dialogue and actions on the promotion of the social dimension of globalisation and decent work in third countries and regions. Technical cooperation in the context of EU enlargement operates in a different institutional setting than the one towards EU neighbourhood policy or towards other third regions and countries. It is therefore important to look at these issues separately.

3.3 Standard setting

The tripartite nature of the ILO is particular relevant for the EU's participation in the area of standard setting. It has an impact on the respective role of national, EU and international social partners. It was also an important element in the Court's opinion 2/91 opinion on the relationship between the EC and the ILO. Three issues merit consideration:

1) the role of the social partners;
2) the treatment of ILO Conventions in areas of Community competence;
3) the Community's role as regards supervision.

3.3.1 *The role of the social partners*

National social partners have the right to be consulted on issues related to the preparation of ILO instruments, their ratification and their possible denunciation. National, regional and international social partners can also use the ILO supervisory procedures towards national governments in case of alleged violations of ratified conventions and of the principles on freedom of association and collective bargaining. How is this organized on EU level, in order to prepare effective participation within the ILO?

Initially, the involvement of social partners in the EC was mainly organized through consultations of representatives of workers, employers and other groups in the European Economic and Social Committee (EESC) after the adoption of a proposal by the Commission. The EC has also established the consultative tripartite committee on health and safety and the single European Act of 1986 recognized the possibility of EC collective agreements (Article 118 EC). The nature of EU social partners' involvement changed dramatically with the European social protocol and its full integration into the EU Treaty by the Amsterdam Treaty that came into force in 1999 (Article 138-139 EC). The Commission has the obligation to promote EU social dialogue (Article 138 EC). Social partners have now to be consulted at a very early stage and they have the possibility to take over the initiative, viz. the negotiation of a framework agreement. The EU's social dialogue includes both bipartite and tripartite dialogue.[24]

These dialogues are also interrelated with national social dialogue in EU Member States as EU social partners have to be composed of national organizations that are part of national industrial relations systems.[25] EU social partners and national social partners are also linked to international or global organizations.[26] All this is of particular relevance for EU-ILO cooperation.

In practice, EU and even global social partners are increasingly consulted and involved on EU-ILO issues including standard setting activities, the promotion of the social dimension of globalisation and of decent work for all. For instance, the consultations are intense in relation to the preparation, the adoption and the follow-up of the ILO consolidated 2006 convention on maritime transport, the ongoing work on an ILO convention on work in the fishing sector and on the promotional framework for health and safety at work as these issues are very relevant for EU policy.[27] EU and global social partners have also expressed an interest towards closer involvement in EU external actions on employment, social cohesion, decent

---

[24] Bilateral EU social dialogue: the cross industry social dialogue committee and the sector social dialogue committees; Tripartite EU social dialogue: the EU tripartite summit on growth and employment.

[25] Criteria for the representativity of EU social partners: Communication (COM) 1998, 322 final; Commission Decision of 20 May 1998 on the establishment of Sector Dialogue Committees promoting the Dialogue between the social partners at European level, OJ (12 August 1998) L-225/27.

[26] The main international organizations of workers are the ICFTU and the WCL. Both are based in Brussels. The ICFTU has its headquarters in the same building as the ETUC (European trade union confederation). ICFTU and WCL are engaged in a process of transforming their organizations into one new global trade union by 2006. The International organization of employers (IOE) organizes the main national organizations of employers (only one for each country) and is based in Geneva while UNICE (European employers federation) is based in Brussels. The historic division of competence between IOE and UNICE (IOE is dealing with ILO and international issues and UNICE with the EU) is not necessarily facilitating the discussions on ILO-EU relations as these are by definition covering at the same time EU, ILO and global issues. EU Member States social partners, global social partners and EU social partners are also involved in the respective OECD consultative committees for workers (TUAC) and employers (BIAC). The good and effective interplay between the different levels of social partners' activity and competences is a challenge in relation to strengthening the policy coherence in a globalised world. EU, national and global authorities are also confronted with this challenge.

[27] The consolidated ILO maritime convention was adopted almost unanimously in February 2006 by the maritime session of the ILC. It consolidates and updates 60 existing conventions and recommendations. An important number of issues included in the new convention are covered by general or specific social or transport policy related EC Directives. The same goes for the ongoing work on a possible future ILO convention (scheduled for adoption at the June 2007 ILC) on work on seagoing fishing vessels and on health and safety at work. The maritime transport sector and the fishing sector have also established EU sector social dialogue committees.

work and the social dimension of globalisation in EU external assistance in third countries and regions, development cooperation, trade and trade related initiatives such as the EU Generalised System of Preferences (GSP) and Sustainable impact assessments (SIA).

3.3.2 *Treatment of ILO Conventions in areas of Community competence*

All EU 25 Member States have ratified the eight ILO core labour standards or have almost completed the ratification.[28] The ILO core labour conventions on the prohibition of child labour, on equal wage between men and women for work of equal value and on the prohibition of discrimination in employment are also covered by EC Directives. The ILO core labour standards on freedom of association and collective bargaining are very relevant for establishing the fundamental principles underpinning EU social dialogue. The large majority of EU Member States have ratified other priority ILO conventions such as labour inspection (No. 81), labour administration (No. 150), tripartite consultations (No. 144), the employment convention (No. 122), the minimum standards on social security(No. 102) and one or more conventions on minimum wage fixing mechanisms (No. 26, 131).

In contrast, the EC itself has not ratified any ILO convention. This is, however, not because of a lack of political will within the Community institutions, but because of the constitutional ILO framework. Regional integration organizations based on voluntary pooling of competences and regional social partners did not exist in 1919. They are by definition not mentioned in the 1919 ILO Constitution. In order to promote the ratification of conventions the Commission has already addressed recommendations to EU Member States requesting the speedy ratification of a convention such as convention 182 on the worst forms of child labour.

ILO international labour conventions, recommendations and resolutions are adopted by a tripartite vote at the ILC. There is no *ad hoc* process of identification of signatory parties depending on the subject and the competences at stake. Under Article 19 of the ILO constitution, regional integration organizations cannot be party to an ILO convention. This explains why the introduction of a classic REIO (regional economic integration organization) or RIO (regional integration organization) clause as used in the UN system and other organizations is not possible in the ILO. However, ILO conventions can refer in their substantive provisions or in the preamble to REIO or RIO. This is for instance the case in the 2006 consolidated maritime convention in relation to the rules for determining the applicable social security scheme (Title IV). Furthermore, the constitutional bar for the EC to become a party to ILO Conventions does not mean that it cannot or does not play a

---

[28] Estonia, Latvia and the Czech Republic were finalizing the ratification of the convention No. 138 or convention No. 182 on child labour. However they were bound by the EC Directive on the protection of young persons at work that also include the minimum age at work.

very significant role in the preparation, the negotiation, the adoption, the implementation or even in the ratification process.

The problem of the EC competence was raised for the first time during the preparation and adoption of the ILO convention No. 153 on working hours and rest periods in road transport (1977-1979). This area was at that time covered by Regulation No. 543/69 EC of 25 March 1969.[29] The Commission referred to the landmark ECJ judgment in the so-called AETR case under which the ECJ confirmed exclusive external EC competence to negotiate international agreements that affect Community law.[30] A similar problem arose during the preparation of convention No. 162 concerning health and safety in the use of asbestos (1983-1986) and in relation to the convention No. 170 concerning safety in use of chemicals at work (1988-1990). The Commission presented proposals for Council decisions defining the EC negotiation mandate and the procedures under which the EC could present its positions at the ILC. The Council did not agree with the Commission. Commission and Council could only reach a satisfactory solution in 1986 on a decision of general scope on the arrangements governing EC participation in negotiations on ILO conventions falling within the exclusive competence of the EC.[31] On 30 November 1989 the Council adopted also a Decision authorizing the Commission to negotiate on the convention Nr. 170. The other issues were not addressed.

The ILO Office was very helpful by presenting documents on 12 February 1981 and 31 May 1989 with a view to facilitate EC participation in various ILO negotiations. These two documents provided amongst other things the possibility that EC Member States could authorize the Commission to present amendments at the ILC and that the ILO conventions affecting EC competences could be submitted to the Council.

Unfortunately, the legal battle between Commission, EC Member States and even national, European and international social partners continued to dominate the relations. In 1991, the Commission requested from the ECJ an opinion on the EC's competence to conclude ILO convention No. 170. The ECJ gave its opinion 2/91 on 19 March 1993.[32] Basically, it took a pragmatic approach and underlined the duty of cooperation between the EC institutions and the EC Member States. As the EC could not become a member of ILO Conventions under the ILO Constitution, the EC had to act through its Member States. The ECJ did not provide operational guidance on how this cooperation between Commission and Member States should or could be organized.

The ECJ also stated that the conclusion of ILO convention No. 170 is a matter which falls within the joint competence of the EC Member States and the EC. The

---

[29] Council Regulation 543/69/EC of 25 March 1969 on the harmonisation of certain social legislation relating to road transport, OJ (29 March 1969), L-77/49.

[30] ECJ, Case 22/70, [1971] *ECR*, p. 263 et seq., paras. 17-18.

[31] Council Decision, 22 December 1986.

[32] ECJ, Opinion 2/91, [1993] *ECR* I-1061, pp. 1077-1080.

ECJ concluded that only parts of this convention fall within exclusive EC competence. In fact, the large majority of EC legislation is setting minimum standards. EC Member States can maintain or impose higher standards under EC law. Similarly, according to Article 19(8) of the ILO Constitution, ILO Member States can always set or maintain a higher level of protection than the international labour conventions. Hence, most of the ILO conventions relate to mixed competences. However, some are touching upon one or more elements affecting exclusive competences such as convention No. 185 on the seafarers' identity documents and specific parts of the ILO 2006 consolidated maritime convention.

The Commission presented in 1994 a communication and draft Council decision on the exercise of Community's external competences at the ILC. The objective was to provide a general procedure for negotiation and conclusion of international labour conventions falling within mixed or joined competences.[33] The Commission took into account the ECJ opinion 2/91 and the need to respect tripartite consultations with organizations of workers and employers. The proposal was only discussed once by the Council social affairs working group. The Member States did not support the proposal. A crucial point of criticism was that the proposed procedures were considered as too formalised and too detailed such as on presenting formal joint replies to ILO questionnaires on future conventions.

At the same time, a number of proposals such as the organization of effective coordination meetings and the presentation of positions and amendments by the EU Presidency are now more and more used in practice.

The Council has adopted on 21 April 2005 a negotiation mandate on the conclusion of the ILO 2006 consolidated maritime convention. The Council has also authorised the EU Member States in 2004 to ratify Convention No. 185 (2003) on the seafarers' identity document in the interest of the Community, as this was touching upon exclusive EC competences on visa.[34]

Another difficult issue was the prohibition of night work for women (convention No. 89) as the ECJ was of the opinion in 25 July 1991 that this prohibition was violating the EC Directive on equal treatment between men and women in employment as the ban was only covering women and not men. The Commission requested the EC Member States to denounce the convention. Social partners, and in particular the workers, argued that this request has not been sufficiently discussed in a tripartite way. They also argued that the EC policy on night work should not be limited to providing a negative message (denunciation) but that it should also include strong positive steps such as recommending the ratification of the convention No. 171 (1990) on addressing the conditions of night work for both men and women and the need to adopt an EC Directive on improving health and safety of night work for both provisions on night work. In the meanwhile the EC adopted in November 1993 a Directive on the organization of some elements of working time including

---

[33] COM (94) 2 final.

[34] Council Decision of 14 April 2005, OJ (30 May 2005) L-136/1.

some provisions on night work.[35] The Commission services and the ILO Office jointly indicated at the 2005 annual high level meeting that EU Member States should also consider the ratification of up-to-date conventions that provide protection for both women and men such as convention No. 171.

3.3.3 *Supervision*

The EU has been more and more active in the ILO's system of supervision as well. It intervenes in the relevant ILC and ILO GB discussions on the situation in certain ILO States. For example, EU positions were presented on the follow-up of the 2000 ILC resolution on forced labour in Burma/Myanmar at the ILC and the ILO GB and in other relevant cases discussed in the tripartite ILC committee for the application of conventions and recommendations in cases such as freedom of association in Belarus, Zimbabwe and Colombia. The EU intervened at the 2004 ILC with a general statement in which it strongly supported the ILO supervisory system following strong criticism on the ILO system by some like minded countries such as Belarus, Cuba and Sudan.

The ILO applied in 2000 its procedure under Article 33 of the Constitution against Burma/Myanmar. By that time the EC had already suspended the EC Generalised System of Preferences (GSP) benefits for Burma/Myanmar since 1998 following a complaint by the European and international trade unions because of serious and systematic violations of the prohibition of forced labour. In addition the EU imposed, after the ILO Resolution, other measures (such as a visa ban for members of the military junta and their families and targeted measures of an economic nature) based on the EU common position that is regularly reviewed. In the case of Belarus the EC has launched in 2004 its internal procedures that could result in the temporary withdrawal of GSP following a complaint by the European and international trade unions because of the systematic and serious violation of ILO conventions Nos. 87 and 98 on freedom of association and collective bargaining.[36]

---

[35] ILO has adopted since 1919 conventions aiming at protection women from dangerous and hazardous work by prohibiting these activities for women and young workers such as conventions No. 41 and 89 on the prohibition of night work for women and convention No. 45 on mining. However this approach has gradually been replaced by ensuring better working conditions for both men and women in line with equal treatment between men and women. In the meanwhile the ILO has classified the old conventions Nos. 41 (1934), 45 (1935) and 89 (1948) as obsolete ones and has adopted convention No. 170 (1990) on night work for men and women and convention No. 175 (1995) on health and safety in mining. The ECJ ruling was confirmed several times and most recently in the case C-203/2003 of 1 February 2005. However the ECJ clarified in this recent ruling that EU Member States that are confronted with conflicting obligations (respect for ratified ILO conventions on the hand and EU law on the other hand) are not violating the EU treaty as long as they cannot denounce the ILO convention. ILO convention can only be denounced every ten years during a limited period of time.

[36] EC GSP can be suspended because of systematic and serious violation of ILO core labour standards. For the 2006-2008 GSP scheme see Article 16(1)(a) of Council Regulation 980/2005/EC of 27 June 2005, OJ (30 June 2005) L-169/1.

The EU intervened at the ILO GB March 2006 session with a statement urging the Belarus government to implement the recommendations of the Commission of Enquiry. The EU statement referred also to the EC GSP as the lack of commitment by Belarus towards the ILO will affect the ongoing GSP procedures in relation to the possible temporary withdrawal of GSP benefits.

3.4 *Policy-making*

EU interventions in the ILO are no longer reserved for standard setting activities. The EU also intervenes in general tripartite debates covering issues with EU relevance such as 2003 ILC general discussion on the employment relation, the 2004 ILC action on migrant workers and the 2005 ILC resolution and action plan on youth employment. The EU expresses agreed positions on the application of standards at the ILC and the GB. Both Member States and the Community participate since 2003 in the debate on the social dimension of globalisation in the framework of the ILO GB working party on the social dimension of globalisation. The EU supports the establishment of closer relations between the ILO and the WTO.[37]

The Commission also intervenes on behalf of the Community whenever necessary in the debates at the ILC and in other meetings with a view to clarify or present relevant EC policy or legislation. These interventions are based on the Community observer status in ILO. The Commission informs and consults the EU Presidency on these interventions as this is part of the duty to cooperate between EU institutions under Article 10 EC.

4. ILO-EU Cooperation on External Assistance to Third Countries

EC-ILO cooperation on external assistance to third countries was very limited before 2001. This was in part due to the different nature of ILO and EC financial regulations. The ILO follows UN rules on contracts, overhead costs and audit. The 2001 renewed exchange of letters, the new EC financial regulation and in particular the adherence in July 2004 of the ILO to the EC-UN Financial and Administrative Framework Agreement[38] contributed to the solution. In addition, employment, social cohesion and decent work were not included in mainstream EC development and external cooperation. All this was not conducive for establishing a wide ranging cooperation although both institutions share from the outset the same values.

[37] Council conclusions of 21.07.2003 and 03.03.2005.

[38] This is also facilitated by the Exchange of Letters of 14 May 2001 between the European Commission and the ILO and by the signature on 8 July 2003 of the adherence of the ILO to the EC-UN financial and administrative framework agreement (FAFA), available at <http://europa.eu.int/comm/employment_social/international_cooperation/ilo_front_en.htm>.

Relations with ILO were very important for the 10 Member States that joined the EU in 2004. In particular the eastern and central European countries had to restructure their entire labour relations system and they had to adjust their social protection systems after 1989. The ILO conventions and technical cooperation contributed to this adjustment at a time where the EU Treaty did not yet include an employment chapter, a method of coordination for social security and social inclusion or an operational social dialogue system. Key EU social legislation was enacted after 1993 after the entry into force of the Maastricht treaty with the social protocol and the Amsterdam treaty. The efforts on the implementation of the *acquis communautaire* were concentrating on the existing legislation such as occupational health and safety and some chapters of labour law. In addition the strong financial and political position of IMF and World Bank the World in the region after 1989 was accompanied by an ideological social agenda on social security and labour relations reform.

The financial capacity and by consequence of the impact of these institutions was much stronger than the ILO (and the EU) in a number of countries. This influence is still ongoing in the current enlargement process although the impact of the EU policies is much stronger now then in 1995. In addition the World Bank has progressively modified its political agenda as it recognizes, at least to a certain extend, the positive role of social protection, of labour administration and of social and economic security in social and economic reform.[39]

5. Conclusion

The EU and the ILO considerably strengthened their cooperation since 2001. That year a renewed Exchange of Letters between the European Commission and the ILO Office established the foundation for the overall cooperation framework covering both EU internal and EU external policies and actions. The agreement highlighted that both institutions pursue similar values, methods of work and approaches through the European social agenda and the EU Lisbon strategy at the one hand and the ILO decent work agenda on the other hand. The cooperation intensified in practice in 2003 with the first annual high level meeting under the 2001 Exchange of Letters and the intensification of EU coordination in the ILO.

---

[39] Enhancing job opportunities, Eastern Europe and the former Soviet Union, World Bank, 2005. However the report is still recommending approaches that are contrary to a number of EU policies such as on the promotion of social dialogue, including collective bargaining, at sector level which is very important for the promotion of the establishment and functioning of employers and workers organizations in countries in transition, in particular in the services sectors (p. 234 of the report). The strengthening of social partners at all levels is a precondition for future responsible and autonomous collective bargaining (this is also recommended by the report) in potential candidate countries and EU neighbouring countries.

The full involvement of the organizations of workers and employers in the ILO decision-making process and the adoption of its conventions and policies under the procedural rules of its 1919 Constitution are unique in the international multilateral context. The implication of the tripartite constituents is not only relevant for the ILC or ILO GB but also for the regional and national level. Therefore, the ILO has to be considered as both a regulator, an actor in development and a knowledge centre. This effective involvement of civil society related to the world of work is a unique feature. The WCSDG and also the Commission have already proposed to strengthen the role of civil society in other international organizations.[40]

The EU is much more than an intergovernmental organization as it is based upon a voluntary transfer and pooling of competences and interests by its Member States. The EC Treaty fully recognizes the role of the organizations of employers and workers in standard setting through social dialogue including collective bargaining, collective agreements and upstream consultation of social partners. The World Commission on the Social Dimension of Globalisation considered the unique model of EU political, social and economic integration as a stepping stone towards strengthening the social dimension of globalisation. The growing role of the EU as a global player and intensification of globalisation have also an impact on the tripartite and bipartite cooperation between national, EU level and international social partners. The EU is not only relevant for standard setting in EU 25 but influences also global standards setting and the broader international employment and social agenda through its positions in international organizations such as ILO and through its external policies and cooperation. All this require closer cooperation and synergies between the national, EU and international social partner's organizations. Evolutions are still ongoing. For instance the two remaining international trade unions, ICFTU and WCL, have decided to establish a new single global trade union according to a pluralistic model in line with that of the European Trade Union Confederation (ETUC).

The ILO Office is already convinced since many years that the EU is a strategic partner. It has contributed to facilitate the exercise of EC external competences in the context of the ILC and the submission of international labour conventions to the competent authority in the context of ratification (this can also be the EC for EU Member States) taking into account the specific historic context and constraints of the ILO 1919 Constitution. The ILO has also adhered to the EC/UN Financial and Administrative Framework Agreement and by doing so facilitated the technical and development cooperation with the EC on the promotion of decent work in third regions and countries.

In recent years the EU was able to go beyond the formal debate on the exercise of EC external competences in the context of the preparation, adoption, submission and ratification of ILO conventions by adopting a pragmatic and political approach

---

[40] Communication on the social dimension of globalisation, 18 May 2004, COM (2004) 383 final.

that takes into account both the global context of the ILO and the increasing interdependence between EU internal and external policies. However the specific historic context of the ILO constitution, adopted in a period without regional integration, cannot be used as an argument by EU Member States or others to ignore the basic nature of the functioning of the EC institutions.

The neglect of the EU context in the past also partly explains why EU Member States still have poor ratification rates of up to date ILO conventions on occupational health and safety (OHS) adopted since 1975. This is regrettable and is not in the interest of the EU, the EU Member States and the global level playing field. It is giving a negative signal to other countries and regions. A specific pragmatic EC effort on facilitating and promoting the ratification of up to date ILO conventions on occupational health and safety (OHS) and working conditions could be helpful. There are no indications whatsoever that these conventions are incompatible with the EC Directives thanks to EC coordination at the ILC. Most of the relevant EC Directives are by the way establishing minimum standards. The same goes for the ILO conventions. This EC initiative could also include proposals for Council Decisions authorizing EU Member States to ratify those conventions that partly affect EC exclusive competences such as convention No. 170 on chemical substances. The implementation of ILO conventions in EC law including trough framework agreements by European social partners can also facilitate the ratification of ILO conventions by EU Member States.[41]

The EU-ILO cooperation can also build on recent good examples such as the work of the World Commission on the Social Dimension of Globalisation, the increasing relevance of ILO work for more and more Commission services, the preparation, adoption and implementation of the ILO 2006 consolidated maritime convention[42] and the provisions of the September 2005 UN Summit outcome on the promotion of decent work for all as part of international and national policies and development strategies. The future EU enlargement and EU neighbourhood policies also offer important possibilities for ILO-EU cooperation as the needs for social and economic reform and for modernizing labour relations are very high in a number of countries. The Commission has adopted on 24 May 2006 an important communication on 'Promoting decent work for all – The EU contribution to the implementation of the decent work agenda in the world'. The communication provides a strategy and orientations for mobilizing the EU internal and external policies in order to contribute to the promotion of the universal objective of decent

[41] See for instance ILO convention No. 180 on working time in the maritime sector and the framework agreement by European social partners', implemented through Council Directive 99/63/EC and accompanied by Directive 99/95 ensuring the supervision of its application by port state control.

[42] Work programme of the European Commission for 2006, COM (2005) 531 final includes a communication on minimum maritime labour standards minimum exploring the possible implementation of the ILO consolidated maritime convention in EC law including by a possible framework agreement by European social partners.

work for all.[43] It uses the ILO definition of decent work. The European Commission also contributed to the July 2006 UN ECOSOC High Level Segment that addressed productive employment and decent work.

The ILO is currently reflecting on strengthening its capacity to assist governments and social partners' efforts on the promotion of decent work in the context of globalisation. The ILO Office has proposed in a document submitted to the March 2006 ILO GB session to strengthen policy coherence and to improve the interplay between standards, social dialogue, analysis, development and technical cooperation and to strengthen the identification of priorities and their effective implementation by decent work country programmes.[44] It also highlights the importance of cooperation with other global institutions, with social partners, the business community and with regional organizations in line with the international obligations of the respective Member States. This initiative could result, through discussions at the 2007 ILC and beyond, in an important updating of the ILO working methods, objectives and authoritative documents. This initiative should be welcomed. The approach is a universal one but it at the same time in line with the EU Lisbon strategy, the EU social agenda, the 2005 European consensus on development policy and EU trade policy options. This opens promising perspectives for the ILO-EU cooperation and for constructive dialogue with social partners, third countries and regions.

---

[43] Communication of 24 May 2006, COM (2006) 249 final and accompanied by a Commission staff working document with annexes to the communication, SEC (2006) 643. Available at <http://europa.eu/rapid/pressReleasesAction.do?reference=IP/06/675&format=HTML&aged=0&language=EN&guiLanguage=en>; <http://ec.europa.eu/employment_social/emplweb/news/news_en.cfm?id=158>.

[44] ILO GB. 295/16/5, available at <http://www.ilo.org/public/english/standards/relm/gb/docs/gb295/pdf/gb-16-5.pdf>.

Chapter 6
UN-EU COOPERATION ON FINANCIAL ISSUES: THE ROLE OF THE EUROPEAN UNION AT THE INTERNATIONAL MONETARY FUND AND THE WORLD BANK

by Carole Garnier, Daniel Daco and Francesca Di Mauro*

1. Introduction

Sixty years after the Bretton Woods Conference of 1944, the International Monetary Fund (IMF) and the World Bank (WB) remain core global institutions in the monetary, financial and development fields. They have adapted to change and are continuously trying to respond with flexibility to emerging issues and changing demands. Though most discussions have focused on how to increase effectiveness and efficiency within and across their areas of activities, the internal governance of the institutions, notably that of the IMF, is increasingly debated in international fora.

A major change over the past sixty years has been the development of the European Union with its current twenty-five Member States, twelve of which use a common currency. The EU is also the world's largest aid donor. The way the EU is represented is considered by many as key to any future reform.

Current representation in the IMF and the WB is examined below. Additionally, we look to the possible options for improved representation of the EU within these organizations. Beyond the institutional aspects, the many facets of cooperation between the EC and WB as leading players in the donor community are reviewed.

2. IMF

There is a widespread perception, both within Europe and outside, that the EU/euro area does not play a role in the international economic, financial and monetary sphere commensurate to its economic weight. Enhancing the external representation of the euro area is an intricate challenge because it is linked to the complexity of the European integration process and because it faces reluctance, if not outright

* European Commission officials, DG ECFIN. The views expressed are those of the authors and do not necessarily represent the Commission's view.

J. Wouters et al., eds., The United Nations and the European Union

opposition, from some of the incumbent actors. Progress on this issue also depends on the broader advances with respect to the common foreign policy.

The completion of the Economic and Monetary Union (EMU) in 1999[1] was recognized as a major change for the international monetary system: it implied the transfer to the Community level of monetary and exchange rate policy of now twelve Member States. EMU was also expected to trigger a sea change in the external representation of EMU in international economic and financial institutions and fora. One has, however, to acknowledge that, six years after its start, progress has been rather limited. The ongoing discussions on the need to improve the governance of the international monetary and financial system, including by giving a greater voice to new global economic players and to the poor countries in the IMF and WB, also provide a context for the debate on the euro area external representation

2.1 Current status of the EC/EMU in IMF

At present, the external representation of the euro area is still fragmented and incomplete. *Ad hoc* arrangements continue to prevail with regard to the different institutions, making it difficult for the EU or the euro area to be seen as speaking with one voice at the international level.

The EC Treaty sets out procedures for deciding both EU common positions and EU representation in international fora regarding economic and monetary issues. Article 111(4) stipulates that 'the Council shall, on a proposal from the Commission and after consulting the ECB, acting by a qualified majority decide on the position of the Community at international level as regards issues of particular relevance to EMU, and acting unanimously, decide on its representation in full respect of competences of the actors involved'. To implement this Article, the Commission proposed to the 1998 Vienna European Council that, as a principle, the Community should be represented by the three relevant Community bodies, notably the euro area's Presidency, the Commission and the ECB.[2]

Member States only agreed to a scaled-down version of this proposal with respect to both its legal basis and its content. Rather than being framed in a Council decision, the agreement was spelled out in the European Council conclusions of Vienna. Its content was also less precise than proposed, in particular with respect to the role of the Commission, which was downgraded to assisting the euro area Presidency in the IMF Board.[3] In practice, even these scaled-down conclusions have only partially been implemented.

---

[1] EU Member States are members of EMU. So far, twelve Member States have adopted the euro and 13 have a derogation.

[2] European Commission, 'Proposal for a Council Decision on the Representation and Position taking of the Community at International Level in the context of the Economic and Monetary Union', COM (98) 637.

[3] The Presidency Conclusions of the Vienna European Council noted: 'The ECB, as the Community body competent for monetary policy, should be granted an observer status at the IMF board.

The euro area/EU dimension is very weak in the IMF. The current membership consists of 184 States. All EU Member States (MS) are members of the IMF and account together for around 32% of the total vote in the IMF. The IMF Board, the IMF decision-making body, counts 24 resident Executive Directors. Germany, France and the United Kingdom each appoint their own Executive Director (ED). The other EU Member States belong to various 'constituencies', representing one or more EU Member States as well as some non-EU members. There are 6/7 EU Executive Directors at the IMF and EU countries are dispersed among 10 constituencies. Executive Directors can only cast their votes as a constituency, but formal voting rarely takes place since decisions are generally taken on a consensus basis. The representation in the International Monetary and Financial Committee (IMFC) and the Development Committee (DC), the main IMF and WB policy orientation bodies, which meet twice a year, is the same as those of the Executive Boards.

Neither the Commission nor the Community has a direct representative on the IMF Executive Board. The Commission, through the Commissioner in charge of Economic and Monetary Affairs, is invited as an observer to both the IMFC and the DC. The euro area Presidency delivers a statement on behalf of the Community in the IMFC twice a year. This statement is subject to long drafting sessions at the Economic and Financial Committee (EFC). Alongside this statement, the Commissioner for Economic and Monetary Affairs submits, on behalf of the Commission, his own IMFC Statement, while the Commissioner for Development and Humanitarian Aid submits his statement to the DC.

The ECB obtained in 1998 an observer status in the IMF board,[4] which allows its representative to attend Board meetings where the euro area economic situation and issues of particular relevance for the euro area are debated.

The external representation at the IMF has been discussed several times by EU Finance Ministers, including during the informal ECOFIN Council in Oviedo on 12-14 April 2002, on the basis of a paper sketching three alternatives for making European coordination in the IMF more effective, namely: (1) improving the existing informal coordination model which involves coordination on *ad hoc* issues and with no pre-commitment to reach a common position; (2) a reinforced coordination model with an *ex ante* commitment to reach agreement on a set of pre-defined issues; (3) a single EU chair, implying a commitment to agree among MS on all issues. While many MS stressed the importance of making progress in coordinating EU positions and some even viewed a single chair as a long-term goal, there was no strong support to move towards a reinforced coordination model. Marginal progress was made at the informal ECOFIN Council of Copenhagen on 6-7 September 2002, which agreed on a more extensive list of IMF issues that could be subject to informal coordination.

The views of the European Community/EMU on other issues of particular relevance to the EMU would be presented at the IMF board by the relevant member of the Executive Director's office of the Member State holding the euro Presidency, assisted by a representative of the Commission'.

[4] Decision No. 11875 (99/1) of the IMF Executive Board, 21 December 1998.

Coordination takes place in both Washington and Brussels. The ECB Observer and a Commission official from the Washington delegation are invited to attend weekly coordination meetings which mostly focus on important policy issues and on EU economic surveillance reports (Article IV). The objective of this coordination is to propose, as often as possible, a common position that will be presented to the Board by the ED representing the Presidency. Other EU EDs are expected to support the Presidency statement, if there is an agreement at the coordination meeting. In order to enhance the visibility and continuity of the representation of EU EDs at the IMF, a troika formula (involving the EDs or Alternate EDs representing the countries holding the current, previous and following Presidencies of the EU) has been used since 2004 to convey common positions on certain matters to the Management of the IMF or other members of the Board.

Coordination on IMF issues is also guided by the Economic and Financial Committee and by its Subcommittee on international monetary and financial issues EFC, created in October 2000. Its aim is to develop common lines on issues of particular relevance for the EU, but there is no obligation to reach a common understanding. The Commission and the ECB provide input through their members in both Committees.

2.2 Options for improved representation

2.2.1 *Constraints of the current situation*

The current arrangements for the external representation at the IMF are not satisfactory for several reasons. Firstly, they rely on voluntary coordination which tends to produce rather weak and defensive position taking. Secondly, they leave aside the relevant EU institutions on issues such as fiscal and macroeconomic surveillance, trade, financial support to crisis countries, international capital liberalisation, financial markets and corporate governance. Thirdly, they are more and more challenged by an evolving international environment.

Coordination has inherent limitations. It risks leading to a position representing the lowest common denominator among EU Member States' positions. Common positions are difficult to adapt to the evolution of the discussions in international fora and/or to new developments, thereby leaving little room for flexibility during negotiations. There is also an intrinsic difficulty in linking consistently the common positions adopted in the course of time on a number of topics. The Community is therefore seriously constrained in designing a more strategic and coherent global position.

The IMF exerts significant and, possibly, growing influence in areas where the Community's competence exists and where strategic interests of the EU are at stake. These competences are manyfold. Firstly, they relate to macroeconomic surveillance. While the ECB is responsible for the definition and implementation of the common monetary policy, the Council and the Commission play a central role in the coordination framework, including in terms of macroeconomic surveillance, by preparing, adopting and monitoring the implementation of the Broad Economic Policy Guidelines and supervising the functioning of the Stability and Growth Pact. The Commission also plays a crucial role in fostering structural reforms in order to achieve the objectives of the Lisbon Agenda. Macroeconomic surveillance is also at the core of the work of the IMF.[5]

Secondly, they concern trade liberalisation and a better set of multilateral trade rules. While trade remains largely peripheral to the core business of the IMF, this institution is pushing for a successful and timely conclusion of the Doha Development Agenda negotiations. While the Commission has the opportunity to present the EU trade policy stance directly to IMF staff in the context of the euro area Article IV consultations, the Community's lack of direct representation in the IMF limits its ability to ensure effective EU representation on trade policy matters. For example, the Commission could therefore not contribute efficiently to the Board discussions on IMF trade integration mechanism.

Thirdly, they pertain to the free movement of capital and progressive financial market integration. The Commission is a major driving force towards achieving free movement of capital between Member States and third countries and the creation of a single financial market. The Commission is also actively involved in the fight against financing for terrorism and anti-money laundering. Through its right of initiative, the Commission has institutional powers to address EU financial stability issues. Financial stability issues have over the last ten years moved closer to the core of the mandate the IMF.

Fourthly, they are linked to the support to some IMF macroeconomic adjustment and structural reform programs: Since 1990 the European Community has committed nearly €6.2 billion of macro-financial assistance to third countries, mainly the current candidate countries, other Eastern European, Mediterranean and Central Asian countries and the Western Balkans,[6] thereby contributing to fill the residual external financing gaps of IMF programmes.

Fifthly, with respect to official development assistance and humanitarian aid, it is worth recalling that the Commission manages one of the world's largest aid budgets, representing 11% of the world total, and plays a key role in development aid worldwide. The Commission is also a significant provider of financial support for major G7/8 initiatives, including the enhanced debt initiative for Highly Indebted Poor Countries (HIPCs).

---

[5] The EMU dimension has been recognized in the IMF surveillance activities: the IMF undertakes, since 1999, in addition to the traditional annual EU national surveillance, a bi-yearly Article IV consultation of the euro area economic policies, with visits to the Commission, the ECB, and the EFC.

[6] The Community's macro-financial assistance takes the form of untied balance of payments assistance, or budget support, in form of medium and long-term loans or grants or a combination of both.

Last but not least, the promotion of an environment conducive to stability, prosperity and peace is a strategic EU interest, which is also shared with the IMF.

The European Union has emerged as the largest world economy with a population of close to 450 million and is also, by far, the largest world trading entity. It represents a highly integrated single market for goods, services and capital. The European Monetary Union, the third stage of EU, brings some EU Member States even closer by having them share a single currency. The number of countries adopting the euro is bound to increase, reinforcing the international use of the euro.

One needs to recognize that the European presence in the IMF is relatively strong, in terms of number of seats and, possibly, voting power. Out of 24 IMF Executive Directors, 6 to 7 come from EU countries and five represent countries belonging to the euro area. Nevertheless, there is a widespread feeling that Europe, despite its number of seats and its voting power in the BWI, is unable to offer a proper counterweight to the United States.

On the other hand, a few emerging market economies with large populations have experienced rapid economic growth and feel increasingly underrepresented in the BWI and international fora. This dissatisfaction has led to the creation of the G20 but has, so far, yielded little response in the IMF.

2.2.2 *Reform proposals*

The external representation of the euro area/EU in the IMF needs to be strengthened not only because the current *ad hoc* arrangements are far from being satisfactory but also because these arrangements impede the Community to fully play the role it has been given by the Treaty. An appropriate representation would need to respect some principles:

- First, the new arrangements for the external representation must improve the practical coordination and representation of Member States' views on issues where a common position is deemed necessary. For transparency reasons, the arrangements should also preferably be consistent across all international institutions and fora.
- Second, the arrangements would need to ensure that the relevant Community bodies are effectively represented and fully participate in international discussions on all areas falling under Community's competence.
- Third, a strengthening of the external representation has to be approached with the perspective of the ongoing debate on the governance of the international financial and economic system. A streamlining of the euro area/EU external representation could allow for a better representation of emerging economic powers in the IMF, while giving more effective power and influence to Europe on IMF decision-making.
- Finally and most importantly, these arrangements should respect the Treaty.

The Commission has made several attempts to give more body to the Vienna agreements. In order to allow the Commission to assist the Presidency representative in the IMF Board effectively, it proposed in 1999 that a Commission official should be appointed in one of the EU Executive Director Offices. The Commission would thereby gain automatic and rapid access to the Fund documents; would participate in all informal meetings that precede IMF Board meetings; and would get direct feedback from these Board meetings. This option remains on the table.

In the IMF, there is at present little chance of obtaining an observer status for the Commission in the Executive Board. Even the regrouping of the 6 or 7 European constituencies into a smaller number of constituencies is strongly opposed by the small 'old' Member States, which fear that those constituencies would become the monopoly of large Member States. Having a Commission official appointed in a European Executive Director office, preferably but not automatically the one holding the euro area Presidency, would be fully in line with the Vienna Council conclusions.

In the longer term, it is clear that a unified or single representation would be the best way for the euro area to be effective and to play a role in the IMF commensurate to its economic power. A membership of the euro area or the EU alongside the membership of EU Member States (the EBRD model) in the IMF would run counter to the IMF Articles of Agreement, since only countries can become Members according to Article II of the IMF statute. Furthermore, as already mentioned, there is a perception that Europe is already over-represented in the IMF. Therefore, the most realistic scenario would entail, either, a regrouping of all euro area countries into a single constituency with a participation of the ECB and the Commission, while maintaining the individual membership of the EU countries, or the outright replacement of the 12 national memberships by a single euro area membership. The latter may require an amendment of the IMF's Articles of Agreement.[7]

Eventually, progress towards a single/unified external representation in international financial and economic institutions and fora will depend on the progress made in the unification of a foreign policy.

3. World Bank

The European Community and the World Bank are leading players in the donor community, with a similar annual aid volume of around $ 8-9 billion (2004 data) and with a global presence among low and middle-income countries. Cooperation between the two institutions is complex and multiform, and this section will try to go through its many facets, be they at the Institutional, policy, financial and operational level.

---

[7] It should be noted that the IMF Articles of Agreement (Article II) leave open the definition of 'countries'.

3.1 Current status of the EC in the World Bank

The perception that the EU does not play a role in the international sphere commensurate to its economic weight also applies to its role in development policy and more specifically in the World Bank Group[8] whose main objective is to fight poverty and improve the living standards of people in the developing world.

The EU is the world's leading partner in terms of aid, trade and direct investment. It is the world's biggest aid donor. The European Community (EC) and its Member States provide 55% (€34.3 Billon in 2004) of all official development aid (ODA). Out of this amount about 20% is managed by the European Commission.

This role is due to further increase. The EU is firmly committed to contribute to the achievement of the Millennium Development Goals (MDGs) through an increase in the volume and quality of its ODA. Building on the commitments undertaken in Monterrey, the EU took in June 2005[9] further steps in agreeing new ODA targets, namely an EU-25 average of 0.56% ODA/GNI target by 2010.

Institutional structures and in particular the set-up and decision-making process of the WB Executive Board are generally considered as a major obstacle to an effective and influential EU representation.

The World Bank's current membership consists of 184 states, including all the EU 25 Member States. The latter account for 28% of the total voting weight compared to 16% for the United States. The two decision-making bodies are the Board of Governors and the Board of Executive Directors. The Board of Governors meets once a year at the Bank's annual meetings. Each of the Bank member countries nominates a Governor and an alternate to the Board. Governors are government officials such as ministers of finance or development. Except on a number of issues such as admission or suspension of members, capital increase (or decrease), distribution of income, arrangements with other international organizations, the Board of Governors delegates authority to the Board of executive directors.

The Board of Executive Directors which consists of 24 EDs is responsible for the conduct of the general operations and exercises all the powers delegated by the Board of Governors. The structures of this main decision-making body do not facilitate the expression of EU common positions.

Membership in the IMF being a pre-requisite for membership in the World Bank, the European Community as such has no legal status and does not have a formal representation in the Board.

---

[8] The World Bank Group is made up of five organizations: The International Bank for Reconstruction and Development (IBRD), the International Development Association (IDA), the International Finance Corporation (IFC), the Multilateral Investment Guarantee Agency (MIGA) and the International Centre for the settlement of Investment Disputes (ICSID).

[9] Agreement by the GAERC of 23-24 May 2005, confirmed by the ECOFIN of 7 June, and the European Council of 16-17 June 2005.

The 184 members, whose voting power is proportional to their share of the Bank's capital and thus proportional to their wealth, are grouped in 24 constituencies. The 25 EU Member States are scattered over 10 different constituencies and chairs. Three Member States, Germany, France and the United Kingdom are among the five members having the largest number of shares. Each has a single chair and an executive Director (ED). Belgium, the Netherlands and Italy lead their respective constituencies where EU and non-EU countries participate. The three Nordic Member States and the Baltics participate in the Nordic-Baltic constituency with a rotating chair between the first three countries. Spain participates in a constituency with Mexico, Venezuela and other Latin American countries. The chair rotates between the first three countries. Ireland and Poland are each in a constituency where others are non-EU members and where the chair is permanently led by a non EU country, respectively Canada and Switzerland. This set-up results from decisions made by each member. For instance, Spain participated in the constituency chaired by Italy until 1978 and so did Poland until 1992.

Such dispersion could theoretically add leverage to the EU position. The participation of non-EU countries in constituencies led by an EU Member State can bring additional voting power in support of the EU position. EU countries could thus dominate 8 of the 24 seats in the World Bank Board, i.e., the three single seats, 4 seats where they have the majority of votes plus eventually the Latin American constituency when Spain has the rotating chair. While EU countries have 28% of the votes, the 8 constituencies together reach 34% of the votes.

However, this theoretical advantage seems rather limited in practice. Each of the constituencies can only express one view. Even if all EU countries agree on a common view some EU members may not be in a position to support it if it differs from the view of the other constituency members and from the view of the country holding the chair. Such a situation was illustrated on the occasion of the first EU joint statement on World Bank budget for 2005 issued in June 2004. This joint statement was signed by EU EDs from the Netherlands, Italy, Germany, France, Austria, and United Kingdom and even by the Swiss ED. Ireland which held the Presidency at that time and had been very active in promoting this common position could not be part of it as it was not supported by the Canadian chaired constituency. This was also the case for Spain, Sweden, Finland and Denmark.

It seems that such difficulties emerge even on relatively benign subjects. Non-EU members have different views which prevail at constituency level.

In any case, EU members do not hold the majority in the World Bank and furthermore, decisions are mainly taken by consensus. This implies alliances and co-operation with other shareholders. Though there may be different groupings depending on the issue at stake, the G7 (G8) positions are widely considered as determinant in both the IMF and the World Bank. EDs representing G7 countries ensure that positions taken are consistent with G7 (G8) consensus which may trigger reluctance from non G7 (G8) members.

3.2 Options for improved representation

3.2.1 *Features and constraints of the current situation*

In the absence of EC legal status in the WB Board, EU representation is based on coordination.

Since the Maastricht Treaty (1992), Member States are bound to coordinate their actions in multilateral organizations and uphold common positions. Special provisions apply to coordination in the development policy of the EU. The Community and Member States have to coordinate their policies including in international organizations and the Commission may take any useful initiative to promote this coordination (Article 180 EC).[10]

However, development policy is an area with very complex decision-making mechanisms at global level, involving a multiplicity of fora, structures and interlocutors. It is a parallel competence of the EC and the Member States. The latter are also bilateral donors and may have different and sometimes divergent interests towards developing countries, depending on their geographical and historical background and their trade relations. Similarity of views, a pre-requisite for common positions, is thus not guaranteed. In addition, fragmentation of the structures in charge at national and EC levels does not facilitate coordination. At national level, different ministries may be responsible for World Bank matters (e.g., finance and foreign affairs, development) and coordination may be difficult both between and within ministries. Again at EC level, there are different departments involved.

The process of coordination between EU members in the World Bank is relatively new since it was launched in 2000. It has been quite significantly strengthened since the end of 2003 and is assessed by the EU EDs as being more effective than in the IMF.[11]

This coordinated approach can lead to two main types of outputs: 'Coordinated statements' and 'Joint statements'. For the former, the EU Presidency prepares a statement which is referred to by other EU Board members in their Board interventions. For the latter which reflect tighter coordination, the EU Presidency prepares a statement that is issued in the names of those who endorse it.

The first joint statement was issued in June 2004 on the World Bank programmes and budget for 2005, as already mentioned. EU coordination advanced further in 2005 under the Luxemburg Presidency. A second joint statement was issued on the World Bank budget for 2006. Joint statements have increased and were also made, for example, on the occasion of the selection of the new World Bank President highlighting the EU EDs understanding of the Bank's missions, on IDA replenish-

[10] T. Lehtinen, 'The Coordination of European Development Cooperation in the field: Myth or Reality?', *ECDMP Discussion Paper 43*, Maastricht, ECDPM, 2003.

[11] L. Keune, *EU coordination in International Organizations: The case of the World Bank*, Mimeo, Washington, 2004.

ment. EU EDs have moreover considered their interventions as decisive in securing the nominations by P. Wolfowitz in September 2005 of two Europeans to senior posts (Chief Financial officer and IFC's executive vice-president).

EU coordination relies on three main mechanisms. The first one is regular consultation between WB EU members and the Commission delegation. Meetings are chaired by the EU Presidency at the World Bank and attended by EDs or their representatives and by the Commission delegation to the United States, in Washington. In November 2003 a framework for this informal coordination process was established. The objectives of such meetings range from exchange of information including on the EU policies to discussion and coordination of positions on strategic topics such as policy issues and country assistance strategies. The frequency of these meetings has drastically increased. Starting from four meetings per year in 2000, they turned into monthly meetings during 2003 and have since 2004 become weekly meetings.

The second recent mechanism more systematically provides EU EDs, through the EC delegation, with the position or views of the EU institutions on key items on the Agenda of the World Bank Board. Written input, aimed at promoting common positions, has thus been provided by the Commission on issues such as trade and conditionality. Input is both demand-driven upon the EDs requests, linked to the Board agenda and supply-driven as the intention of the Commission is to make known its position on some strategic themes which are not (yet) on the Board Agenda.

The third means of coordination between the EU EDs and the EU Institutions is through their annual visits to Brussels. The first visit in January 2004 was followed by two others in March 2005 and 2006. These visits seem to have been highly appreciated also because they enhanced confidence between the World Bank Board Members.

Though quite significant progress had been achieved since 2004, there remain deficits in the current EU coordination process. These deficits impinge on the actors and on the mechanisms of coordination.

As far as actors are concerned, the EU Presidency plays an important role in communication and in the issuance of common positions. The change every six months of the Member State holding the Presidency does not favour continuity nor EU visibility in the World Bank. In addition, action may be especially difficult when the Member State that holds the Presidency is part of a mixed constituency led by a non-EU country. While a permanent role for the Presidency at World Bank level would likely be rejected, the idea of a Troika has been evoked as a possible improvement, in line with the provisions of the Constitutional Treaty.

The role of the Commission's delegation in Washington is equally important, not least because World Bank EU EDs may not be aware of all aspects of EU policies. The absence of the Commission on the World Bank Board makes its coordination role particularly difficult. The Commission has no automatic and rapid access to World Bank documents, reports and papers for Board deliberations. Nor can it have direct feedback on Board discussions and positions taken. There is thus ample scope for greater systematic and more in-depth communication and feedback, a prerequisite for strengthening the coordination role of the delegation.

Ultimately, the intensity of coordination is dependent upon the willingness of the EU EDs to act in a concerted way. Many EU EDs are convinced of the advantages of a cooperative strategy and are willing to further improve intra-EU coordination. Others may be more reluctant.

There are also deficits in the mechanisms of coordination. First of all, these are still limited and informal and do not internalise as an *ex ante* target the goal of achieving common positions.

In addition, the gap in coordination at the level of Member States, often cited as a complication for stronger EU coordination, has not been addressed. Paradoxically, the significant progress evidenced in EU coordination may result from the absence of formal structures for coordination with capitals.

The creation of a committee at EU level conducting work on World Bank issues as done by the so-called EFC Subcommittee on IMF and related issues (SCIMF) lacks consensus. Many consider that such a mechanism would be too complex for World Bank matters which involve different ministries in different countries, as compared to IMF matters which only involve Ministries of Finance and Central Banks. For similar reasons there is no consensus either on the desirability of an informal network. The added value of new mechanisms, on top of the existing regular informal meetings between directors general for development from all EU Member States and the Commission still has to be demonstrated.

Further improving coordination with the EU Institutions, in particular the Commission, through more binding coordination structures, also faces limits in the absence of EC representation and membership in the World Bank.

3.2.2 *Reform proposals*

The institutional constraints and the inherent limitation of coordination have led to the formulation of options for improved EU representation. The objective is to increase the effectiveness of the EU role in the World Bank and more generally in development matters. The criteria are broadly similar to those mentioned for the IMF.

A unified representation would *a priori* appear as an appropriate way to ensure a strong EU presence in the World Bank. Indeed, for the first time, the Treaty establishing a Constitution for Europe (TCE) had paved the way for such a solution. Its' Article III-196 stipulates that the Council, on a proposal from the Commission, may adopt appropriate measures to ensure a unified representation within the International Financial Institutions.

There are mainly two options for a unified representation, depending on whether or not the European Community substitutes Member States. In the first option, all EU countries would remain members of the World Bank but would share a constituency casting a single vote. There would be strong reasons for the constituency to be chaired by the European Commission, since it already represents the EU in trade policy, a matter tightly linked to development issues. Nevertheless, the constituency could also be chaired through rotation between the Member States.

This option faces two main obstacles likely to be raised respectively by EU and non-EU members. One is the reluctance of various Member States to give up their own seat. Member States have their own development policies. They contribute substantially to IDA (nearly $9 Billion for IDA 14) and guarantee a large part of the capital of IBRD. In return, they want to influence the decision-making of the World Bank Group. Such influence would be reduced by sharing one seat. Furthermore, a unified constituency might not retain the same voting power as the EU 25 currently have. This voting power is already considered excessive by several non-EU members, notably the United States and developing countries. A better representation of the latter in international fora is among the priorities of the Millennium Development Goals. At present 46 African Countries share 2 seats in the World Bank. Together their two constituencies represent 5.4% of total voting power.

The second option would be to transfer competence to the European Community (EC), e.g., represented by the Commission. The EC would have a single seat, would take over the shareholding of EU Member States in the IBRD and replace them as donor to IDA. Though a single EU chair would signal strong visibility and impact for the EU coalition, it raises issues similar to those of the first option, namely Member States' willingness to do so and recalculation of voting power. EU EDs are likely to argue that having six EU EDs in the Board (Germany, France, United Kingdom, Italy, the Netherlands, Austria) leads to much more influence on decision-making than a single EU constituency with a reduced share and voting power. Furthermore, the incidence of EC shareholding might create a significant burden on the EU budget.

A third option might also be worth further consideration. It does not lead to a unified representation. It improves EC representation without substituting the EC to Member States, which may be more easily acceptable in the short to medium term. The option is to have EC shareholding next to shareholding by individual Member States. This option would mimic EU representation in the European Bank for Reconstruction and Development (EBRD) where the EC, represented by the Commission, holds 3% of the Bank's shares and has a seat in the Boards of Governors and Executive Directors, alongside the EU Member States. This option could be easier to accept for Member States and would have smaller implications for the EU budget. Since an additional seat in the World Bank might be difficult to obtain, there might be a need for some reshuffling of EU Member States constituencies to free up an EC Commission seat.

The process for a unified or improved representation may take some time. In the first option where EU Member States share the same constituency, the IBRD articles of Agreement would need to be amended as Article V, Section 4 foresees that the five largest countries are represented individually. A majority of 3/5 of the members representing 85% of the voting power would be needed. EC membership also requires a change in the articles of Agreement of the IMF and the EBRD which only attribute full membership to sovereign states. This may be the reason why some have advocated a reshuffling of EU constituencies as a means to increase consistency in the short-term. Clearly, a unified representation and/or EC membership would be a driving force to strengthen the current coordination and turn its informal and relatively *ad hoc* basis into a more systematic *ex ante* process. Still whatever the option, intra-EU coordination will continue to be required.

While EC representation in the World Bank is the ultimate goal and a pre-requisite to enhance the EU position and influence as a global player, there are nevertheless various mechanisms of cooperation, interaction and joint initiatives between the EC/European Commission and the World Bank.

3.3 Cooperation between the EC and the World Bank

Enhanced cooperation with the IFIs is explicitly foreseen in the recent 'Joint EU Development Policy Statement' (the so-called 'European Consensus' of November 2005),[12] as a way to improve the effectiveness of multilateral aid. Cooperation with the World Bank is part of this wider cooperation. It is encapsulated in three Memoranda of Understanding (MoUs) signed by the Commission over the past five years with the World Bank, the European Investment Bank (EIB), and other IFIs. They cover coordination of activities in respectively Central and East European countries, Cyprus, Malta and Turkey (including the Western Balkans since 2005); Eastern Europe and Southern Caucasia, Russia and Central Asia and as of 2004 the Middle East and Southern Mediterranean/North Africa Region. The MoUs seek to provide a practical framework for an enhanced cooperation in terms of economic dialogue, technical assistance, institutional building and financial assistance.

Moreover, relations with the World Bank which have been long-standing and intense, notably in support of developing countries, go beyond such frameworks. They encompass policy, financial and operational cooperation with specific processes and mechanisms.

3.3.1 *Policy coordination*

One form of EC-WB collaboration concerns the policy strategy level, which is especially relevant for developing low-income countries: both institutions share a common objective of poverty reduction and the attainment of the Millennium development Goals (MDGs). Their assistance is fully inscribed within the Poverty Reduction Strategy Paper (PRSP) approach, which was launched in 1999 by the

[12] Joint Statement by the Council and the representatives of the governments of the Member States, meeting within the Council, the European Parliament and the Commission on European Union Development Policy: 'the European Consensus', OJ (24 February 2006) C-46/1.

World Bank and the IMF, and which aims at federating donors around a nationally-owned medium-term development strategy. The key features of this approach are: country ownership; a strong focus on results; and partnership among donors and civil society in shaping the country-owned strategy. The PRSP is a comprehensive approach, incorporating macroeconomic, structural and social reforms.

Since its launch, the EC has been in close contacts with the World Bank to define common interest within PRSPs with high-level meetings and 'intellectual' contribution on the policy design of PRSPs. To further enhance coordination, the EC decided to base its Country Strategy Papers on country PRSPs. Moreover, similarly to the World Bank creation of a specific Poverty Reduction Support Credit (PRSC) to facilitate implementation of PRSPs, the EC established a Poverty Reduction Support Grant (PRSG) to complement the financial contributions of the Bretton Woods institutions. Collaboration in this field continues, with regular meetings at headquarters level to discuss the reviews of the PRSP and find ways to improve this tool.

The two institutions are also committed to the international aid effectiveness agenda, as endorsed in the Paris Declaration in February 2005, notably on applying the principles of national ownership, partnership, donor coordination and harmonisation, alignment to the recipient country systems and results-orientation.[13] In practice, the Paris Declaration identifies 12 indicators to measure progress on aid effectiveness, together with a number of targets for 2010, which should be monitored by the OECD-Development Assistance Committee. It should therefore become easier over time to actually evaluate the degree of cooperation among institutions, including between the EC and the World Bank.

One of the processes which somehow formalises the EC-WB policy collaboration described above is the so-called 'Limelette' process, a series of joint annual high-level meetings that combine upstream policy dialogue with downstream collaboration in the field. These have been held since April 2003 in Brussels or Paris, bringing together staff from country offices and headquarters in an open and frank discussion. The objective is to identify ways to achieve greater collective development impact in PRSP countries, by working together more effectively. A number of principles have been agreed over time for an effective collaboration, and the meetings usually end with a joint EC-WB Action Plan, as well as a joint letter signed by the management of both institutions and sent to respective country offices, encouraging them to implement the agreed principles and actions.[14] The agreed principles are the following:

---

[13] Paris Declaration on Aid Effectiveness, Paris, 28 February-2 March 2005, available at <http://www1.worldbank.org/harmonization/Paris/FINALPARISDECLARATION.pdf>.

[14] Joint Note on Supporting the PRSP Process in Africa, available at <http://old.developmentgateway.org/download/249469/WB-EC_paper_-_Supporting_PRSP_Process.doc>.

1. National lead in the PRS process and national ownership of the PRSP. Centrality of the PRSP and the annual PRS reviews in country and donor processes – including clear links to the national budget cycle and the use of the PRSP and annual review as a foundation for domestic accountability and donor support.
2. Clear links in the PRSP between sectors and the macro framework and national budget. The budget should include all sector programs and so-called global programs.
3. Greater results orientation of PRSP support, and continued emphasis in the PRS process on the development of appropriate indicators and measurement systems.
4. All donor country assistance strategies and support based on the PRSP and APR.
5. Increased use of programmatic support instruments along the spectrum of projects to sector programs to budget support, in accordance with the readiness of the country.
6. Government lead in sector coordination and budget support groups. Both WB and EC should participate in the latter and in groups in the sectors where they are engaged.
7. Complementarity between the two institutions respected and exploited. Duplication of work avoided. The role of EC in political dialogue recognized.
8. Mission timing synchronised with country processes. Mission size reasonable. Information on mission planning and results shared among donors.
9. HQ decision-making and support to local offices consistent with these principles, including in particular the principle of country ownership.

This 'Limelette' process also allows for an open discussion on issues where the two institutions have more divergent opinions. This is for example the case for trade liberalisation: while the EC broadly follows a regional approach to trade liberalisation, the WB very much supports a *multilateral* one. The current policy dialogue tries precisely to find ways to design EC policies to minimise potential drawbacks.

Overall, EC-WB collaboration on the countries of sub-Saharan Africa is rather good. The adoption in 2005 of the respective strategies on Africa (the WB Africa Action Plan and the Commission EU strategy for Africa), where approaches and priorities converge and/or complement each other, is a good example of the harmonious tone between the two institutions.

In other regions, such as the Western Balkans or the Mediterranean (North Africa and Middle East), the EC-WB relationship has faced a more distinctive evolution. Here, the EU approach may be different, either more political, e.g., driven by EU accession, or more strategic, with priorities that do not totally overlap with the PRSP agenda. In the Western Balkans in particular, the relations with the WB have been substantially modified over time. From a deep EC-WB collaboration during the post-conflict years in the mid-1990s, with the creation in 1999 of a 'joint WB-EC office' for the reconstruction of South-East Europe, the countries of the regions have slowly moved towards the accession aspiration. The initial focus on physical infrastructure and post-conflict poverty alleviation, which made the division of tasks somehow easier between the two institutions has gradually evolved. The framework launched in 1999 by the EC, the so-called 'Stabilisation and Association Process' (SAP),[15] served as the main driving force for reforms in the region, and became their priority, with a view to obtaining the 'candidate country' status from the EU.

This meant in particular that in the early stages the activity of each institution had to be adjusted to a new setting, bringing a differentiation between the priorities to be set under the SAP and the PRSP/MDGs processes. This process was accompanied by a shared feeling that a multiplication of donors' initiatives could strain scarce local administrative capacity and financial resources. The focus of WB/EC assistance naturally started to diverge. WB aid kept being focused upon reconstruction and poverty alleviation (also through programmatic lending), guided by the MDG agenda, while the EC assistance was increasingly geared towards capacity and institution-building, with a view to legal approximation to the 'EU acquis'. Over time, as a result of close dialogue at headquarter and country level, the two institutions recognized the complementarity and substantial convergence of goals and measures embodied in the two strains (PRSP/SAP), and the need to bring them together into a single nationally-driven development framework.

3.3.2 *Financial cooperation*

There are two main modalities of financial cooperation between the Commission and the World-Bank: co-financing and EC/Commission's participation in the World Bank Trust Funds.[16]

The Commission's assistance to World Bank Trust Funds is framed in a Trust Fund Agreement signed in 2001 and amended in 2003. The EC/Commission has participated in more than 100 Trust Funds. 32 are currently active and benefit from a total EC grant contribution of more than € 500 million. Among the visible examples are the Global Funds to fight Tuberculosis, HIV/AIDS and Malaria or specific funds such as the Afghanistan Reconstruction Trust Fund.

A specific mention should be made in the context of the Heavily Indebted Poor Countries (HIPC) Initiative launched in 1996, which aims at reducing both the bilateral and multilateral debt burden of poor countries. In this context, the World Bank established the 'HIPC Trust Fund', a channel used by bilateral donors to help

---

[15] The Stabilisation and Association process is a progressive partnership, in which the EU offers a mixture of trade concessions (Autonomous Trade Measures), economic and financial assistance (CARDS Programme) and contractual relationships (Stabilisation and Association Agreements).

[16] The tables and graphs in annex give an overview and a breakdown by main geographical areas and thematic of programmatic and co-financing collaboration (EC/EIB/WB).

finance the multilateral debt relief (excluding the IMF and the WB), e.g., that of the African Development Bank. Since the beginning, the Community has taken an active part in the Initiative and as a donor has contributed substantially to the HIPC Trust Fund: it provided up to €934 million, making it the single largest donor. Given the importance of its financial contribution, in 2000 the EC was exceptionally allowed to participate in some World Bank Board meetings. Moreover, the EC has since the beginning managed to make its voice heard at the regular Multilateral Development Banks (MDBs) meetings held in Washington. The outcomes of these meetings, synthesised in a 'Chairman's Summary', have often shaped policy directions in the implementation of the initiative, and fed into WB/IMF staff papers presented to the Boards, so this is an area where the EC had an opportunity to directly influence the policy debate.

The World Bank has some strength as a manager of the Trust Funds financed by EC and bilateral contributions. It has a quasi-global coverage of both donors and beneficiaries. It is well placed to support initiatives requiring macro-economic (links with the IMF) or private sector (links with the IFC) inputs.

However, there is a widespread and growing perception that the EC does not have a role in the use of the funds and a visibility commensurate to its financial contribution. Concerns have also been expressed on the feed-back it receives in terms of financial control, quality and timing of reports, perceived strategy and results of projects.

With a view to becoming a strategic and visible partner, a possible approach would be to prioritise and concentrate financial means on fewer Trust Funds and to request EC membership in their steering committees.

EC role and visibility have by definition been hampered by the dispersion and fragmentation of contributions in many trust funds, some of which received very limited financial amounts. A more strategic use of these Trust Funds would imply a streamlining based on their respective usefulness and on the EU priorities.

Trust Funds are considered to be helpful instruments in specific situations. This is the case in crisis, post-conflict and other sensitive situations (e.g., Tsunami; Gaza/West Bank). They foster coordination which would otherwise be difficult to achieve and allow assistance to be disbursed quickly. They may also have advantages in addressing financing for global goods and new challenges (e.g., AIDS) where donors and beneficiaries have neither the resources nor the technical expertise to address the problem.

EU priorities (e.g., focus on Africa, some post conflict areas, trade related assistance) have to be taken into account in order to concentrate finance on a few 'priority' Trust Funds and/or to assess whether there could not be another implementation solution.

The latter option has recently been retained in the context of the EU strategy to Africa. To provide EU financial support for transborder infrastructure projects, notably in energy, transport and water, which will improve inter-connections and reduce gaps in regional infrastructure networks, the EC has signed in February 2006 a MoU with the EIB. It establishes an EU-Africa Infrastructure Partnership and a Trust Fund to which the EC and the Member States will contribute grant resources. The EC/EIB Trust Fund will channel additional resources to Africa, as implied by the ODA commitments undertaken by the EU. And so will the new Africa Catalytic Growth Fund announced by the WB on 21 February 2006 whose complementarity has been welcomed by the Commission. It is also to be viewed as a strengthening of EU coordination, a necessary condition for enhanced coordination of all donors, called for by the Paris Declaration.

3.3.3 *Cooperation in the field*

It is clear that for an effective EC-WB cooperation, this should eventually take place at country level, where policies and strategies are implemented. Indeed, the 'Limelette' process described above emphasises the need to put in practice at country level the principles and policy directions agreed, so that these can feed back to headquarters level and be adjusted accordingly. To this effect, a number of countries in Africa are designed as pilot cases where strengthened cooperation is implemented (currently Burkina Faso, Ethiopia and Zambia).

But collaboration in the field also works rather well outside the 'Limelette' process. The EC and the World Bank collaborate closely within the so-called 'Consultative Group meetings', donor meetings that prepare a concerted donor (financial) response for a certain country, as well as in joint donor assessments (evaluation of needs).

Finally, one of the most promising areas of cooperation between the EC and the World Bank is on the assessment of public expenditure management, through the Joint Public Expenditure and Financial Accountability (PEFA) programme, which started in December 2001. Beyond the World Bank and the European Commission, PEFA includes the UK's Department for International Development, the Swiss State Secretariat for Economic Affairs, the French Ministry of Foreign Affairs, the Royal Norwegian Ministry of Foreign Affairs, the IMF and the Strategic Partnership with Africa. The objective is to facilitate closer coordination among donors and between donors and partner countries in assessing public expenditure, procurement and financial accountability systems, which leads to the identification of follow-up measures for related policy reforms and capacity building. This is especially relevant for the delivery of aid through budget support, i.e., direct grant/loan resources to the government budget, and contributed to aid effectiveness by improving donor harmonisation.

Examples of activities include the following: the elaboration of a common approach for supporting the development and implementation of country-led reform strategies and action plans in a coordinated and integrated manner with a focus on the results; the development of a number of performance indicators that provide consistent information for assessing and monitoring country public finance management performance; funding support in selected countries for integrated collaborative diagnostic assessments and actions plans.

4. Conclusion

In sum, effectiveness and efficiency in dealing with the challenges of the global economy require an efficient organization. Whether current governance in the IMF (and WB) is best suited to achieve their objectives is part of an on-going debate. There have been significant changes in the configuration and role of international actors over the past sixty years. Emerging economies and developing countries consider that they are under-represented in the decision-making process and have triggered discussions on representation. The development of the EU and the creation of the euro area have not been reflected in the governance structures of the IMF and the WB. Informal arrangements have been developed to strengthen the EU voice and cooperation between the EC and the WB has been extended and reinforced in the policy, financial and operational fields. There is certainly scope for improving the EU profile in all these dimensions. However, there are also inherent limitations to coordination and cooperation. For the Community to fully play the role it has been given by the Treaty its external representation will have to be strengthened.

Chapter 7
THE EUROPEAN COMMUNITY AT UNESCO: AN EXCEPTIONALLY ACTIVE OBSERVER?

by Lucia Cavicchioli*

1. INTRODUCTION**

In April 2005, the Executive Board of UNESCO[1] adopted an unprecedented decision in the history of the relations between the Organization and the European Union.[2] It invited, 'on an exceptional basis', the European Community, while maintaining

* Assistant Legal Officer, Office of International Standards and Legal Affairs, United Nations Educational, Scientific and Cultural Organization (UNESCO). The views expressed in this article are those of the author in her personal capacity and do not necessarily represent the views of, and should not be attributed to, UNESCO.

** All UNESCO documents referred to in this paper, unless otherwise indicated, are available on the UNESCO website at the following address <http://unesdoc.unesco.org/ulis/index.html>.

[1] The Executive Board is the executive organ of the Organization. It is composed of 58 members elected by the General Conference from among the Conference delegates appointed by Member States. It meets twice a year. The Board prepares the agenda for the Conference and is responsible for the execution of the programme adopted by the General Conference. Under the internal procedure for the elaboration of conventions and recommendations, upon proposals of the Director-General, the Executive Board is the convening authority for the meetings of technical and legal experts at which the content of preliminary draft instruments is negotiated. See Article 10.4 of the *Rules of Procedure concerning recommendations to Member States and international conventions covered by the terms of Article IV, paragraph 4, of the Constitution*, and Articles 18 et seq. of the *Regulations for the general classification of the various categories of meetings convened by UNESCO*, in UNESCO, *Basic Texts* (Paris, UNESCO Publishing 2004) p. 113 et seq.

[2] The reference made to the 'European Community' (instead of the 'European Union') throughout this paper, although contrary to the general trend shown in external and internal EU documents as well as in the international practice, is intended to reflect the legal situation, since this paper is primarily focused on the participation of the Community, according to the competences conferred thereon by its Member States, in the elaboration of UNESCO standard-setting instruments. This also reflects the terminology used in the relevant UNESCO documents. While leaving aside the issue of the international personality of the Union, as distinguished from that of the Community, reference to the 'European Union' is made only when describing in general its relations with UNESCO. For a recent analysis of the participation of the EC and the EU in international organizations in the perspective of the EU constitutional reform, see I. Govaere, J. Capiau and A. Vermeersch, 'In-between Seats: the Participation of the European Union in International Organizations', 9 *European Foreign Affairs Review* (2004) pp. 155-187. See also more in general E. Cannizzaro, 'Fragmented sovereignty? The European Union and its Member States in the International Arena', 12 *Italian Yearbook of International Law* (2003) pp. 35-57.

J. Wouters et al., eds., The United Nations and the European Union

its observer status, to participate actively in the work of the intergovernmental meeting of experts convened to elaborate a preliminary draft of the Convention on the protection and promotion of the diversity of cultural expressions.[3]

Agreement on this decision was reached after long discussions that had started already in September 2004, at the previous session of the Board, when the Member States of the European Union represented therein had asked that the European Community be granted 'extended rights' in the context of these negotiations, in view of the direct impact that several provisions of the draft Convention could have on Community competences.

As a result of a difficult negotiation process in which the European Union had an unusual visibility, in October 2005, the UNESCO General Conference adopted the final text of the Convention on the protection and promotion of the diversity of cultural expressions (hereinafter 'Cultural Diversity Convention').[4] Following an EC drafting proposal, this is the first UNESCO Convention[5] that contains a final clause allowing regional economic integration organizations to become a party to it (Article 27).

Apparently, the relations between the Organization and the European Union are at a turning point. A clear procedure for coordination between the EU Members States and the European Commission has been defined for the first time with regard to the negotiation of a UNESCO convention, and a more active role of the European Community in the procedure for the elaboration of standard-setting instruments has been expressly recognized by a UNESCO governing body.

In giving a general overview of the relations between the two organizations, the focus of this paper will be on the notion of 'active' observer as defined within UNESCO with specific reference to the European Community, a status that seems to have been granted to it on an exceptional basis in the context of the negotiation of the Cultural Diversity Convention. The paper will try to assess the potential relevance of the UNESCO Executive Board's decision in consolidating the role of the Community as a special observer endowed with additional rights in the elaboration process of UNESCO's future standard-setting instruments that could potentially affect the *acquis communautaire*.

The second part of the paper examines the implications of the new final clause allowing the participation of the European Community in the new Convention from

[3] See Decision 171 EX/60, in UNESCO Doc., *Decisions adopted by the Executive Board at its 171st session* (12 April-28 April 2005) pp. 71-72.

[4] The Convention on the protection and promotion of the diversity of cultural expressions had a different title during the negotiation phase. All UNESCO documents and EU documents relating to this phase referred to a 'draft Convention on the protection of the diversity of cultural contents and artistic expressions'. To avoid confusion, throughout this paper, we use the abbreviated title 'Cultural Diversity Convention'.

[5] The term 'UNESCO conventions' is used technically to refer only to those conventions adopted by the UNESCO General Conference in accordance with the standard rules of procedure. It does not include a number of conventions, which have been adopted by international diplomatic conferences convened under the auspices of UNESCO.

the perspective of the UNESCO legal framework and tries to figure out how this participation would be implemented in practice. The clause in question has been modeled on the corresponding provisions found in previous international conventions adopted under the auspices of the United Nations and other UN agencies.[6] However, the Cultural Diversity Convention, like other UNESCO conventions, provides for a monitoring mechanism under which the parties have specific reporting obligations that are a reflection of those generally provided for under the constitutive treaty with regard to all standard-setting instruments elaborated within the Organization. How the European Union will fulfill these obligations in parallel with the EU Member States that will be parties to the Convention and how the participation of the Community in the work of the follow-up bodies created under the Convention will be structured is difficult to tell. These are the questions which the paper seeks to examine with a view to providing preliminary answers.

2. Evolution of the Relations Between the European Union and UNESCO Since the 1964 Cooperation Agreement

In 1964, UNESCO accorded observer status to the European Economic Community by way of an exchange of letters between the President of the Commission of the then European Economic Community and the UNESCO Director-General.[7] The content of the 1964 agreement was very general. It had the primary objective of coordinating the action of both organizations in pursuit of their common aims through the exchange of documents and information, the presence of observers at their respective meetings, and the establishment of joint working groups on specific technical questions of common interest. Under this agreement, subject to the due observance of existing rules and regulations, the UNESCO Director-General invites the President of the Commission to send observers to any technical meetings and conferences of UNESCO at which questions of common interest are to be examined. Similarly, the President of the Commission invites the Director-General of UNESCO to be represented by observers at the pertinent EC technical meetings and conferences.

---

[6] The text of the clause was elaborated following similar provisions set forth in the UN Framework Convention on Climate Change, the Convention on Biological Diversity, and the WHO Framework Convention on Tobacco Control. See *infra*, section 4.

[7] The conclusion of the agreement was authorized by the Executive Board in 1962. See Decision 63 EX/6.9, in UNESCO Doc., *Resolutions and decisions adopted by the Executive Board at its sixty-third session* (26 October-12 December 1962) p. 49. At the same time, even before the signature of the agreement, the Board authorized the European Economic Community to send observers to the 12th session of the General Conference. See Decision 63 EX/14.2 (III) and Decision 63 EX/15.1, ibid., pp. 13 and 15. For the text of the agreement see UNESCO Doc. 67 EX/29, *Draft Agreement with the Commission of the European Economic Community (EEC)* (20 April 1964) Annex I, p. 2 (document not available on Internet).

Cooperation was further developed in another exchange of letters of 12 December 1972 and 14 February 1973, which identified the fields of action that were of common interest for both organizations.[8] The collaboration was focused on a number of priority areas, such as environment, higher education, the creation of a world system of scientific and technical information, the fight against analphabetism in Africa, and aid to development in the field of education, science, culture and media. Following the intensification of the cooperation between the two organizations, another agreement including more details on modalities for the implementation of joint programmes and projects was concluded in 1996,[9] and more recently, in 2004, the European Commission and UNESCO signed a financing and administrative agreement with the aim of strengthening and facilitating all forms of technical assistance between the two institutions through harmonization of their administrative and financial procedures.[10]

The European Union is nowadays a major contributor to UNESCO's project activities in all fields of the Organization's competence, and particularly in the area of education.[11] Furthermore, UNESCO is often associated by the Community in the execution of Community-funded projects in partner countries, for example in view of providing support to national reforms in the field of higher education or technical expertise in the restoration of monuments or archaeological sites. Other potential areas of cooperation have been identified recently with reference to water management at global level (in collaboration with the UNESCO Intergovernmental Oceanographic Commission), protection of the world heritage, bioethics, intercultural dialogue, protection of human rights in UNESCO's fields of competence.

---

[8] The text of the 1972-1973 agreement is unpublished. For an analysis of the relations between the two organizations at the time of the conclusion of this agreement see D. Hymans, 'Les relations de la CEE et de l'UNESCO', 164 *Revue du marché commun* (1973) pp. 160-162.

[9] See UNESCO Doc. 147 EX/44, *Cooperation between the European Commission and UNESCO* (16 August 1995).

[10] This agreement was concluded on 23 February 2004 to complete the previous exchanges of letters. It extends to UNESCO as a UN specialized agency the Financial and Administrative Framework Agreement signed in 2003 between the European Commission and the United Nations. The text of the agreement between the European Union and the UN is available on the EU web portal at the following address <http://europa.eu.int/comm/europeaid/tender/gestion/cont_typ/onu/un_ec_fwc_en.pdf>. In this regard see *Communication from the Commission to the Council and the European Parliament. The European Union and the United Nations: The choice of multilateralism*, COM (2003) 526 final (10 September 2003).

[11] UNESCO receives financial contributions from the European Commission in the form of extra-budgetary voluntary contributions (since the European Community is not a member of UNESCO, it does not contribute to its ordinary budget). The most recent contributions have been mainly concentrated on the Education Sector of UNESCO. In 2005, 11,4 million USD have been destined to this sector, including a contribution of 3,2 million USD to support secondary education in Iraq. Other contributions have been made for supporting professional teaching and improvement in the quality of school textbooks in developing countries. See Délégation permanente du Royaume Uni, Mission permanente d'observation de la Commission européenne, *Note d'information. L'Union Européenne et l'UNESCO* (décembre 2005) (unpublished document).

Since the conclusion of the 1964 Cooperation Agreement, there has been a significant extension of the competence of the European Community. As a result, the rights attached to the status of observer have apparently become inadequate to allow the Commission to fully negotiate on behalf of the Community when it comes to matters that fall within the EC exclusive competence or within shared competences between the Community and its Member States.[12]

However, until recently, the limits inherent in the observer status with respect to the participation in the elaboration of standard-setting instruments were not perceived by the Community as diminishing its role during the negotiations. In the latest agreement with UNESCO, the status of the representative of the Community is left unchanged: UNESCO recognizes the status of observer to the Commission before its governing bodies and encourages its participation in the technical meetings organized by its departments.[13]

While the European Community obtained additional rights before UN bodies having specific competence over matters falling within the *acquis communautaire* and in several international conferences convened under the auspices of the United Nations for negotiating important international instruments partially affecting its competences, it submitted an explicit request for playing an active role in the process for the elaboration of UNESCO normative instruments only during the procedure for the preparation of the preliminary draft Convention on cultural diversity.

During the negotiations concerning previous UNESCO conventions, the modalities for the participation of the Community had been defined according to a practice developed before other UN agencies with standard-setting activities, of which the EC is not a member. Usually, the Community is represented by the Commission and may participate without vote in meetings of UNESCO governing bodies, internal commissions and technical bodies. The representative of the Commission or an EC Member State government (usually the State holding the Presidency of the Council) may speak on behalf of the Community if they so agree, but only a gov-

---

[12] The Commission holds that the European Community has to ensure the unity of its representation in international organizations, also when shared competences are involved. See European Commission, *Recommendation from the Commission to the Council to authorize the Commission to participate, on behalf of the Community, in the negotiations within UNESCO on the convention on the protection of the diversity of cultural contents and artistic expressions*, SEC (2004) 1062 final (1 September 2004) p. 5, para. 3. This assertion is based on the general duty of cooperation provided under Article 10 of the EC Treaty and on Opinion 2/91 of the European Court of Justice, *Convention No. 170 of the International Labour Organization concerning safety in the use of chemicals at work* [1993] *ECR* I-1061. See also ECJ, Opinion 1/94, *WTO* [1994] *ECR* I-5967, paras. 107-108. For a recent review of the issue of the Community competence, whether exclusive or not, to conclude an international agreement, see ECJ, Opinion 1/03, *Competence of the Community to conclude the new Lugano Convention on jurisdiction and the recognition and enforcement of judgments in civil and commercial matters* (7 February 2006) para. 120-133. The text of this opinion is available on line on the website of the Court at the following address <http://www.curia.eu.int/en/content/juris/index.htm>.

[13] See para. 1 of the Agreement of 23 February 2004 between UNESCO and the European Commission (unpublished document).

ernment of an EC Member State may submit proposals or amendments to proposals on behalf of the Community.

Given the subject-matters covered by UNESCO conventions in line with the broad terms of the Organization's mandate, which touches upon normative areas in which the European Community generally has shared competences (education and vocational training, cultural and natural heritage, natural and social sciences, including human rights related aspects),[14] the limitations linked to the status of observer were not felt as irremediably affecting the possibility for the EC to safeguard its interest during the negotiation process.

The only occasion on which the question of the modalities for the participation of the Community was raised was in 1976, during the negotiations concerning the Protocol to the 1950 Agreement on the Importation of Educational, Scientific and Cultural Materials (the so-called 'Florence Agreement'), which had a potential bearing on circulation of goods.[15] At a meeting of government experts on the preliminary draft of the Protocol, the Commission and the EC Member States present at the meeting expressed the wish that the Community could introduce proposals for amendments on its own behalf. This possibility was excluded as incompatible with the EC observer status, and the draft amendments were presented on behalf of the Community by the State holding the EC Presidency. However, during the debate on substantive issues, it was only the representative of the Commission that intervened on behalf of the EC and its Member States present at the meeting.[16]

The negotiations on the 1976 Protocol to the Florence Agreement concerned matters close to those covered by the more recent Cultural Diversity Convention, i.e., the circulation of cultural, scientific or educational goods.[17] Aimed at overcoming economic obstacles to the free flows of ideas, the Florence Agreement regulates the importation of educational, scientific and cultural materials in order to facilitate the circulation of books, newspapers, periodicals and printed materials, works of art, visual and auditory materials, scientific instruments and equipment for educational purposes. The Protocol was adopted to remove some forms of dis-

---

[14] The conventions adopted by the UNESCO General Conference during the past twenty years concern mainly cultural and educational issues.

[15] See the Agreement on the Importation of Educational, Scientific and Cultural Materials, with Annexes A to E and Protocol annexed (Florence, 17 June 1950) and its Protocol, with Annexes A to H (Nairobi, 26 November 1976). The texts of UNESCO standard-setting instruments are available for consultation on the UNESCO website at the following address <http://www.unesco.org/legal_instruments>.

[16] The legal issues relating to the participation of the Community in the debates on the elaboration of the Protocol and the possibility to allow the EC to become a party to this instrument are examined in a internal note of the Legal Office, dated 25 March 1976, prepared by the then UNESCO Legal Adviser, Claude Lussier (unpublished document).

[17] At the early stage of the preparation of the Convention in 2003, one of the options considered by the UNESCO Secretariat for developing a new instrument on cultural diversity was a new Protocol to the Florence Agreement. See UNESCO Doc. 166 EX/28, *Preliminary study on the technical and legal aspects relating to the desirability of a standard-setting instrument on cultural diversity*, Executive Board, 166th Session (12 March 2003) p. 6, para. 22.

crimination with respect to the content, nature or purpose of films, works of art and other cultural products still permitted under the Florence Agreement and to extend the scope of the latter to other cultural goods and materials such as sports equipment, musical instruments, and materials and machines used for the production of books.[18]

As shown below, things went differently during the negotiation concerning the draft Cultural Diversity Convention. This time, the Community formally requested and obtained to be granted rights beyond those of an observer.

3. The Negotiations Concerning the Cultural Diversity Convention: An Exceptional Request for Participation

The elaboration process of the Cultural Diversity Convention started when the UNESCO General Conference decided at its 32nd session, in October 2003, that it was advisable to adopt an international legal instrument on cultural diversity.[19] The drafting of a binding international instrument on cultural diversity generated a growing interest in UNESCO Member States.[20] The future Convention would have established principles concerning the recognition of the distinctive nature of cultural goods and services, the preservation of the right of States Parties to adopt cultural policies and appropriate measures for the protection and promotion of cultural expressions, and the strengthening of international cooperation so as to improve developing countries' capacity to promote the diversity of cultural expressions throughout the world. The new instrument would have also addressed the issue of cultural policies, with inevitable repercussions on the links between culture and trade.[21]

For the elaboration of the new Convention, the Director-General opted for a multi-stage procedure in line with the practice developed for the preparation of other standard-setting instruments relating to the protection of cultural heritage. A first phase, in which a restricted group of independent experts appointed by the Director-General had several meetings to develop recommendations for drafting the outline of the future convention, was followed by a second phase where meet-

[18] See UNESCO, *A Guide to the Operation of the Agreement on the Importation of Educational, Scientific and Cultural Materials*, 4th edn. (Paris, UNESCO Publishing 1969).

[19] The UNESCO General Conference asked the Director-General to submit at the next session of the Conference, to be held in 2005, a preliminary report accompanied by a preliminary draft convention. See Res. 32 C/34, *Desirability of drawing up an international standard-setting instrument on cultural diversity*, in UNESCO Doc., Records of General Conference, 32nd session (Paris, 29 September to 17 October 2003) Vol. 1: Resolutions, p. 64.

[20] The only existing instrument of universal character on this issue was at that time the UNESCO Declaration on Cultural Diversity adopted in 2001.

[21] On the state of the global 'culture and trade' debate see R.J. Neuwirth, 'Culture and Trade? A European Way Towards an International Instrument on Cultural Diversity', 13 *Italian Yearbook of International Law* (2003) pp. 97-129.

ings of government experts were convened by the Director-General with a view to reaching an agreement on a preliminary text.[22]

The intention to play an active role in the negotiations was expressed by the European Commission even before the UNESCO General Conference had made a decision on the desirability of adopting a convention on cultural diversity. In an early communication to the Council and the European Parliament issued in August 2003, the Commission stated that it would seek consistency between European internal and international action regarding cultural diversity in the exploratory discussions concerning the drawing-up of a convention and 'cooperate with the Member States to develop common positions in order for the EC to be united in its proposal and conduct at the General Conference'.[23]

After the end of the first phase of negotiations[24] and in view of their continuation at the intergovernmental level, the European Commission issued a recommen-

---

[22] The procedure for the preparation of conventions and recommendations is established in a set of rules adopted by the UNESCO General Conference in 1950. Since the Conference meets every two years, the preparation of an instrument is usually completed during a corresponding lapse of time. The decision to adopt a standard-setting instrument is based on a preliminary study prepared by the Secretariat, which has been previously submitted to the Members States for comments. On the basis of this study and the observations of the Executive Board, the General Conference makes a decision on the advisability to elaborate an instrument. Subsequently, the Director-General may decide to convene meetings of independent experts to assist him in preparing a first draft. At the end of this first phase, a preliminary report of the Director-General, which may be accompanied by a preliminary draft, is sent to Member States for a first round of observations. In the second phase, several meetings of government experts may be convened by the Director-General upon decision of the Executive Board or the General Conference. These meetings are not diplomatic conferences. The meeting of government experts is open to all Member States of UNESCO. It has the task to assist the Director-General in elaborating the draft instrument that has to be communicated to Member States seven months before the opening of the General Conference at which the text is to be adopted. In the recent past, a practice has been developed to convene additional intergovernmental meetings, if necessary, after the transmission of the draft to Member States, in order to make progress in the negotiation. An updated version of the text is then submitted to the General Conference for final adoption. See *Rules of Procedure concerning recommendations to Member States and international conventions covered by the terms of Article IV, paragraph 4, of the Constitution*, *supra* n. 1, Chapters II to V. On the procedure for elaborating UNESCO standard-setting instruments, see H. Saba, 'L'activité quasi-législative des institutions spécialisées des Nations Unies', 111 *Hague Recueil* (1964-I) pp. 603-690. In the recent practice, UNESCO has developed another type of normative instruments, namely declarations or charters, for which a simplified procedure has been approved by the Conference. See Res. 33 C/87, *Multi-stage procedure for the elaboration, examination, adoption and follow-up of declarations, charters and similar standard-setting instruments adopted by the General Conference and not covered by the Rules of Procedure concerning recommendations to Member States and international conventions covered by the terms of Article IV, paragraph 4, of the Constitution*, in UNESCO Doc., *Records of the General Conference*, 33rd session, Paris, 3-21 October 2005, Vol. 1: Resolutions, pp. 141-142.

[23] Cf., *Communication from the Commission to the Council and the European Parliament. Towards an international instrument on cultural diversity*, COM (2003) 520 final (27 August 2003) p. 8.

[24] A group of fifteen independent experts chosen by the UNESCO Director-General met three times between December 2004 and May 2005 and elaborated a text constituting a basis for the pre-

dation to the Council seeking for the authorization to participate, on behalf of the Community, in the negotiation process within UNESCO.[25] In the Commission's view, the preliminary draft convention was likely to affect the *acquis communautaire* and the Community policies in a number of areas, namely in the cultural field, cultural and audiovisual policies, freedom of movement for cultural goods and services, intellectual property, and cultural aspects of the EC development policies. It was clear that the draft convention touched upon areas coming within the Community exclusive competence[26] as well as shared competences.[27] The Council granted this mandate to the Commission in November 2004.

A request to grant the Community 'extended rights', going beyond the formal rights of an observer, at the forthcoming negotiations on the draft Convention, was submitted for the first time by the EU Member States represented at the UNESCO Executive Board right after the end of the first intergovernmental meeting held in September 2004. The EU Presidency, on behalf of the Member States, asked that regional economic integration organizations, such as the Community, be given 'the right to speak at any time as full participants and the right to introduce proposals and amendments to the texts under consideration'.[28] The request was based on the

liminary draft convention, which was transmitted by the Secretariat to Member States in July 2004. See UNESCO Doc., *Preliminary draft convention on the protection of the diversity of cultural contents and artistic expressions, Preliminary report of the Director-General*, CLT/CPD/2004/CONF.201/1 (Paris, July 2004).

[25] See *Recommendation from the Commission to the Council to authorize the Commission to participate, on behalf of the Community, in the negotiations within UNESCO on the convention on the protection of the diversity of cultural contents and artistic expressions*, SEC (2004) 1062 final (1st September 2004).

[26] The EC exclusive competence on commercial policy (Article 133 of the EC Treaty) was likely to be particularly affected, especially in connection with the proposal to include a clause providing that the Convention could prevail over the rights and obligations of the parties deriving from any existing international instrument 'where the exercise of those rights and obligations would cause serious damage or threat to the diversity of cultural expressions'. See UNESCO Doc., *Preliminary draft of a convention on the protection of the diversity of cultural contents and artistic expressions*, CLT/CPD/2004/CONF-201/2 (Paris, July 2004) p. 10. Only agreements on intellectual property rights would have been excluded from the application of this rule, but any other agreement concluded within the World Trade Organization (WTO) framework could have been affected.

[27] EC exclusive and shared competences are often inextricably linked in the matters covered by the Convention. Several examples are mentioned in the document of the Commission: a) the free circulation and mobility of artists and creators, a question touching upon the free movement of workers in the EU internal market, immigration issues and the opening of the EC market to temporary cultural workers, for which negotiations are still ongoing in the context of the WTO; b) the facilitation of access to global markets for works from developing countries, an issue susceptible to affect customs policy instruments, namely in view of a possible reduction of duties on the imports of certain cultural products into the EC market, c) trade matters, in particular the commitments entered into by the EC and its Member States under WTO instruments; d) intellectual property, with particular reference to the treaties concluded under the auspices of the World Intellectual Property Organization (WIPO). For a detailed description of the EC competences involved see R.J. Neuwirth, loc. cit. n. 21, pp. 97-129.

[28] See UNESCO Doc. 170 EX/PLEN/DR.2 (12 October 2004) para. 4, in which the Board was requested to decide that 'regional economic integration organizations constituted by sovereign

fact that an observer's rights were considered insufficient for the Commission to be able to safeguard the interests of the European Community in matters falling within its exclusive competence, which the provisions of the draft Convention were likely to affect.[29]

In presenting the proposal, the representative of the EU Presidency asserted that the request for the EC to be an active observer could appear unusual within UNESCO, but not for the international system as a whole. A reference was made in particular to the negotiations within the World Health Organization (WHO) concerning the 2003 Framework Convention on Tobacco Control, where regional economic integration organizations were permitted to participate actively in the drafting of the instrument within the competent intergovernmental bodies. In fact, the decision proposed to the UNESCO Executive Board reflected very closely the text of the World Health Assembly resolution on the same issue, but it included a precise description of the additional rights to be granted to regional economic integration organizations.[30]

States, Members of UNESCO, to which their Member States have transferred competence over matters within the purview of the intergovernmental meeting of experts on the preliminary draft convention [...], including the competence to enter into treaties in respect to these matters, may actively participate in the work of the intergovernmental meeting while maintaining their observer status. Such active participation shall consist of the right to speak at the same time as full participants, and the right to introduce proposals and amendments to the text under consideration'. In its very first request, formulated in a letter to the Deputy Director-General, the European Commission had proposed to insert an 'assimilation clause' into the rules of procedure of the intergovernmental meeting granting to the EC the same procedural rights as Members States elected at the Board. See a letter dated 16 September 2004 from the Permanent Delegation of the European Commission to OECD and UNESCO to the UNESCO Deputy Director-General (unpublished document). This idea was abandoned, as it would have implied a status of 'full participant' without the right to vote.

[29] UNESCO Doc. 170 EX/37, *Participation of the European Commission in the intergovernmental meeting of experts (category II) on the preliminary draft convention on the protection of the diversity of cultural contents and artistic expressions* (29 September 2004). This request was formulated when the EU Council had still to make a decision in order to authorize the Commission to negotiate on behalf of the Community. The decision was made on 16 November 2004, after the first intergovernmental meeting on the Convention, and contained specific negotiating directives for the Commission. See Council of the European Union, Doc. 13840/04 CULT 103, *Draft Council Decision authorizing the Commission to participate, on behalf on the Community, in the negotiations within UNESCO on the convention on the protection of the diversity of cultural contents and artistic expressions* (29 October 2004), and *EU Bulletin*, 11-2004, point 1.4.24.

[30] See Resolution of the World Health Assembly, WHA52.18, *Towards a WHO framework convention on tobacco control*, 24 May 1999, para. 1(3), according to which regional economic integration organizations constituted by sovereign States, Members of WHO, to which their Member States have transferred competence over matters governed by this resolution, including the competence to enter into treaties in respect to these matters were allowed to 'actively participate' in the drafting and negotiations of the intergovernmental negotiating body and working group established by the World Health Assembly. The same active observer status has been granted to regional economic integration organizations in the context of the revision of the International Health Regulations by an intergovernmental working group, see Decision WHA56.28, *Revision of the International Health Regulations*, 28 May 2005. The Resolutions of the World Health Assembly are available on the WHO website at <http://www.who.int./gb/e/index.html>.

The UNESCO Legal Adviser's intervention, prompted by the novelty of the request within UNESCO's legal framework, confirmed that the granting of extended rights to regional economic integration organizations under similar circumstances was not unusual in the practice of international organizations, especially in the United Nations system, and made it clear that there were no obstacles in the UNESCO Constitution nor in its internal regulations that would prevent the Board from granting the EC the status of active observer.

He delimited clearly the content of the 'active observer'[31] rights as identified in the EC proposal, *vis-à-vis* the procedural rights at meetings usually accruing from membership. He noted that in most cases certain procedural rights such as the right to raise points of order, to move procedural motions, the right to be elected as an officer or to be a full-fledged member of a drafting group were not usually extended to 'active observers'.[32] With reference to the practice of UNESCO, the Legal Adviser recalled that in the context of recent negotiations, concerning in particular the Convention on the protection of the underwater cultural heritage adopted in 2001, the rules of procedure had been interpreted with a certain flexibility so as to grant certain observers, on an informal basis, the right to speak at the same time as full participants and to make proposals, provided that their proposals were seconded by a full participant.[33]

Despite the explanations received, the representatives of the UNESCO Member States serving on the Board reacted negatively to the request of the Community, mainly because there was a fear to set a precedent,[34] but also because many of them seemed not to be familiar enough with the concept of regional economic integration organizations nor with the practice developed within the UN system as to the Community participation in meetings. Hence, the decision was postponed to the following session of the Board in order to allow its members further reflection on the issue. The European Commission could therefore participate in the first two inter-

---

[31] The expression 'active' or 'enhanced' observer is sometimes used in EU documents to define the special observer status enjoyed by the Community during the negotiations of conventions in conferences convened under the UN auspices or before the international organizations of the UN system, see for example, *Communication from the Commission to the Council and the European Parliament. Building an effective partnership with the United Nations in the fields of development and humanitarian affairs*, COM (2001) 231 final (2 May 2001) p. 17, note 7, where the term is defined with reference to the EU participation in UN bodies and specialized agencies as meaning 'participation in and contribution to the work of governing bodies including contribution to decision-making'.

[32] See the intervention of the UNESCO Legal Adviser, A.A. Yusuf, in UNESCO Doc. 170 EX/SR.1-10, *Summary records of the 170th session of the Executive Board* (4-14 October 2004) pp. 259-260, para. 18.

[33] These rights were recognized in particular to representatives of non-Member States and non-governmental organizations. See UNESCO Doc.170 EX/SR 1-10, Ibid., p. 263, para. 28.1.

[34] The representatives of the United States and Australia also contested the assumption that the EC competences were directly affected by the provisions of the draft Convention. Ibid., p. 254, para. 3 and pp. 256-257, para. 9.

governmental meetings on the draft Convention only with the role of a traditional observer.[35]

At the following session of the Board in March 2005, the European Community reiterated its request referring to 'the right to actively participate in the same manner as full participants in the work of the intergovernmental meeting, excluding the right to vote'.[36]

The proposal was first examined by a subsidiary body of the Executive Board competent for discussing matters concerning the Board's working methods, which decided to establish an *ad hoc* informal working group on the controversial issue. An agreeable solution was reached only after long discussions that continued on an informal basis until the very moment of the discussion of the issue before the Board. The text eventually submitted to the Board for decision did not contain a general reference to economic regional integration organizations nor a list of the additional rights qualifying the status of active observer, as originally drafted. The decision recognized only to the European Community 'on an exceptional basis' the right to 'participate actively and as fully as appropriate' in the next intergovernmental meeting, which was the last one scheduled for the elaboration of the draft Convention.

The decision of the UNESCO Board was clearly inspired by the decision made on the same issue by the World Health Assembly in connection with the drafting of the Framework Convention on Tobacco Control. But the UNESCO decision concerned specifically the European Community and not regional economic integration organizations in general, and there was a clear intention to underline its exceptionality in connection with the very special circumstances under which it was made.

Nonetheless, in contrast with the very general wording chosen for the decision of the Board, a statement made by the EU Presidency immediately thereafter specifically enumerated the rights considered by the Community as being inherent in its status of 'enhanced observer':

> 'The European Union considers that this active participation shall consist within the negotiation of the convention of the ability to speak as other participants. Such active participation shall also consist of the ability to reply, to put forward proposals and amendments on issues for which it has competence at the formal meetings. It shall also include the ability to take part in the discussion of procedural issues within the context

[35] Two meetings of government experts were organized from 20 to 24 September 2004 and from 31 January to 11 February 2005 respectively. Moreover, a drafting committee established at the first meeting met in December 2004 to revise the preliminary draft convention in the light of Member States' comments.

[36] The proposal included not only the right to speak, to reply, and to put forward proposals and amendments at formal meetings, but also the right to take part in committees, working groups, formal and informal meetings, and the right to have a nameplate. See UNESCO Doc. 171 EX/47 Add., *Participation of the European Community in the intergovernmental meeting of experts (category II) on the preliminary draft convention on the protection of the diversity of cultural contents and artistic expressions* (17 March 2005).

> of the draft cultural diversity convention and the ability to take part in the committees, working groups, formal or informal meetings set up in the course of the work relating to negotiation of this convention.
>
> The European Community shall have its own nameplate. The European Community may not chair committees or subcommittees or serve as *Rapporteur* unless there is full consensus. The European Community shall not have the right to vote nor break or block consensus'.[37]

The UNESCO Member States represented in the Board took note of this statement and did not object to it. The Chairman made it very clear that the statement reflected the definition of the EC 'active participation' as agreed between the members of the Board.[38]

The European Community had the possibility to effectively take advantage of its status of enhanced observer only during the last intergovernmental meeting convened by the Board in view of the preparation of the final draft. When the draft Convention was examined by the UNESCO General Conference for adoption, there was no debate on substantive issues. The majority of Member States expressed their favour for the text as agreed upon at the end of the last meeting of government experts. Therefore, the General Conference was not requested to decide on the issue of the participation of the European Community in the negotiations at their final stage, before the competent Conference commission and then within the plenary.[39]

This by no means diminishes the relevance of the decision of the Board, which definitely sets a precedent that could have a bearing on the elaboration process of future UNESCO conventions, should the European Community claim that either its exclusive competences or shared competences could be affected by the draft instrument concerned.

An active role of the European Community in the UNESCO standard-setting process has now been officially recognized. For the first time, within a UN agency having a wide normative activity, the notion of 'active' or 'enhanced' observer in

---

[37] It must be noted that the EU Presidency requested that the statement be put into the records *in extenso*. See UNESCO Doc. 171 EX/SR.1-10, *Summary records of the 171st session of the Executive Board* (18-28 April 2005) pp. 292-293. At this stage, a code of conduct had already been agreed between the Council, the Member States and the Commission for defining the *modus operandi* to be adopted during the negotiations. See Council of the European Union, Doc. 5518/05, *Draft code of conduct between the Council, the Member States and the Commission on the UNESCO negotiations on the draft convention on the protection of the diversity of cultural contents and artistic expressions* (21/28 January 2005). The code of conduct contained indications on the distribution of tasks between the Presidency and the Commission.

[38] See UNESCO Doc. 171 EX/SR.1-10, *supra* n. 37, p. 295, para. 88.

[39] In its decision, the Board had recommended that 'the General Conference, at its 33rd session, take this decision into account with respect to its consideration of the item relating to the preliminary draft convention on the protection of the diversity of cultural contents and artistic expressions'. See Decision 171 EX/60, *supra* n. 3.

connection with the special nature of the European Community was given, in the context of the negotiation of this specific Convention, a clear definition through an interpretative declaration.[40]

Quite surprisingly, despite the initial opposition shown by several UNESCO Member States before the Board, the Community has obtained on this occasion procedural rights, which, even though they may not correspond to those of a 'full participant' awarded to the EC before some UN bodies,[41] granted it a highly developed active observer status. The extensive discussions on the issue over two sessions of the Board served as a useful learning process for non-EU UNESCO delegates, who have now become more aware of the peculiar repartition of powers between the EC and its Members States over the matters governed by the Convention.

Clearly, the European Community has been acquiring a unique role of special observer within the UN system and the development of the active observer status in a multiplicity of fora could be very important to ensure that the Community could

[40] The procedural rights claimed in this declaration, such as the ability to take part in the discussion of procedural issues, and the ability to take part in committees, working groups, formal or informal meetings, go beyond those of a traditional observer. According to the traditional notion, 'observers do not have the right to vote and are not entitled to sponsor or co-sponsor substantive proposals (including amendments) or procedural motions, or to raise points of order or challenge rulings'. See the guidelines on observer status issued by the UN Secretariat, *United Nations Juridical Yearbook* 1975, p. 167, para. 21. In general on the rights of observers and in particular on their participation in meetings as far as procedural issues are concerned, see E. Suy, 'The status of observers in international organizations', 160 *Hague Recueil* (1978-II) pp. 147-148. See also S. Marchisio, 'EU's Membership in International Organizations', in E. Cannizzaro (ed.), *The European Union as an Actor in International Relations* (The Hague, Kluwer 2004) p. 231, at p. 255. The UN General Assembly has recognized the special nature of the Community as an organization having special powers and responsibilities in international economic relations when granting to it the status of permanent observer. See UN Resolution 3208 (XXIX), *Status of the European Economic Community in the General Assembly* (11 October 1974) and the *Memorandum to the Secretary of the Second Committee of the General Assembly*, prepared by the UN Secretariat, on the request by the EEC Council to be invited to attend the deliberations of the Second Committee with observer status, in *UN Juridical Yearbook 1971*, pp. 197-198.

[41] Before the UN Commission on Sustainable Development, the European Community is entitled 'to participate fully, within its areas of competence, in the work of the Commission or any subsidiary body thereof, in accordance with the present decision. Such full participation shall include the right to speak and the right of reply, as well as the right to introduce proposals and amendments. Such full participation shall also include the right to raise as a point of order the fact that consultations are continuing among the Community and its Member States on a matter on which a final decision is about to be made and for which the Community is the representative on the Commission in accordance with the present decision, provided that the right to raise this point of order shall not include the right to challenge the decision of the Chairman in response to that point of order. The Community shall not have the right to vote but may submit proposals that shall be put to the vote if any member of the Commission so requests'. See the UN Economic and Social Council Decision 1995/201, *Full participation of the European Community in the Commission on Sustainable Development*, available on line on the UN website at the following address <http://www.un.org/documents/ecosoc/index.html>.

make its voice heard in those organizations where membership is not a feasible option.

4. The Participation of the European Community in UNESCO Conventions

Another true novelty concerning the Cultural Diversity Convention is the inclusion of a final clause according to which regional economic integration organizations may become parties to it.[42]

Under the UNESCO Constitution, the standard-setting activity is addressed only to Members States, which are requested to submit to the Organization reports on the action taken upon conventions and recommendations.[43] Nonetheless, there is

---

[42] Article 27 (Accession), paragraph 3, of the Convention reads as follows:
'The following provisions apply to regional economic integration organizations:
(a) This Convention shall also be open to accession by any regional economic integration organization, which shall, except as provided below, be fully bound by the provisions of the Convention in the same manner as States Parties;
(b) In the event that one or more Member States of such an organization is also Party to the Convention, the organization and such Member State or States shall decide on their responsibility for the performance of their obligations under the Convention. Such distribution of responsibility shall take effect following completion of the notification procedure described in sub-paragraph (c). The organization and the Member States shall not be entitled to exercise rights under the Convention concurrently. In addition, regional economic integration organizations, in matters within their competence, shall exercise their rights to vote with a number of votes equal to the number of their Member States that are Parties to the Convention. Such an organization shall not exercise its right to vote if any of its Member States exercises its right, and vice-versa;
(c) A regional economic integration organization and its Member State or States which have agreed on a distribution of responsibilities as provided in subparagraph (b) shall inform the Parties of any such proposed distribution of responsibilities in the following manner:
(i) in their instrument of accession, such organization shall declare with specificity, the distribution of their responsibilities with respect to matters governed by the Convention;
(ii) in the event of any later modification of their respective responsibilities, the regional economic integration organization shall inform the depositary of any such proposed modification of their respective responsibilities; the depositary shall in turn inform the Parties of such modification;
(d) Member States of a regional economic integration organization which become Parties to this Convention shall be presumed to retain competence over all matters in respect of which transfers of competence to the organization have not been specifically declared or informed to the depositary;
(e) 'Regional economic integration organizations' means an organization constituted by sovereign States, members of the United Nations or of any of its specialized agencies, to which those States have transferred competence in respect of matters governed by this Convention and which has been duly authorized, in accordance with its internal procedures, to become a Party to it.'

[43] See Articles IV.B, paragraph 4, and VIII of the UNESCO Constitution. See also *Rules of Procedure concerning recommendations to Member States and international conventions covered by the terms of Article IV, paragraph 4, of the Constitution*, *supra* n. 1. While several UNESCO conventions provide for autonomous monitoring bodies which examine reports sent by the States Parties, the monitoring action on the implementation of the other standard-setting instruments only rely on the reporting obligation imposed on Member States under the Constitution. The general reporting

no apparent incompatibility between the constitutional obligations linked to the adoption and follow-up of standard-setting instruments and the potential participation in a UNESCO convention of the European Community, as an organization to which some UNESCO Member States have transferred their competences over matters falling within the purview of that specific instrument.[44] Moreover, the Cultural Diversity Convention, as many other UNESCO conventions, establishes a special monitoring mechanism that can function independently from, and in parallel with, the general reporting obligation set forth in the UNESCO Constitution.[45]

In the past, the European Community had already formulated a request to become a party to a UNESCO Convention, in the context of the negotiations concerning the 1976 Protocol to the Florence Agreement on the Importation of Educational, Scientific and Cultural Materials.[46] Several drafting proposals had been submitted by the Community to this end, but were rejected. Although the possibility of a participation of the European Community was considered in principle as feasible within the UNESCO legal framework, this solution was not retained in the case at stake. The negotiated instrument had been conceived as having the form of a protocol linked to a previous convention, to which only Member States were entitled to accede.[47]

When presenting its proposal concerning accession of regional economic integration organizations to the Cultural Diversity Convention, the European Community made it clear that in the absence of a specific clause allowing EC participation,

---

mechanism provided under the Constitution is implemented only with respect to UNESCO conventions which do not provide for a special mechanism: all Member States, including those which have not ratified them, are periodically requested to submit reports. As regards non-binding instruments (recommendations, declarations and charters), despite the general obligation set forth in the Constitution, for many UNESCO recommendations there is no monitoring mechanism due to the absence of a specific decision of the General Conference asking Member States to report on their implementation. However, the application of some recommendations in the field of education and of the most recent declarations is monitored by special supervisory bodies.

[44] The case could be different for other international organizations with relevant law-making activity. For instance, within the legal framework of the International Labour Organization (ILO), there are major obstacles at the constitutional level, which would make it difficult to allow the ratification of a convention by the European Community. The ILO Constitution sets out provisions envisaging a complex reporting system and special supervisory mechanisms, which are applicable only to Member States. Moreover, the tripartite nature of the Organization imposes the participation of social partners in the elaboration of standard-setting instruments and in the follow-up on their implementation. A ratification of an ILO convention by the EC could not be possible without first amending the ILO Constitution.

[45] See Article 23 of the Convention establishing an Intergovernmental Committee competent for examining the reports from the Parties (Article 23.6(c)) and transmitting them, with its observations, to the Conference of Parties for further examination.

[46] See *supra* section 2.

[47] See the note prepared by the then UNESCO Legal Adviser, Claude Lussier, in 1976, loc. cit. n. 16, in which he asserted that 'une telle situation n'est pas sans précédent et serait sans doute acceptable en droit international des traités, s'il s'agissait d'un instrument entièrement nouveau, non lié à un accord existant.'

neither the Community nor its Member States could become parties to the Convention, given the fact that they had transferred to the Community their competences on some of the issues governed by the instrument, including the competence to conclude treaties on those issues.[48]

While the initial proposal was modeled on the corresponding provisions of the WHO Framework Convention on Tobacco control,[49] the clause as adopted in its final version is more detailed and combines the wording of previous provisions in treaties adopted under UN auspices,[50] by which the WHO clause was inspired, together with other provisions in treaties adopted within the World Intellectual Property Organization (WIPO).[51]

The wording of this final clause reflects the widely accepted solution of the alternative exercise of rights under the instrument on the basis of a general declaration of competence, which may be modified in order to adapt to the progressive extension of the Community competences. Nonetheless, the fact that it is incorporated for the first time in a UNESCO convention aimed at setting standards on a highly sensitive normative area raises several questions as to how the EC would exercise its rights before the bodies established under the Convention, namely the Conference of Parties.[52]

---

[48] See *Communication de la Commission européenne et de ses États membres à l'UNESCO sur l'avant-projet de Convention de l'UNESCO sur la protection et la promotion de la diversité des contenus culturels et expressions artistiques* (15 novembre 2004) (unpublished document). In its initial request, the Community had expressed also the wish to insert in the Convention a 'disconnection clause', a clause which is often included in the treaties of the Council of Europe admitting the participation of the European Community. By virtue of this clause, the States Parties that are members of the European Community may apply, in their mutual relations, Community rules instead of rules arising from the Convention except in so far as there is no Community rule governing the subject concerned. The use of this clause reflects the interest of the European Community to avoid that Member States might invoke their international treaty obligations as an obstacle to the further development of Community law. On this specific subject see J. Polakiewicz, *Treaty-making in the Council of Europe* (Strasbourg, Council of Europe Publishing 1999). In the context of the negotiations within UNESCO, the request for inserting the clause was not pursued further, probably because it was too innovative and it would not have been easily accepted.

[49] See Article 35 of the WHO Convention, the text of which is available at <http://www.who.int/tobacco/framework/en/>.

[50] The Convention on Biological Diversity (Article 34) and the Framework Convention on Climate Change (Article 22) both adopted in 1992. See UNESCO Doc., *Appendix 2 to the Preliminary Report of the Director-General containing two preliminary drafts of a Convention on the protection of the diversity of cultural contents and artistic expressions. Consolidated text prepared by the Chairperson of the intergovernmental meeting*, CLT/CPD/2005/CONF.203/6 – Add. (29 April 2005) (unpublished document). The texts of these treaties are available on the following websites <http://www.biodiv.org/convention/default.shtml>; <http://unfccc.int/essential_background/convention/background/items/2853.php>.

[51] See the 1996 WIPO Internet Treaties, namely Article 17 of the WIPO Copyright Treaty (WCT) and Article 26 of the WIPO Performances and Phonograms Treaty (WPPT). The texts of these instruments is available on the WIPO website at the following address <http://www.wipo.int/treaties/en/>.

[52] Under Article 22 of the Convention, the Conference of Parties is competent to examine the reports submitted by the parties to the Convention, to approve operational guidelines and to take any

Although some diverging opinions about the scope of the Convention appear to have been eventually overcome as a wide agreement was reached on the final text of the Convention,[53] the definition of certain notions which are fundamental to determine its scope of application, as for example the notions of 'cultural activities, goods and services', appears far from being uncontroversial.[54]

What might render the EC participation problematic is, on the one hand, the potential disagreement between the UNESCO Member States parties to the Convention as to the precise scope of the Convention *vis-à-vis* trade matters, and, on the other hand, the fact that the distinction between matters falling within the exclusive competence of the Community and those pertaining to the shared or concurrent competence of the EC and its Members is undoubtedly blurred. Divergent views might emerge when the Conference of Parties will be called to approve guidelines for the implementation of the Convention or other measures judged as being necessary to further the objectives of the instrument. In such situations, the exercise by the EC of its rights under the Convention could be rendered difficult.

Although the coordination process does not appear to have raised problems during the negotiation phase and the EC position was uniformly expressed with regard to the adoption the Convention, on specific issues concerning its implementation, positions of EC Member States might be diversified and the coordination process could be much more complicated.

The European Commission launched quickly the ratification process within the Community. To this end, it submitted a proposal for a Council decision[55] that was eventually adopted in May 2006. In this decision, the ratification by all Member States together with the Community is recommended in order to guarantee a uniform application of the Convention.[56]

If the European Community becomes a party to the Convention before the ratification by some EC members, the Community could be called to participate in the decision-making of the follow-up bodies of the Convention without having the certainty to have those decisions implemented in the EC Member States non-parties to

other measures necessary to further the objectives of the instrument. An intergovernmental committee with a restricted composition is also established under Article 23. Regional economic integration organizations may not participate in the work of this body, as only States Parties may be elected as members of the Committee. The European Community would supposedly participate in the work of this body through the EC Member States represented in the Committee.

[53] 148 UNESCO Member States voted in favour of the adoption of the Convention.

[54] See Article 1(g) of the Convention asserting the dual nature (cultural and economic) of cultural activities goods and services, and the definition of these terms in Article 4.4.

[55] See *Proposal for a Council Decision on the conclusion of the UNESCO Convention on the Protection and Promotion of the Diversity of Cultural Expressions*, COM (2005) 678 final (21 December 2005).

[56] The decision was adopted at the 2729th Council Meeting (18-19 May 2006). See Doc. 8668/1/06 REV 1(en), *Council Decision on the conclusion of the Convention on the Protection and Promotion of the Diversity of Cultural Expressions* (11 May 2006) p. 3; see also Doc. 9148/1/06 REV 1 (Presse 131), p. 14. A similar decision was approved for the WHO Framework Convention, to which the EC is a party since February 2005.

the Convention in areas where competences are shared and closely interlinked. Furthermore, the declaration of competence included in this document, which refers in detail to EC legislation, risks to be too difficult to be comprehended by UNESCO Member States which are not members of the EC.[57] This could seriously affect the decision-making process of the follow-up bodies, if divergences arise as to the existence or the nature of the EC competences.[58]

5. Concluding Remarks

Through the decision of the Executive Board, the European Community has been formally recognized as having a role in the UNESCO standard-setting process in relation to a specific convention. Although its participation has been considered as exceptional and limited to the negotiations concerning the Cultural Diversity Convention, the Community could perhaps claim to play a similar role during the elaboration process of other instruments aimed at governing matters falling within its competences.

Much will depend upon the interest that the Community will show towards the normative activity of the Organization insofar as there is a risk that it touches upon its competences. It is true that special attention has been paid by the EC to conventions the object of which covered trade-related aspects or copyright issues, whereas other recent instruments in the area of culture, concerning in general the protection of underwater cultural heritage and of intangible cultural heritage, appear not to have so far attracted the interest of many EC Member States.[59]

Seen from a more general perspective, the decision made by the UNESCO Executive Board might also have an indirect impact on the practice of other UN agencies. The status of the Community within the UN system no longer reflects the level of integration the Community has attained. However, the UN and its specialized agencies have been sometimes reluctant to take an explicit decision recognizing a special observer status to the Community on the basis of the fragmentation of sov-

---

[57] The decision adopted by the Council also contains a unilateral declaration to be annexed to the EC instrument of approval that would allow EC members not to apply the Convention in their mutual relations as far as Community provisions exist in the fields covered by the instrument. See Doc. 8668/1/06 REV 1(en) Annex 2, *supra* n. 56.

[58] At the time of the adoption, a declaration by the Council and the Commission has been included in the minutes of the Council, in which they agree that a proposal for a code of conduct between the Council, the Member States and the Commission on certain aspects of the implementation of the UNESCO Convention will be prepared by the Commission. See Annex to Doc. 8953/06, *Proposal for a Council Decision on the conclusion of the UNESCO Convention on the Protection and Promotion of the Diversity of Cultural Expressions* (11 May 2006).

[59] Only Spain and Lithuania have ratified the 2001 Convention on the Protection of Underwater Cultural Heritage and not many EU Member States (nine, as of August 2006) have so far ratified the 2003 Convention on the Safeguarding of the Intangible Cultural Heritage, which entered into force in April 2006.

ereignty characterizing the relations with its Member States. In the past, pragmatic solutions have been elaborated on an *ad hoc* basis without taking formal decisions. The fact that some UN agencies operating in areas relevant to the competences of the Community have now expressly recognized this anomaly may represent a first step towards a more general recognition of the need to grant the EC a status of observer endowed with more extensive rights, which may vary according to each specific situation.

With regard to the Cultural Diversity Convention, the controversies about its scope of application due to its potential overlapping with international instruments on trade matters risk to create difficulties for the implementation of the Convention, especially if it is not ratified by all EC Member States together with the Community.

Cultural policy is an issue on which the competence of the Community still has to be consolidated.[60] The relevant role that the EC had in the adoption of the Cultural Diversity Convention and the large support expressed by its members could represent an important step towards such consolidation. Future standard-setting instruments adopted by UNESCO in this domain could see a greater involvement of the Community as far as the exercise of its competences on cultural issues develops.

[60] Under Article 151 of the EC Treaty unanimity is required for Council's deliberations over cultural matters. This Article was included by the 1992 Maastricht Treaty in order to define the main objectives of Community action in the cultural field. Although having only a programmatic character, Article 151 has permitted the development of cultural actions at the European level, but has also guaranteed that cultural aspects are taken into account in other areas of Community action.

Chapter 8
UN-EU COOPERATION ON PUBLIC HEALTH: THE EVOLVING PARTICIPATION OF THE EUROPEAN COMMUNITY IN THE WORLD HEALTH ORGANIZATION

by Barbara Eggers* and Frank Hoffmeister**

1. Introduction

The World Health Organization (WHO) and the European Community (EC) have cooperated since the early 1980s, when they established formal relations. Over the last twenty years, this cooperation has significantly increased. With an ever growing body of Community legislation fostering a high level of public health, the European Community has become an important actor for the promotion of international public health standards. Against this background, the EC has played an important role in the WHO negotiations of the Framework Convention on Tobacco Control (FCTC) from 1999-2003 and the revised International Health Regulations (IHR) from 2003-2005.

This article begins with a brief summary of the mission and structure of the WHO. We then analyze how the Community as a non-Member fits into this organization. The central focus of this contribution is on the EC's recent participation in practice within the WHO. What practical arrangements have allowed the EC to present positions in the WHO with one voice? Finally we review the ordinary participation in the meetings of the World Health Assembly and the Executive Board as well as the negotiations on the two above-mentioned agreements (FCTC and IHR) with a view to identifying the decisive factors for efficient EC participation in these traditional inter-state negotiations. We conclude with some lessons learnt and an outlook for the future.

* Dr. iur., LL.M., Member of the Legal Service of the European Commission.

** Dr. iur., Member of the Legal Service of the European Commission; Professor (part-time) at the Free University of Brussels. The authors wish to thank Nicholas Fahy of the European Commission's Directorate General for Health Matters (SANCO) and Laura Pignataro Nolin (Legal Service) for helpful comments on the draft. The opinions expressed in this article are purely personal.

J. Wouters et al., eds., The United Nations and the European Union

2. Mission and Structure of the World Health Organization

Established in July 1946 as a specialized organization of the United Nations, the WHO enjoys distinct international personality. Under Article 1 of its Constitution,[1] the WHO's mission is to foster the attainment by all peoples of the highest possible level of health around the globe. As can be seen from Article 2 and the preamble of its Constitution, the WHO is thus preoccupied with the fight against diseases as well as supporting Member States in putting in place health services and measures to promote public health. Reflecting the state of international law after the Second World War, membership of the WHO is open to states only (Article 3). To date, 192 states have become members of the organization.

The members meet in annual sessions of the WHO's plenary organ, the World Health Assembly (the 'Assembly'). As the WHO's highest body, the Assembly determines the policy of the organization and has the power to adopt multilateral conventions (Article 19) or regulations (Article 21). Furthermore, it adopts non-binding resolutions containing recommendations to Members or statements of a political character. Apart from these norm-setting activities, the Assembly also promotes and conducts research in the field of health by personnel of the Organization or by cooperation with other institutions (Article 18(k)). Different voting patterns apply in the Assembly depending on the substance matter to be decided.[2]

As a restricted body, the Executive Board (the 'Board') consists of 32 elected members reflecting an equitable geographical distribution. The Board acts as the preparatory and executive organ of the Assembly. It gives effect to the latter's decisions and policies, but may also take on its own emergency measures to deal with events requiring immediate action. The Board meets twice a year and decides on important matters with a two-thirds majority (Rule 43 of its Rules of Procedure). Both the Assembly and the Board may establish specialised committees. Finally, the Director-General of the WHO conducts the ordinary business of the organization and acts as the head of the Secretariat, composed of the Geneva headquarters and six regional offices in other parts of the world. Currently, over 3.500 health experts and supporting staff work for the WHO secretariat.

3. The European Community's Evolving Role in the WHO

3.1 Community powers in the area of public health

Community powers in the area of public health have gradually evolved.[3] Since the adoption of the Single European Act in 1987 the Community enjoys a broad power

[1] Constitution of the World Health Organization, 14 *UNTS* p. 185.

[2] See Articles 72 and 73 of the Assembly's Rules of Procedures. Decisions on 'important questions' shall be made by a two-thirds majority of the Members present and voting, whereas other decisions shall be made by a majority of the Members present and voting.

[3] See *M.* v. *Schwanenflügel*, Gesundheit in Europa, *Europarecht* 1998, p. 210 et seq.

to adopt legislation aiming at the completion of the internal market. Community measures for the approximation of laws and regulations of Member States that concern, *inter alia*, health, shall respect a high level of protection (Article 95(3) EC). For example, the Community enacted legislation to regulate the ingredients of tobacco products and labelling,[4] as well as to ban tobacco-advertising.[5] Furthermore, legislation adopted under Article 175 EC in the field of environment may contribute to the protection of public health, in particular, when related to the ban of dangerous substances.

The 1992 Maastricht Treaty introduced a new specific Community policy on public health. Article 3(1)(p) sets out that Community activity shall include a contribution to the attainment of a high level of health protection. A 'horizontal clause' requires that this objective be ensured when defining and implementing action in all areas where the Community has competence.[6] In narrowly defined circumstances the Community may also legislate directly on public health matters. Due to an amendment brought about by the Amsterdam Treaty in 1997, the Community may, in particular, adopt related measures setting high standards of quality and safety of organs and substances of human origin, blood and blood derivates (Article 152(4)(a) EC). Furthermore, on the basis of new powers in the veterinary and phytosanitary fields (Article 152(4)(b) EC), the Community adopted a far-reaching regulation on the principles of food stuff safety.[7] However, specific Community action on most public health matters is primarily construed as complementary to Member State action (Article 152(1) 2nd subparagraph EC). Hence, the main part of this shared competence under Article 152 EC still remains with the Member States.

Notwithstanding this somewhat restricted internal Community powers in the specific field of public health, the Treaty calls upon the Community and the Member States to foster cooperation with third countries and the competent international organizations in the sphere of public health (Article 152(3) EC). This provision envisages in particular EC-WHO cooperation. It is also noteworthy that the European Court of Justice has interpreted the notion 'public health' under Community law in light of the WHO's preamble as encompassing a state of complete physical, mental and social well-being.[8]

---

[4] See Directive 2001/37/EC, OJ (18 July 2001) L-194/26, abrogating the previous Directives 89/622/EEC and 90/239/EC.

[5] See Directive 2003/33/EC, OJ (20 June 2003), L-152/16; the previous Directive 98/43/EC, OJ (30 July 1998) L-213/9, was annulled by the European Court of Justice upon German application because the legislator had not demonstrated that it would contribute to the elimination of trade barriers (ECJ, Case C-376/98, *ECR* 2000, I-2247). The present directive is, again, being attacked by the German government (Case C-380/03), pending before the Court.

[6] For a discussion of the practical application of this clause see the Communications of the Commission COM (95) 196 final; COM (96) 407 final; COM (98) 34 final; COM (99) 587 final.

[7] Regulation No. 178/2002 of the European Parliament and the Council of the European Union, OJ (1 February 2002) L-31/1.

[8] ECJ, Case C-84/94 *United Kingdom* v. *Council* [1996] *ECR* I-5755, para. 15.

Furthermore, the Community enjoys exclusive competence to negotiate international agreements in all areas where it covered a field by internal legislation (*ERTA*-principle).[9] Thus, the EC's internal market legislation involving high health standards, for example, creates an external power of the Community to negotiate corresponding international standards. Importantly, under the common commercial policy the European Community has the power to regulate imports and exports of goods (including animals and plants). Article 133 EC includes a power to adopt sanitary and quarantine requirements and other safeguards to prevent the spread of disease into the Community. Furthermore, the Treaty of Amsterdam of 1997 which entered into force during May 1999, introduced a Community power to regulate the short-term entrance of third-country nationals into the Schengen area (Article 62(2) EC). Immigration into the Community may be subjected to certain standards and procedures if and insofar as there is reason to believe that human beings may be infected with dangerous diseases. Finally, inside the Community, secondary legislation on the free movement of workers also touches upon similar questions.[10]

This large body of legislation in the field of public health qualifies the European Community under its own legal rules to actively engage in international negotiations aiming at the protection of public health in those areas. Where Community competence exists, the Council may authorize the Commission to negotiate, on behalf of the EC, in cooperation with a Committee to be appointed by the Council (Article 300(1) EC). The final agreement is then concluded by the Council (Article 300(2) EC). Depending on the characteristics of the agreement, the European Parliament is either consulted or asked for its assent.

In short, over time, the EC gained an exclusive external competence to negotiate international agreements on numerous public health matters. In areas which are not yet covered by treaty powers or internal Community legislation, the EC and its Member States either have a shared competence to conduct relations on health issues or such competence remains with the Member States.

3.2 Community status in the WHO

3.2.1 *WHO rules on effective relations with other international organizations*

The WHO Constitution of 1946 only mentions States as Members (Article 1). Non-sovereign territories are invited to become Associate Members (Article 8 WHO Constitution). Since the European Community does not qualify for being an (Associate) Member, it has to seek a different constitutional status.

[9] ECJ, Case 22-70 *ERTA* [1971] *ECR* 263, 274, para. 16. Confirmed in the so-called 'open-skies' cases: ECJ, Case C-476/98 *Commission./.Germany* [2002] *ECR* I- 9855, paras. 103-113 with annotation by F. Hoffmeister, 98 *AJIL* (2004) pp. 567-572.

[10] Directive 2004/38/EC of the European Parliament and of the Council of 29 April 2004 on the right of citizens of the Union and their family members to move and reside freely within the territory of the Member States, OJ (30 April 2004) L-158/77.

However, the WHO Constitution does not contain express rules on participants or observers. Rather, it refers to the 'establishment of effective relations' with other intergovernmental organizations on several occasions.

First, Chapter XVI mandates the WHO to establish relations with the UN and other specialised agencies (Article 69 WHO Constitution) or with other intergovernmental organizations (Article 70 WHO Constitution). The WHO can also conclude formal agreements with the latter, requiring a two-thirds majority in the Assembly. In practice, such agreements have been concluded mainly with specialised agencies of the UN.[11]

Second, under Article 18(h) the Assembly has the power to 'invite any organization, international or national, governmental or non-governmental, which has responsibilities related to those of the Organization, to appoint representatives to participate, without right of vote, in its meetings or in those of the committees and conferences convened under its authority, on conditions prescribed by the Assembly'. Rule 3 of the Assembly's Rules of Procedures provides that invitations for a regular session shall be sent to all participating intergovernmental organizations. Under Rule 48 the invited intergovernmental organization participates in the deliberations of the plenary and the main committees. Participation in sub-committees or other subdivisions requires an additional decision of the Assembly. Likewise, the Board may invite 'representatives of other intergovernmental organization with which the Organization has established effective relations under Article 70 of the Constitution' to participate without a vote in the deliberations of the Board and its committees. The Board may extend this invitation also to the meetings of its subcommittees or other subdivisions (Article 4(1) of the Rules of Procedure of the Board).

Third, under the second sentence of Article 33 of the WHO Constitution, the Director-General may 'establish direct relations with international organizations whose activities come within the competence of the Organization'.

It follows that WHO rules offer three possibilities of granting the status of a participant to an intergovernmental organization: either the WHO concludes a comprehensive agreement with specialized agencies or other intergovernmental organizations covering participation in the two main organs and all subsidiary bodies thereof,[12] or each of the two main WHO bodies grants access to its own work only according to its own rules of procedure, or the Director-General opens the WHO for direct participation of another international organization.

---

[11] There are agreements between the WHO and the UN, the ILO, the FAO, the UNESCO, the IAEA, the UNIDO (presumably concluded under Article 69 WHO-constitution) as well as agreements between the WHO and the 'Pan American Health Organization' (presumably concluded under Article 70 WHO-constitution).

[12] See, e.g., Article II(1) of the WHO/ILO Agreement: 'Representatives of the ILO shall be invited to attend the meetings of the Executive Board of the World Health Organization and the World Health Assembly and to participate without a vote in the deliberations of each of these bodies and their commissions and committees with respect to items on their agenda in which the International Labour organization has an interest'.

3.2.2 *Relations between the WHO and the European Community*

The European Community and the WHO chose the third possibility to establish effective relations. By way of an exchange of letter of 28 April 1982, Commissioner Richard and the WHO's Director-General Mahler concluded an 'arrangement establishing relations between the European Community and the World Health Organization'. Paragraph 3 of that arrangement provided that

> 'the World Health Assembly shall invite a representative of the European Communities to participate as observer in sessions of the World Health Assembly, the Executive Board and the Regional Committee for Europe, and, where appropriate, in the work of their committees, with respect to items on their agenda on which the European Communities and the Word Health Organization have a common interest.'[13]

This arrangement was replaced by another exchange of letters between Commissioner Byrne and WHO Director-General Brundtland of 14 December 2000.[14] Although the later exchange of letters used a different wording (referring to the Commission rather than to a representative of the Community) the WHO continued to invite the European Community alongside other WHO related organizations to the regular meetings of the Assembly and the Board.[15] Under their relevant rules of procedures, this triggers a right for the EC to be present and to speak in the formal meetings as well as in the main committees.[16] However, the EC may only be present in the deliberations of the meetings of subcommittees or other subdivisions of the Assembly and the Board, if so invited by them.[17] Furthermore, the Community's general participation rights may fall short of the prerogatives of other WHO Members, which may cause a disadvantage for the Community in situations of treaty negotiations. This may relate to the order of speaking, the right to propose amendments, the right to chair committees and finally the right to vote.

The 2000 exchange of letters also prepared the ground for high-level political contacts between the WHO Secretariat and the Commission. As the letters identify various priority areas, including health information, communicable diseases, to-

[13] Exchange of letters between the European Communities and the World Health Organization laying down the procedure for cooperation between the two organizations, OJ (28 October 1982).

[14] Exchange of letters between the World Health Organization and the Commission of the European Communities concerning the consolidation and intensification of cooperation, OJ (4 January 2001) C-1/7.

[15] See, e.g., the letter of the WHO of 28.11.2005, registered with the Commission Delegation in Geneva, 2.12.2005: 'The Director-General of the WHO has the honour to invite the specialized agencies, the IAEA, the World Trade Organization, the World Tourism Organization, *and the intergovernmental organizations*, to appoint representatives to attend the 117th session of the Executive Board....'

[16] Article 48(1) 1st sentence of the Assembly's Rules of procedures; Article 4(1) 1st sentence of the Board's Rules of Procedures.

[17] Article 48(1) 2nd sentence of the Assembly's Rules of procedures; Article 4(1) 2nd sentence of the Board's Rules of Procedures.

bacco control, environment and health, sustainable health development or health research, annual meetings between the WHO Director General and the relevant Commissioners have been organized since 2001. They have been organized alternately by the WHO and the Commission and have led to an intensive exchange of views as regards policy priorities, as well as prompting intensified contacts at technical level.[18]

4. Community Participation in the WHO in Practice

While bilateral contacts between the executive branches of the WHO and the Community may be seen as a mixture of administrative and political activities, Community participation in the WHO may also involve norm-setting. In this most important area, three cases merit a detailed review: the regular participation of the Community in meetings of WHO bodies (1), the participation in the negotiation of international conventions under the auspices of the WHO as exemplified by the Framework Convention on Tobacco Control (2) and the EC's participation in the adoption of secondary WHO law, namely the 2005 International Health Regulations (3).

4.1 **Meetings of the Assembly and the Board**

Acting on the basis of the 1982 arrangement, Commission officials representing the European Community have been invited to the meetings of the Assembly and the Board. Until recently the Commission has not played a very visible role. This was partly due to a lack of Community competence on the specific topics under discussion, and partly due to a lack of EC coordination to achieve a Community position. Member States' health attachés in Geneva were not well connected with Brussels, thus no common understanding between them was developed resulting in the EU Member States attachés failing to act with a single voice in the WHO on Community matters. Nor was there considerable effort to harmonize national positions on matters of Member States' competence to come to common positions. If the Commission spoke, it did so as observer after several EU Member States already had delivered their statement, sometimes with a comparable content.

This deplorable situation is on the verge of being improved. Spurred on by the refusal of the United States to let a Community representative participate in the meetings of an Executive Board's drafting committee in January 2005, the Commission and the Council have systematically reviewed the Community status in these meetings. Following intensive discussions up to COREPER level, Commissioner Kyprianou and the Austrian Federal Minister for Health and Women (as

---

[18] For summaries of the high-level meetings of April 2001, June 2002, May 2003 and July 2004 see the web-page of DG Health and Consumer Protection <http://europa.eu.int/comm/health/ph_international/int_organisations/who_en.htm> (visited 3 May 2006).

Presidency) wrote a joint letter to the Chair of the Executive Board informing about the Community's intention to participate fully in the deliberations of the Board's 117th session in January 2006. The relevant request in the Executive Board was presented by the four EU Member States sitting in this body (France, Lithuania, Portugal, and the Czech Republic) and accepted by the Board. Accordingly, the European Commission was allowed to participate as EC representative not only in the main meetings, but also in the sub-committees or other sub-divisions. This is essential, as in practice most detailed drafting of resolutions is done outside the formal meetings of the Board.

Australia and the United States pressured initially for a clear definition of Community powers and for no overlap of Commission and Member States interventions. However, in the course of the deliberations the United States encouraged the Community as a whole to actively intervene (i.e., the Commission and the 4 EU Member States) on issues where there was transatlantic agreement in substance. In practical terms, EU coordination was organized by the Austrian Presidency. Agreed Community positions were then put forward by Portugal (replacing Austria, which at that time was not a Member of the Board). On one occasion the Commission delivered on behalf of the EC an additional statement to the intervention of the Member States on pandemic influenza preparedness and the EC's response to it.

A similar exercise of strengthening EU coordination took place for the preparation of the World Health Assembly in May 2006. The EC asked the Assembly at the beginning of the session for an invitation to all meetings. EU coordination was organized in Geneva, with some additional input from the Council working group in Brussels on positions for areas of particular Community competence, such as the proposed resolution on international trade and public health. This reflects the situation in the World Trade Organization where the Community represents those positions as well. In the medium-term, the Commission and Council may also come up with an internal code of conduct on which items on the WHO agenda (both Assembly and Board) common positions should be prepared (and delivered by the Presidency) and on which items Community positions could be elaborated (and mainly delivered by the Commission).

4.2 Framework Convention on Tobacco Control

4.2.1 *Community status in the negotiations*

The second important example of EC participation in the WHO relates to the negotiations of the Framework Convention on Tobacco Control (FCTC).[19] In May 1999, the Assembly established an intergovernmental negotiation body and a related work-

---

[19] The text of the Convention can be found in the Annex to Council Decision 2004/513/EC of 2.6.2004, OJ (15 June 2004) L-213/8.

ing group open to all WHO Member States in order to prepare this international convention. It further decided

> 'that regional economic integration is constituted by sovereign States, Members of the World Health Organization, to which their Member States have transferred competence over matters governed by this resolution, including the competence to enter into treaties in respect to these matters, may actively participate, in accordance with Rule 55 of the Rules of Procedure of the Health Assembly, in the drafting and negotiations of the intergovernmental negotiating body (...) and in the preparatory working group (...).'[20]

In September 1999 the Commission recommended to the Council to grant it a negotiation mandate under Article 300(1) EC. Having regard to the relevant *acquis* in the area of tobacco control,[21] the Council agreed with qualified majority and asked the Commission to strive for harmonized standards against tobacco consumption in separate protocols. The Commission should also ensure that the Convention would be open to accession by the Community itself. Upon request from the United Kingdom a common Council/Commission declaration was made that the mandate would only cover Community matters under Articles 95 (internal market) and 152 (public health) of the Treaty. The Council extended this mandate in April 2001 to cover all areas of Community competence, including such issues as taxation, smuggling and tobacco growing subsidies.

Being duly authorized, the Commission hence participated on behalf of the Community in the relevant negotiations of the working group and the intergovernmental body. Although Rule 55 of the Assembly's Rules of Procedure only grants a right to speak upon permission of the Assembly's President, the above-mentioned resolution paved the way for full and effective participation of the Community alongside its Member States. The Commission was seated next to the Member State holding the Presidency and was able to speak on behalf of the Community without any restrictions based on the status issue.

4.2.2 *Community coordination during the negotiations*

Internal Community coordination was, however, more cumbersome. Of course, Member States were aware of their duty under Article 10 of the EC Treaty to strive for common positions even in an area of mixed competence flowing from the requirement of unity in external representation.[22] Yet, in the absence of a written procedural mechanism for achieving this, divergences had therefore to be brought

---

[20] Resolution of the Fifty-Second World Health Assembly, A 52/38 of 24 May 1999; acting upon the second report of Committee A <http://ftp.who.int/gb/pdf_files/WHA52/ew38.pdf> (visited 3 May 2006).

[21] See *supra* nn. 5-7.

[22] ECJ, Opinion 1/94, [1994] *ECR* I-5483, para. 108.

before COREPER[23] or before the Council of Ministers. However, even these efforts depend on the political goodwill of all Member States. Against this background, the Community presented a united position in many crucial tobacco control areas during the negotiations, which was also supported by the acceding countries. However, in certain other areas, like passive smoking and duty free sales, no agreement on a meaningful Community position could be reached. Incidentally, these issues were at the same time subject to internal dispute, as Germany had successfully attacked the first tobacco advertising Directive in September 2000. Following the European Court of Justice's ruling in September 2000,[24] the German delegation was generally less cooperative in the negotiations on that point. Even at COREPER level in October 2002, Germany resisted, in particular, establishing any Community position on a total ban of tobacco advertising in the Convention. After tough negotiations in Geneva among WHO members in the final round in February 2003, a narrowly described exception was finally agreed to accommodate the German preoccupation. Under Article 13(3) the FCTC,[25] Parties would be allowed not to enact a total ban on tobacco advertising if its constitution would not so permit.

4.2.3 *Community ratification of the Convention*

In May 2003, the WHA adopted the draft FCTC Convention with the support of the Community and its Member States. Since the Convention touches both Member States and Community competence, simultaneous ratification was desirable.[26] For the Community, the Council did so on 2 June 2004 after having received the opinion of the European Parliament in April 2004. It approved the Convention on the basis of Articles 95, 133 and 152 EC with the necessary declaration on competence as required by Article 35(3) of the FCTC.[27] The Council also reassured Germany by making an interpretative declaration that an EC Member State, whose national constitution or constitutional principles do not permit the introduction of a comprehensive ban on all tobacco advertising, promotion and sponsorship may make use of Article 13(3) of the Convention. Despite this speedy action by the Community, three Member States did not ratify in due time. Hence, in the first meeting of the Parties in February 2006 (one year after the entry into force of the Convention on 27 February 2005), the Commission was present and could express positions on

---

[23] Under Article 207 EC, COREPER is the committee consisting of the Permanent Representatives of the Member States. It is responsible for preparing the work of the Council and for carrying out the tasks assigned to it by the Council. Once the Council Working Group on Health reaches an agreement on an EU position, COREPER and subsequently the Council would endorse it. In case the Working Group cannot reach a common position, the issue 'goes up' to COREPER with a view to reaching a decision at the higher political level.

[24] See *supra* n. 5.

[25] <http://www.who.int/gb/fctc/PDF/inb6/einb65.pdf> (visited 3 May 2006).

[26] See Recital 4 of Council Decision 2004/513/EC of 2.6.2004, OJ (15 June 2004) L-213/8.

[27] Council Decision 2004/513/EC of 2 June 2004, OJ (15 June 2004) L-213/8.

behalf of the Community. However, if an item touching Community competence were to be voted on, the Commission did not have 25 votes but only 22, in accordance with Article 32(2) of the Convention.

4.3 International Health Regulations

4.3.1 *Community status in the negotiations*

A third example of the evolving role for the European Community in the WHO concerns the International Health Regulations (IHR), a sort of WHO secondary law. Under Article 21(a) WHO Constitution, the Assembly has the power to adopt regulations concerning sanitary and quarantine requirements and other procedures designed to prevent the international spread of disease. Such regulations shall come into force for all WHO Members, unless they opt out by notifying the Director-General through rejection or reservations (Article 22 WHO Constitution). Historically, these regulations were first used in 1969 to address a limited number of most eminent diseases like plague, cholera and tuberculosis. They were revised in 1973 and 1983. Today the IHR covers any disease irrespective of its origin, including, e.g., SARS, Asian Flu or Bird Flu. Given the importance of the subject-matter and the vast array of Community border measures in place, the Commission signalled to the WHO its wish to be included in the revision process. Inspired by the precedent relating to the FCTC, the Assembly adopted on 28 May 2003 a resolution in which it allowed full participation for regional economic integration organizations in the work of the intergovernmental working group.[28] In Brussels, the Council granted a negotiating mandate to the Commission on 1 December 2003, authorizing it to negotiate on behalf of the European Community with regard to all matters within Community competence. During the course of the negotiations the Council added in May 2004 specific points on substance to this mandate. It furthermore recalled that the Commission shall closely coordinate with the Member States to ensure that the uniformity of international representation of the Community is respected. Again, after having fixed the legal framework with a proper authorization from the Council and a broad invitation from the Assembly, the Commission experienced an encouraging working atmosphere on the ground. Despite being relegated to sit among the observers due to US insistence (rather than next to the EU Presidency as in the FCTC negotiations) the Commission could fully participate in the discussions. Indeed, its desk between the Holy See and the Palestinian Authority became a frequent meeting point for delegates to discuss compromises. Depending on the substance matter, either the Presidency or the Commission put forward Community positions without being hampered by the 'status' issue.

---

[28] Resolution of the Fifty-Sixth World Health Assembly, WHA56.28 of 28 May 2003.

4.3.2 *Community coordination*

As regards the substance of Community positions, the situation differed from the experience in the FCTC negotiations. Following intensive coordination over several months, agreed positions and fall-back positions had been developed on all points. To achieve this, the Commission regularly distributed working documents with a 'Matrix' listing all Community positions in an Annex. These matrices were discussed with the Member States both in the Brussels-based Council Working Group on Public Health and in a series of technical experts' meetings in Luxembourg. These positions were then endorsed by the Members of the Council Working Group on Public Health in good time before the negotiations started (with an understanding that flexibility and further coordination in Geneva was needed to respond effectively to negotiating positions of other WHO Members). Drawing on this preparatory work, the Community was in an excellent position to rely on the previously agreed fall-back positions where necessary. This made fine-tuning on-the-ground a lot easier. In Geneva, up to two formal EU-coordination meetings took place every day, supplemented where necessary by *ad hoc* coordination in the WHO working groups. Member States were represented by their health-attachés and technical experts; the Commission by officials from the Health and Consumer Protection Directorate-General (SANCO) and the Legal Service.

To efficiently coordinate the presentation and negotiation of Community positions in Geneva, the 'matrix' was accompanied by a 'speaking-plan'. It indicated on which articles either the Commission or the Presidency would intervene. Such division proved easy for topics like military or diplomatic activities (Member States) or data protection or border measures (Community). However, many of the articles could not be properly deemed to fall within either Community or Member States competence only. Therefore, a pragmatic approach was taken in designating these mixed topics as 'Presidency and Commission'. This allowed for a case-to-case decision who should speak without prejudice to the legal division of powers. The Dutch and later Luxembourg Presidency were empowered to deliver the opening speeches for the entire Community on all points, with the Commission developing more and more into the central spokesperson and negotiator for the Community in the mixed areas.

Another field showing good internal cooperation, concerned Community representation in the corridors and working groups. The Presidency agreed that the Commission should speak and negotiate in informal contacts including on matters of Member States competence, especially on legal issues and sometimes even take the floor in the Plenary when these issues were raised. At the same time, the Commission authorized diplomats of Member States with particular knowledge of certain technical issues or countries to discuss agreed Community positions with other negotiating partners in order to gather support. Once such negotiations would enter into their final stage, they informed the Commission and the Presidency to join and finalise the points. In a similar vein, a representative of one Member State with high-level experience and recognition was authorized to head a working party notwithstanding the fact that the subject-matter of this working party exceeded Member States' competence. Thanks to this pragmatic approach making best use of all Community resources and experience, the EC became the key promoter of joint compromise proposals on the main sticking points that were developed with one or several of the other main players (the African Group, Canada, China, the Montevideo Group and the United States). Generally, the EC positions found support from the WHO European region (all European States including Russia), in their separate meetings.

The only point which could have threatened the unity of the Community position and the achievement of the ultimate goal to allow the Presidency to finally vote on behalf of all 25 EU Member States in favour of the adoption of the IHR was draft Article 44bis IHR, entitled 'armed forces'. Under that provision State Parties were required to ensure that their military personnel, conveyances, containers, etc., meet the requirements of the Regulations 'consistent with their national security laws'. Lithuania was concerned that this qualifier could limit its right to control Russian troops in transit over Lithuanian territory to Kaliningrad and opposed the draft article. Although Lithuania's concerns were legally not shared by other Member States and the Commission, the Commission and Lithuania both thoroughly analysed the issue with a view to developing compromise positions to further safeguard Lithuania's rights that could be proposed to other WHO Members. After many meetings between the Commission, Presidency and Lithuanian experts in Brussels, the Lithuanian delegation accepted a Community position and a number of fall-back positions. The Community would strive in the first place for the deletion of Article 44bis, but could accept it as a fall-back position subject to textual modifications. In the final negotiations in Geneva, it was mainly the United States that insisted on maintaining the original formulation of the article and African countries suddenly requested the introduction of articles on ground crossings which also touched upon Lithuania's concern. This caused much upheaval in the EC delegation because Lithuania felt forced to refuse adopting the IHR. However, since the Commission had already obtained an early harvest in achieving the key Community positions on all other issues, the Commission and Presidency could put the full EC negotiating power to serve the interest of this one Member State. Thus, in the final negotiating hours the United States accepted to delete Article 44bis and the African group agreed to modify the articles on ground crossings. Thanks to the excellent cooperation of all Member States, the Commission and Presidency, the Community was, therefore, able for the first time to present itself as fully united to the other WHO Members throughout the entire negotiation of a WHO instrument.

4.3.3 *Adoption of the IHR*

When the IHR were due for adoption by the World Health Assembly on 17 May 2005, the question came up as to how the Community should express its support for the final draft. As the regulations were a sort of secondary WHO law (and not a separate international convention as in the case of the FCTC), only WHO Members were entitled to vote on them under Article 2(k) and 21 of the WHO Constitution. On the other hand, some parts related to Community competence, where Community positions should normally be expressed by the Commission after internal determination of the Council under Article 300(2) 2nd sub-paragraph EC. However, as the Community may not vote in the WHO, this internal rule would lead effectively to the absence of any Community position in the adoption phase. Accordingly, upon a proposal from the Commission, the Council authorized the Member States in early May 2005 to accept the final text in the interest of the Community, unless it significantly departs from the final Community position. Internally, the Community has still the power to decide whether to oblige Member States to trigger the objection procedure under Article 22 of the WHO Constitution or to express its (indirect) consent to be bound by remaining silent.[29]

5. Conclusion

UN-EU cooperation on public health matters manifests itself in the WHO in a remarkable fashion. Albeit largely unknown, the European Community has acquired an unwritten status of participant in the WHO. Responding positively to two invitations from the World Health Assembly, the Community played an active role in the negotiations on the Tobacco Framework Convention and the International Health Regulations. To the satisfaction (and surprise) of other WHO members, the Community did so by applying the principle of 'maximal internal coordination' and 'unity of external representation' in health matters. The latter principle can include the alternate designation of the Presidency and the Commission as spokespersons and may even involve a re-delegation to Member States' delegates. Such a pragmatic approach is inspired by a wish to maximise the technical expertise with benefit for the WHO at large. It does not constitute an attempt to over-represent Europe or to seize undue negotiation advantages with regard to other partners. The ever-evolving role of the European Community in the WHO may in the long run also be felt in the ordinary meetings of the Assembly and the Board. Whereas this encouraging experience of the last decade may lay the ground for the conclusion of a formal agreement between the Community and the WHO under Article 70 of the Constitution in the mid-term, a long-term perspective could include full membership of the European Community in the WHO as another option as well.

---

[29] As a non-Member to the WHO, the European Community is not *eo ipso* bound by the International Health Regulations. However, since Member States also expressed consent to be bound in the interest of the Community, the Community has itself (unilaterally) declared to fully apply the IHR.

Part Three

UN-EU Cooperation on Human Development Issues

Chapter 9
UNHCR, THE EU AND REFUGEES

by Judith Kumin*

1. Introduction

Europe's relationship to refugees is a complex one, with deep roots spanning the continent's experience as both a refugee-producing and refugee-receiving region, as well as a major source of humanitarian aid. The cooperation between the European Union and the Office of the United Nations High Commissioner for Refugees (UNHCR) reflects this complexity.

Refugees have been an integral part of modern European history, and Europe has played an important role in the history of the UN refugee agency. Immediately following World War II, Europe faced the settlement needs of millions of refugees and displaced persons. UNHCR was created in 1951 to deal with that still-unresolved problem, along with new refugee flows which were emerging on the divided continent.

The origins of contemporary international refugee law are essentially European. European States spearheaded the Conference of Plenipotentiaries which adopted the 1951 Geneva Convention relating to the Status of Refugees.[1] That Convention has been recognized ever since as the cornerstone of international refugee law. Until it was broadened by the New York Protocol of 1967,[2] the refugee definition contained in the 1951 Convention focused on persons with a well-founded fear of persecution as a result of events occurring in Europe.[3]

During the Cold War, Western European countries welcomed refugees from Eastern Europe with open arms, and also took in tens of thousands of Indo-Chinese refugees in the late 1970s and 1980s. After the Berlin Wall came down, large numbers of refugees from war and ethnic cleansing in the former Yugoslavia found safety in other parts of Europe. The European Union's Charter of Fundamental

* UNHCR's Regional Representative in Brussels. This article represents her personal views and does not represent the opinion of the United Nations or the UNHCR.

[1] Geneva Convention relating to the Status of Refugees 1951, 189 *UNTS* no. 2545. Of the 26 participating States, 17 were European countries. The initial definition of 'refugee' contained in the 1951 Convention focused on persons having a well-founded fear of persecution 'as a result of events occurring in Europe'.

[2] New York Protocol of 1967, 666 *UNTS* no. 8791.

[3] Article 1(B) Geneva Convention relating to the Status of Refugees 1951, 189 *UNTS* no. 2545.

Rights,[4] which was solemnly proclaimed by the Presidents of the European Commission, Council and Parliament on 7 December 2000, incorporates the right to asylum in Article 18.

Today, the European Union is playing a key role in determining Europe's position towards refugees, both within and beyond the Union. Inside the EU's borders, the Member States have set for themselves the aim of establishing a Common European Asylum System by 2010. At the same time, EU institutions are engaged in the *external* dimension of European refugee policy, which encompasses humanitarian assistance to refugees and other forcibly displaced people in third countries, as well as programmes to build the capacity of third countries to protect refugees and to find long-term solutions to their plight. The European Commission is a major donor of humanitarian assistance and of official development assistance, although to reach the level of aid provided by the United States, the world's single largest donor country, one must tally aid from the Commission and the 25 EU Member States.[5]

This article offers an overview of the wide-ranging interaction between UNHCR and the European Union. Although it deals both with the internal and external dimensions of EU refugee policy, it touches more briefly on the latter, as Europe's role as a source of humanitarian aid is dealt with elsewhere in this volume.

2. UNHCR and the European Institutions: An Evolving Relationship

UNHCR's Representation in Brussels is one of the organization's six original branch offices. It was opened in 1951 to address refugee protection matters in the Benelux countries. After the establishment of the European Communities, relations with the European Institutions were initially handled out of UNHCR's Headquarters in Geneva. Over time, it became apparent that closer monitoring of and more direct involvement in EU affairs would be necessary.

In early 1991, UNHCR appointed its first staff member in Brussels tasked with following EU asylum policy developments and cooperation with the Commission's Directorate-General for Justice and Home Affairs (later re-baptized Justice, Freedom and Security). Nearly ten years later, UNHCR's relationship with that Directorate-General was formalized through an exchange of letters signed in July 2000 between the then, UN High Commissioner for Refugees Sadako Ogata and the then, European Commissioner for Justice and Home Affairs António Vitorino.[6]

---

[4] European Union's Charter of Fundamental Rights, 7 December 2000, OJ (18 December 2000) C-364/1.

[5] Development Initiatives, 'Global Humanitarian Assistance Update 2004-2005', Somerset (2005), available on <www.globalhumanitarianassistance.org>.

[6] This text has been superseded by the exchange of letters signed in February 2005 between High Commissioner Lubbers and EC Commissioner Frattini, see *infra* n. 10.

The two institutions agreed to strengthen cooperation on refugee and asylum issues, in particular by establishing regular channels for exchange of information, mutual assistance in the study and implementation of programmes on refugee and asylum questions, and regular senior-level consultations in accordance with a standard agenda.

While UNHCR focused on asylum policy developments in the European Union, it was also working to develop its relations with the European Commission as a source of financial support for UNHCR's programmes, which are funded nearly entirely through voluntary contributions. The European Commission has consistently been a major donor, ranking most years in third place after the United States and Japan. From 1995 to 2005, the Commission provided 9.17% of UNHCR's income, compared with 31.82% donated by the United States and 12.22% by Japan. Over the past decade, the European Commission's annual contribution to UNHCR's activities has fluctuated from a high of US$ 117.3 million or 14.5% of all contributions in 1997, to a low of US$ 40.8 million or 5.8% in 2000. In 2005, Commission sources covered around 7.92% of UNHCR's budget. Taken together, contributions from the Commission and the EU Member States supply over half of UNHCR's funding each year.

In September 1999, UNHCR decided to transfer from UNHCR Headquarters to Brussels the entire unit responsible for donor relations and resource mobilization with the European Commission. This unit collaborates extensively with the Directorates-General for External Relations, Humanitarian Aid, and Development, *inter alia*, coordinates UNHCR funding submissions to the EC, and manages the related contracts and reports.

In February 2005, UNHCR and the European Commission signed a Memorandum establishing a 'strategic partnership'[7] in the field of protection and assistance to refugees and other persons of concern to UNHCR in third countries. This was one of a series of agreements promoted by the Commission in implementation of its 2001 Communication on 'Building an effective partnership with the United Nations in the field of Development and Humanitarian Assistance'[8] and its 2003 Communication on 'The European Union and the United Nations: the choice of multilateralism'.[9]

However, the limitation of the UNHCR-EC strategic partnership agreement to the *external* dimension of EU refugee policy reflects the difficulty the Commission

---

[7] Memorandum concerning the establishment of a strategic partnership between the Office of the United Nations High Commissioner for Refugees and the Commission of the European Communities in the field of protection and assistance to refugees and other people of concern to UNHCR in third countries, Brussels, 15 February 2005 available on <http://www.unhcr.org/cgi-bin/texis/vtx/home/opendoc.pdf?tbl=RSDLEGAL&id=42135e6c4>.

[8] Communication from the Commission to the Council and the European Parliament of 20 May 2001, 'Building an effective partnership with the United Nations in the fields of development and humanitarian affairs', COM (2001) 231.

[9] Communication from the Commission to the European Parliament of 10 September 2003, 'The European Union and the United Nations: the choice of multilateralism', COM (2003) 526 final.

has faced in reaching a cohesive approach, linking the external and internal dimensions of its refugee policies. As a result of this limitation, it was necessary to complement the agreement with a revised exchange of letters between UNHCR and the European Commissioner for Justice, Freedom and Security concerning cooperation with respect to the *internal* dimension of refugee policy. A principal objective set out in that exchange of letters is 'cooperation in addressing the challenges of the Common European Asylum System and in the monitoring and evaluation of the application of the instruments of the Common European Asylum System by Member States.'[10]

Beyond its relations with the Commission, UNHCR has sought to expand its contacts with other EU bodies, and in particular with the European Parliament, which in 2005 gained the right of co-decision on asylum policy matters. Dialogue with the European Court of Justice, which may be called upon to assess the compatibility of European asylum instruments with international law, the Council, the External Borders Agency and other institutions remains important to UNHCR. In parallel, the European Commission has sought to increase its influence within the UNHCR.

As the European Union gained competence on matters covered by UNHCR's mandate, the Commission sought an enhanced role within UNHCR's governing body, the Executive Committee (ExCom). Currently made up of 70 Member States, the ExCom meets in plenary session in Geneva annually. It reviews and approves UNHCR's programmes and budget for the coming year, and advises and adopts conclusions on international protection as well as decisions on financial, operational and administrative matters. A wide range of refugee issues are discussed within the ExCom in the presence of governmental and non-governmental partners. In addition, ExCom's Standing Committee meets several times during the year to carry work forward in-between the plenary sessions.

Only States may be members of the Executive Committee.[11] As an observer, the Commission is able to take part in all the work of the Committee except for the drafting of the Executive Committee's Decisions and Conclusions. The Commission also wishes to participate in that process and has therefore sought a status or arrangement which would also enable it to do so. This parallels broader EC efforts to strengthen participation in the governance of UN funds, programmes and humanitarian bodies, a move which has been supported by the Council.[12]

---

[10] Available on <www.unhcr.org/cgi-bin/texis/vtx/news/opendoc.pdf?id=42135cba4&tbl=RSD LEGAL>.

[11] The General Assembly and ECOSOC Resolutions establishing UNHCR's Executive Committee stipulate that the Committee will consist of representatives from States members of the United Nations or of the specialized agencies (UN Doc. A/RES/11166; E/RES/672(XXV)). This precludes membership for a body that is not a State. The question of observers is regulated by the Executive Committee's Rules of Procedure (UN Doc. A/AC.96/187/Rev.5).

[12] See Joint Council/Commission statement to Minutes of the Council of 11 March 2002. The Commission's Communication on 'The European Union and the UN: The Choice of Multilateral-

3. Harmonization of European Asylum Policy: The Backdrop

The need for a harmonized approach to asylum became evident as soon as internal controls on movement within the European Union started to be removed, a process which began in 1985 with the conclusion of the Schengen Agreement abolishing checks at the internal borders between the Benelux countries, France and Germany. Over the past two decades, UNHCR has been closely associated with the efforts to develop a common European asylum policy. Contacts with the Presidency, Commission, Council and Parliament became progressively more intensive, as UNHCR's advice on proposed European asylum instruments was sought by these actors, as well as by Member States.

Consultations on asylum questions among EU Ministers of Interior and Immigration took place at regular intervals from the mid-eighties onwards. In 1990 the Dublin Convention regarding allocation of responsibility for dealing with asylum claims was adopted,[13] although it took seven years to enter into force. The first non-binding Council Resolutions on a common approach to asylum issues were adopted in 1992.[14] The Maastricht Treaty,[15] which entered into force in November 1993, established a formal mechanism for intergovernmental cooperation in the area of justice and home affairs, but because competence in those areas, including asylum, continued to rest with the Member States, this could result only in the adoption of non-binding resolutions with a general content.

It was not until 1997, with the adoption of the Treaty of Amsterdam, that a political decision was taken to establish a Common Area of Freedom, Security and Justice, including a Common European Asylum Policy, the building-blocks for which would consist of binding instruments in a number of key areas. This decision is reflected in Article 63 of the Amsterdam Treaty,[16] which also stipulates that measures on asylum must be in accordance with the Geneva Convention of 28 July 1951. UNHCR's responsibility for supervising the application of that Convention is set out in its Article 35, and is reinforced by Declaration Number 17 to the Amsterdam Treaty which states: 'Consultations shall be established with the United Nations High Commissioner for Refugees ... on matters relating to asylum policy'.[17]

---

ism' (COM (2003) 526) recommends that 'The EC should be given the possibility to participate fully in the work of UN bodies where matters of Community competence are concerned ...', at p. 22.

[13] Convention determining the State responsible for examining applications for asylum lodged in one of the Member States of the European Communities (entry into force: 1.9.1997), OJ (19 August 1997) C-254/1-12.

[14] These Resolutions concerned manifestly unfounded applications for asylum and the notion of host third countries and of 'safe' countries of origin.

[15] Treaty on European Union, OJ (20 July 1992) C-191/0109.

[16] Treaty of Amsterdam amending the Treaty on European Union, the Treaties establishing the European Communities, and Related Acts, OJ (10 November 1997) C-340.

[17] Ibid.

The agenda set by Article 63 of the Amsterdam Treaty was given decisive political impetus in October 1999, when the European Council held a special meeting in Tampere, Finland, on the creation of an area of freedom, security and justice in the European Union. In its Conclusions, the Council set out the main lines of a Common EU Asylum and Migration Policy, including partnership with countries of origin, management of migration flows, and establishment of a common European asylum system. Once again the importance of consulting UNHCR was stressed, along with the fact that this system should be based on the 'full and inclusive application of the Geneva Convention'.[18]

4. The First Phase of Harmonization: Focus on the Internal Dimension

The European Union has completed the first phase of its planned harmonization of asylum policy. In substance, this has involved the adoption of four Directives and two Regulations. UNHCR followed the drafting of these instruments closely, and has published comments on all of them. The four Directives set out minimum standards on temporary protection to be granted in situations of mass influx;[19] on reception conditions for asylum-seekers;[20] on the definition and status of refugees and other persons in need of protection;[21] and last but not least, on asylum procedures.[22] The two Regulations are the Dublin II Regulation,[23] which designates the Member State responsible for determining an asylum claim, and the Eurodac Regulation,[24] which establishes a common database of fingerprints to facilitate the implementation of the Dublin II Regulation.

---

[18] Presidency Conclusions, Tampere, 15-16 October 1999, paras. 13 and 14.

[19] Council Directive 2001/55/EC of 20 July 2001 on minimum standards for giving temporary protection in the event of a mass influx of displaced persons and on measures promoting a balance of efforts between Member States in receiving such persons and bearing the consequences thereof, OJ (7 August 2001) L-212.

[20] Council Directive 2003/9/EC of 27 January 2003 laying down minimum standards for the reception of asylum-seekers, OJ (6 February 2003) L-031.

[21] Council Directive 2004/83/EC of 29 April 2004 of Minimum Standards for the Qualification and Status of Third Country Nationals or Stateless Persons as Refugees or as Persons who otherwise need International Protection and the Content of the Protection Granted, OJ (30 September 2004) L-304.

[22] Council Directive 2005/85/EC of 1 December 2005 on minimum standards on procedures in Member States for the granting and withdrawing of refugee status, OJ (13 December 2005) L-326.

[23] Council Regulation (EC) No. 343/2003 of 18 February 2003 establishing the criteria and mechanisms for determining the Member State responsible for examining an asylum application lodged in one of the Member States by a third-country national, OJ (25 February 2003) L-050.

[24] Council Regulation (EC) No. 2725/2000 of 11 December 2000 concerning the establishment of 'Eurodac' for the comparison of fingerprints for the effective application of the Dublin Convention, OJ (15 December 2000) L-316.

UNHCR has welcomed the EU's effort to harmonize its approach to asylum. Like the Commission, it wanted texts which were not only in accordance with international refugee law, but which were of the highest possible standard. A critical look at the legislation which has been adopted, however, reveals that the balance sheet is quite mixed. In some cases, the EU legislation is leading to improved standards of refugee protection. In others, however, it seems to be serving as an incentive for States to align their policies around the lowest common denominator.

UNHCR expressed satisfaction with the Directive setting minimum standards for the granting of temporary protection when there is a mass influx of persons in need of refuge. The Directive was a direct result of the disparate and sometimes chaotic approach taken by Europe toward the mass influx of persons from the former Yugoslavia during the 1990s. It provides for consultations with UNHCR on the establishment, implementation and termination of a common EU temporary protection regime. Further positive aspects include the fact that the Directive is placed squarely within the framework of the 1951 Convention and that temporary protection does not prejudge or prevent recognition of refugee status under that Convention.

However, the Directive on temporary protection has yet to be tested in practice, and it does not address the politically sensitive issue of burden-sharing. This topic was the source of considerable acrimony during the 1990s when Germany, which took in hundreds of thousands of persons fleeing war and ethnic cleansing in the former Yugoslavia, was unable to persuade other Member States to agree to a formal burden-sharing mechanism. It is fair to wonder what would happen today, were there to be a new mass influx of people seeking protection in the EU in the security-conscious, post-September 11, 2001 environment. Moreover, although all Member States were required to have transposed the temporary protection Directive into national law by the end of 2002, a number of EU Member States had not done so.

The second Directive adopted by the Council sets out minimum standards for the reception of asylum-seekers. This is a topic on which the 1951 Convention is silent. The 1951 Convention addresses the social and economic rights of persons recognized as refugees, but does not govern the treatment of people while they are waiting for a decision on their asylum applications, although international human rights law is certainly applicable to them.[25] Moreover, if the basic needs of asylum-seekers are not met, they may be impeded from pursuing their claims.

The deadline for States to transpose the Reception Conditions Directive expired on 6 February 2005. However, a significant number of Member States did not meet this deadline. Conditions of reception remain extremely variable within the EU, and seriously problematic in some Member States.

---

[25] UNHCR, 'Reception of asylum-seekers, including standards of treatment, in the context of individual asylum systems', UN Doc. EC/GC/01/17, 4 September 2001.

Of the Directives included in the first phase of European asylum harmonization, it is the third instrument, known as the 'Qualification Directive', which relates most directly to UNHCR's mandate for refugee protection. It incorporates into Community law the refugee definition as contained in the 1951 Convention, and takes international protection one step further by establishing an obligation for all States to provide subsidiary protection to persons who would not meet the refugee definition, but would nonetheless face serious harm on return. This is an important advance, since State practice in this respect has varied widely. It is also significant that under the terms of this Directive, the persecution or serious harm may be at the hands of State or non-State agents. In addition, the Directive specifically refers to gender and child-specific forms of persecution as grounds for protection.

UNHCR remains concerned, however, that the Qualification Directive may be interpreted to exclude individuals from the scope of protection if they are fleeing from situations of generalized violence. This concern arises from the wording of Article 15(c), which requires an *individual* threat to a civilian's life or person by reason of *indiscriminate* violence in the context of *international or internal armed conflict* [emphasis added]. Time will tell how Member States (and perhaps the European Court of Justice) will interpret this vital but ambiguous passage.

A further concern is the fact that the rights accorded by the Qualification Directive to beneficiaries of subsidiary protection are significantly less extensive than those accorded to 1951 Convention refugees. UNHCR fears that States may therefore be tempted to grant subsidiary protection even when an individual is eligible for refugee status. Such an approach would not only cause hardship to the individuals concerned, and could provoke unnecessary judicial appeals, but would not be conducive to integration and social harmony, if the rights of beneficiaries of subsidiary protection to employment and family reunification, for example, remain limited.

The most recently adopted – and most controversial – piece of asylum legislation is the Asylum Procedures Directive. It sets out minimum norms on how decisions on asylum claims in EU Member States should be made, and will apply to all applications for asylum lodged after 1 December 2007, the deadline for transposition of its provisions into national law. The Directive is the only international law instrument to address how an asylum procedure should be conducted, a matter which is not dealt with in the 1951 Convention.

The negotiation of the Asylum Procedures Directive was particularly difficult. It finally received 'political approval' at the eleventh hour, on 29 April 2004, the deadline for adoption of the first phase instruments having been set at 1 May 2004 by the Treaty of Amsterdam. Final approval was not obtained until 1 December 2005, when the Council of Ministers of Justice and Home Affairs adopted the Directive. It did so without debate and in particular without considering the lengthy, and quite critical, report on the text presented by the European Parliament, which had adopted the report by a margin of just two votes at the end of September 2005.[26]

During the negotiation process, UNHCR repeatedly expressed its concerns about this Directive, which still contains serious deficiencies in its final version. UNHCR is especially unhappy about rules allowing for the designation of 'European safe third countries' to which asylum-seekers may be turned back with no examination of their individual situation. The text also fails to spell out clearly that asylum-seekers should not be sent back to their countries of origin during the appeal process.

5. The Second Phase of Harmonization of EU Asylum Policy: The Hague Programme

Even though the first phase instruments have not yet been implemented by all Member States, the European Commission and the Council have pressed ahead with work on the second phase of the asylum harmonization process. In November 2004, the Council adopted a new multi-annual programme in the area of freedom, security and justice, known as the Hague Programme.[27] This Programme foresees ambitious asylum policy measures, both inside and outside the EU. One of the stated objectives of the Programme is to improve the capability of the Union and its Member States 'to provide protection in accordance with the Geneva Convention on Refugees…'.[28] However, it calls for UNHCR's involvement only with respect to actions *outside* the EU. UNHCR is not mentioned in the Hague Programme with respect to any of the steps to be taken *within* the European Union. The significance of this omission remains to be seen; it could be argued that the European Commission and Member States wish to keep UNHCR at arm's length, where domestic measures are concerned.

The Hague Programme reaffirms the goal of a common European asylum procedure and a uniform status throughout the EU for persons who are recognized as refugees or granted subsidiary protection. UNHCR welcomed the renewed commitment of the Union to ensuring that this will be based on the 'full and inclusive' application of the 1951 Convention. In reality, however, there is no consensus as to what a 'common asylum procedure' means. Does this mean a supranational procedure carried out by a European body, or simply the alignment of 25 national procedures? It does not seem likely that Member States will be prepared, in the foreseeable

[26] European Parliament legislative resolution on the amended proposal for a Council directive on minimum standards on procedures in Member States for granting and withdrawing refugee status (14203/2004 – C6-0200/2004 – 2000/0238(CNS)).

[27] 'The Hague Programme: strengthening freedom, security and justice in the European Union', OJ (3 March 2005), C-53.

[28] Ibid., Introduction.

future, to yield any sovereignty with respect to decision-making in such a sensitive area.

In an effort to facilitate practical cooperation among Member States, the Hague Programme instructs the Commission to establish, in 2005, 'appropriate structures involving the national asylum services of the Member States'.[29] This objective was not achieved by the end of the year. The Hague Programme intends that such structures would eventually be transformed into a 'European support office' for all forms of cooperation relating to the Common European Asylum System. The Commission is also to conduct a study on the feasibility of 'joint processing' of asylum applications within the EU.[30] No deadline is given for this study, and no Member States are pressing for its early completion, a further sign of a minimalist approach to the Common European Asylum System.

The Programme also instructs the Commission to complete, in 2007, an evaluation of the 'first phase' instruments and to present proposals for 'second phase' measures with a view to their adoption by the Council and the Parliament before the end of 2010. However, it is not clear at this stage what the content of second phase instruments might be, and Member States are showing little enthusiasm for further European legislation in the asylum field.

There is much more interest among the Member States for the Hague Programme's external dimension. Refugee advocates fear that the interest of Member States is in deterring and deflecting asylum-seekers from EU territory, as much as in building the refugee protection capacity of third countries. This apprehension was strengthened by the fact that the Hague Programme calls on the Commission, 'in close consultation with the UNHCR', to complete a study of the 'merits, appropriateness and feasibility of joint processing of asylum applications outside EU territory'.[31]

Whatever the underlying motives of the Member States, the Hague Programme places significant emphasis on partnerships between the European Union and third countries with respect to refugee protection, including countries of origin, countries of first asylum and countries of transit. It calls on the Commission to develop EU 'Regional Protection Programmes' in partnership with third countries and in close consultation and cooperation with UNHCR.[32] Pilot programmes were to be launched by the end of 2005 to enhance the protection capacity of third countries, and were to include a joint EU resettlement scheme. The latter, however, would be limited to voluntary participation of Member States.

As of the end of 2005, two regions had been identified for pilot Regional Protection Programmes: Tanzania, which is host to over half a million refugees from Burundi, the Democratic Republic of Congo, and other countries; and the Western Newly Independent States of Belarus, Moldova and Ukraine. However, the budget

---

29 Ibid., 1.3.

30 Ibid.

31 Ibid.

32 Ibid., 1.6.2. The European Council also adopted General Conclusions on improving access to durable solutions at its session of 2-3 November 2004.

allocated to these programmes is quite modest and the budgetary and implementation methodology complex. The full coordination of these Programmes with other initiatives remained a challenge, and consultation with the countries concerned had only just started. UNHCR repeatedly reminded the EU that the countries concerned must be fully-fledged owners of these Programmes and they must see the benefits – otherwise the Programmes will fail. The EU may have made a tactical as well as conceptual mistake, in casting external dimension activities as part of the EU's asylum policy. The so-called 'Regional Protection Programmes' are intended to benefit refugees staying in non-EU countries. Rightly or wrongly, these programmes are seen by many advocates as part of an EU effort to 'externalize' its asylum responsibilities. UNHCR has consistently emphasized that the external dimension of EU refugee policy must be a complement to, and not a substitute for, Member States' obligations toward asylum-seekers arriving directly on their territory. A clear distinction needs to be made between burden-sharing, which is welcome, and burden-shifting, which is not. Moreover, Europe's actions have a clear 'export value', as countries around the world follow Europe's lead.

6. Conclusion

UNHCR's position *vis-à-vis* the European Union is more complex than that of the large number of advocacy organizations which monitor and comment on EU refugee policy, or of the large number of humanitarian agencies which receive Commission funding. The agency must fulfill its mandated functions, which include monitoring the compliance of governments with their obligations under the 1951 Convention, without 'biting the hand that feeds it'.

UNHCR has been consulted during the past twelve years of work on the harmonization of EU asylum policy, though its recommendations have not always been followed. Indeed, some observers worry that the agency may serve as alibi for EU actions in the 'internal' dimension of refugee policy, rather than as a genuine partner. Perhaps not surprisingly, UNHCR's advice is more rigorously followed with regard to the 'external' dimension, an area where Member States feel they have less at stake.

Collaboration between UNHCR and the Commission in the field varies quite considerably from one country to another. The Commission has delegations in 118 third countries around the world. Its Humanitarian Aid Department, ECHO, has a network of technical experts present in 36 countries. Traditionally, UNHCR field offices have tended to regard ECHO as their natural partner, though the need for political and developmental synergies, and the Commission's increasing involvement in asylum capacity-building, make broader and closer collaboration essential, with other parts of the Commission as well.

One of the challenges to this collaboration is the perception that each partner has of the other. EC staff tend to regard UNHCR as a contracting partner, implementing the Commission's programmes in much the way as NGO partners do. UNHCR field staff tend to regard the Commission as a donor to UNHCR's programme. The reality lies somewhere in between. One key to closer collaboration, both in the field and in Brussels, lies in improved cross-pillar coordination within the Commission, which the Commission itself has recognized is needed 'to ensure coherence of the EU's external activities'.[33]

UNHCR's cooperation with different parts of the Commission puts the agency in a good position to encourage inter-service coordination on refugee policy. This has become increasingly necessary, as Europe tackles the challenge of protecting refugees within broader migration movements, and as the Directorate-General for Justice, Freedom and Security is increasingly involved in actions outside the territory of the EU. The Directorates-General for External Relations, Development, Humanitarian Aid, and Enlargement are also engaged in refugee protection and assistance activities outside the European Union, and UNHCR cooperation with each of them remains essential. It is UNHCR's hope that the Strategic Partnership Agreement it signed with the European Commission in February 2005 will serve as the umbrella for this broader relationship.

[33] Communication from the Commission: A strategy on the External Dimension of the Area of Freedom, Security and Justice, 12 October 2005, COM (2005) 491 final.

Chapter 10
THE EU'S HUMAN RIGHTS POLICY IN THE UN: AN EXAMPLE OF EFFECTIVE MULTILATERALISM?

by Hadewych Hazelzet*

1. INTRODUCTION

During the UN General Assembly's Third Committee in New York members of the Group of 77 developing countries (G77) used to make bets that 'the stronger the EU statement, the more likely that the EU will either abstain or unravel'. Lack of EU unity is often equated with lack of EU effectiveness, or vice-versa 'if the EU is united they cannot be defeated'.[1] Is this so, and if so why? During the Commission on Human Rights in Geneva, some countries would make bets that the longer the EU would spend in its so-called 'blue box' (the EU offices), the more the EU position would be fixed and the more difficult it would be to negotiate with the EU and reach any result. What does 'effective multilateralism' concretely mean in the field of human rights? How effectively is the EU pursuing its human rights policy and how could it do better? How can the EU respond to the call by the High Commissioner for Human Rights for a 'new culture' needed for the newly established Human Rights Council?

This chapter sets out the EU's human rights policy and its activities in the UN in the field of human rights. It analyses a number of specific cases in which the EU pursued human rights objectives through the UN, exploring the question under which conditions the EU was a more or a less effective actor and whether the degree of EU unity was a decisive factor. It concludes by making a number of suggestions on how the EU could build on successes of the past and pursue new avenues to increase the effectiveness and visibility of its human rights policy through the UN, notably through the new Human Rights Council.

---

* Dr. Hadewych Hazelzet works as an EU official at the Council of the European Union, General Secretariat, Directorate-General for External Relations and Politico-Military Affairs. This article is written in a personal capacity and does not reflect official EU positions.

[1] K.V. Laatikainen and K.E. Smith, 'Introduction – The European Union at the United Nations: Leader, partner or failure?', in K.V. Laatikainen and K.E. Smith, *The European Union at the United Nations: intersecting multilateralisms* (Basingstroke, Palgrave 2006), pp. 1-23, at p. 16. See also K.E. Smith, 'Speaking with One Voice? European Union Coordination on Human Rights Issues at the United Nations', 44 (1) *Journal of Common Market Studies* (2006), pp. 113-138.

J. Wouters et al., eds., The United Nations and the European Union

2. EU Human Rights Policy

What are the main priorities of the EU's human rights policy? A range of provisions in the Treaty on European Union (TEU) and the Treaty Establishing the European Community (TEC) are designed to promote human rights in the EU's external relations and development cooperation.[2] Over the years, these provisions have perhaps been most prominently translated into EU action in multilateral fora (notably the UN, OSCE and Council of Europe), the EU human rights dialogues and consultations with third countries, as well as in various EU human rights guidelines.[3] The EU moreover publishes an annual report on its actions in the field of human rights.[4]

The EU has a variety of instruments at its disposal to promote the protection of human rights, which range from common analysis on the basis of human rights fact sheets, confidential demarches, political dialogue with third countries, human rights clauses in partnership agreements, public declarations, technical cooperation, or in ultimate resort, restrictive measures – such as financial or travel sanctions.[5] More and more, crisis management operations and rule of law missions have been initiated as a way of preventive diplomacy in situations were human rights protection and the rule of law needed strengthening.[6]

Who are the 'masterminds' behind the EU's human rights policy? The EUs human rights policy is developed and monitored by the human rights directors of all Member States, who meet regularly in the so-called Council Working Party on Human Rights (COHOM). One of the main objectives is to 'mainstream' human rights throughout the EU's foreign policy, but also in Community policies such as trade

---

[2] For example, Articles 6, 11, and 40 TEU and 177 TEC.

[3] Since 1995, the EU holds a bi-annual human rights dialogue with China, since 2002 with Iran (irregular). In 2003 the EU and the Russian Federation commenced human rights consultations. The EU holds Troika consultations on human rights with the United States, Canada and others. The EU human rights guidelines are the following: death penalty (1998), torture and ill-treatment (2000), human rights dialogues (2002), children and armed conflict (2003), human rights defenders (2004).

[4] Available at <http://www.consilium.eu.int/human-rights>.

[5] On the legal bases and the use of these various instruments, see for instance P. Alston, *The EU and Human Rights* (Oxford, OUP 1999); B. Brandtner and A. Rosas, 'Human Rights and the External Relations of the E.C.: an Analysis of Doctrine and Practice', 9 *EJIL* (1998), pp. 468-490; A. Casese, C. Lalumiere, P. Leuprecht and M. Robinson, *Leading by example: a human rights agenda for the European Union for the year 2000* (San Domenico di Fiesole, Italy, Academy of European Law, European University Institute, 1998); H. Hazelzet, *Carrots or Sticks? EU and US reactions to Human Rights Violations (1989-2000)* (San Domenico di Fiesole, Italy, European University Institute, Ph.D. dissertation 2001); H. Hazelzet, *Suspension of development cooperation: an instrument to promote human rights?* (Maastricht/Brussels, European Union Development Policy and Management Institute (EUDPM) 2005); F. Hoffmeister, *Menschenrechts- und Demokratieklauseln in den vertraglichen Außenbeziehungen der Europäischen Gemeinschaft* (Berlin, Springer 1998); H.J. Steiner and P. Alston, *International Human Rights in Context: Law, Politics and Morals* (Oxford, OUP 2000, 2nd edn), Chapter 13, p. 2117 et seq.

[6] See Chapter by Jim Cloos in this book; see also H. Hazelzet, 'Human Rights Aspects of EU Crisis Management Operations: from Nuisance to Necessity', in N. White, R. Murphy and K. Mansson (eds.), *Human Rights and Peace Operations*, published by Frank Cass, forthcoming. Examples of rule of law missions are for instance training of judges and lawyers in Georgia and Iraq.

and development. Therefore, ongoing efforts are undertaken to ensure that human rights issues are incorporated into all regional, bilateral and thematic policy areas and relations of the EU where appropriate.[7] The Presidency, the Council Secretariat and the Commission play an important role in this regard. The Presidency, assisted by Council Secretariat and Commission, has an important steering role. The Presidency, Council Secretariat, Commission, and in practice the incoming Presidency, take part as members of the Troika in human rights dialogues and consultations. In addition, the Commission manages the European Initiative for Democracy and Human Rights (EIDHR), is responsible for election observation missions and the implementation of the agreements with human rights clauses with third countries.[8] The EU's and Member States' representations in Geneva and New York play a crucial role in carrying out EU's human rights policy in the UN.

The European Parliament (EP) takes an active interest in human rights protection, both inside and outside the EU. Largely through its re-instituted Sub-Committee on Human Rights, it holds regular public hearings and urgency debates, prepares resolutions for adoption at Plenary, issues an annual report on human rights, arranges for briefings with the Presidency and the Commission and its members pose numerous written and oral questions to the Council and the Commission to keep them alert and accountable. The biggest « stick » of the EP in the field of human rights is the delay or refusal to sign cooperation or association agreements with third countries on the basis of lack of respect for human rights.[9] Such deference can have important financial implications for third countries. Its biggest 'carrot' is its approval of the budget and the money earmarked for human rights, as well as the annual reward of the Sakharov price to individuals for their human rights defender activities.[10]

NGOs are actively involved in the EU's human rights policy, through regular briefings to COHOM and the Troika, frequent contacts on urgent issues of concern, implementation of EIDHR projects, participation in legal seminars associated with the human rights dialogues, and the Annual EU NGO Human Rights Forum.

3. UN Human Rights Fora and Instruments

The UN is arguably the most important multilateral forum through which the EU seeks to promote the protection of human rights.[11] The main bodies through which

[7] Available at <http://www.consilium.eu.int/human-rights/>.

[8] Available at <http://europa.eu.int/comm/external_relations/human_rights/intro/ >.

[9] In the nineties, cooperation agreements were deferred in a number of cases: Algeria (1998), Croatia (1995), Morocco (1996), Pakistan (1999), Russia (1995), Syria (1992-1993) and Turkey (1995). See Hazelzet 2001, op.cit., *supra* n. 5, at p. 76.

[10] Available at <http://www.europarl.eu.int/committees/droi_home_en.htm>.

[11] This chapter does not cover EU cooperation in the Council of Europe or the OSCE, which are of course extremely important regional organizations in the field of human rights protection and promotion.

the EU has in the past sought to express concerns about country situations and to promote certain thematic issues are the UN General Assembly's Third Committee and the Commission of Human Rights (CHR).[12] The EU has been one of the main actors in these bodies over time, initiating a large number of initiatives during both bi-annual meetings.

In the past few years, the EU successfully tabled resolutions on, *inter alia*, the human rights situation in Burma/Myanmar, Democratic People's Republic of Korea, Democratic Republic of Congo, Sudan, Turkmenistan, Belarus (together with the United States), religious intolerance, death penalty and rights of the child (together with Latin American countries). Draft resolutions and EU statements on all agenda items are prepared by COHOM and finalised in New York and Geneva where necessary. In the last few years Member States have also started to coordinate questions to the UN Special Procedures. The Presidency speaks on behalf of the EU in these bodies, although on some issues Member States also take the floor in their national capacity, such as during the High Level Segment for Ministers. In cases where the Presidency was not a member of CHR an arrangement was found in which the Presidency could still speak on behalf of the EU.[13] Council Secretariat and Commission have observer seats in UNGA and CHR.

In March 2006, after months of intensive negotiations in the context of UN reform, the UN General Assembly adopted a resolution on the establishment of a Human Rights Council (HRC), which will replace the CHR.[14] The fact that countries with a notorious human rights record could be members of the CHR and even Chair it had lead over time to a loss of credibility of this body.[15] The context of UN reform was used as an opportunity to replace the CHR with a more credible organ with a stronger mandate. The President of the General Assembly managed to get a 'compromise text' adopted before the next session of CHR started. The EU was actively involved in this process and ultimately voted in favour of the text which it saw as a compromise which largely met its key priorities, even though it had aimed for a more ambitious result.

---

[12] For EU initiatives and statements on human rights made over time in the UN, see the EU Annual Report on Human Rights as well as:<http://www.europa-eu-un.org/articles/articleslist_s9_en.htm>.

[13] For procedural questions, where only Member are allowed to speak, the incoming Presidency or in case of a BENELUX Presidency, the Netherlands, Belgium or Luxembourg would speak on behalf of the EU. The Commission usually makes a statement in its capacity of observer on issues within its competence such as technical cooperation or electoral observation under the appropriate agenda item. Some Presidencies, for instance the United Kingdom, have on some occasions encouraged Member States to take the floor in support of EU positions to add to the number of voices during the meeting. This was important in particular during the negotiations on the establishment of the HRC and review of Special Procedures, where many countries in the room took positions that were contrary to EU positions.

[14] Available at <http://www.ohchr.org/english/bodies/hrcouncil/>.

[15] See Kofi Annan's speech at the 61st session of CHR in April 2005, available at <http://www.ohchr.org/english/bodies/chr/sessions/61/speeches.htm>.

An important activity connected to these two main human rights fora is the promotion of cooperation with the UN Special Procedures and Treaty Bodies and follow-up to their recommendations and concluding observations. The EU systematically raises these issues during political and human rights dialogue meetings and consultations with third countries. The High Commissioner for Human Rights as well as a number of Special Representatives have been invited for briefings with the Political and Security Committee of the EU, as well as to Council Working Parties.[16] The EU and its Member States also take active part in standard-setting, for example *vis-à-vis* the negotiations on a UN Convention on the effective enjoyment of human rights by persons with disabilities[17] and the Convention on Enforced Disappearances. The EU and its Member States are among the largest voluntary contributors to the budget of the OHCHR.[18]

EU cooperation on human rights within the UN goes beyond the two main human rights fora. First, the EU is actively involved in major UN Conferences including for instance the World Conference on Women (Beijing, 1995), the World Conference Against Racism (Durban, 2001), the UN Special Summit on Children (New York, 2002), and, more recently, the World Summit on the Information Society (Tunis, 2005). The EU prepares common positions for such meetings. Second, in pursuit of the EU Human Rights Guidelines on Children and Armed Conflict, regular contacts are maintained with UNICEF, the Special Representative of the UN Secretary-General and the UN Department for Peace Keeping Operations. These contacts are of more general importance in the context of EU-UN cooperation in the field of crisis management.[19]

4. Analysis of EU Positions at UN Human Rights Fora

This section briefly analyses the level of unity and effectiveness of EU country and thematic initiatives at CHR and UNGA, EU positions towards initiatives taken by third countries, negotiations on the Human Rights Council and cooperation on human rights with other UN agencies.

As far as initiatives taken by the EU at the CHR are concerned, lengthy internal negotiations were often necessary to reach agreement on which country situations would merit a resolution, and if so, under which agenda item: the more 'confrontational' item 9 or the more 'cooperative' item 19.[20] The introduction of Council

[16] For instance from 2004-2006 the HCHR and UN Special Representatives on Human Rights Defenders, Burma, Belarus and Violence Against Children visited Brussels, as did the UNSG's Special Advisors on the Prevention of Genocide and on Children and Armed Conflict.

[17] Available at <http://www.un.org/esa/socdev/enable/>.

[18] See annual report of the OHCHR at <http://www.ohchr.org/english/about/fundraising.htm>.

[19] See Chapter by Jim Cloos in this book, also see Hazelzet – forthcoming (*supra* n. 6).

[20] Item 9 was the item under which country resolutions were introduced of a more condemnatory nature, sometimes leading to the appointment or prolongation of a mandate of a UN Special Rappor-

conclusions in which the EU highlighted not only which initiatives it was planning to take in CHR but also other country situations of concern helped reaching agreement. Although the EU adopted internal guidelines on how to prepare and prioritise its actions in CHR and UNGA during 2004, these were of limited direct value once decisions had to be made on which countries to table a resolution. The main difficulties usually concerned the situations in Iran, China, Chechnya and to some extent Zimbabwe.[21] These conclusions have thus served more to assure internal EU cohesion than to tell the world which human rights concerns were among the EU priorities. The general EU statements on country situations have also helped to assure EU Member States that all topics of concern could be mentioned in one way or another. Preparations for the UNGA Third Committee have tended to be smoother given the lower number of initiatives and the fact that no Council conclusions have been needed. It is important to note that the last country initiative taken bilaterally by an EU Member State was the Danish resolution on China in 1997.[22] The repercussions were that some trade missions were cancelled so that afterwards EU Member States generally seemed to consider that country resolutions are best done by the EU as a whole.

On EU thematic initiatives, discussions have been marked by coherence from the outset. The initiative on religious intolerance used to be run by Ireland. Over time it had become more and more difficult to negotiate due to heated debates and exposure by various major religious groups which were lobbying for singling out the 'phobias' directed against each religion – while the EU wanted the resolution to focus on religious intolerance in general. When Ireland assumed the Presidency in 2004, it was felt that it would perhaps be inappropriate to run a national initiative and more effective if the EU as a whole would put its weight behind it. Since then, the EU has continued to run the resolution, albeit that Member States have taken turns in taking over the lead from the Presidency as so-called 'burdensharer'. Negotiations have continued to be difficult but even after the initial outburst of the cartoons issue the text was unanimously adopted in the UNGA Third Committee in November 2004. The EU would have been ready to run the initiative again at the

teur, item 19 addressed the human rights situation in a country aiming at establishing some sort of technical cooperation.

[21] The introduction of resolutions on Iran by Canada and on China and Cuba by the United States and on Belarus together with the United States have facilitated EU coordination to some extend, but discussions on co-sponsorship have still not always been easy. The EU has always maintained that having a human rights dialogue or consultations with a country does not prejudge it taking a public stand in the UN human rights fora on these countries.

[22] Following lack of progress on a list of benchmarks agreed in 1995, the EU again tabled a resolution on the situation in China in 1996 in the CHR, following which China cancelled the dialogue in 1996. That year, China once again succeeded in getting majority support for a no-action motion, hence preventing a vote on the resolution. In 1997 Denmark tabled the resolution in its national capacity, supported by all EU Member States except France, Germany, Spain, Italy and Greece. Once again, the resolution was defeated by a no action motion. China 'retaliated' by cancelling several, mostly trade-related, visits by delegations from Denmark, the Netherlands and Austria.

next session of CHR following the eruption of reactions to the cartoons during early 2006.[23] A similar development had occurred years earlier over the resolution on the death penalty which used to be run by Sweden and Finland. On this resolution, the EU has managed to attract an increasing number of co-sponsors over time. The resolution on torture, traditionally run by Denmark, would seem a likely candidate to follow suit given the EU Guidelines on torture. However, due to national priorities, this has not yet been considered. Some Member States also continue to introduce national initiatives on certain themes.[24] EU Member States go to great lengths to assure that all EU Members can co-sponsor their resolutions.[25]

As regards initiatives taken by third countries, Presidencies as well as outsiders have tended to judge their success in the UNGA and the CHR by the degree of EU unity achieved during their term. This is measured by the number of split votes on resolutions introduced by third countries, and to a lesser degree by the number of common co-sponsorship of others' resolutions. The EU seeks only to coordinate co-sponsorship on resolutions of great political importance, such as country resolutions or some thematic ones such as the Mexican resolution on Human Rights and Counter-terrorism. On other resolutions, usually Member States merely inform each other of their plans to co-sponsor. Sometimes, the EU uses the possibility of common EU co-sponsorship in its negotiations on the text with third countries. Consultations behind the scenes, often before texts are introduced, have been crucial in this regard. The table om page 190 shows the number of split votes and common co-sponsorship over time, in absolute numbers and as a percentage of the total number of resolutions.

We see that little pattern can be deduced from the number of split votes over time, but that there is a clear trend towards more common co-sponsorship both in terms of the number of common EU initiatives and in terms of the percentage of the total number of resolutions tabled at the EU. EU enlargement has thus not weakened EU unity in this regard. Creative use of statements as well as increased use of burdensharing – an informal system in which EU Member States agree to take the lead on certain resolutions and coordinate positions or lobby – has helped to increase common EU positions on third country resolutions, as well as to increase votes in favour of EU initiatives.[26] The large number of resolutions makes it impos-

[23] The issue became linked to the negotiations on the HRC resolution where members of the Organization of Islamic Conference (OIC) had wanted an operational paragraph on defamation of religion and cultural diversity. This was unacceptable to the EU. There were also proposals to see if the OIC and the EU could come forward with a joint initiative on religious intolerance at CHR. The challenge here was that the OIC would have wanted to take the Pakistani-lead resolution on defamation of religion as a basis and the EU its resolution on religious intolerance. In the past, the EU has called for a vote and voted against the Pakistani resolution. In the end, the issue is mentioned in the preamble of the resolution establishing the HRC.

[24] For instance Austria on minorities, Denmark on torture, France on enforced disappearances, Sweden/Finland on extra-judicial and summary executions.

[25] The resolution on torture has been particularly challenging in this regard.

[26] The peak in 1997 is presumably caused by the split regarding the resolution on the human rights situation in China.

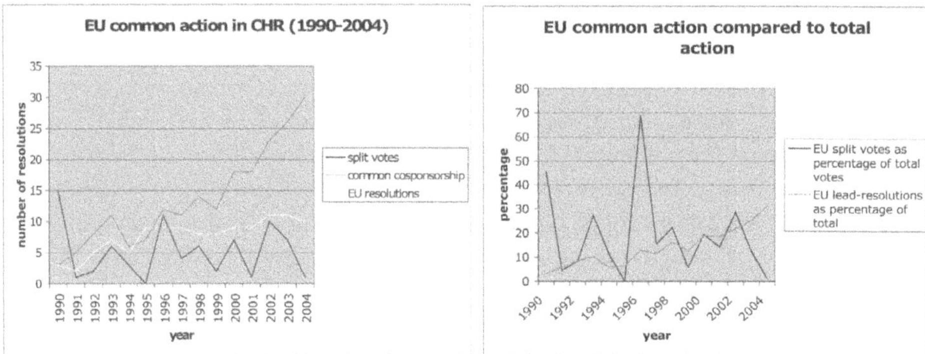

Table 1: EU common action in CHR (1990-2004). Calculated on the basis of data collected by Smith (*Journal of Common Market Studies*, 2006).

sible for any delegation to follow detailed discussions on each and every one of them, in particular for smaller delegations or Presidency teams. Elaborated lobby schemes have also been prepared to ensure that each EU Member States reaches out to a number of countries to seek support for EU positions and initiatives.

On what issues does the EU tend to split? Despite many hours of internal negotiations in the « blue box » the EU has tend to split in the past on some resolutions on the Middle East, introduced by third countries, as well as on the right to development and racism (follow up to Durban). Other examples include the resolution on mercenaries, toxic waste, unilateral coercive measures, and some issues related to the UN budget. On country situations other than the Middle East there have usually been common positions. In recent years there has been a tendency to encourage third countries, in particular African countries, to 'take ownership' by introducing resolutions themselves, such as on Zimbabwe, DRC and Sudan, with varying success. This has also been a way to postpone or avoid an EU decision on whether the EU should take the lead on these initiatives.

Sometimes the split was caused by one vote only, such as on the right to development where Sweden has traditionally voted against. So-called 'three-way splits' are considered the worst, with some countries abstaining, some voting in favour and others voting against. In such cases the Presidency tries to find a common middle ground, often in a common abstention, by presenting an EU explanation of vote which encompasses all positions in some way. The less cooperative the introducer of a controversial text or the more extreme and emotional the wording, the easier it has been for the Presidency to get all Member States to take the same position, albeit for different motivations. As a corollary, the more moderate these texts, or the more willingness from the third party to negotiate, the easier it has been to get EU proposals into the text and to make it acceptable to all.

A prominent example of difficult internal negotiations to reach a common position has been the vote on the Cuban-lead resolution on Guantanamo Bay at CHR in 2005. The fact that Cuba – a country that has refused to cooperate with the UN

Special Procedures – called on the United States to cooperate with them, as well as grave concerns about the human rights situation in Cuba, made some EU Member States take a position against the resolution from the outset. On the other hand, the fact that the draft resolution used language from a resolution recently adopted by the European Parliament, coupled with strong public opinion at home, made it difficult for some other Member States to vote against. The fact that the United States publicly stated it would work with the UN Special Rapporteurs (UNSRs) with a view to a visit to Guantanamo Bay finally facilitated a common EU vote against the resolution. This decision was difficult to explain to public opinion in many EU Member States. On the other hand, it gave the EU a hook to continue to press for a visit by the UNSRs to the US at all political levels. When such a visit did not materialise in line with the standard UN terms of reference for such visits, it became clear that the EU could probably not take the same position should a resolution be put forward again. Agreement on the Human Rights Council and the procedural last session of the CHR meant neither the EU nor the United States was confronted with that situation as of yet.

The process of negotiations on the Human Rights Council could by and large be characterised as EU unity on key issues leading to an effective EU role during the negotiations. The EU aimed for a standing body, with good quality of membership and a strong mandate to effectively address country situations. Given the strong positions of other UN Member States, the fact that the EU managed to have its key objectives reflected in the resolution, albeit not in every detail and not at the same level of ambition, was due to active lobbying behind the scenes and engagement with all relevant players, not the least the President of the General Assembly. Hick-ups in the final days of the negotiation which aimed at achieving consensus on the text and avoiding a vote, were finally solved by a strong EU explanation of vote, the same method as often adopted at the CHR and the UNGA Third Committee. In this case, the EU was too late to express its support for the 'final' compromise text presented by the President of the General Assembly in February. When the United States came out publicly against the compromise, some Member States started to change position and argued in favour of further negotiations. In the end, the situation was solved by an EU statement issued in New York which indicated EU support for the text. The overriding aim remained to avoid attempts by others to re-open the text and to avoid a vote. Still, for internal political reasons, the United States called for a vote and voted against, while the EU and 170 other countries voted in favour. Crucially, and under strong pressure from the EU and others, the United States did however express its support for the HRC and its intention to cooperate with it, so that another ICC situation was avoided.

The first elections of the HRC on 9 May were a potential source of internal divergence, given the fact that EU Member States were to some extent competing against one another in trying to obtain a seat in the 47-member body. Yet, the spirit in which the EU – for the first time – tried to reach an internal understanding on Member States' approaches towards these elections set an important tone for the future.[27] This question was of particular importance to incoming Presidencies and their role, according to the Treaty, to effectively represent the EU in multilateral fora. Therefore, understanding was reached on certain guiding principles regarding expectations towards candidates. In the end, not all incoming Presidencies that posed their candidature were elected. Some members were elected only for one or two years, therefore they can run again next year. Since the ballot was secret, the extent in which EU Member States adhered to the just agreed EU guiding principles when seeking support for their candidatures and when supporting others, cannot be verified.

EU cooperation within the UN in other human rights related areas perhaps catches less of the public attention but is no less significant. Active EU collaboration with the UN agencies and the UN Special Procedures is widely and strongly supported within the EU and attempts are made to do more and be more effective. Examples are the recent EU paper on the implementation of UN Security Council Resolution (UNSCR) 1325 on Women, Peace and Security and on UNSCR 1612 on Children and Armed Conflict. Implementation of these resolutions, as well as EU-UN cooperation in the field of crisis management, are discussed in the bi-annual EU-UN Steering Committee. The EU sought advice of UN experts at UNICEF and elsewhere for the elaboration of the EU Guidelines on Children and Armed Conflict and subsequent follow-up, *inter alia*, in a checklist on the integration of children and armed conflict into ESDP operations.[28] Last but not least, negotiations on the establishment of the Rome Statute on the International Criminal Court could not have been successfully concluded without the active and united support of the EU.

5. Concluding Observations

Literature on the role of the EU within the UN as well as the EU Presidencies tend to measure the EU's effectiveness by the degree of unity within the EU. This chapter explored whether the degree of unity is indeed a decisive factor for EU action to be effective, and what explained a lack of unity at certain occasions. Given the EU's codified commitment to human rights one would expect to find a large degree of unity in this policy area and consequently an effective EU contribution to UN work in the field of human rights.

---

[27] The EU historically, does not coordinate electoral matters within the UN. Since 1995 it started to coordinate elections of high level officials to a certain extent, which was reinforced in 1998 and again in 2000. Given the EU public statement at the adoption of the resolution on the HRC, which said that EU Member States would not vote for certain candidates, the ground was cleared for some level of coordination. Since, however, the EU had also advocated during the negotiations that more candidates should be presented than seats and that candidates should be judged on their human rights record, it would be difficult to go as far as to pre-arrange which EU Member States could present their candidatures when. The ballot is secret and Member States vote, not the EU as such. The outcome of the elections can be found at the following website <http://www.un.org/ga/60/elect/hrc/>.

[28] Relevant documents can be found at <http://www.consilium.europa.int/human-rights>.

Why would the EU be more effective if it is united in pursuing its human rights policy? One argument would be that once the EU arrives at a common position, given the common denominator of 25 Member States, it tends to adopt a rather moderate position which is likely to gather support within the UN. This middle-ground position is subsequently carried out by 25 UN Member States. It is more difficult for third countries to try and drive a wedge between Member States. On the other hand, united EU positions are very difficult to negotiate. This does not always lead to reaching EU goals. It could be more effective if Presidencies are given a certain mandate with margin of manoeuvre to negotiate with third parties.

A brief analysis of EU action in CHR and the UNGA Third Committee as well as a number of human rights related policies suggests that, indeed, the EU is more effective when it is united, but only up to a certain extent. There is a trade-off between the time it takes to agree, the inflexibility of resulting EU positions and resources that could meanwhile have been used elsewhere. We saw that the use of Council conclusions or explanations of vote, as well as encouraging ownership by others, are used as instruments to reach an EU common position, in particular where public denunciation of country situations is concerned. Paradoxically, denunciation of country situations is on the one hand the area where the EU could make most difference, and where it is most appealing to Member States not to go it alone. On the other hand, country resolutions are also the most difficult to agree on, not so much on the obvious cases such as Burma/Myanmar and DPRK, but more for the cases in between. Discussions are then not so much about whether or not a certain situation needs to be mentioned, but how best to address it, which could be outside the CHR/UNGA. Within the EU, agreement on substance can be trying, but agreement on tactics is even more difficult and therefore largely (but perhaps not enough) left to the Presidency. On thematic initiatives, we saw EU concerted action on some themes, but not on others, explained perhaps by the degree of willingness or opportunity of the national 'owner' of the resolution to hand it over to the EU.

From the point of view of third countries, the EU internal dynamics can at times be rather trying. Countries that are sensitive to naming and shaming may be more attentive to EU public statements than countries that look at how EU action will ultimately affect them in real terms of trade, security or negotiations in other fields. The EU has in the past not used its trade or financial weight in UN fora on human rights to force or induce countries to cooperate. This is perhaps one reason why discussion in the CHR and UNGA has been relatively isolated from developments ongoing elsewhere. The relative lack of linkages thus far between the UN human rights fora and other activities clearly touches on the question of how much more effective the EU could be, and whether the degree of unity is really the most determining factor when seeking to measure EU effectiveness. The EU could perhaps get more out of these fora if it were to spend less time on forging unity in certain areas, if it were to pick its battles and would make better use of its diversity and resources. How much of a difference did split votes make once CHR was over? How much lobbying on human rights issues or meetings with human rights defenders could have been done in the time needed to arrive at a common EU position? How much of a difference on the ground did EU resolutions or statements make? The answers to these questions are perhaps more indicative of EU effectiveness than the level of unity within the EU.

The Human Rights Council offers plenty of opportunities to do things differently and to have a real impact on the ground. It will meet throughout the year and, like the CHR, it has the possibility to convene special sessions. Its members should 'abide by the highest human rights standards' and make pledges and commitments thereto. They will also be subject to peer review and are expected to fully cooperate with the HRC and its mechanisms. They can only serve for two consecutive terms which ensures more rotation than was the case in the past. Mainstreaming of human rights issues, human rights education and technical cooperation will be important means to improve human rights situations on the ground and through the UN. The relationship with the UNGA Third Committee will be reviewed but should avoid duplication as was to some extent the case until now. The agenda of the HRC will be shorter and more flexible and perhaps the role of the OHCHR will be more prominent. NGOs will participate. The HRC can make recommendations throughout the UN system, including to the UN Security Council. Crucially also, the budget of the OHCHR was doubled as part of UN reform which defined human rights protection as one of the principal pillars of the UN, together with security and development.

The HRC offers opportunities to the EU to prepare itself in a different way to the sessions of the HRC and the UNGA Third Committee. Obviously it should continue to strive for unity, but perhaps pick its battles more selectively and take a longer term view at which kind of initiatives should be taken when and where, with whom, and keep their results under regular review. Many see the HRC as an opportunity to move away from a 'confrontational' approach towards a more conciliatory one. Taking a holistic approach towards its initiatives, and ensuring mainstreaming of human rights throughout EU policies would perhaps be easier and more imperative with the new HRC due to its regular sessions. More use could be made of burdensharing arrangements among EU Member States to effectively use all the resources at the disposal of the EU and its Presidency. It could also have an impact on COHOM's working procedures and the role played by the Council Secretariat and the Commission.

Human rights policy has all the potential to be a true example of effective multilateralism. History will judge the level of effectiveness not by the degree of unity or number of initiatives adopted in multilateral fora, but by tangible progress in human rights protection on the ground.

Chapter 11
EU-UN COOPERATION FOR SUSTAINABLE DEVELOPMENT

by Jochen Jesinghaus*

1. Introduction

Sustainable Development has become a high-level objective for the European Union. Article 2 of the EU Treaty, as amended by the Treaty of Amsterdam (1997), stipulates:

> '*The Union shall set itself the following objectives*:
>
> – to promote economic and social progress and a high level of employment and to achieve balanced and **sustainable development**, in particular through the creation of an area without internal frontiers, through the strengthening of economic and social cohesion and through the establishment of economic and monetary union, ultimately including a single currency in accordance with the provisions of this Treaty.'[1]

Furthermore, the Amsterdam Treaty revised Article 6 of the EC Treaty as follows:

> 'Environmental protection requirements must be integrated into the definition and implementation of the Community policies and activities referred to in Article 3, in particular with a view to promoting **sustainable development**'.

So can we lean back and watch progress towards a more sustainable society? The official 'Questions & answers on the Amsterdam Treaty' website[2] explains why the EU needs the Amsterdam Treaty, and what its consequences are for the European citizen; does it tell us something about true priorities that the word 'sustainable' can not be found in almost ten-thousand words of text?

* European Commission, DG Joint Research Centre (JRC). The views expressed in this text are those of the author and do not necessarily reflect the official European Commission's view on the subject.

[1] Article 2 of the Treaty of Amsterdam amending the Treaty on the European Union, the treaties establishing the European Communities and related acts (Amsterdam treaty), OJ (10 November 1997) C-340.

[2] 'Questions & answers on the Amsterdam treaty', available at <http://europa.eu.int/abc/obj/amst/en/qa.htm>.

J. Wouters et al., eds., The United Nations and the European Union

This contribution explores the current sustainable development agendas in the international discourse (section 2). Section 3 is dedicated to the role of the European Union as a 'sustainable development player' at the UN. Priorities for sustainable development in the future are dealt with in section 4, leading to a conclusion in section 5.

2. Sustainable Development Agendas

2.1 The Rio process

The term 'Sustainable Development' was coined around 1972, presumably by René Dubos and Barbara Ward (*Only One Earth*, 1972). However, the recognition that Earth's resources are limited, and therefore might not sustain overexploitation, can be traced back to earlier origins, such as the writings of Robert Malthus (*An Essay on Population*, 1798), Harold Hotelling (*The Economics of exhaustible Resources*, 1931), Fairfield Osborn (*Our Plundered Planet*, 1948), Harrison Brown (*The challenge of man's future*, 1954), Kenneth Boulding (*The Economics of the Coming Spaceship Earth*, 1966), Garrett Hardin (*The Tragedy of the Commons*, 1968) and many others.

The Sustainable Development debate left the academic sphere with the first report to the Club of Rome titled 'Limits to Growth' (1972). The book, full of complicated graphs and formulas that no ordinary citizen could possibly understand, sold twelve million copies in 37 languages. Saying it was controversial would be an understatement: from this moment on, the World was neatly divided in those who believed in doomsday scenarios and those who believed that technological progress would eventually bring prosperity to everybody. And still, it took a long time until Sustainable Development ('SD') became a prominent *political* framework.

As early as 1972, the United Nations Conference on the Human Environment in *Stockholm* promoted some remarkably familiar ideas: 'Principle 2: The natural resources of the earth … must be safeguarded for the benefit of present and future generations'; 'Principle 26: Man and his environment must be spared the effects of nuclear weapons .. of mass destruction…';[3] finally principle 21 emphasized the prohibition of cross-border environmental damage under international law, thereby serving as a precedent for much of the environmental diplomacy of the past two decades.[4]

However, the 1972 Stockholm conference did not attract enough media attention to push environmental themes into the mainstream of politics. Fifteen years

[3] Declaration of the United Nations Conference on the Human Environment, UNEP, 16 June 1972, available at <http://www.unep.org/Documents.multilingual/Default.asp?DocumentID=97&ArticleID=1503>.

[4] P. Haas, M. Levy, and T. Parson, 'Appraising the Earth Summit: How should we judge UNCED's success?', 34 (8) *Environment* (1992), pp. 6-11, 26-33.

later, the World Commission on Environment and Development, better known as the *Brundtland Commission*, gave SD a short and crispy definition that is still the most widely used formula:

> 'The General Assembly,
> Believing that **sustainable development**, which implies **meeting the needs of the present without compromising the ability of future generations to meet their own needs**, should become a central guiding principle of the United Nations, Governments and private institutions, organizations and enterprises, ...'[5] [emphasis added]

The political breakthrough for Sustainable Development came five years later, with over one- hundred heads of state meeting in Rio de Janeiro at the June 1992 United Nations Conference on Environment and Development (UNCED). The assembled leaders signed the Convention on Climate Change[6] and the Convention on Biological Diversity,[7] endorsed the Rio Declaration on Environment and Development[8] and the Forest Principles,[9] and adopted *Agenda 21*, a 300 page plan for achieving sustainable development in the 21st century.[10] In December 1992, the UN created the Commission on Sustainable Development (CSD) to monitor the implementation of the Earth Summit agreements, today the most active 'functional Commission' in the UN system, and the stage for most of the cooperation between the European Union and the Member States of the United Nations.

Another five years later, the UN convened a 'Special Session of the General Assembly to Review and Appraise the Implementation of Agenda 21' from 23-27 June 1997, a session that, according to the International Institute for Sustainable Development,[11] acted as a sober reminder that little progress had been made in implementing Agenda 21 and ended without significant new commitments.

Ten years after Rio, the Johannesburg World Summit on Sustainable Development (WSSD) added further to the new soberness; in the absence of political enthusiasm, the only major innovation of the Summit was the introduction of 'partnerships' as a means to promote sustainability outside the official government activities. In the meantime, the European Union announced the EU Energy Initiative (EUEI),

---

[5] UN General Assembly Resolution A/RES/42/187: Report of the World Commission on Environment and Development.

[6] United Nations Framework Convention on Climate Change, 9 May 1992, 1992, 31 *ILM* 848.

[7] Convention on Biological Diversity, 5 June 1992, 1992, 31 *ILM* 818.

[8] Rio Declaration on Environment and Development, 12 August 1992, UN Doc. A/CONF.151/26 (Vol. I).

[9] Non-Legally Binding Authoritative Statement of Principles for a Global Consensus on the Management, Conservation and Sustainable Development of All Types of Forests, 14 August 1992, UN Doc. A/CONF.151/26 (Vol. III).

[10] Agenda 21, June 1992, at <*http://www.un.org/esa/sustdev/documents/agenda21/english/Agenda21.pdf*>.

[11] IISD, The sustainable development timeline', at <http://www.iisd.org/pdf/2006/sd_timeline_2006.pdf>.

the EU Water Initiative (EUWI), and the EU Action Plan on Forest Law Enforcement, Governance and Trade (FLEGT); they are today, in terms of budgets and participation, the most important partnerships created in the wake of the WSSD.

This 'Sustainable Development timeline' concentrated on the 'big events', and most SD experts are quite familiar with them. But what about the Millennium Development Goals (MDGs), the Doha Development Agenda (DDA) and the Monterrey commitments?

2.2 The Millennium Development Goals

In *September 2000*, the UN *Millennium Summit* formulated the United Nations Millennium Declaration.[12] The largest-ever gathering of world leaders agreed to a set of eight timebound and measurable goals, to be achieved by 2015.

The World Trade Organization's fourth Ministerial Conference in Doha (Qatar) in *November 2001* aimed to improve conditions for worldwide trade and investment, focusing on better international governance as a precondition for development. The Ministerial Declaration launching the Doha Development Agenda (DDA) mandated negotiations on agriculture, industrial products, services, intellectual property (geographical indications, TRIPs and Health), the 'Singapore issues' (investment, competition, transparency in government procurement and trade facilitation), WTO rules (anti-dumping, subsidies, regional trade agreements) and trade and environment (relationship between existing WTO rules and trade obligations set out in Multilateral Environmental Agreements).[13]

At the *March 2002* International Conference on *Financing for Development* in Monterrey, donors and partner countries met to discuss how the MDGs could be achieved, and agreed on a global deal called the '*Monterrey Consensus*' in which sustained political and economic reform by developing countries (i.e., good governance) would be matched by direct support from the developed world in the form of aid, trade, debt relief and investment.

2.3 The value of a single framework

For an outsider who is not so familiar with the recent history of development policy, it might look as if there were two important parallel but independent political agendas:

1. The 'from Rio to Johannesburg' *Sustainable* Development agenda;
2. The Millennium Summit, Monterrey and Doha *Development* agenda.

---

[12] UN General Assembly Resolution A/RES/55/2, 18 September 2000, UN Millennium Declaration.

[13] See 'The Doha Development Agenda', available at <http://europa.eu.int/comm/trade/issues/newround/doha_da/index_en.htm>.

There are indeed two communities of actors: one is anchored around keywords like *Kyoto Protocol, biodiversity, ecological footprint*; the other is more familiar with *Lomé, Cotonou, GATT, Doha*, etc. – most readers of this book will easily recognize both families of keywords.

Officially, there should be no such categories, and *all* development should be sustainable. But in political reality, members of the SD community are easily put into the 'environmentalists corner', and members of the MDG community are suspicious of ignoring the warnings of Mother Nature. Merging the two historically grown frameworks into one global agenda for *sustainably eradicating poverty* remains a formidable challenge for the diplomatic corps who gather in the General Assembly, at ECOSOC and CSD.

One might ask: Does it really matter if there are two political frameworks around? The world has seen major changes in the last decade. Sustainable Development is now mainstream; globalisation is the engine of the world's economy; fighting poverty has moved centre stage through the Millennium Development Goals. The attack on the World Trade Center in September 2001, and the 'clash of civilisations' that followed the publication of some cartoons in a right-wing Danish newspaper illustrate once more the need for the United Nations, as a global institution where dialogue can promote understanding, and where binding commitments such as the MDGs and the Monterrey outcome can be negotiated.

2.4 **Implementing the goals: A culture of words, or performance indicators?**

For structuring the global dialogue, and avoiding that it turns into talking for the sake of talking, an analytical framework is essential. The emergence of the Sustainable Development and MDG frameworks have already contributed a lot to streamline and structure the dialogue between rich and poor states.

Merging the MDG and CSD frameworks, and their respective communities, would help to focus the work at the United Nations, and to advance jointly towards achieving the goals that have been set, explicitly or implicitly, in the two development-oriented movements that shaped the last decades. The European Union has reaffirmed, in the December 2005 *European Consensus on Development*,[14] that 'the primary and overarching objective of EU development cooperation is the eradication of poverty *in the context of sustainable development*, including pursuit of the Millennium Development Goals (MDGs).' [emphasis added]. How can this somewhat vague formula be translated into action?

---

[14] Joint statement by The Council and the Representatives of the Governments of the Member States meeting within the Council, the European Parliament and the Commission on The European Union Development Policy, OJ (24 February 2006) C-46/1.

Table 1: Two slightly different agendas for development

The MDG agenda	The Sustainable Development agenda [15]
1 Eradicate extreme poverty and hunger 2 Achieve universal primary education 3 Promote gender equality and empower women 4 Reduce child mortality 5 Improve maternal health 6 Combat HIV/AIDS, malaria and other diseases 7 Ensure environmental sustainability 8 Develop a global partnership for development	1 Social issues *Equity, Health, Education, Housing, Security, Population* 2 Environmental issues *Climate Change, Ozone Layer Depletion, Air Quality, Agriculture, Land, Forests, Desertification, Urbanization, Oceans, Seas and Coasts, Fisheries, Water, Biodiversity* 3 Economic issues *Economic Structure, Trade, Financial Status, Material and Energy Use, Consumption and Production Patterns, Waste Generation and Management, Transportation* 4 Institutional issues *Strategic Implementation of SD, International Co-operation, Information Access, Communication Infrastructure, Institutional Capacity, Science and Technology, Disaster Preparedness and Response*

At first sight (see Table 1) there seem to be major differences between the two agendas. However, for merging the CSD into the MDG framework, only a few corrections are needed:

- Among the eight MDGs there is already an 'environmental pillar' (Goal 7) that might be fleshed up to reflect the complexity of the subject as shown in the CSD version of 'environmental issues'.
- The other MDGs and their underlying targets would profit from a systematic analysis of the *sustainability* of the means provided to reach them. Or, paraphrasing the *European Consensus*, 'the overarching objective ... is the *eradication of poverty*, in its multiple faces described in the MDGs, *in a sustainable way*'.
- Alternatively, the MDGs could be merged into the CSD framework, thus maintaining the four-pillar structure that has been so successful in communicating Sustainable Development to a wider public (e.g., in the context of the numerous 'Local Agenda 21' initiatives):

[15] Adopted from the CSD Theme Indicator Framework, available at <http://www.un.org/esa/sustdev/natlinfo/indicators/isdms2001/table_4.htm>.

- Goal 1, fighting poverty, could be expanded and enriched to fill the economic cluster of the CSD with less 'environmental' subjects (mainstream economists might be relieved if *material use, waste*, etc. would disappear from this pillar);
- Goals 2 (education), 4 (children), 5 (mothers) and 6 (HIV/AIDS, malaria, tuberculosis and other diseases) would constitute the social pillar;
- Goal 7 would fill the environmental pillar, with some more detail;
- Goals 3 (gender) and 8 (global partnership) would form the basis for the fourth pillar, which might be renamed 'Culture & Governance' to reflect a more recent notion of 'institutions'.

It is not the author's intention to decide which 'merger' would be the better one. However, for advancing the political agenda from *formulating* goals to *implementing* measures and *reaching* targets, it would be helpful if the international community could agree on one single framework.

Of particular importance are the *indicators* attached to the two frameworks. Usually, UN resolutions are solemn declarations, pledging to take gender equality or the fight against poverty seriously; but these declarations of good intentions are only rarely monitored in terms of success or failure. Not surprisingly, the United Nations sustain a 'culture of words', rather than a 'culture of figures and benchmarking' as, in particular, in the business sector. The success of negotiations at the UN is often measured in terms of 'agreed text' – phrases, sometimes fragments of phrases, that have been elaborated in long nights of negotiations between groups of nations that were initially very far apart. The treasure of *agreed text* can be found in many UN resolutions and conference outcome documents, reflecting 'consensus capital' accumulated jointly by parties with hugely diverse agendas and interests.

The value of *agreed text* should not be underestimated. In most cases, such text has been *unanimously* adopted by governments (majority voting is a pretty rare event in the General Assembly and the CSD). Any citizen of the world can stand up and say 'my government has agreed that I have the right X'. However, principle is not practice, and rarely does the citizen have a chance to prove that the government did not fulfil the commitments.

This is why *indicators* mark the difference between the political stages of *agreement in principle* and *implementation*. Words are helpful when agreeing on principles, but figures are needed to manage the implementation of our good intentions.

For the CSD framework, a set of indicators has been elaborated since 1993. The current set of approx. 60 indicators, structured by social, economic, environmental and institutional themes is under revision. Overall and without blaming anybody in particular, it is probably fair to say that it was not a great political success.

In contrast, the MDG indicators, a set of 48 indicators closely matching the eight goals and sixteen targets, has been widely accepted as a tool to monitor the implementation of the Millennium Development Goals. The United Nations Statistics

Division has made the MDG database available to the public,[16] and many organizations in the UN (and Bretton Woods) system make extensive use of these indicators. There are signs that the *culture of words* is slowly being complemented by a *culture of figures*. More and more, partner countries have started to structure their Poverty Reduction Strategy Papers (PRSPs) by MDGs, and to underpin their analyses with the MDG indicators provided by the UNSTAT. Donor countries, and in particular the European Union, invest substantial efforts in making these indicators part and parcel of country strategies, knowing that 'you cannot manage what you cannot measure'.

3. The European Union as 'Sustainable Develoment Player' at the UN

When describing the relations of the EU with the UN, one should first recall some basic rules of participation (a) Furthermore, two diverse ways of cooperating should be distinguished: the role of the EU as a donor organization in UN agencies, funds and programmes (b), and the cooperation between EU and non-EU Member States in political UN fora such as the General Assembly and CSD (c).

3.1 The status of the EU in the UN system

Despite their similar underlying values, the EU and the UN have always been awkward partners, because of their structures. The EU is a unique arrangement in the world, and does not fit so well in the UN system of nations, states and international organizations. Outsiders can easily be confused by the different hats and names we give to the institutions of the EU: the European Commission, the European Community, the European Parliament, the European Council (not to be confused with the Council of Europe).

In practice, the EU is represented at the United Nations by its Member States, in their individual capacities, and two of the above-mentioned institutions: The EU Presidency and the European Commission. The latter takes the floor in the General Assembly and other UN fora only when issues are treated for which the European Community has competence, such as trade, fisheries and agriculture. In addition, the EC has been granted a special 'full participant' status to a number of important UN conferences, like the Rio 'Earth Summit', the Cairo (population), Copenhagen (social), Beijing (women) and Kyoto (climate change) conferences, the Intergovernmental Forum on Forests (IFF). Most importantly, the European Community

[16] Millennium Development Goal Indicators Database, available at <http://unstats.un.org/unsd/mi/mi_goals.asp>; for an easy-to-use version of this complex database, see the MDG Dashboard provided by IISD and the European Commission's Joint Research Centre (JRC) at <http://esl.jrc.it/envind/mdg.htm>.

fully participates in the UN Commission on Sustainable Development (UN CSD). Represented by the Commission, the Community may take the floor like other members and act on the same footing with the exception of voting rights.

In most other cases, 'the Presidency' – i.e., the EU Member State in charge of EU policies for the current six month period – speaks collectively for all EU Member States *and* the Community.[17]

3.2 The European Union in its role as a donor

The EU is the world's biggest donor to development assistance. According to OECD, compared to 2004, the combined ODA of the fifteen members of the Development Assistance Committee (DAC) that are EU members rose 27.9% in real terms to USD 55.7 billion, equivalent to 0.44% of their combined GNI (United States: net Official Development Assistance (ODA) in 2005 USD 27.5 billion, 0.22 % of GNI, with major increases in Iraq and Afghanistan).[18] European Union Member States are thus overall on track towards the EU target of 0.39% by 2006, although four of them still need to increase their ODA substantially to reach the minimum country target of 0.33%. EU members committed themselves to these targets before the 2002 Monterrey International Conference on Financing for Development.[19] It should be noted, though, that even the 0.44% achieved by the EU is far below the 0.7% target pledged 36 years ago in a 1970 UN General Assembly Resolution.[20]

Again, it is useful to recall the different actors in the EU. Most of the 25 Member States have their own development cooperation programmes, coordinated at EU level through regular meetings of the respective Director Generals. A major part of the Official Development Assistance, however, is channelled through the European Commission (around USD 9.6 billion according to OECD/DAC), in particular through the European Development Fund (EDF). The EDF is the main instrument for development cooperation in the ACP countries and aims at granting technical and financial assistance to African, Caribbean and Pacific countries that were European colonies or with which certain countries have historical ties.

Apart from the contributions of EU Member States to the general UN budget (accounting for 37% of the total), substantial amounts of ODA flow into the UN system, in particular to specialized agencies such as UNDP, WHO and FAO. Most EU Member States are full members in the governing bodies of these agencies. The EC, although a major 'stand-alone donor', is not a sovereign state, has observer status in most parts of the UN system and does not contribute to the general budget.

---

[17] See 'Description of the European Commission Delegation in New York', available at <http://europa-eu-un.org/articles/en/article_458_en.htm>.

[18] OECD, 'Aid flows top USD 100 billion in 2005', 4 April 2006, available at <http://www.oecd.org/document/30/0,2340,en_2649_201185_36418344_1_1_1_1,00.html>.

[19] Source: OECD, 11 April 2005.

[20] Millennium Project, 'The 0.7% target: An in-depth look', available at <http://www.unmillenniumproject.org/involved/action07.htm#01>.

Nonetheless, it is one of the principal donors to specialized UN agencies, funds and programmes (UN AFP) and thus plays an important role in the implementation of their policies, in close but far from perfect coordination with EU Member States. In order to improve this coordination, and to move towards a more efficient cooperation with the UN system, several efforts have been launched:[21]

- multiannual programming instruments aimed at ensuring greater visibility and coherence in EC programming. This relates in particular to country strategy papers;
- the ongoing recasting of the Financial Regulation of the European Community. The Commission has proposed greater flexibility in terms of financing UN activities. The Commission proposal would allow the Commission to recognise the equivalence of auditing and accounting procedures, *inter alia*, with its own rules;
- the framework agreement between the EC and the UN and its reform. The agreement on the principles for financing or cofinancing by the EC of programmes and projects administered by the UN was signed in August 1999 and was followed by 'a standard grant agreement with international organizations' in December 2000. These two initiatives provided a pragmatic solution to practical problems. In the context of the renegotiation of this agreement, the Commission aimed to ensure principally some form of permanent representation in the programming and administrative organs. It also wished to amend the verification clause in order to grant the Commission a more important role in controlling and auditing programmes and projects. After lengthy negotiations and approval procedures on both sides, the reform Financial and Administrative Framework Agreement (FAFA) was finally signed on 29 April 2003 by Deputy Secretary-General Fréchette and Commissioner Nielson. It applies to all contribution specific agreements between both organizations since then.[22]

For the European Commission, 'strategic partnerships' are a central element for enhancing the cooperation with the UN.[23] The EC is engaged in a process of establishing strategic partnerships with individual UN agencies and programs, such as UNDP, WHO, ILO, FAO and others. The Commission has pre-selected a number

---

[21] Quoted from SCADPlus: 'Building an effective partnership with the United Nations', available at <http://europa.eu.int/scadplus/leg/en/lvb/r12600.htm>.

[22] Financial and Administrative Framework Agreement between the European Community and the United Nations, 29 April 2003, at <http://europa.eu.int/comm/europeaid/tender/gestion/cont_typ/onu/index_en.htm>.

[23] See also Communication from the Commission to the Council and the European Parliament, 'Building an effective partnership with the United Nations in the fields of development and humanitarian affairs', 2 May 2001, COM (2001) 231 final, available at <http://europa.eu.int/eur-lex/lex/LexUriServ/site/en/com/2001/com2001_0231en01.pdf>.

of UN organizations based on their mandate and capacities, and their relevance to the Community's Development Policy priorities, and will try to build a closer and more stable relationship with them. The main features of these partnerships are policy dialogues on specific targeted issues. The EC tries to step up the involvement of the European Commission in the governing bodies of these UN organizations, and to provide more stable financial cooperation in operational activities.

3.3 The European Union in negotiations with other UN Member States

The European Union strongly supports the notion of *effective multilateralism*, as one of the defining principles of the EU's external policies. The EU has a clear interest in supporting the evolution and improvement of the system of global governance, and sees the UN system as very much in the core of that multilateral approach. This position has been formalised in two recent Communications from the Commission to the Council and the European Parliament, 'Building an Effective Partnership with the UN in the field of Development and Humanitarian Affairs'[24] and 'The European Union and the United Nations: The choice of multilateralism'.[25]

Work in the General Assembly and the functional commissions such as CSD differs very much from the above-mentioned role of the EU as a donor. For example, the Commission on Sustainable Development (to focus on the UN body that is most relevant for Sustainable Development) works as follows: The CSD meets every spring in New York to discuss in two weeks the World's Sustainable Development agenda. In 2003, at its eleventh session, the CSD (i.e., the delegates of all present UN Member States) agreed on a multi-year programme of work on the basis of seven two-year cycles, with each cycle focusing on selected thematic clusters of issues:

Cycle	*Thematic cluster*
2004/2005	Water Sanitation Human Settlements
2006/2007	Energy for Sustainable Development Industrial Development Air Pollution / Atmosphere Climate Change
2008/2009	Agriculture Rural Development

[24] Ibid.

[25] Communication from the Commission to the Council and the European Parliament, 'The European Union and the United Nations: the choice of multilateralism', 10 September 2003, COM (2003) 526 final, available at <http://europa.eu.int/comm/external_relations/un/docs/com03_526en.pdf>.

Cycle	*Thematic cluster*
2008/2009 (cont.)	Land Drought Desertification Africa
2010/2011	Transport Chemicals Waste Management Mining A Ten Year Framework of Programmes on Sustainable Consumption and Production Patterns
2012/2013	Forests Biodiversity Biotechnology Tourism Mountains
2014/2015	Oceans and Seas Marine Resources Small Island Developing States Disaster Management and Vulnerability
2016/2017	Overall appraisal of implementation of Agenda 21, the Programme of Further Implementation of Agenda 21 and the Johannesburg Plan of Implementation

Each CSD cycle is split in a 'review' and a 'policy' year. In the *review* year, the CSD will discuss the scientific state of the art, monitor progress, identify obstacles, best practices, etc., in the *policy* year it shall take political decisions to advance the Sustainable Development agenda.

The above listed thematic clusters will be addressed in an integrated manner, taking into account economic, social and environmental dimensions of sustainable development. Furthermore, in all cycles, *means of implementation* (ODA) and a number of 'cross-cutting issues' will be addressed:

> 'Poverty eradication, Changing unsustainable patterns of consumption and production, Protecting and managing the natural resource base of economic and social development, Sustainable development in a globalizing world, Health and sustainable development, Sustainable development of SIDS, Sustainable development for Africa, Other regional initiatives, Institutional framework for sustainable development, Gender equality, and Education'.[26]

---

[26] Multi-year Programme of Work of the Commission on Sustainable Development, available at <http://www.un.org/esa/sustdev/csd/csd11/CSD_mulityear_prog_work.htm>.

It goes without saying that in two weeks there cannot be a thorough debate of all the issues mentioned above. On the other hand it would be unfair and overly pessimistic to call the CSD a 'talk shop'. Delegates come together to exchange their views and concerns, to increase the world's 'diplomatic capital' by adding 'agreed text' to conference outcome documents and General Assembly resolutions, and to establish contacts and form coalitions around areas of common interest.

The European Union is one of several more or less stable coalitions in UN fora. Other groups with particular relevance to Sustainable Development are JUSCANZ (Japan, the United States, Canada, Australia and New Zealand – a group that shares common views in particular in climate change negotiations), the Group of 77 & China (G77, currently over 130 Developing Countries) and the Small Island Developing States (SIDS/AOSIS, over 40 low-lying island states particularly threatened by climate change). In this setting, the EU has generally a positive and progressive image. Often the EU is able to build bridges between groups whose positions are far apart; and, being the largest donor, the EU has usually good relations with the largest group, the G77. For example, in the wake of the Rio Summit, the EU established close links with the SIDS group (a sub-set of G77), thus advancing the Kyoto process and establishing a global platform around the issue of climate change (but not limited to the latter). When Good Governance is on the agenda, the EU is more likely to join forces with the JUSCANZ group; when Human Rights and Gender Equality are being discussed, the EU will be the most progressive group of countries, and will find individual supporters in others.

Coalitions are not always predictable – as the CSD's multi-year programme of work shows, the Sustainable Development agenda is a broad one. Progress on this agenda depends, *inter alia,* on the willingness of all actors to agree on a common framework, preferably (but this is strictly the author's private opinion) the already widely accepted MDG framework 'fleshed up' with more detail from the environmental and institutional pillars of Agenda 21. Even more important, given the ever growing complexity of the Sustainable Development agenda, would be the transition from a pure 'culture of words' expressing vague preferences in non-binding UN resolutions, to a 'culture of indicators'. The growing acceptance of the MDG indicator set as a guiding tool in development cooperation is a very positive sign. However the MDG set needs to be strengthened, in terms of data availability, quality and comparability.

4. Priorities for Sustainable Development: The New Energy Crisis?

The long list of issues in the CSD's multi-year programme of work is not exactly what journalists and politicians want when they address the public. Are there not any priorities that we could work on in the coming years? What about poverty, Africa, globalisation, HIV/AIDS, terrorism, nanotechnology?

Picking a priority from the list is not particularly difficult. The author, for example, would choose the new *energy crisis* as a top priority in advancing Sustainable Development. We had energy crises in 1973/74 and 1980/81, with known consequences for the World economy, but the current price of 60 US$ per barrel (March 2006) is still a little bit below the 1981 peak price. However, previous crises were short-lived phenomena – the oil price dropped very quickly to one third of the 1981 value, until it began rising again in 2001. In contrast, the current crisis is only at its beginning. The World is very close to 'Peak Oil', the point where oil supply can no longer match demand due to exhaustion of resources. Given the quickly growing demand from the Chinese and other economies, several safe predictions can be made:

- The oil price will never drop back to the low levels of the last two decades. On the contrary, it will continue rising. This entails a *massive* transfer of wealth from oil-consuming to oil-producing countries.
- US citizens will pay the highest price. With 20 tons of CO_2 per year, their *per capita* oil consumption is over twice as high as the EU average (and twenty times as high as the African average).
- Europeans, with about 8 tons of CO_2 *per capita* and year, are in a much more comfortable position – high fuel taxes have forced the European economies to develop and use modern technologies, like small energy-efficient cars and an extensive system of public transport. Renewable energies are on the rise, and may compensate some of the economic loss.
- Poor oil-exporting Developing Countries will experience sudden wealth – and only the wisest governments will be able to keep corruption under control.
- Poor oil-importing Developing Countries will experience even more poverty. Many of them currently use around three quarters of their export revenue for paying their oil bill (the quota is only about 25% for the United States), and even a modest rise in oil prices distorts their trade balance. Rough calculations show that the *additional* yearly burden due to recent oil price increases is about *ten* times as high as the generous debt relief that was decided at the Gleneagles G-8 in 2005.
- Some nations will try to solve the problem by reverting to nuclear energy. Although this is economically unsound, given the much higher rates of return of investments in energy-saving technologies, this 'solution' will be popular, especially if subsidies start flowing. As a consequence, nuclear technologies and material will be more easily available (we may need a new security debate).
- Other nations will solve the problem by going back to coal. Given its high carbon content, emissions of CO_2 will rise drastically, with obvious consequences for the Earth's climate and for the credibility of the Kyoto process.

These arguments may look convincing, and may underline the plausibility of choosing the new energy crisis as 'the' priority in Sustainable Development; however, the author might be completely wrong. Perhaps the loss of biodiversity is much more threatening? Why not choose globalisation, terrorism, genetically modified organisms, nanotechnology, the acidification of the oceans, or avian flu?

If there is one important lesson that we should have learnt in the thirty-five years since the publication of 'Limits to Growth', then it is that we should look at the *whole* picture. Picking a priority *seems* what politicians like – but a successful politician knows very well that she or he has to advance a dozen agendas in parallel, and in a cautiously balanced way, to meet the expectations of a majority of voters.

We have eight MDGs, sixteen targets and 48 indicators. In global databases, about one-hundred indicators are available, even for poor nations that have more urgent things to do than collecting data. If the poor still collect such detailed statistics, it is often an indication that the information was needed for managing an important political agenda. For moving towards Sustainable Development, we need to accept the complexity of the SD agenda, rather than asking for 'priorities' and simple fixes. Surrendering in front of the complexity is not a solution; instead, we should continue to develop, enrich, refine and improve the MDG framework, so that it can become a tool for structuring and managing the global (sustainable) development agenda. Effective multilateralism needs a strong framework.

5. Conclusion

The European Union has always underlined the importance of a multilateral approach, and has always given support to the United Nations. Europe is a prosperous place; after World War II, no war has devastated the Member States of the European Union. Peaceful cooperation, a rich cultural diversity, a strong belief in democracy and respect for human rights are values that Europe is proud of, and wants to promote in the rest of the World. When US Defence Secretary Donald Rumsfeld lamented in January 2003 the reluctance of 'old Europe' to fight the war in Iraq, he certainly did not intend to launch a debate on the richness of 'old' European culture. But for many Europeans, his remarks provoked a reflection on the value of doing things 'the European way'… old Europe, new pride?

The European Union is a unique institution. In a process that is without historic precedence, first 6, then 12, 15 and now 25 nations have come together to practice 'effective multilateralism'. It has established a cooperation that is seen by many observers as a model for those regions of the World that still suffer from poverty, as a consequence of mutual mistrust, isolationism, military interventions and civil wars. It is a major achievement that the European Union Member States have abandoned, once and forever, the military option among themselves, and that they speak, with rare exceptions, with one voice in the United Nations.

Sustainable Development, in a World threatened by unfettered globalisation, a still rapidly growing population, rampant poverty, terrorism and growing mistrust between Christians and Muslims, needs this willingness to work together in an atmosphere of mutual understanding and respect. The United Nations is the ideal place to do so.

Chapter 12
THE EU: GREENING THE UN? ENVIRONMENTAL COOPERATION BETWEEN THE EU AND THE UN

by Aurore Maillet*

1. INTRODUCTION

Environment has been one of the fastest evolving areas of multilateral diplomacy, and has grown to be, in just a few decades, a fully-fledged field of international cooperation. The United Nations has played a key role in this development. Indeed, the major stepping stones of international policy in the environmental arena, from the 1972 Stockholm Conference on the Human Environment[1] to the 1992 Rio Conference on Environment and Development[2] or the 2002 World Summit on Sustainable Development,[3] all took place under UN auspices. All the major Multilateral Environmental Agreements (the so-called 'MEAs') on issues such as climate change, desertification or biodiversity, albeit autonomous legal instruments with their own conference of parties and secretariats, are part of the UN family.

Yet, environment is another area where UN reform is badly needed if the organization is to deliver on its ambitious, global, sustainable development agenda. The jury is out as to whether the complex web of treaties and organizations that comprise the UN's reach in environmental policy are realistically equipped to tackle an ever growing degradation of the Earth's common resources. Environmental issues in the UN are still handled piecemeal and mostly by institutionally weak structures. The environment is still often seen as the UN's poor child.

The EU sees itself as a global leader in environmental policy. It has been a consistent supporter of the UN's role in the environmental field and is generally perceived in the UN as a champion of sustainable development and environmental protection, as well as a real – if sometimes starry eyed – force in greening the UN agenda.

This contribution will first review the foundations of EU support to UN environmental action. How far and how is the EU exercising leadership? Secondly, it will

---

* Desk Officer, European Commission, DG Environment. The opinions expressed in this article are entirely personal.

[1] United Nations Conference on the Human Environment, Stockholm, 5-16 June 1972.

[2] United Nations Conference on Environment and Development, Rio de Janeiro, 3-14 June 1992.

[3] The World Summit on Sustainable Development, Johannesburg, 26 August-4 September 2002.

J. Wouters et al., eds., The United Nations and the European Union

analyse how the EU sees environment issues in the wider framework of UN Reform.

2. Current UN-EU Cooperation on Environmental Issues

2.1 The root of EU positions in the UN on environmental issues

EU positions in the UN on environmental issues find their roots in the EU's belief in multilateral diplomacy, in its long experience in environmental management and its commitment to a high level of environmental protection but also to a certain extent in its will to ensure the competitiveness of European businesses.

The EU's strong commitment to effective multilateralism translates especially well to the field of environment where global initiatives are often the only solution to environmental challenges of a transboundary nature, such as air pollution, water management or the preservation of biodiversity. 'In the years to come', said former European Commission President Romano Prodi,

> 'only a new concept of sovereignty that puts the interests and welfare of the individual at the centre and seeks to strengthen international environmental law and the authority of multilateral organizations, starting with the United Nations, can offer the instruments needed for balanced and effective action.'[4]

The European Commission addressed the links between the EU and the UN:

> 'An active commitment to an effective multilateralism means more than rhetorical professions of faith. It means taking global rules seriously, whether they concern the preservation of peace or the limitation of carbon emissions; it means helping other countries to implement and abide by these rules; it means engaging actively in multilateral forums, and promoting a forward-looking agenda that is not limited to a narrow defence of national interests.'[5]

This commitment to multilateralism is re-enforced by specific EU know-how in environmental matters, which it is eager to share at UN level and which, most importantly, supports the EU's credibility when internationally advocating higher levels of environmental protection.

Sustainable development, as well as a 'high level of protection and improvement of the quality of the environment'[6] feature among the core tasks of the Com-

[4] Romano Prodi, in a speech at San Rossore, 'Climate change, the real threat to global peace', 15 July 2004, p. 4, available at <http://europa.eu.int/comm/archives/commission_1999_2004/prodi/index_en.htm>.

[5] Communication from the Commission to the European Parliament of 10 September 2003, 'The European Union and the United Nations: the choice of multilateralism', COM (2003) 526 final.

[6] Article 2 of the Treaty establishing the European Community (EC Treaty), OJ (24 December 2002) C-325/40.

munity. The EC Treaty requires that environment protection be integrated into EU policy/making[7] and establishes that one of the key objectives of Community policy on the environment is to promote measures at international level to deal with regional or worldwide environmental problems.[8] While applying this ambitious policy framework, the EU has gained extended experience of environmental management. In the field of water for instance, the EU Water Framework Directive,[9] which aims to comprehensively address all the components of water management, is one of the most advanced in the world and is used as a reference in the UN and as a basis for many countries wishing to develop similar policies. In a number of environmental fields, the EU is also a front-runner in implementing international agreements, and illustrating how they can work. This is the case in the fight against climate change, with many countries looking to the EU and its advanced Emissions Trading Scheme, developed in the framework of the Kyoto Protocol.[10]

In addition to factors of a strictly environmental nature, economic considerations also play a structural role in EU international environmental policy. Firstly, the EU's environmental policies are among the most advanced in the world and its standards of environmental protection among the most stringent. European standards therefore often, as is the case for car manufacture standards, benchmark global standards. This gives a distinct advantage to EU businesses when exporting goods, and significantly contributes to the creation of a level playing field for European firms. There is also a growing global market for green businesses, a domain in which some EU companies, for example in the areas of water or renewable energies are highly competitive. An ambitious global EU policy supports their efforts. Secondly, the EU is increasingly dependent on resources imported from the rest of the world. Decoupling resource use from economic growth and moving away from unsustainable patterns of consumption and production (essential global commitments made under UN auspices) are first and foremost the responsibility of developed countries, and therefore crucial for the EU's economy in the long-term.

Nevertheless, despite efforts to ensure a high level of environmental protection, the EU itself, still figures among the world's biggest polluters. Along with other developed countries, it still consumes a disproportionate share of the world's resources and is a major source of global pollution, and global warming. The EU represents only 7% of the world's population. But it is estimated that it uses 17% of the biosphere regenerative capacity, and that its 'footprint', i.e., its demands on

---

[7] Article 6 EC Treaty.

[8] Article 174(4) EC Treaty.

[9] Directive 2000/60/EC of the European Parliament and of the Council of 23 October 2000 establishing a framework for Community action in the field of water policy, OJ (22 December 2000) L-327/1.

[10] The Kyoto Protocol is an amendment to the United Nations Framework Convention on Climate Change (UNFCCC). It was negotiated in Kyoto, Japan, in December 1997, opened for signature on 16 March 1998 and closed on 15 March 1999. As of February 2006, a total of 162 countries have ratified the agreement.

nature, more than doubles its own biological capacity,[11] placing a high demand on its environment as well as that of third countries. The EU's ability to compensate for its exaggerated use of natural resources and to reduce the impact of its growth on other economies through developing sustainable patterns of consumption and production is more and more a condition of its ability to maintain a leadership role. If not, it risks loosing all credibility on the international scene.

2.2 The EU as a key financial contributor to UN environmental institutions

Arguably, the close partnership between the EU and the UN is best measured in terms of finance – the EU being the main contributor to UN's environmental efforts.

To start with, collectively, the EU and its Member States are the largest donor to the United Nations Environment Programme (UNEP), through UNEP′s Environment Fund. Four EU countries (the United Kingdom, Germany, the Netherlands and France) figure in the top five donors to the Environment Fund, with the United Kingdom and Germany being the largest world donors in the list. In total, 12 EU Member States figure in the top 20 largest donors.[12] Considering both the fact that UNEP's donor base is very thin (over 95% of the total contributions to the Environment Fund come from only 20 countries) and the voluntary nature of contributions, continued EU support to UNEP's budget is essential to its relative stability and therefore, to the proper functioning of the United Nations Environment Programme.[13] In an effort to further ensure stable resources for UNEP, to enable long-term planning, four countries, including three EU Member States: Belgium, the Netherlands and Ireland have entered into Partnership-agreements with UNEP,[14] which aim to consolidate funding for UNEP's priority activities.

Moreover, the EU and its Member States all together provide half of the basic funding for three essential multilateral environmental agreements, the so-called 'Rio Conventions', which address desertification, climate and biodiversity.[15] They are in addition, major contributors to other multilateral environmental agreements such

---

[11] WWF's Report 'Europe 2005: The Ecological Footprint', 14 June 2005, Global Footprint Network available at <http://www.footprintnetwork.org/gfn_sub.php?content=europe2005>.

[12] Figures for 2003-2005, in UNEP Annual Report 2005, UNEP Funding 2004, available at <http://www.unep.org/Documents.multilingual/Default.asp?DocumentID=67&ArticleID=5125&l=en>.

[13] United Nations Environment Programme, Environment Fund, Contributions, available at <http://www.unep.org/rmu/en/Financing_of_UNEP/Environment_Fund/index.asp>.

[14] Over the period 2001-2004, UNEP signed partnership agreements of different types with Norway (US$ 13 million for 2002-2004), Belgium (US$ 9.4 million for 2001-2003), Ireland (€ 3 million for 2002-2004) and the Netherlands (€12.3 million for 2002-2004).

[15] The three 'Rio' conventions are the 1992 UNFCCC (UN Framework Convention on Climate Change), the 1992 UNCBD (UN Convention on Biological Diversity) and the 1994 UNCCD (UN Convention for Combating Desertification).

as the Montreal Protocol Fund[16] (dealing with ozone depleting substances) as well as to the UN Forum on Forests.[17]

Finally, the involvement of the European Union in the Global Environment Facility (GEF),[18] an innovative form of international financing, is also worth mentioning, since EU countries do not only largely contribute to it, but have also played a central role its creation. Indeed, France and Germany took the lead in setting up an experimental GEF in 1991. At the time, the GEF was inspired by new developments during discussions on the protection of the ozone layer, a field in which it was difficult for developed countries, including the EU Member States, to convince their counterparts from the South to limit CFCs (substances which contributed to the depletion of the ozone layer). Protecting the ozone layer was largely perceived as a Northern Agenda, mostly caused by developed countries, and first and foremost benefiting them. Therefore, it was necessary to find a specific way to finance the incremental cost of measures that were good for the global environment, but not in the direct interest of the countries concerned, without diverting from much needed development aid budget.

As momentum built towards the Rio Summit, the debate widened and discussions began on the need for similar mechanisms in other sectors of the environment: an experimental GEF was set-up in 1991. After its formal creation in 1994, GEF has become the largest source of funding for the global environment. It has been allocated 5 billion dollars in direct grants, and leverages 16 billion US dollars through co-financing. It assists developing countries and countries with economies in transition to fund projects and programmes in six areas: biodiversity, climate change, international waters, land degradation, the ozone layer and persistent organic pollutants and serves as the de facto financing mechanism for several multilateral environmental conventions. The GEF has three implementing agencies: the World Bank, UNEP and the UN Development Programme (UNDP). It also involves a number of other UN agencies and Regional Development Banks in its operations.

A number of EU Member States (France, Germany, Italy, the United Kingdom and the Netherlands) have permanent seats in the GEF Council, the power centre of GEF governance, while the European Commission was awarded observer status. The EU is normally loosely coordinated in matters related to the GEF, with Member States eager to preserve their independence on the issues. However, coordinated EU positions on the GEF, within the conference of the parties of environmental conventions financed by it, are now the norm, and it can be argued that they have played a key role in maintaining a coherent line of requests from the conference of the parties to the GEF. In terms of finance, here again, the EU is one of the largest donors, and EU Member States figure high in the list of biggest donors.

[16] Multilateral Fund for the Implementation of the Montreal Protocol, established in 1991.

[17] United Nations Forum on Forests (UNFF) established in October 2000 by Resolution 2000/35 of the UN Economic Social Council (ECOSOC).

[18] Instrument establishing the Global Environmental Facility, done at Geneva, 16 March 1994, *ILM* 1994, 1273ff.

Because of its flexible structure as well as its specific role GEF is an innovative example of global environmental finance. It has helped developing countries agree to multilateral environmental agreements and to meet their new environmental obligations. It has also helped developed countries to save money by avoiding the development of separate financing mechanisms, for each environmental convention. Conversely, critics of the GEF have argued that the lack of funding mechanisms for each individual convention has in fact generated lower levels of overall financial commitments, as well as concentrated the power away from developing countries and into the hands of donors and of Bretton Woods institutions.

2.3 The EU's involvement in many multilateral environmental agreements (MEAs)

The EU's involvement in the UN's environmental activities is not limited to financial support. It is active in a number of MEAs to which it is a party. The European Community has already ratified many international environmental agreements, whether at global level (multilateral agreements negotiated under the auspices of the UN), or at regional level (e.g., in the context of UN Economic Commission for Europe, UNECE). Matters addressed by these cover a wide span including biodiversity and nature protection, climate change, protection of the ozone layer, desertification, management of chemicals and waste, transboundary water and air pollution, environmental governance, or maritime and river protection.[19]

The specific set-up for EU involvement in environmental agreements needs to be underlined, since it sometimes influences the EU's strength. Generally, the Community and its Member States are jointly competent to conclude environmental agreements. Both can become parties to MEAs and both participate in negotiations. Member States and the Community institutions must closely cooperate when the subject-matter of an agreement partly falls within the competence of the Community and partly within that of the Member States.

Sometimes though, the role of the EU in a specific MEA is limited when an old convention did not allow the European Community to become a party as a 'regional economic integration organization' (the 'REIO clause') therefore weakening the Community's ability to influence decision-making in the field covered by the agreement.[20] In such cases, the European Council can authorize Member States to act jointly in the interest of the European Community to remedy this obstacle. Still, the situation remains far from ideal, especially when the subject-matter is covered by Community policy, which is frequent in the environmental field. Since the European Commission holds most of the information and concentrates most of the ex-

---

[19] See <http://www.europa.eu.int/comm/environment/international_issues/pdf/agreements_en.pdf> for a list of MEAs to which the Community is a party or a signatory.

[20] CITES, the Convention on International Trade in Endangered Species is an example of an old convention where the EC could not become a party.

pertise the EU's ability to properly represent its point of view can be damaged as a consequence.

Nonetheless, the EU remains a driving force in many MEAs. This can be understood by looking at the European involvement in climate change negotiations in the last few years. Within the UN Framework Convention on Combating Climate Change (UNFCCC)[21] the EU played a determining role in the negotiation and entry into force of the Kyoto Protocol, a binding addendum to the UNFCCC, whose ultimate objective is to stabilise global greenhouse gas emissions at a level that would prevent dangerous human-induced interference with the climate system.[22] Currently, the EU is heavily engaged with partners in discussions on the future of Kyoto and climate change policy, the so-called 'post 2012' discussions.

The EU sees Climate Change as both a major global environmental threat and as a danger to security and development. It has been consistently calling for a strong, ambitious and multilateral answer to climate change within a UN framework. With keen media and public attention given to the issue of global warming, the EU also saw the climate change negotiations, which picked up in the nineties, as an opportunity not only to meet an imperative environmental challenge, but also as an occasion to strengthen European integration, taking advantage of the newly adopted Maastricht Treaty, and speaking with a single EU voice on the world stage.[23] This further strengthened the EU stance. It is also worth noting that Europeans had sent their environment ministers as their representatives at the Kyoto Protocol negotiations. They were more prone to defending a tough EU line, all the more so since some of them originated from Green Parties (Juergen Trittin from Germany or Dominique Voynet from France for instance, were very active during the sixth conference of the parties of UNFCCC in The Hague). The United States and Canada conversely were represented by their less environmentally minded Foreign Offices.[24] In fact, the EU position was sometimes accused of antagonising other countries by being too inflexible and pro-active.

The Kyoto Protocol, finally adopted in December 1997, reflects a compromise between two visions. In climate negotiations, the EU position had been, and remains today, led by two essential considerations; first, promote concrete targets for greenhouse gas emission reductions backed up by domestic action. Second, make sure that the global policy on climate changes involves all actors and remains under UN auspices. Other countries, such as the United States, joined by Australia or New Zealand, advocated more flexibility with mechanisms to carry out emissions reduc-

---

[21] 11th Conference of the UN Framework Convention on Climate Change, Montreal, 28 November- 9 December 2005.

[22] Under the Kyoto Protocol, the EU-15 has committed to reduce its overall emissions of the six greenhouse gases controlled by the Protocol to 8% below the 1990 level by 2012, see Memo/02/120 at <http://europa.eu.int/rapid/pressReleasesAction.do?reference=MEMO/02/120&format=HTML&aged=0&language=EN&guiLanguage=en>.

[23] R. Wilkinson, et al., *The Global Governance Reader* (London, Routledge 2005) p. 277.

[24] Ibid.

tion abroad and crediting the so-called 'carbon sinks'.[25] Those countries now also favour more voluntary, pick and choose frameworks outside the UNFCCC framework, which they consider too inflexible.

After the adoption of the Kyoto protocol the challenge moved from negotiation to implementation. The EU immediately took the lead by ratifying the Kyoto Protocol in spring 2002,[26] sending a strong signal to the World Summit on Sustainable Development in Johannesburg which took place between 24 August and 4 September 2002. It indicated its intention to proceed despite the United States' decision not to ratify. This demonstrated to others that the EU wanted the Kyoto Protocol to come to life independently of US involvement. The EU also promptly undertook domestic action in order to meet Kyoto targets, notably adopting the pioneering EU Emissions Trading Scheme,[27] therefore showing that it was possible to deliver. The EU emissions Trading Scheme is the largest multi-national, multi-sector greenhouse gas emission trading scheme worldwide. Finally, the EU also played a key role in convincing other countries to ratify the Kyoto Protocol, notably Russia whose backing was vital to its entry into force. At the EU-Russia Summit in 2004, for instance, the EU and Russia re-affirmed their joint commitment to the Kyoto Protocol, and some implied that the EU had put the ratification of the Kyoto Protocol as a condition for its support for Russia's joining the World Trade Organization (WTO). President Putin's declaration, following EU-Russia agreement on the WTO, points to such a trade-off:

> 'The EU has met us half way in talks over the WTO and that cannot but affect positively our position on the Kyoto Protocol. We will speed up Russia's movement toward the Kyoto Protocol's ratification.'[28]

Now that the Kyoto Protocol is up and running, the next challenge for global climate policy is to decide what will happen after 2012, in the 'post Kyoto' period. In December 2005, in Montreal, an agreement was reached to launch talks under the UN Framework Convention on Climate Change to which non-Kyoto signatories Australia and the United States are also parties. This is a good step forward for the EU which reiterated its support for a UN-based, multilateral approach to climate change. The United Kingdom Environment Minister Margaret Beckett, who headed the EU delegation in Montreal, wrote in the Canadian journal Globe and Mail:

---

[25] Carbon sinks are 'forests and other ecosystems that absorb carbon, thereby removing it from the atmosphere and offsetting CO2 emissions'. EEA glossary <http://glossary.eea.eu.int/EEA Glossary>.

[26] Council Decision 2002/358/EC of 25 April 2002 concerning the approval, on behalf of the European Community, of the Kyoto Protocol to the United Nations Framework Convention on Climate Change and the joint fulfilment of commitments thereunder, OJ (15 May 2002) L-130/1.

[27] Directive 2003/87/EC of the European Parliament and of the Council of 13 October 2003 establishing a scheme for greenhouse gas emission allowance trading within the Community and amending Council Directive 96/61/EC, OJ (25 October 2003) L-275/32.

[28] 'Putin U-turn could rescue Kyoto', BBC News Europe, 21 May 2004.

> 'Voluntary measures can be helpful, but compulsory action is a surer way of delivering results. Without mechanisms in the form of compulsory action, such as targets to cut emissions, existing and new technologies will never be rolled out on the scale we need'.

The key challenge for the EU now lies in showing that it can deliver on its Kyoto emission reduction targets. This will not to be an easy ride for European Member States. According to the European Environment Agency (EEA), five EU-15 Member States (Denmark, Ireland, Italy, Portugal, Spain) do not project that they will meet the target.[29]

2.4 UNEP-EU: partners for the environment

A large part of the UN Membership now share the view that the way environmental issues are dealt with in the UN is not only confusing but also largely inefficient, suffering from several drawbacks.

First, the United Nations Environment Programme (UNEP) is too weak. It was established as a UN Programme in 1972 to be a coordination organ and saw its tasks grow on an *ad hoc*, piecemeal basis. UNEP's ability to meet its responsibilities is hampered by its status as a simple programme, not being a specialized agency or organization. As seen above, the lack of sufficient budget is also a stumbling block, along with the lack of scientific capacity available to UNEP and its location in Nairobi, away from other international organizations (UNEP officials need to travel on average more than 3000 miles to visit the seat of another UN agency).[30]

Second, the increased fragmentation of the UN system, with specialized organizations, agencies, funds and programmes as diverse as UNESCO, UNDP, the FAO or UNIDO, all undertaking environmental activities remains an important issue particularly through the lack of any real coordination efforts which results in many gaps and inconsistencies.

Third, the great number of Multilateral Environmental Agreements (MEAs) with separate conferences of the parties, secretariats and embedded interests, in fields which sometimes overlap do not develop sufficient synergies.

This has prompted some to say that

> '[d]espite a congested institutional terrain and the appearance of much activity, the pace of climate change, species loss and desertification has called into question the ability of the global machinery for delivering on the environment'.[31]

---

[29] 'Green house gases emissions trends and projections in Europe, 2005', EEA Report 8:2005 available at <http://reports.eea.eu.int/eea_report_2005_8/en/>.

[30] M. Ivanova, 'Can the anchor hold? Rethinking the United Nations Environment Programme for the 21st Century'. Report Number 7, *Yale School of Forestry and Environmental Studies Publication Series*, 2005, p. 37.

[31] R. Wilkinson, et al., *The global governance reader* (London, Routledge 2005) p. 2.

Indeed, despite successful and welcome efforts by UNEP's executive Director Klaus Toepfer to improve finance, programming and the profile of UNEP, the UN still lacks a real 'home for environment'. Many have argued that UNEP should be turned into a proper UN agency, or even, into a World Environment Organization, taking the WTO as a model. Turning UNEP from a simple 'programme' into an 'agency' would have important consequences. In the UN system, a programme has its hands tied: it is a subsidiary organ of the General Assembly and answers to it. An 'Agency', on the other hand has much wider margins of manoeuvre. It is a separate international organization, with a governing body, independent of the UN Secretariat and the General Assembly.[32] An upgraded UNEP would therefore have more political weight, accompanied by the more regular resources that accompany the status of 'agency'.

In March 2003, the European Council considered the drawbacks of international environmental governance and the need to create a UN Environmental Agency and opted for an evolutionary approach, recommending 'to strengthen UNEP including through upgrading it into a specialized agency'. The EU pursues this option through seeking to implement the so-called 'Cartagena Package',[33] adopted by UNEP in 2002. The agreement on the package, one of the highest points of the debate on international environmental governance so far, calls for a number of improvements to international environmental governance, giving preference to improved use of existing structures, while keeping open the possibility of upgrading UNEP into an autonomous Agency. The EU believes that this evolutionary option is a good way to strengthen UNEP politically and financially, and is set to make it happen sooner rather than later. Of the six elements for improvement of international environmental governance outlined in Cartagena,[34] which are all complementary, a number are key to the EU:

- Universal membership of UNEP's Governing Council along with a reinforced Global Ministerial Environment Forum (GMEF) is a good way to reinforce UNEP's credibility.
- UNEP's financing needs to be more stable and predictable, and the donor base must continue to broaden.
- Coordination and the improved effectiveness of MEAs also has full EU support. The EU is, in fact, open to suggestions that would go further than the framework established at Cartagena, such as strengthening the interlinks between MEAs with a comparable focus or area, exploring synergies through

[32] M. Ivanova, loc. cit. n. 30, at p. 31.

[33] The Cartagena Protocol on Biosafety to the Convention on Biological Diversity was adopted on 29 January 2000. By date, the Protocol has received 103 signatures. The Protocol entered into force 11 September 2003.

[34] The six elements of the Cartagena package are: the issue of universal membership, the role of the Governing Council/Global Ministerial Environment Forum, finance, coordination and effectiveness of MEAs, capacity building and technology transfer, and the Environment Management Group.

'back to back' meetings of the UN's conferences of the parties, universal participation in MEAs as well as regrouping and co-locating MEA secretariats.

It is also worth noting that the European Commission has recently stepped up its cooperation with UNEP, through a memorandum of understanding. The Memorandum signed in 2002, aims to strengthen cooperation and dialogue between the European Commission and UNEP, and envisages regular meetings at various levels, strategic policy discussions and financial cooperation.[35] The various fields envisaged for cooperation so far include sustainable consumption and production, capacity development on trade, environment and sustainable development, implementation of MEAs, water and energies, or environmental assistance for countries with economies in transition.

There has been good progress on the Cartagena package since 2002, but addressing comprehensively all its aspects still remains incomplete, and keeping all the elements together still promises to be an up-hill fight. At first restrained to environment experts, the debate on international governance reform has now widened as the debate on UN reform picked up, ahead of the UN World Summit in September 2005.

3. Engaging in the 21st Century: EU Ambitions for UN Reform

The UN needs urgent and profound reform in order to fulfil its role, and the field of environment is no exception to that. The EU, in the run up to the UN World Summit and after has made environmental issues an essential item of the debate on how UN reform can improve the way we globally address the threats and challenges of the 21st century. Most of the EU proposals were set out in two sets of documents: the so-called 'Millennium Development Goal package',[36] which addressed development issues, and the 2005 Commission Communication 'Addressing the global challenges and making a success of the reformed UN',[37] both later endorsed by the European Council. There were four entry doors to discuss environmental issues at the UN World Summit.

---

[35] M.M. Buckens, 'The New International Environmental Governance: the EU and multilateralism', Supplement to Europe Information Environment, Europe Information Service, October 2004.

[36] The MDG package comprises the following Commission Communications on 'Speeding up progress towards the Millennium Development Goals. The European Union's contribution', COM (2005) 132; 'Accelerating progress towards achieving the Millennium Development Goals: financing for development and aid effectiveness', COM (2005) 133; 'Policy coherence for development. Accelerating progress towards attaining the Millennium Development Goals' COM (2005) 134.

[37] Commission Communication: 'The 2005 UN Summit, addressing the global challenges and making a success of the reformed UN', COM (2005) 259, 15.06.2005.

3.1 A broad definition of security

The first entry door was the UN debate on the concept of security. UN Secretary-General Kofi Annan in his Report 'In Larger Freedom'[38] argued that

> 'The threats to peace and security in the 21st century include not just international war and conflict [...]. They also include poverty, deadly infectious diseases and environmental degradation since these can have equally catastrophic consequences'.

In line with this assessment, the EU took the view that the Summit should recognise the primary role of environment for global security.[39] It therefore proposed to fully integrate environmental issues at the programming and policy level in UN conflict prevention, humanitarian assistance, peace-building and reconstruction activities. Post-conflict activities should consider the need to restore the environment and ensure that economic reconstruction is not done at the expense of the environment. The European Commission also proposed to give further consideration to the monitoring of natural resources, especially in areas where they could lead to conflict. This proposal included setting up a UN structure to examine the link between natural resource exploitation and conflict and to encourage donors to work more closely with commodity producing countries to improve governance, traceability and transparency in commodity sectors connected to conflict. Finally, it encouraged leaders at the UN summit to consider the issue of environmental refugees and internally displaced people who have had to move for environmental reasons. Indeed, climate change effects such as global warming could put at risk 200 million people, and already by 2010, the number of environmental refugees is likely to double that of 2005.

3.2 Environment plays a role in the fight against poverty

The second entry door for an environmental agenda at the Summit was the debate on the global development agenda, which the EU aimed at greening. It is the poor who suffer the most from environmental degradation and whose lives depend most on natural resources such as soils, forests, water, etc. This is why the EU supported the proposal of the UN Secretary-General's report to formulate poverty reduction strategies that would integrate economic, social and environmental concerns.

Vulnerability to natural disasters, likewise, is a key concern, as illustrated by the impact of recent natural catastrophes since environmental degradation can increase the occurrence of disasters and their consequences. At the Summit, the EU pro-

---

[38] Report of the Secretary-General, 'In larger freedom: towards security, development and human rights for all', 21 March 2005, UN Doc. A/59/2005.

[39] Commission Communication: The 2005 UN Summit, addressing the global challenges and making a success of the reformed UN', COM (2005) 259 final.

moted the need to take into account environmental management issues in disaster readiness and prevention and in poverty reduction strategies. It also supported the creation of worldwide early warning systems for all natural hazards.

3.3 Foster environment protection

The third entry door was more obvious, and laid in the Summit's commitment to foster environmental protection. The EU focused its efforts in calling for a strengthening of the three Rio Conventions. In particular it called for reinforcement of the UN Convention on Biodiversity (CBD) and of the UN Convention to combat desertification, calling there for the adoption of measurable targets. In the field of climate change, one of the most controversial issues at the Summit, the EU called for

> 'the widest possible cooperation by all countries and their participation in an effective, cost efficient and appropriate international response, in accordance with their common but differentiated responsibility and respective capabilities.'[40]

It called upon all partners to consider discussing a more inclusive international framework to combat climate change beyond 2012.

3.4 The UN reform agenda: how to help the UN deliver on environmental goals

The fourth entry door was the UN's reform agenda in general, the field in which the EU made its most ambitious proposals. First, the EU supported the strengthening of the Economic and Social Committee (ECOSOC), in its role of coordination and follow-up to major UN conferences and summits, addressing jointly all the three economic, social and environmental pillars of sustainable development. Second, it called for a review of the mandate of UN agencies, funds and programmes with the aim to further integrate environment across the UN system. Third, and perhaps more importantly, the EU went a step further from its previous position on international environmental governance by advocating the creation of a UN Environmental Organization (UNEO). The European Council so defined its views on how UNEO should be dealt with at the Summit:

> 'initiate a process, as part of UN reform, which will lead to negotiations on the establishment of a UN agency for the environment, based on UNEP, with a revised and strengthened mandate, supported by stable, adequate and predictable financial contributions and operating on an equal footing with other UN specialized agencies. This agency, based in Nairobi, would make it possible to develop the environmental dimension of sustainable development in an integrated and consistent manner, and would co-

[40] Ibid.

operate closely with multilateral agencies, each using its comparative advantages to best effect.'[41]

3.5 Implementing the Summit outcome: looking at the future

The Summit outcome, though far from groundbreaking in the field of environment, has taken on board some European views. For instance, the role of ECOSOC as a forum for dialogue and action on sustainable development is reaffirmed.

In the field of governance, the Summit calls for greater coherence in the UN system in the development, humanitarian and environmental fields and Heads of State and Government propose improving environmental governance in the UN, recognizing

> 'the need for more efficient environmental activities in the United Nations system, with enhanced coordination, improved policy advice and guidance, strengthened scientific knowledge, assessment and cooperation, better treaty compliance, while respecting the legal autonomy of the treaties, and better integration of environmental activities in the broader sustainable development framework at the operational level, including through capacity building, we agree to explore the possibility of a more coherent institutional framework to address this need, including a more integrated structure, building on existing institutions and internationally agreed instruments, as well as the treaty bodies and the specialized agencies.'

Consequently, discussions are now taking place under auspices of the UN General Assembly, seeking to analyse gaps and overlaps and to propose improvements. The UN Secretary-General Kofi Anan has just nominated a High Level Panel which will make proposals on how to improve coherence in the UN system, including in the humanitarian field.[41] The High Level Panel will propose options for reform in the autumn of 2006. One of the solutions, among others, could be the creation of UNEO, advocated by the EU and others.

However, opposition to UNEO is still the norm among key UN groups and Member States. The United States and likeminded countries oppose UNEO both in principle and for budgetary reasons (their contribution to a UNEO might increase) as well as for fear of adding another inefficient layer of UN bureaucracy to that which already exists. The United States stresses the specific difficulties they would face should Congress be asked to approve the establishing Treaty for UNEO. They might however warm to the idea of realising economies of scale within UNEO. Many G-77 countries, including Brazil or India oppose UNEO for similar reasons but also for fear that negotiations on UNEO would distract from the current environmental agenda, and that a stronger norm setting body in the field of environment might hide a protectionist agenda.

---

[41] Presidency Conclusions, Brussels European Council, 16-17 June 2005, p. 11, para. 39.

4. Conclusion

The UN and the EU are now at the crossroads. Environmental norm setting has developed extremely fast in the past 30 years. It has seen major successes. But the onus is no longer on lengthy negotiations, but on concrete implementation of what was agreed. This calls for structural adaptations in the UN.

An agreement can be found that will strengthen the UN's environmental arm, and reinforce the capacity of the system to implement the agreements that were negotiated in under its auspices. Failure to do so may result in discussions getting lost in the intricacies of UN decision-making and international diplomacy. If the EU is to succeed in helping the UN adapt to the new challenges at hand, it now needs to ensure that a number of conditions are met.

First, it must develop a capacity to better bring developing countries on board on the agenda for UN reform, notably by better taking into account the links between environmental and development policy. It must continue to try and convince the United States to remain a strong multilateral player. As demonstrated in the climate change talks, no sensible global environment policy can be fully effective without US participation. This will require a constant and persistent political will from the EU. It will also require a flexible, non-doctrinal approach to issues. Most of all, it will require not just words, but action. The European capacity to address at home its own environmental problems and to meet, in the EU, international environmental targets is the key that will allow the EU to keep a strong voice on environmental issues in the UN, and the very basis to the EU's credibility when claiming a leadership role.

Part Four

UN-EU Cooperation on Security Issues

Chapter 13
UN-EU COOPERATION IN CRISIS MANAGEMENT

by Jan Wouters* and Tom Ruys**

1. INTRODUCTION

When it comes to crisis management, both the European Union and the United Nations learned hard lessons at the end of the 20th century. The emergence of consecutive hotbeds of instability at the EU's backdoor dramatically exposed Europe's lack of military capacity. Without US support, European States had no response to stop the ongoing murdering in the Balkans, or to stop hundreds of thousands of fugitives from flooding their borders. The United Nations experienced a similar feeling of powerlessness with regard to the crisis in the former Yugoslavia and the Rwandan genocide, events that – in the words of the Secretary-General – would haunt the UN forever.[1]

Fortunately, the UN has done more than merely apologize. The peacekeeping department (DPKO) underwent a sweeping makeover on the basis of the recommendations of the *Brahimi Report*.[2] Furthermore, the UN increasingly appealed to regional and sub-regional organizations for assistance, so as to meet the growing demand for peacekeeping, peacemaking and peacebuilding activities. Similarly, the EU drew its conclusions after the mid-1990s. It revitalized plans to develop a European Security and Defence Policy (ESDP) as part of its Common Foreign and Security Policy (CFSP), setting ambitious capacity-building goals in order to become an autonomous crisis management actor. Early 2003, the EU launched its first police mission in Bosnia-Herzegovina. This mission was soon followed by other military and civilian missions, *inter alia*, in the DRC and the former Yugoslav Republic of Macedonia (FYROM).

Both developments have stimulated cooperation between the UN and the EU with regard to crisis management, a cooperation from which each can benefit. The

* Professor of International Law and the Law of International Organizations, Leuven University, *Of Counsel,* Linklaters De Bandt, Brussels.

** Research Fellow, Fund for Scientific Research Flanders, Institute for International Law, Leuven University.

[1] 'Annan apologizes for UN failure to stop Bosnian massacre', *UN Wire,* 12 October 1999; 'Annan apologizes for Rwanda genocide', *CNN*, 26 March 2004.

[2] *Report of the Panel on United Nations Peace Operations*, UN Doc. A/55/305-S/2000/809, 21 August 2000.

J. Wouters et al., eds., The United Nations and the European Union

EU could provide the UN with the necessary capacities to fulfil its complex tasks, thus considerably lightening the latter's financial and logistical burden. A stronger engagement of the EU with regard to peacekeeping and peace enforcement would also enable it to establish itself as a 'global actor' and security provider on the international level.

Since 2003, the two organizations have entered into a more structural relationship through the conclusion of a Joint Declaration on UN-EU Cooperation in Crisis Management and the subsequent creation of a joint consultative mechanism.[3] More changes are underway. In the meantime the time is ripe for an appraisal of the *status questionis*.

First, we will examine in general terms the increased cooperation between regional organizations and the UN with regard to peacekeeping and peacemaking (section 2). We will then provide an overview of the EU's emerging role in crisis management, by discussing its capacity-building process as well as past and present EU crisis management operations (section 3). Hereafter, we will give an overview of the emerging partnership between the EU and the UN, both on the structural and on the operational level (section 4). Finally, we will point to some assets and shortcomings of the said cooperation (section 5).

2. Cooperation Between the UN and Regional and Intergovernmental Organizations in Crisis Management

Although Chapter VIII of the UN Charter endows them with a special – albeit subsidiary – role with regard to the maintenance of peace and security,[4] cooperation between the UN and so-called 'regional arrangements or agencies' was virtually non-existent throughout the Cold War. Until 1988, the Security Council referred to regional organizations only twice.[5]

This situation changed in the early 1990s as a growing demand for blue helmets plunged the United Nations into a number of highly complex and expensive operations. Deploying some 80.000 peacekeepers in over 30 different operations, the UN's capacity was seriously overstretched. Moreover, as operations in volatile regions (e.g., Somalia) suffered considerable losses, several UN members began to perceive DPKO as unfit for the job and grew reluctant to submit troops. As a result, the UN turned to regional organizations for support.

[3] Joint Declaration on UN-EU Cooperation in Crisis Management, New York, 24 September 2003, available at <http://europa-eu-un.org/articles/lt/article_2768_lt.htm>.

[4] Article 52 allows them to take initiatives for the peaceful settlement of disputes within their region. Article 53 foresees the possibility to undertake enforcement actions, provided that these are duly authorized by the Security Council.

[5] R. Sonnenfeld, *Resolutions of the United Nations Security Council* (Dordrecht, Nijhoff 1988), at p. 103.

Already in 1992, Secretary-General Boutros-Ghali pointed out that cooperation with regional organizations could lighten the burden on the UN and contribute to a deeper sense of participation, consensus and democratization in international affairs.[6] He argued that regional organizations had a potential that should be utilized for preventive diplomacy, peacekeeping, peacemaking, and post-conflict peacebuilding. This plea was repeated in the 1995 *Supplement to an Agenda for Peace*,[7] in which Boutros-Ghali raised the possibility of diplomatic and operational support, co-deployment and joint missions.

At the same time, the UN could appeal to a much larger group of potential partners than was the case in 1945. Indeed, whereas the OAS and the League of Arab States were the only regional organizations in the early Charter era, the number of cross-, sub- and regional organizations increased exponentially in subsequent decades. Moreover, several organizations gradually expanded their scope of activities from collective defence (e.g., NATO) or economic cooperation (e.g., ECOWAS) to the domain of conflict prevention and crisis management.

As a result of these developments, regional peacekeeping – which had been rare and controversial during the Cold War[8] – was taken up by a large number of organizations. In similar vein, the Security Council, no longer crippled by the East-West divide, on numerous occasions authorized regional and intergovernmental organizations to undertake enforcement action. Thus, the UN worked together with the OAU (now AU) in Western Sahara, the Great Lakes Region, Sierra Leone, Ethiopia and Eritrea; with ECOWAS in Liberia and Sierra Leone; with the OSCE in Yugoslavia, etc.

Regional peacekeeping and subcontracting of enforcement action inevitably led to the question as to what specific institutions meet the criteria to be considered as 'regional' in the sense of Chapter VIII, a matter which has given rise to incessant doctrinal debates. The UN Charter notoriously does not provide a definition of regional organizations, but merely states that such organizations have the task of taking care of the peaceful settlement of disputes within their own region (Article 52). Only a small number of organizations have explicitly identified themselves as 'regional', either in their constituent Charter (e.g., the OAS) or in later declarations (e.g., the Arab League, the OSCE and the CIS). Others, such as NATO or the EU, have avoided being qualified as such. The Security Council, however, seems to have adopted a very pragmatic, flexible approach and has started to cooperate with the 'able and willing' irrespective of this doctrinal controversy. Relevant Council resolutions sometimes refer to Chapter VIII, on other occasions to Chapter VII. Finally, the Council has sometimes avoided explicitly designating the organization envisaged.

---

[6] *Agenda for Peace*, Report of the Secretary-General 17 June 1992, UN Doc. A/47/277 – S/24111.

[7] *Supplement to an Agenda for Peace*, Report of the Secretary-General 3 January 1995, UN Doc. A/50/60 – S/1995/1.

[8] C. Gray, *International Law and the Use of Force* (Oxford, OUP 2nd edn. 2004), at p. 283.

The same flexible approach is also apparent from the practice of biennial high-level meetings between UN representatives (including the Secretary-General) and representatives of regional organizations, the first of which was convened in 1994.[9] The list of participants has doubled over the years, from 10 in 1994 to 20 in 2005. The fifth high-level meeting (2005) for example was attended amongst others by the Caribbean Community, the EU, Interpol, the League of Arab States, NATO and the Pacific Islands Forum.[10] The high-level meetings have led to some interesting results, such as the adoption of 'modalities for conflict prevention'[11] or 'guiding principles' for cooperation in peacebuilding.[12] During the fifth high-level meeting, a distinction was drawn, for the first time, between regional organizations and other inter-governmental organizations, albeit without actually identifying participants as falling within a particular category. At the same meeting, it was decided to organize the high-level meetings on a yearly instead of biennial basis. A Standing Committee was established in order to prepare the meetings and streamline the process.[13]

In the meantime, representatives of regional and intergovernmental organizations have also met with the UN Counter Terrorism Committee.[14] A small number of organizations moreover met with the Security Council itself in 2003, 2004 and 2005.[15] Despite the fact that the wide diversity in aims, means and methods of regional and similar organizations forces the UN to adopt a pragmatic approach, these evolutions illustrate the emergence of a rudimentary framework for cooperation in conflict prevention and crisis management.

In all likelihood, global-regional cooperation in crisis management is bound to increase in the future. More and more regional and related organizations are pressing for an autonomous role with regard to crisis management.[16] As long as these organizations respect the primary role of the Security Council and the need for an authorization for enforcement action, this evolution should be welcomed. Whereas regional organizations need the UN's legitimacy, the UN on the other hand increasingly depends on the former's resources. However, despite the recent formalization of high-level meetings, one cannot deny the *ad hoc* manner in which global-re-

---

[9] See B. Boutros-Ghali, 'Secretary-General's Statement at opening of Second Meeting between United Nations and Regional Organizations', Press Release SG/SM/5895, 15 February 1996.

[10] K. Graham and T. Felício, *Regional Security and Global Governance* (Brussels, VUBPress 2006), at p. 69.

[11] UN Doc. AS/52/1021, S/1998/785, 21 August 1998, Annex § 7.

[12] UN Doc. S/2001/138, 14 February 2001, Annex I.

[13] UN Doc. A/60/341, S/2005/567, 8 September 2005, Annex I.

[14] 'Outcome document of the special meeting of the Counter-Terrorism Committee with international, regional and subregional organizations', 6 March 2003, UN Doc. S/AC.40/2003/SM.1/4.

[15] See Meeting Record of the Security Council's 4739th meeting, 11 April 2003, S/PV/4739; Statement by the President of the Security Council, 20 July 2004, S/PRST/2004/27; Meeting Record of the Security Council's 5282nd meeting, 17 October 2005, S/PV/5282.

[16] E.g., ECOWAS has recently adopted a Protocol for Conflict Prevention, Management, Resolution, Peace-keeping and Security. The African Union has established a Peace and Security Council and has promulgated a Common African Defence and Security Policy.

gional cooperation has been organized up-to-day. Thus far, only one organization, namely the OSCE, has concluded a framework agreement with the UN dealing with consultation and cooperation.[17] Such an improvised approach is not sustainable in the long-term, since it lacks efficiency and continuity. For this reason, the September Summit Outcome Document (2005) called for an expanded consultation and cooperation between the UN and regional and sub-regional organizations 'through formalized agreements between the respective Secretariats, and, as appropriate, involvement of regional organizations in the work of the Security Council'.[18] The latter call was repeated by the Security Council,[19] which invited the Secretary-General to submit a report on the challenges and opportunities facing global-regional cooperation in peace and security and which encouraged him to explore the possibility of concluding framework agreements. In this context, viz. the quest for a more structural relationship between the UN and its partner organizations, the rapidly developing partnership between the UN and the EU could well serve as a model for closer cooperation with other organizations.

3. THE EUROPEAN UNION AS AN AUTONOMOUS ACTOR IN CRISIS MANAGEMENT

3.1 The build-up of EU operational capabilities

The origins of the ESDP can be traced back to the amendment in 1954 of the Brussels Treaty, establishing the Western European Union (WEU).[20] For several consecutive decades, the WEU played an active role, e.g., concerning arms control, yet by 1973 the organization lay more or less dormant. During the 1980s, attempts were made to revitalize the organization, but it was the year 1992 that proved to be the landmark for the European Security and Defence initiative. In that year, the initiative was brought within the ambit of the newly founded European Union by the Maastricht Treaty. A 'Declaration on Western European Union' was attached to the Treaty, in which WEU Member States agreed to 'strengthen the role of WEU, in the longer term perspective of a common defence policy within the European Union, which might in time lead to a common defence'.[21] Moreover, the role of the WEU

[17] UN Doc. A/48/185, 1 June 1993, Appendix.

[18] 2005 World Summit Outcome, GA Res. 60/1, 24 October 2005, § 170. Similar recommendations can be found in the report of the High-Level Panel on Threats, Challenges and Change, 29 November 2004, UN Doc. A/59/565 (§272) and Kofi Annan's report 'In Larger Freedom', 21 March 2005, UN Doc. A/59/2005 (§ 213).

[19] SC Res. 1631 (2005) of 17 October 2005.

[20] Treaty on Economic, Social and Cultural Collaboration and Collective Self-Defence, Brussels, 17 March 1948, amended by the Paris Agreements, Paris, 23 October 1954.

[21] Declaration on Western European Union, 1 May 1992, OJ (29 July 1992) C-191/0105.

was expanded as a result of the Petersberg Declaration.[22] This declaration shifted its emphasis from contributing to common defence toward the so-called Petersberg Tasks, dealing with different types of crisis management: 'humanitarian tasks, peacekeeping tasks, and tasks for combat forces in crisis management, including peacemaking'. In 1997, the Amsterdam Treaty[23] incorporated the Petersberg tasks into the CFSP (Article 17(2)EU).

The actual EU capacity-building process took off shortly after the British-French diplomatic summit at Saint Malo, where both countries declared that the EU 'must have the capacity for autonomous action, backed up by credible military forces, the means to decide to use them and a readiness to do so, in order to respond to international crises'.[24] This diplomatic breakthrough was subsequently Europeanized by the Kosovo crisis. Indeed, the latter crisis opened the eyes of the European leaders to Europe's continuing lack of a military fist; no EU Member State even remotely possessed the capacity to set-up a mission the size of the 1999 NATO operation in Kosovo. As a result of this catalyst, the idea of a European defence capability – which had been taboo for four decades – promptly gained acceptance among the different EU Member States. Within a period of months a first historical meeting of the European Ministers for Foreign Affairs and Ministers of Defence was organized. In June 1999, at the European Council in Cologne, a 'Declaration on Strengthening the Common European Policy on Security and Defence' was adopted, copying the language of the Saint-Malo Declaration, while adding that the EU would 'increase its ability to contribute to international peace and security in accordance with the principles of the UN Charter.'[25]

Six months later, at the December 1999 Helsinki Summit, this commitment was given substance by endorsing the Saint Malo proposal aimed at creating a 50.000- to 60.000-strong Rapid Reaction Force (RRF), supported by corresponding air and naval resources, as a 'Headline Goal' to be achieved by the year 2003. These troops should be able to deploy within a period of 60 days and then sustain forces capable of fulfilling the full range of the Petersberg tasks for at least one year. The RRF would not constitute a European army, but rather a pool of national units. Member States would retain the ultimate choice regarding engagement in a specific operation. Still, theoretically, the RRF would be able to execute crisis management operations anywhere in the world under UN auspices. Command and control would remain with the Member States, although the High Representative would coordinate the workings of the different brigades.

---

[22] Western European Union, Council of Ministers, Petersberg Declaration, Bonn 19 June 1992.

[23] Treaty of Amsterdam amending the Treaty on European Union, the Treaties establishing the European Communities and certain related acts, 2 October 1997, OJ (10 November 1997) C-340/1.

[24] Joint Statement by the British and French Governments, Franco-British Summit, Saint-Malo, France, 4 December 1998.

[25] European Council, Conclusions of the Presidency, Cologne, 3-4 June 1999, § 28.

In order to coordinate the ESDP efforts three new bodies were established in the course of 2000:[26] the Political and Security Committee, which monitors the international situation and exercises political control and strategic direction of crisis management operations; the EU Military Committee (EUMC), composed of the national Chiefs of Defence, and responsible for giving military advice, developing an overall concept of crisis management and conducting military relations with third States and organizations; and finally the EU Military Staff, which provides early warning and strategic planning of the Petersberg tasks and which is charged with implementing the decisions of the EUMC. Another crucial step took place in December 2002 when the EU and NATO adopted the so-called 'Berlin Plus' Agreements. These agreements assure EU access to NATO operational planning and resources and provide for consultation between the two organizations. Thus, a necessary step was taken in order to implement the ESDP and avoid duplication of NATO capabilities. The implication is, however, that ESDP strongly relies on NATO assets and will continue to do so in the future.

In the first half of 2003, the European defence ministers agreed that the Helsinki Headline Goal had been attained and that the European Rapid Reaction Force was henceforth a reality.[27] Shortly afterwards, a new military Headline Goal 2010 was spelled out.[28] Its central feature is the creation of thirteen small, rapidly deployable 'battlegroups' by 2007. 'Battlegroups' should each consist of some 1.500 troops, including appropriate supporting elements, and should be deployable within 15 days. These forces are designed primarily, though not exclusively, for higher intensity operations in response to UN requests. During the June 2005 summit, the European Council concluded that Member States' commitments will enable the desired goal for the Initial Operational Capability in 2005 and 2006 – i.e., to have the capacity to undertake one battlegroup-sized operation – to be achieved.[29] During the Full Operational Capability, from 2007 onwards, the EU should have the capacity to undertake two concurrent single battlegroup-sized rapid response operations.

So far we have concentrated on the creation of the EU's military capacities, yet EU Member States have also recognized that the fulfilment of the Petersberg tasks requires civil crisis management capabilities. In this regard, four priority areas were identified at the European Council in Santa Maria da Feira on 19 and 20 June 2000: civilian policing, promoting the rule of law, strengthening civilian administrations and ensuring protection for civilian populations. In May 2000, EU Member States

---

[26] Provisionally established by Council Decisions of 14 February 2000, OJ (22 February 2000) L-49/1; permanent establishment by Council Decisions of 22 January 2001, OJ (30 January 2001) L-27/1.

[27] 'Declaration on EU military capabilities', General Affairs and External Relations Council, 19 May 2003.

[28] Presidency conclusions Brussels, 17-18 June 2004, § 62.

[29] Presidency conclusions Brussels, 16-17 June 2005.

agreed to establish a Committee for the Civilian Aspects of Crisis Management.[30] An Action Plan was also adopted in order to create a pool of 5.000 police officers, 1.400 of whom can be deployed within 30 days; 300 judges, prosecutors and prison officers; other experts with regard to civil administration and; with regard to civil protection, two or three assessment and/or coordination teams, consisting of 10 experts, who could be dispatched within three to seven hours, as well as intervention teams of up to 2.000 persons for deployment at short notice.[31] The Ministerial Civilian Crisis Management Capability Conference held on 19 November 2002 confirmed that the concrete targets in the four priority areas had been reached and even exceeded through States' voluntary commitments.[32] Consequently, the European Council endorsed the Civilian Headline Goal 2008, which set forth new goals in order to enable the EU to deploy concurrent civilian missions at short notice and to work in close cooperation with the military.[33]

Finally, in October 2003, a proposal was launched by France, to establish a European Military Police Force to be employed in peace support operations. This led to an Agreement between the Netherlands, France, Italy, Spain and Portugal to establish a 3.000-strong European Gendarmerie Force, which will be first and foremost at the disposal of the EU.[34] Other countries were invited to join the initiative.

ESDP implementation has led to remarkable results. Basic operational capabilities are now in place, as well as a decision-making and coordination structure. Some 200 peoples are currently accredited to Brussels as permanent ESDP staff. The EU has also been working on training, financing, rapid deployment concepts and civil-military coordination.[35] Four military crisis management exercises have been held, one of which was carried out together with NATO in November 2003.

Nevertheless, the results are tempered by a number of continuing shortfalls. This was recognized by subsequent Capability Improvement Conferences, as well as by the European Council at its session of June 2003 in Thessaloniki.[36] First, whereas EU Member States have some 1.8 million persons under arms, and spend some 160

---

[30] Council Decision 2000/354/CFSP of 22 May 2000 setting up a Committee for civilian aspects of crisis management, OJ (27 May 2000) L-127/1.

[31] H.-B. Weisserth, 'The European Headline Goal', in K. Von Wogau (ed.), *The path to European Defence* (Antwerpen, Maklu 2004), at p. 116.

[32] Speaking Points of Javier Solana, High Representative for CFSP, at the Civilian Crisis Management Capabilities Conference at ministerial level, Brussels, 19 November 2002.

[33] Presidency conclusions Brussels, 16-17 December 2004.

[34] See 'European Gendarmerie – Declaration of Intent', Brussels, 17 September 2004, available at <http://www.iss-eu.org/chaillot/chai75e.pdf>.

[35] See, e.g., Council Joint Action 2005/575/CFSP of 18 July 2005, establishing a European Security and Defence College (ESDC), OJ (26 July 2005) L-194/15. See C.R. Earle, 'European capacities for peace operations: taking stock', March 2004, available at <http://www.stimson.org/fopo/pdf/Earle-EuropeanCapacitiesforPeaceOperations-TakingStock.pdf>.

[36] Presidency Conclusions June 2003 at Thessaloniki: 'The EU has operational capability across the full range of Petersberg tasks, limited and constrained by recognized shortfalls, which can be alleviated by the further development of the EU's military capabilities', § 56.

billion euros a year on their cumulative defence budgets, the EU still underachieves on deployability, mobility, sustainability, effective engagement and command and control.[37] This even led one author to conclude in July 2004 that despite official declarations to the contrary, the original Helsinki Headline Goal had not really been met.[38] The lion's share of the European defence budget is traditionally spent on personnel and infrastructure, rather than on new equipment and research. This makes it hard for Europe to keep up with ongoing military-technical developments. As regards deployability, EU Member States can only deploy 10 to 15 % of their forces for missions abroad, because most of them rely primarily on conscripts and still focus on territorial defence.[39] If implemented as planned, the battle group concept will fill one of the most crucial capability gaps. Furthermore, as regards mobility, the EU would need to improve its heavy airlift capabilities. The establishment of the European Defence Agency[40] will hopefully provide a powerful tool to achieve a more functional and cost-effective capability development.

A second shortfall lies in the diversity in military manpower, budget and capabilities among EU Member States.[41] Only a handful of European States possess the means to conduct military operations both at the strategic and operative level. This situation leaves heavy responsibilities to a limited number of countries (France, Germany, Italy and the United Kingdom) to push for further development of capabilities at different levels. Finally, it should not be forgotten that the ESDP is organized on a purely intergovernmental basis, meaning that all decisions have to be reached by unanimity of EU Member States. So far, the impetus in the ESDP's development has been most remarkable. Yet the disagreement over the Iraq crisis illustrates the difficulty in reaching consensus. The recent EU enlargement and the difficulties regarding the ratification of the European Constitution are not likely to make this any easier.

3.2 **The EU's first missions**

Although ESDP was declared operational in 2001,[42] it actually took off in 2003, when a number of police missions and military crisis management missions were launched on behalf of the European Union.

---

[37] See A. Dumoulin, R. Mathieu and G. Sarlet, *La politique européenne de sécurité et de defense (PESD): De l'opératoire à l'identitaire* (Bruxelles, Emile Bruylant 2003), at pp. 493-521.

[38] J.Y. Haine, 'A new impetus for ESDP', (2004) 11 *I.S.S. Bulletin*.

[39] B. Schmitt, 'European capabilities: how many divisions?' in N. Gnesotto, *EU Security and Defence Policy: the first five years (1999-2004)* (Paris, Institute for Security Studies 2004), pp. 89-102, at pp. 97-99.

[40] Council Joint Action 2004/551/CFSP on the establishment of the European Defence Agency, 12 July 2004, OJ (17 July 2004) L-245/17-28.

[41] See Y. Boyer, 'The ESDP and its challenges', September 2003, available at <http://www.csm.org.pl/pl/files/raporty/2003/rap_i_an_1203.pdf>, at 8.

[42] Declaration on the operational capability of the Common European Security and Defence Policy, Annex II to the Presidency Conclusions, Laeken, 14-15 December 2001, SN 300/1/01

The first test case was the Police Mission in Bosnia-Herzegovina (EUPM), which started on 1 January 2003. EUPM was established by a decision of the Council on 11 March 2002,[43] and was welcomed by the Peace Implementation Steering Board and by Security Council resolution 1396.[44] EUPM replaced the UN's International Police Task Force (IPTF), set-up under the 1995 Dayton Peace Accord, and sought to establish sustainable policing under ownership of Bosnia and Herzegovina, through monitoring, mentoring and inspection activities. The original mission, which was set to run until the end of 2005, was composed of some 554 police officers from 24 EU Member States and from 9 other countries. However, following an invitation by the Bosnian authorities, the EU decided to establish a scaled-down follow-on mission for another two-year period.[45]

On 31 March 2003, the EU undertook its first military operation, Operation Concordia in FYROM. This operation was set up by the Council in January 2003,[46] following a request by the FYROM President, and was subsequently endorsed by the Security Council.[47] Concordia took over from NATO's Operation Allied Harmony, established to facilitate the implementation of the Ohrid Framework Agreement, which settled the conflict in Macedonia in 2001. The operation was carried out with recourse to NATO resources under the Berlin Plus Agreements. Twenty-six countries, including all EU Member States except Ireland and Denmark, provided 357 lightly armed troops. More than a third of the troops were supplied by France, which acted as 'framework nation' during the first six months of the operation. When the mission's mandate was extended on 21 July 2003, the responsibilities of the framework nation were transferred to EUROFOR. Shortly afterwards, on 15 December 2003, Operation Concordia was brought to an end.

The EU launched a second military operation, operation Artemis, on 12 June 2003. Contrary to the two previous missions, operation Artemis was not located within regional proximity of the EU, but in the Democratic Republic of Congo, in and around the city of Bunya. The operation was based both on a decision of the Council[48] and on a formal authorization by the UN Security Council.[49] Operation Artemis was meant to be an interim emergency mission, to improve the humanitarian situation and to end fighting between ethnic militias, in close coordination with the UN Mission in the DRC (MONUC). The operation comprised some 1800 troops. The bulk of these (some 1700) were provided by France, which again acted as

REV 1: 'the EU is now able to conduct some crisis-management operations. The Union will be in a position to take on progressively more demanding operations, as the assets and capabilities at its disposal continue to develop'.

[43] Council Joint Action 2002/210/CFSP of 11 March 2002, OJ (13 March 2002) L-70.

[44] SC Res 1396 of 5 March 2002.

[45] Council Joint Action 2005/824/CFSP of 24 November 2005, OJ (25 November 2005) L-307/55.

[46] Council Joint Action 2003/92/CFSP of 27 January 2003, OJ (11 February 2003) L-34.

[47] SC Res. 1317 (2000).

[48] Council Joint Action 2003/423/CFSP of 5 June 2003, OJ (11 June 2003) L-143.

[49] SC Res. 1484 (2003) of 30 May 2003.

framework nation. There were 13 EU Member States and 3 other non-European States providing troops, logistics or other support. Artemis was shut down on 1 September 2003, when a strengthened MONUC peace-keeping force led by Bangladesh took over its tasks.

A second police mission, Operation Proxima in the FYROM, was approved by the Council in September 2003.[50] Operation Proxima became operational on 15 December 2003, as a follow-on mission to the military operation Concordia. Proxima is composed of some 200 EU police experts and aims at monitoring, mentoring and advising the country's police to help fight organized crime and promote European policing standards. Contrary to its predecessor, operation Proxima no longer operates by means of NATO assets. After the operation ended in December 2005,[51] it was immediately succeeded by a smaller EU police advisory team (EUPAT), consisting of some 30 police advisors, for a duration of 6 months.[52]

On 16 July 2004, the European Union established the EU Rule of Law Mission to Georgia (EUJUST THEMIS),[53] a small-scale operation, comprised of 8 international experts, plus local staff, foreseen to last 12 months. The aim of the operation was to support the Georgian authorities in addressing urgent challenges in the criminal justice system and assisting in the reform process. As such, it was the first mission aimed at strengthening the rule of law, one of the four priority areas of the European Union with regard to civilian crisis management. The operation was completed on 14 July 2005.

On 12 July 2004, the Council furthermore adopted a Joint Action establishing another military mission, notably Operation Althea in Bosnia and Herzegovina,[54] which replaced the NATO Stabilization Force (SFOR) on 2 December 2004.[55] This mission, which was explicitly authorized by the Security Council,[56] is carried out under the auspices of the Berlin Plus Agreements and will last three years. The goal is to deter hostilities and contribute to the consolidation of peace in Bosnia-Herzegovina. The operation consists of approximately 7000 troops, compared to a total of some 3000 personnel in the ESDP's five preceding missions. Operation Althea will undoubtedly represent the most serious challenge for the EU's crisis management capabilities to date.

Numerous smaller operations have been set up throughout 2005 and 2006. These include:

---

[50] Council Joint Action 2003/681/CFSP of 29 September 2003, OJ (1 October 2003) L-249.

[51] 2608th General Affairs Council meeting, Luxembourg, 11 October 2004, Press Release 275 No. 12767/04.

[52] Council Joint Action 2005/826/CFAP of 24 November 2005, OJ (25 November 2005) L-307/61.

[53] Council Joint Action 2004/523/CFSP of 28 June 2004, OJ (3 July 2004), L-234.

[54] Council Joint Action 2004/570/CFSP of 12 July 2004, OJ (28 July 2004), L-252.

[55] 2608th General Affairs Council meeting, Luxembourg, 11 October 2004, Press Release 275 No. 12767/04.

[56] SC Res 1575 (2004).

- two EU operations in the DRC in order to contribute to security sector reform, transition and stabilisation.[57] The first mission (EUPOL Kinshasa), counting approximately 30 persons, was launched in April 2005 and aims at monitoring and advising on the setting-up of an Integrated Police Unit in Kinshasa. The second operation (EUSEC DR Congo) was launched on 8 June 2005. It consists of 8 experts that will provide practical support for the integration of the Congolese army.
- EUJUST LEX, an integrated rule of law mission for Iraq, which became operational on 1 July 2005 for a period of twelve months.[58] This mission was set-up to provide training for senior officials and executive staff from the judiciary, the police and the penitentiary.
- EU support for the AU mission in Darfur (AMIS II), including a civilian and a military component. This action was established in July 2005 and provides for important financial, political and logistical support (e.g., strategic airlifts, communications equipment) as well as for the deployment of a small number of EU officers for training and planning purposes.[59]
- the Aceh Monitoring Mission (AMM), designed to monitor the implementation of the peace agreement between the Indonesian government and the Free Aceh Movement.[60] The AMM became operational on 15 September 2005 and counts some 199 unarmed personnel. Roughly half of these comes from EU Member States, Norway and Switzerland. The other half is seconded by the five participating ASEAN countries.
- two operations in the Occupied Palestinian Territories. The EU Border Assistance Mission for the Rafah Crossing Point (EU BAM Rafah) was launched on 26 November 2005. The operation aims at monitoring and evaluating the performance of the PA's border control, while contributing to Palestinian capacity-building.[61] EU BAM Rafah includes approximately 70 personnel and will last for a period of 12 months. The second operation is the EU Police Mission for the Palestinian Territories (EUPOL-COPPS), comprised of 33 unarmed personnel.[62] EUPOL-COPPS became operational in January 2006 for a period of three years and aims at contributing to effective policing under Palestinian ownership in accordance with international best standards.

---

[57] Council Joint Action 2004/847/CFSP of 9 December 2004, OJ (14 December 2004), L-367/30; Council Joint Action 2005/355/CFSP of 2 May 2005, OJ (3 May 2005), L-112/20.

[58] Council Joint Action 2005/190/CFSP of 7 March 2005, OJ (9 March 2005), L-62/37.

[59] Council Joint Action 2005/557/CFSP of 18 July 2005, OJ (20 July 2005) L-188/46.

[60] Council Joint Action 2005/643/CFSP of 9 September 2005, OJ (10 September 2005) L-234/13; Memorandum of Understanding between the Government of the Republic of Indonesia and the Free Aceh Movement, Helsinki, 15 August 2005.

[61] Council Joint Action 2005/889/CFSP of 12 December 2005, OJ (12 December 2005) L-327/28.

[62] Council Joint Action 2005/797/CFSP of 14 November 2005, OJ (14 November 2005) L-300/65.

- a two-year EU Border Assistance Mission to Moldova and Ukraine, including border police and customs officials from 16 EU Member States.[63] The operation was launched in December 2005 and aims at preventing smuggling, trafficking and customs fraud by providing advice and training to improve the capacity of the Moldovan and Ukrainian border and customs services.

Most recently, the Security Council, acting under Chapter VII, authorized the deployment of the autonomous EU military operation EUFOR RD Congo, in order to support MONUC during an initial period of four months following the first round of presidential and parliamentary elections in the DRC.[64] The EU operation was mandated to take all necessary measures, *inter alia*, to support MONUC in stabilizing the situation, to contribute to the protection of civilians under imminent threat and to execute operations to extract individuals in danger. EUFOR RD Congo, established with the support of the DRC government, would comprise some 400-450 troops within Congolese borders, as well as a battalion-size 'over-the-horizon' force outside the country, to be deployed if need arose.

When considering the overall picture of the ESDP's first missions, it seems that the EU has followed a 'gradualist' approach on crisis management.[65] The EU first engaged in a nearby police mission (EUPM), subsequently followed by a nearby military operation in FYROM (Concordia). It is important to note that Operation Concordia took place in a relatively stable climate, where ethnic tensions were not likely to rise again.[66] The same cannot be said for operation Artemis, which took place in a much more volatile and hostile environment. This became clear on 16 June 2003 when EU troops came under attack from armed militiamen.[67] Two militiamen were killed during the incident. Operation Artemis moreover raised the bar in two other ways. Firstly, the operation no longer relied on NATO assets under the Berlin Plus Agreements. Secondly, for the first time the European Union acted beyond its own geographical proximity. Nevertheless, the operation was very limited in time and scope. This led to criticism from humanitarian agencies. Indeed, whereas conditions in Bunya had improved as a result of the intervention, the situation in the surrounding countryside, where the EU had no mandate, remained extremely unstable.[68] By launching Operation Althea in December 2004, the European Union has again raised the bar. Although this mission still relies on NATO assets, its size definitely makes it a crucial test for EU capabilities.

---

63 Council Joint Action 2005/776/CFSP of 7 November 2005, OJ (8 November 2005) L-292/13.

64 SC Res. 1671 (2006)of 25 April 2006, followed by Council Joint Action 2006/319/CFSP of 27 April 2006, OJ (29 April 2006) L-116/98.

65 G. Lindstrom, 'On the ground: EDSP Operations' in N. Gnesotto, op. cit., *supra* n. 39, at p. 111.

66 R. Stefanova, 'Implications for ESDP from the unfolding of operation Concordia', 14 March 2004, available at <http://www.weltpolitik.net/print/1002.html>.

67 C. Mace, 'Operation Artemis: Mission improbable?', (2003) *European Security Review*, No. 18.

68 Ibid.

So far, the ESDP's curriculum is rather impressive. The EU has proven its willingness and capability to engage in a wide array of civilian and military crisis management functions, including the promotion of the rule of law, border control, training activities for security personnel, monitoring of the implementation of peace agreements, assistance in combating organized crime, et cetera. In 2005, the EU for the first time incorporated a human rights component in one of its operations (AMM), a novelty that will hopefully set a precedent for future action. Training programmes and 'lessons-learned' evaluations are starting up.[69] Financing problems have been partially tackled as a result of the Council decision to create a permanent mechanism for handling common costs of EU missions ('Athena'),[70] although it is widely acknowledged that the CFSP requires more money to deliver.[71] Finally, the EU has also devised useful practices to facilitate deployment and coordination, such as the identification of a 'framework nation' taking a lead role in a particular operation – as France did for Concordia and Artemis –, or the deployment of advance elements on the ground to prepare for full operability. On the other hand, it should be conceded that most EU operations have been modest in scope as well as size, the only exception being operation Althea (7.000) troops, which depended on NATO assets. The combined troop strength of past and present operations is indeed relatively low when compared to for example NATO's operations in Afghanistan (ISAF – 9.000 troops) and Kosovo (KFOR – 16.000 troops) or with UN operations in the DRC (MONUC – 17.000 troops), Haiti (MINUSTAH – 9.000 troops) or Liberia (UNMIL – 19.000 troops). Furthermore, the larger ESDP operations in Bosnia-Herzegovina and the FYROM may suggest that the EU prefers taking over existing (NATO or UN) operations rather than establishing operations that are led by it from the outset. In all, the EU has made enormous headway in becoming a global security provider, although it still has a lot to prove. Operation Althea and EUFOR RD Congo will provide just that opportunity.

4. Interaction between the UN and the EU

4.1 The first steps

Since the 1990s, as the EU has become increasingly involved in matters relating to peace and security, new opportunities for EU-UN cooperation have emerged. An

69 A. Missiroli, 'ESDP – How it works', in N Gnesotto, op. cit., *supra* n. 39, pp. 55-72, at p. 66.

70 Council Decision 2004/197/CFSP of 23 February 2004, OJ (28 February 2004), L-63/68. Remark: in accordance with Article 28 § 3 TEU, expenses which do *not* arise from operations *having military or defence implications* shall be charged to the budget of the European Communities and not to the Member States. This provision has important implications for the voting requirements (qualified majority or unanimity) for the creation of EU crisis management operations as well as for the respective competences of the Commission and the Council.

71 See G. Grevi, 'The Aceh Monitoring Mission: towards integrated crisis management', December 2005, available at <http://www.iss-eu.org/occasion/occ61.pdf>.

important pre-requisite in this regard was the EU's continuous commitment to the primary role of the UN in maintaining international peace and security.[72] This dedication is most ardently expressed in the European Security Strategy, which declares that: 'Strengthening the United Nations, equipping it to fulfill its responsibilities and to act effectively, is a European priority'.[73]

The first appeal to develop a more systematic relationship with regard to crisis management was made in 2000 by the French Presidency of the General Assembly.[74] At this occasion the UN Secretary-General was invited to meet with EU institutions, which he did that very month. Concrete proposals were spelled out by the EU General Affairs Council on 11 June 2001 in its draft conclusions on EU-UN cooperation in conflict prevention and crisis management,[75] which affirmed the 'determination to develop and strengthen cooperation in the areas of crisis management and conflict prevention'. The following areas for cooperation were emphasized: conflict prevention, particular regional issues (such as the Balkans and Africa) and civil and military crisis management. As regards the latter, the document emphasized the need to ensure that the EU's evolving military and civilian capacities provide a real added value for the UN, e.g., by enhancing compatibility of training standards, exchange of information and coordination in the field. The document also foresaw the creation of new points of contacts to improve understanding between the two organizations. Previously, consultation had been limited to 1) the biennial high-level meetings between the Secretary-General and the representatives of various regional organizations (cf., *supra*), and; 2) informal meetings between the Secretary-General and the EU High Representative since October 2000. Information exchange and consultation was drastically enhanced after the Göteborg Summit, through the establishment of a 'platform for intensified cooperation', which led to an intensification of desk-to-desk dialogue on different levels.[76] Although this evolution certainly marks a closer cooperation between the UN and the European Union, EU-UN relations in terms of crisis management remained mostly symbolic until the beginning of 2003. By contrast, 2003 was a landmark year, both on the structural and operational level.

---

[72] E.g., Article 11 Consolidated version of the Treaty on European Union, OJ (24 December 2002), C-325/1.

[73] 'A Secure Europe in a Better World' – a European Security Strategy, adopted by the European Council on 12 December 2003.

[74] Speech of 12 September 2000, available at <http://www.un.int/france/eu/speeches/debat/0912F.htm>.

[75] Draft Council conclusions on EU-UN cooperation in conflict prevention and crisis management, Doc. 9528/2/01 REV 2, 7 June 2001, later approved by the European Council.

[76] A. Novosseloff, 'EU-United Nations Partnership in Crisis Management: Developments and Prospects', IPA, June 2004, available at <http://www.ipacademy.org/PDF_Reports/EU_UN_PARTNERSHIP.pdf>, at pp. 3-4.

4.2 Structural cooperation

As regards the structural level, the Council in July 2003 called for the development of comprehensive guidelines[77] to identify areas for possible EU-UN cooperation, 'the importance of which calls for a proper framework for closer dialogue and consultation'. In the military domain, the Council suggested a stronger cooperation in crisis management exercises and training activities as well as the exchange of 'lessons learned' and 'best practices' and the establishment of more regular contacts between military experts from both organizations. In the civilian domain, similar proposals were made. Moreover, the Council set out six different scenarios for civil crisis management operations: 1) National contributions to an operation led by international organizations, without any EU coordination; 2) National contribution to such an operation, but following EU consultations aimed at, e.g., identifying opportunities to pool resources; 3) A coordinated EU contribution; 4) A whole EU component in an operation under the overall lead of an international organization; 5) An EU-led operation with some components provided by international organizations, and; 6) Autonomous EU operations (which could also precede or follow a UN operation). Finally, the Council invited the Presidency to make proposals for a comprehensive MoU with the UN.

On 10 September 2003, the European Commission presented a new strategy for EU-UN relations, calling for further collaboration.[78] The Commission reaffirmed the EU's commitment to multilateralism, stressing that: 'providing active and early support to UN-mandated or UN-led operations is a clear track for the progressive framing and deployment of the EU's security and defence policy and capabilities'. The Commission expounded several practical recommendations to enhance EU-UN relations, for example by means of joint planning and desk-to-desk dialogue on conflict prevention and crisis management. Further steps were needed to make the standards of training for EU and UN field personnel compatible and to promote the exchange of personnel and joint training activities. Both organizations should, moreover, coordinate systematically with other regional organizations, active in the field of conflict prevention and crisis management. The Commission's call for closer cooperation led to intensified working relations and the creation of integrated EU-UN teams to 'pilot' an exchange of early warning information on five countries.[79]

The next step was to follow very soon. On 24 September 2003 the UN Secretary-General Kofi Annan, and Silvio Berlusconi, then president of the EU Council,

---

[77] 'EU Cooperation with the UN: Practical aspects of EU contributions to civilian crisis management operations and activities led by the UN', Doc. 11022/1/03, 4 July 2003, available at <http://register/consilium.eu.int>.

[78] Commission of the European Communities, 'The European Union and the United Nations: the choice of multilateralism', 10 September 2003, COM (2003) 526 final.

[79] D. Manca, 'Follow-up to the European Security Strategy: Effective Multilateralism', (2004) *European Security Review,* No. 23.

concluded a Joint Declaration on EU-UN cooperation in Crisis Management, covering both civilian and military operations.[80] In this Declaration, both organizations agreed to establish a joint consultative mechanism to examine ways and means to enhance mutual coordination and compatibility in the following areas: 1) planning, including reciprocal assistance in assessment missions and greater contact and cooperation between mission planning units; 2) training: the establishment of joint training standards, procedures and planning for military and civilian personnel, the synchronization of pre-deployment training; and the institutionalization of training seminars, conferences and exercises; 3) communication: greater cooperation between situation centres; exchange of liaison officers whenever required; establishment of desk-to-desk dialogue through the respective liaison offices in New York and Brussels; and 4) best practices: regularized and systematic exchange of lessons learned and best practices information, including information on mission hand-over and procurement. By establishing a joint consultative mechanism, the Joint Declaration deals with the basic requirements needed for crisis management cooperation and formalizes the steps taken by the EU and the UN since 2000-2001.[81]

After the breakthrough of September 2003, the European Council approved a number of measures to implement the Joint Declaration with regard to military crisis management.[82] Two models of rapid deployment in support of the UN were put forward: firstly, the 'bridging model', which aims at providing the UN with time to mount a new operation or to reorganize an existing one by deploying an autonomous EU force (as was the case with Operation Artemis); secondly, the 'Standby model', which would consist of an EU component – an 'over-the-horizon reserve' or an 'extraction force' – in support of a UN operation. The 'bridging model' involves a rapid deployment EU operation for a short duration with a clear end state. The exit strategy of such an operation consists of the arrival of UN forces to take over. Therefore, the deployment of EU troops should be complemented by political efforts in the UN framework to ensure that the UN force would have the appropriate mandate and capabilities, as well as technical assistance and exchange of information with the UN and TCCs to facilitate the hand-over. Early deployment of UN troops before the actual handover is furthermore recommended. The 'Elements of Implementation' also suggest the re-hatting of forces to assist transition; either by participation of EU troops in a subsequent UN operation, or by maintaining a number of enabling capabilities after the end of the EU operation. In short, close coordination is considered the key to the successful use of such a force.[83]

---

[80] Joint Declaration on UN-EU Cooperation in Crisis Management, loc. cit., *supra* n. 3.

[81] A. Novosseloff, loc. cit., *supra* n. 76, at p. 13.

[82] 'EU-UN Cooperation in Military Crisis Management Operations: Elements of Implementation of the EU-UN Joint Declaration', adopted by the European Council on 17-18 June 2004, available at <http://ue.eu.int/ueDocs/cms_Data/docs/pressData/en/misc/81343.pdf>.

[83] F. Cameron and G. Quille, 'ESDP: The State of Play', EPC Working Paper No. 11, September 2004, available at <http://www.theepc.net>, at p. 15.

The document also emphasizes that national military capabilities are in no way 'frozen' for ESDP purposes and can voluntarily be assigned to UN operations. The Council indicates that here too the EU could play a supporting role by providing a framework for information exchange and coordination of national contributions in the form of a 'clearing house process' among Member States. Such a process would be activated at the request of one Member State willing to contribute to a UN operation and desiring to share this commitment with other Member States. Finally, the elements of implementation include several proposals regarding assistance to UN operations by the EU Satellite Centre and the Institute for Security Studies, enhanced intelligence sharing and reinforcement of liaison offices with crisis management experts.

A similar document on the implementation of the Joint Declaration albeit with regard to civilian crisis management was adopted by the European Council in December 2004.[84] Here, three main scenarios for practical cooperation are identified. The first option concerns the exchange of information on the European level to improve efficiency. Thus, consultations within the Political and Security Committee could inform the UN of EU Member States' willingness to offer support to an operation and could identify opportunities for efficiency measures, such as pooling resources. Secondly, the EU might function as a 'clearing house' to coordinate Member State contributions in order to meet the UN's needs and to avoid shortfalls in the overall EU effort. Last but not least, practical cooperation in civilian crisis management could take the form of an EU contribution consisting of: 1) evaluation, assessment and monitoring of a crisis in advance of an UN operation, through the rapid provision of experts; 2) a component of a larger UN operation; 3) an autonomous operation within the UN framework; 4) an autonomous operation launched before or after an UN operation (such as EUPM), or; 5) simultaneous EU-UN operations. The document stresses that both organizations would benefit from further cooperation in civilian crisis management; the UN by relying on the EU's qualitative and quantitative capabilities, especially in situations where rapid deployment is required; the EU by acquiring greater external visibility. Although the final recommendations are mainly concerned with the European capability build-up, the document also contains some general suggestions regarding the development of appropriate 'clearing house' processes, information exchange and expertise sharing, etc.

It should finally be noted that the joint consultative mechanism became operational in February 2004.[85] It is led by a EU-UN Crisis Management Steering Committee which meets two to three times a year at senior level and more frequently at officials' level. It brings together officials from the EU Council and the UN Secre-

---

[84] 'EU-UN cooperation in civilian crisis management', Annex IV of the Presidency report, Council Document 16062/04, 13 December 2004, available at <http://register.consilium.eu.int/pdf/en/04/st16/st16062.en04.pdf>.

[85] D. Manca, loc. cit., *supra* n. 79.

tariat (most notably from DPKO and DPA), as well as a range of other actors, such as UNDP, OCHA or ECHO, thus stressing the need for a comprehensive approach to crisis management. The Steering Committee has held a number of meetings to identify joint initiatives in the areas of disarmament, demobilisation and reintegration.[86]

4.3 Operational cooperation

As the EU became engaged in crisis management operations throughout 2003, the significant structural progress concerning EU-UN cooperation has also been tested on the operational level, as a result of EUPM in Bosnia-Herzegovina and Operation Artemis in the Democratic Republic of Congo. With regard to Bosnia-Herzegovina, the transition from the UN International Police Task Force (IPTF) to EUPM was carefully planned and executed.[87] Firstly, nine months before the actual handover, an EU planning mission was sent to the area. Secondly, the Dane Sven-Christian Frederiksen was consecutively appointed as head of IPTF and then as head of EUPM. Thirdly, the High Representative in Bosnia-Herzegovina simultaneously acted as Special Representative of the EU. Finally, after the handover in January 2003, a UN liaison office remained in place for several months.

The temporary reinforcement of MONUC (the UN mission in the DRC) by an EU-led interim emergency force (Operation Artemis) went equally well.[88] At this occasion, the UN Secretary-General made an urgent appeal for assistance in order to avoid a Srebrenica-like tragedy in the volatile Bunya region in the eastern DRC. His appeal was answered with remarkable swiftness. In the words of Claude-France Arnould, the Defence Aspects Director of the General Secretariat of the Council of the EU:

> 'between Javier Solana and the French government and Kofi Annan, there was a clear understanding that transforming a French operation into an EU operation did not cost one day, which is positive because one day could mean a massacre, and it did not cost anything in terms of military efficiency'.[89]

Another important aspect was the fact that the EU High Representative reported directly to the UN Security Council on developments in the field. Albeit largely a matter of improvisation,[90] coordination between the EU and DPKO was facilitated through common patrols, attendance of briefings by MONUC liaison officers, pro-

---

[86] Ibid.

[87] A. Novosseloff, loc. cit., *supra* n. 76, at p. 11.

[88] See, e.g., DRC Spokesperson from the Ministry of Foreign Affairs, 16 September 2003, available at <http://www.un.int/france/documents_anglais/030916_mae_presse_afrique.htm>.

[89] C.F. Arnould, 'The United Nations and the European Union: an ever stronger partnership', 18 May 2004, available at <http://www.irri-kiib.be/speechnotes/EU-UN/EU%20UN%20intro-key.pdf>.

[90] C.-F. Arnould, loc. cit., *supra* n. 89.

gressive hand-over of points of control, etc.[91] Analogous to the case of EUPM, the MONUC representative in the Ituri sector was also a French officer.

Following Operation Artemis, EU and UN officials alike agreed on the desirability of extending consultation and cooperation beyond the confines of a concrete operation. Thus, Artemis provided the direct inspiration for the creation of the joint consultative mechanism in 2003-2004. Drawing on the aforementioned operations, the European Union moreover organized a crisis management exercise (EST 05) in April 2005, which focused on the modalities of EU-UN cooperation in the field in three different scenarios: 1) a UN military operation taking over an EU operation; 2) an EU police operation taking over a UN operation, and; 3) health and medical support for a UN operation.[92] The exercise made it possible to clarify certain issues related to planning, chains of command, rules of engagement, liaison officers and information-sharing.

A last test-case is EUFOR RD Congo, created in order to support MONUC during the period following the Congolese elections. Security Council Resolution 1671 (2006) explicitly requested the European Union and the Secretary-General to ensure a close cooperation from the preparation of the operation until its disengagement. It also requested the EU to report regularly to the Security Council on the implementation of the mission's mandate.

These examples suggest that EU-UN cooperation on crisis management has successfully become operational, through simple and transparent procedures. This development could well serve as a precedent for relations between the UN and other international organizations.

5. Evaluation of the Emerging UN-EU Partnership Regarding Crisis Management

5.1 EU commitment to peacekeeping and peace enforcement

5.1.1 *Some figures*

The emerging EU-UN partnership in crisis management is clearly a desirable evolution. By building up military and civilian capabilities, the EU now has great potential to contribute to UN crisis management in areas where the latter is traditionally weaker, such as rapid deployment, and to considerably lighten the UN's financial and logistical burden. The EU has used this potential in Bosnia-Herzegovina – where

[91] A. Novosseloff, loc. cit., *supra* n. 76, at pp. 12-13.

[92] T. Tardy, 'EU-UN cooperation in peacekeeping: a promising relationship in a constrained environment', in M. Ortega (ed.), *The European Union and the United Nations – partners in effective multilateralism* (June 2005, ISS-EU Chaillot Paper No. 78), available at <http://www.iss-eu.org/chaillot/chai78.pdf>, at p. 64.

it took over from the IPTF, thus allowing the UN to redeploy elsewhere –, and in the DRC – where the EU twice played a crucial role in support of MONUC.

Nevertheless, EU-UN cooperation is not without shortcomings or dangers. The first and foremost criticism relates to the question whether the EU's commitment is reality or merely lip service. Traditionally, UN officials have complained about EU Member States' low participation in UN peacekeeping. Indeed, whereas the 25 EU Member States provide almost half of the peacekeeping budget, in April 2006 they accounted for only 4.008 (or 6.4%) out of 62.656 military observers, civilian police and troops engaged in UN peacekeeping missions.[93] There is, moreover, an unmistakable downward trend in EU troop contributions when we consider the contributions of the current 25 Member States (EU-25) over the past years.[94] Since 2001, these numbers have consistently declined. In 2001, for example, the EU-25 provided 7.246 civilian, military and monitoring personnel. In 2002, they accounted for only 5.932 troops. The situation has continued to worsen: 4.757 troops in 2003; 4.607 in 2004; 4.245 in 2005, and finally; 4.008 in April 2006.

EU contributions to UN peace-keeping operations
in terms of military observers, civilian police and troops

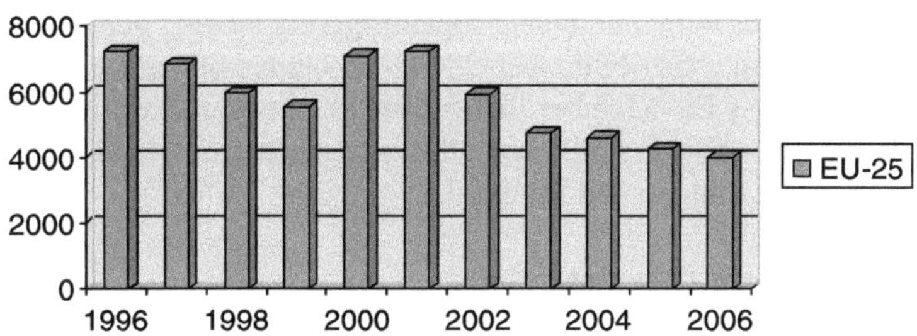

This picture becomes even gloomier when we look at relative instead of absolute numbers. A comparison of EU troop contributions to the UN peacekeeping total shows a steep fall in EU participation since 1998, notably the inception of the ESDP. Whereas the current 25 EU Member States were good for 41.4% of the 14.394 UN peacekeepers in 1998, this number declined year after year to 38.4% of 14.447 peacekeepers in 1999; 18.7% of 37.967 peacekeepers in 2000; 15.4% of 46.957 peacekeepers in 2001; 13.4% of 44.359 peacekeepers in 2002; 12.4% of 38.287 peacekeepers in 2003, 7.4% of 62.307 UN peacekeepers in 2004, and, finally 6,2 % of 68.513 peacekeepers in 2005.

A third demonstration of this downward slope concerns the list of the largest UN peacekeeping troop contributors.[95] In 1998, four of the current EU Member States

[93] As of May 2005, available at <http://www.un.org/Depts/dpko/dpko/contributors/2004/>.

[94] Data collected from Global Policy Forum <http://www.globalpolicy.org/security/peacekpg/data/> and DPKO <http://www.un.org/Depts/dpko/dpko/contributors/>. Data 2001-2005 are collected for the month of September, data 1996-2000 for the month of October.

[95] Data collected from Global Policy Forum <http://www.globalpolicy.org/security/peacekpg/data/>.

Percentage of EU troops in United Nations peace-keeping operations
in terms of military observers, civilian police and troops

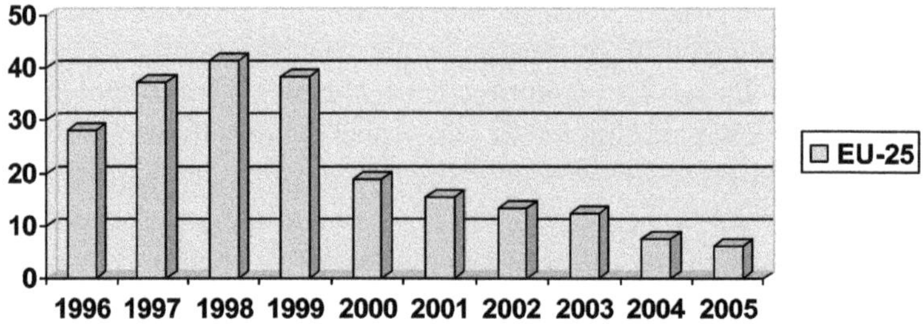

were among the top ten contributors, notably Poland (first), Austria (third), Finland (fifth) and Ireland (sixth). As of 2000, only Poland made it to the top ten. Since 2002, no European country has reached the top ten list. Prominent among the new donors are developing countries such as Bangladesh, Ghana, India, Nigeria and Pakistan. Pakistan for example, provided 9.880 troops in May 2005, thereby doubling the total EU-25 contribution.

Sadly enough, the EU seems to have joined the ranks of Russia and the United States, two countries with unmatched capabilities but lacking genuine commitment to UN peacekeeping (contributions in 2004: 365 United States personnel, 332 Russian personnel). Few EU Member States have demonstrated a true commitment to DPKO over the past five years. Among the exceptions are Poland, Ireland, Austria, Slovakia, Sweden, Finland and Portugal.

5.1.2 *The European response*

In response to these allegations, EU Member States argue that they contribute by far the most troops to other peace missions under the authority of the Security Council, thereby referring to the preponderance of European personnel in both SFOR in Bosnia-Herzegovina and KFOR in Kosovo. Non-UN-led operations indeed account for a much larger part of the European troops abroad than actual UN peacekeeping missions. As of June 15 2004 for example, ISAF counted 4.223 personnel from 22 different EU Member States, or 65.3% of the total mission strength,[96] exceeding the total amount of EU personnel in current UN peacekeeping operations. Moreover, in July 2003, the EU-15 provided 6.211 personnel to the Stabilization Force in Bosnia-Herzegovina (now taken over by operation Althea) and 16.173 personnel to the Kosovo Force (KFOR), or respectively 53% and 69% of the total mission strength. Finally, one should not forget that several EU Member States have engaged intensively in national or multinational peacekeeping and peacemak-

[96] NATO fact sheet available at <http://www.nato.int/issues/afghanistan/040628-factsheet.htm#troop_contributions>.

ing abroad, especially with regard to their former colonies (cf. the UK sent troops to Sierra Leone from 2000 to 2002; France sent troops to Côte d'Ivoire in 2004; Portugal sent troops to East-Timor in 2006).

Still, this argument is not wholly convincing. A glance at the annual 'Allied Contributions to the Common Defence' for example, published by the American Department of Defence, shows a rather conflicting image.[97] Besides the obvious finding that EU participation in UN operations has declined drastically, this publication also demonstrates that the total EU personnel contributions to multinational peace operations (whether UN-led or not) have diminished as well. Thus in 2000, the United States' European Allies provided 44.611 troops to multinational peace operations worldwide. This figure dropped to 41.986 in 2001, 33.659 in 2002, and no more than 22.812 in 2003. These numbers must be dealt with cautiously, as they only cover EU Member States that are also Member States of NATO, i.e., the following countries: Belgium, the Czech Republic, Denmark, France, Germany, Greece, Hungary, Italy, Luxembourg, the Netherlands, Poland, Portugal, Spain and the United Kingdom. Moreover, the figures for 2004 and 2005 have not yet been released. Contributions of those EU Member States that joined NATO throughout 2004 are therefore not included. Neither do the results cover the substantial amount of European troops currently active in Iraq. Estimates of August 2006 indeed suggested that coalition troops in Iraq included some 12.000 European personnel from 9 Member States (8.500 of which originate from the United Kingdom).[98] Still, these figures cover all the largest EU Member States. They contradict the suggestion that the swift development of European military and civilian capabilities has led to a significant broader share in peacekeeping and peacemaking. The reality of EU troop contribution is thus not wholly reconcilable with the European Security Strategy's declaration that:

> 'The increasing convergence of European interests and the strengthening of mutual solidarity of the EU makes us a more credible and effective actor. Europe should be ready to share in the responsibility for global security and in building a better world'.

5.1.3 *Evaluation*

These observations lead to two concerns about the emergence of EU crisis management capabilities. Firstly, some States and UN officials fear that the ESDP will only serve egocentric or 'eurocentric' purposes, concentrating on Europe's own neighbourhood. This fear has been proven wrong as a result of Operation Artemis, AMM, EUFOR RD Congo as well as some smaller operations such as EUPOL

---

[97] United States Department of Defence, '2004 Statistical Compendium on Allied Contributions to the Common Defence', available at <http://www.defenselink.mil/pubs/allied.html>.

[98] 'Iraq coalition troops. Non-US forces in Iraq – 23 August 2006', available at <http://www.globalsecurity.org/military/ops/iraq_orbat_coalition.htm>.

KINSHASA, EUJUST LEX and EU BAM Rafah. By conducting operations both in Europe, Africa, Asia and the Middle East, the European Union has indeed demonstrated its commitment to peace and security in other parts of the world.[99] Especially with regard to the African continent, the EU has time and again affirmed its willingness to contribute to the prevention and resolution of violent conflicts, in particular through enhanced dialogue with and support for the AU and sub-regional organizations.[100]

Secondly, the UN is concerned that the EU crisis management policy might be developed at the expense of EU contributions to UN peace operations.[101] Three aspects can be discerned; troop contributions, mission control and EU policy on UN mandates. The preferences of the UN are obvious: 1) the EU should only undertake enforcement action after obtaining a UN mandate,[102] 2) the EU should preferably participate in UN peacekeeping operations (by augmenting troop contributions to DPKO), instead of creating EU-led operations; 3) finally, undertaking EU-led operations, close EU-UN coordination should be ensured. Whether these wishes will be fulfilled remains to be seen.

As regards enforcement action, the EU has not spelled out a clear policy on obtaining UN mandates. Documents such as the European Security Strategy only refer to 'conformity with the Charter of the United Nations'. EU practice suggests that a UN mandate will be sought, except for non-coercive operations carried out in Europe.[103] However, one should not forget that many EU Member States took part in the unauthorized NATO-operation Allied Force in 1999. The EU's ambivalent posture in relation to humanitarian intervention is furthermore evident from the submission to the High-level Panel on Threats, Challenges and Change.[104] On the one hand, this document declares that: 'the EU is of the view that military action going beyond the lawful exercise of the right to self-defence should be taken on the basis of Security Council decisions'. On the other hand, it states that 'there is a need

[99] C.F. Arnould, loc. cit., *supra* n. 89.

[100] See, e.g., Council Common Position 2004/85/CFSP of 26 January 2004 concerning conflict prevention, management and resolution in Africa and repealing Common Position 2001/374/CFSP, OJ (28 January 2004), L-21/25; Political and Security Committee, 'Action Plan for ESDP support to Peace and security in Africa', Brussels, 16 November 2004, Doc. 10538/4/04 REV 4.

[101] T. Tardy, 'Limits and opportunities of UN-EU relations in peace operations: implications for DPKO', GCSP External Study, September 2003, available at <http://www.gcsp.ch/e/about/News/Faculty-articles/Academic-articles/Tardy_UN_EU_Peac_Ops.pdf>, at p. 8.

[102] See for example the foreword of UN Under-Secretary-General for Peacekeeping Operations Jean-Marie Guéhenno in M. Ortega (ed.), *The European Union and the United Nations: partners in effective multilateralism*, EU-ISS Chaillot Paper No. 78, June 2005, available at <http://www.iss-eu.org/chaillot/chai78.pdf>, pp. 7-12, at p. 9: 'I believe that the starting point (...) is recognition that effective multilateralism builds on legitimacy. (...) UN Security Council authorization should ideally be sought for any operation carried out by regional organizations. This recommendation in fact goes beyond the Charter, which only requires authorization for forceful action.'

[103] Loc. cit., *supra* n. 101, at pp. 9-10.

[104] General Affairs and External Relations Council, 'Paper for the submission to the High-Level Panel on Threats, Challenges and Change', 17-18 May 2004, at p. 12.

to clarify the international principles that would authorize, in exceptional circumstances, outside intervention in the territory of a sovereign country to prevent a humanitarian catastrophe'.

As regards troop contributions, the figures listed above leave no doubt that EU Member States prefer participating in EU-led or NATO-led operations rather than submitting troops to UNDPKO. Despite the *Brahimi* Report and its follow-up,[105] EU Member States are still influenced by the Srebrenica fiasco and continue to perceive the UN Secretariat as incapable of adequately leading multinational operations.[106] This makes it all the more remarkable that EU Member States agreed to provide the bulk of troops for a beefed up UNIFIL presence in Southern Lebanon following the Israeli intervention in July 2006.[107] For Belgium, for example, this marked the first substantial participation in a UN operation since ten Belgian blue helmets were murdered in Rwanda in 1994. Should the present UNIFIL mission prove to be a success, this might well lead to a more positive attitude of EU Member States *vis-à-vis* participation in UN missions in the future.

The idea that the UN will be allowed to play a substantial role in EU-led operations is improbable. This is especially true for military operations, where the EU Political and Security Committee (PSC) exercises 'political control and strategic direction' of the EU's military response to the crisis.[108] But also with regard to civilian crisis management operations, 'autonomy of action' is stressed as one of the core concepts.[109] UN consultation in EU-led peacekeeping operations will most likely remain limited to informal contacts. For EU-led peace enforcement operations, direct reporting by the CFSP High Representative to the Security Council – as was done during Operation Artemis – is likely to be repeated. However, from a legal perspective, one may wonder whether this practice is sufficient, given that the Security Council must at all times retain overall control of enforcement operations.[110] But even with regard to peacekeeping, informal and improvised contacts are hard to bring in line with the original Charter framework, which foresaw that 'regional arrangements or agencies' would only act in relation to their own region – which contrasts strongly with the EU's manifold out-of-area operations – and that they

[105] Follow-up reports available at <http://www.un.org/peace/reports/peace_operations/>.

[106] A. Novosseloff, loc. cit., *supra* n. 76, at p. 8.

[107] The following EU Member States agreed to contribute to UNIFIL: France – 2.000 extra troops; Italy – 2.500-3.000 troops; Spain – one mechanised battalion; Denmark – at least two ships; Poland – 500 troops; Belgium – 400 troops; Finland – 250 troops; Germany – maritime/border patrols. See 'China ups Lebanon force to 1.000', *BBC News*, 18 September 2006.

[108] See 'Political and Security Committee', Annex III to Presidency Report on ESDP, Annex VI to the Council conclusions, Nice European Council, December 2000.

[109] See 'EU cooperation with international organizations in civilian aspects of crisis management', Presidency Report on ESDP, Annex V, Göteborg European Council, June 2001.

[110] See E. De Wet, 'The relationship between the Security Council and Regional Organizations during Enforcement Action under Chapter VII of the United Nations Charter', (2002) 71 *Nordic JIL* at p. 20.

would at all times keep the Security Council fully informed of their activities undertaken for the maintenance of peace and security (Article 54 UN Charter).

In this context, the opportunities and dangers of the EU's capacity in crisis management are illustrative of the arguments raised by proponents and opponents of regional peacekeeping and peace enforcement.[111] On the one hand, regional and similar organizations may dispose of larger resources and greater support to undertake a certain operation. On the other hand, such organizations may lack the experience of UNDPKO and may be perceived as partial or as dominated by a regional hegemon. More fundamentally, they lack the unique legitimacy of the 192-Member United Nations. For this reason, erosion of the UN's primary role in peacekeeping and peacebuilding should be avoided; regional peacekeeping should remain the exception.

5.1.4 *The UN Standby-Arrangement System*

UN officials' reservations about the EU's new crisis management vocation are not entirely unfounded. If the EU wants to support its pledge of commitment with deeds, personnel contributions to UN operations should go up. One potential act of faith would be for the EU to participate in the UN Standby Arrangement System (SBAS).

The Standby Arrangement System is a database of individual states' agreements to provide the UN with specific resources within an agreed timeframe for UN peacekeeping operations.[112] Although actual participation in a particular UN operation remains contingent on national approval, the SBAS facilitates mission planning and actual force generation by giving UNDPKO a precise understanding of available resources and capabilities.

Originally, the SBAS consisted of three conventional levels of commitment: the provision of a list of capabilities; more detailed information in the form of Planning Data Sheets, and; the conclusion of a generic Memorandum of Understanding. States signing up to either of these commitment levels agree to maintain their resources on standby and fully trained. In 2000, a fourth level of readiness – the Rapid Deployment Level (RDL) – was added to indicate resources deployable within 30/90-days of a Council mandate, again with appropriate national approval.[113] According to the most recent status report, some 83 states currently participate in the SBAS, including 13 EU Member States.[114]

---

[111] See, e.g., W. Dorn, 'Regional peacekeeping is not the way', (1998) 27 *Peacekeeping in International Relations*, pp. 1-4; P.F. Diehl, 'Regional alternatives to UN Peacekeeping operations', available at <http://www.acdis.uiuc.edu/Research/S&Ps/1994-Wi-Sp/S&P_VIII-2/regional_alterna tives.html>.

[112] Council for a Livable World Education Fund, 'Developing a rapid deployment capability: an old idea for troubled times', available at <http://www.clw.org/archive/un/rapreac.html>.

[113] W.J. Durch, V.K. Holt, C.R. Earle and M.K. Shanahan, *The Brahimi Report and the future of UN Peace Operations* (Washington DC, Henry L. Stimson Center 2003), at p. 72.

[114] Member States in the UNSAS as of 15 April 2005, information available at <http://www.un.org/Depts/dpko/milad/fgs2/unsas_files/status_report/statusreport15april05.pdf.pdf>.

The SBAS Military Handbook expressly foresees regional or sub-regional participation, stressing this would reduce the response times as well as the costs for the UN.[115] Regional participation in SBAS is moreover recommended by the September Summit Outcome Document.[116] At present, states participating in the SBAS submit mostly infantry.[117] To be effective, the arrangement would need more personnel in the areas of strategic airlift/sealift, communications, multi-role logistics, transport, health services, engineering, mine clearing and transport utility aircraft, as well as more civilian police personnel. EU participation would therefore enable the UN to make proper use of the EU's developing rapid deployment capacity and to tackle some of the present deficiencies in the SBAS framework.

Unfortunately, the aforementioned 'Elements of Implementation' illustrate the lack of enthusiasm for the Standby model.[118] Operations under this Model are considered to be very demanding, as they would require complicated coordination between the EU and the UN, and carry considerable risks. The Council document notes that the Standby Model is of limited usability and would be particularly relevant in an African context. Further analysis under the development of the Battle Group Concept is deemed necessary. Consequently, EU participation in the SBAS is highly unlikely in the near future, and is denounced as 'wishful thinking' by EU officials.

5.2 Other concerns

Apart from reservations concerning the EU commitment to UN peacekeeping, a number of other shortcomings have to be addressed as well. The first of these relates to the wide variety of actors in the ESDP. More than 30 years ago, US Secretary of State Henry Kissinger posed the following question: 'Who do I call when I want to get Europe on the phone'? Despite the emergence of EU-UN meetings on different levels, the same question now puzzles UN officials. The quest for a single EU contact point would partly be resolved if the Treaty establishing a Constitution

---

[115] 'UN SBAS Military Handbook', edition 2003, available at <http://www.un.org/Depts/dpko/milad/fgs2/unsas_files/UNSASHandbook2003.pdf>. Remark: in this regard, mention should be made of the SHIRBIG initiative, created by Denmark in 1995. SHIRBIG, the Standby High Readiness Brigade, is a multinational brigade designed to complement the UNSAS, and to provide approximately 5000 troops, within 15-30 days for up to six months. SHIRBIG, which consists of a Steering Committee, a Planning Element and a Brigade Pool of Forces, was declared available to the UN in January 2000. Since then, it has participated in UN Missions in Ethiopia-Eritrea, in Ivory Coast and in Liberia. As of today, 16 nations have signed on to one or more SHIRBIG documents, with five more nations participating as observers. Although most of them are European states, SHIRBIG is not an EU initiative and also counts members such as Argentina and Canada.

[116] 2005 World Summit Outcome, GA Res. 60/1, 24 October 2005, § 170.

[117] See J. Hule, '81 States ready to join UN peacekeeping system', *Panafrican News Agency*, 2 April 1999.

[118] 'EU-UN Cooperation in Military Crisis Management Operations: Elements of Implementation of the EU-UN Joint Declaration', loc. cit., *supra* n. 82.

for Europe were to enter into force.[119] This Treaty would transform the High Representative for CFSP into the newly created post of EU Minister for Foreign Affairs (Article I-28), with a broader mandate. In the future, the EU Minister for Foreign Affairs would 'conduct the Union's common foreign and security policy'. The signature of the Treaty was therefore rightfully welcomed by the UN Secretary-General as an opportunity to strengthen cooperation between the UN and the EU.[120] In light of the negative outcome of the referenda in France and the Netherlands, however, it is unlikely that the Constitution will ever enter into force in its present form.

A second issue relates to the question of whether the EU should claim the status of a regional organization in the sense of Chapter VIII of the UN Charter. As mentioned before, the Charter does not provide a definition of regional arrangements, thereby enabling organizations to proclaim themselves as such, as was done by the OAS in 1948. In 1990, Boutros-Ghali already hinted at the possible emergence of new regional arrangements in Europe:

> 'efforts of regional agencies should be in harmony with those of the UN and in accordance with the Charter. This applies equally to regional arrangements in all areas of the globe, including those that might emerge in Europe'.[121]

Two important implications would follow from the transformation of the EU into a 'Chapter VIII organization'. On the one hand, the EU would become the primary organization responsible for the pacific settlement of local disputes. The EU would then have to adopt new procedures to secure internal security. Referral to the Security Council would become a last resort. The second difference would be the obligation contained in Article 54 of the Charter to keep the Security Council informed of all activities 'undertaken or in contemplation under regional arrangements or by regional agencies for the maintenance of international peace and security'. The EU's possible transformation had long been an issue of controversy, and is not likely to be solved in the near future. Although such transformation would not cure all problems, it could arguably institutionalize the EU's attachment to the UN and contribute to a more structured and more organized relationship between the UN and other regional organizations.[122]

---

[119] *Treaty establishing a Constitution for Europe*, Rome 29 October 2004, OJ (16 December 2004), C-310/1.

[120] UN News Service, 'New European Constitution should offer chance to boost cooperation with UN – Annan' available at <http://www0.un.org/apps/news/story.asp?NewsID=12397&Cr=European&Cr1=Union>.

[121] Report of the Secretary-General on the Work of the Organization, *Secretary Gen. Rep.* 21, 1990, at p. 21.

[122] J. Wouters and F. Naert, 'Linking global and regional organizations: the Case of the United Nations and the European Union', available at <http://www.kuleuven.ac.be/iir/eng/wp/title.html>, at p. 5.

6. Concluding Remarks

Since 1998, the EU has developed an extensive pool of military and civilian operational capacities. The EU's aspirations to become an autonomous security provider have, moreover, been put to the test in different EU-led operations. Although most of these have been limited in scope and size, and although the operational capacity still suffers from deficiencies in terms of mobility and deployability, this progress can undoubtedly be called a success and can serve as a precedent to develop regional and sub-regional capacities in Africa and elsewhere. Parallel to the development of the ESDP, the European Union and the United Nations have engaged in closer cooperation, for example by installing regular contacts at different levels and establishing a joint consultative mechanism. The UN-EU partnership has also been successfully tested on the operational level during EUPM and Operation Artemis, and, most recently, EUFOR RD Congo. EU crisis management supports UN activities in several ways. It enables peacekeeping or peacemaking when the United Nations itself is not fit for the job. This may be for technical or logistical reasons, for example when rapid deployment capacities are needed. It may also occur when States are reluctant to address the United Nations for political reasons. This was the case with regard to the situation in Aceh: the Indonesian government was reluctant to bring in the UN in order not to internationalize the situation (and raise the Security Council's attention), instead consenting in the deployment of the EU Aceh Monitoring Mission. Secondly, EU-led operations sometimes serve to reinforce UN operations when the going gets rough (as they did in the DRC) or allow the UN to redeploy its assets elsewhere. As mentioned earlier, the latter took place in Bosnia-Herzegovina, when the EU relieved the guard in 2003. A similar exercise seems underway with regard to Kosovo, as the EU is considering a civilian operation to take over from UNMIK in 2007. Finally, the EU provides a crucial contribution to crisis management through its logistical and financial support for regional peacekeeping in Africa. Without such support, the African Union would perhaps not have been able to deploy in the Sudanese Darfur region.

The newborn partnership, flawed as it may yet be, should be encouraged as an example for UN cooperation with other regional and related organizations. In the words of the Irish EU Presidency:

> 'Drawing from our positive experiences (…) we recommend that DPKO expand and deepen its contacts with regional organizations and their sub-regional partners, especially at the working level, in order to identify and implement practical means of tapping this potential for cooperation'.[123]

[123] EU Presidency Statement – United Nations Peacekeeping Operations, 17 May 2004, Statement by H.E. ambassador Richard Ryan.

One concern must nevertheless be emphasized. EU Member States should not consider EU crisis management as an alternative for support for DPKO. Hence, it is vital that EU crisis management is not developed at the expense of the UN. Neither should the EU Member States see financial or logistic assistance to regional organizations, for example through the creation of the African Peace Facility, as an alternative to actual crisis management.

On 14 October 2004, the Secretary-General expressed similar concerns during an address to the National Forum on Europe.[124] In his declaration, Kofi Annan recognized that strengthened EU capacities could make a unique contribution to UN peacekeeping, as the EU is capable of rapid deployment and can provide specialized skills that the largest troop contributors do not possess. Annan nevertheless noted that EU contributions were low, too low; only one in ten UN peace-keepers is from an EU country, in Africa this proportion even drops to less than one in twenty. He therefore warned that the ESDP's development should not mean a weakening of the commitment to provide troops for UN peacekeeping missions, since 'our starting point must be one of commitment to the Charter and solidarity with our fellow men and women, regardless of whether they live in Kosovo or Darfur or Afghanistan or the Congo'.[125] In this respect, the European participation in the reinforced UNIFIL operation is of paramount importance. If the mission goes as planned, this could somewhat ease EU Member States' negative attitudes towards UN command and control, inspiring them to augment contributions to DPKO.

In all, as 'the new kid on the block', the EU should be applauded for the potential realized through the development of the ESDP over recent years. At the same time, EU Member States should take some time to reflect on where the road will lead them. If the European Union really wants to gain credibility as a security provider, it must in any event do more than paying the bill.

---

[124] Secretary-General's address to the National Forum on Europe, 14 October 2004, Dublin, available at <http://www0.un.org/apps/sg/sgstats.asp?nid=1131>.

[125] Ibid.

Chapter 14
EU-UN COOPERATION ON CRISIS MANAGEMENT – PUTTING EFFECTIVE MULTILATERALISM INTO PRACTICE

by Jim Cloos*

1. INTRODUCTION

Relations between the UN and the EU have undergone fundamental changes during recent years. This is due both to changes in the international environment and to internal developments within the EU. The end of the Cold War has made it possible for the UN to play a greater role. Between 1946 and 1990, there were 683 Security Council resolutions; in the fifteen years since then, this number has more than doubled. The multiplication of local crises and wars has increased the relevance of UN interventions, particularly in Africa. As a result, the UN has nearly 80,000 uniformed and civilian personnel deployed in 18 peacekeeping and related field operations. This has, however, stretched the UN peacekeeping capacities to its limits. The UN needs the assets that are required for complex and occasionally robust peacekeeping. More than troops, the UN needs a rapid reaction capacity and 'enabling assets', such as strategic airlift, medical units, intelligence or logistics.

At the same time, the gradual transformation of the European Community into a more political European Union has given it an increased role in foreign policy. The emergence of the European Security and Defence Policy (ESDP) is of particular relevance. The development of the ESDP is in many ways geared towards providing the UN with services in order to help it fulfil its increasing burden.

This article concentrates on crisis management, one of the most important and promising areas of EU-UN cooperation. It first sets out the conceptual background, the EU vision of its role and responsibility in international affairs, and then secondly gives a brief account of a number of aspects related to the development of the concrete EU-UN cooperation in crisis management. Finally, a number of comments are made on the way forward. It is important to underline that crisis management should be seen as part of broader approach. Therefore, the article also touches on a number of other areas where the EU is able to support UN action, ranging from conflict prevention to its multifaceted involvement in the peacebuilding phase.

* Director at the Council General Secretariat. He writes here in a personal capacity.

J. Wouters et al., eds., The United Nations and the European Union

2. The EU Philosophy

The European Security Strategy adopted in December 2003[1] sets out the EU vision of a stronger international society, well functioning international institutions and a rules-based international order. It strongly emphasises the role of the United Nations and states that

> 'the fundamental framework for international relations is the United Nations Charter. The United Nations Security Council has the primary responsibility for the maintenance of international peace and security. Strengthening the United Nations, equipping it to fulfil its responsibilities and to act effectively is a European priority.'[2]

The EU reiterated its strong support of the UN in the conclusions of the European Council on 15-16 December 2005.

The EU is in itself a structure for peace and security in its region. It was created to overcome the legacy of two world wars and to prevent future wars in Europe. The founding idea of the EU was to create a zone of peace built on the voluntary pooling of sovereignty, common institutions and the rule of law. The EU wants to extend this zone of peace and prosperity to its neighbouring countries. One of the most important recent successes of the EU is the enlargement process. Since the fall of the Berlin wall, eight of the countries from the former Soviet-bloc, in addition to Cyprus and Malta, have been integrated in the European Union, committing themselves to the values embodied by the EU.[3] Europe's positive transformative power in its immediate neighbourhood has undoubtedly been a decisive factor for the peaceful system change in Eastern Europe. Seen in this perspective, the recent EU history is a success.

The EU emphasises the same values in wider international relations. Strengthening the international order and the organization that best illustrates these ideals, that is the UN, is a fundamental objective for the EU and its Member States. Building on its own experience, the EU is an active proponent of effective multilateralism. The European Security Strategy states that 'the best protection for our security is a world of well-governed democratic states. Spreading good governance, supporting social and political reform, dealing with corruption and abuse of power, establishing the rule of law and protecting human rights are the best means of strengthening the international order.'[4] These principles also provide the background for the EU new neighbourhood strategy.

The EU, however, does not confine itself to the 'post-modern paradise' of today's Europe. The European Security Strategy acknowledges that there can be a need for

---

[1] *A secure Europe for a better world – European Security Strategy (ESS)*, European Council, 12-13 December 2003, Presidency conclusions, p. 21.

[2] *European Security Strategy*, op. cit. n. 1, at p. 9.

[3] Treaty of Accession, OJ.(23 September 2003) L-236/16.

[4] *European Security Strategy*, op. cit. n. 1, at p. 10.

intervention in other parts of the world where 'pre-modern' states are faced with the threat of collapse, chaos and decomposition. State failure is one of the main concerns addressed in the European Security Strategy. It is an alarming phenomenon, often associated with threats such as organized crime and terrorism. State failure undermines global governance and adds to regional instability. If multilateralism is to be effective, there is a need for crisis management tools and mechanisms to enforce global governance. The European Security Strategy emphasises the need to 'develop a culture that fosters early, rapid and when necessary, robust intervention.'[5] The EU is already putting this into practice. Since the beginning of 2003, the EU has successfully engaged in more than a dozen military or civil ESDP operations in three continents. An important aspect of the EU crisis management capabilities is the close cooperation with the UN.

It should finally be underlined that the EU is completely in line with the comprehensive approach underlying the report of the High Level Panel on Threats, Challenges and Change[6] and supported by Kofi Annan in his report 'In Larger Freedom'[7] as well as by the world's Heads of State and Government in the outcome document adopted at the World Summit on 14-16 September 2005.[8] Kofi Annan eloquently stated that 'we will not enjoy development without security, we will not enjoy security without development, and we will not enjoy either without respect for human rights. Unless all these causes are advanced, none will succeed.'[9] The EU has warmly welcomed this approach, including at the level of Heads of State and Government. The EU-UN cooperation should be seen in this broader perspective. In this context, it is worth mentioning that the EU – the European Community and EU Member States taken together – provides more than half of the Official Development Assistance in the world. In the framework of the 2005 World Summit, the EU has undertaken very substantial commitments to delivering even more and better aid.

3. The UN-EU Cooperation in Crisis Management

The relations between the EU and the UN in the field of crisis management began to develop at a time when the UN was looking at the reform of its peace operations in the framework of the Brahimi report process, which coincided with the laying of the foundations of the ESDP. The UN, confronted with the changing nature of peacekeeping, sought increased support from regional actors. At the same time, the EU started creating crisis management capacities.

---

[5] Ibid., at p. 11.

[6] 'A more secure world: Our shared responsibility', Report of the Secretary-General's High-level Panel on Threats, Challenges and Change, 29 November 2004, UN Doc. A/59/565.

[7] 'In larger freedom: towards development, security and human rights for all', Report of the Secretary-General, 21 March 2005, UN Doc. A/59/2005.

[8] 2005 World Summit Outcome, 24 October 2005, GA Res. A/RES/60/1.

[9] 'In larger freedom', loc. cit. n. 7, at p. 6, para. 17.

The first two ESDP operations in 2003 were successful tests for the EU-UN relationship:

- The EU Police Mission in Bosnia and Herzegovina[10] took over the UN International Police Task Force in a seamless transition, thanks to close cooperation in the planning phase.
- Operation Artemis was a rapid EU military deployment in support of the UN mission in the Democratic Republic of Congo (MONUC),[11] at the UN's request and under a UN mandate.[12] EU and UN activities were intimately linked throughout the planning and the deployment of the operation. The EU intervention in Ituri, strictly limited in time, allowed the UN to strengthen MONUC and to expand its mandate.

These examples of cooperation on the ground were a major breakthrough in the relations between the two institutions. It forced them to work together on the ground and to get a better knowledge of each other's working methods. A framework for regular consultation between the two organizations was set-up by the September 2003 'Joint Declaration on UN-EU Cooperation in Crisis Management'[13] which identified four areas for further cooperation: *planning*, *training*, *communication*, and *best practices*. A consultative mechanism, the Steering Committee, was established to enhance coordination in these areas between the UN (in particular DPKO and DPA) and EU staff (Council Secretariat and Commission). The Steering Committee meets twice a year. This is a quite novel approach, lending a new quality to the relationship between the UN and the EU.

The new relationship with the UN has without any doubt stimulated and energized the EU efforts at improving its crisis management capacity. Two further developments will further enhance this capacity. The first relates to the setting up in Brussels of a civil-military cell with the aim of improving the overall planning capacity in an integrated fashion. The second concerns the creation of some 18 'battle-groups, i.e., battalion-sized forces of 1,500 troops, fully equipped, rapidly deployable, with force headquarters, pre-identified logistics and transport elements.

4. THE WAY FORWARD

After a very promising start the time has now come to consolidate the work done and to move to a higher level. There are seven concrete lines of action that I would like to advocate.

---

[10] Council Joint Action 2002/210/CFSP of 11 March 2002, OJ (13 March 2002) L-70/1.

[11] Council Joint Action 2003/423/CFSP of 5 June 2003, OJ (11 June 2003) L-143/50.

[12] SC Res. 1484 of 30 May 2003.

[13] Joint Declaration on UN-EU Cooperation in Crisis Management, New York, 24 September 2003, available at <http://europa-eu-un.org/articles/lt/article_2768_lt.htm>.

First, we should develop the Steering Committee approach and continue to work on all four priorities identified in the 2003 declaration. The recently concluded agreement on exchange of classified information and the deployment of an EU military liaison officer to the Council's New York Liaison Office will further facilitate cooperation.

Second, lessons identified from operations and modalities underlying the possible scenarios will have to be looked at. Issues such as the information-sharing mechanisms in pre-deployment phases, the compatibility of standards and rules of engagement, the re-hatting of EU forces into an UN operation by individual nations, the possible double-hatting of the Head of the mission, the financing of operations, the recourse to joint participation and evaluation missions all need to be examined in detail. These issues are necessary conditions for smooth transitions between EU and UN deployments.

Third, it will be important to examine in a very pragmatic way how the EU battle groups or other rapid reaction forces can be used to respond to UN demands. The latter refer to concepts such as 'reserve force', 'over-the-horizon standby force', 'enhanced rapid deployable forces'. The EU is ready to look into these demands, but with two very clear conditions: the EU will always insist on its political autonomy and on an EU chain of command, with the political and the strategic control being exercised by the Political and Security Committee. The EU cannot guarantee a decision that ultimately depends on national decisions to provide troops. The recent debate in Germany about assuming a lead role for the setting-up of a mission to support the election in the DRC underscores this point. This mission provides an interesting illustration of an innovative EU contribution following a UN request.

Fourth, the 'EU Strategy for Africa' adopted at the meeting of the European Council on 15-16 December 2005[14] will be an important framework for much of the work involving the African continent. It is a comprehensive strategy, based on shared values and agreed UN principles, which includes development, security and human rights. Covering all African countries, it entails a prioritised approach aiming at the promotion of peace and security and sustainable economic and social development in Africa. The Strategy sets out a medium and long-term perspective, including measures to be taken during the next 10 years. It also foresees the continuation of the highly successful Africa Peace Facility mechanism.

Fifth, one of the promising areas for EU-UN cooperation is assistance to regional organizations such as the African Union in order strengthen their crisis management capacity. As current examples show in Congo or Sudan, there is scope for an intensified UN/EU/AU cooperation. In Darfur, the EU, working in close coopera-

[14] Brussels European Council, Presidency conclusions, 15-16 December 2005, p. 2.

tion with the UN and other partners such as Canada and the United States, has consistently supported the AU AMIS mission in terms of financing (via the Africa Peace Facility), planning and command structures. Work is presently ongoing to prepare smooth transition from AMIS to an UN operation. The case of the DRC shows how a variety of EU missions have helped the UN (MONUC) to stabilize the situation and to support the transition process to a political settlement: ARTEMIS as a quick response and a bridging operation, EUPOL Kinshasa for police training, EUSEC Congo for security sector reform, and a chain of payment project to ensure effective payment of the reformed armed forces. The election support mission mentioned above will be another important contribution in that respect.

Sixth, our organizations should develop their efforts to look together at crisis management as a continuum involving conflict prevention, military and civil peace-keeping and peace building. It is important to develop both a comprehensive and coherent approach, involving civil and military aspects. In this regard, the concept of integrated missions is very promising: EU operations are planned in an integrated way both from a military and civilian perspective, so that post-conflict reconstruction is taken into account from the start. This integrated approach is in line with UN thinking, in particular the Brahimi report and the setting up of the Peacebuilding Commission (PBC). As mentioned above, the EU has already established a civil-military cell[15] in order to strengthen the coherence between military and civilian components in operations.

Finally, the setting-up of a PBC[16] will further strengthen the efforts to ensure a comprehensive approach. The PBC will fill the present gap between the end of peace-keeping operations and the return to the path of development. The EU is presently looking into ways of improving its contributions to Security Sector Reform (SSR) and Disarmament, Demobilisation and Reintegration (DDR) in order to assist in the transition from peacekeeping to peacebuilding, areas that fall within the PBC's future area of responsibility. The establishment of the PBC has consistently been an EU priority, and the EU intends to participate constructively and actively through an integrated approach, taking into account both crisis management tools and longer term development aid. The EC has every intention to provide support to the Peacebuilding Fund that will be set-up.

5. Conclusion

Crisis management, both military and civilian, has become a major new element in UN-EU relations. We have gone a long way since the first contacts of the year

[15] Brussels European Council, Presidency conclusions, 17-18 June 2004, p. 20.
[16] GA Res. 60/180 of 20 December 2005 and SC Res. 1645 of 20 December 2005.

2000, moving from an *ad hoc* dialogue to a structured cooperation. This cooperation has begun to yield good results in terms of knowledge of respective functioning and activities, as well as in terms of an institutionalised yet un-bureaucratic framework for practical cooperation. None of the relationships between the UN and the other regional organizations has gone as far as the UN-EU relationship – even though the EU is not a traditional regional organization in the sense of Chapter VIII of the UN Charter. This cooperation offers promising prospects. We need to think both operationally and strategically about our relations. The EU is willing to take a pro-active approach and remain a front-runner in both regards.

Chapter 15
THE EUROPEAN SECURITY STRATEGY: CONFIRMING THE CHOICE FOR COLLECTIVE AND COMPREHENSIVE SECURITY

by Sven Biscop and Edith Drieskens*

1. Introduction

In this chapter, we focus on the conceptual convergence in EU-UN security thinking, as manifested by the European Security Strategy (ESS). We will first discuss the genesis of this document, starting by recalling its policy context. We will then turn to the substance of the document, in which the EU Member States expressed their attachment to effective multilateralism, including by confirming their choice for a collective and comprehensive definition of international security. Our focus on both these dimensions will lead to our conclusion.

2. A Security Strategy for the European Union

The EU's Common Foreign and Security Policy (CFSP) is said to have reached its low point in the spring of 2003, when a rift became visible between the opponents and advocates of military intervention in Iraq, controversially described by US Defense Secretary Donald Rumsfeld in terms of the 'old' and 'new' Europe.[1] Symbol of the disunity displayed was the open letter 'United We Stand', which was published in *The Times* on 30 January. By way of this letter, eight European leaders – José María Aznar, José-Manuel Barroso, Silvio Berlusconi, Tony Blair, Vaclav

* Sven Biscop is senior research fellow at the Brussels-based Royal Institute for International Relations (IRRI-KIIB) and Professor of European security at Ghent University (Belgium). Edith Drieskens works as doctoral researcher of the Research Foundation Flanders (FWO-Vlaanderen) at the Institute for International and European Policy at Leuven University (Belgium). Both authors contributed equally to this chapter.

[1] When Rumsfeld was asked at the foreign press corps meeting in Washington on 22 January why Europe was not supporting US policy on Iraq, he answered as follows: 'You're thinking of Europe as Germany and France. I don't. I think that's *old Europe*. If you look at the entire NATO Europe today, the centre of gravity is shifting to the east and there are a lot of new members. The vast numbers of other countries in Europe, they're not with France and Germany, they're with the United States.' [emphasis added].

J. Wouters et al., eds., The United Nations and the European Union

Havel, Peter Medgyessy, Leszek Miller and Anders Fogh Rasmussen[2] – expressed their support for the enforcement of UN Security Council Resolution 1441 and, as a consequence, also for the Bush Administration's Iraq policy. A few days later, on 6 February, the labels 'old' and 'new' Europe gained an additional meaning, when the foreign ministers of the *Vilnius Ten* signed a similar letter of support, despite most of their countries' desire for EU membership.[3] Then President of the European Commission Romano Prodi declared after a special meeting of the European Council on 17 February that Europe was 'united'.[4] Yet, as 18 European governments endorsed US policy, most of them going against their public opinion, the evidence was otherwise.

This open rift not only had repercussions on EU decision-making, but also on the proceedings within NATO and the UN. Belgium, France and Germany broke the *silence procedure* at NATO, because they were not willing to approve the deployment of preventive measures to protect Turkey. They feared that by doing so, they would not only consent with the protection of Turkey, but also with a military campaign against neighbour Iraq. Similarly, at the UN Security Council, France and Germany refused to join the American camp, in contrast to Spain and the United Kingdom who co-sponsored a resolution authorizing military action. While CFSP High Representative Javier Solana was convinced that this poor performance could have been avoided by EU membership of the UN Security Council,[5] Belgian Prime Minister Guy Verhofstadt concluded that a credible EU foreign policy is impossible without a viable defence component. At his invitation, Gerhard Schröder, Jacques Chirac and Jean-Claude Juncker gathered in Brussels on 29 April to give the development of the European Security and Defence Policy (ESDP) a new impulse. To this end, the statement issued afterwards included a number of principles to be incorporated in the *Draft Treaty establishing a Constitution for Europe,* as well as seven concrete initiatives to improve military cooperation.[6] Most (media) attention went, however, to the creation of what was formulated as a 'a nucleus collective capability for planning and conducting operations for the European Union', as this was considered to imply the creation of an EU operational headquarters separate from NATO in the Brussels suburb of Tervuren. Since the United Kingdom was not invited and the Dutch and Italian governments did not show up, for most commentators, the 'Praline Summit' was another indication of a divided European continent.

[2] 'United We Stand', *The Times*, 30 January 2003. At the time, Aznar, Barroso, Berlusconi, Blair, Medgyessy, Miller en Fogh Rasmussen were Prime Minister of respectively Spain, Portugal, Italy, the United Kingdom, Hungary, Poland and Denmark. Havel was president of the Czech Republic.

[3] The *Vilnius Ten* are Albania, Bulgaria, Croatia, Estonia, Latvia, Lithuania, Macedonia, Romania, Slovakia and Slovenia.

[4] Press Conference, Brussels, 17 February 2003.

[5] 'Solana: Einheit Iraks muss erhalten bleiben', *Die Welt*, 24 March 2003.

[6] *Meeting of the Heads of State and Government of Germany, France, Luxemburg and Belgium on European Defence*, Brussels, 29 April 2003.

Developments in the field indicated nevertheless that the Iraq crisis did not mark the end of CFSP/ESDP.[7] Although this was largely overshadowed by the events in Iraq, on 31 March, the EU launched its first military operation, in the Former Republic of Macedonia ('Concordia'), taking over command from NATO. Earlier that year, it had already deployed its first police mission in Bosnia-Herzegovina ('EUPM'). And while France and the United Kingdom clashed in the UN Security Council over the question whether or not military action was justified, at their summit meeting in Le Touquet on 4 February, Chirac and Blair had agreed to take ESDP to a new stage.[8] Moreover, like past crisis situations had turned out to be *cathartic* experiences for European integration in security and defence, also the divisions over Iraq seem to have positively influenced the development of ESDP, by underlining the necessity of a strategic vision and a security strategy, and more specifically, of a definition of the overall policy objectives that could serve as a reference framework for everyday decision-making. While the Iraq crisis underlined the necessity of such strategy, the promising proceedings of the *Convention on the Future of Europe* created a favourable policy context.[9] Indeed, while the EU Member States were divided over Iraq, within the Convention, they agreed on a number of proposals to strengthen the EU's external profile, including the creation of an EU Minister for Foreign Affairs supported by a European External Action Service (EEAS) and EU legal personality.

The ESS was drafted by a small team headed by Solana. Rather unexpectedly, he was mandated to elaborate a 'European strategic concept' at the informal meeting of the EU foreign ministers in Kastellorizo on 3 May. Bailes notes that France, Germany and the United Kingdom pushed the idea of a mandate in an attempt to close the ranks after the Iraq debacle.[10] In June, Solana presented a first draft at the meetings of the External Relations Council (Luxembourg, 16 June) and the European Council (Thessaloniki, 19-20 June), where he was asked to draft an 'EU security strategy' for adoption at the next European Council meeting. In the following months, the text was discussed at expert seminars in Rome (19 September), Paris (6-7 October) and Stockholm (20 October). Deliberations with the Member States and the Commission were also organized. On 12 December, the European Council formally adopted the text – a 14-page document entitled *A Secure Europe in a Bet-*

---

[7] See, for example, Nicole Gnessotto's preface to A. Missiroli, *From Copenhagen to Brussels. European defence: core documents* (Paris, European Union Institute for Security Studies 2003); A. Menon, 'From crisis to catharsis: ESDP after Iraq', 80(4) *International Affairs* (2004), pp. 631-648; D. Dinan, *Ever Closer Union. An Introduction to European Integration* (Houndmills, Basingstoke, Hampshire, Palgrave MacMillan 2004).

[8] *Declaration on Strenghtening European Cooperation in Security and Defence*, Le Touquet, 4 February 2003.

[9] A.J.K. Bailes, *The European Security Strategy. An Evolutionary History* (Stockholm, SIPRI 2005), at p. 10.

[10] Ibid.

ter World and subtitled *European Security Strategy.*[11] Solana was 'warmly congratulated for the work accomplished' and, like the incoming Dutch Presidency, asked to elaborate concrete proposals for its implementation. This follow-up was to focus on four topics, including 'effective multilateralism with the UN at its core'.[12]

From a substantive point of view, the ESS mainly codifies policy praxis, like the Single European Act (1986) did with the framework of European Political Cooperation (EPC). But by way of this document, the development of CFSP/ESDP moved from an *institutional* to a *conceptual* level. Such thinking had been taboo, as it was feared that entering a strategic debate could bring to light differences of opinion between the Member States and paralyse the momentum created by the Franco-British Saint-Malo summit of December 1998. For this reason, the development of ESDP in particular had been focusing on the establishment of structures and institutions. As an exception to the rule, however, the 2001 Belgian EU Presidency suggested that the Paris-based European Union Institute for Security Studies (EUISS) should draft a strategic concept. Because some Member States strongly opposed this idea, the Laeken European Council ended up tasking the EUISS with making an assessment of the capabilities that the EU needs to deal with the crisis scenarios that it could face, and this to inform public opinion.[13] From an operational point of view, the resulting report was a stimulating contribution to the debate on ESDP. Yet, as also stated by Bailes, it refrained from the larger political and institutional questions which are typical of the drafting of a security strategy.[14]

A number of scholars have indicated that, although the Solana paper was renamed a security *strategy*, it is not a strategy according to the strategic studies definition of the term, as it does not connect political objectives to the actual use of force.[15] Indeed, political rather than military considerations are at the basis of the

---

[11] *A Secure Europe in a Better World. European Security Strategy*, Brussels, 12 December 2003. As the ESS is a declaration of the European Council and not a 'common strategy' as defined by Article 13 of the *Treaty on European Union*, it is only politically binding. Toje states here that Robert Cooper, who is said to have actually written the ESS, wanted to sidestep the cumbersome decision-making process typical of common strategies. See A. Toje, 'Europe's Consensus-Expectations Gap' (Munich, Research Note, Centrum for Applied Policy Research 2005), at p. 6.

[12] *Presidency Conclusions*, Brussels European Council, 12-13 December 2003.

[13] The *Presidency Report on European Security and Defence Policy* instructed the EUISS to 'work in particular on a publication on European Defence in the framework of the Petersberg tasks'. The resulting report was published in May 2004. See European Institute for Security Studies, *European Defence. A Proposal for a White Paper* (Paris, European Institute for Security Studies 2004).

[14] A.J.K. Bailes, op.cit., *supra* n. 9, see notes 26 and 54.

[15] See, for instance, Basil Henry Liddell Hart's often-cited definition: 'the art of distributing and applying military means to fulfill the ends of policy'. See B.H. Liddell Hart, *Strategy: the indirect approach* (London, Faber and Faber 1967), at p. 335. See, for instance, also A. Toje, 'The 2003 European Union Security Strategy: A Critical Appraisal', 10(1) *European Foreign Affairs Review* (2005), at pp. 120-121; S. Everts, L. Freedman, C. Grant, D. Heisbourg, D. Keohane and M. O'Hanlon, *A European Way of War* (London, Centre for European Reform 2004); S. Duke, 'The European Security Strategy in a Comparative Framework: Does it make for Secure Alliances in a Better World', 9(4) *European Foreign Affairs Review* (2004) pp. 459-481.

objectives set. The text only refers explicitly to the use of military force with regard to failed states, saying that 'military instruments may be needed to restore order'. In addition, 'military assets and effective policing may be needed in the post conflict stage' in case of regional conflicts. Furthermore, although it reaffirms the transatlantic relationship, the ESS does not make real choices on its nature, while some authors argue that this was exactly the issue at stake in the spring of 2003.[16] Categorising the Solana paper as a *strategy* was nevertheless important as to give an apposite answer to the US National Security Strategy (NSS), which had been released by the Bush Administration in September of the previous year.[17] More importantly, in the broader, public management meaning of the term, the ESS can be considered a strategy. Starting from the security threats facing the EU, it outlines the long-term policy objectives and the instruments that can be applied to achieve them. By confirming collective and comprehensive security as guiding principles for the use of force, it could indeed serve as a reference framework for day-to-day policy-making, defining also the legitimacy of actions and leading the development of capabilities within the EU.

3. The Choice for Collective Security

The ESS starts from the idea that 'as a union of 25 states with over 450 million people producing a quarter of the world's Gross National Product (GNP), and with a wide range of instruments at its disposal, the European Union is inevitably a global player'. For this reason, it should be ready 'to share in the responsibility for global security and in building a better world'. As indicated above, by defining its security identity in this way, the EU not only intended to close ranks, it also aimed to send a clear political message to the US government, namely that despite the fact that some of its Member States had turned away during the Iraq crisis, it should still be seen as a credible partner that considers the transatlantic relationship of paramount importance:

> 'The transatlantic relationship is irreplaceable. Acting together, the European Union and the United States can be a formidable force for good in he world. Our aim should be an effective and balanced partnership with the USA. This is an additional reason for the EU to build up further its capabilities and increase its coherence'.

By calling the proliferation of weapons of mass destruction (WMD) 'potentially the greatest threat' and terrorist groupings acquiring such weapons the 'most frightening scenario', the ESS recognised the US security agenda as defined by the NSS.

---

[16] See, for instance, Nicole Gnessotto's preface in A. Missiroli, op.cit., *supra* n. 7, at pp. 9-10.
[17] *The National Security Strategy of the United States of America,* September 2002.

Besides terrorism and the proliferation of WMD, the EU is said to face threats linked to regional conflicts, state failure and organized crime. Addressing these threats is seen as a strategic objective, next to 'building security in our neighbourhood', and 'an international order based on effective multilateralism'. Recognizing that geography remains important also in an era of globalisation, the EU aims to extend the zone of security in a Southern and Eastern direction by promoting 'a ring of well governed countries' with whom it enjoys close and cooperative relationships. Moreover, a world of global threats, markets and media requires a 'stronger international society', with well 'functioning institutions and a rule-based international order'. An international order based on effective multilateralism with the UN at its core is the aim here: 'Strengthening the United Nations, equipping it to fulfil its responsibilities and to act effectively, is a European priority'.

As the threat analysis was similar, but the suggested approach different, both the EU Member States supporting and opposing US policy on Iraq could find something to suit them within the document that Solana presented. Indeed, in contrast to the US, the EU supports a *multilateral* approach of the threats defined, based on international law and institutions. While the NSS puts the UN in the same category with the WTO, the OAS and NATO, and mentions it merely as a partner for rebuilding Afghanistan, the ESS sees the UN as the 'fundamental framework for international relations'. If for the US, the UN seems to be a forum which *could* be used, especially if it serves its national interest, for the EU it *should* be used, as a matter of principle. Because it has been trying to counterbalance the selective interpretation that the Bush Administration has given to the notion of multilateralism, including by putting it forward as both a means and an end in policy documents like the ESS, authors like Jorgensen have been writing here that the EU has been on a *rescue mission,* with the aim of putting multilateralism back on track.[18] Most of them explain this by saying that multilateralism is an inherent part of European integration, referring to the creation of the EU as a cooperation project between European states with the aim of preventing another major war.

Some scholars argue that by placing the threats first in the discussion of the strategic objectives – in the Thessaloniki draft they came last – the EU once more tried to appease the US government. Yet, in comparison with the Thessaloniki draft, the analysis of the security environment has been extended and toned down.[19] As it put a stronger emphasis on the dangers of terrorism and WMD, the Thessaloniki

[18] K.E. Jorgensen, 'A multilateralist role for the EU?', in O. Elgström and M. Smith (eds.), *European Union's Roles in International Politics. Concepts and analysis* (London, New York, Routledge 2006) at pp. 30-46; K.E. Jorgensen, 'Intersecting Multilateralisms: The European Union and Multilateral Institutions', in K. Smith and K. Laatikainen (eds.), *Intersecting Multilateralisms: The European Union and the United Nations* (Houndmills, Basingstoke, Hampshire, Palgrave Macmillan 2006), at pp. 195-211.

[19] S. Biscop, 'The European Security Strategy. Implementing a Distinctive Approach to Security', 82 *Sécurity et Stratégie* (2004), at pp. 15-18.

draft was much more in keeping with the NSS than the text that was finally approved. The latter no longer makes a distinction between 'old' and 'new' terrorism. The proliferation of WMD is no longer seen as 'the single most important', but rather as 'potentially the greatest' threat. A sentence saying that deterrence would fail against small groups having acquired WMD was deleted. Moreover, while the NSS sees terrorism purely as an external threat, the ESS recognizes that Europe is 'both a target and a base'. In addition, in the final version of the text, state failure and organized crime have become separate entries in the list of threats and regional conflicts have been added. Also, more attention is paid to the negative effects of globalisation, like poverty, disease and global warming.

Although these threats are 'more diverse, less visible and less predictable' than the 'large-scale aggression' that faced the EU Member States in the past, they are considered to require a powerful attitude and a 'strategic culture that fosters early, rapid, and when necessary, robust intervention'. Observers have been focusing here on the fact that in comparison to the text discussed in Thessaloniki, the notion of 'pre-emptive engagement' was replaced by, some say watered down to, 'preventive engagement', to be understood in terms of 'conflict prevention and threat prevention'. Nevertheless, the ESS also stresses that the EU should be 'ready to provide assistance' to make sure that countries that have placed themselves outside the bounds of the international society rejoin it. Those unwilling to do so should understand that there is 'a price to be paid', including in 'their relationship with the EU'. The same line should be followed at the international level. As it states that international organizations, regimes and treaties can only be effective if the EU is 'ready to act when their rules are broken', for the EU, 'effective multilateralism' seems to imply *enforceable* multilateralism.

Although the ESS confirms that the UN Security Council has the 'primary responsibility for the maintenance of international peace and security', it does not explicitly require that the EU or its Member States should seek a mandate from the UN Security Council to legitimate military action. One could see this as an illustration of the fact that the EU rather than the UN sets the agenda for EU-UN security cooperation and that there is, as pointed out by Tardy, a divide between what the UN wants and the EU is willing to offer.[20] Indeed, while the UN wants the EU to abide by its rules as a matter of principle, making its operations dependent upon a resolution from the UN Security Council, the EU Member States seem reluctant to give up their *autonomy* and *visibility* and to condition their actions to the decision-making dynamics within this framework, especially to a veto of Russia and China.[21] However, past practice learns that they consider such a resolution a *conditio sine*

[20] T. Tardy, 'EU-UN cooperation in peacekeeping: a promising relationship in a constrained environment', in M. Ortega (ed.), *The European Union and the United Nations. Partners in Effective Multilateralism* (Paris, European Union Institute for Security Studies, Chaillot Paper 78, 2005), at pp. 49-50.

[21] T. Tardy, *Limits and Opportunities of UN-EU Relations in Peace Operations: Implications for DPKO* (Geneva, Geneva Center for Security Studies 2003), at pp. 7-10.

qua non for coercive operations as defined by Chapter VII of the UN Charter as well as for missions outside the European continent. So, even if the wording of the ESS leaves room for a military intervention without a mandate of the UN Security Council – the so-called *Kosovo scenario*, this should be seen as an exception to the rule. This might also explain why the *EU Strategy against Proliferation of Weapons of Mass Destruction*, which was adopted at the same European Council meeting, explicitly refers to the UN Security Council as 'the final arbiter on the consequences of non-compliance'.[22] Here, 'coercive measures under Chapter VII of the UN Charter and international law', including 'the use of force', could be considered when political and diplomatic instruments fail. This message of what Haine calls *soft power plus* can also be seen as a message to the US government: the EU recognizes that an 'effective multilateralist response' may include the use of force, but as a last resort.[23] In such cases, the UN Security Council should play 'a central role'.

In the following months, the EU made this commitment to *collective security* explicit through its contribution to the proceedings of the *High-Level Panel on Threats, Challenge and Change*. This panel of eminent persons was set-up following Kofi Annan's address to the UNGA on 23 September 2003 and finished its proceedings in early December 2004. It was instructed to recommend clear and practical measures for ensuring effective collective responses to common security problems and challenges. In May 2004, the EU submitted the *EU Paper for Submission to the HLP on Threats, Challenges and Change.*[24] In this contribution, the EU confirmed its adherence to the principle of effective multilateralism, stating that 'multilateralism alone is no guarantee of an effective response' and 'collective tools and collective will to use them must be built together'. Here, the UN Charter remains 'the basis for any legitimate response to threats to international peace and security'. More specifically, in view of the EU, it should remain for the UN Security Council, in accordance with its primary responsibility for the maintenance of international peace and security, 'to decide on the appropriate response to the risks in any situation that is brought to its attention, and to form a judgment on the appropriate course of action in any given situation'. The UN Security Council should resort to military intervention only if, 'in its judgment', 'there are no other valid options'. This may be the case when a state is 'unwilling or unable to deal with the threat posed by a non-state actor on its territory'. In other words, without explicitly saying that a mandate from the UN Security Council is necessary in order to ensure the *legality* and *legitimacy* of every crisis management operation they might start, by entrusting this multilateral forum with the decision on the use of force, the EU

[22] *EU Strategy against Proliferation of Weapons of Mass Destruction*, Brussels, 12 December 2003.

[23] J. Haine, 'Venus without Mars: Challenges Ahead for ESDP', in S. Biscop (ed.), *Audit of European Strategy* (Brussels, IRRI-KIIB, Egmont Paper 3, 2004), at pp. 18-27.

[24] *Paper for Submission to the High-Level Panel on Threats, Challenges and Change,* Brussels, 17-18 May 2004. The EU also submitted a second, confidential paper, which is said to be more operational in nature.

Member States have been confirming their adherence to the notion of collective security in various strategic documents in the aftermath of the Iraq crisis.[25]

4. The Choice for Comprehensive Security

In its report, the High-Level Panel wrote that the UN needs a 'new security consensus', based on a 'comprehensive vision of collective security'.[26] Unlike in the early years of the UN, the threats we face today, as well as in the decades ahead, 'go far beyond states waging aggressive war'. They originate from 'non-state actors' as well as 'states' and they endanger 'state security' as well as 'human security'. Moreover, they are interconnected. In the same vein, UN Secretary-General Kofi Annan recognized in the report he presented on 21 March 2005 that present-day threats include not just war and conflict, but also poverty, deadly infectious diseases and environmental degradation: security ('freedom from fear'), development ('freedom from want') and human rights ('freedom to live in dignity') are interrelated.[27] By integrating the politico-military dimension of security in this kind of framework, Annan too subscribed to the *holistic* or *comprehensive* approach to security that the EU has been following for years. This is not to say that the European members of the High-Level Panel (Robert Badinter and David Hannay) or the EU documents submitted have dominated UN proceedings.[28] Because of the secret nature of these proceedings, it is, at least for an outsider, not possible to conclude whether this was the case. However, as the approach presented strongly resembled the traditional EU one, it was no surprise that the EU leaders at their European Council meeting of 20 and 21 March 2003 called Annan's report a 'prime contribution' to the preparations of the UN Millennium Review Summit later that year.[29]

Although it already inspired the drafters of the UN Charter, the notion of comprehensive security was put on the forefront by the CSCE/OSCE during the Cold War period. At a time when it was primarily defined in military terms, the 1975 Helsinki Final Act broadened the concept of security by dividing it in three baskets: politico-military aspects of security; cooperation in matters relating to economy,

---

[25] For this interpretation of collective security, see J.G. Ruggie, 'Multilateralism: the Anatomy of an Institution', 46(3) *International Organization* (1992), pp. 561-598.

[26] *A more secure world: Our shared responsibility, Report of the Secretary-General's High-level Panel on Threats, Challenges and Chang*e, 2 December 2004.

[27] *In Larger Freedom: towards Development, Security and Human Rights for All, Report of the Secretary-General*, 21 March 2005. Annan was asked to report on the implementation of the Millennium Declaration in preparation of the *Millennium Review Summit* of September 2005.

[28] S. Biscop and E. Drieskens, 'Effective Multilateralism and Collective Security: Empowering the UN', in K. Smith and K. Laatikainen (eds.), *Intersecting Multilateralisms: The European Union and the United Nations* (Houndmills, Basingstoke, Hampshire, Palgrave Macmillan 2006), pp. 115-132.

[29] *Presidency Conclusions,* Brussels European Council, 20 and 21 March 2003.

science, technology and the environment; and human rights and freedoms.[30] According to the CSCE/OSCE's comprehensive definition, economic and social progress, environmental protection and human rights are essential building blocks of (state) security. Yet, as also noted by Dunday, the distinctiveness of the OSCE's security approach has been crumbling in recent years.[31] Organizations with no or little relevance during the Cold War period have been entering the field, including the EU and the Council of Europe, while organizations like NATO, which had been addressing security threats in a traditional politico-military way, decided to broaden their scope. As a result, today the European continent is a patchwork of geographically and functionally overlapping security organizations.[32] Within this framework, the EU has become a *trendsetter*, promoting not only the reaffirmation of a comprehensive approach to security, but also translating it into actual policy-making and integrated civil-military structures.[33] In what follows, we apply the notion of global public goods (GPGs) to conceptualise the comprehensive notion of security which underlies the ESS.[34] This way, we define effective multilateralism in terms of effective global governance, and more specifically, in terms of ensuring access to GPGs.

The notion of GPGs was put to the forefront by Kaul, Grunberg and Stern in their 1999 publication on *Global Public Goods*.[35] Supported by the UN Development Programme (UNDP), this volume was written with the aim of taking the concept of public goods 'across the national level'. In many public policy areas, the issues that had been considered national, 'spilled across borders' and were 'global in reach and impact'. In line with what *Human Development Reports* had been indicating, the contributors argued that trans-border threats require 'a new framework for international cooperation', of which the theory of GPGs would be an 'essential part'. GPGs are defined as *public* goods – goods that are *non-rival* in consumption and *non-excludable* – with benefits that are strongly *universal* in terms of countries, people and generations.[36]

Already in its first paragraph, the ESS recognizes that not everybody enjoys the benefits of globalisation to the same extent. The process of globalisation has not

---

[30] F. Evers, M. Kahl and W. Zellner, *The Culture of Dialogue. The OSCE Acquis 30 Years after Helsinki* (Hamburg, Centre for OSCE Research 2005).

[31] P. Dunday, *The OSCE in crisis* (Paris, European Institute for Security Studies, Chaillot Paper 88, 2006)

[32] S. Biscop, 'The EU, the OSCE and the European Security Architecture: Network or Labyrinth?', paper paper presented at the *Helsinki Monitor Conference: OSCE's Future after 30 Years*, Vienna, 9 September 2005.

[33] S. Biscop, *The European Security Strategy – A Global Agenda for Positive Power* (Aldershot, Ashgate Publishing 2005).

[34] S. Biscop and R. Coolsaet, *The World is the Stage – A Global Security Strategy for the European Union* (Paris, Notre Europe 2003).

[35] I. Kaul, I. Grunberg and M.A. Stern, *Global Public Goods. International Cooperation in the 21st Century* (Oxford, Oxford University Press 1999).

[36] Ibid., at pp. 2-3.

only generated insiders but also outsiders. Or, in terms of access to GPGs, it has generated *haves* as well as *have nots*: '[f]lows of trade and investment, the development of technology and the spread of democracy have brought freedom and prosperity to many people', while others see globalization as 'a cause of frustration and injustice'. To deal with this growing gap, the ESS suggests a comprehensive approach to security:

> 'Spreading good governance, supporting social and political reform, dealing with corruption and abuse of power, establishing the rule of law and protecting human rights are the best means of strengthening the international order'.

In the same vein, the *EU Strategy against Proliferation of Weapons of Mass Destruction* states that 'the EU will continue to address the root causes of instability including through pursuing and enhancing its efforts in the areas of political conflicts, development assistance, reduction of poverty and promotion of human rights'. In its contribution to the HLP as well, the EU recognized that 'a wide-ranging collective response is the best way to deal with complex, inter-connected threats'. Based on the notion of GPGs, such a comprehensive approach equals an *integrated* approach, in terms of *instruments*, *time* and *actors*.

First, the ESS states that present-day threats call for a 'mixture of instruments'. More specifically, they require an active approach regarding the 'full spectrum of instruments for crisis management and conflict prevention at our disposal, including political, diplomatic, military and civilian, trade and development activities', thus effectively integrating a number of *policy fields*, including both intergovernmental and Community ones. At the same time, each policy domain should continue to operate according to its own rationale and dynamics. In other words, 'securitization', or the instrumentalization of non-military dimensions of foreign policy in function of 'hard' security concerns only, must be avoided. Threats should only be addressed as security threats if they pose an effective threat of violence. For this reason, the ESS is not merely a security strategy, but even more a *foreign policy* strategy.

Secondly, several passages in the ESS indicate that a comprehensive approach to security entails an integrated approach in time, focusing not only on actual crisis management, but also on prevention and reconstruction. Underlining the importance of (structural) conflict prevention, the text states that 'conflict prevention and threat prevention cannot start too early' and that the EU 'should be ready to act before a crisis occurs'. The EU should 'be able to act before countries around us deteriorate, when signs of proliferation are detected, and before humanitarian emergencies arise'. Also, 'preventive engagement can avoid serious problems in the future'. As for reconstruction, the text says that the EU needs 'greater capacity to bring all necessary civilian resources to bear in crisis and post-crisis situations', as well as that 'regional conflicts need political solutions but military assets and effective policing may be needed in the post conflict phase'.

Thirdly, the ESS underlines that a comprehensive approach to security involves cooperation of different actors at different levels. As there are 'few, if any' problems that the EU can deal with on its own, international cooperation is considered a 'necessity'. To pursue its strategic objectives, the EU will work together with a number of regional and international organizations and partner countries. In addition to the UN, the ESS lists the WTO, NATO, the OSCE, ASEAN, MERCOSUR and the AU as key institutions for international cooperation. In addition to the United States, it names Russia, Japan, China, Canada and India as key partners. Like *human security*, a comprehensive approach to security based on the notion of GPGs takes the individual as point of reference. Yet, by saying that '[t]he best protection for our security is a world of well-governed democratic States', the ESS recognizes that the state remains the primary partner in achieving effective multilateralism. Therefore, third states are seen as partners for cooperation rather than as subjects of EU policy. By referring to the *Barcelona Process* and by stating that '[t]rade and development policies can be powerful tools for promoting reform', the ESS indicates that the EU aims to *influence* rather than to *coerce*, using the *carrot* rather than the *stick*. As a policy approach based on GPGs is often intrusive, target countries may not always be willing to accommodate.[37] One could argue, however, that it is in the very nature of GPGs that pursuing them is in the mutual interest of all those involved. As the question *for whom* rather than *against whom* determines policy-making, a GPGs based approach is a *positive* approach that could enhance the legitimacy of the policies pursued, including policies implying the use of force.

5. In conclusion

Since the Iraq crisis of early 2003 and in the following debate on the role of the UN, the EU has emerged as one of the strongest advocates of multilateralism, at the least on a conceptual and theoretical level. As indicated in this chapter, also by way of the ESS, the EU confirmed its attachment to collective and comprehensive security, making 'effective multilateralism' the *adagium* of its foreign and security policy. What it comes down to is translating this support on paper into policy practice. Here, it can fall back on a number of documents, papers and conclusions, including the Communication that the Commission presented on 10 September 2003.[38] This Communication suggested that the EU should become a 'front-runner' within the UN, developing and implementing multilateral instruments and commitments. As its real influence within the organization still falls short of its economic and combined political contribution, and especially of its financial contribution, the EU

[37] A. Hurwitz and G. Peake, *Strengthening the Security-Development Nexus: Assessing International Policy and Practice Since the 1990s* (New York, International Peace Academy 2004).

[38] COM (2003) 526 final, *The European Union and the United Nations: The choice of multilateralism,* Brussels, 10 September 2003.

itself would also benefit from such an approach, living up to its potential. From this perspective, maybe as important as the question to what degree the EU has been able to leave a mark on the UN reform debate in the last few years, is the conclusion that this debate has provided the EU with a unique opportunity to position itself as a global security actor embracing the principles of collective and comprehensive security.

Chapter 16
UN-EU COOPERATION ON SECURITY: IN SEARCH OF 'EFFECTIVE MULTILATERALISM' AND A BALANCED DIVISION OF TASKS

by Kennedy Graham*

The international community in the early 21st century CE is undergoing dynamic change to the point of serious upheaval.[1] The traditional tenets of the international security system – sovereign equality, territorial integrity, and the non-use of force save in the common interest – are under challenge. A new paradigm of threat perception has been recognized. Reform of the UN system, both institutional and managerial, is underway. The relentless process of globalisation and its intensifying discontents, generating, *inter alia*, heightened tensions between culturally-diverse civilizations, continues apace. And the burgeoning threat of climate change with the coming socio-economic and psychic stress on all of humanity casts such change in stark, and unremitting, relief. The citizenry of the world are, in a word, worried about, even fearful of, the future.

It is a distortion of reality to describe, as is often done, the United Nations as encountering a 'mid-life crisis' at sixty years of age. The evolutionary experience of the UN cannot be assessed in terms of the human life-cycle – measurable within the finite span of a few decades more. The world organization may conceivably end peremptorily with a 'bang' in the form of a major terrorist event and/or related 'preventive' conflict conducted *ultra vires* its legal scope and beyond its capacity to handle. It may linger with a 'whimper' through marginalization in the calculus of strategic security, left to concentrate on technical projects of a humanitarian and developmental nature. Or – on a more positive note – it might simply mutate, through adaptation to a fast-changing world by displaying a 'legal creativity' – involving a dynamic interpretation of the Charter along teleological lines to common purpose that will serve not only the major powers but the broader membership.

---

* Dr. Kennedy Graham is Project Director at the UN University's comparative regional integration studies programme and Visiting Professor at the College of Europe (Bruges), Senior Consultant to the UN's Dept. of Political Affairs (New York), and Research Fellow at the School of Law, University of Canterbury (Christchurch).

[1] In this chapter the Christian calendar is adopted for ease of reference. In deference to inter-cultural sensibilities, the term CE (Common Era) is employed. At some stage in the future, the international community would benefit from a commonly-agreed universal calendar.

J. Wouters et al., eds., The United Nations and the European Union

Whichever fate it is, a universal global body will continue to exist or will reincarnate – in whatever form, with whatever name, under whatever normative framework and for whatever redesigned political goals. The overwhelming military might of the current superpower notwithstanding, the global village has no room today for unilateralist instinct to sustain strategic policy for any length of time. Multilateralism will continue to evolve, in varying degrees of effectiveness. The real challenge for the 'global community' (of peoples) is to ensure that the 'international community' (of states) sustains an effective multilateralism and that unilateralist instinct, whether emergent from America or Asia, Africa or Europe, is constructively re-directed towards that end.

This chapter considers the challenge of strengthening 'effective multilateralism', the nature of the present cooperation between the United Nations and the European Union to that purpose, and the goal of striking a balanced division of tasks between these two proud organizations in the foreseeable future.

The principal thesis advanced is that three prerequisites remain to be satisfied before substantive progress can be made:

- consensus over the 'legitimacy' of legislative, executive and judicial action at the global level;
- clarification of the structural paradigm that governs the partnership between the UN and 'regional and other intergovernmental organizations'; and
- coherence within the EU itself over its true nature and destiny.

None of these three requirements is easily met. Each will take decades to evolve to any satisfactory conclusion.

1. 'Effective Multilateralism' and Global Legitimacy

The 20th and 21st centuries are proving to be a time of transition. The Westphalian era of three centuries – from the 17th to the 19th – witnessed the rise and apogee of the nation-state, with full and untrammelled sovereignty, the right to initiate war and engage in conquest, to enslave fellow humans, and to exploit the planet's natural resource base for national self-aggrandisement unencumbered by any prescient notions of global unsustainability.

The 20th century witnessed the birth and early growth of international organization, ranging alongside the nation-state as its natural constituency, with the latter remaining dominant through retaining the gravitational pull on military and political influence. Sovereign equality remained the cardinal principle in theory yet had suffered significant practical erosion by the end of the century. The right to war was circumscribed steadily in theory, if weakly in practice, to the point of total proscription – the use of armed force being confined today to that undertaken in self-defence or authorised by the UN Security Council. And territorial integrity remained largely intact. Essentially the century ushered in a transition period of 'hybrid sovereignty' – shared uneasily at national and global levels with the former retaining control of the strategic heights of statecraft.

The 21st century has already witnessed, in its early years, a dynamic replay of the prevailing legal and political precepts of the LON-UN era. The metamorphosis in inter-state relations, inter-civilizational mood, and global sustainability has produced a completely new paradigm of global perception and response mechanism, affecting the three cardinal principles themselves.

Until the debate over the future definition of these principles is settled, there can be no truly 'effective multilateralism'. The global community, acting officially through the governments of UN Member States, does not agree on three fundamental issues which, taken together, amount to what is best termed a 'global legitimacy crisis'. These are:

- differences in regional priority accorded to the global threat perception;
- dispute over the institutional legitimacy of the UN Security Council as the principal response mechanism for those threats; and
- contestation among different civilizational belief patterns over the philosophical legitimacy for all action by, and for, the global community as a whole.

1.1 Differences in threat perception

The current articulation of 'global threat perception' is captured succinctly in the UN Secretary-General's 2004 High-Level Panel. The Panel's report identified six threat clusters, viz. inter-state aggression, intra-state instability, WMD proliferation, terrorism, trans-national crime, and socio-economic stress.

This threat paradigm reflects a judicious perception by a globally-representative group of eminent people. Yet the Panel's report had recommendatory status only. The current official statement by the international community – the 2005 World Summit Outcome Document – was confined to a much broader observation that effectively leaves the debate ongoing:

> 'We recognize that we are facing a whole range of threats that require our urgent, collective and more determined response. We also recognize that, in accordance with the Charter, addressing such threats requires cooperation among all the principal organs of the United Nations within their respective mandates. We acknowledge that we are living in an interdependent and global world and that many of today's threats recognize no national boundaries, are interlinked and must be tackled at the global, regional and national levels in accordance with the Charter and international law. We therefore reaffirm our commitment to work towards a security consensus based on the recognition that many threats are interlinked, that development, peace, security and human rights are mutually reinforcing, that no State can best protect itself by acting entirely alone

and that all States need an effective and efficient collective security system pursuant to the purposes and principles of the Charter.'[2]

Differences in threat perception are, in fact, profound across regions. North America and Europe rate what they perceive as terrorism and WMD proliferation to be the highest security threats of all. Latin America, and to some extent Asia, rate trans-national crime to be the highest security threat. Africa, and to some extent Asia, rates epidemic disease and absolute poverty as the highest threats.

This dilemma is illustrated in Table 1 which gives an impressionistic portrayal of regional priorities pertaining to the six threat clusters.[3]

Table 1. Incidence in Regional Threat Perception (2006)

	Nature of Threat to Regional Peace and Security (Perception of Region)						
	Inter-State Aggression	Intra-State Instability	Inter-Region Instability	Terrorism	WMD Proliferation	Organized Crime	Socio-Economic Instability
North							
Nth. Americ	D	D	A	A	A	B	D
Europe	B	C	A	A	A	B	C
South							
SS Africa	B	A	C	C	D	D	A
Arab World	C	A	A	B	C	D	B
Asia	A	C	C	B	C	C	C
Pacific	D	B	D	C	D	C	A
Car/Lat Americ	C	C	C	C	C	B	B

Key: A = primary threat; B = significant threat; C = modest threat; D = minor threat

1.2 Dispute over institutional legitimacy

Given the inter-locking nature of the threats, the lack of a global consensus on threat perception thwarts a collective unity over a resolute response.[4] Yet the skewed distribution of Security Council membership, reflecting the dominant position of

[2] A/RES/60/1, paras. 69-72.

[3] The judgments entered in the table are those of the author alone. No official exercise has been undertaken that illustrates the regional variation in threat perception. The judgment rests on an analysis of the patterns of statement by regional leaders and resolutions of regional organizations.

[4] Political dispossession breeds *anomie* which spawns terrorism which generates inter-civilizational tension which prompts aspirations for WMDs which prompts selective strategic policies that perpetuate and highlight political dispossession.

the West at the creation of the United Nations and since, results in a largely Western threat perception prevailing in the Council.

This skewed threat perception influences global policy-making at a time when the Council is undergoing far-reaching self-empowerment in the post-Cold War era. Designed to be an executive agent for combating inter-state aggression in the mid-1940s, the Council has interpreted its own powers in an expansive manner, unfettered by any judicial constraint on what is widely recognized to be an essentially political body. The three 'elements of power' accorded to the Council under the Charter – determination of aggression, breach of the peace, or threat to the peace, are fundamentally different:

- The first two accord 'traditional' powers on the Council to deal principally with inter-state conflict on a territorially-specific basis on issues involving 'objective' fact.
- The third accords the Council a vehicle of self-empowerment through subjective judgment on issues that may be generic and territorially non-specific.

The Council has in fact used its third 'discretionary power' in the past two decades to range widely across the spectrum of global affairs. In January 1992, for example, the Council at its first summit meeting agreed that the proliferation of weapons of mass destruction constituted a 'threat to international peace and security'.[5] In 2001 it identified terrorism as another 'generic threat'. Security Council Resolution 1373 was also an example of the Council legislating international law rather than simply executing it.[6] Other examples include the creation of *ad* hoc criminal tribunals, and targeted sanctions on groups (Taliban, 1999; bin Laden and associates, 2000), individual sanctions and arrest warrants (Somalia, 1993).

In taking these actions, the Council is demonstrating its readiness to transform from its original role as enforcer of international law into a prototype body of global governance. This raises the *ante* of the institutional legitimacy of the Council in terms of its global representational integrity. Yet repeated attempts at enlarging its composition in a manner that more accurately reflects the distribution of humanity across regions have perished on the rocks of national ambition and rivalry. The failure of the most recent attempt, in 2005, based on the alternative models offered by the High-Level Panel[7] and endorsed by the Secretary-General in his report of

---

[5] Statement by the President of the Security Council at the Meeting of Heads of State and Government, S/23500, 31 January 1992. This presidential statement is not binding, but was subsequently cited in Council Resolution 1540 (2004) in which the Council, acting under Chapter VII, *decided* that States shall refrain from assisting non-state actors to acquire WMD.

[6] SC Res. 1373 (2001) of 28 September 2001.

[7] Report of the Secretary-General's High-level Panel on Threats, Challenges and Change, 'A more secure world: our shared responsibility', 1 December 2004, available at <http://www.un.org/secureworld/>.

March 2005,[8] has soured the scene for any constructive move forward in the foreseeable future. As long as the majority of the global community remains resentful at the skewed distribution of power arrayed in the form of permanent membership of the Security Council, the ultimate attainment of 'effective multilateralism' through the United Nations machinery will remain a mirage.

1.3 Contest over philosophical legitimacy

Beneath these surface battles lies a more fundamental, and more ominous, contestation – a multifaceted difference over what, in fact, constitutes the legitimacy of policy-making and execution for the global community as a whole. The Huntington theory of inter-civilizational clash was repudiated so strenuously in the mid-1990s principally because of the sensationalism that surrounded the debate – rather than the partial truth it enunciated. In fact, events both before and since have illustrated that there are three fundamentally-opposite beliefs over the legitimacy of global policy and action:

- the traditional belief that legitimacy is to be found in *secular universalism*, the notion that, however much one civilizational belief pattern may disagree with another, the ultimate route to global redemption is through respect and accommodation of the other; and that the institutional vehicle for this is the United Nations which acts as the sole bestower of global legitimacy;[9]
- the revolutionary belief that legitimacy is not be found in universalism which masks 'regressive' and 'rogue' regimes, but is to be found in *democratic liberalism*; and that the vehicle for this is the Community of Democracies rather than the United Nations, the latter acting merely as a forum in which the struggle is to be played out;[10]

---

[8] Kofi Annan, 'In larger freedom: towards development, security and human rights for all. Report of the Secretary-General', 21 March 2005, available at <http://www.un.org/largerfreedom/>.

[9] 'When States decide to use force, not in self-defence but to deal with broader threats to international peace and security, there is no substitute for the unique legitimacy provided by the United Nations Security Council. States and peoples around the world attach fundamental importance to such legitimacy, and to the international rule of law.' UN Secretary-General Kofi Annan, Address, Williamsburg, Virginia, 8 February 2003 <http://www.una-uk.org/iraq/iraqkofisspeech.html >. After the adoption of SCR 1441 in November 2002, the Secretary-General praised the Council for uniting on the basis of consensus, adding that the resolution gave the international community the strategy it needed with the universal legitimacy that only the United Nations could extend.

[10] In a 1999 article in the *Weekly Standard* titled 'Kofi Annan's Power Grab,' current US ambassador to the UN, John Bolton laid out the neoconservative position on US military supremacy with respect to what the neocons regarded as the outdated UN Charter. Bolton took issue with Annan's description of the United Nations as 'the sole source of legitimacy on the use of force.' According to Bolton, 'If the United States allows that claim to go unchallenged, its discretion in using force to advance its national interests is likely to be inhibited in the future.' In mounting the challenge to Annan and the United Nations, Bolton also criticized President Clinton for 'his implicit endorsement of the Annan doctrine' during his speech opening the General Assembly session that year. In

- the ancient belief (packaged in various post-modern forms) that legitimacy is exclusively derived from *divine revelation*, the vehicle for which remains ancient spiritual texts interpreted in fundamentalist ways; and that the United Nations is either an irritant or an outright evil standing in the way of a preordained end.[11]

The struggle between these three belief systems adumbrates the increasingly intense power struggle between UN Member States, and also between governments and non-state actors. It is a struggle being played out in the corridors of the United Nations, in the military headquarters of major powers, in the universities and *madrassahs* around the world, and in the rural and urban killing fields. Until some form of truce is signalled and a genuine dialogue is generated to find common ground at a fundamental philosophical level, a global political accord will prove illusory and military confrontation will continue.

This has significance for the partnership between the United Nations and the European Union and a balanced division of tasks between them. The United Nations has no single 'global soul'. It is, and will remain for as long as one can foresee, simply a forum for debate in the General Assembly. Yet the Security Council carries out far-reaching action, including authorisation of military action, in the Assembly's name.[12] If the international community of States cannot agree on the underlying source of legitimacy for global action, then the General Assembly evinces no agreed basis of action. Yet the Security Council acts as if there is one. In an important underlying sense, the United Nations mirrors the global schizophrenia that afflicts humanity in our lifetime.

In contradistinction, the European Union reflects essentially one cultural viewpoint on world affairs. While minority issues are increasingly important on the

---

Bolton's view, Annan had put his own legitimacy at risk by expressing his concerns about the NATO bombing campaign over the former Yugoslavia. When visiting the war zone, Annan said: 'Unless the Security Council is restored to its preeminent position as the sole source of legitimacy on the use of force, we are on a dangerous path to anarchy.' Subsequently, in the Secretary-General's annual report to the UN membership, Annan wrote that 'enforcement actions without Security Council authorization threaten the very core of the international security system. ... Only the [UN] Charter provides a universally legal basis for the use of force.' Bolton wrote that these were 'sweeping – indeed, breathtaking – assertions'. Available at <http://rightweb.irc-online.org/profile/97>.

[11] 'Those who claim they are the leaders of Arabs and are still in the United Nations have renounced the message of Muhammad. Those who resort to international legitimacy are renouncing the legitimacy of the Holy Book and the legacy of the Prophet Muhammad. .... Muslims should understand the nature of this struggle, and the truth about this struggle, so they can decide in which ranks they stand. .... In essence, this war is a religious war. ... Those who take our tragedies today and want to solve them in the United Nations are hypocrites, deceiving God and his prophet and deceiving the believers.' Statement by Osama bin Laden, reported by Associated Press, 3 November 2001, available at <http://multimedia.belointeractive.com/attack/binladen/1103binladen.html>.

[12] The General Assembly, elects the non-permanent Council members (Article 23.1) and the Council reports annually to the Assembly (Article 24). The Council acts on behalf of all the UN membership (Article 24.1).

domestic agenda of EU countries, there never has been any question of what the founding belief pattern of Europe is.[13] Unlike the UN, the EU evinces no cultural schizophrenia. Its view of what should constitute 'effective multilateralism', therefore, remains less complex, to an order of magnitude. Yet, by the same token, the EU also is simply one actor on the UN stage. Being a 'global actor' does not endow oneself with the whole stage, or even the right to remain centre-stage for any undue length of time.

Until these complex and inter-related issues of 'legitimacy' are also resolved, the attainment of a true 'effective multilateralism' will prove difficult, if not illusory.

2. The UN-Regional Partnership: Paradigmatic and Structural Change

In determining some form of global governance, the international community has struggled for almost a century now to strike the correct balance between regionalism and 'globalism' – all in the name of universalism. For the architects of the first experiment at international organization – the League of Nations – the issue was clear-cut. In what was a remarkable and largely unrecognized phenomenon, the world took not one but two steps up in political self-governance, however inchoate and fragile, from the national to the global – essentially leap-frogging the regional level. This was done in a rather absent-minded manner – President Wilson having concluded that the American hemispheric model of collective security in the Monroe Doctrine should serve as a model for war-torn Europe, and by implication and rather as an afterthought, the world as a whole. Global centralism was born with the congenital weakness of a universal veto through the principle of consensus but was, nonetheless, recognisable for what it was.

2.1 The Charter framework: primacy of global governance

The second cut at the same experiment – the United Nations barely twenty-five years later – revisited the global-regional issue in the light of a more globalised world and the need for tighter constraint on national military freedoms. An intensive debate ensued between those in favour of regional security councils (led by the United Kingdom and the Commonwealth under Churchill, but prosecuted equally vigorously by the Latin America, Arab and Soviet groups) and those preferring a centralised global security council (led by the United States with the moderate support of China). Fears from the Latin Americans of a combined Soviet aggression plus veto prompted an assertive move to develop some form of regional collective

[13] The debate over a reference to Christianity as the spiritual heritage of Europe in the draft European Constitution, the policy-exchange over Turkish membership, and the controversy over Pope Benedict's Regensburg address are reflections of this issue.

security that could also be compatible with a strong UN Security Council. The resulting compromise proved fateful – the introduction at a late stage in the negotiation process of the self-defence provision in the UN Charter plus the creation of Chapter VIII on regionalism. But the final Charter signalled a victory for centralism and what was characterised as a 'mild discouragement' of regionalism in the maintenance of international peace and security.

That characterisation, however, is something of an overstatement. The Charter bestows some reliance on regional 'arrangements or agencies' to play a role alongside the UN Security Council. In particular they are 'encouraged' to take initiatives in pacific settlement without any advance authorization of the Security Council. So there was an implicit recognition by the framers of the Charter that, in the (peaceful) prevention and resolution of conflict, regional organizations had a collaborative role to play with the centralised global body. Yet, when it came to enforcement, the Charter is clear: the Security Council 'shall, where appropriate, utilize' regional organizations, but no enforcement may be undertaken by them without Council authorization. Although it is not explicitly stated, grammatical logic requires that this means advance authorization. On this basis, the stage was set for the second attempt at collective security, with a strong centralised global body and weaker (and hitherto largely anticipated) regional organizations playing a significant though supporting role.

The early onset of the Cold War, however, killed the concept of global collective security shortly after birth. The Cold War saw two regional entities of entirely different kinds:

- The first kind involved mirror-images of collective security, but at the regional rather than the global level (the Arab League, the OAS). Such organizations envisaged regional collective security supplementing global collective security.
- The second kind were regional collective defence alliances (NATO, SEATO, CENTO, Warsaw Pact, ANZUS), justified under the self-defence provision of the UN Charter,[14] yet armed to the teeth with nuclear weapons and, at least from the West, a first-use policy. These developments tended to undermine, if anything, the concept of global collective security.[15]

The popular mind, and to some extent the official mind, has scarcely bothered to acknowledge the qualitative difference that exists between global collective secu-

---

[14] Article 51.

[15] This is not to assert that regional collective defence alliances were antithetical to the UN Charter. Such agencies affirmed their compatibility with the purposed and principles of the UN Charter. But that compatibility pertained to the principle of self-defence, a last-minute recruit by way of compromise, and not to the central provisions of global collective security. By according primary responsibility to (regional) self-defence alliances rather than the Security Council for peace and security, this tended to undermine the central tenet of the United Nations.

rity and regional defence alliance as the guarantor of international peace and security. The former assumes a closed global system within which a universal majority responds to aggression in a unified manner. The latter assumes a fragmented world in which two adversarial sides of broadly equal military weight engage in a global balance of power, largely independent of the UN Charter and partially blind to international law. In any event security regionalism of the Charter kind remained largely stunted through this period.

In the post-Cold War period this problem has effectively disappeared. With a few exceptions, regional defence alliances have themselves been dissolved. And the principal exception, NATO, has devoted strenuous effort at mutating into a subcontractor to the United Nations for global collective security – offering itself and its 'assets' to the United Nations not only in enforcement but also in conflict prevention and resolution.

At the sub-regional level, economic organizations have been obliged, in the course of the 1990s and since, to undertake a security function as well, including enforcement. This has included ECOWAS, IGAD, SADC, ECCAS and CARICOM, while some regional organizations (CIS, PIF) had similar experiences as well.

The post-Cold War world, however, has encountered two major and inter-related issues:

- how to respond to the 'new security threats' beyond the traditional inter-state aggression (the other five 'threat clusters' identified earlier); and
- the extent to which the vehicle for responding should remain the global body (the UN Security Council) or regional and sub-regional bodies.

2.2 Post-Charter reality: trend towards security regionalism

The immediate post-Cold War period carried great expectations of a reinvigorated Security Council tackling all security crises around the world on the basis of political consensus and military collaboration. Plans were called for by the 1992 Security Council summit and laid out in the ambitious *Agenda for Peace* of the Secretary-General.[16] Two developments spelled an early demise to such ambitions. The refusal of the Member States in general to provide the financial resources, or to commit sufficient troop and logistical support (including either a standing or rapidly deployable force) handicapped the UN's ability to police the world effectively. And the debacle of the Somali campaign, together with the shame of Srebenica and Rwanda, resulted in a withdrawal of US support for UN peacekeeping or peace-enforcement. In such straitened circumstances the conclusion was inescapable: the United Nations had no choice but to rely on regional (and sub-regional) organizations for cooperation in the maintenance of international peace and security.

---

[16] *Agenda for Peace*, Report of the Secretary-General 17 June 1992, UN Doc. A/47/277 – S/2411.

The international community has responded to this logic. Since 1994, a series of high-level meetings has been convened by the UN Secretary-General, the most recent being the 7th HLM in September 2006. These meetings have focused on particular themes – cooperation in conflict prevention, and peace-building, and responding to new threats. For its part the Security Council has also, rather belatedly, responded to the same prompt. It has now convened four thematic debates on cooperation with regional organizations in peace and security (April 2003, July 2004, October 2005, September 2006). At its third meeting, the Council adopted a resolution, in which it expressed its determination to take:

> 'appropriate steps to the further development of cooperation between the United Nations and regional and sub-regional organizations in maintaining international peace and security, consistent with Chapter VIII of the United Nations Charter'.[17]

The Council also urged all States 'and relevant international organizations' to contribute to strengthening the capacity of regional and sub-regional organizations in conflict prevention, crisis management and post-conflict stabilization, including through the provision of human, technical and financial assistance.[18,19]

The Council's call for a strengthened regional-global partnership for peace is echoed in the broader membership of the UN. Responding to the recommendation of the Secretary-General's High-Level Panel[20] and the Secretary-General's own report,[21] the General Assembly at its 60th session, meeting at summit level, determined that:

> 'We support a stronger relationship between the United Nations and regional and sub-regional organizations, pursuant to Chapter VIII of the Charter, and therefore resolve: (…) to expand consultation and cooperation between the United Nations and regional and sub-regional organizations through formalized agreements between the respective secretariats and, as appropriate, involvement of regional organizations in the work of the Security Council.'[22]

Thus, the structural framework for strengthening the partnership between the UN and regional and sub-regional organizations is steadily being put into place. But what does this mean for EU-UN cooperation? And what are the impediments to progress in this regard?

---

[17] SCR 1631 (2005), 17 October 2005.

[18] Particular regard is to be given to African regional and sub-regional organizations.

[19] A report is expected to be submitted to the 4th thematic debate of the Security Council in September 2006.

[20] A/59/565, 29 November 2004. See especially recommendation 86(b).

[21] A/59/2005, 21 March 2005. See especially para. 213.

[22] A/RES/60/1, 24 October 2005. See especially para. 170.

2.3 Looking ahead: challenges for a regional-global security mechanism

The problems facing the UN-regional partnership and therefore, EU-UN cooperation, are essentially three-fold:

- the lack of definitional clarity on the central concepts involved;
- the lack of clarity over the constitutional nature of the 'partner organizations' or the nature of the relationship between them and the UN;
- the skewed capacity of such partner organizations around the world, in financial and thus human and military terms.

2.3.1 *Definitional imprecision*

Although the Charter describes the United Nations itself as an 'international organization', it does not refer to 'regional organizations'. Yet this phrase has become commonplace in the international community. The relevant chapter in the Charter is entitled 'Regional Arrangements' and the chapter's content refers to 'regional arrangements or agencies' without defining either or distinguishing between them in any operational sense. A definition of a 'regional agency' offered by Egypt at the San Francisco Conference was rejected, although it was quite sound and potentially useful.[23] The UN has made no effort to develop a working definition of a 'regional agency' or 'organization', even in the course of its high-level meetings.

It is, in fact, becoming increasingly important that a conceptual clarification and some definitional precision be introduced into the process if the UN-regional partnership is to be strengthened for operational purposes and realise the potential comparative advantage of each partner. Some twenty organizations attend these meetings, only about half of which are genuinely regional or sub-regional organizations. In the high-level meetings, the fundamental distinction officially used is two-fold: regional (including sub-regional) organizations and 'other intergovernmental organizations'.

The practical significance of this classification is that only the regional and the sub-regional organizations would partner with the UN under Chapter VIII of the Charter. The other organizations attending the high-level meetings would partner with the UN under the other relevant provisions of the Charter.

---

[23] 'There shall be considered, as regional arrangements, organizations of a permanent nature grouping in a given geographical area several countries which, by reason of their proximity, community of interests or cultural, linguistic, historical or spiritual affinities make themselves jointly responsible for the peaceful settlement of any disputes which may arise (...) as well as for the safeguarding of their interests and the development of their economic and cultural relations.' UNCIO XII, pp. 850, 857, 8 June 1945; quoted in B. Simma, et al. (eds.), *The United Nations Charter: A Commentary* (Oxford, OUP 1995) pp. 688-689.

Does this legal, as opposed to terminological distinction matter in the real world? The potential significance was alluded to earlier – namely, the difference between those agencies that focus on their own jurisdictional area of their membership and those that are prepared and able to act on behalf of the UN on an 'out-of-area', global basis. Essentially, the former are acting as executive agents for the UN within the context of regional collective security, and the latter are acting as executive agents for the UN within the context of global collective security. In this way the basic aims of the Charter are realised more effectively, and the tension between universalism and regionalism in the maintenance of international peace and security is, to some extent, resolved.

The nature of the partnership arrangement with the UN in peace and security rests on two main issues: geographical and functional:

- does the partner organization act exclusively within the jurisdictional zone of its own Member States ('regional focus') or does it act also 'out-of-area' (global focus);
- does the partner organization undertake action in one or more of the measures of peace and security: conflict prevention, peacemaking, enforcement and peace-building?

Clarification of these questions paves the way for an effective operational partnership with the United Nations that would respond to the inherent comparative advantage of all.

Which, then, are which? Of the 21 organizations that have attended recent high-level meetings, the likely taxonomy is shown in Table 2.

Seven regional and five sub-regional organizations would partner with the United Nations under Chapter VIII of the Charter. Eight (or nine) other intergovernmental organizations would partner with the UN under the other relevant chapters (VI, VII and IX).

What might be the practical significance of such a distinction? It rests on the nature of the partnership with the Security Council. Regional and sub-regional partners would act under chapter VIII but would be responsible only for maintaining peace and security within their regional jurisdictional zones. All such organizations would take initiatives in the first instance in pacific settlement (conflict prevention and peacemaking) under Article 52 of the Charter. And they are able, indeed encouraged, to take such initiatives by themselves without reference to the Security Council. All such regional and sub-regional organizations identified in the table above do engage in pacific settlement measures.

Some of them – those that are constitutionally empowered by their founding document to do so – would also be prepared to undertake enforcement action within their region under Article 53, but only in the event that the UN Security Council decided to utilize them and authorized such action. Those that have shown a capa-

Table 2. Possible Taxonomy of Regional, Sub-Regional and Other Intergovernmental Organizations*

Organization Type	Regional	Sub-Regional	Other Intergovernmental
Charter Provision	Chapter VIII		Chapters VI, VII, & IX
	AU	ECOWAS	NATO**
		IGAD	EU**
		ECCAS	SCO
		SADC	CSTO
	LAS		Commonwealth
	COE		OIF
	CIS		CPLP
	ASEAN		OIC
	PIF		
	OAS	CARICOM	

* OSCE has been omitted from this table. It has declared itself to be a 'regional agency' for the purposes of Chapter VIII of the UN Charter. Yet its membership is cross-regional, spanning North America, Europe and Central Asia. Any formal decision on whether OSCE is a regional agency or one of the 'other intergovernmental organizations' would require legal advice and a consensus within the high-level process.
** Both NATO and the EU have, in fact, indicated that they do not see themselves as regional organizations for the purposes of Chapter VIII of the Charter.

bility and a willingness to undertake such enforcement action to date are the AU, LAS, CIS, PIF and ECOWAS.[24]

The other intergovernmental organizations would partner with the United Nations under other chapters of the Charter. They would be free to take similar initiatives in conflict prevention under Chapter VI (Article 33) of the Charter, not only for their own members but for all UN Member States – that is, not only within their jurisdictional zones but beyond, on a global basis.

Some of these – those that are constitutionally empowered by their founding document to do so – would also be prepared to undertake enforcement action within their region under Chapter VII (Article 42), but only in the event that the UN Security Council decided to utilize them and authorized such action. Those that have shown a capability and a willingness to undertake such enforcement action to date, on a global basis, are NATO and the EU.

Is it necessary to draw such a fine distinction? The reason is that the regional and sub-regional organizations would naturally become the 'partners of first instance'

[24] OAS also authorized enforcement action against Cuba in 1962. But it has taken the political decision ever since not to engage in enforcement action.

to undertake such actions since they are directly responsible for the peace and security in their own regions and sub-regions, within the overall 'primary responsibility' of the UN Security Council. But if the regional or sub-regional organization is unable or unwilling to undertake such action (i.e., enforcement action), then the Security Council might call upon a 'global executive agent' such as NATO or the EU to assume the responsibility – including in 'out-of-area' zones.

For the Security Council meeting of September 2006, both the UN Secretary-General and the Council President for the meeting (the Foreign Minister of Greece) made far-reaching observations about the need for a 'clarification of roles'. The SG's report stressed that one of the two major challenges facing UN-regional cooperation was such a clarification, and it recommended that the Council discuss the desirability of partner organizations identifying themselves either as regional organizations acting under Chapter VIII or as other intergovernmental organizations acting under other Charter provisions.[25] A concept paper by Greece explored the distinction between Chapter VIII (for regional organizations) and Chapters VI and VII (for other organizations), with criteria to assist (*viz.* membership and mandate).[26]

In the Council debate itself the Secretary-General forewarned that 'the reality of the next decade is that the demand for peacekeeping and [conflict prevention and resolution, and peace-building] will continue to grow. And we must be ready. That means the time has come for us to take the regional-global mechanism to a new level of clarity, practicality and seriousness. Chapter VIII exists for reasons that are as valid today as they were 61 years ago. Cooperation between the United Nations and regional organization offers a framework for doing this with the requisite flexibility, accountability and legitimacy.' Endorsing this view, Greece saw a need 'to identify regional and sub-regional agencies and to clarify the criteria on the basis of which these agencies are distinguished, for the purposes of applying Chapter VIII of the Charter from other international organizations. Such clarity will give real meaning to the envisaged global-regional mechanism and should restore more authority to the Security Council and greater reliance on constitutionally-delegated executive functions to genuine regional agencies under Chapter VIII of the Charter.'

2.3.2 *Constitutional uncertainties*

A second problem concerns the legal capacities of the partner organizations to enter formalized agreements with the UN. The past few years have seen a growing conviction on the part of the international community that a stronger partnership between the regional and other intergovernmental organizations is necessary for an operational efficiency to be attained and the comparative advantage of each partner maximised. In short, in times of crisis it is imperative that, under the leadership and

---

[25] UN doc. A/61/204—S/2006/590, 28 July 2006

[26] UN doc. S/2006/719, 20 September 2006

authority of the United Nations, there is a clear understanding of who does what when. Too many times in the past problems in conflict prevention and resolution have been characterised by a lack of coordination.

Accordingly the 2005 World Summit supported a 'stronger relationship between the United Nations and regional and sub-regional organizations, pursuant to Chapter VIII of the Charter', through, *inter alia*, formalized agreements between the respective secretariats.[27]

There is no clear understanding of the legal nature of some of the organizations – whether they have legal personality in international law, what legal competence and capacities they have to accept binding commitments and formal responsibilities *vis-à-vis* the United Nations. The definitional imprecision discussed earlier does nothing to assist: while it is generally accepted that a regional organization is a 'regional agency' (as opposed to a 'regional arrangement'), it is less clear when a regional organization is properly constructed. It is generally accepted that a constitutive document of a binding legal nature and a standing organizational structure separate from that of the Member States are the two principal conditions. Based on these criteria, it might be possible to classify the group of 21 partners participating in the high-level process as being composed of five regional agencies, three regional arrangements, seven other intergovernmental agencies and one intergovernmental arrangement.[28] The capacity of the 'arrangements' to enter binding agreements with the United Nations is uncertain. It would be necessary for legal advice to be sought on this issue.

2.3.3 *Skewed capacities*

A third problem concerns the skewed resource capacities of the regional organizations – both human and financial. It is clear that the capacity of regional organizations to act in international peace and security is skewed, particularly in financial capacity. This compares with the tremendous capacities of the EU and NATO. This raises the question of the extent to which the EU's role in the 'regional-global security mechanism' (as well as NATO's) is to act as an executive 'global actor' on behalf of the UN in 'out-of-area' locations or as a supporting 'enabler' to the regional and sub-regional organizations. In the former scenario, it is possible to envisage 'hybrid' operations with the regional/sub-regional organizations in peace missions; and in the latter scenarios it is likely that financial, plus logistical support only will be offered.

---

[27] A/RES/60/1, 24 October 2006, para. 170(a)

[28] See K. Graham, T. Felicío and R. Tavares, *Legal Personality of Regional, Sub-Regional, and Other Intergovernmental Organizations* (UNU-CRIS Background Paper for UN-DPA/UNU-CRIS Seminar, April 2006).

3. Internal Clarification: What Destiny for the EU?

Within the past half-century, Europe has qualitatively changed in a political manner of historic significance. It has metamorphosed from a divided and war-torn assemblage of sovereign nation-states, weary of the past and distrustful of the future, into a dynamic and integrating region in which the absolutism of national sovereignty is ceding ground to a complex and multi-layered jurisdictional system of potential governance. Sovereign authority is being stretched, on the basis of the subsidiarity principle, from the nation down to the province and the county, and up to the sub-region and the region.

3.1 **Developing the CFSP**

From the ECSC through the EEC and the EC to the EU, Europe has steadily merged its common industrial and agricultural base, and then its social and service sectors. Today it aspires to develop a common foreign and security policy (CFSP). The Maastricht Treaty of 1992 established the EU as an entity and laid out ambitious criteria by which the EU's actions as a global player were henceforth to be judged. Milestones along the way have been:

- the Common Foreign and Security Policy (CFSP), introduced in the Maastricht Treaty and including the European Security and Defence Policy;
- the folding of the Western European Union into the operational security mechanism of the EU's ESDP (June 1999);
- the EU Council's Programme for the Prevention of Violent Conflicts ('Goteborg Programme') of 2001, which reaffirmed that 'conflict prevention [was] one of the main objectives of the EU's external relations and should be integrated in all its relevant aspects, including the ESDP….';[29]
- development of cooperative links with NATO through a series of agreements over the past decade;[30]
- the UN-EU Joint Declaration on Crisis Management which defines their respective roles in military and civilian relief operations and disaster situations;[31]
- the EC Communication (September 2003): 'The EU and the UN: The Choice of Multilateralism';[32]

---

[29] Available at <http://www.eu2001.se/static/eng/pdf/violent.PDF>.

[30] See <http://www.nato.int/issues/nato-eu/index.html>.

[31] Joint Declaration on UN-EU Cooperation in Crisis Management, New York, 24 September 2003, available at <http://europa-eu-un.org/articles/lt/article_2768_lt.htm>.

[32] Commission of the European Communities, 'The European Union and the United Nations: the choice of multilateralism', 10 September 2003, COM (2003) 526 final.

- the completion of the European Security Strategy (December 2003) which proclaims 'effective multilateralism' as the EU's guiding principal in its foreign policy;[33]
- the submission of an EU policy brief (June 2004) to the UN High-Level Panel on Threats, Challenges and Change;[34]
- the signing of the European Constitution (October 2004) which lays out the future structure of the EU's foreign and security policy.[35]
- Elements of Implementation of the Joint EU-UN Declaration?[36]

Under the new Constitution, the EU's common security and defence policy is to be an integral part of the CSFP, providing the Union with an 'operational capacity' that draws on European civilian and military assets. The EU may use such assets 'outside the Union' for peacekeeping, conflict prevention and strengthening international security, but only in accordance with the principles of the UN Charter.[37]

In addition, the EU will engage henceforth in the 'progressive framing' of a common defence policy, with decisions made being recommended for implementation by Member States in accordance with their respective constitutional requirements. Member States are to progressively improve their military capabilities. Armed aggression against any Member State will incur an obligation of assistance from all Members (in accordance with Article 51 of the UN Charter pertaining to individual and collective self-defence). This collective defence arrangement, however, is not to prejudice 'the specific character of the security and defence policy of certain Member States' – thus acknowledging the relationship between allied and neutral Member States.

The CFSP has been a stated aspiration of the Union since 1992, and there has been some criticism that a fully-fledged common policy is not yet in place. In fact, much of the foreign policies of Member States do already reflect a high degree of commonality, as recorded in voting behaviour at the UN General Assembly.[38] But

---

[33] 'A Secure Europe in a Better World' – a European Security Strategy, adopted by the European Council on 12 December 2003.

[34] General Affairs and External Relations Council, 'Paper for Submission to the High-Level Panel on Threats, Challenges and Change', 17-18 May 2004, available at <http://ue.eu.int/uedocs/cmsUpload/EU%20written%20contribution2.pdf>.

[35] *Treaty establishing a Constitution for Europe*, Rome 29 October 2004, OJ (16 December 2004) C-310/1.

[36] 'EU-UN Cooperation in Military Crisis Management Operations: Elements of Implementation of the EU-UN Joint Declaration', adopted by the European Council on 17-18 June 2004, available at <http://ue.eu.int/ueDocs/cms_Data/docs/pressData/en/misc/81343.pdf>.

[37] The Constitution of the European Union, Article I-41.

[38] The level of concurrence in voting pattern is 80% to 90% – see J. Wouters, 'The European Union as an Actor within the United Nations General Assembly', in V. Kronenberg, *The European Union and the International Legal Order: Discord or Harmony?* (The Hague, TMC Asser Press 2001), pp. 375-404. Also P. Adriaenssens (University of Ghent), research thesis *Cooperation between the EU and the UN from an Historical Perspective (1974-2005)* (unpublished).

the more contentious issues, such as the Iraq crisis of 2003, give a surface impression of a region of peoples divided by national foreign policies. This is exacerbated, and to some extent sensationalised, by the historical quirk that two of its Member States, Britain and France, have permanent membership of the UN Security Council with veto rights.

Some of these issues were expected to be resolved with the adoption of the draft European Constitution, involving the creation of an EU foreign minister and diplomatic service. Yet the fate of the draft document, ratified by fourteen Member States but rejected by two, is currently unknown. This development holds implications for Europe that go beyond the fate of the document itself. It brings to the surface hitherto subterranean issues of Europe's self-identity in multifaceted ways – political and cultural – that are driven by a set of unpredictable societal forces of immigration, urban living, unemployment and religious affiliations.

3.2 Alternative future identities

The jury is still out. Europe has yet to decide what it is to be – a fully-integrated 'global actor' forging a new reality on the world stage, or a loose association of sovereign states operating as a traditional intergovernmental organization.

One possible future is articulated in the European Parliament which resolved in January 2004 that, once the EU attains a legal personality, it should secure a permanent seat on the UN Security Council, and be represented by its (future) foreign minister.[39] Although this remains a distant goal in light of the current constitutional hiatus, there appears to be increasing public sympathy around the world for stronger regionalism at the UN in peace and security. Yet an innovation of the kind envisaged by the EP – an actual seat for a regional organization in the Council as opposed to such organizations acting as partners with the Council – raises far-reaching constitutional issues for the international community. The cardinal principle of the contemporary era – the sovereign equality of nation-states as the constituent membership of the UN – would need revision. The Charter would require amendment to allow regional organizations to become members of the United Nations (all principal organs?) and range alongside nation-states also acting as members.

Even if this revolutionary change were enacted, further questions arise.

- What degree of integration would be required of such 'regional organizations' before they gain entry and act internally as a 'UN member', as opposed to a 'regional arrangement or agency' cooperating externally under Chapter VIII? Would the EU be followed by the AU and others?

---

[39] Report on the relations between the European Union and the United Nations Organisation (2003/2049(INI)). The report was adopted by the EU Parliamentary Committee by a vote of 32-5 (2 abstentions). See <http://www.epp-ed.org/Activities/pday03/day159_en.asp>.

- If they were members, how to avoid duplication of effort, and ensure rationalisation and compatibility of policy? If, for example, the EU were a member of the Council in February-March 2003, what would have been its policy and voting behaviour?

These problems are complex and profound. It would appear almost inevitable that, in the event a truly integrated regional organization became a member of the UN, the price would be a constitutional merger of its own 25 Members States in terms of UN representation, even if they do not complete a total political merger themselves back home in Europe.

An alternative future for the EU is that preferred by the United Kingdom and some of the new members – the loosening of its internal cohesion and a trend back to the traditional concept of an intergovernmental organization – with power to cooperate on, but not decide, regional policy in an integrated sense. If this occurs, the EU will simply act in similar manner to that of 'other intergovernmental organizations' – the second category of UN partners that attend the high-level meetings.

The choice will not be made in such a precise and exclusionary manner as is implied with these two alternatives, nor will it be made solely, or even significantly, on the basis of foreign policy considerations. The future of the EU will be the product of decision-making on the myriad regional issues, by political leaders reflecting the broader sway of public opinion.

3.3 A balanced division of tasks

Meanwhile, the EU represents itself at the UN as a 'global actor' of a *sui generis* character, with global reach and interests,[40] and not a 'chapter VIII regional agency'. This the EU of the type that the UN deals with and which relates to the UN. Taking this as a given, what is the 'balanced division of tasks' between the UN and the EU that most effectively serves the common interest of humanity?

Two kinds of task are involved – the theoretical dimension and the practical dimension – and potential exists for a mutually-reinforcing division of labour in both. But it must always be borne in mind that it is the United Nations, as the universal organization of the international community, that is the superior institution under whose auspices all others cooperate. Every regional and other intergovernmental organization must fully respect international law, and in particular none may contravene the UN Charter. This accords primary responsibility to the Security Council for peace and security, and no other Member State (including the United States) or organization (including NATO and the EU), may resort to armed force without the Council's authorization other than in self-defence.

[40] The EU currently accounts for over 50% of UN operational funding and over 60% of UN development funding.

This is clearly recognized in the emerging EU foreign policy.[41] What might be called the first 'strategic policy' of the EU is spelt out in the twin documents of 2003: the EC Communication in September and the EU Security Strategy three months later. These two documents will prove seminal in the annals of EU foreign policy development. The EU's overarching 'strategic objective' is the strengthening of an international order based on 'effective multilateralism'. The 'fundamental framework' for international relations remains the UN Charter. Strengthening the UN, equipping it to fulfill its responsibilities and act effectively, was necessarily a European priority. The challenge accepted by the EU is to help the multilateral system deliver on its key objectives. Two aspects of its contribution to effective multilateralism could, the EU believes, be further developed: its ability to act as a 'front-runner' in developing multilateralism; and its support for capacity-building in other countries and regions. And EU efforts should also focus on UN reform, especially of the Security Council.[42]

In making its contribution to effective multilateralism, the EU recognized that it needed to become 'more active, more coherent and more capable' as a single actor. It has accordingly sought a delicate balance between too precipitate and too belated a resort to force in crisis management. In adopting a concept that distinguishes it from the US doctrine involving the 'pre-emptive use of force', the EU is essentially seeking to position itself optimally between the United States and the rest of the international community. 'Preventive engagement', says the EU, can avoid more serious problems in the future. Yet, when the chips are down, 'we need to develop a strategic culture that fosters early, rapid and when necessary, robust intervention'.[43]

Thus, in a doctrinal sense, the EU can contribute to a balanced division of tasks with the UN by stressing, and demonstrating by its action, that it will respect both the judgment and the authority of the universal body with respect to the maintenance of international peace and security, and particularly with respect to the use of armed force.

It could also take the lead in the question of WMD disarmament which is a long-standing goal of the United Nations. The Charter bestows on the Security Council the responsibility for devising a system for the regulation of armaments and submitting this to the General Assembly.[44] As noted; two of the EU Member States are nuclear weapon powers and permanent members of the Council. They are therefore

[41] Parts of this section are adapted from K. Graham, *The EU and the UN: Partners in Crisis Management* (EPC Policy Brief European Policy Centre: Working Paper No. 13, November 2004).

[42] 'The EU should adopt a determined "front-runner" approach to the negotiation and implementation of important UN initiatives in the fields of sustainable development, poverty reduction, and international security, taking a more proactive approach to the development of international instruments and specific EU implementing actions. Moreover, the EU should give renewed impetus to the UN reform.' EC Communication COM (2003) 52246, September 2003, p. 9.

[43] 'A Secure Europe in a Better World: European Security Strategy', Brussels, 12 December 2003, p. 11.

[44] Article 26.

well-placed, and have the constitutional duty under the Charter, to initiate moves, albeit belatedly, towards fulfilment of this responsibility.

The second division of task concerns operational action in the field. It is often contended that Europe has been slow to develop an operational capability in crisis management. Yet it should be recalled that, only a decade ago at the time of the Balkans crisis, the EU did not even exist as an entity. The EC's capacity to undertake an operational deployment in the Balkans was, inevitably, seriously limited.

In the past five years the EU has begun to develop its operational capability, and this is starting to show practical results in the field. To date, the crisis management actions by the EU are seen in Table 3.

Table 3. EU Crisis Management Actions (2003-06)

Operation	Location	Troop Level	Mission Type	Duration
EUPM	Bosnia-Herzegovina	930	Police	Jan 03 – Dec 05
Concordia	Macedonia	350	Military	Apr 03 – Dec 03
Artemis	DR Congo	1800	Military	Jun 03 – Sept 03
Proxima	Macedonia	200	Police	Jan 04 –
EU JUST Themis	Georgia	10	Rule of law	Jun 04 – July 05
Althea	Bosnia-Herzegovina	7000	Military	Dec 04 –
EUPOL Kinshasha	DR Congo	30	Police	Dec 04 Dec 05
EUSEC DR Congo	DR Congo	8	Security sector reform	Jun 05 – Jun 06
EU JUST Lex	Iraq	24	Rule of Law	Jul 05 – Jun 06

Source: http://ue.eu.inty/cms3_fo/showPage.asp?id=268&lang=en&mode=

The EU is now working to create a 60,000-strong rapid reaction force for future humanitarian and peacekeeping missions. EU officials have considered the possibility of the EU sending a preventive force to Sudan to assist in the Darfur crisis. Deployment to date, however, has been confined to African Union peacekeeping forces and present thinking is for a UN replacement force.

Recently the UN has recognized the far-reaching potential of relying on a more active, capable and coherent EU as an operational partner committed to 'effective multilateralism'. The UN Secretary-General has visited EU headquarters in October 2000, January 2004 and July 2006 and remains in constant contact with the EU High Representative. In June 2001 the EU General Affairs Council agreed on a 'platform for intensified cooperation' at four levels:[45]

- EU ministerial meetings in troika format with the UN Secretary-General;

[45] Draft Council conclusions on EU-UN cooperation in conflict prevention and crisis management, Doc. 9528/2/01 REV 2, 7 June 2001, approved by the European Council.

- Meetings and contact between the EU High Representative and the EC External Affairs Commissioner with the UN Secretary-General and his Deputy;
- Political and Security Committee meetings with the UN Deputy and Under-Secretaries-General;
- Contact between the Council Secretariat and Commission with the UN Secretariat.

These plans have been thoroughly implemented in the past two years. Effective contact between the two secretariats commenced with DPKO officials on peacekeeping in May 2001. Since April 2002 the UN-DSG has led an annual mission to Brussels. The EU military staff has identified UN-DPKO as its UN partner, and the EU Policy Unit has identified UN-DPA (Europe branch). Joint task forces have been established to coordinate interaction over police and military missions, and foster training, with a 'steering committee' now meeting biannually. Liaison offices have been strengthened in New York and Brussels. It is clear that, as far as the UN is concerned, the EU is in business as a 'global actor', underpinning it with extensive financial, human and potentially military support.

4. Conclusions

Both the United Nations and the European Union are experiencing a time of reflection and reform. Both enshrine the same strategic and doctrinal goal of 'effective multilateralism'. Both regard the other as essential to the realisation of their stated goals. But the UN, as a universal organization, has a broader constituency which accords it a global legitimacy role while making the task of delivering that legitimacy in specific situations immeasurably more complex. The two organizations are by no means identical or interchangeable.

A 'balanced division of tasks' requires that the EU, having settled certain critical issues pertaining to its own self-identity and internal coherence, proceed to identify its position and role within the UN-regional partnership, and faithfully support the UN within that broader context.

This is no minor challenge. But if it is successfully met, the EU still has the potential to become the single most potent and effective 'global actor' on the world stage, and to play a crucial, perhaps indispensable role in the reform and revival process of the UN.

Chapter 17
COOPERATION BETWEEN THE EUROPEAN UNION AND THE UNITED NATIONS IN COUNTERTERRORISM

by Gijs de Vries*

1. INTRODUCTION

Terrorism is a global phenomenon that requires a global response. As UN Security Council Resolution 1566 states, acts of terrorism are under no circumstances justifiable by considerations of a political, philosophical, ideological, racial, ethnic, religious or other similar nature. Although many countries increasingly work together, much remains to be done to strengthen the global alliance against terrorism.[1]

This article first briefly recalls the EU counterterrorist strategy. It then presents a survey of EU support for UN action against terrorism. The penultimate section is dedicated to the role of human rights in counterterrorism before providing a succinct conclusion.

2. THE EU COUNTERTERRORIST STRATEGY

Terrorism in the EU is not a new phenomenon. The people of Europe have long suffered from the bombing campaigns of groups such as the IRA, ETA and the Red Brigades. Well before the attacks of 9/11, the European Council stated on numerous occasions its determination to fight terrorism, which it affirmed 'constitutes a threat to democracy, to the free exercise of human rights and to economic development'.[2]

After 9/11, the EU adopted an action plan[3] to deliver a series of measures directed specifically at countering terrorism and, following the Madrid attacks in March 2004, an EU Counterterrorism Coordinator was appointed to ensure implementa-

* Counterterrorism Coordinator of the European Union.

[1] UN SC Res. 1566 (2004) of 8 October 2004.

[2] La Gomera Declaration on Terrorism, Annex 3 to the Presidency Conclusions, European Council, Madrid, 15-16 December 1995, available at <http://www.europarl.eu.int/summits/mad2_en.htm#annex3>.

[3] Conclusions and Plan of Action of the extraordinary European Council meeting on 21 September 2001, available at <http://www.consilium.europa.eu>.

J. Wouters et al., eds., The United Nations and the European Union

tion. The current EU counterterrorism strategy, adopted in December 2005,[4] sets out the EU's commitment 'to combat terrorism globally while respecting human rights, and make Europe safer, allowing its citizens to live in an area of freedom, security and justice.' This strategy focuses the efforts of the EU on four main objectives:

- *First,* to prevent people from turning to terrorism by tackling the factors and root causes which can lead to radicalisation and recruitment, in Europe and internationally;
- *Second,* to protect citizens and infrastructure and reduce our vulnerability to attack, including through improved security of borders, transport and critical infrastructure;
- *Third,* to pursue and investigate terrorists across borders and globally; to impede planning, travel and communications; to disrupt support networks; to cut off funding and access to materials, and to bring terrorists to justice; and
- *Fourth,* to prepare ourselves, in the spirit of solidarity, to manage and minimise the consequences of a terrorist attack, by improving the capabilities to deal with: the aftermath; the coordination of the response; and the needs of victims.

As the strategic commitment states, the EU is determined to fight terrorism globally. Indeed, none of the four objectives can be achieved without international cooperation because terrorism is a global challenge and the security of Europe is indivisible from that of the whole world. This is why working with international partners, and in particular the UN, is so important.

3. EU Support for UN Action Against Terrorism

The UN is central to the fight against terrorism because it provides the framework in which all countries of the world can work together on the basis of common values and a common understanding of what the threat of terrorism means for us all. The UN fulfils a threefold function in the counterterrorism arena. Firstly, it provides legitimacy for this work by setting moral and legislative standards, serving as the primary venue for the creation of a worldwide normative framework. Moreover, the UN Security Council has in recent years devised mechanisms that are crucial to tackle the terrorist threat, *inter alia,* through the creation of subsidiary bodies. Last but not least, working within the UN framework should ensure that, while all states have a duty to fight terrorism, their actions must always be in accordance with international human rights, humanitarian law and refugee law.

---

[4] The European Union Counterterrorism Strategy, approved by the Council on 1-2 December 2005, available at <http://register.consilium.eu.int/pdf/en/05/st14/st14469-re04.en05.pdf>.

3.1 Counterterrorism and standard-setting

A central part of the EU's foreign policy relates to supporting the UN's role in setting standards in the field of counterterrorism. That is why, for instance, the EU pushed strongly for the recent adoption of the UN Convention on Nuclear Terrorism[5] and is currently active in promoting a Comprehensive Convention against International Terrorism to complement the 13 sectoral conventions which have already been adopted. In its relations with third countries, the EU stresses the importance of ratifying these conventions and of implementing the relevant UN Security Council Resolutions. There is a direct correlation between a state's record on implementation and its effectiveness in the fight against terrorism. The EU also provides technical assistance and support to those countries which have the will to implement UN Conventions and Resolutions but lack the means to do so. Ratification by itself is not enough. The EU aims to support the UN by ensuring that signatures are turned into effective measures on the ground.

Member States are also keen to see the adoption of a Comprehensive Convention on Terrorism. Discussions on this matter have not always been easy. Considerable differences of opinion still exist about key issues, such as the definition of terrorism, the notion of state terrorism, and what the right to self-determination entails, but we should use the stimulus provided by the recommendations of the UN High Level Panel[6] on terrorism, and endorsed by the UN Secretary-General in his 2005 speech in Madrid,[7] to push these talks to a conclusion.

As part of its global strategy in the fight against terrorism the EU is now mainstreaming the issue of terrorism in its relations with third countries. The Union has been intensifying the dialogue on counterterrorism with third countries and counterterrorism clauses are being introduced into all EU external agreements. Chapters on counterterrorism have been included in all the Action Plans agreed between the EU and its neighbours under the European Neighbourhood Policy (ENP), from Morocco to Jordan and Israel.

Furthermore, the EU is working hard to promote the universal ratification of all 13 UN Conventions in the fight against terrorism.[8] In recent years, the rate of ratification has gone up and the Counterterrorism Committee (CTC) can take much of the credit for this. For example, the number of parties to the Convention for the

---

[5] International Convention for the Suppression of Acts of Nuclear Terrorism, adopted by the General Assembly on 13 April 2005 (by consensus), available at <http://untreaty.un.org/English/Terrorism/English_18_15.pdf>.

[6] Report of the Secretary-General's High-level Panel on Threats, Challenges and Change, 'A more secure world: our shared responsibility', 2 December 2004, available at <http://www.un.org/secureworld/>.

[7] Secretary-General's keynote address to the closing plenary of the International Summit on Democracy, Terrorism and Security, 'A Global Strategy for Fighting Terrorism', Madrid, 10 March 2005, available at <http://www.un.org/apps/sg/sgstats.asp?nid=1345>.

[8] The texts of these Conventions are available at <http://www.un.org/sc/ctc/law.shtml>; details on ratification can be consulted at <http://www.un.org/sc/ctc/documents/treatytable.pdf>.

Suppression of Terrorist Bombings (1997) has increased almost six-fold between September 2001 and January 2006 (from 22 countries to 145); adherence to the Convention for the Suppression of the Financing of Terrorism (1999) grew even more (from 4 countries to 145). Nevertheless, of the 192 Member States of the UN many are not yet a party to all original 12 instruments. To improve this record is one of the objectives of the EU's common foreign policy and security policy. The EU's own record in this field is not perfect. Of the 25 Member States, 21 have ratified all 12 'old' conventions. Belgium, Poland, and Sweden still need to ratify one and Luxembourg four. Poland and Sweden are in the process of completing ratification. As mentioned, EU Member States strongly supported the agreement in 2005 about the International Convention for the Suppression of Acts of Nuclear Terrorism. All Member States have signed this instrument. On 23 March 2006, Slovakia became the first EU country to ratify it.

In addition to promoting the existing 13 UN Conventions and additional instruments,[9] the EU attaches importance to ensuring the ratification of the UN Conventions against Corruption[10] and Transnational Organized Crime,[11] as well as the additional protocols to the TOC Convention, in particular the Protocol against the Illicit Manufacturing of and Trafficking in Firearms, their Parts and Components and Ammunition.[12]

The EU also provides aid and technical assistance to countries lacking the capability to implement the common legal framework set out by UN Resolutions and Conventions. The EU is working closely with several countries in order to help them build up their capacity to fight terrorism. Much of this aid and technical assistance is aimed at helping these countries to meet their commitments under UN Security Council Resolution 1373.

3.2 Security Council Resolutions on counterterrorism

UN Security Council Resolutions 1267, 1373 and 1540 have considerably enhanced the role of the UN.[13] The three resolutions established the Al-Qaida and Taliban Sanctions Committee (1267), the Counterterrorism Committee (1373) and the Committee to combat the proliferation of weapons of mass destruction (1540). The EU is committed to ensuring that these instruments are effective yet for this to be the

---

[9] Notably the Amendment to the Convention on the Physical Protection on Nuclear Material, the Protocol to the Convention for the Suppression of Unlawful Acts against the Safety of Maritime Navigation and the Protocol of 2005 to the Protocol for the Suppression of Unlawful Acts against the Safety of Fixed Platforms Located on the Continental Shelf.

[10] UN Convention against Corruption, UN GA Res. 58/4 of 31 October 2003.

[11] UN Convention against Transnational Organized Crime, UN GA Res. 55/25 of 8 January 2001.

[12] UN GA Res. 55/255 of 8 June 2001.

[13] UN SC Res. 1267 (1999) of 15 October 1999; UN SC Res. 1373 (2001) of 28 September 2001; UN SC Res. 1540 (2004) of 28 April 2004.

case, it is important that all the work in this field is joined up. Current working relations between the responsible committees and agencies within the UN still leave a lot to be desired. UN Security Council Resolution 1566 called for closer cooperation between all the UN committees involved in counterterrorism work, as did the 2005 World Summit. The EU would like to see such cooperation put into effect and is keen to play a part in bringing it about. Coordinated country visits by the three aforementioned Committees, consolidated country reporting procedures, and joint assessments of developing countries' needs would go a long way to enhancing the effectiveness of the United Nations in fighting terrorism.

Coordination and cooperation are necessary not only among the various committees but also among the different bodies of the UN. The United Nations Office on Drugs and Crime (UNODC), for instance, has an important role to play in implementing international action against terrorism, particularly in reviewing and helping to improve domestic legislation and providing training to national criminal justice systems. The European Commission and UNODC have concluded a memorandum of understanding to enhance cooperation. And in 2005 the EU invited the UN Interregional Crime and Justice Research Institute (UNICRI) to Brussels for discussions with experts of the Member States on cooperation between their institute and the EU. Numerous UNICRI projects in the field of police cooperation involve the active participation of Europol and the law enforcement agencies of the Member States. All UN bodies which share responsibility in the fight against terrorism should make sure their activities are properly coordinated and mutually supportive. In all, some 23 organizations, departments, agencies, units and groups in the United Nations system and among its partners are actively involved in building State capacity to prevent terrorism, and the EU welcomes Secretary-General Annan's proposals to improve coordination among them.[14] The Counterterrorism Committee (CTC) and its Executive Directorate (CTED) have a particularly important role to play in improving the coordination, coherence and efficiency of delivery of technical assistance in the field of counterterrorism.

Synergy and cooperation are not only important objectives within the UN system, but also at the level of Member States. Member States of the UN need to ensure that they properly coordinate not only at international level, but domestically as well. To fight terrorism effectively national departments and agencies need to be prepared to share information and work together, at home as well as abroad. Strong and timely coordination among relevant national agencies is also necessary to ensure effective delivery of external technical assistance (counterterrorism capacity building). To encourage its Member States to identify best practices and learn from each other the European Union has conducted a peer evaluation of domestic anti-terrorism legislation, and particularly of national counterterrorism coordinating mechanisms in the Union. As non-EU states might find the EU findings

---

[14] 'Uniting Against Terrorism: Recommendations for a global counterterrorism strategy', Report of the Secretary-General available at <http://www.un.org/unitingagainstterrorism/contents.htm>.

of interest, the public version of the EU's peer review has been shared with the UN Counterterrorism Committee and the CTED.[15]

3.2.1 *Implementation of UNSCR 1373*

Resolutions 1267 and 1373 were remarkable in that they gave the UN teeth in its fight against terrorism. They imposed obligations on Member States to respond to the global threat of terrorism and, by establishing the Counterterrorism Committee and, subsequently, the Counterterrorism Executive Directorate, the UN showed that on this issue it meant business. The CTC has since played a leading role in creating and sustaining momentum against terrorism and it is a tribute to its work that all UN Member States have reported on their domestic efforts on counterterrorism. The EU is committed to support the work of both committees.

In its report to the CTC in May 2003, the European Union listed the wide range of legislation it had adopted in the areas covered by UNSCR 1373, including Common Positions which commit the EU as a whole to full implementation of the resolution and provide the basis for more specific measures aimed at cutting off terrorist funding.[16] In particular, a Council Regulation of December 2001 'freezes funds, financial assets and economic resources of, and prohibits the provision of financial services to, persons, groups and entities involved in terrorism'.[17] This Regulation stipulated that the Council should establish and maintain a list of persons, groups and entities involved in terrorism and that this list would be constantly updated. The list is drawn up on the basis of investigations carried out by the competent judicial and police authorities of the Member States. It includes European-based groups such as ETA and the IRA, as well as other groups such Hamas and the Palestinian Islamic Jihad.

The EU is constantly looking to update best practice in light of the experience gained and further clarifications from the Financial Action Task Force (FATF). New legislation on money laundering, with specific application to terrorist financing, and on cash remittances has been approved and will shortly come into force. The EU is also working on a code of conduct for charities in line with FATF Special Recommendation VIII.

Looking more generally at the international aspects of UNSCR 1373, the reports submitted to the CTC by UN Member States show that many of them have the will

[15] Final report on the evaluation of national anti-terrorist arrangements: 'Improving national machinery and capability for the fight against terrorism', available at <http://www.consilium.europa.eu/cms3_fo/showPage.asp?id=406&lang=EN>.

[16] Report to the CTC, 'European Union activities in the field of counterterrorism', 20 May 2003, available at <http://www.un.org/spanish/docs/comites/1373/eu-ctc-rev4may03.doc>.

[17] Council Regulation No. 881/2002 of 27 May 2002 imposing certain specific restrictive measures directed against certain persons and entities associated with Usama bin Laden, the Al-Qaida network and the Taliban, and repealing Council Regulation No. 467/2001 of 27 May 2002, OJ (29 May 2002) L-139/9.

to wage an effective fight against terrorism, but that they lack the legislative, institutional or technical means to do so. The EU is keen to work together with the CTC and the CTED to redress this balance. Counterterrorism assistance is already part of the aid strategy of the EU and its Member States and the Council has resolved to further enhance the contribution of the Union. Both the EU and several Member States, for example, support Indonesia's Centre for Law Enforcement Cooperation in Semarang.

In 2005 the EU Counter-Terrorism Coordinator accompanied Ambassador Ruperez on a CTED mission to Kenya. Furthermore, EU technical experts have taken part in the CTED's needs assessment missions to Albania, Algeria, Morocco, and Tanzania to identify specific needs in the fields of judicial capacity, customs, and financial investigation and legislation. EU Member States and the Commission have subsequently developed counterterrorism capacity building aid packages for Algeria and Morocco, and others. These efforts, which cover areas from financial intelligence to border protection and judicial and police cooperation, are aimed at enabling these countries to meet their obligations under Resolution 1373. The European Council has invited the European Commission to increase funding for capacity-building projects in third countries and to ensure that there is sufficient flexibility in the budgetary procedures to allow funds to be used imaginatively.

A regular dialogue has also been set up with the Gulf Cooperation Council (GCC) countries to explore cooperation in the field of terrorist financing. As a consequence of the 2005 EU-GCC meeting the countries of the GCC expressed their commitment to ratifying the UN Convention on the financing of terrorism.[18]

The EU has also reinforced cooperation within the Asia-Europe Meeting (ASEM) and the ASEAN Regional Forum. Europol, the organization charged with improving cooperation between the competent law enforcement agencies of the EU Member States, has concluded agreements with several countries and is expanding its link with others. Eurojust, which is tasked with the coordination of investigations and prosecutions, is moving in a similar direction.

3.2.2 *Implementation of UNSCR 1267*

Two years ago the team charged with monitoring the implementation of UN Security Council Resolution 1267 warned that the sanctions imposed by the Security Council on the Taliban, Al-Qaida and their associates had begun to lose credibility. The effect of the financial and economic sanctions was unclear, and no state had reported stopping anyone on the 1267 Committee Consolidated List from travel-

[18] See Joint Communiqué, adopted at the 15th GCC-EU Joint Council and Ministerial Meeting, Manama, 5 April 2005, available at <http://europa.eu.int/comm/external_relations/gulf_cooperation/intro/finaldecl_050405.pdf>, at 6.

ling, or reported taking action against them in respect of the arms embargo.[19]

The reports of the 1267 Monitoring Team[20] contain important recommendations for improving the effectiveness of the sanctions against Al-Qaida, the Taliban and their allies. Some of the recommendations have been taken on board by the 1267 Committee. It is important that the three areas of asset freezing, travel ban and arms embargo are properly covered, while ensuring that due process is observed because sanctions can only serve the cause for which they were set-up if their implementation is consistent with the protection of human rights.

The EU has fully implemented the Al-Qaida and Taliban sanctions regime set out in this Resolution, and those which followed, in its internal legal order, thus ensuring uniform application throughout the EU Member States of the different measures to be taken in relation to those designated on the consolidated list as belonging to or associated with either organization. Unlike in the case of Resolution 1373, where the EU established its own autonomous list to fulfil its obligations, the list adopted by the 1267 Committee is transposed automatically into Community legislation.

Listing – especially of groups – clearly has an important political and psychological impact. Furthermore, these measures have reduced the possibilities for terrorists and terrorist organizations to misuse the financial sector and have made it more difficult for organizations to raise and move funds. But it is of primary importance to ensure that the consolidated list is as operational and as effective as possible. It is worth noting that the transition from applying asset freezing measures primarily as a political measure against governments or persons linked to them (the original aim of most UN and EU sanctions regimes prior to 9/11) to freezing as a preventive measure, targeting terrorist individuals and groups, has led to a series of legal questions. These questions range from the criteria which should be applied and the evidence which is needed for administrative freezing, the relation of administrative freezing to judicial freezing, seizure and confiscation, to matters of due process, availability of de-listing procedures and the role of intelligence in the designation process. Effective freezing action will require the preparation of designations that are based on solid intelligence and information from competent authorities which comply with the agreed criteria for freezing. This will be the case whether those designations are being decided by the UN in the 1267 Committee, or by the EU itself for terrorist individuals, groups and entities not linked to Al-Qaida and the Taliban. This will require enhanced information sharing both within and between states, while respecting legal safeguards.

Pursuant to Resolution 1617 (2005)[21] all UN Member States were to report by 1 March 2006 on the measures taken to implement the latest requirements in relation

---

[19] First report of the Analytical Support and Sanctions Monitoring Team appointed pursuant to Resolution 1526 (2004) concerning Al-Qaida and the Taliban and associated individuals and entities, UN Doc. S/2004/679, para. 29

[20] Available at <http://www.un.org/Docs/sc/committees/1267Template.htm>.

[21] UN SC Res. 1617 (2005) of 29 July 2005.

to the sanctions list, including the invalidation of lost and stolen passports and the sharing of information on such documents with other Member States through Interpol's database. The requirement to share information on lost and stolen passports with Interpol has equally been included in the EU Council Common Position (2005/69/JHA) on exchanging certain data with Interpol of 24 January 2005.[22] While the Interpol database has been growing strongly it still only stores data about one third of the more than 35 million passports that are estimated to have been lost or stolen worldwide. The Union will therefore continue to encourage third states to submit all relevant data to Interpol, and to make sure that all competent domestic authorities have access to the database.

It is essential to provide adequate identifying information concerning those on the list and those about to be listed, in order to allow proper enforcement of the sanctions. At the same time, the EU also attaches great importance to the respect for fundamental rights in the context of listings, including due process considerations. In this context, the EU considers that the recommendations concerning de-listing mentioned in the Monitoring Team's report deserve detailed examination, both in relation to de-listing procedures in general, including the possible justifications for de-listing, as well as in relation to a possible specific procedure concerning deceased persons. It is important that we get this list right. States will only add to it if they are confident that it is consistent with basic human rights. As the Second Monitoring Team's report points out, the list is a living document, relying on constant input from Member States. Upgrading its content and image can only help make the sanctions more effective. Although the 1267 Committee has approved a partial revision of its Guidelines, improving decision-making procedures, clarifying rules concerning the updating of the list and the application of exemptions pursuant to Resolution 1452 (2002), there remains scope for further reform, particularly with respect to listing and delisting procedures. As was emphasised by the World Summit, there should be fair and clear procedures for placing individuals and entities on sanctions lists and for removing them, as well as for granting humanitarian exemptions. Two EU Member States co-sponsored a report on 'Strengthening Targeted Sanctions through Clear and Fair Procedures' which has been submitted to the 1267 Committee.[23]

On the arms embargo, EU legislation has been in place for some time to regulate the traffic, acquisition, storage and trade in arms. After the adoption of Resolution 1390,[24] establishing the arms embargo in relation to individuals and groups linked to Al-Qaida and the Taliban, the EU was therefore able to apply the experience already gained in this field to fulfilling its obligations in respect of the Resolution. This aspect of the 1267 Committee's work is the least highlighted, perhaps because

---

[22] Council Common Position 2005/69/JHA of 24 January 2005 on exchanging certain data with Interpol, OJ (29 January 2005) L-027/61.

[23] Report on 'Strengthening Targeted Sanctions Through Clear and Fair Procedures', available at <http://watsoninstitute.org/pub/Strengthening_Targeted_Statement.pdf>.

[24] UN SC Res. 1390 (2002) of 16 January 2002.

it is non-contentious and, in comparison with some of the other issues, more easily implemented. But it is nevertheless an important part of the overall measures being taken to restrict terrorism. Shoulder-launched missiles (Man-Portable Air Defence Systems or Manpads) for instance continue to pose a serious threat to civil aviation. The Monitoring Team's recommendations for establishing effective national controls on these devices deserve close examination. Looking more widely at measures to reduce the access of terrorists to arms, we have undertaken a number of actions which are helpful in this cause. The EU has for instance worked closely with the Russians to reduce their chemical and nuclear stockpiles. It has also established various instruments regulating the transfer of light weapons, such as the Code of Conduct on Arms Exports, the common position on arms brokering and the Programme of Action to Prevent, combat and eradicate the illicit trade in small arms.

Clearly, there is a link between the Monitoring Team and the work of the Committee established under Resolution 1540 introducing measures to prevent non-State actors gaining access to weapons of mass destruction. Although the prospect of, for instance, a bio-terrorist attack at present may seen remote, terrorist networks such as Al-Qaida have researched the materials for such an attack and some remain keen on acquiring chemical, biological, radiological and nuclear weapons. However small, the chance of a terrorist group being able to conduct a CBRN attack,[25] the consequences of such an attack would be devastating. We need to ensure that our work on terrorism and on WMD is joined up to prevent this from happening.

Several EU instruments and policies serve to implement the travel ban. The purpose of the Schengen Convention is to enhance the security of our citizens. Its provisions are designed to ensure that, while in principle allowing the freedom of movement within the territory of the Member States, strict and effective controls are applied at the external borders. The objective of these controls is to deny listed individuals entry to the territory of any of the Member States of the EU. A major issue in this context is that sufficient identifiers must be provided to allow for accurate targeting of the individuals concerned. Further consideration is needed on how best to improve the identifying information provided concerning the individuals listed.

The reliability of travel documents also plays an important role. We must make it more difficult for terrorists and those who support them to travel using forged documents. This is why the EU has adopted new standards for security features and biometrics in travel documents.[26] As indicated, the EU has also agreed rules for the exchange of passport data by Member States with Interpol. The more effective

---

[25] A CBRN attack stands for an attack by means of a chemical, biological, radiological or nuclear agent.

[26] Council Regulation on standards for security features and biometrics in travel documents, 13 December 2004, OJ (29 December 2004) L-385/1.

Interpol's database will become, the better we will be able to combat identify fraud by terrorists and other criminals.

Two special categories of individuals in relation to the area without border controls are those who are nationals of a Member State or are in possession of a residence permit issued by a Member State. In principle, such individuals cannot be the subject of an alert in the Schengen Information System (SIS) for the purposes of refusing entry. However, under certain strict conditions it is possible for Member States to deny such individuals entry into their territories for reasons of public policy or public security. Therefore, if they are found within the territory of another Member State they can be returned to their state of origin or residence. Their state of origin or residence can also monitor or otherwise restrict their movement in accordance with national rules. It would be interesting to compare examples of practices developed by other States in relation to the treatment of their own listed nationals or listed foreign nationals to whom they have issued a residence permit.

Within the EU in general and in the Schengen area in particular, a wide range of measures have been developed to ensure maximum cooperation between police and judicial authorities. The sophistication of the Schengen Information System allows data on a range of issues to be shared in real time between the law enforcement agencies of the Member States. SIS allows a policeman on the beat to connect electronically to the central data base. As a result, a minor infringement of the law (e.g., a parking or speeding offence) would lead to identification as a designated individual where that individual has been made the subject of an alert in the SIS and a return to his country of origin or residence.

3.2.3 *Implementation of Resolution 1540*

It is not easy to assess the effect the adoption of Resolution 1540 has had worldwide. The 1540 Committee and its group of experts have done useful work in developing a matrix and building a legislative database on the basis of the State reports examined and other relevant information received. The database will be an important tool of information for Member States. However, many countries have not yet informed the UN about their measures of implementation. As of February 2006, almost two years after the 1540 Committee was created, more than one third of the UN membership (67 states) had yet to submit any report. While some of the backlog in reporting may be explained by 'reporting fatigue', there also appears to be considerable divergence in national appreciations of the urgency of combating the spread of weapons of mass destruction. As Al-Qaida and other terrorist networks continue their search for WMD, the threat of non-conventional terrorist attacks is a serious one, and the EU is committed to combat it both in Europe and globally. The EU has urged all States, which have not yet done so, to submit their reports to the Committee and it is prepared to consider any request for assistance or advice to such States as might be required. The Union has also decided to support the three regional seminars (in China, Ghana and Peru) which will be organized by the 1540 Committee in the second half of 2006.[27]

In its own report to the UN on implementation of Resolution 1540,[28] the EU highlighted the European Union Strategy against the proliferation of weapons of mass destruction[29] as the cornerstone for EU policies and activities in areas covered by the Resolution. The Strategy is based on the belief that the EU must seek an effective multilateralist response, including through the UN, to the new threat of terrorism and weapons of mass destruction. The EU approach is guided by:

> 'the conviction that a multilateral approach to security, including disarmament and non-proliferation, provides the best way to maintain international order and hence our commitment to uphold, implement and strengthen the multilateral disarmament and non-proliferation treaties and agreements;
> the conviction that non-proliferation should be mainstreamed in our overall policies, drawing upon all resources and instruments available to the EU;
> the determination to support the multilateral institutions charged respectively with verification and upholding of compliance with these treaties;
> the view that increased efforts are needed to enhance consequence management capabilities and improve coordination;
> the commitment to strong national and internationally-coordinated export controls of dual use items;
> the conviction that the EU in pursuing effective non-proliferation should be forceful and inclusive and needs to actively contribute to international stability;
> the commitment to cooperate with partners who share the same objectives.' (para. 14)

The EU policy is to pursue the implementation and universalisation of the existing disarmament and non-proliferation norms. To that end, the EU will seek the universalisation of the Non-Proliferation Treaty (NPT), the IAEA Safeguard agreements and protocols additional to them, the Chemical Weapons Convention (CWC), the Biological and Toxin Weapons Convention (BTWC), the Hague Code of Conduct against the Proliferation of Ballistic Missiles (HCOC), and the early entry into force of the Comprehensive Test Ban Treaty (CTBT). If the multilateral treaty regime is to remain credible, however, it must be made more effective. The EU places particular emphasis on a policy of reinforcing compliance with the multilateral treaty regime. Such a policy must be geared towards enhancing the ability to detect significant violations and strengthening enforcement of the prohibitions and norms

---

[27] Council Joint Action 2006/419/CFSP in support of the implementation of the United Nations Security Council Resolution 1540 (2004) and in the framework of the implementation of the EU Strategy against the proliferation of weapons of mass destruction, 12 June 2006, OJ (17 June 2006) L-165/30.

[28] European Union Report on the implementation of Security Council Resolution 1540 (2004), 15 November 2004, UN Doc. S/AC.44/2004/(02)/48.

[29] EU Strategy against proliferation of Weapons of Mass Destruction, 12 December 2003, available at <http://ue.eu.int/uedocs/cmsUpload/st15708.en03.pdf>.

established by the multilateral regime, including by providing for criminalization of violations committed under the jurisdiction or control of a state.

The EU is committed to strengthening export control policies and practices within its borders and beyond in coordination with partners. A peer review of Member States' implementation of export controls of dual use items has been completed and its recommendations will lead to improved export controls in the EU. Within our own borders, a series of measures to account for and secure the production, use and storage or transport of WMD materials and to ensure effective physical protection of nuclear material, as required by Resolution 1540, have been put in place within the framework of the Euratom Treaty.

The EU also provides assistance to third countries to help them fulfil their obligations under multilateral conventions and regimes. It has also enhanced its political, financial and technical support for agencies in charge of verification, such as the International Atomic Energy Agency and the Organization for the Prohibition of Chemical Weapons. At the practical level, the EU has been a longstanding provider of assistance directly or indirectly related to threat reduction. For instance, 1 billion Euros have been committed over a 10-year-period to support the G8 Global Partnership. Projects currently underway include enhancing nuclear safety and security, chemical weapons destruction, the re-employment of former scientists, export control and border security.

4. Counterterrorism and Human Rights

The protection of the most basic human right – the right to life – is at the heart of the struggle to prevent terrorism. Terrorists hope that by their actions they will provoke a repressive response from governments which will in turn feed the cycle of violence. But security should not be sought at the expense of liberty. We must not fall into the trap of 'undermining or even destroying democracy on the grounds of defending it', to quote the words of the European Court of Human Rights, expressed in the context of the Red Army and Baader-Meinhof terrorism in Germany in 1978 and reaffirmed each time the Court has dealt with cases concerning terrorism. Abraham Lincoln's words, stating that 'those who are ready to sacrifice freedom for security ultimately will lose both', were true then and are still true today. That is why, for instance, the EU is in the process of strengthening rules on data protection, so that information can be used where justified to improve our security while at the same time protecting the rights of the individual against abuse. And in its relations with third countries the Union aims to promote good governance, the rule of law and respect for human rights in the fight against terror. A lack of good governance, including inadequate protection of human rights, is one of the factors underlying radicalisation and recruitment into terrorism. This is one more reason why states must be reminded of their responsibility to implement counterterrorism measures in conformity with international human rights and humanitarian law, consistent with

Security Council Resolution 1456.[30] Respect for human rights is not only compatible with fighting terrorism; it is an indispensable dimension of a successful counterterrorism strategy. Without justice there can be no lasting security.

Clearly it is important for the Member States of the United Nations not only to ratify the international conventions against terrorism, but to ratify and implement the international human rights instruments as well. The EU has committed itself to promoting the universal ratification and implementation of the ICCPR.[31] In addition, through its political dialogue with third countries the EU has prioritised the universal ratification and implementation of the 1977 Additional Protocols to the Geneva Convention and the Statute of the International Criminal Court.[32]

Torture is abhorrent and illegal in all circumstances – including in the struggle against terrorism. Regrettably, one quarter of the Member States of the UN are not yet a party to the Convention against Torture. Efforts to achieve universal ratification and implementation urgently need to be intensified. Diplomatic initiatives are also required to encourage states to sign, ratify and implement the Optional Protocol to the Torture Convention, which allows for on-site country visits by the UN Committee against Torture. The EU has been encouraging all states which have not yet done so to ratify the UN Convention against Torture and to abide by its provisions. All EU Member States have ratified this essential Convention. The Optional Protocol has thus far been signed by 17 EU Member States and ratified by 5, thus signalling that the EU still needs to improve its own record.

In addition, the EU Framework Decision establishing the European Arrest Warrant explicitly stipulates that '(n)o person should be removed, expelled or extradited to a State where there is a serious risk that he or she would be subjected to the death penalty, torture or other inhuman or degrading treatment or punishment'.[33] The more states respect human rights, the easier international judicial cooperation will become. Indeed, it is not a state's determination to respect human rights which is a stumbling block to closer cooperation in the fight against terrorism, but rather the failure of states to respect human rights. Technical assistance to reinforce the independence of the judiciary and ensure the respect of fair trial rights could become an important component of the work of the UN in supporting international cooperation.

Building on the Barcelona Declaration (1995) the European Union is developing its New Neighbourhood Policy. Working with each partner individually the EU has agreed several Action Plans to deepen relations. The European Neighbourhood

---

[30] UN SC Res. 1456 (2003) of 20 January 2003.

[31] Guidelines to EU Policy towards third countries on torture and other cruel, inhuman or degrading treatment or punishment (April 2001), available at <http://ue.eu.int/uedocs/cmsUpload/TortureGuidelines.pdf>.

[32] EU Guidelines on promoting compliance with international humanitarian law (December 2005), OJ (23 December 2005) C-327/4.

[33] Council Framework Decision of 13 June 2002 on the European Arrest Warrant and the surrender procedures between Member States, OJ (18 July 2002) L-190/1.

Action Plans devote a central part to political dialogue and reform, strengthening democratisation and the rule of law.[34] Furthermore, in these agreements the partners explicitly commit themselves to respect human rights in the fight against terrorism. In the Action Plan with Israel, for example, the EU and Israel agreed to strengthen their cooperation in the fight against and prevention of terrorism 'while ensuring the safeguarding of human rights in that pursuit'. Similar provisions have been included in the Action Plans with Jordan and the Palestinian Authority. Critics have argued, however, that the EU is better at formulating commitments than at implementing them.[35]

Some countries appear to be using the struggle against terrorism as a pretext for silencing non-violent expressions of opposition to their national government. This was particularly clear in the case of Uzbekistan. On 23 May 2005 the EU's Council of Ministers characterised the use of force by President Karimov against demonstrators as being excessive and disproportionate, and repeated calls for an independent inquiry. On 3 October 2005, the Council imposed sanctions on Uzbekistan, including a partial suspension of the EU Partnership and Cooperation Agreement. This is the first time the EU has suspended a Partnership and Cooperation Agreement.

In this context, implementation of UN Security Council Resolution 1624 by UN Member States needs to be scrutinized with particular attention. This Resolution condemns the incitement of terrorist acts and repudiates attempts at the justification or glorification (*apologie*) of terrorist acts that may incite further terrorist acts. It is clear, however, that states have different understandings of what is meant by incitement,[36] and there is a risk that abusive governments will invoke this resolution to restrict free speech or muzzle opponents.

Fundamental principles of fair trial must apply in all circumstances, including while countering terrorism. Even in a state of emergency the right to be tried by an independent and impartial tribunal should be upheld, as well as the right to be heard and to challenge the legality of one's detention; the right to a defence, and the presumption of innocence. Indefinite detention without trial is clearly incompatible with fundamental human rights.

The EU has committed itself to urge its partners to ban secret places of detention and ensure that all persons deprived of their liberty are held in officially recognized places of detention. The European Union has also called on the United States to close the Guantanamo detention facility. Other objectives include ensuring that all statements obtained through torture and ill-treatment shall not be invoked as evi-

---

[34] The Action Plans are available at <http://europa.eu.int/comm/world/enp/documents_en.htm#6>.

[35] See for example Amnesty International, 'Reaffirming the primacy of human rights. A ten-point programme for the Austrian Presidency of the European Union', available at <http://www.amnesty-eu.org>.

[36] UN News Service, 'States tackling speech that "incites" terrorism but have different ideas of word's meaning, UN official says', 15 June 2006, available at <http://www.un.org>.

dence in any proceedings, except against a person accused of torture as evidence that the statement was made.[37] The European Parliament has created a committee to investigate the alleged use of European countries by the CIA for the transport and illegal detention of prisoners.

The EU therefore welcomes the UN Secretary-General's own commitment in this field when he said that 'in the long-term we shall find that human rights, along with democracy and social justice, are one of the best prophylactics against terrorism'.[38] The CTC itself has been in close dialogue with the Office of the High Commissioner for Human Rights in pursuing its mandate, according to the provisions of UNSCR 1535, and the CTED has enlisted the help of a human rights expert. The European Union has strongly promoted the adoption by the UN Human Rights Commission of a resolution providing for the appointment of a Special Rapporteur on the protection of human rights while countering terrorism.[39] Both the CTC and the CTED should make sure the human rights dimension is fully integrated in their work. For its part, the new UN Human Rights Council should pay careful attention to the reports by the Special Rapporteur.

5. Conclusion

In many parts of the world people continue to suffer horrendous and indiscriminate violence at the hands of terrorists. In Europe, Madrid (11 March 2004) and London (7 July 2005) have been the target of major terrorist attacks. Indeed, in some respects the world is now facing a more complex and dangerous challenge than it did after 9/11. While governments have been successful in degrading the capabilities of Al-Qaida, the threat has become more complex and in some ways more challenging as the ideological message of Osama Bin Laden provides inspiration to smaller and less well-known groups, which are more difficult to track and suppress.

In countries that have been spared attacks in recent years there is a risk that the public commitment to the fight against terror may weaken. Terrorists, however, are known to exploit situations where they expect to meet least resistance. Countries that would allow themselves to become a weak link in the global chain against terrorism would not only endanger the lives of their own citizens, but the lives of people elsewhere in the world. This is why the fight against terrorism is, and must remain, everybody's business.

---

[37] Guidelines to EU Policy towards third countries on torture and other cruel, inhuman or degrading treatment or punishment (April 2001), available at <http://ue.eu.int/uedocs/cmsUpload/TortureGuidelines.pdf>.

[38] Secretary-General address to Security Council meeting on Counterterrorism, 18 January 2002, Press Release, SG/SM/8105.

[39] Commission on Human Rights, Resolution 2005/80, available at <http://ap.ohchr.org/documents/E/CHR/resolutions/E-CN_4-RES-2005-80.doc>.

The European Union therefore supports Secretary-General Annan's call for a clear 'principled, comprehensive strategy' in the global fight against terrorism based on the recommendations of the High Level Panel. The different elements of this strategy provide a framework for action to counter the threat of terrorism on a global basis, while ensuring that human rights and the rule of law are always respected. The principles of the strategy,[40] and the values underlying it, are ones to which the EU is fully committed. What is needed now is for the General Assembly to adopt a short and concise document, highlighting concrete actions and measures flowing from the Secretary-General's report. This UN Counterterrorism Strategy should be operational and action-oriented. It should focus on steps to enhance cooperation among states and regional organizations against terrorism, on strengthening the capacity of the UN system in assisting states to fight terrorism, and on enhancing coordination of UN activities. The strategy should also highlight the central role of the rule of law and human rights in countering terrorism. In line with the multi-track approach foreseen at the World Summit, and to secure the necessary broad support in the General Assembly, the strategy should not deal with issues related to the comprehensive convention, such as the definition of terrorism, the right of self-determination and state terrorism, which should continue to be discussed in other fora.

The UN and EU have similar agendas in addressing factors underlying the recruitment and support for terrorism. There is general recognition that regional conflicts, bad governance and state failure can provide fertile ground for recruitment into terrorism. Efforts to resolve regional conflicts and to promote human rights and good governance must therefore be at the heart of international counterterrorism strategies. The EU and its Member States are already providing most of the world's official development aid. The EU Development Ministers recently announced agreement to increase the collective aid target for the EU to 0.56% of GNI by 2010. This would result in an additional € 20 billion a year in official development aid – a significant boost aimed at moving faster towards the UN Millennium Goals and to attain the internationally agreed target of 0.7%. Reducing poverty in the world is not only a moral duty but it also contributes in a practical way towards ensuring our own security. Efforts to prevent military conflict and terrorism are equally important to promote equity and growth. Development and security are two sides of the same coin. We need a joined up approach. This is why efforts to promote good governance, for instance in Iraq and Afghanistan, are an integral part of the EU's counterterrorism activities. This is also why the EU and its Member States play an increasingly prominent role in peace-keeping operations in various parts of the world. In a more secure and more just world, we will be better able to reduce the breeding grounds of terrorism and address the root causes of the problem. The European Union is committed to work with like-minded partners across national and religious boundaries and to engage with moderate Muslims to defend the fundamental

---

[40] See *supra* n. 14.

rights of our citizens: the right to live in a humane and democratic society, free of terrorism and free of Islamophobia, anti-semitism and other forms of prejudice.

It is imperative that the United Nations and its Member States continue to show their unity and resolve in the global fight against terrorism. To that end, the European Union supports the 2005 World Summit's call to conclude a comprehensive convention on international terrorism during the Assembly's 2006 session. It also looks forward to the speedy adoption and implementation of a comprehensive United Nations counterterrorism strategy, based on the Secretary-General's proposals. The 'Freedom from Fear' element of the Secretary-General's report[41] puts the fight against terrorism firmly into context. The European Union agrees that 'no State, however powerful, can protect itself on its own; no country weak or strong, can realize prosperity in a vacuum'. The European Union is determined to promote an effective multilateral approach to terrorism with the UN as its heart.

[41] K. Annan, 'In larger freedom: towards development, security and human rights for all. Report of the Secretary-General', 21 March 2005, available at <http://www.un.org/largerfreedom/>.

Chapter 18
THE UNITED NATIONS AND THE EUROPEAN UNION IN KOSOVO – THE CHALLENGES OF JOINT NATION-BUILDING

by Michael Karnitschnig*

1. Introduction: Kosovo as a Test Case

The tectonic changes that the international order underwent in the 1990s were particularly visible in South Eastern Europe. Notably this region experienced the partial shift from *inter-* to *intra-*state conflicts, the 'export' of insecurity by 'failing' entities or authoritarian states and the blurring lines between political security risks and organized crime.

These challenges were especially serious for the United Nations, which despite the checks and balances on nation-states enshrined in its Charter is essentially based on the 'Westphalian' concepts of sovereignty, non-intervention in 'internal affairs' and the sanctity of borders. The UN struggled to come to terms with these new conflicts.[1] On the ground, UN sanctions were not properly implemented; UN forces were walking the tightrope between a role as 'peacekeepers' and as 'dividers' of 'ethnically cleansed' territories. As a result, the UN, despite all diplomatic and security efforts under its auspices, was sidelined in the end-phase of the Bosnian and Croatian wars in 1995 and during the Kosovo crisis of 1998/1999.

Similarly, the problems of Europe's still nascent foreign and security policy were also laid bare in the post-Yugoslav crises. The lack of a common strategic vision and of credible policy tools meant that the EU was largely reduced to an *ex post* provider of humanitarian and reconstruction aid, while European states played vary-

---

* The author serves as speechwriter to EU External Relations Commissioner Ferrero-Waldner. From 2001-2004, he was Desk Officer for Serbia and Montenegro including Kosovo in the European Commission. Before that, he had worked on security policy and Western Balkans affairs in the Austrian Ministry of Foreign Affairs, i.a. during the Kosovo crisis. This article solely reflects his opinions and does not engage the European Commission.

[1] One argument used in favor of a rapid recognition of Slovenia's, Croatia's and Bosnia and Herzegovina's independence (they joined the UN in May 1992) was that this 'internationalization' of the conflicts would help to resolve them in the UN framework. This attempt failed due to the lack of consensus in the Security Council.

J. Wouters et al., eds., The United Nations and the European Union

ing but not decisive roles in the political and military actions.[2] The 1990s thus demonstrated the double limitations of the UN's 'ineffective multilateralism' and of Europe's flawed 'diplomacy of equidistance', lacking political will and the ultimate means of outright force.

In mid-1999, however, both organizations got the chance to redeem themselves as political vehicles. The UN returned to the fore as the most acceptable framework for post-conflict governance in Kosovo. Political circumstances after NATO's contentious air campaign required a broad multilateral arrangement. In particular, Russia's and China's assent to a strong civil and military presence in Kosovo depended on making the UN with its universal mandate and legitimacy the lead agency.[3] This requirement for international consensus did, however, not mean that the field mission stuck to the lowest common denominator. Although one reason for its creation was undeniably to 'freeze' the status issue and leave Kosovo in a legal limbo, the mission gradually evolved into the most far-reaching international state-building exercise ever. This rather unintended 'constitutionalization' of the UN Mission in Kosovo created several challenges, as shall be seen below.

The European Union reinforced its presence in the Balkans, too. This was based on the recognition of the region's strategic centrality. The EU could not afford another foreign policy 'failure' in its own backyard, and stabilizing the powder-keg Kosovo, in many ways a 'mini-Yugoslavia', was a key to that. The earlier Yugoslav crises had already been a catalyst for the development of Europe's external instruments, and in 1999 the EU adopted an ambitious political framework for the 'Western Balkans' as a whole,[4] the Stabilization and Association process (SAP). This policy bundles and develops the Union's instruments (trade preferences, financial assistance, contractual ties and policy advice) inspired by the tools of EU enlargement. Most importantly, it offers the ultimate perspective of EU membership – a major anchor for political and economic reforms.[5]

As a result, Kosovo's international interim administration is a reflection of the 'new world disorder' and, at the same time, a test case for the capacity of both the UN and the EU and their members to deal with it. In particular, Kosovo is an example of the changing nature of sovereignty (with the international community holding a territory 'in trust') and of the critical importance of 'state-building', i.e.,

---

[2] The major contribution of NATO's European members to the military campaign over Kosovo in 1999 reflected Europe's changing attitude towards the region. Still, arguments within the Alliance persisted over the conduct and objective of that campaign. Cf., General Wesley Clark's account in *Waging Modern War* (New York, Public Affairs 2001), 240 p.

[3] For more detail, cf., I.H. Daalder and M.E. O'Hanlon, *Winning Ugly: NATO's war to save Kosovo* (Washington, Brookings Institution Press 2000), p. 174 et seq. Note also that UN Security Council Resolution 1244 ensures that any decision on Kosovo's final status has to run via the Security Council, i.e., requires Russia's and China's agreement. This is a revolutionary step for the UN, as it comes close to envisaging the imposition of territorial boundaries on a state.

[4] This region includes Croatia, Bosnia and Herzegovina, Albania, the FYRO Macedonia, Montenegro and Serbia incl. Kosovo under UNSCR 1244.

[5] For Kosovo's position under the SAP, cf., below.

the creation of viable democratic institutions, the fundaments of the rule of law and the basics of a market economy on a territory.

This article attempts to sketch the challenges encountered in this context and analyzes the evolving UN-EU relationship therein. It will review the functioning of the UN Interim Administration in Kosovo and the role Kosovo plays in the EU Stabilization and Association Process before and during a status settlement. Finally, some tentative conclusions for international state-building missions are drawn.

2. A New Leviathan? The UN Interim Administration Mission in Kosovo

2.1 The establishment of UNMIK

UN Security Council Resolution 1244, adopted on 10 June 1999, is an innovative, quasi-constitutional basis for the most far-reaching UN operation in the organization's history: The United Nations Interim Administration Mission in Kosovo (UNMIK). UNSCR 1244 authorized the UN Secretary-General to create an 'international civilian presence in Kosovo' and to establish substantial autonomy and self-government *within* the Federal Republic of Yugoslavia (FRY), pending the determination of Kosovo's future status. This 'partial international sovereignty' created by UN law is different from the post-war set-up in Bosnia and Herzegovina. There, the General Framework Agreement for Peace (the 'Dayton Agreement') is not as such based on a UNSCR, but a trilateral agreement between the Republic of Bosnia and Herzegovina, the Republic of Croatia and the late Federal Republic of Yugoslavia.

UNMIK has two main tasks: Acting as a transitional administration and overseeing the development of provisional institutions to which it could progressively transfer its responsibilities, without, however, prejudging Kosovo's final status, as UNSCR 1244 reaffirmed the FRY's sovereignty and territorial integrity. This compromise creates two dilemmas at the heart of UNMIK: The contradictions between state-building[6] and a 'status freeze', and between territorial and popular sovereignty, i.e., the right to self-determination.[7]

It is important to note the complex relationship between the scope of UNMIK's powers, the mission's 'calendar' and its objectives which follows from this sovereignty dilemma: Firstly, the mission has competences normally attributed to a state government, as 'the situation in the region continues to constitute a threat to international peace and security' in terms of Article 39 of the UN-Charter. More specifi-

[6] The notions of 'nation-building' and 'state-building' are used interchangeably. The term 's*tate*-building' does not necessarily imply that Kosovo will become a 'state' in the constitutional sense of the word.

[7] UNMIK is thus balancing 'between the Scylla of Kosovo's independence and the Charybdis of Yugoslavia's sovereignty'. A. Yannis, 'The UN as Government in Kosovo', 10 *Global Governance* (2004) p. 67.

cally, UNMIK Regulation 1/1999[8] vested '*all* legislative and executive authority with respect to Kosovo' in UNMIK and hence suspended all competences of the Federal Republic of Yugoslavia. The Security Council thus reduced the FRY's (now Serbia's) sovereignty to an empty shell, a 'nudum ius'.[9]

Secondly, UNMIK's mandate, while being set *ad interim*, is open-ended. The mission shall perform basic civilian functions 'where and as long as required'.[10] Pursuant to UNSCR 1244, its task is to 'facilitate a political process designed to determine Kosovo's future status' and 'in a final stage, overseeing the transfer of authority from Kosovo's provisional institutions to institutions established under a political settlement'. However, the Resolution did not define a precise calendar, neither for the transfer of powers nor for a status decision, and did not set out any details of such a final settlement. UNMIK was set-up to create institutions, but not to promote a claim of statehood or self-determination (unlike, e.g., the UNTAES mission in East Timor under UNSCR 1272 (1999)). As a result, UNMIK faced 'a governance challenge wrapped in a sovereignty enigma'[11] from its very inception. Its bi-cephalous nature as a transitional administrator and facilitator (but not judge) of final status became increasingly difficult.

2.2 UNMIK's 'Pillar structure' – a recipe for confusion?

The United Nations and the European Union were well-suited to create synergies in Kosovo. The EU, a champion of effective multilateralism,[12] had gained some experience in assisting transition countries elsewhere in the Balkans, while the UN provided global legitimacy, especially among the permanent members of the Security Council, and contributed its expertise in administrating territories.

UNSCR 1244 explicitly recognized the contribution to be made by other international organizations. It authorized the UN Secretary-General to establish the civil presence 'with the assistance of relevant international organizations'. UNMIK, headed by the Special Representative of the UN Secretary-General[13] (SRSG), thus

[8] UNMIK Regulation 1999/1 'On the Authority of the Interim Administration in Kosovo'. The Regulation declares most of FRY and Serbian law enacted before 1999 inapplicable. The law of the land was laid down in greater detail in UNMIK Regulation 1999/24.

[9] Cf., Report of the Secretary-General on the United Nations Interim Administration in Kosovo, S/1999/779, 12 July 1999, para. 41: 'UNMIK is the only legitimate authority in Kosovo.' Its institutional basis was spelt out in greater detail in May 2001 in the Constitutional Framework for Provisional Self-Government (cf., UNMIK Regulation 2001/9). The Constitutional Framework sets out which powers will be transferred to the PISG under the SRSG's oversight and which remain 'reserved' (e.g., the 'sovereignty-sensitive' fields of justice and law enforcement, monetary policy and budgetary control and international affairs).

[10] UNSC Res. 1244, Article 11(b).

[11] B. Knoll, 'From Benchmarking to Final Status', 16 *EJIL* (2005) p. 638.

[12] Cf., The Commission's Communication on Effective Multilateralism, COM (2003) 526.

[13] The first SRSG, Dr. Bernard Kouchner of France, served from July 1999 to January 2001. He was succeeded by Denmark's former Minister of Defense Hans Hækkerup (February 2001 to De-

has four different components called 'Pillars', headed by Deputy SRSGs and supported by specific partner organizations: Pillar I originally organized refugee return under the auspices of UNHCR. It was later reorganized to deal with police and justice issues. Pillar II managed civil administration, Pillar III is the Organization for Security and Cooperation in Europe (OSCE) Mission in Kosovo and responsible for democratization and institution-building. The fourth UNMIK Pillar, commonly but inaccurately referred to as the 'EU Pillar', deals with economic development. The UN thus tried to pool resources while keeping control of the mission's operation.

The EU contributed to UNMIK through significant financial support and 'in kind'. Firstly, it covers the major part of Pillar IV's operational expenditure.[14] Without this support to UNMIK's budget, rising to € 20 million per year, the Pillar could not operate.

In addition to this financial support, both the EU institutions and Member States detached experts to UNMIK and funded locally contracted manpower.[15] Pillar IV's respective Heads[16] were suggested by the EU, but appointed by UN SG Annan as Deputies of the SRSG. These personal linkages between the Union, its Member States and the mission initially helped to guide Pillar IV's policies. The EU's and particularly the Commission's expertise played a critical role in jump-starting reforms, not least in the first phase of economic institution-building when senior functions in the Pillar where taken by seconded EU officials.

However, the high staff fluctuation common to international field missions gradually led to loser 'personal ties' between the Pillar and the EU, between which there was never a formal chain of command but only the grant agreement. As a result, the EU's and in particular the Commission's indirect influence was affected. Key projects

---

cember 2001), German diplomat Michael Steiner (Germany, January 2002 to July 2003) and former Finnish PM Harri Holkeri (August 2003 to June 2004). Søren Jessen-Petersen (Denmark, July 2004 to June 2006). The current SRSG is Joachim Rücker of Germany.

[14] Cf., Council Joint Action 1999/522/CFSP of 29 July 1999, prolonged by Joint Actions 1999/864/CFSP of 21 December 1999 and 2000/175/CFSP, by which the EU undertook to support 'the installation of an UNMIK component for economic reconstruction, rehabilitation and development'. These short-term acts adopted in the context of the EU's Common Foreign and Security Policy (CFSP) were soon replaced by Council Regulation (EC) No. 1080/2000 of 22 May 2000, amended by Council Regulation (EC) No. 2098/2003 of 27 November 2003. The details of the EU grant to UNMIK's budget are laid down in a Financing Agreement between the European Community and UNMIK, signed by the Commission and the SRSG (as of 2005, Pillar IV's DSRSG signs this agreement after the SRSG's approval). The EU grant also covers main parts of the costs of the Kosovo Trust Agency (KTA), the privatization body which is formally independent but linked to Pillar IV (cf., below).

[15] The growing use of consultants in key positions did, however, loosen UNMIK's political command chain.

[16] The Pillar's first head, Joly Dixon, had served as Director in the EU Commission's Directorate-General for Economic and Financial Affairs prior to his appointment, while his successors Andrew Bearpark, Nikolaus von Lambsdorff, Joachim Rücker and Paul Acda were detached by their respective Member States.

of UNMIK's Pillar IV – notably privatization – were caught in the complex channels of the mission's bureaucracy and, more fundamentally, between the all-encompassing political authority and legal responsibility of the UN under UNSCR 1244 and the EU's financial support and reform advice.

It is therefore critical to note that the United Nations' authority in Kosovo was not diluted by the pillar-structure. The organization could not 'outsource' or subcontract its powers under a Chapter VII Resolution. The Pillars are not separate missions. Their legal and political ownership lies with the UN. This is reflected in Regulation (EC) 1080/2000 which provides for an EC financial 'contribution to the establishment and operation of the UNMIK (fourth Pillar)', but not for the creation of an EU mission. Consequently, UNMIK's so-called 'EU Pillar' is not an EU-agent. On the contrary, it is an integral part of a UN mission with a command chain running from the UNSC and the UNSG through the SRSG to the pillars,[17] but with financial input and political support from the EU. This principle of UNMIK's global authority was repeatedly emphasized by UN lawyers when UNMIK was set-up.

While the pillar-architecture was both logical and innovative under the unusual circumstances in Kosovo, Pillar IV's increasingly contested ownership started to pose problems. The 'EU' was held responsible for economic policy issues on which it had no direct influence, in particular the privatization process. Also, the EU as such did originally not have a strong role in the definition and monitoring of the UN's Kosovo 'standards'.

Some astute observers within Pillar IV ironically described this set-up as 'organized irresponsibility'. While this is too harsh an assessment, it is true that the creative ambiguity in the quadrangle between UNMIK's leadership, Pillar IV, UN HQ and the EU did not produce optimal results, especially after UNMIK's early successes gave way to the difficulties of day-to-day administration. This was not so much a matter between the UN and the EU as organizations, but rather an issue between various parts of 'Planet UNMIK', and between Pristina, with its practical policy pressures of running a quasi-state, and UN HQ in New York, with its often more orthodox and status-conscious reading of UNSCR 1244.

This multitude of actors was aggravated by the fact that the EU itself is not a unitary foreign policy actor. Important competencies for Kosovo's development lie with the EU Commission: Aid programming, trade preferences, and last but not least the daily management of gradual EU rapprochement. Vice versa, Member States and the High Representative/Secretary-General of the Council take the lead on political mediation.[18] In the run-up to a settlement, it became clear that this division of labor had to be improved (cf., below).

---

[17] Pillar III, however, is made up by a distinct OSCE Mission in Kosovo (OMiK) which also reports to the OSCE's Permanent Council. This dual chain of command repeatedly led to issues, in particular regarding OMiK's independent human rights monitoring which also covered UNMIK's action.

[18] Some Member States – France, Germany, Italy and the United Kingdom – are members of the Balkans Contact Group, which also comprises the United States and Russia.

2.3 UNMIK's performance – Pillar IV successes

Many observers tend to forget the institutional and economic vacuum that UNMIK found in mid-1999. Serbia had maintained an authoritarian presence but no functioning administration in the years before, while the underground structures built by the Kosovar Albanians were not fit to govern the province. Furthermore, economic neglect and the immediate war-damage had produced serious hardship, with the shadow and partly criminal economy reigning.[19] In addition to avoiding a humanitarian disaster, UNMIK's mission was thus twofold: To fill the institutional vacuum and to lay the foundations for self-administration and a market economy.

After basic services and supplies had been secured and the reconstruction of houses and infrastructure had seen rapid success, Pillar IV started to build a macroeconomic framework. It regularized the use of currencies and created a payments system as the economy's backbone. An entire banking system was set-up, overseen by a Banking and Payments Authority. Kosovo's Consolidated Budget was created, initially managed by the Central Fiscal Authority, and taxation was regularized to give Kosovo's institutions a transparent revenue basis. Pillar IV also set-up the Kosovo Customs Service which was trained by an EU-funded customs assistance mission and which executed the trade policy devised by the Pillar on the ground. A policy dialogue with local experts in all these fields was also started.

In a second phase, the Pillar moved from laying the groundwork of an economy to regulatory reform and private sector development, in the agricultural, industrial and especially the services sector. This meant to build a favorable investment climate through a liberal legislative framework, in particular rules on business registration, bankruptcy, contracts and property rights. Also, new rules for capital lending were enacted. Finally, UNMIK's Pillar IV started a privatization program (cf., below) which, however, became a political testing ground for perceived status issues and a point of discord between parts of the UN system and the EU.

To strengthen the coherence of these policies, to improve local ownership and to produce a joint economic development strategy, Pillar IV and the Provisional Institutions of Self-Government (PISG) established the Economic Strategy and Project

---

[19] Despite the international community's efforts and partial successes, Kosovo's economy remains weak and structurally hampered, with low income levels (a per capita-GDP of 1200 Euros), widespread poverty (affecting one third of the population) and a significant shadow business sector. The official unemployment rate reaches 40-50%, but is *de facto* much lower due to the sizeable informal economy. GDP growth over the last years has been patchy and even negative in 2002/3 under IMF estimates. The logical decline in international donor's support (from 36% of GDP in 2002 to 22.7% in 2005), the lack of FDI inflows and the ensuing growing current account deficit (approx. 30% of GDP in 2005) are among the most pressing challenges (cf., below), as is the curbing of public expenditure due to the exhaustion of deposits and the impossibility to have recourse to public borrowing under the current mandate. Updated statistics available at <http://www.ks-gov.net/esk/index_english.htm>.

Identification Group in March 2003.[20] This group does not have powers of its own, but acts as a catalyst for the work of the PISG and UNMIK. UNMIK's Pillar IV thus succeeded in bringing together the key actors without getting entangled in the omnipresent status sensitivities – the right strategy in Kosovo's complex polity.

On balance, Pillar IV performed remarkably well under extreme conditions and high political volatility. It kept basic services going and started a system of economic governance.[21] It succeeded on the basis of an initially clear agreement with UNMIK's and local leaders and good EU-UN cooperation, with the UN setting out the political course and the EU providing economic and financial expertise. However, this trilateral consensus started to unravel, mainly between UNMIK's core team and the PISG and most visibly in the context of privatization.

2.4 **Reforms versus status? – Privatization as a testing ground for UNMIK's mandate**

The entanglement of reforms, final status, local interests and questions of competences between UN, the PISG and the EU was particularly acute in Kosovo's privatization process. This case is instructive inasmuch as it reflects both difficulties in the UN-EU relationship in Kosovo and broader structural challenges of international state-building.

While Kosovo built institutional autonomy under UNSCR 1244 and achieved relative macro-economic stability, structural economic problems continued to loom in the background. The lack of a socioeconomic perspective was easily abused by local powerbrokers and 'ethnic entrepreneurs' during the riots of March 2004.[22] The accusation 'You gave us freedom but not a future', launched by an angry student against UNMIK, reflected this politically explosive sense of deception.

Boosting micro-economic reforms and attracting foreign investment was therefore a vital task for the international presence. To this end, Pillar IV, supported by the EU and the United States, created a specific privatization policy,[23] enforced through a special body, the Kosovo Trust Agency (KTA). While UNMIK, in line with its trustee obligations under UNSCR 1244, manages *publicly*-owned enterprises such as public utilities without transferring their assets, its role on *socially*-

[20] Co-chaired by Pillar IV and the Office of the Prime Minister, ESPIG includes staff from various PISG Ministries as well as the World Bank and the IMF. It is supported through a project funded by the European Agency for Reconstruction.

[21] This was accomplished in addition to UNMIK's overall achievements of institution-building, strengthening the rule of law, organizing free elections and fostering the emerging political system.

[22] In March 2004, unfounded allegations of Serbs drowning Albanian children sparked fighting in the divided northern town of Mitrovica, leading to two days of Kosovo-wide riots that killed 19 and wounded 900 and led to the 'ethnic cleansing' of entire minority villages and neighborhoods. The Kosovo-Albanian mob, a mixture of disaffected youth and politically organized criminals, exposed KFOR's and UNMIK's structural weaknesses and seriously harmed the credibility of the international presence.

[23] Cf., the 'KTA Regulation', UNMIK Regulation 2001/9.

owned enterprises (SOEs) goes further. Its KTA has the power to liquidate SOEs, by initiating bankruptcy proceedings, and to spin-off of their assets to subsidiaries, so-called 'newcos', whose shares are subsequently sold to investors through competitive tenders.[24]

This sophisticated system of 'indirect privatization' maximizes asset value and helps to release the latent potential in Kosovo's economy and create jobs. At the same time, it preserves the rights of both potential owners claiming title and of creditors, keeping the balance between the status of enterprises and UNMIK's obligation to promote economic reforms. Furthermore, privatization actually reduces opportunities for crime by channeling investment through transparent tenders. Most of Kosovo's productive capacity had *already* been taken up by the shadow and criminal economy before the KTA started its work. The question faced by UNMIK was therefore not *whether* to privatize but *how.*[25]

The privatization project thus tried to navigate between the seemingly conflicting concepts at the center of UNSCR 1244: Structural reforms and formal status preservation. However, it soon had its very own 'status issues'. The property of the SOEs to be 'spun-off' was difficult to establish. More specifically, Serbia had already 'privatized' various Kosovar companies in the early 1990s. The KTA had originally not taken these transactions into account, judging them to be generally discriminatory in both intent and substance.[26] This policy was reversed by the new Pillar IV/KTA leadership in mid-2003, which, under UN HQ's guidance, proceeded to a detailed case-by-case analysis of all SOEs. Still, despite this vetting, doubts remained on a number of firms, which in turn led to the question of immunity of the international KTA Board members in case of lawsuits.[27] Due to this legal insecu-

---

[24] The proceeds from tenders and liquidations are held in trust by the KTA and, after the deduction of possible debts, distributed to the former SOE owners (mainly workers and management). A large number of SOEs are, however, candidates for liquidation, operating – if at all – far below capacity. Their primary value is their real-estate which, after liquidation and asset sales, can be developed by the private sector.

[25] 'UNMIK's failure to regulate privatization did not mean that it did not happen.' see D. Eyre and A. Wittkowsky, 'Privatization in Kosovo', 4 *Südosteuropa-Mitteilungen* (2002) p. 25.

[26] This 'clean-slate' approach was also favored by the PISG. However, although most of these pre-1999 transactions were dubious, often with mass lay-offs of Albanian workers and payments to the Belgrade regime, it was possible that property had been validly transferred in some cases.

[27] The Board, the KTA's main decision-making body, includes four Kosovan and four international members. The Head of Pillar IV who chairs the Board is covered by the UN Convention on the Privileges and Immunities as Deputy SRSG. Vice versa, his Deputy and the KTA Managing Director do not have such protection. They feared that they could be sued *ad personam* for KTA decisions in any jurisdiction worldwide. Note that the KTA Regulation (which binds UN members as an act adopted under a Chapter VII Resolution) gives the Kosovo Supreme Court exclusive jurisdiction for all privatization-related lawsuits, thus in principle protecting Board members from suits in UN member countries. Also, KTA officials benefit from specific functional immunities. These guarantees were, however, deemed insufficient by the Board. A first lawsuit had been filed in a US court against UN, UNMIK and the KTA in late 2003. UN and UNMIK had invoked their immunities for themselves, but not for the KTA.

rity, the third wave of tenders was suspended in fall 2003, bringing a key element of Kosovo's economic reforms to a halt.

The following delay of nearly a year provoked serious accusations against 'the EU' (sic) by the PISG, who wrongly assumed the Pillar and the KTA were EU agents.[28] The UN's refusal to pursue privatization thus put a strain on its ties with the EU and the PISG respectively. Beyond that privatization became a sign for UNMIK's 'unfulfilled promises'.

Privatization had always been a contentious project within the UN. Parts of the mission and of UN HQ had only grudgingly accepted the KTA Regulation, with the aforementioned belts and braces. They considered privatization 'a bridge too far', fearing it could in extremis violate the FRY's formal 'sovereignty guarantee' and the status freeze under UNSCR 1244 through wrongful sales of assets. This caution reflected the deeply-engrained sense of political neutrality that had grown in traditional UN peacekeeping operations.

UNMIK's Legal Adviser and UN Headquarters argued that 'the KTA was not a UN body' and refused to grant legal protection. Consequently, the international Board members turned to the EU for support, stating that the Union's role in financing Pillar IV and the KTA engaged its responsibility. This point was, however, entirely inaccurate, for several reasons. Firstly, the United Nations could not simply abandon a key responsibility of a mission mandated by the Security Council under Chapter VII. As set out above, the EU's support to Pillar IV and to privatization in particular does not make it an EU venture. There is no EC legal responsibility for the KTA, whose actions remain entirely attributable to UNMIK, nor an obligation to extend immunity coverage to non-EU personnel.[29]

Secondly, the UN's attempt to deny its principal-agent relationship with the KTA was flawed. The creation of the KTA as a distinct legal person[30] has no impact on the UN's overall responsibility. UNSCR 1244 itself explicitly defines the 'reconstruction of key infrastructure and other economic reconstruction' as a core task of the international civil UN presence. This is specified in the Constitutional Framework.[31] The KTA itself was set-up by virtue of an UNMIK Regulation and key KTA managers are appointed by the SRSG who may also modify and repeal KTA

[28] The local elites were not helpful throughout this debate. Many of them considered privatization a political tool rather than an instrument of economic reforms. This played into the hands of those in the UN (and in Serbia) who accused the KTA of 'ethnic privatization'.

[29] Granting EC immunity to KTA Board Members would in fact have led to problems under EC law. Accepting liability for acts committed by non-EC agents would have gone beyond Article 288(2) EC on the Community's extra-contractual responsibility, which is limited to actions of officials of its institutions.

[30] Section 1 and 18 of Regulation UNMIK 2002/12 on the Establishment of the Kosovo Trust Agency use the term 'legally separate from UNMIK'. The KTA is an agency under public law, capitalized with € 10 million, and notably has the 'capacity [...] to sue and be sued in its own name'.

[31] Cf., Section 11(g) of UNSCR 1244. Section 8.1(q) of the Constitutional Framework defines the 'authority to administer public and socially-owned property' as a reserved power.

Board decisions.[32] In consequence, any *infra vires* action by KTA staff with the relevant authority is performed on behalf of the UN.

After several rounds of discussions, the EU Commission, who represented the EU on this matter, argued successfully for a re-start of the process under UN responsibility and for more procedural transparency.[33] At that point, UN Headquarters had seen that freezing privatization until the start of final status talks was untenable. Politically, further delays would have deepened the rift with the PISG after the riots of March 2004, endangering the credibility of the mission as such. Economically, procrastination would have lead to unregulated growth and the entrenchment of illicit activities. Legally, 'outsourcing' or 'freezing' privatization did not insulate the UN against liabilities anyway, as it could have constituted a dereliction of its fiduciary duties under UNSCR 1244. Finally, the UN had come under pressure from both the EU and the United States who refused to let their political and financial 'investment' lie idle.

A solution for the SOE status determination was found by inserting the power of 'eminent domain' into the KTA Regulation. The KTA can now 'spin-off' assets in the general interest even if property is *not yet* fully established.[34] KTA tendering rules were tightened to avoid money laundering and collusion. At the time of writing, privatization is in its successful 18th 'wave'.[35] This spin-off of hundreds of SOEs has strengthened Kosovo's economic fabric.

The privatization debate negatively affected the UN-EU relationship in Kosovo. However, this was not a matter of diverging economic policy choices in Brussels and New York, but a reflection of the more fundamental mismatches between urgent reform imperatives on the ground and a more conservative, status-oriented approach by UN Headquarters.

The saga sketched above teaches several lessons for policy-makers in interim administrations. Firstly, the lack of clear political lines of command and the dilution of responsibility in UNMIK were main sources of delays. The UN, increasingly afraid of the potential (but ultimately overrated) status implications of privatization, tried to duck its mandate under UNSCR 1244. It wanted to outsource a key policy to the seemingly 'independent KTA', which it then abandoned politically and legally. In turn, the EU as the main fundraiser of the KTA and an early

[32] One of the more ironic details of this affair was that SRSG Holkeri eventually fired the controversial KTA Managing Director, Marie Fucci, thus implicitly admitting UNMIK's responsibility in privatization matters.

[33] More bizarre UN proposals had been the demand for EU *ex post* compensation in case of lawsuits against the UN, and transferring most privatization powers to the PISG, which would have been both legally and politically problematic.

[34] This shifts the emphasis from cumbersome SOE-vetting *ex ante* to quicker spin-offs and judicial review and compensation *ex post.* The rule of 'eminent domain' thus covers the KTA against *ultra vires* tort claims and instead opens the path to expropriation compensation. The option of annulling *all* post-1989 transformations in the KTA Regulation was discarded. This would have provoked allegations of transgressing UNSCR 1244.

[35] Privatization 'waves' are groups of tenders launched together by the KTA.

proponent of privatization tried to help, but did not have a direct say on the matter and thus unjustly bore the blame among Kosovo's population. A clearer division of labor, especially *within* the UNMIK universe, would have reduced political obstacles and would have avoided that Pillar IV and the KTA were left in limbo by the rest of UNMIK.

Secondly, this episode reflected the growing gap between UNMIK's actions and political oversight by UN Headquarters. While mission micro-management needs to be avoided – a point rightly made by UN HQ – a functioning protectorate needs backing at the highest political level, especially in key areas such as economic reforms. UN HQ, however, only entered the privatization fray *after* the process had become bogged down and thus had to untie this Gordian knot at a higher political cost. *Ex ante* guidance and sufficient capacity to implement policy priorities are vital. Neither did exist abundantly in support of the KTA.

Thirdly, the privatization process showed yet again that economic recovery is the key for successful transition. Trade liberalization and international aid cannot have the desired impact without structural reforms *within* a territory. Some observers have therefore advocated an earlier and clearer definition of property rights through arbitration and compensation – even at a political cost – to avoid permanent blockades and bargaining chips in the status endgame.[36]

Most fundamentally, the issue illustrated the entanglement between the mission's task to strengthen the economy and the 'long shadow' of status. It is true that UNMIK's dilemma of building quasi-state institutions without a clear prospect of statehood created problems, especially in the field of property and economic governance. However, Pillar IV, supported by the EU and the United States, created a viable system under UNSCR 1244 to unleash the potential of unused assets. Reforms and a temporary status freeze are thus not *per se* irreconcilable. Ironically, it was not privatization but UN HQ's orthodox stance, compounded by the PISG's attitude, which started to undermine UNMIK's mandate – the opposite of what this cautious approach tried to achieve.

In conclusion, it is wrong to assume that Kosovo's economic woes are simply the result of its status, as argued by the PISG. It is true that legal uncertainty scared off some investors and that status barred access to many IFI funds. Still, political volatility, the lack of an industrial basis, the weak rule of law and not least endemic corruption are equally key factors. They can only be cured through structural reforms.[37] Self-determination will not do the economic trick.

---

[36] Cf., A. Wittkowsky, 'Modelfall Kosovo?', 2 *IPG* (2002) pp. 29-42, at p. 4. The European Stability Initiative also points out that it is 'simply not possible to defer difficult property questions until after a resolution of Kosovo's status' ESI Report, 'The Ottoman Dilemma – Power and Property in Kosovo', Pristina 2002, p. 4.

[37] Beyond privatization, there were other policy areas where similar issues of 'reforms v status' played. For example, the EU Commission helped to extend the European Investment Bank's lending mandate to projects in Kosovo. This was all the more important as Kosovo – not being a state – has practically no access to the funds of International Financial Institutions. However, UNMIK lawyers

2.5 UNMIK's policy – standards *before* status?

The 'standards before status' doctrine, invented by SRSG Steiner, tried to reenergize UNMIK and bridge its two key dilemmas: That the interim mission was perceived as quasi-permanent, and that the lack of a status perspective provided disincentives for good governance. The new policy therefore aimed to overcome the wait-and-see attitude of the PISG, who knew that time worked in their favor. It wanted to accelerate the building of institutions which are indispensable for Kosovo regardless of its specific future status. In short, it shifted UN policy from temporarily 'freezing' status to making the PISG 'earn' status talks. Only after compliance with the 'standards' could such talks be opened. The underlying rationale was that Kosovo could only make headway towards political and economic sustainability if some minimal conditions were met.

In October 2002, UNMIK presented this policy based on eight standards,[38] which were subsequently endorsed by the Security Council.[39] A complex machinery comprising both international and local representatives was created to flesh out the standards and monitor their implementation. The Kosovo Standards Implementation Plan (KSIP), adopted in early 2004, defined the concrete actions, aiming at a truly 'multi-ethnic, stable and democratic Kosovo which is approaching European standards'.[40] The standards process was therefore in principle mutually reinforcing with the EU's Stabilization and Association Process.

However, there were several structural flaws in it from the outset. Firstly, the standards were initially not 'quantifiable' enough, an issue later corrected in the KSIP. This meant that benchmarking and hence political pressure on the PISG was rather weak in the beginning.

Secondly, some standards were *de iure* under UNMIK's and even under *de facto* Serbian control. For instance, the dismantling of Serbian parallel structures in Northern Kosovo could hardly be demanded from the PISG. The standards thus involun-

---

unduly delayed this EIB access with their doubts over a new PISG Law on International Financial Agreements (IFAs), fearing that the UN (via the SRSG who signs the IFAs) would incur obligations to repay defaulting loans. This was solved through a 'roll-over clause' by which the local institutions take political responsibility for payments *after* a status settlement. Similarly, UNMIK's hypersensitivity that the conclusion of Free Trade Agreements 'on behalf of Kosovo' would transgress its mandate and prejudge final status (even though the Constitutional Framework provides for the conclusion of international agreements by the SRSG), briefly delayed Kosovo's vital inclusion into the free trade network in South Eastern Europe.

[38] These basics of good governance in Kosovo are: Functioning democratic institutions, rule of law, freedom of movement, returns and reintegration, economy, property rights, dialogue with Belgrade, and the Kosovo Protection Corps. The policy built on an earlier UNMIK exercise of 'benchmarking' reforms.

[39] Security Council Presidential Statement S/PRST/2003/1 of 6 February 2003.

[40] The KSIP set out in detail *what* actions are designed ('Action'), *who* is responsible for them ('Responsible Actor'), *who* will act in support ('Supported by') and *when* the action is planned ('Timeline'). This degree of detail was only reached in early 2004, with a set of 109 action points, six working groups and quarterly reviews.

tarily gave the PISG a chance to oscillate between demanding more power and asking that status talks be held rapidly, even *before* real progress on the standards. Vice versa, Serbia undermined the implementation by organizing a partial Kosovo-Serb boycott of the PISG.

Most critically, UNMIK could not guarantee under UNSCR 1244 that progress would actually lead to the locally desired status *outcome* (i.e., undoubtedly independence). It is not the territorial status as such that is linked to the fulfillment of the conditions, but only the *commencement* of status talks. However, the conditionality doctrine of 'earned status' that appears to underpin the Kosovo-standards logically presupposes that the 'earnable' status be defined in advance. Due to this basic flaw in its incentive structure, the standards were initially an UNMIK-driven exercise, an internal bookkeeping tool that lacked local ownership.

Finally, despite the agreement to make the standards and the EU's SAP mutually compliant, the EU's role in their formulation and monitoring was initially problematic. While some key standards are not directly related to the EU '*acquis*' (but part of the EU's political conditionality, such as democratic practices, the rule of law and human and minority rights), others, notably in the economic field, have a strong EU dimension, which was, however, not taken up in the early phase. Moreover, it is difficult to link specific EU norms to a status settlement – the nexus around which this policy was built. The EU's policy of drawing an entity closer through the SAP until membership corresponds more to a 'standards *beyond* status' philosophy.

To frame the UN-led standards process within the context of Kosovo's EU perspective and to ensure that the two enterprises were complementary, both the SAP Tracking Mechanism and the reform agenda of the European Partnership – both of which are critical for institution-building – gradually integrated the UN standards. They are now part of the European Partnership and hence subject to EU evaluation under the SAP report and STM, which gives them more leverage.

In 2003 the international Contact Group[41] – and not UNMIK – proposed a 'Review Mechanism' to correct some of the problems mentioned above, notably the flawed incentives. Progress on implementing the standards would be the subject of a comprehensive assessment around mid-2005. If sufficient progress had been made by the time of the review, the Contact Group pledged to initiate a process, yet undefined, to determine Kosovo's future status.

Despite these mid-way improvements, the standards-policy never fully achieved its objective. It became a textbook example of UNMIK's 'transfer-responsibility gap'. The political responsibility of the PISG could only have been engaged through stronger devolution within the boundaries of UNSCR 1244, of which UNMIK remained skeptical.

---

[41] The 'Standards for Kosovo' plan flowing from this initiative created five UNMIK-PISG working groups to coordinate implementation, which were then evaluated by UNMIK in quarterly reports to the SC.

More fundamentally though, UNMIK suffered from the inbuilt contradictions of its mandate. Nation-building *in vacuo*, i.e., without the guarantee of eventual statehood cannot function but is rather made more difficult. The standards exercise was therefore a turning point for Kosovo as it undeniably showed that the province risked entering 'a hybrid limbo between statehood and disempowered neo-trusteeship'.[42] The international presence, brought in both as a 'status freezer' and reform catalyst, risked becoming part of Kosovo's problems instead of part of the solution. Generally, one can distinguish three phases in state-building: A period of stabilization and reconstruction, in which the international community had great accomplishments in Kosovo; a phase of institution-building with an equally positive balance-sheet; and gradual empowerment, in which UNMIK could not overcome its basic dilemma.[43]

This structural paralysis was recognized in a report prepared by UN Special Envoy Kai Eide in summer 2004. The Eide Report[44] noted that the 'standard before status' strategy 'lacked credibility' and recommended that it be replaced immediately with a more 'dynamic' approach. In June 2005, this led to the appointment of a Special Envoy (Eide himself) to conduct a standards review and assess the next steps – i.e., the possibility of launching status talks. This gradual paradigm shift does, however, not mean that the standards are 'dead' or overtaken by status discussions (as parts of the PISG seem to believe). On the contrary, accelerated status talks can, if handled properly, provide new incentives for progress on the standards. This was reflected in Special Envoy Ahtisaari's initial strategy of focusing on sectoral substance and not just legalistic formal status.[45]

3. The EU 'Beyond UNMIK' – Kosovo in the Stabilization and Association Process

3.1 The use of SAP tools *vis-à-vis* Kosovo

The EU's contribution to UNMIK was not its only support to Kosovo. To draw the province into the European mainstream, it was also covered by the Stabilization

[42] B. Knoll, *supra* n. 11, p. 238.

[43] F. Fukuyama, *State building: Governance and world order in the 21st century* (New York, Cornell University Press 2004), p. 135 et seq.

[44] 'The Situation in Kosov', Report to the UN SG. Summary and Recommendations, undertaken by the Head of the DPKO Political Assessment Mission on Kosovo, Amb. Kai Eide (S/2004/932, Annex I, Brussels, 15 July 2004). The renewed international focus on Kosovo was a reaction to the 'wake-up call' of the March 2004 riots.

[45] The eight rounds of talks between February and summer 2006 focused on decentralization, economic issues and the protection of cultural and religious sites. However, this bottom-up, incremental approach soon showed its limits. Pristina did not move as long as the bigger 'status picture' was not clear, while Belgrade wanted to limit the talks to 'status-neutral' issues. Therefore, Ahtisaari moved to direct status discussions in July 2006 in a so-called 'Elephant Round' of Serbia's and Kosovo's Presidents and Prime Ministers. Even though they merely reiterated their well-known, contradictory positions, the top-level talks show that the status process is nearing the endgame.

and Association Process (SAP) ever since 1999. Thus, the EU stabilizes and reforms Kosovo with the SAP's tools already *during* its interim status, linking these levers to its support to UNMIK in a complementary fashion. The only SAP element not yet applied to Kosovo is the option of contractual relations.[46] The final SAP objective of EU membership, while in principle open to Kosovo, depends on the prior determination of final status and massive progress in the political, economic and administrative fields.

EU policies have booked major successes in Kosovo: As early as June 1999, the Commission established a 'Kosovo Task Force' on the ground to implement its reconstruction program. The Task Force was phased out once the European Agency for Reconstruction was operational.[47] The Agency implements the EU's massive aid in Kosovo, the main framework being the 'Community Assistance for Reconstruction, Development and Stabilization' (CARDS). Since 1999 this aid totaled over € 1.6 billion, making the EU by far the single largest donor and Kosovo the biggest per capita recipient of EU aid worldwide in 1999-2001.[48] Assistance gradually shifted from 'hard' reconstruction, e.g., the re-building of houses and the regeneration of energy supplies, to 'softer' issues such as institution-building and the rule of law. This became even more important as the PISG lacked the capacity to manage their growing 'transferred powers'.

Aid priorities are programmed by the EU Commission on the basis of a consultation process with both EU Member States and other donors. Also, the EU's aid dovetails with UNMIK's and the PISG's political priorities. It gives the EU leverage as the lead donor in the shaping and implementation of policy reform goals. Without this support, the financial sustainability of Kosovo's interim administration would have been put into jeopardy.

Still, the linkage between UNMIK's policy goals and EU aid was not always as effective as it could have been. As UNMIK and the PISG entered a phase of more sophisticated state-building – and thus inevitably had disputes on competences and ultimately status – there was a growing risk of mismatches between Europe's long-term reform investments and the medium-term stagnation in the Kosovar polity. To improve the interplay between the EU dimension and reforms on the ground, the Commission created the Kosovo SAP Tracking Mechanism (STM) in 2002 (cf., below).

On a more negative note, Kosovo's reliance on donor funds is dangerously close to aid dependency. As international support declines and moves into sectors such as institution-building, remittances from the strong Kosovar Albanian diaspora abroad

[46] For issues and options regarding contractual relations with Kosovo, cf., below.

[47] Created by Council Regulation (EC) No. 2667/2000 of 5 December 2000, OJ (7 December 2000) L-306/7, the Agency's mandate was later extended to Serbia, Montenegro and the Former Yugoslav Republic of Macedonia.

[48] € 59.5 million have been committed for 2005 and € 54.5 million have been earmarked for 2006.

replaced its role as financial lifeline. This is, however, clearly unsustainable in the long-term.[49]

The SAP's second component[50] was therefore particularly important for Kosovo. The EU's autonomous trade measures (ATMs) provide for practically unlimited and duty-free access to the EU of nearly all products originating in Kosovo, which is a separate customs territory performing its own trade policy independently from Serbia. The ATMs give Kosovo a major outlet, the world's largest market, to stabilize the economy and foster export-led growth. Today, the EU is a key trading partner for Kosovo.[51] However, the possibility of market access alone does not *per se* lead to more growth and employment. It would therefore be wrong to criticize the ATMs for an alleged 'lack of success'. The key to structural reforms in Kosovo and a growing economy is privatization. This shows the linkages between UN and EU policies. A delay in one policy backfires on the other organization's activities.

In the regional context, the EU ensured Kosovo's inclusion into the network of bilateral free trade agreements under the auspices of the Stability Pact for South Eastern Europe.[52] This regional trade network does not only improve export opportunities and good-neighborly political relations, but equally boosts Kosovo's investment climate.

The third major element of the Stabilization and Association Process is reform advice. In line with Kosovo's long-term perspective of rapprochement with the EU, both UNMIK and the PISG need to follow EU-compatible practices. The evolving body of Kosovo's legislation should broadly comply with EU rules.[53] Moreover, a detailed policy dialogue with EU experts enables Kosovo to tap the wealth of experience that the EU Commission developed in helping transition in Central and Eastern Europe from 1989 onwards. In these countries, political advice, benchmarking and (later) treaty obligations had supported the domestic reform agenda and sustained the local integration momentum that had proven so critical. The SAP intends to recreate this momentum in South Eastern Europe.

---

[49] A peculiar form of 'aid dependency' was the 'capacity sucking-out' (as opposed to 'capacity-building') by the international presence, including richly endowed NGOs. They attracted scarce local talent and thus crowded out the PISG. Cf., M. Ignatieff as quoted in F. Fukuyama, *supra* n. 43, at p. 139.

[50] Cf., Council Regulation (EC) No. 2007/2000 of 23 September 2000, OJ (23 September 2000) L-240/1 as last amended by Council Regulation (EC) No. 1946/2005 of 14 November 2005, OJ (29 November 2005) L-312/1.

[51] 28.7% of Kosovo's exports went to the EU. 35.6% of its imports came from the EU (2004). Still, Kosovan producers have difficulties in using the ATMs due to high EU product standards and problems in finding specific outlets.

[52] Kosovo has FTAs with Albania, the FYRO Macedonia and Bosnia and Herzegovina. In addition, trade with Serbia is free as it is intra-state commerce, although practical obstacles occur repeatedly. Kosovo now also participates in the talks on a regional free trade agreement.

[53] Specific obligations to approximate legislation would only be laid down in a future agreement. However, Kosovo's unique position with a clean legal slate (cf., above, UNMIK Regulation 1/1999) enables it to adopt European standards from the beginning rather than engage in difficult and costly adaptations at a later stage.

Originally, Kosovo was covered by the 'Consultative Task Force' (CTF) with the late FRY, which 'screened' policy areas and developed recommendations. However, UNMIK acted *de facto* only in an observer role in the CTF, given the sensitivity of a common framework with the FRY. As reforms in Kosovo broadened and the PISG took a bigger role in them, the Commission therefore created a specific Kosovo SAP Tracking Mechanism (STM) in November 2002. Regular STM meetings, bringing together EU, UNMIK and PISG experts, discuss practically all areas of reforms and establish joint recommendations to drive progress. More fundamentally, these seemingly 'technical' meetings help to de-politicize and move touchy subjects below the radar-screen of the 'status-conscious' PISG. The STM's advice was thus the final piece in the jigsaw puzzle of reforms, complementing the policy development and management by UNMIK and the aid devised and implemented by EU.

The STM was also a first step to 'Europeanize' the PISG. The organization and management of the STM meetings and their recommendations led to the creation of EU coordination structures in the various local Ministries, overseen by a 'European Integration Office' attached to the Prime Minister's Cabinet which is now being transformed into a stronger 'Agency for European Integration'. This Agency and its counterparts in the line-Ministries play a crucial role, for they drive the technical work of adapting to European policy reform standards. Such a system of transmission belts, implementing political decisions, was a recipe of the success of the new EU Member States that joined in 2004.

To strengthen the 'European flavor' of Kosovo's structural reforms even further, the EU decided to adopt a European Partnership for Kosovo[54] in 2004. This new instrument, inspired by the Accession Partnerships used for the candidate countries and proposed for the Western Balkans in the run-up to the Thessaloniki Summit in 2003, contains detailed short- and medium-term priorities which the entities need to address. EU aid is then targeted on these priorities. The beneficiaries draw up a national action plan for implementation, which serve as a domestic agenda. Progress is assessed by the Commission in the following Annual Report.

Given this major EU support, it is inaccurate to demand a 'European perspective' for Kosovo, as some critics do. EU policy did include incentives ever since 1999. However, it is true that the various 'stepping-stone' tools of the SAP were more difficult to manage once Kosovo moved from post-war reconstruction to a more complex political set-up. The EU's *short-term* instruments were insufficient to 'tempt' local elites and overcome the growing status conundrum. Secondly, the *longer-term* 'carrot' of membership, the gravitational pull that has so successfully guided transition in other countries, was too far away for Kosovo's leaders and people and not credible enough to resolve the statehood dilemma either.[55]

---

[54] As part of a package with Serbia and Montenegro, cf., Council Decision 2004/520/EC of 14 June 2004, OJ (26 June 2004) L-227/21, later replaced by Council Decision 2006/56/EC of 30 January 2006, OJ (7 February 2006) L-35/32. The European Partnership, drawn-up by the EU Commission in discussion with the entity addressed, is formally adopted by the EU Council of Ministers.

[55] It is one of the fundamental ironies of Europe that integration, i.e., the pooling and partial transfer of sovereignty, presupposes a functioning nation-state that can validly conclude and imple-

Instead, the local powerbrokers in the PISG centered their attention on the *medium-term* status question,[56] with less stamina for reforms on the ground, which could also have conflicted with vested interests. Still, forging and sustaining domestic – as opposed to international – political will is indispensable to drive reforms, as amply demonstrated by the successful transformation of other post-Communist countries. The challenge faced by the EU is therefore threefold: To make the existing SAP incentives more palpable and even more effective, to ensure that the European dimension is properly taken into account in a final status settlement, and to help create a broad domestic platform to carry Kosovo's integration.

3.2 **Improved EU presence and policy**

In its first phase, UNMIK was based on a relatively effective division of labor. However, the deepening and differentiation of its policies, increasingly tense relations with the PISG and growing fears of touching status-sensitive issues led to the tunnel-vision criticized by Special Envoy Eide. At the same time, the EU's uncomfortable position as an *outside* actor through the SAP and an indirect *'insider'* as Pillar IV's main fundraiser became problematic, too.

Pillar IV was increasingly caught between the institutional lines of fire. As described, this was mainly a UN-internal problem, with the EU bearing a minor part of the blame for not having stepped in earlier. Privatization showed that the Pillar needed a clearer mandate, not least to justify EU funding. Also, the ongoing transfers of power to the local institutions required a stronger EU flavor. Most crucially, the status process as such needed substantial EU input. The EU suggested improvements in all these fields, building on the existing SAP, in order to strengthen the effectiveness, coherence and visibility of its action in Kosovo.

A first institutional step was the creation of a separate EU Commission Office in Pristina. This is all the more important as many of the EU's substantial levers are managed by the Commission, e.g., the SAP Tracking Mechanism, the monitoring of the European Partnership, overall political advice on the SAP and trade preferences. The Liaison Office represents the Commission in all these matters. Also, the Office helps to clarify the – admittedly complex – EU presence on the ground, cooperating closely with HR/SG Solana's personal envoy. It also improves coordination with UNMIK – a point rightly raised in the Eide report. Furthermore, the lifetime of the European Agency for Reconstruction was prolonged until the end of

---

ment its EU obligations. The integration problems created by the 'baroque federalism' of the late Serbia and Montenegro and Bosnia and Herzegovina demonstrate this. Some observers have therefore argued that Kosovo has no choice but to go through its nation-building phase before being truly able to enter the EU's 'post-national' space.

[56] The author vividly recalls a conversation with Kosovo lawmakers as early as 2002, who argued that Kosovo *was 'already* independent' and 'just waiting' for the international community to recognize this.

2006,[57] so that EC aid for the period 2000-2006 is implemented without disruption.

In addition to these organizational changes, the EU stepped up its pace to substantiate Kosovo's European future. The Commission published a Communication on this matter in April 2005,[58] which provided input for a Joint Report by the Commission and HR/SG Solana in June 2005,[59] by which the two bodies jump-started the EU-internal debate on the Union's role. This report was further refined in joint papers in December 2005 and July 2006.[60]

The Commission's Communication reaffirms the various SAP instruments as enriched by the 2003 Thessaloniki Summit, notably the STM and the European Partnership. It places particular emphasis on economic development. It foresees support for Kosovo's Economic Development Plan, for the creation of a better expenditure framework to redress the unsustainable budget deficit, for strengthened customs and taxation services and targeted action to help small and medium-sized enterprises. Furthermore, the Commission pledges to continue aiding Kosovo's integration into regional structures. Pillar IV, its partners in the PISG and the Commission had already successfully pursued this, avoiding all status traps, notably in the fields of trade, energy, transport and the environment. Thirdly, building institutional capacity remains high on the EU agenda, supported by continued aid, access to twinning and TAIEX, and new aid possibilities under the Union's Pre-Accession Instrument (IPA) as of 2007. Finally, the Commission suggests action to bring the EU perspective closer to the Kosovar people, through visa facilitation and better access to EU education programs.[61]

The Commission/Council Joint Paper of June 2005 builds on these policies, focusing on the EU's contribution to the standards implementation process, the restructuring of UNMIK and most importantly the status talks and a redefined international presence after a settlement.

As to the Kosovo standards, the Commission suggests to pursue a dual policy of reinvigoration and streamlining with EU standards. In this vein, it is proposed to progressively merge the KSIP process with the EU approximation venture under the SAP, to give local reforms a stronger European dimension and to put the Union's political weight behind them. This gradual 'European take-over' of reform monitoring has progressed further through the assessment made in the Commission's SAP Progress Report 2005 and the amendments to the European Partnership fol-

---

57 Council Regulation (EC) No. 2068/2004 of 29 November 2004, OJ (3 December 2004) L-358/1. From 2007, the Commission Office will absorb the EAR's functions, notably regarding the implementation of aid projects under the new Pre-Accession Instrument.

58 COM (2005) 156 of 20 April 2005.

59 'The Future EU Role and Contribution in Kosovo', 7 June 2005 (unpublished). Commission and Council had submitted a first paper in February 2004, focusing on the EU presence in Kosovo and support for the standards.

60 Endorsed by the Council on 12 December 2005, and 17 July 2006 (unpublished).

61 Note that Kosovo is also fully covered by the latest 'SAP upgrade' in the Commission's Communication 'The Western Balkans on the road to the EU: consolidating stability and raising prosperity', COM (2006) 27 final, of 27 January 2006.

lowing from it. The Action Plan drafted between the PISG and UNMIK in response to the Partnership is a crucial part of this 'fusion process'. Also, the STM is being expanded to strengthen economic and sectoral advice. As a result, the EU has gradually assumed the international lead-role in setting Kosovo's reform agenda, which helps to devise long-term reforms beyond status and improves the political incentive structure.[62]

A second important field for the Union is its support to UNMIK's restructuring and to the accompanying transfer of powers to the PISG. This is progressing through three phases – before, during and after a status settlement. To strengthen UNMIK's architecture, the EU has particularly underlined the need for a clearer mandate for Pillar IV. The draft mandate negotiated between UNMIK and the Commission emphasizes the 'leadership of the UN' and stresses the SRSG's 'ultimate authority for Pillar IV as an integral part of UNMIK'. This helps to increase its effectiveness within the mission.[63]

The EU suggests redefining the Pillar's tasks: This would mean to transfer most executive powers and to assume a 'role of oversight and advice to the PISG'.[64] In turn, the EU proposes further PISG capacity-building and pledges to program aid accordingly. However, the mission's downsizing must obviously not affect its ability to exercise its *reserved* powers. Also, as a key lesson from the privatization conundrum, the EU stresses that it 'cannot take over reserved powers entrusted to UNMIK' itself and that 'the UN has to retain full responsibility under UNSCR 1244'. The EU thus declines the dubious honor to morph UNMIK into a EUMIK.[65] The Union will not be in the lead of an international presence in Kosovo until a final settlement is reached.

3.3 The EU's stake in the status settlement: intervention versus integration?

Beyond the support to the revitalization and 'Europeanization' of the standards and to the restructuring of UNMIK, the EU plays a crucial role in the status settlement itself, given Kosovo's geopolitical importance and its European perspective.

Firstly, *during* the status talks EU and particularly the Commission hold several short- to medium-term 'deliverables' which could in principle facilitate the pro-

[62] On the PISG's side, the Office (now Agency) for European Integration has been reinforced to coordinate the implementation of the 'Europeanized' standards.

[63] The accountability of Pillar IV for EU support remains governed by the bilateral Financing Agreement.

[64] This would include the transfer of UNMIK's reserved powers relating to the KTA upon a settlement. On the other hand, the second Joint Paper hints at remaining EU oversight in the field of monetary policy (not least as the Euro is Kosovo's legal tender), fiscal policy and trade. The exact nature of this involvement is open.

[65] The Paper adds that EU-executive powers under UNSCR 1244 'could only complicate the set-up and the chain of command, threatening the credibility [...] of the international presence and the EU in particular.'

cess, such as political pressure, aid, transition advice, a security presence and a 'leap forward' towards EU membership, both for Kosovo and for Serbia proper.[66] This could help to cushion the status impact in Belgrade and Pristina to some degree, especially as the international community may have to impose a specific status deal in the absence of a negotiated agreement between Belgrade and Pristina.

On the other hand, the 'European perspective' is neither a panacea nor a straight-jacket. While the SAP already provides key advantages, others – especially the 'big prize' of EU membership itself – accrue only *after* and not *during* the status talks. They are not decisive levers for a settlement, as could be seen in Serbia and Kosovo over the last months. Moreover, it is unlikely that the 'unconvinced Europeans' in Belgrade's and Pristina's elites could easily 'sell' a trade-off between 'Europe' and 'status' to their voters. Latent enlargement fatigue in several EU countries is a further complicating factor. Still, making all these EU bargaining chips palpable is critical to facilitate the talks. Also, watering down the 'EU perspective' at this critical juncture would be self-defeating for the Union.

Secondly, *after* a settlement, the EU will in any event have to deal with the longer-term 'status fall-out' as the region progresses towards the Union. In particular, the EU is expected to bear a major share of a follow-on presence on the ground. For both reasons, it is vital to ensure that the outcome is fully compatible with EU integration requirements. A result delaying post-status Kosovo on its European journey would be extremely destabilizing. The perspective of EU accession must be respected by any status settlement.[67]

The EU is therefore working very closely with the UN Special Envoy for the status talks, former Finnish President Matti Ahtisaari, ever since his appointment by the UN Secretary-General in October 2005. He has been authorized by the UN Security Council 'to start a political process to determine Kosovo's future status'. Ahtisaari has considerable freedom of operation. The most important road signs for his diplomatic efforts are the Contact Group's Guiding Principles agreed in November 2005. They outline the fundaments that a settlement should include and promote, including stability, non-partition, multi-ethnicity, democracy and human rights. Importantly, they emphasize that the settlement should 'conform with European standards' and 'contribute to realize the European perspective of Kosovo, in particular Kosovo's progress in the Stabilization and Association process'.[68]

---

[66] The start of SAA negotiations with Serbia and Montenegro in 2005 has to be seen in this light, too.

[67] The EU's mediation efforts between Serbia and Montenegro, leading to the genesis of the now disbanded 'State Union', show how necessary short-term crisis management can create obstacles for long-term integration.

[68] These principles are echoed in the Commission/Council Secretariat Joint Papers of June and December 2005 and in the European Council Declaration on Kosovo of 16/17 December 2005. They were politically endorsed in the UN framework by a letter of UN Security Council President Denisov to SG Annan (UN Doc. S/2005/709 of 10 November 2005).

The EU has nominated a Special Representative to liaise with Ahtisaari's team.[69] In addition, there are permanent contacts between the 'status' team and the EU Commission that provide expertise on political, economic and sectoral issues. Both the Commission and the Council Secretariat work closely with the Contact Group whose EU members have converging views on status – a remarkable difference when compared to the disagreements of the 1990s. Also, an Informal Steering Group on future arrangements in Kosovo has been set-up by UNMIK, which has commenced detailed planning. Besides the EU, it includes the OSCE, NATO, UNHCR, the Council of Europe and key players like the United States.

As a result of this close involvement, the EU can channel political pressure on both sides and support the status process through its various instruments under the SAP, which is of course not suspended during the talks but enhanced. Still, despite this input, the EU as such is not in the driving seat of the status process. The talks are UN-led (as set out in USNCR 1244) and ultimately subject to a Security Council decision, which therefore also depends on a mutual understanding of the United States, Russia and China and could even be subject to political trade-offs with other current international issues. Therefore, there is a residual possibility that a – necessarily complex – settlement would be partly incoherent with the SAP's rationale and create issues for Kosovo's and/or Serbia's long-term integration. In theory, the EU 'could end up holding a big, ugly baby of uncertain parentage'.[70]

To avoid such a potential contradiction between 'intervention' and 'integration', Kosovo must in particular acquire a functional government structure which is able to externally conclude and internally enforce far-reaching EU-obligations, in the Stabilization and Association process and beyond, even in case of a residual international presence. Kosovo does not need a revamped *transitional* sovereign. EU enlargement cannot easily accommodate blurred competencies between international and local bodies.

This essential EU-need for a functioning partner government is particularly strong for possible contractual relations with Kosovo. For *political* reasons, it is unlikely that there will be a 'traditional' Stabilization and Association Agreement (SAA) with Kosovo as such in the foreseeable future. The European Community and its Member States are unenthusiastic about concluding full-fledged associations with non-state entities, fearing that this is seen as 'prejudging' statehood.[71] It is there-

---

[69] HR/SG Solana's Balkans Adviser Stefan Lehne serves in this role as EU Representative to the Kosovo future status process. He was appointed by the GAERC Conclusions of 7 November 2005, point 10.

[70] 'Kosovo – The Challenge of Transition', Crisis Group Europe Report No. 170, 17 February 2006, p. 14.

[71] For example, the 'Interim Association Agreement on Trade and Cooperation between the EC and the PLO (for the benefit of the Palestinian Authority)' does not create a formal association under Article 310 EC – contrary to its rather baroque title – but a less integrated relationship. *Legally* however, even though Article 310 mentions 'states' (and international organizations) as contracting partners, it does not seem to preclude association treaties with *other* entities such as Kosovo provided they possess *all* necessary treaty-making powers, i.e., have 'material statehood' for the purposes of the agreement in question.

fore more probable that the EU will start preparing the ground for far-reaching *sui generis* bilateral treaty relations with Kosovo, which would be tailored to its specific reform needs, include political conditions, commercial measures and legislative approximation requirements, but stop short of a formal SAA. Kosovo's institutions must obviously obtain the legal powers to conclude such an agreement under a settlement, and book major progress on the reform front to qualify.[72]

In this vein, the June 2005 Commission/Council Paper already mentions the need of granting Kosovo (at least partial) treaty-making powers under a settlement so that it can 'benefit fully from its involvement in the SAP'. This is mirrored in the Contact Group's Guiding Principles, which note that 'the settlement should ensure that Kosovo [...] can cooperate effectively with international organizations and international financial institutions.'[73] At the same time, the Commission/Council papers note that an international presence could retain some external relations competencies, too. In short: Kosovo could, e.g., be enabled to conclude an agreement with the EU and regional treaties (and succeed to all agreements undertaken by UNMIK on its behalf), but could be temporarily barred from full diplomatic relations and UN membership, also known as 'a flag on the East River'.

Beyond the issue of contractual relations, the EU must avoid creating a contradiction between its possible roles *on the ground* as an enforcer of last resort and, vice versa, as an *outside* partner and center of gravity for Kosovo. Overstretching the EU's post-status executive role would run counter to the principles of partnership, cooperation and conditionality that underlie the SAP and enlargement. The Council has therefore reaffirmed that 'Kosovo's future status must be fully compatible with European standards and norms'.[74] In this vein, the 2006 Joint Paper astutely distinguishes between limited international intervention powers (i.e., both corrective and executive functions), overall international monitoring of the settlement and – most importantly – increased support for good governance and economic reforms.

Europe's exact role in post-status Kosovo can only be determined once status is clear. Still, there is an emerging consensus on three main components of the EU's engagement. Firstly, there will be an EU contribution to an international civilian mission (ICM), notably by 'double-hatting' its head as EU Special Representa-

---

[72] Cf., COM (2005) 156 p. 4. The Commission notes that, while contractual relations are key to achieve the SAP's goals, 'a fully-fledged SAA with Kosovo is not on the table at present'. Still, it would 'explore creative ways' to help Kosovo, including 'in due course [...] contractual relations [...] as appropriate'. The July 2006 Joint Paper appears to go one step further, noting that 'the aim should be to include all areas which are covered in SAAs with other countries in the region'. Note that the European Community has *already* accepted Kosovo under UNSCR 1244 as a contracting partner to the (multilateral) Treaty establishing the Energy Community between the EU and South Eastern Europe, and has facilitated its inclusion into the regional FTA network.

[73] More specifically, the July 2006 Commission/Council paper mentions 'full membership of the WTO, the IMF, the World Bank and other IFIs'.

[74] GAERC Conclusions of 7 November 2005, point 13.

tive.[75] An EU team to support the ICM's creation has been established. Secondly, the rule of law will be further core areas of EU involvement. Here the EU's role would lie in enhanced capacity-building with SAP instruments and in managing an EU police mission under the European Security and Defence Policy (ESDP), notably to oversee the Kosovo Police Service's senior staff in sensitive areas.[76] A first EU planning team (EUPT Kosovo) has already been deployed to analyze the specific rule of law needs in Kosovo.[77] Further EU intervention powers may be necessary in the judiciary where limited progress was made under UNSCR 1244.[78] Thirdly, the EU will deepen the aforementioned SAP tools to draw Kosovo closer. In this regard, the monitoring of SAP conditionality through the European Partnership and policy dialogue will be key. The EU will also enhance Kosovo's integration in the region, mobilize further aid[79] and work towards contractual relations (cf., above). As to economic policy, the EU foresees a mere guidance role, with the goal 'to transfer powers as far as possible to the local authorities'.

The financial implications of a settlement are a critical subject for the EU, too. In line with the above tasks, the Commission distinguishes between the EU's financial contribution to an international presence, including the possibly largest CFSP/ESDP mission ever conducted; aid for Kosovo's future development under the Pre-Accession Instrument; and funding linked to the status settlement as such. As to the latter, the EU assumes there will be a call to donors to partly alleviate the resulting burden, even though the financial impact of the status needs to be borne by the parties concerned (Kosovo and Serbia) to the largest degree possible.[80]

In conclusion, the Joint Papers provide a first sketch of an EU presence in Kosovo, around the 'trinity' of limited intervention powers, monitoring and substantial institution-building. Any such presence will therefore not resemble a full-fledged 'EUMIK', but would remain much leaner. Not only would a broad management and enforcement role on the ground be alien to the Union's philosophy of transformational empowerment. The EU institutions themselves also lack the practical ex-

---

[75] This 'double-hatting' is met with skepticism by some EU Member States. Such 'political schizophrenia' already exists in Bosnia, where the international High Representative also serves as EUSR. In a way, the EU is thus negotiating a Stabilization and Association Agreement 'with itself'. This 'clash of foreign policy philosophies', i.e., intervention v. integration, is especially delicate in areas relating to the Copenhagen criteria of democracy and human rights. It is hard to imagine the EU assessing, e.g., 'its own' human rights record.

[76] Over € 35 million of EC assistance are already being implemented in these fields. The nucleus of the EU police mission itself could be ready by January 2007.

[77] Council Joint Action 2006/304/CFSP of 10 April 2006, OJ (19 April 2006) L-112/19.

[78] Such 'reserved EU powers' could cover war crimes, inter-ethnic crimes and high-level corruption.

[79] A further successful donor meeting was co-chaired by the Commission and the World Bank in April 2006. The pledges made at this meeting are critical to bridge Kosovo's considerable budget shortfalls in 2006 and 2007.

[80] For example, unofficial estimates put Kosovo's share of SCG's external debt (which Kosovo does not serve at present but may have to cater for in the future) at € 1 billion, i.e., 50% of Kosovo's GDP.

pertise and the administrative capacity to run daily policies (and politics) in a (quasi)state. A heavy EU mission with powers well beyond its internal treaty-based competencies could hence easily damage the EU's credibility.

Fostering local capacity and ownership will therefore remain a key motive of the EU's support to Kosovo. Democratic accountability cannot work without them. The necessary pressure on Kosovo policy-makers to comply with the conditions of a settlement and to pursue reforms should rather be channeled through the enlargement method and clear SAP conditionality. That is where 'the EU's comparative advantage lies', as pointed out in the Joint Papers. This approach is more promising than intrusive policy substitution by a resident European viceroy, who would possibly lead the Union into a neo-colonial trap of liberal imperialism. In this vein, the Union stresses that 'the future international presence should not be open-ended, but provide for an eventual exit strategy, possibly linked towards Kosovo's progress towards the EU'. The goal of this process – EU accession – remains clear. But its speed is difficult to judge in the light of Kosovo's enormous developmental challenges.

4. Conclusion: Some Tentative Lessons for EU-UN Cooperation in State-building

UNMIK is the most far-reaching civilian UN Mission ever. In an era in which the occurrence of 'failing states' and international post-conflict missions are increasingly likely, its successes and challenges are therefore instructive. In particular, UNMIK's story provides lessons for the architecture of missions, their mandate, the role of economic issues and the primordial importance of a political exit strategy:

Firstly, clear lines of command and shared strategic priorities are vital. UNMIK's Pillar structure was initially useful to pool resources for reconstruction and basic reforms, but became confusing for internationals and locals alike once policies became more complex and had longer timelines. The partly unguided growth of UNMIK led to a lack of inter-pillar coordination. In some instances, this led to 'institutional overkill', in others to the abandonment of core responsibilities, as with privatization. Instead of strengthening the mission across the board, UNMIK's complexity partly diluted both international ownership and leverage. To create more synergies and to safeguard political ownership, the clear authority of a lead organization and joint 'cross-pillar' policy formulation are needed. This is a lesson to be learnt for any international field mission and for EU-UN relations in particular.

Similarly, relations between headquarters and the mission itself need to be clear. Some components of UNMIK were on the verge of becoming 'quasi-states' on a relatively lose leash from UN HQ, who could not easily adjudicate in disputes. The intra- and inter-pillar discussions over privatization illustrate this need for guidance.

A clearer vertical and horizontal division of labor is not only a matter of institutional clarity and legal responsibility. It has a direct impact on the ground. The privatization delays affected economic reforms, the use of EU funds and ultimately the uptake of the trade preferences. On a similar note, the problems around the UN standards for Kosovo meant that the EU's STM and the implementation of the European Partnership could not function optimally either.

A second, more practical lesson is the need for more staffing stability. High personnel fluctuation and the outsourcing of key posts to international consultants affected the mission's longer-term effectiveness. A permanent pool of civilian peacekeepers and administrators to bridge the gap between post-war reconstruction and state-building could therefore be helpful. However, neither the UN nor the EU have such a standing corps of 'transition managers' who could achieve in the civilian field what modular 'battle groups' accomplish in the military realm. Even a much reduced post-status presence will have to tackle this issue. The EU may therefore have to reflect on how to develop its political management capacity on the ground, beyond its current instruments of institution-building in transition countries, twinning and TAIEX, but without substituting local capacity and political will.[81]

A third essential lesson from UNMIK's work is the central role of economic reforms in state-building. Laying the basis for future prosperity is not only an end in itself. A lack of socioeconomic perspectives also creates a reservoir of political unrest and entrenches crime. These issues came together in UNMIK's privatization project, which also reflected the importance of clarifying property issues early on in a post-conflict mission. At the same time, the international community must recognize its limited means (both in political and financial terms) in overcoming structural economic problems. Also in this context, enhancing local ownership is critical. Therefore, the present efforts of building a local political platform for a long-term economic policy planning and enhancing domestic support for structural reforms are crucial.

Most fundamentally, UNMIK had problems wherever institution-building depended largely on changed behavioral patterns of local powerbrokers and/or on Kosovo's formal status. International field missions acting as quasi-sovereigns therefore need clear entry and exit perspectives. They must not be forced into a double-act as an administrator of a protectorate and, at the same time, a future status arbiter without clear 'deliverables'.

Unfortunately, UNMIK 'was the victim of [this] lack of a clear political perspective'.[82] It suffered from its multiple personalities as institution-builder in chief, defender of the status quo under UNSCR 1244 and coach for a – yet undefined –

[81] 'Twinning' means the long-term secondment of EU experts to candidate countries to help reform their public administrations from within. TAIEX is the Technical Assistance and Information Exchange Instrument through which the approximation and enforcement of reform legislation is supported. Both instruments apply to Kosovo.

[82] The 'Eide Report', p. i.

future status.[83] Unsurprisingly, it could only bridge these contradictions between an open-ended nation-building mission and an unclear political settlement for a while. As a result, the mission could not provide the necessary long-term incentives to local elites – whose formalist 'status *before* standards' policy, blind to the substantial requirements of constructing statehood, was not helpful either. This was UNMIK's basic flaw, built into the fabric of UNSCR 1244 and fully visible as its mandate entered the post-reconstruction phase. The mission is now gradually overcoming these problems as the status talks have created a new framework of reference and new conditionality options for the international community.

The vicious circle of 'reforms versus status' created a political ownership gap at the very center of Kosovo's polity. The local elites could all too often hide conveniently behind UNMIK, due to the broad definition of the reserved powers and the logical misconceptions of the 'standards before status' policy set out above. UNMIK's attempts to forge a shared reform agenda did only succeed in some fields. More transfers of power to the PISG, within the limits of UNSCR 1244, and a more cooperative attitude by UNMIK would probably have helped to alleviate this to some degree. Still, the fundamental dilemma of institution-building under a status freeze, politically necessary in 1999 and hence enshrined in UNSCR 1244, was ultimately inevitable, despite UNMIK's undeniable successes. The EU's 'standards *beyond* status' policy which supported UNMIK's work tried to tackle these problems through financial aid and policy advice. Still, Europe's successes on the ground were also eclipsed by the macro-political situation.[84]

It is therefore highly questionable whether any future international institution-building effort can be made sustainable without a clearer transfer of powers to local bodies and without a remote perspective of status taking account of the right of self-determination.

This fundamental crux will be less relevant *after* a status settlement, which will untie the Gordian knot to a large degree. Still, as thinking of decision-makers evolves towards a form of 'conditional independence' with a residual international presence on the ground,[85] it remains vital to engage the local institutions more strongly, to build responsibility from within and to create incentives through clearer conditionality. Any reserved powers need to be exercised without installing a new international Leviathan. Political and economic conditionality cannot work without domestic demand for reforms.[86]

---

[83] The distinction between President Ahtisaari's role as status negotiator and UNMIK's continued managerial presence on the ground is thus an important tactical improvement.

[84] Again, it is important to note that the status issues were more political in nature than legal.

[85] Most commentators see 'conditional independence' as a status under which Kosovo would possess most attributes of statehood, but without full international sovereignty and UN membership, and with a remaining international presence in key areas (security, justice, minority protection) as sketched above. Full independence could be achieved through progress on a set of governance conditions – i.e., sort of 'independence on probation'.

[86] Cf., F. Fukuyama, *supra* n. 43, at p. 48.

This is one of the key lessons from prior successful rounds of EU enlargement: Political consensus among domestic elites is crucial. Disagreements between local leaders around and after a status settlement would therefore not only backfire on Kosovo's stability but also impede its rapprochement with the Union.

Given Kosovo's geopolitical position, its European vocation and the EU's self-interest in avoiding negative spill-over effects, the EU will assume a critical role in Kosovo's future. It will need to deploy all of its soft power to channel the transformation of the province into a democratic, law-based, multi-ethnic and economically viable entity. Striking the right balance between local responsibility and international oversight will thus remain a key task.

Whatever Kosovo's final status is, its future clearly lies in Europe. The Union must therefore be prepared to conduct an active policy with its entire arsenal of 'carrots and sticks', without disenfranchising local elites and without accidentally morphing into a 'EUMIK'. Europe must avoid the 'sovereignty trap' into which UNMIK stepped under UNSCR 1244. This is the most critical lesson to be drawn from Kosovo for future international state-building efforts.

Part Five

Outlook

Chapter 19
REGIONAL GROUPS WITHIN THE UN POST-EU ENLARGEMENT

by Roman Kirn*

1. Introduction

Regional groups are not the object of much public debate. Yet they constitute an important reality within the UN system. Their establishment is not rooted in the UN Charter but has resulted from UN practice. Their role has been strengthened throughout the years. The present contribution shall address the origins and functioning of regional groups, as well as their relationship with the European Union (EU). Emphasis will be placed on the EU's capacity to exert influence and to act as a major player within the UN, in light of the fact that its Member States are represented in three different regional groups. Finally, taking account of new realities, in particular the recent EU enlargement from fifteen to twenty-five Member States in May 2004 – with eight out of the ten new Member States belonging to the Eastern European Group (EEG), we shall examine whether this has or should have any effect on the existing UN structure of regional groups.

2. Regional Groups in the UN

2.1 Origins

The founding fathers of the UN never had in mind the establishment of regional groups as they exist today. Well before the negotiations about the future organization started at the conference of Dumberton Oaks, ideas had been mooted as to whether or how to secure a kind of a regional representation within the future United Nations by creating a number of blocks of countries to be represented in the UN's General Assembly. Yet, regionalism proved to be a highly divisive issue, reflecting two opposing concepts on the future of the UN. Some saw a regional approach as the best way to establish and maintain the balance of power within a global organization. Others, however, saw regional groupings – and consequently regional alli-

* Ambassador, Permanent Representative of Slovenia to the United Nations, New York.

J. Wouters et al., eds., The United Nations and the European Union

ances – as a danger. They could assume the role of furthering 'spheres of influence', a phenomenon that was considered to be one of the decisive failures of the League of Nations. In the end, the idea of regional groupings is reflected in the concept of the permanent members of the Security Council (SC) bearing primary responsibility for world peace and security, accompanied by (originally six, later ten) non-permanent members broadly representative of different regions. Indeed, Article 23 of the UN Charter, dealing with the composition of the Security Council, states that the ten non-permanent members of the Security Council shall be elected by the General Assembly 'due regard being specifically made (…) to equitable geographical distribution'. Interestingly enough, no mention is made of 'equitable geographical distribution' in relation to other principal organs of the UN.

When, starting in the 1960s, UN Membership began to increase considerably as a result of the decolonization process, the composition of the main UN organs and bodies was enlarged so as to ensure their representative character on the basis of a balanced geographical distribution among its Member States. In addition to the principle of 'equitable geographical *distribution',* referred to in Article 23 of the UN Charter, another principle was introduced, namely the principle of 'equitable geographical *rotation'* of the office of the President of the General Assembly among the four following regions: African and Asian States; Eastern European States; Latin American States, and Western European or other States.[1] The introduction of this principle of rotation was partly due to the existing political circumstances, largely related to the Soviet Union and the EEG. The above distinction was applied for the election of all members of the General Committee of the General Assembly (i.e., the President and Vice-Presidents of the General Assembly and the Chairmen of the Main Committees).

The General Assembly reaffirmed the principle of regional representation also with regard to the enlargement of the Security Council and the Economic and Social Council (ECOSOC), and, again in 1971, when ECOSOC membership was further expanded.[2] By virtue of these resolutions, UN regional groups were recognized for the first time, though not formally established.

Only in 1978 were the existing regional groups formally endorsed by the General Assembly[3] (by separating the groups of African and Asian States), thus introducing the five following regions: Africa, Asia, Eastern Europe, Latin America, Western Europe and Other States.

2.2 Composition

Currently the five regional groupings are as follows:

---

[1] See GA Resolution 1990 (XVIII), and its Annex, dated 17 December 1963.

[2] See GA Resolution 2847 (XXVI) dated 20 December 1971.

[3] See GA Resolution 33/38, and Annex, on the question of the composition of the relevant organs of the UN: amendments to rules 31 and 38 of the rules of procedure of the General Assembly, dated 19 December 1978.

- the African Group consists of all 53 States in Africa, including island States of the Eastern Atlantic Ocean and Western Indian Ocean.
- the Asian Group is composed of 52 States from Asia and the Pacific Island Countries.
- the Eastern European Group (EEG) includes 23 States from Central and Eastern Europe.
- the Group of Latin American and Caribbean Countries (GRULAC) covers 33 States.
- the Western European and Others Group (WEOG) includes 28 States and is composed of Western European States, CANZ (Canada, Australia, New Zealand), Israel (granted temporary membership in 2000) and the United States.

All but three UN Member States belong to one of the five regional groups. The membership to a specific regional group is primarily a matter of geography, but also of other criteria (as is illustrated by the case of Israel).

2.3 **Purpose**

The regional groups serve primarily for *election* and *consultation* purposes. The fact that the regional groups first and foremost serve as electoral groups is not a valid argument to question their relevance. As we have seen, regional groups evolved progressively throughout a period of time, as a result of UN practice, in order to protect the needs and interests of its Member States and with a view to ensure the representative character of the UN. All decisions related to the composition of the main UN organs and bodies are based on the principle of a balanced and equitable geographical distribution among its Member States. This principle continues to be relevant today and it is very likely to remain important in the future. In addition, two of the regional groups (African Group and GRULAC) also act as a caucus group.

2.4 **Practice**

The principle of equitable geographical distribution among the existing five regional groups is applied not only in all main UN organs, but also in numerous subsidiary and *ad hoc* advisory and expert bodies of the General Assembly, as well as in most specialized UN agencies, funds and programmes. Let us mention just a few examples:

- Regional groups decide who fills the ten rotating/non-permanent seats at the Security Council. Five non-permanent members are elected each year, proposed by the regional groups and confirmed by the General Assembly. Distribution of non-permanent seats among regional groups is as follows: the African Group, the Asian Group, GRULAC and WEOG are each accorded two seats; one seat is reserved for the Eastern European Group and, finally, one rotating seat is divided between Africa and Asia. At present, reform of the Security Council is blocked in part due to the inability of the African Group to agree upon its own representation in an enlarged SC. Expansion of SC membership is, moreover, unlikely to happen without an additional non-permanent seat of the EEG, which claims that it is under-represented in the Council.

- The General Committee of the General Assembly is composed of the President and 17 Vice-Presidents of the General Assembly, as well as the Chairmen of the Main Committees. Its key task is to consider the provisional agenda of the General Assembly and to decide which items are to be included and which are to be rejected. Apart from the fact that the five permanent members of the Security Council (the so-called P-5) each provide one of the Vice-Presidents of the General Assembly, the composition of the General Committee properly reflects equitable geographical distribution.[4] Thus, of the 12 remaining Vice-Presidents, 7 are chosen from African and Asian States, one from Eastern European States, 3 from Latin-American States, and two from Western European and other States. Likewise, before the conclusion of each session of the General Assembly, regional groups are to agree among themselves on the distribution of the Chairmanship of the six Main Committees for the following session. These Committees relate to the major fields of responsibility of the General Assembly. They consider agenda items referred to them by the GA and propose recommendations and draft resolutions for submission to the GA Plenary. All the substantial General Assembly work is done by those six Committees. Chairmanship of the Committees is equally divided among the regional groups (with one rotating between GRULAC and Africa). Finally, rotation among the regional groups ensures equitable geographical representation in the case of the GA President.
- The Advisory Committee on Administrative and Budgetary Questions (ACABQ) is responsible for the expert examination of the regular and peacekeeping budgets and the accounts of the UN, as well as the administrative budgets of the specialized agencies. Its sixteen members are selected on the basis of a 'broad geographical representation' that includes all regional groups.

The electoral chart of each regional group includes over sixty instances where candidates for different posts are elected due to their affiliation to the respective regional groups. Such a wide application of the principle of equitable geographical distribution and rotation demonstrates the current relevance of the regional groups and the importance of the role Member States are able to play through their affilia-

[4] See GA Resolution 1990 (XVIII), and its Annex, dated 17 December 1963.

tion to the regional groups. From time to time, today as in the past, Member States claim that their respective regional group is under-represented in certain UN organs and bodies. The relevance of the existing regional groups was most recently reconfirmed and reinforced by the decisions, adopted in the aftermath of the UN World Summit of September 2005, establishing two new UN bodies, namely the Peacebuilding Commission[5] and the Human Rights Council.[6] For both bodies, a balanced regional representation served as a source of greater legitimacy.

3. The EU and Regional Groups

The EU Member States are represented in three different regional groups:

- Sixteen of them belong to the Group of Western European and Other States. These are: Austria, Belgium, Denmark, Finland, France, Germany, Greece, Ireland, Italy, Luxembourg, Malta, the Netherlands, Portugal, Spain, Sweden and the United Kingdom;
- Eight belong to the Eastern European Group. These are: the Czech Republic, Estonia, Hungary, Latvia, Lithuania, Poland, Slovakia and Slovenia;
- Finally, one EU Member State, Cyprus, is part of the Asian Group.

EU membership should, therefore, never be equated with membership of the WEOG; the EU has various Member States that do not belong to the WEOG and vice versa. One should indeed not neglect, nor underestimate, the fact that, out of the EU Member States, nine belong to other regional groups (EEG, Asian group).

While addressing the position of the EU within the regional groups of the UN, it is important to stress, again, that regional groups serve primarily for electoral purposes and perhaps also for consultations. They can never discuss matters of substance, let alone exercise the function of coordination. As a result, the division in different regional groups does not, in any way, affect the efficiency of EU coordination or the ability of the European Union to demonstrate its political strength. It is the Member States that can make a difference. In this perspective, the EU enlargement of May 2004 from 15 to 25 Member States, with ten new Member States belonging to three different regional groups, has clearly augmented the overall role, influence and strength of the EU within the UN system.

We have already put forward some examples to demonstrate the linkage between the regional groups and the principle of equitable geographical distribution. Let us now examine the effects of this relationship on the European Union's position in the UN, in particular, in relation to the combined WEOG and EEG membership in the main UN bodies as of 2006:

[5] GA Resolution 60/180 of 20 December 2005; SC Resolution 1645 of 20 December 2005.
[6] GA Resolution 60/251 of 3 April 2006.

- In the Security Council, the EU is currently represented by five Member States: two permanent members – the United Kingdom and France – and three non-permanent members – two from the WEOG (Denmark and Greece) and one from the EEG (Slovakia). This means that the EU currently occupies a third of the Council's 15 seats, a pattern which is likely to persist in the future. Theoretically, as mentioned elsewhere in this book,[7] the EU could even gain a sixth seat in the SC, were Cyprus elected a member on behalf of the Asian Group.
- The Economic and Social Council (ECOSOC), another of the UN's principal organs, has a total of 54 members, out of which – again based on the principle of equitable geographical distribution – 13 are members of the WEOG and 6 are members of the EEG. Their joint membership again potentially strengthens the role of the European Union in ECOSOC.
- Of the General Committee's 27 members, 5 are from the WEOG and three from the EEG. Following the principle of geographical rotation for the election of the GA President, the likelihood that an EU candidate is elected for the post is doubled (provided that the elected President is from an EU Member State from the EEG). Moreover, out of six Main Committees, the WEOG and the EEG have one chairman each, so that the EU would, potentially, be in charge of two Main Committees.

These examples, like many others reflected in the electoral chart of the regional groups, show that there are many advantages for the EU in being represented in three different regional groups. This fact adds to the effects of EU presence at the UN, increases its influence and strengthens its power. Therefore, the issue raised in the context of EU enlargement[8] is not whether or how to overcome EU Member States' dispersion among regional groups by suggesting their eventual revision or amalgamation. Rather, the question is how to take advantage of this situation in the context of the EU's common foreign and security policy and its future role in the UN. The European Union should, therefore, recognize the advantages of its presence in different regional groups and acknowledge the fact that the principle of equitable geographical distribution does not necessarily run against EU interests.

4. The Way Forward

After EU enlargement in 2004 – with eight new Member States from the EEG and one from the Asian group – ideas have been surfacing on the eventual need to rearrange the existing regional groups in order to deal with the growing number of

[7] See the Chapter by Ambassador Johan Verbeke on the Security Council.

[8] The EU and the UN: The Choice of Multilateralism; COM (2003) 526, Brussels, 10 September 2003.

EEG countries that have become EU Member States. These ideas have been taken over in other parts of the world by those who see no rationale in maintaining the EEG and who suggest merging it with the WEOG. These ideas are inspired by different motives and interests, yet they tend to neglect the fact that the regional groups primarily serve the electoral purposes of their respective members. Proposals for a merger of the WEOG and the EEG lack sustainable argument as they fail to recognize that neither the WEOG nor the EEG can be equated with the European Union. Therefore, the issue of eventual re-arrangement of the regional groups requires a broader approach, taking account of the UN in its entirety, and addressing *all* existing regional groups. In this regard, there are three possible solutions to move forward: partial re-arrangement of some regional groups; comprehensive re-arrangement of all regional groups; or *status quo*.

Partial re-arrangement of some Groups seems tempting but tends to be too selective and lacks a broader perspective. It could, perhaps, undermine the basic concept of geographical balance as a source of legitimacy for the United Nations. Injustice would be done to the EEG if such a proposal were limited to its abolishment or to a merger with the WEOG. Since the early 1990s, the membership of the EEG has more than doubled, from ten to twenty-three.[9] The Group, as such, has undergone a wide range of political and economic transitional processes that are valuable not only for EEG members themselves but also for the wider UN membership. These processes have reinforced the identity of the group, in addition to its geographic origins. The argument of a 'split identity' of the EEG (because eight of its members are also EU Member States) is not sustainable: first, because neither the EEG nor the WEOG can be equated with the European Union and, secondly, because other regional groups also lack internal cohesion and undisputed identity.[10]

Comprehensive revision of all regional groups would be the most appropriate solution, provided that the modalities of such an approach were acceptable to all UN Member States. Since current regional groups were not established by a formal decision, the question remains how to find an appropriate approach in revisiting the existing regional groups. Moreover, however imperfect existing Groups may be, they still mirror a balance between different regional groupings in the wider UN system that is politically significant. If comprehensive re-arrangement of the regional groups were to put into question the basic principles enshrined in the UN Charter, such an undertaking could seriously affect multilateralism, as it is being exercised through a universal organization. In the absence of a common under-

[9] In July 2006, Montenegro was the last country to join the EEG.

[10] The WEOG includes countries from different continents, apart from Europe, namely the USA and Canada from America and Australia and New Zealand from Asia. The African Group is *de facto* divided into three subgroups. The Asian Group, likewise, experiences difficulties in exercising its unity and identity as one Regional Group: it includes five Central Asian countries that are members of the Organization for Security and Cooperation in Europe.

standing on the need, scope and modalities of a comprehensive re-arrangement of the regional groups, maintaining the *status quo* thus seems to be the most harmless and realistic option for the time being.

Maintaining the status quo may have some advantages for the EU, at least in the present circumstances. The presence of EU Member States in three regional groups could help expand EU influence in the United Nations, increase its ambitions in the elections for intergovernmental bodies and strengthen the efficiency of its lobbying for different candidacies within the UN system. However, maintaining the *status quo* will of course require enhanced consultation and coordination among the EU Member States. Moreover, it will also require getting rid of the continuous misconceptions that the EU and the WEOG are one and the same.

Chapter 20
THE EUROPEAN UNION AND THE REFORM OF THE UNITED NATIONS

by Danièle Smadja*

1. Introduction

The ongoing debate on UN reform goes beyond the mere enhancement of the efficiency of the World Organization's organs. Prompted, in particular, by Secretary-General Kofi Annan's report 'In Larger Freedom: towards Development, Security and Human Rights for All',[1] the discussion extends to the 'vital importance of an effective multilateral system … in order to better address the multifaceted and interconnected challenges and threats confronting our world.'[2] In other words, the debate strikes at the core of a defining principle of the EU's external policy.

As a staunch supporter of 'effective multilateralism', the EU was by definition called upon to be an important player in the process of UN reform. All the more so, since the UN Summit negotiations were permeated by the general acknowledgment – subsequently embodied in the Outcome Document – that 'development, peace and security and human rights are interlinked and mutually reinforcing',[3] thus bringing together the various areas of UN activities with respect to which the EU is playing an increasing role as discussed in previous chapters.

Did the EU rise up to the challenge? It was clearly one of the major actors; but was its action *instrumental* in bringing the process forward? And if so, in what fields? These are important questions as the impact of the EU in the ongoing UN reform process is in fact quite revealing as to its role as a global actor in the framework of the UN, with its strengths and limitations, but also its potential.

* Director at the European Commission – Directorate General for External Relations – in charge of Multilateral Affairs and Human Rights. The views expressed in this article are however her personal views and do not necessarily represent the official view of the European Commission.

[1] 'In Larger Freedom: Towards Development, Security and Human Rights for All', UN Doc. A/59/2005. This report in turn is inspired in particular by the following two documents: the report of the High-Level Panel on Threats, Challenges and Change set up by the Secretary-General entitled 'A More Secure World: Our Shared Responsibility', UN Doc. A/59/565 and the report entitled 'Investing in Development: A practical Plan to Achieve the Millennium Development Goals' (Sachs report).

[2] 2005 World Summit Outcome, GA Res. 60/1, 16 September 2005, para. 6.

[3] Ibid., para. 9.

J. Wouters et al., eds., The United Nations and the European Union

2. A Visible Actor on UN Reform

With the notable exception of the question of Security Council reform, the EU presented, to a very large extent, a united front on the major issues of the 2005 UN Summit. Through sustained coordination, it was able to engage in the process as *a* key player, delivering much more than a common statement of a general character.

The EU adjusted its efforts to circumstances and adapted its posture to needs. At times the EU chose to act in a discrete way providing some important actors with informal inputs or lobbying a number of targeted capitals; at other times it went public by making common statements, adopting EU Council conclusions or inviting the UN Secretary-General to meetings in Brussels so as to show its support at a difficult juncture.

In the very early days of the Summit preparation – when the High Level Panel of Eminent Persons nominated by UNSG Kofi Annan was preparing its report – the EU submitted contributions to the members of the Panel. Two elements deserve to be mentioned in this context: (a) these inputs were coordinated within the EU working structures so as to represent a common view and were also brought to the attention of the highest political level;[4] (b) there was a strong consensus within the EU for these inputs to be informal. Similarly, the EU offered additional contributions before the Secretary-General issued his report.

All this is current practice in multilateral diplomacy and many actors tend to influence the process behind the scene. What may be worth noting is that it is fairly new for the EU to integrate a systematic approach of reaching out to other actors in the way it operates within the UN. For years – and still now – the EU was known for its intense internal coordination mechanism at the end of which it was regularly or most of the time too late to enter into real interacting with other actors.

When the time to negotiate and position itself came in spring 2005, the EU offered fairly detailed proposals on both principle and drafting regarding the various sections of the Outcome Document, through the Presidency and/or Troika – and, where appropriate, the Commission representing the European Community. All this was backed up with an intense lobbying effort to garner third States' support on EU priorities. Action on both the negotiating and lobbying front naturally has continued as regards the Summit follow-up.

The importance attached to dynamic EU involvement in the UN reform process as an expression of its strong support for effective multilateralism and recognition of the pivotal role of the UN was repeatedly confirmed at the highest political level. Thus, in the run-up to the Summit, the European Council highlighted EU priorities,

---

[4] EU Foreign Affairs Ministers meeting within the General Affairs and External Relations Council were asked to take note of these documents before they were transmitted to the Panel. See General Affairs and External Relations Council, 'Paper for the submission to the High-Level Panel on Threats, Challenges and Change', 17-18 May 2004.

with a special emphasis on EU commitments on development assistance.[5] This was the result of a clear determination expressed a year in advance by both the Commission and the Member States to not only show the importance attached within the EU to the development aspect of the Summit outcome but also to be as visible as possible very early on in the negotiating process. The Commission further presented a Communication specifically on the Summit, emphasizing the need for clear and action-oriented decisions on UN reform.[6] Following the adoption of the Outcome Document, the General Affairs and External Relations Council underlined the EU's continued engagement as regards both implementation of Summit decisions as well as efforts to achieve 'important reforms in the UN system on issues not covered at the Summit', also setting out relevant EU priorities.[7]

Conclusions adopted at EU level as regards UN issues are not a new tool and over the years they have covered specific aspects. However, it has been a relatively new practice for the General Affairs and External Relations Council or the European Council to adopt conclusions of a comprehensive nature as regards the UN. It dates from 2003[8] when promotion of effective multilateralism with the UN at its core was confirmed as a key component of EU external and foreign policy, with the EU demonstrating a clear will to be more present and more visible on the UN scene.

All the steps described above were the result of intense EU coordination. Clearly, there were internal divisions with respect to certain aspects of the topics under discussion which remained unresolved. For instance, where questions of seat distribution/representation are involved, national interests inevitably resurface. It is also undeniable that when the interests of the P5 are at stake, France and the United Kingdom react primarily in that capacity rather than as EU members, including as regards an otherwise consensual issue at EU level such as the establishment of the Peacebuilding Commission.[9] Nevertheless, throughout the process, the EU has remained a highly recognizable actor for third States and for the negotiators/facilitators, with clear positions on most issues.

This is of course not a novel development. As discussed elsewhere in this book, EU visibility at the UN and UN-sponsored conferences is a reality. The EU delivers

---

[5] Presidency conclusions, European Council, Brussels, 16 and 17 June 2005, paras. 21-40. The Commission adopted on 12 April 2005 a 'development package' set out in three Communications, respectively on 'Speeding up progress towards the Millennium Development Goals: The European Union's contribution' (COM (2005) 132 final); 'Accelerating progress towards attaining the Millennium Development Goals – Financing for Development and Aid Effectiveness' (COM (2005) 133 final); and 'Policy Coherence for Development – Accelerating progress towards attaining the Millennium Development Goals' (COM (2005) 134 final).

[6] Communication entitled 'The 2005 UN Summit – Addressing the global challenges and making a success of the reformed UN', COM (2005) 259 final of 15 June 2005.

[7] 13737/1/05/Rev 1, adopted on 7 November 2005.

[8] Communication entitled 'The European Union and the United Nations: The choice of multilateralism', COM (2003) 526 final of 10 September 2003.

[9] For instance the question whether the P5 should be guaranteed a seat and the relation of the Peacebuilding Commission to the Security Council.

common statements – to which acceding, candidate and potential candidate countries routinely associate themselves as well as other specific EU partners -- on an ever-increasing number of issues. The instances of split EU votes are decreasing. EU-sponsored resolutions and EU-level reactions to resolutions sponsored by others are commonplace.

Still, the high visibility of the EU as an important actor on UN reform deserves special emphasis as it eloquently demonstrates that the EU is not only a global actor as regards major thematic and geographical issues of our times (from peacebuilding to the environment, and from Africa to the Middle East) but also has a say on the multilateral process itself. The question however remains, to what extent it can actually steer this process in the desired direction, in other words what influence the EU actually wields.

3. An Influential Actor on UN Reform?

It was tempting to write the title of this section without the question mark. However, the EU influence on UN reform is indeed a question which, unlike the issue of EU visibility, does not lend itself to a general answer, given the wide-ranging spectrum of issues addressed in the context of the UN Summit. Nevertheless, some conclusions can be drawn on the basis of the evaluation of the EU's role with respect to specific aspects of the UN reform process.

3.1 **The Peacebuilding Commission**

The EU most certainly invested a great deal of energy and political will in ensuring that the Summit Outcome Document contained provisions on the establishment of the Peacebuilding Commission (PBC),[10] and thereafter, spared no efforts for the adoption of the implementing resolutions[11] before the critical deadline of 31 December 2005. Internal coordination, submission of numerous and hopefully constructive proposals as well as intense lobbying were clearly elements of a successful approach.

Yet characterising the EU contribution to the establishment of the PBC as a manifestation of actual *leadership* would seem to be an overstatement. Indeed, the EU was not alone in supporting the setting-up of a dedicated mechanism to address the special needs of countries emerging from conflict towards recovery, reintegration and reconstruction and to assist them in laying the foundation for sustainable development. The United States was also in favour, as were a number of other countries, in particular African States. However significantly divergent views were expressed by UN Member States in particular on the mandate of the PBC, its rela-

[10] World Summit Outcome, paras. 97-105.

[11] GA Resolution 60/180 and SC Resolution 1645 (2005) of 20 December 2005.

tionship to other UN organs – especially the Security Council, the General Assembly and ECOSOC – and last but not least its composition. The negotiations were moreover complicated by a tactical factor: several States were tempted to link agreement to an early decision on the PBC to guarantees on other aspects of UN reform.

It is not certain that the EU's influence in bringing about a successful outcome derived so much from the weight of its arguments on the usefulness of the PBC. To a large extent, it seems that the EU reaped on this matter the benefits of its 'front-runner commitment'[12] in the area of development. The EU took indeed a pro-active approach in May 2005, by deciding, among other things, to increase Official Development Aid (ODA) and to enhance quality and effectiveness, with a view to ensuring achievement of the Millennium Development Goals. In particular, a timetable was adopted for Member States to achieve 0.7% of GNI by 2015, with an intermediate collective target of 0.56% by 2010, which should see annual EU aid double to over €66 billion in 2010, with at least 50% of such increase intended for Africa.[13]

This action confirmed the responsible attitude of the EU as a major donor and showed the EU determination to have a balanced approach by ensuring that development was as important as security in the Summit agenda and outcome. As a result, it also granted the EU considerable credibility; it allowed the EU to play a decisive role in the negotiation of the development section of the Summit Outcome Document,[14] notwithstanding the skeptical US attitude towards an increase of development assistance. Obviously, the result of the Summit on development is not as ambitious in all aspects as the EU would have wanted, but nevertheless overall it remained satisfactory.

The EU thus came into the more detailed negotiation on the PBC in the follow-up to the Summit as an actor who has demonstrated the potential and willingness to deliver. While this factor alone did not of course lead to the establishment of this new organ, it did play an important role in securing agreement. But so did US engagement on the PBC – despite certain misgivings in allowing progress on this issue before management reform.

3.2 The Human Rights Council

Despite the efforts deployed by the EU at the time, the result obtained at the Summit did not go much beyond a 'resolve to create' the Human Rights Council (HRC).[15] However, in the follow-up negotiating process of a detailed resolution on the estab-

---

[12] For a more detailed discussion of the EU as a 'front-runner', see, e.g., the Communication of the European Commission entitled 'The European Union and the United Nations: The choice of multilateralism', COM (2003) 526 final, 10 September 2003.

[13] General Affairs and External Relations Council conclusions of 23-24 May 2005.

[14] World Summit Outcome, section II.

[15] Ibid., paras. 157-160.

lishment of this new organ, the EU has emerged as a crucial player on this aspect of UN reform.

The EU, as discussed by other contributors to this publication,[16] has been a major actor in the context of the UN human rights machinery, especially the former Commission on Human Rights and the Third Committee of the General Assembly. While not all its initiatives command the same degree of support, the EU enjoys overall significant credibility on human rights, both *vis-à-vis* developing countries and the United States, probably because human rights issues are an important element of its bilateral relations whether through a specific clause – named the 'essential clause' – included in almost all its bilateral agreements, or other dialogue or consultation mechanisms.

Throughout the process leading to the creation of the HRC, the EU has maintained a coherent and unified line – in spite of the looming internal divisions on participation/distribution of seats – and has lobbied consistently. The wavering degree of US engagement and the latter's sometimes non-constructive approach have further contributed to the EU assuming a central role in the process.

Several times during the process, all those actively involved in the negotiation and attached to the creation of this new organ looked to the EU as the possible driving force capable of reconciling a number of divergent views, including those of countries not convinced that a solution was necessary before the 62nd session of the Commission on Human Rights. Although the EU had a number of red lines on which it was not ready to compromise, its commitment to finding a solution was well established. When the time came to decide whether or not to accept the draft tabled by General Assembly President Eliasson, the decision was not easy and required some internal discussion at the EU political level in Brussels. While the United States clearly stated its opposition to the draft and other actors declared their dissatisfaction with many aspects of the text, the jury was still out for a couple of days. When the EU decided to go along with the text and made its decision known, this opened the door to an agreement which was eventually reached on 15 March 2006.

All actors have since recognized that the EU posture was *the* key to the successful outcome. The entire UN membership, including the United States, was influenced by this move. While voting against the text of the resolution,[17] the United States made a statement indicating that it 'will work cooperatively with other Member States to make the Council as strong and effective as it can be'.[18] This was made possible by discussions between the EU and the United States which allowed the EU to confirm that it was not reducing its level of ambition as regards some

---

[16] See in particular chapter 5.

[17] The resolution was adopted by 170 in favour to 4 against (Israel, Marshall Islands, Palau, United States), with 3 abstentions (Belarus, Iran, Venezuela).

[18] Explanation of vote by Ambassador John R. Bolton, USUN Press Release, #51(06).

important credibility aspects of the new organ.[19] Several like-minded countries were also encouraged to follow suit in their declaration after the vote.

This is a clear-cut case where the EU made the difference, although one should add that it will take more than mere influence for the EU to make the HRC a credible and operational machinery.

3.3 International environmental governance

The EU is generally a 'front-runner' in the environmental field, as demonstrated in particular by its engagement leading to the entry into force of the Kyoto Protocol and by the impressive number of multilateral conventions and agreements to which the European Community has become a party. Its support for a more integrated international environmental governance structure, based on existing institutions such as the United Nations Environment Programme (UNEP), therefore comes as no surprise. It has been a longstanding EU policy to push for improved international management of environmental issues within the UN system, in particular through the reform of UNEP. Until recently this objective was pursued through a reform package agreed at the 2002 meeting of the Governing Council of UNEP in Cartagena.

In the run-up to the Summit,[20] the EU agreed on a common position to support the establishment of a UN specialized agency for the Environment to be known as the United Nations Environment Organization (UNEO). It believes that if such an organization were supported by stable, adequate and predictable financial contributions, it would advance the environmental dimensions of sustainable development in an integrated and consistent manner.[21]

In this area as well, the EU undertook a number of outreach activities well in advance of the Summit. In the end, however, the Summit Outcome Document fell short of its expectations, with only an agreement to 'explore the possibility of a more coherent institutional framework (…) including a more integrated structure, building on existing institutions, and internationally agreed instruments, as well as the treaties bodies and the specialized agencies.'[22] This gives the international community a further opportunity to discuss international environmental governance, including the EU proposal for a specialized agency or UNEO and should therefore not be interpreted as a failure. The EU itself had recognized that progress would take time, by setting as a Summit objective the 'initiation of a process' which would lead to negotiations on the establishment of UNEO.[23]

---

[19] See EU statement delivered on 15 March 2006 in the General Assembly, whereby the EU Member States 'commit[ed] themselves not to cast their vote for a candidate that is under sanctions imposed by the Security Council for human rights related reasons'.

[20] See European Council conclusions, 16-17 June 2005, para. 39.

[21] Ibid. See also Commission Communication on Summit, *supra* n. 5, p. 16.

[22] World Summit Outcome, para. 169.

[23] See European Council conclusions, 16-17 June 2005, para. 39.

If it pursues its outreach strategy aimed at encouraging countries to discuss in an open and constructive manner and is ready to continue to adopt a dynamic approach the EU is likely to succeed. There is of course always the risk that negative developments on other aspects of UN reform considerably delay the process. However it is interesting to note that the mandate of the High-Level Panel nominated by the Secretary-General on 15 February 2006 to study the system-wide coherence covers also environment and not just development and humanitarian assistance.

3.4 Management reform

Unlike the establishment of new organs which requires – albeit after lengthy negotiations – a one-time decision, management reform is in fact a process which entails several different actions, as agreed at the Summit.[24] Following some 'early wins' such as the establishment of the ethics office[25] and the promulgation of a whistleblower protection policy,[26] the follow-up process is engaged on issues such as review of rules, regulations and policies, mandate review and enhancing flexibility for the Secretary-General while ensuring more accountability to Member States.

The United States considers management reform as a top priority, while the G77 is taking a defensive approach, fearing that proposed reforms will considerably weaken the control of the General Assembly – and hence their own control – over the Secretariat. The EU, for its part, has consistently expressed support for the reforms proposed by the Secretary-General[27] and is therefore largely in agreement with the United States on substance, although it uses more subtle language. Given its recent experience as regards management reform, the European Commission has been approached by the UN Secretariat to exchange some lessons learned.

As a result of the above and its balanced agenda – development, security, human rights, management reform –, the EU has the opportunity to act as a bridge-builder in UN management reform. Given the importance attached to this issue by the United States, a successful outcome could be an additional demonstration of EU influence. However, this is becoming an increasingly difficult endeavour, given the confrontational atmosphere surrounding the debate, and the escalation brought about by the uncompromising stance of the G77 which called for a vote against many of the Secretary-General's proposals.[28]

---

[24] World Summit Outcome, paras. 161-167.

[25] UN Doc. ST/SGB/2005/22 of 30 December 2005.

[26] UN Doc. ST/SGB/2005/21 of 19 December 2005 on 'Protection against retaliation for reporting misconduct and for cooperating with duly authorized audits or investigations.'

[27] See, e.g., speaking points of EU Presidency on Secretariat and Management Reform, 7 and 14 February 2005, available at <http://www.eu2006.at/en/News/Statements_in_International_Organisations/UN/index.html>.

[28] The vote took place in the Fifth Committee of the General Assembly on 28 April 2006.

3.5 Security Council reform

Aside from the Secretariat, reform of the three other main organs, namely the General Assembly, ECOSOC and, last but not least, the Security Council is also part of the debate. As far as the General Assembly is concerned, the term 'revitalization' actually used is quite revealing as to the extent of the exercise, in which the EU of course participates, but without a particularly high profile – maybe reflecting the rather limited attention for this aspect of the reform process. On ECOSOC reform, the EU is an important player, reflecting its weight in the relevant areas of UN activities – although the subject is not one that makes the headlines either.

This brings us to the question of Security Council reform. For obvious reasons, EU Member States hold widely divergent views on the matter. As long as the EU cannot position itself with a united front on such a central element of the architecture of the international system, this will remain *the* issue which most eloquently shows the limits of the EU's role in the UN reform process in general.

4. Conclusion

The considerable efforts and energy invested by the EU in supporting the UN reform process, both pre- and post-Summit, have certainly borne tangible fruits. Its ambitious commitments in the development area have generally given it more clout and leverage, showing the potential it has as a key actor in the UN context. EU successes, however, tend to continue to be assessed on a case-by-case basis.

For decades observers of the UN scene have been unanimous in saying that the EU was a visible entity addressing an ever-increasing number of issues with a common position. Subsequently and in particular over the last years, the debate has been about the semantic question of visibility versus influence, which in itself underlines that the latter element was not absolutely obvious, possibly because the EU still lacked a global and long-term strategy on the issues involved.

The Summit and its follow-up may well have consolidated the EU capacity to exert influence and confirmed that whatever terminology is used to qualify the EU – a global actor, a major player or a soft power – the centre stage of the multilateral system is occupied by a visible force able to influence a process and to engage the UN membership when necessary. It is interesting to note in this context that many people do not like or do not want to talk about the EU as a *leader.* Promoting effective multilateralism does not necessarily mean that a single leadership is what the UN needs. It needs the engagement of key actors in a sustained way and the capacity of its main bodies to deliver when action is required.

Chapter 21
THE FUTURE OF THE UNITED NATIONS: A VIEW FROM THE EUROPEAN PARLIAMENT

by Jo Leinen*

1. Introduction

The cooperation between the EU and the UN concerns several questions at the crossroads of the development and security policy agenda's, such as the fight against terrorism, proliferation of weapons of mass destruction and the implementation of sanctions of the UN Security Council. More and more, the EU is also engaged in the area of conflict prevention and crisis management, a topic on which the EU and the UN signed a common declaration in September 2003.[1] The fight for human rights is another issue on which Europe and the United Nations are working closely together, as is the support of the EU for the implementation of a UN Peacebuilding Commission, a body intended to help countries emerge from conflicts by seeking to overcome the difficulties of the transition period to stability and development.

Thus, there is a strong link between the United Nations and the European Union, both organizations relying on the system of multilateralism to achieve their goals and sharing a common set of values as well as the common belief that together they will achieve more than any member country alone. However, when it comes to democratic representation and legitimisation, the European Union is in the lead.

This article will first recall the reasons why there is a need to reform the UN system. Based on this analysis, the views of the European Parliament for a stronger UN will then be presented. A short assessment of the Outcome Document of September 2005 will follow before concluding.

2. The Need to Reform the UN System

The governance of the UN system is still largely a process between governments alone. An international representation of citizens or a mechanism of parliamentary

* Member of the European Parliament, Chairman of the Committee on Constitutional Affairs.

[1] Joint Declaration on UN-EU Cooperation in Crisis Management, New York, 24 September 2003, available at <http://europa-eu-un.org/articles/lt/article_2768_lt.htm>.

J. Wouters et al., eds., The United Nations and the European Union

control of international governmental action does not exist. This is one of the few areas where the powerful force of globalisation has not yet had much impact.

As the most prominent and most powerful of all international organizations, the United Nations not only faces a problem of lack of control by the peoples of the world. The UN needs general reform. The Report of the 'High-level Panel on Threats, Challenges and Change' of 1 December 2004[2] makes more than a hundred recommendations on change and the need for reform of the UN in order to address challenges and threats ranging from poverty, infectious diseases, environmental damage and civil violence to terrorism, weapons of mass destruction and nuclear non-proliferation. For sure, in the years since its creation, the UN has been reformed time and again – on average once every eight years. Changes have involved both membership as well as institutional structure. The 'enemy state clause' does not apply anymore, and the Trusteeship Council has ceased to play an active role. Even the Security Council underwent reform in 1965, when it was enlarged to include four new members, thus increasing its membership to 15. In particular, the system of the 'United Nations' has expanded: new specialized organizations have emerged, and new special programmes and funds have been set-up. The United Nations has dealt with hunger, provided humanitarian aid to refugees, and has policed ceasefires. The UN has set-up rules in important domains like trade, protection of human rights and environmental protection. It supervises the implementation of international treaties negotiated under its auspices and gives credit to developing countries, to name but a few of its most important activities.

There are, however, also darker sides to this bright picture. Serious internal problems and the lack of powers of policy implementation have contributed to the perception that the United Nations is a poorly managed debating club. In his report 'In larger freedom: towards development, security and human rights for all', the Secretary-General,[3] points out the urgency in the need to review policies and institutions of the United Nations in order to rise to the challenge of meeting new threats and to avoid its erosion in the face of increased discord between states and unilateral action by them.

This need of a profound reform is becoming ever more necessary. Breakthroughs in biology and genetics as well as challenges in the fields of environmental protection, biodiversity, climate change, terrorism, ethnic and religious conflicts, proliferation of weapons of mass destruction, demographic development, and unequal distribution of resources and prosperity have made the stability of the international community and its capacity to act a critical issue for the future. Furthermore, global industrial progress is coupled with a threat to the ecological foundations of life on

[2] Report of the High-Level Panel on Threats, Challenges and Changes set-up by the Secretary-General: 'A More Secure World: Our Shared Responsibility', 29 November 2004, UN Doc A/59/565.

[3] Report of the UN Secretary-General: 'In larger freedom: towards development, security and human rights for all', 21 March 2005, UN Doc A/59/2005.

earth and therefore makes it a necessity to ensure the survival of future generations. The effects of an ever-proceeding and accelerating globalisation already arrived like a storm. If we do not wish this storm to turn into a hurricane, we have to be prepared to cope with these effects.

3. European Parliament Proposals to Strengthen the UN

While there is widespread agreement on the need to reform the UN system, there is sharp disagreement on what kind of reform is needed and for what purpose.

In 2004 the European Parliament ('EP') set-up a working group on UN relations to keep the EP updated and informed about the work of the UN and to have high-level exchanges of experience with UN officials. The working group, a sub-organ of the Committee on foreign affairs, holds regular meetings and aims to strengthen the ties between the European Parliament and the UN as well as getting a better insight into the challenges and tasks of the UN and its sub-systems. This way of exchanging information and experience convinced the European Parliament that on an institutional level the UN-system must be strengthened, be better coordinated and made more transparent. The envisaged reforms and the successful implementation of the Millennium Development Goals will be the most crucial tasks for the UN to ensure that it continues to play a leading role in today's international system.

The European Parliament has passed several resolutions on the strengthening of the UN, outlining that it must be democratized through greater direct representation of citizens, underlining that citizens have a right, as well as a responsibility to become equal participants in the governance of their own global community. The most elaborate resolution dates from September 2005 and is dedicated specifically to the reform of the UN.[4] The Members of the European Parliament reaffirmed their commitment to a strong UN, reiterating that genuine multilateralism is the most appropriate tool for solving the challenges, problems and threats faced by the international community. In the view of the Parliament, several dimensions can be identified in the reform debate.

3.1 Improving the EU status in the United Nations

From the European perspective, the creation of a single European seat in the Security Council which could be taken up by the European Foreign Minister is desirable in the long run. Such a seat would be the logical consequence of the EU's ambition to conduct a common foreign and security policy and to speak with one voice in

[4] European Parliament, Resolution on the outcome of the United Nations World Summit of 14-16 September 2005, Strasbourg, 29 September 2005, P6_TA(2005)0362, available at <http://www.europarl.europa.eu/omk/sipade3?L=EN&OBJID=101077&LEVEL=3&MODE=SIP&NAV=X&LSTDOC=N>.

world affairs. At the moment, however, this EU seat cannot be realised because the European Union does not yet have legal personality. The necessary legal changes to modify this are envisaged by the European Constitution and would come into effect once it enters into force. Therefore, more short-term aims have to be set for the impending reform efforts.

As long as the conditions are not in place for an EU-seat, we have to discuss how the European Union can participate in the decision-making of the UN Security Council. The easiest way to achieve this would be to assign one of the existing, or newly created 'European' seats to the EU. One or several Member States would thus act as a sort of 'representative' of the EU in the Security Council and would be supported herein by the European Commission, the Council and by the future European External Action Service in close cooperation with the other institutions of the Union, notably the European Parliament. The European Council should work out possible steps for such a scenario.

It is quite obvious that the regional representation in the Security Council has to be improved. All regions of the world must have a permanent place in this important world-institution, including Africa and Latin America. It is equally clear that participation in the world organization must be 'worthwhile' for the countries in question, as the High-Level Panel underlined in its report. The European Parliament stressed the same idea in the report which it adopted on 9th June 2005,[5] in the following words:

> 'The European Parliament is convinced of the need to change the composition of the Security Council in a way that takes into account the changed state of the international system as well as current geopolitical realities, by increasing the number of developing countries in the Council, by ensuring that its members are willing and able to act when action is needed, and by employing more effective and transparent working methods.'

3.2 Adding a democratic dimension to the UN system

To achieve real acceptance and legitimacy of decisions taken by the United Nations, its decision-making processes have to be democratised. Global developments have taken such dimensions in daily life that they cannot be solved any longer without taking into account the will, ideas and initiatives of the people of the world. The participation of the people is not only needed for the planning of lasting solutions of the world's problems, but also to transform the UN into an effective instrument of global governance. Moreover, experience has shown that for people to become active and support a cause, the feeling of ownership of the issue is of high importance. Only when people see that they are involved in the decision-making

---

[5] European Parliament, Resolution on the reform of the United Nations, 9 June 2005, P6_TA-PROV(2005)0237, available at <http://www.cipresearch.fuhem.es/pazyseguridad/EU_parliament_resolution_9June05.pdf>.

processes will they more actively support and take part in the implementation of the decisions.

The possibilities for citizens to participate in UN processes must be improved and enlarged. It is to be regarded as very positive that the UN already includes numerous NGOs in its work, in particular when it comes to implementing policies and strategies. Nonetheless, a more structured approach for democratization is necessary. In its January 2006 part-session, the Parliamentary Assembly of the Council of Europe adopted Resolution 1476 (2006) on the Parliamentary dimension of the United Nations[6] calling for a step-by-step approach to a closer involvement of parliamentarians in UN activities, with a view to redressing the democratic deficit in global governance and bridging the distance between the UN and the people.

Thus, several international actors have come to the conclusion that it is necessary to create a parliamentary dimension of the United Nations system. It must therefore be examined in which areas this would be possible. Then the question of the most suitable institutional form arises. In this regard, a 'Parliamentary Assembly' for the citizens' chambers of the world should be set-up. Such an assembly would be a link between the United Nations, the national governments and civil society, and could act as a political catalyst for the development of global cooperation and international law, and thus contribute to shaping globalisation in a positive way. It should be authorized to establish inquiry commissions and to question staff and officials of the United Nations.

As outlined in the Council of Europe resolution, such a step-by-step strategy could, *inter alia*, include the following stages:

- setting-up a network of regional parliamentary assemblies to discuss emerging UN priorities, with consultative functions for one or more General Assembly committees;
- setting-up a parliamentary committee to discuss issues of special global or regional importance and/or the UN budget;
- adopting clear rules for the involvement of parliamentarians in its work, setting out their rights and responsibilities, as well as the obligations for parliamentary delegations to ensure a fair representation of the political parties or groups in their parliament.

The rights and tasks of this newly created Parliamentary Assembly could include:

- submission of its own opinions/resolutions to the General Assembly, the ECOSOC, the Secretary-General, the Security Council, and to the organs and other institutions of the UN system;

---

[6] Council of Europe, Parliamentary Assembly, Resolution 1476 (2006), 23 January 2006, available at <http://assembly.coe.int/Main.asp?link=/Documents/AdoptedText/ta06/ERES1476.htm>.

- consultation by the General Assembly, by ECOSOC and the other institutions of the UN system with regard to important questions;
- the right to address questions to the Secretary-General, the Presidents of the General Assembly, to ECOSOC and to the Security Council as well as to the heads of other institutions of the UN system;
- rights of information and participation in relation to the activities of the institutions of the UN system including the still independent international financial institutions;
- readings of draft resolutions of the General Assembly and of ECOSOC with the right to submit suggestions for amendments;
- the right to submit to the General Assembly and to ECOSOC draft resolutions for further negotiation and adoption;
- co-decision with regard to the adoption of the UN budget;
- co-decision with regard to the election of the UN Secretary-General;
- the right to be integrated into all treaty negotiations which are conducted under the auspices of the United Nations to found or modify international institutions;
- the right also to be integrated into the remaining multilateral treaty negotiations at the international level and;
- the right to submit legal questions to the International Court of Justice, in accordance with Article 65 of its Statute.

3.3 **Identifying policy priorities**

The main concern of the European Parliament lies with the protection of human rights worldwide. The Parliament, being convinced that human rights and fundamental freedoms are the prerequisites for the development of democracy and strong civil societies, once more made clear in a hearing in February 2006 that it wants more effective and strict implementation of the human rights and democracy clauses that have been obligatory in EU agreements with non-EU countries since 1995.[7] The EU must use its political and economic weight to promote democratic change abroad. The EU is the biggest aid donor in the world, accounting for 55% of development assistance and the largest market for products from the developing world. This financial capacity must be translated into political influence and needs to be controlled effectively.

With its Common Foreign and Security Policy (CFSP), the EU has a tool for supporting the UN's activities to achieve and promote peace and security on an international level. However, once the Constitutional Treaty enters into force and the EU Foreign Minister and the European External Action Service assume their

[7] See Radio Free Europe, 'EU: Parliament debates role of rights in foreign policy', 14 February 2006, available at <http://www.rferl.org/featuresarticle/2006/02/74f25628-dfbc-487d-9bb5-f9d927a7d2c6.html>.

functions, the EU would be much better equipped to follow-up and implement these policy areas, giving the EU a greater weight in the international arena. Furthermore, the European Foreign Minister will have to report and inform the European Parliament about the developments in the foreign policy area, thus providing the European parliamentarians with an effective instrument to monitor the EU's UN-related activities on behalf of the European citizens.

Apart from the fight for human rights, the European Parliament gives high priority to combating terrorism. In its 2005 resolution on 'Reform of the UN'[8] the Parliament supports the forging by the United Nations of a strategy of counter-terrorism which is respectful of human rights and the rule of law, which involves civil society and which is based on the five pillars of dissuading persons from resorting to terrorism or support thereof, denying terrorists access to funds and material resources, deterring states from supporting terrorism, developing state capacity to combat terrorism, and defending human rights. At the same time it stresses that a comprehensive convention on terrorism must be based on a clear and agreed definition, respecting human rights and democratic freedoms.

When implementing these policies, the European Parliament emphasises the need for a multilateral approach as opposed to the US' rather unilateralist stance. For the Parliament, the UN's primary task is to promote peace in the world. In this context, the EP has already suggested concrete measures for European countries, such as transforming the EU Member States' armies into units suitable for deployment in peace operations and placing contingents on stand-by for UN purposes.

4. Assessment of the Outcome Document

Decisions taken at the 2005 World Summit in GA Resolution 60/1 call for a stronger UN system-wide coherence.[9] At the policy level, the resolution urges the UN to strengthen linkages between its normative work and operational activities. It also proposes greater coordination at the level of the governing boards of various agencies to ensure a coherent policy in assigning mandates and allocating resources.

At the country level, the resolution calls for a more effective, efficient, coherent and coordinated UN system with strong Resident Coordinators with the necessary authority, resources and accountability structures to be able to have a common management, programming and monitoring framework in every country. The resolution also seeks to ensure that human rights, gender and sustainable development are mainstreamed in UN decision-making across the board.

To achieve these goals new bodies, such as the Peacebuilding Commission, were set-up. Others, such as the Human Rights Council (HRC) underwent substantial

---

[8] Loc. cit., *supra* n. 5.

[9] UN GA Res. 60/1, 15 September 2005.

reforms. The European Parliament believes that members of the new Human Rights Council should abide by the highest human rights standards and that membership of the Council is a privilege and not a right. With its new structure and membership regulations, admitting only countries that themselves strictly implement human rights, the HRC can act with higher credibility than its predecessor. However, the reformed body now has to stand the test of reality and needs to ensure that its members act in accordance with their commitments. Especially the European members of the HRC have to take on a leading role in transforming the Council into a powerful instrument, capable of acting quickly and effectively for the defence of human rights.

The European Parliament endorses multilateralism as the 'most appropriate tool for solving the problems and threats faced by the international community'.[10] Against this background, the European Parliament highly welcomes the proposal to create a Peacebuilding Commission as well as a Peacebuilding Support Office within the UN Secretariat, in order to rebuild states devastated by violence, and supports calls for the establishment of a civilian peace corps (*white helmets*) for performing non-military functions. The European Parliament 'recognises that peace-building requires an entirely different set of skills to peace-keeping and considers that there is a need for regional and global peace-building commissions to develop the necessary skills and capabilities, backed by a support office and a standing fund, thereby raising the UN's profile in crisis and post-conflict areas.'[11] The establishment of the Commission can be seen as a sign of an emerging sense of collective international responsibility to protect in the event of genocide and other large-scale killing. From the EP point of view, the International Criminal Court is a very important institution in this context, prosecuting perpetrators of any of these crimes. The international community and the EU in particular have recognized that unstable states, weak economies and poor prospects for the future are some of the main reasons for people to leave their countries and look for a better life, *inter alia*, in the EU Member States. The creation of a tool that helps countries in post-conflict or post-war situations, based on best-practice examples and past experiences, gives rise to the hope that more and more countries will overcome their political, economical and social weakness, and develop into stable entities within the world community, based on human rights and democracy. But the UN must be able to rely on its members – the organization can only be as strong as the members allow it to be. Thus, it is of the utmost importance that the United Nations receives the necessary financial and human resources to deal with the tasks given to it. Here, the EU is exemplary – committing itself in its security strategy to provide civil, police and military forces

---

[10] European Parliament, Motion for a resolution, 21 September 2005, PE 361.932v01-00, available at <http://www.europarl.europa.eu/omk/sipade3?SAME_LEVEL=1&LEVEL=2&NAV=S&LSTDOC=Y&DETAIL=&PUBREF=-//EP//TEXT+MOTION+B6-2005-0510+0+DOC+XML+V0//EN>.

[11] Joint motion for a resolution, PE 361.932v01-00} RC1, 26 September 2005, available at <http://www.europarl.europa.eu/registre/seance_pleniere/textes_deposes/prop_res_commune/2005/0483/P6_RC(2005)0483_EN.pdf>.

to the UN. The entire European Security and Defence policy is designed to act in accordance with the UN charter and contribute to the UN peace-building missions. This is the multinational approach that Europeans have learned to estimate highly in the past 5 decades.

As regards institutional reform, the EP had stressed the need for adapting the composition of the Security Council to the changed state of the international system. First, it is necessary to increase the representation of developing countries in the Council, since all geographic areas should be represented in this body. According to this guiding principle, a single EU seat remains the aim to be pursued by the European Parliament. The European Constitution, in creating a legal personality for the EU and a European Foreign Minister, opens the way for this.

Furthermore, it is important to strengthen the democratic dimension of the UN. The organization has only united the governments of the world but not its citizens. This is a serious democratic deficit. As discussed above, the EP has been calling for the establishment of a United Nations Parliamentary Assembly (UNPA) with genuine rights of information, participation and control, and competent to adopt recommendations directed at the UN General Assembly. Such a step would increase the democratic profile and internal democratic process of the organization and would allow world civil society to be directly involved in the decision-making process. The European Parliament regrets that the outcome of the Summit falls short of these ambitions. The EP moreover deplores that no firm commitment was made with a view to granting substantially more authority to the UN Secretary-General as Chief Administrative Officer of his secretariat.

In other areas as well, the Outcome Document received severe criticism from the European Parliament.[12] Indeed, while it is positive that there has been a renewed commitment by the international community to achieving the Millennium Development Goals and promoting sustainable development, one cannot deny the lack of a precise timetable committing all developed countries to the pursuit of the intermediate and final MDG targets. Furthermore, the Summit has not issued a further appeal to those donor countries which have not yet formally committed themselves to the goal of allocating 0.7% of their GNI to Official Development Assistance (ODA) by 2015. Finally, the EP sees it as a serious failure that the September Summit did not produce any agreement on a comprehensive definition of terrorism and urges the UN Member States to rectify this without delay. The same holds true for the failure to reach agreement on measures with regard to nuclear non-proliferation and disarmament.

---

[12] Ibid.

5. Conclusion

The UN must continue its reform efforts. The Summit in September 2005, although it can be seen as a step forward, falls short of reaching all the necessary agreements for a new structure of the organization and falls short of transforming it into a body fit for the new requirements of globalisation and changed world order. Ideas for a stronger, more effective and more democratic multilateral system must be communicated and discussed and turned into reality over the coming years.

UN reform has to be based on the principles of democracy, multilateralism and transparency, principles that also guided the European integration process. The European Parliament calls for the establishment of one seat for the European Union in the Security Council. The sooner the European Constitutional Treaty enters into force, the earlier the EU will have the legal basis to become *one* strong actor within the United Nations. This holds true not only for the structural questions, but also for the European Parliament's prioritized policy areas, such as safeguarding human rights, creating peace and democracy and fighting terrorism. With its proposals for new bodies or reform of existing institutions, the UN is on the right track. If, for example, the members of the new Human Rights Council really live up to the high aims and principles of the new body, also in cooperation with the International Criminal Court, the UN stands a chance to be perceived by the public as an important, powerful and, most important of all a trustworthy actor on the international scene. The establishment of the Peacebuilding Commission is a further step in the right direction, helping countries and their peoples to overcome the difficult post-war or post-conflict situations and offering a perspective to the people.

Overcoming the democratic deficit of the United Nation's institutional set-up is the other priority for the European Parliament. Based on experiences from its own history, the European Parliament and the EU can prove that the involvement of the people in the decision-making is necessary for creating a sense of ownership and generating the will for commitment to certain values and tasks. A more inclusive participation in UN deliberations and decision-making is an indispensable part of the process of democratization of the UN organizations. The achievement of the crucial Millennium Development Goals will only be possible in cooperation with civil society and the people of the world themselves. For this, 'we the peoples' should have a stronger say in international affairs. For this reason, the creation of a 'United Nations Parliamentary Assembly' should be an integral part in reforming the UN, symbolizing that we are not merely living in a world of states but in a true world community in which human beings are fellow citizens.

Chapter 22
EPILOGUE: THE UN AND THE EU – THE ROAD TO PARTNERSHIP

by Jan Wouters, Frank Hoffmeister and Tom Ruys

The EU's input into the United Nations and the common output of both organizations in several policy fields constitutes the central focus of this volume. We believe it is our privilege and task as editors to put together the common threads of all contributions. Can we detect overarching patterns as regards EU status and coordination in the main bodies and specialized agencies? What is the impact of UN-EU cooperation in the various policy fields of human development and security? Drawing from the various contributions and some additional own research, we would therefore present briefly the main findings of this volume and share our conclusion.

1. EU Status and Coordination at UN Bodies, Programmes and Agencies

A first striking finding is the difference of EU statuses at various UN bodies. Whereas, in 1964, the European Commission first established a tiny information office in New York, ten years later, this office was upgraded to the official EC delegation to the United Nations following the granting of observer status to the European Community in the General Assembly. Presently, six such EC delegations exist: one in New York (accredited, *inter alia*, to the General Assembly, the Economic and Social Council, UNDP and UNICEF), one in Geneva (accredited to specialized bodies there such as OCHCHR, UNHCR, ILO, WHO), one in Vienna (accredited to IAEA, UNODC), one in Paris (accredited to UNESCO), one in Rome (accredited to the FAO, WFP and IFAD), and one in Nairobi (accredited to UNEP and Habitat).[1] Moreover, the EU Council has established Liaison Offices in New York and Geneva. These offices have no autonomous political function, but serve first and foremost to support the Member States, in particular the EU Presidency, in the day-to-day running of EU business at the United Nations. This includes the provision of information and the circulation of documents (through the electronic mailing network CIREU) as well as the facilitation of coordination among EU Member States.

[1] Information on all these delegations is available at the website of EU@UN, see <http://www.europa-eu-un.org/home/index_en.htm>.

J. Wouters et al., eds., The United Nations and the European Union

Further to this proliferation of EU delegations at the various UN seats, there is a trend of upgrading the formal status of the EC within certain UN bodies, ranging from a mere observer over an active participant to a full member.[2] Next to the well-known observer status of the European Community in the General Assembly since 1974, the Community became a member of the FAO in 1991.[3] Since 2002, the Community has acted as a Member in the context of the World Food Summit, and in 2003, following lengthy negotiations, the Community became a Member of the Codex Alimentarius Commission,[4] established under FAO auspices. Furthermore, throughout the entire UN system, remarkable developments have taken place as regards the granting of full participant status to the Community. Such status was granted during many UN Conferences, such as the United Nations Conference on Environment and Development (Rio, 1992) or the World Summit on Sustainable Development (Johannesburg, 2002). The Community also enjoys full participant status in the Commission for Sustainable Development since 1993, and last but not least, in the context of international treaty negotiations under the auspices of the WHO (1999, 2003)[5] and UNESCO (2005).[6] With regard to UNHCR, an EC request for full participation is pending.

It is a commonplace that EU coordination at the UN is increasing. However, what could be astounding – and this constitutes our second finding – is the mere frequency and the variety of the covered fields. For example, for the New York office alone it is estimated that around 1.300 coordination meetings take place every year. These meetings cover all six main committees of the General Assembly and its subordinate bodies, as well as ECOSOC and its functional commissions. With regard to the activities of the Security Council, weekly Article 19-meetings (named after the coordination obligation laid down in Article 19 TEU) are organized. Even though the latter meetings cannot be said to constitute a genuine consultation process, they do supply EU Member States that are not members of the Security Council with valuable inside information on what was discussed in closed consultations of the Council and provide some insight in the Council's future activities. Another 1.000 EU coordination meetings are organized each year in Geneva. Coordination meetings concerning the activities of the main UN bodies are chaired by the EU Presidency, which sits at one end of the table, the Council Secretariat and the European Commission sitting at the opposite end. EU Member States are seated at the long sides of the table and move up one place every six months (see Figure 1).

Although policy formulation and positioning on UN decision-making is principally done in national capitals and Brussels-based EU institutions, these coordination meetings nevertheless play an important complementary and corrective role,

---

[2] See chapter 1 by Frank Hoffmeister and Pieter-Jan Kuijper.

[3] See chapter 4 by Joergen Maersk Pedersen.

[4] Ibid.

[5] See chapter 8 by Barbara Eggers and Frank Hoffmeister.

[6] See chapter 7 by Lucia Cavicchioli.

Figure 1. European Union coordination at the UN, seating order under the Finnish Presidency Coordination Meetings (second half of 2006)[7]

allowing the EU to cope with the time difference between Brussels and New York as well as with the dynamism of activities 'on the ground'.[8]

The coordination process has intensified over the years and has now become well-entrenched in the practice of EU Member States. The net result has been twofold. On the one hand, there has been an increase in voting alignment, evidenced by the fact that EU cohesion now stands around 95% of all resolutions adopted by the General Assembly, which is significantly higher than the general voting cohesion of *circa* 76%.[9] This means that the EU votes unanimously on four out of five General Assembly resolutions that are actually voted on. Split votes mainly concern

---

[7] Source <http://www.europa-eu-un.org/articles/en/article_1245_en.htm>.

[8] See chapter 2 by Esa Paasivirta and Dominic Porter.

[9] 'The enlarging European Union at the United Nations: making multilateralism matter', January 2004, available at <http://ec.europa.eu/comm/external_relations/un/docs/brochure0104.pdf>, at p. 11-12. See also J. Wouters, 'The European Union as an actor within the United Nations General Assembly', in V. Kronenberger (ed.), *The European Union and the international legal order: discord or harmony?* (The Hague, TMC Asser Press 2001) pp. 375-404; H. Young and N. Rees, 'EU Voting behaviour in the UN General Assembly, 1990-2002: the EU's Europeanising Tendencies', 16 *Irish Studies in International Affairs* (2005) pp. 193-207.

dossiers that are politically (e.g., nuclear disarmament, decolonization or the Middle East) or ethically sensitive (e.g., human cloning). Although such split votes have become rather rare, they still tend to undermine the credibility of the EU as an international actor. On the other hand, the number of common EU and EC statements has grown considerably. Common positions mainly deal with peace and security matters, followed by economic and development issues, and are mostly presented by the EU Presidency. Common statements in the General Assembly are rarely delivered by the European Commission, even on areas for which it is directly responsible. This is partially due to the fact that the European Commission, because of its observer status, can only speak after all UN Member States. Thus, the Commission presents only some 5-7 statements a year to the Assembly, compared to the hundreds issued by the EU Presidency.[10] This, however, does not withhold the Commission from playing an active role in informal Assembly sessions or in the drafting of common positions presented by the Presidency.

The presentation of common statements is now a widespread practice, whether in open debates of the Security Council (in the form of EU Presidency statements with which the EU members of the Security Council will usually align), in General Assembly sessions or in the many UN Conferences and Summits. Often candidate countries which are expected to gradually align their foreign policy with the EU's CFSP and other non-EU countries with treaty links to the EC to subscribe to the EU statement. This renders support to the voice of the EU Presidency to sometimes up to 37-38 States.[11]

Both the upgrading of EU status at various UN entities and the increase of EU coordination reflect the increased competences of the Community in a wide range of policy areas, viz. the important evolution of the Union's CFSP and ESDP and contribute to the visibility and influence of the European Union at the United Nations. Despite these positive trends, however, a lot of work remains to be done in our view, both with regard to EU status and EU coordination.

Firstly, EC status remains unsatisfactory in a variety of UN bodies and agencies, such as the ILO[12] or the Bretton Woods institutions,[13] often undermining the efficient exercise of Community powers. Sometimes, the refusal to grant the EC adequate status is based on non-EU countries' fear of an increase in EU power, or

---

[10] M. Farrell, 'EU representation and coordination within the United Nations', in K.V. Laatikainen and K.E. Smith, *The European Union at the United Nations* (Basingstroke, Palgrave 2006), pp. 27-46, at p. 38.

[11] Apart from the 25 EU Member States, up to thirteen other States may align themselves with EU Presidency Statements. These are first and foremost the Acceding Countries, Bulgaria and Romania, as well as the Candidate Countries, Turkey, Croatia and the Former Yugoslav Republic of Macedonia. Other possible subscribers are the countries of the Stabilisation and Association Process and potential candidates: Albania, Bosnia and Herzegovina and Serbia. A third category consists of the EFTA countries Iceland, Norway and Liechtenstein. Last but not least, alignment is common for Ukraine and the Republic of Moldova.

[12] See chapter 5 by Rudi Delarue.

[13] See chapter 6 by Carole Garnier, Daniel Daco and Francesca Di Mauro.

their unfamiliarity with the division of competences between EU Member States and the European Commission. Thus, in the context of the Convention on Cultural Diversity, States stressed the exceptional basis of the EC's active participation in the negotiation process.[14] On other occasions, poor EC status stems from political resistance from its own Member States to hand over important representational tasks to Brussels. Such attitude is hard to reconcile with the duty of loyal cooperation enshrined in Article 10 EC Treaty, which may include an obligation for Member States to promote EC membership within international organizations.[15]

Furthermore, the coordination process still suffers from a number of shortfalls. Firstly, coordination is not always pursued with the same vigour. In the Security Council, for example, where the EU has not yet any formal status, coordination through Article 19-meetings is rather an exchange of information than a true discussion.[16] Admittedly, the quality of these meetings has improved in recent years, turning from largely retrospective to more prospective and more interactive briefings. Still, several improvements, such as the inclusion of representatives from the EU Presidency or the Council Secretariat in the delegations of EU Security Council Members, remain possible.[17] Moreover, EU coordination in many UN programmes, funds and specialized agencies remains very restricted. Only recently have 'information rounds' been introduced and then only for the New York-based agencies.[18] With regard to the ILO for instance, although EU Member States have been more and more recognizing the added value of timely upstream and on-the-spot coordination, EU coordination has not yet reached its full potential.[19] Indeed, often EU Member States tend to give priority to preparatory discussion and statements in informal groups. In several other bodies, including the Bretton Woods institutions, coordination remains very restricted or even absent, due to EU Member States' prioritization of national positions.

Apart from the aforementioned 'gaps' in the coordination process, coordination also comes at a price. Obtaining consensus among 25 States requires an enormous amount of time and energy, taking up a large share of the workload of national representations of EU Member States.[20] Moreover, this investment does not always

---

[14] See chapter 7 by Lucia Cavicchioli.

[15] ECJ, Case 3, 4 and 6/67, *Kramer* [1976] *ECR* 1279 concerning the Community's exclusive competence in the field of fisheries. A similar duty to promote EC accession may be argued in areas of shared competence. In this sense: see I. Govaere, J. Capiau and A. Vermeersch, 'In-between seats: the participation of the European Union in international organizations', 9 *European Foreign Affairs Review* (2004), pp. 155-187, at pp. 173-174.

[16] See chapter 3 by Johan Verbeke.

[17] Ibid.

[18] S. Biscop, 'Security and development: a positive agenda for a global EU-UN partnership', in M. Ortega (ed.), *The European Union and the United Nations: partners in effective multilateralism* (EUISS Chaillot Paper No. 78, June 2005), available at <http://www.iss-eu.org/chaillot/chai78.pdf>, at p. 27.

[19] See chapter 5 by Rudi Delarue.

[20] See chapter 2 by Esa Paasivirta and Dominic Porter.

guarantee a productive outcome. Indeed, often coordination only results in a least-common-denominator position, contributing little to the substantive debate at the UN and leaving EU Member States frustrated. The time and energy needed to reach agreement may also lead to rather rigid positions, difficult to adapt to the dynamism of the diplomatic process, and thus acting as a brake on negotiations. With regard to EU positions concerning human rights protection, these drawbacks could be remedied if the EU were to 'pick its battles' selectively, so as to make better use of its diversity and resources, instead of attempting a common position on every single issue.[21] It may also be more effective to grant the EU Presidency greater flexibility to negotiate with third parties, instead of binding it to detailed EU statements, as was already suggested in the European Commission's Communication on 'the choice of multilateralism'.[22] All in all, however, the EU coordination process has become a key feature of EU-UN relations, allowing the EU to speak with a more unified voice.

The recognition of 'enhanced observer status' in several UN agencies and conferences, and the increase in EU coordination have allowed the European Union to pragmatically improve its visibility and influence at the United Nations in spite of the EU's inherent institutional complexities. In the longer term, however, these complexities, due to the variety of EU actors and the untransparency and ever-evolving nature of its division of competence, have to be addressed.[23] Indeed, the present situation whereby EU positions are often presented by the EU Presidency, even on matters where the Community is competent and would normally be represented by the Commission, is very confusing for other countries, which tend to confuse the way the EU expresses its positions with the nature of the competences.[24]

2. UN-EU Cooperation on Human Development and Security Issues

Recent years have witnessed increased consultation between the UN and the EU to improve areas of actual cooperation. For example, EU representatives now meet the UN Secretary-General at ministerial level annually in New York. Moreover, the UN Deputy Secretary-General and other senior UN officials regularly visit EU institutions in Brussels, Strasbourg and Luxembourg. Other examples include meetings between senior UN officials and the EU Political and Security Committee or increased participation by Members of the European Parliament. Daily working contacts between the EU Council and Commission on the one hand and the UN

[21] See chapter 10 by Hadewych Hazelzet.

[22] Ibid.; European Commission, Communication on 'The European Union and the United Nations: the Choice of Multilateralism', 10 September 2003, COM (2003) 526.

[23] See, e.g., I. Govaere, J. Capiau and A. Vermeersch, loc. cit., *supra* n. 15, pp. 155-187.

[24] See, e.g., chapter 5 by Rudi Delarue.

Secretariat on the other hand have likewise developed considerably. Two areas have seen a particular rise of EU-UN cooperation and consultation: human development and security issues.

In the field of human development, one cannot ignore the vital financial EC contribution to the workings of the UN, or the recent surge in EC funding to UN programmes and specialized agencies. As a member of FAO the EC's record on supporting worldwide programming and projects on food security, food safety and quality as well as rural development has led to a close relationship between the two organizations, a relationship that can be labelled a partnership, rather than mere donorship.[25] Moreover, the EU has frequently acted as a front-runner with regard to, for example, environmental protection,[26] the protection and promotion of human rights,[27] international labour standards[28] or support for the International Criminal Court. In the context of the Commission on Sustainable Development, the EU has generally a positive and progressive image, allowing the EU to build bridges whose positions are far apart. Furthermore, the EU's support of the UNESCO Convention for cultural diversity[29] and the WHO Tobacco Framework Convention[30] was vital for their successful adoption.

On the other hand, some areas of cooperation show a more mixed result. The EU's role as a driving force behind many environmental treaties and the main donor to UNEP, cannot hide the fact that European countries still figure among the world's largest polluters.[31] Furthermore, as regards asylum policy, the EC and EU Member States tend to keep UNHCR at arm's length, making it hard for the latter body to monitor compliance with refugee instruments, without 'biting the hand that feeds it'.[32] It also remains unclear whether the EU's concept of sustainable development copes with the one advocated by different UN bodies.[33] Finally, the internal lack of financial discipline of EU Member States seems to hamper firm EU positions in the Bretton-Woods institutions to revitalize world economy.

EU-UN cooperation in the broader field of development and humanitarian affairs is another topic that needs further research. The European Union has long been an important provider of Official Development Assistance (ODA). In 2004,

---

25 See chapter 4 by Joergen Maersk Pedersen.

26 See chapter 12 by Aurore Maillet.

27 See chapter 10 by Hadewych Hazelzet.

28 See chapter 5 by Rudi Delarue.

29 See chapter 7 by Lucia Cavicchioli.

30 See chapter 8 by Barbara Eggers and Frank Hoffmeister.

31 See chapter 12 by Aurore Maillet.

32 See chapter 9 by Judith Kumin. See also UN Secretary-General Annan's address to the European Parliament on 29 January 2004, where he declared that: 'The [European] public has been fed images of a flood of unwelcome entrants, and of threats to their societies and identities. In the process, immigrants have sometimes been stigmatized, vilified, even de-humanized', available at <http://www.europa-eu-un.org/articles/>.

33 See chapter 11 by Jochen Jesinghaus.

for example, EU Member States and the European Commission together provided some € 35 billion in ODA, accounting for 54% of worldwide development aid (compared to circa 20% by the United States and 9% by Japan). This figure is bound to rise in the future as EU donors have subscribed to the long-standing target of 0,7% of GNP by 2015 and have set an interim target of 0,56% of GNP to be implemented by 2010. Whether this target will be achieved remains to be seen; at present only five EU Member States have reached the said level of ODA (Denmark, Luxembourg, Sweden, the Netherlands and Portugal). If all EU donors would implement the target, this would imply an increase in EU ODA from the present € 35 billion to € 55 billion by 2010, a figure which is estimated to represent some 63% of ODA in that year.[34]

A large share of the EU's development aid and humanitarian assistance is borne by the European Community. In 2002, for example, the European Community provided € 6,5 billion in ODA, or roughly one fifth of the total ODA of EU Member States, and € 538 million for humanitarian assistance, or some 45% of all EU humanitarian assistance (EC aid included).[35] Of the latter amount, which is distributed through the European Commission's Humanitarian Aid Office (ECHO), almost a third is devoted to UN projects, especially those run by UNHCR. Similarly, of the development aid funded by the European Community (mainly distributed through EuropeAid), a considerable share flows to UN programmes, funds and specialized agencies, especially to the United Nations Development Programme (UNDP), the World Food Programme (WFP) and the UN Relief and Works Agency for Palestine Refugees in the Near East (UNRWA). What is particularly remarkable is that EC contributions to UN programmes and agencies have grown significantly since 2002. With regard to the WFP, for instance, EC contributions have gone from $ 179 million in 2002 to $ 264 million in 2005, thus firmly establishing the European Community as the second largest contributor (after the United States).[36] EC contributions to UNDP have also increased from $ 226,5 million in 2004 to $ 427 million in 2005.[37] Another illustration is the augmentation of funding to UNHCR from $ 71 million in 2002 to $ 86 million in 2005, making the European Community the third largest donor (after the United States and Japan).[38]

Since the EC is a major contributor to UN funds and agencies, the European Commission has in past years attempted to use this financial leverage to improve coordination with the various UN agencies involved. In this regard, the European

---

[34] See European Commission and OECD, *EU Donor Atlas 2006: Volume I*, February 2006, available at <http://ec.europa.eu/comm/development/body/publications/docs/eu_donor_atlas_2006.pdf#zoom=100>, at 2.

[35] Loc. cit., *supra* n. 9, at p. 14, 33.

[36] Information on WFP funding is available at <http://www.wfp.org/appeals/Wfp_donors/>.

[37] See UNDP Annual Reports of 2006 and 2005, available at *http://www.undp.org/publications/annualreport2006/index.shtml*.

[38] Data on UNHCR funding is available at <http://www.unhcr.org/cgi-bin/texis/vtx/partners?id=3b963b874>.

Commission in 2001 issued a Communication in which it criticized the existing case-by-case cooperation between the EC and UN agencies, funds and programmes, and called for a more effective partnership with the United Nations in the fields of development and humanitarian affairs.[39] The Communication deplored the lack of a clear overall approach to cooperation, and of a general evaluation of that cooperation. The document also complained of difficulties in reaching agreement on principles for financial control and audit, as well as of inadequate reporting by UN entities. Last but not least, it criticized the lack of visibility of EC financing for UN operations. Indeed, if one looks at the pre-2005 Annual Reports of UNDP for example, the European Commission is not included in the ranking of top contributors. Instead, a footnote merely declares that the Commission 'is a major source of non-core funding to UNDP'. In order to 'improve the effectiveness of [the EC's] development and humanitarian assistance as well as the quality of UN delivery', the Communication contained a number of proposals, such as the identification of 'strategic UN partners' or the improving of operational guidelines for cooperation with UN entities. Several of these recommendations have been implemented in the meantime, leading to an intensification of UN-EC cooperation in development and humanitarian affairs.

An important step was taken on 29 April 2003, when UN Deputy Secretary-General Fréchette and European Commissioner for Development and Humanitarian Aid Nielson signed the Financial and Administrative Framework Agreement between the EC and the UN (FAFA).[40] This agreement addresses procedures and conditions regarding EC funding to the United Nations. It focuses on a results-oriented approach, based on objective indicators of achievement and provides for the participation of Commission representatives in the main monitoring and evaluation missions relating to the performance of EC-funded actions. It regulates UN reporting requirements, for example by setting a broad timeframe or by determining that expenditures must be converted into Euro. The FAFA also contains detailed provisions on what direct costs are considered eligible, the extent to which indirect costs are disbursable, the procurement of goods and services, payment schedules, etc. Another section of the Agreement deals with the issue of EC visibility, viz. the use of the EU logo in UN publications or on equipment and supplies purchased by means of EC funds. Finally, the FAFA stresses that UN procedures should conform to internationally accepted standards and reproduces in annex the contents of an agreement of November 2001 on the application of the financial control clause included in all contracts and financing agreements between the UN and the European Commission.

---

[39] Communication from the Commission to the Council and the European Parliament, 'Building an effective partnership with the United Nations in the fields of Development and Humanitarian Affairs', Brussels, 2 May 2001, COM (1002) 231 final.

[40] Financial and Administrative Framework Agreement between the European Community and the United Nations, 29 April 2003, available at <http://ec.europa.eu/comm/europeaid/tender/gestion/cont_typ/onu/un_ec_fwc_en.pdf>.

The Financial and Administrative Framework applies to all contribution-specific agreements with the UN secretariat and UN Funds and Programmes (e.g., UNICEF, UNDP). Moreover, as foreseen in the FAFA, numerous UN specialized agencies (ILO, FAO, UNIDO, WHO, WMO, UNESCO, IAEA, IFAD and ICAO) have acceded to the Agreement through an exchange of letters. As a result, a single set of rules now applies to a whole array of EC-UN projects, thus facilitating cooperation and disbursement. In accordance with the Agreement, a Working Group was established to oversee implementation and agreement through yearly meetings. These meetings have allowed to clarify and supplement the FAFA rules. Thus, during the third meeting, which took place in April 2006, the European Commission presented draft guidelines on FAFA reporting obligations. EC and UN representatives moreover decided to develop a joint action plan and joint operational guidelines with regard to the visibility of EC financing and underscored the need to comply with internationally accepted standards on accounting, audit and procurement procedures. Both sides 'took note' of the increasing scale of Commission contributions to UN-managed activities and delivered a positive appraisal of the operation of the FAFA.

Another novelty is the conclusion of Memoranda of Understanding (MoU) establishing Strategic Partnerships between the EC and selected UN partners. An example hereof is the MoU concluded on 28 June 2004 between the EC and UNDP.[41] This non-binding document sets out possible areas of cooperation, which may be used for elaborating a commonly agreed multi-annual work programme. It also provides for regular policy dialogue, *inter alia*, through regular High-Level bilateral meetings or yearly senior level meetings. Furthermore, the two parties agreed on a number of working principles, for example with regard to exchange of information or informal consultation on a desk-to-desk basis and between representatives at the field level. UNDP's Brussels office serves as a focal point for the Strategic Partnership. On the EC side, the MoU foresees the appointment of a similar focal point within the Directorate-General for Development. Similar partnerships were set-up with WHO, FAO, ILO and UNCHR, leading to an intensification of cooperation and consultation, both on the strategic and operational levels.

The conclusion of the FAFA and the creation of strategic partnerships have fuelled a closer, more uniform and more efficient cooperation between the EC and the UN with regard to development and humanitarian assistance. Both developments have moreover strengthened the EC's influence and visibility. However, they do not address some of the constraints on EC efficiency and visibility identified in the 2001 Commission Communication, namely the weak status of the Community in most UN agencies or the low-key EU coordination on development and humanitar-

[41] Memorandum of Understanding concerning the establishment of a strategic partnership between the European Commission and the United Nations Development Programme, 28 June 2004, available at <http://europeandcis.undp.org/WaterWiki/images/8/88/MoU_EC_UNDP.pdf>.

ian issues.[42] In this regard, we can refer to what was mentioned earlier, i.e., on the one hand, that EC participation in certain specialized agencies is improving through the recognition of enhanced observer status, although the EC still lacks significant status in others, and that, on the other hand, EC coordination with regard to specialized agencies remains much more restricted than for example coordination with regard to General Assembly matters.

Crisis management is arguably the area where UN-EU relations have made most progress in recent years: it has transcended mere statements like the September 2003 Joint Declaration on UN-EU cooperation in crisis management, covering both civilian and military operations,[43] and practical cooperation on the basis of an institutionalised but unbureaucratic framework has become routine business by now.[44] The beginning of this important development can be traced back to the 1997 Amsterdam Treaty, which incorporated the so-called Petersberg Tasks in the EU's Common Foreign and Security Policy (Article 17(2) TEU). These tasks concern 'humanitarian tasks, peace-keeping tasks, and tasks for combat forces in crisis management, including peacemaking'. In subsequent years, EU Member States engaged in an ambitious capability-building programme on the basis of consecutive Headline Goals. This led to the creation of a 60.000-strong 'Rapid Reaction Force' (RRF), consisting of pools of national units, and of a number of smaller rapidly deployable 'battlegroups'. Likewise, on the civilian crisis management side, EU Member States contributed to a reserve pool of police officers, judges, prison officers, etc. Since 2003, as the initial capability targets were achieved, the EU has engaged in a growing number of military and police operations, both in the European region (e.g., Bosnia-Herzegovina, the former Yugoslav Republic of Macedonia) and elsewhere (e.g., Democratic Republic of Congo, Aceh). These operations have gradually established the EU's reputation as a security provider and peacebuilder. Moreover, ESDP crisis operations have rendered important support to United Nations peacekeeping activities. EU-led operations bear some of the UN's logistical and financial burden – currently stretched to its limits as a result of the deployment of some 75.000 troops in 15 different peacekeeping operations –, especially in areas where UN peacekeeping is traditionally weaker (e.g., rapid deployment). In Bosnia-Herzegovina, for example, the EU Police Mission (EUPM) took over from the International Police Task Force, thus allowing the UN to redeploy elsewhere. In the Democratic Republic of Congo, the EU sent troops to Bunya when violence in the region escalated, thus allowing the UN operation in the DRC (MONUC) the necessary time to beef up its presence. Most recently, the European Union moreover sent troops to the DRC (EUFOR RD Congo) to support MONUC in its functions during the election process. Finally, as regards peace building, the EU's contribution to the

---

[42] Loc. cit., *supra* n. 39, at p. 4.

[43] Joint Declaration on UN-EU Cooperation in Crisis Management, New York, 24 September 2003, available at <http://europa-eu-un.org/articles/lt/article_2768_lt.htm>.

[44] See chapter 14 by Jim Cloos.

civil UN Interim Mission in Kosovo since 1999 may serve as a stunning example of a joint nation-building process, where institutional and personal intertwining between the two organizations reached an unprecedented peak.[45] This mission serves as an illustration both of the potential benefits of UN-EU cooperation and the challenges thereof, allowing important lessons to be drawn for future cooperation on the ground.

These examples illustrate the important contribution EU crisis management can make to UN peacekeeping and peacebuilding. It can assist UN peacekeeping in important ways, while strengthening EU visibility as a global actor. It can also set a precedent for closer relations between the United Nations and other regional, sub-regional or 'quasi-regional' organizations, such as the African Union or ECOWAS, especially in light of the World Summit Outcome's call for more formalized cooperation with partner organizations.[46] On the other hand, some caution is needed when assessing this evolution. Firstly, it should be emphasized that most EU-led operations have been of modest size and that EU capabilities are still rather limited (the latter is *a fortiori* true for the African Union and ECOWAS). Furthermore, the creation of numerous EU-led operations should not divert attention from the fact that EU personnel contributions to UN-led peacekeeping operations are extremely low.[47] Indeed, although EU Member States account for two fifths of UN peacekeeping funding, at present only one out of fifteen blue helmets comes from an EU country. In this regard, EU Member States should carefully consider the UN Secretariat's plea for participation of EU battle groups in a UN 'Strategic Reserve' and for cooperation in the establishment of a UN Standing Police Force.[48] On a broader level, the growing role of regional, sub-regional organizations and the like (e.g., the EU, NATO, AU) in crisis management raises the fundamental question as to where lies the appropriate division of tasks between the latter organizations and the United Nations. In this regard, there is a growing need for constitutional clarity, which will have to be addressed in the years to come.[49]

Another important milestone for EU-UN cooperation on security issues was the adoption of the European Security Strategy ('ESS') in December 2003 with its emphasis on comprehensive security.[50] Putting the strengthening of international rule of law and the United Nations at the centre of EU foreign policy objectives,

---

[45] See chapter 18 by Michael Karnitschnig.

[46] 2005 World Summit Outcome, UNGA Res. 60/1, 16 September 2005, para. 170.

[47] See chapter 13 by Jan Wouters and Tom Ruys.

[48] See the foreword of UN Under-Secretary-General for Peacekeeping Operations Jean-Marie Guéhenno in M. Ortega (ed.), *The European Union and the United Nations: partners in effective multilateralism* (EU-ISS Chaillot Paper No. 78, June 2005), available at <http://www.iss-eu.org/chaillot/chai78.pdf>, pp. 7-12. Remark: the creation of an intial operating capability for a standing UN police capacity was endorsed in the 2005 World Summit Outcome Document: see UNGA Res. 60/1, 16 September 2005, para. 92.

[49] See chapter 16 by Kennedy Graham.

[50] See chapter 15 by Sven Biscop and Edith Drieskens.

reassured the United Nations in a rough post-9-11 climate. The ESS clearly takes a different position with regard to the role of the United Nations than the US National Security Strategy (NSS). Indeed, whereas the NSS puts the UN in the same category with other organizations such as the WTO, the OAS and NATO, the ESS sees the UN as '*the* fundamental framework for international relations' (emphasis added).[51]

Furthermore, as the European Security strategy identified the threats arising out of terrorism as one of the key challenges for the international system, the European Union put its means at the disposal of the UN to implement relevant Security Council resolutions. In this regard, the European weight is also important in shaping further normative UN standards and in fine-tuning UN targeted sanctions against individuals.[52] It may also well be the case that European Courts will be among the first to balance the need to comply with UN Security Council resolutions with fundamental human rights, including the right to judicial review and a fair trial.[53]

3. Crisis, Reform and Enlargement

A final, more contextual finding concerns the fact that both the EU and the UN are currently both experiencing a crisis in their respective histories, a fact which should be kept in mind when examining UN-EU relations. On UN side, the loss of credibility of a number of organs such as the (now-abolished) Commission on Human Rights, sexual abuse by blue helmets, mismanagement evidenced most amply as a result of the oil-for-food scandal, the divisions created by the Iraq war in 2003 and profound dissatisfaction with the lack of representativeness and transparency of the Security Council have fuelled a call for fundamental reform of the world organization. The European Union, on the other hand, is struggling to cope with the arrival of ten new Member States. Whereas the EU has thus 'widened' considerably and is set to further enlarge in upcoming years, the 'deepening' of EU integration has grinded to a painful and unpromising halt as a result of the negative outcome of referenda on the EU Constitution in France and the Netherlands in June 2005.

Some progress has been made on UN reform as a result of the World Summit in September 2005 and subsequent implementation of its recommendations. With significant input from the EU[54] a Peacebuilding Commission was created,[55] and a

---

[51] Ibid.

[52] See chapter 17 by Gijs de Vries.

[53] See notably Court of First Instance, judgments of 21 September 2005 in Cases T-306/01 *Yusuf and Al-Barakaat International Foundation* v. *Council and Commission* and T-315/01 *Kadi* v. *Council and Commission*, not yet published in the *ECR*; judgments of 12 July 2006 in Cases T-253/02 *Ayadi* v *Council* and T-49/04 *Hassan* v. *Council and Commission*, not yet published in the *ECR*.

[54] See chapter 20 by Danièle Smadja.

[55] Established by UNGA Res. 60/180 and SC Res. 1645 (2005), both adopted on 20 December 2005.

Human Rights Council replaced the discredited Commission on Human Rights.[56] However, UN reform is far from complete. Thus, whereas the two new bodies were almost universally welcomed, both have very high expectations to live up to. If anything, the disappointing first session of the Human Rights Council in June 2006 illustrated the challenges for EU coordination and the need for vigilance with regard to the operation and output of this new organ. Secondly, implementation of several other aspects of the September Summit Outcome has given rise to considerable disagreement mainly between western and developing States. This was most evident in the General Assembly's Fifth Committee, dealing with budgetary and administrative matters, where a six-month spending cap was imposed on the UN budget in order to increase pressure for management reform, the latter being opposed by developing States. Only at the very last minute was the spending cap lifted, thus averting a major financial crisis at the United Nations. Furthermore, several controversial issues (e.g., nuclear proliferation, a definition on terrorism) were not addressed in the September Summit Outcome. The most remarkable lacuna in the Outcome Document is the lack of proposals on Security Council reform. This matter has for decades given rise to fierce debates among UN Member States and continues to hang over the United Nations like the sword of Damocles. It is also a highly divisive issue for the European Union (mainly because Italy opposes a permanent seat for Germany), hindering a comprehensive unified EU position on UN reform.

On the EU side, the enlargement to 25 Member States has arguably strengthened the EU's influence and voting power, without substantially undermining EU coordination at the United Nations.[57] Indeed, coordination meetings have continued as usual. Moreover, voting cohesion remains high, given the fact that the ten newcomers already aligned with EU voting in the vast majority of cases in the years preceding their actual accession. Still, enlargement implies that coordination becomes more time-consuming and inevitably increases the potential for split votes on politically or ethically sensitive dossiers. Furthermore, the negative referenda on the EU Constitution have dramatically exposed the uncertainty on the future course of European integration. This also affects UN-EU relations in several ways. For instance, the EU Constitution contains several provisions on the appointment of an EU Minister for Foreign Affairs and the establishment of a European External Action Service.[58] In cases where the EU has defined a position on an item which is on the agenda of the Security Council, the EU Constitution states that 'those Member States which sit on the Security Council shall request that the Union Minister for Foreign Affairs be asked to present the Union's position.'[59] Article III-196(1) more-

[56] Established by UNGA Res. 60/251, adopted on 15 March 2006.

[57] See chapter 19 by Roman Kirn; see chapter 2 by Esa Paasivirta and Dominic Porter.

[58] E.g., Articles I-28 and III-296(1) and (2) (EU Minister for Foreign Affairs), Article III-296(3) (the European External Action Service), Treaty establishing a Constitution for Europe, OJ (16 December 2004) C-310/1.

[59] Article III-305 EU Constitution.

over declares that the Council, on a proposal from the Commission, shall, by qualified majority, adopt common positions within the competent international financial institutions and conferences on matters of particular interest for the economic and monetary union. The Council may also, again by qualified majority vote, adopt 'appropriate measures to ensure unified representation' within these institutions (Article III-196(2)). These measures could assist the EU in speaking with a unified voice and would certainly further EU visibility at the United Nations. Moreover, the EU Constitution explicitly endows the EU with legal personality.[60] Such a development would obviously have far-reaching consequences for EU participation in the UN's principal organs, funds, programmes and specialized agencies. This again illustrates that underlying linkages exist between the two dossiers of UN reform and EU reform and enlargement; linkages that have repercussions for UN-EU relations. This being said, the EU Constitution should not be seen as a panacea for the EU's position and role in the UN. The introduction of a 'double-hatted' EU Minister for Foreign Affairs, sitting in the Commission and as well as in the Council, carries a number of complexities and uncertainties with it,[61] and the decision-making procedures for CFSP matters remain largely based on unanimity. One should not forget either that, even if the institutional mechanisms at EU side become better attuned to an efficient coordination and representation in the UN and UN family of organizations, the EU's position and role in the latter will remain subject to constraints proper to the work of intergovernmental bodies and organizations, including the need for acceptance of an enhanced EU position by the other Member States of these bodies and organizations.

4. Concluding Remarks

'What is Europe's role in this changed world? Does Europe not, now that it is finally unified, have a leading role to play in a new world order, that of a power able both to play a stabilising role worldwide and to point the way ahead for many countries and peoples?' This rhetorical question sets the tone of the Laeken Declaration on the future of the European Union.[62] In recent years, EU Member States have affirmed their wish to pursue such goal through a multilateral policy, a policy

[60] Article I-7 EU Constitution. Remark: Contrary to the EC Treaty (Article 281), the Treaty on European Union does not explicitly endow the EU with international legal personality. However, on the basis of the EU's treaty-making power under Article 24 TEU, it is generally assumed that the EU already possesses legal personality, although this remains somewhat controversial. Article I-7 of the EU Constitution would end this controversy.

[61] See, *inter alia*, J. Wouters, 'The Union Minister for Foreign Affairs: Europe's Single Voice or Trojan Horse?', in J.W. de Zwaan, J.H. Jans and F.A. Nelissen (eds.), *The European Union. An Ongoing Process of Integration. Liber Amicorum Alfred E. Kellermann* (The Hague, T.M.C. Asser Press 2004) pp. 77-86.

[62] Laeken Declaration on the future of the European Union, December 2001, available at <http://www.euconvention.be/static/LaekenDeclaration.asp>.

which puts the United Nations at its very heart. But does the European Union also live up to its commitments in its actual practice? This consideration brings us back to the two core questions we posed at the very outset of the present volume and to our findings of this epilogue: firstly, to what extent does the growing EU-UN partnership further the aims and activities of the United Nations, and; secondly; to what extent does the EU manage to speak with one voice and influence UN decision-making?

The former question is fairly easy to answer. True, in some areas the EU still suffers from a lack of credibility. Thus, despite the surge in Official Development Assistance, EU Member States still dump massive amounts of subsidized agricultural products on the world market, to the detriment of developing countries' national economies. Likewise, continuous lip service to the UN Charter cannot hide the fact that some EU Member States participated in recent military campaigns against the Federal Republic of Yugoslavia and Iraq without authorization from the UN Security Council. However, if we look at the whole picture of EU-UN cooperation in areas such as environmental protection, human rights promotion, counterterrorism, etc., the EU's support for the principles and purposes of the UN outweighs the more questionable effects of some of its policies and of the military actions of some of its Member States.[63] It is therefore safe to assert that the EU and the UN are, indeed, true partners in multilateralism.

The second question is harder to tackle. On the one hand, the EU constitutes a Union of 25 States, covering over 450 million people, producing a quarter of the world's GNP. On the other hand, it is generally assumed that the EU's influence on the world stage falls short of its economic and political weight. This is probably true as regards international security issues, where the EU is only just establishing itself as a 'global actor'. However, in other areas, the EU has achieved significant successes (e.g., the entry into force of the Rome Statute on the International Criminal Court or the Kyoto Protocol) and is generally perceived as a key player. This goes first and foremost for the economic sphere, but also in the environmental and aid-related arenas.[64]

As many authors in the present volume demonstrate, the key to EU influence on UN decision-making lies in speaking with a single voice – even though it is probably overoptimistic to believe that 'if the EU is united, they cannot be defeated'.[65] In this regard, it should be welcomed that EU coordination in UN fora has increased significantly over the past years. The UN reform process serves as a good example hereof where EU Member States facilitated through close intra EU-coor-

---

[63] B. Fassbender, 'The better peoples of the United Nations? Europe's practice and the United Nations', 15 *EJIL*(2004) pp. 857-884, at p. 883.

[64] See, e.g., N. Chaban, O. Elgström and M. Holland, 'The European Union as others see it', 11 *European Foreign Affairs* Review (2006), pp. 245-262, at p. 262.

[65] See K.V. Laatikainen and K.E. Smith, 'Introduction – The European Union at the United Nations: leader, partner or failure?' in K.V. Laatikainen and K.E. Smith, op. cit., *supra* n. 10, p. 16.

dination the establishment of the Human Rights Council and the Peacebuilding Commission.[66]

EU influence and visibility would further increase if the coordination process, which is now firmly entrenched at the UN's main bodies, would spread consistently to the activities of all of the UN's funds, programmes and specialized agencies. In this regard, there certainly remains room for improvement. EU Member States must also do better in 'selling' the EU and the EC to non-Members. This means first and foremost that the EU must abide by its own rules on who is to represent the EU/EC in different circumstances and that EU Member Status must promote EU accession to international organizations where appropriate. In the longer term, the EU must provide an answer to Kissinger's question as to 'who to call when I want to speak with Europe?' The EU must work for a more transparent division of competences and a clearer external representation. The EU Constitution does offer a step in the right direction. It remains to be seen whether some of the Constitution's novelties cannot be realized through formal inter-institutional agreements, informal codes of conduct or constant practice.

In the end, we believe it would be wrong to explain the limits and shortcomings of current EU-UN relations solely in the light of the aforementioned crises and lack of institutional reforms. At least as important, it is submitted, is the lack of political will, leadership and vision of the EU's current leaders. Thus, the lack of an EU position with regard to such a central issue of the UN's architecture as Security Council reform painfully shows the severe limits of the EU's role in the UN. Much more political courage and vision will be needed to strengthen the role of the EU in the UN system and fill the 'leadership gap' that currently enfeebles and undermines the UN and the accomplishment of its objectives.

[66] See chapter 20 by Danièle Smadja.

Annex
INVENTORY OF THE EUROPEAN COMMUNITY STATUS AT UN BODIES AND CONFERENCES[1, 2]

UN BODIES

---

[1] This inventory is not exhaustive.
[2] Source: A substantial part of this table reproduces an internal document of the European Commission of 2006, which has been slightly modified by the editors with the authorization of the Commission.
[3] From 1992 until January 2005.

	UN BODY	EC STATUS
UN PRINICIPAL ORGANS		
I.1	UNGA United Nations General Assembly	**Observer**
I.2	ECOSOC Economic and Social Council	**Observer**
I.3	Security Council	**None**
I.4	ICJ International Court of Justice	**None**
UNGA PROGRAMMES AND FUNDS		
II.1	UNCTAD United Nations Conference on Trade and Development	**Observer**[4]
II.2	UNEP United Nations Environment Programme	**Observer**
II.3	UNICEF United Nations Children's Fund	**Observer**
II.4	UNDP United Nations Development Programme	**Observer**
II.5	UNFPA United Nations Population Fund	**Observer**
II.6	UNHCR United Nations High Commissioner for Refugees	**Observer**
II.7	WFP World Food Programme	**Observer**
II.8	UNRWA United Nations Relief and Works Agency for Palestine refugees in the Near East	**Observer**
II.9	UN-Habitat United Nations Human Settlements Programme	**Observer**
ECOSOC: FUNCTIONAL COMMISSIONS		
III.A.1	CHR Commission on Human Rights	**Observer**
III.A.2	CND Commission on Narcotic Drugs	**Observer**
III.A.3	CCPCJ Commission on Crime Prevention and Criminal Justice	**Observer**
III.A.4	Commission on Science and Technology for Development	**Observer**
III.A.5	CSD Commission on Sustainable Development	**Full Participant**
III.A.6	CSW Commission on the Status of Women	**Observer**
III.A.7	Commission on Population and Development	**Observer**
III.A.8	CSOCD Commission for Social Development	**Observer**
III.A.9	Statistical Commission	**Observer**

[4] Sometimes party to UNCTAD agreements and thus as member to the Conferences of the Parties.

	UN BODY	EC STATUS
ECOSOC: REGIONAL COMMISSIONS		
III.B.1	ECA Economic Commission for Africa	**Observer** (subject to invitation)
III.B.2	ECE Economic Commission for Europe	**Observer** (subject to invitation)
III.B.3	ECLAC Economic Commission for Latin America and the Caribbean	**Observer** (subject to invitation)
III.B.4	ESCAP Economic and Social Commission for Asia and the Pacific	**Observer** (subject to invitation)
III.B.5	ESCWA Economic and Social Commission for Western Asia	**Observer** (subject to invitation)
ECOSOC: OTHER BODIES		
III.C.1	United Nations Forum on Forests	**Observer**
SPECIALIZED AGENCIES		
IV.1	ILO International Labour Organization	**Observer**
IV.2	FAO Food and Agriculture Organization of the United Nations	**Member**
IV.3	UNESCO United Nations Educational, Scientific and Cultural Organization	**Observer** (full participant as regards treaty negotiations)
IV.4	WHO World Health Organization	**Observer** (full participant as regards treaty negotiations)
IV.5	ICAO International Civil Aviation Organization	**Observer** (subject to invitation)
IV.6	IMO International Maritime Organization	**Permanent Observer**
IV.7	WIPO World Intellectual Property Organization	**Observer**[5]
SPECIALIZED AGENCIES (BRETTON WOODS)		
V.A	World Bank	**None**[6]
V.B	IMF International Monetary Fund	**None**[7]
OTHER BODIES		
VI.1	IAEA International Atomic Energy Agency	**Observer**
VI.2	Codex Alimentarius Commission	**Member**

[5] Full participation of the EC in 3 WIPO experts committees (SCCR, STC and SCIT), no right to vote.

[6] The European Commission has observer status at the 'Joint Ministerial Committee of the Boards of Governors of the World Bank and the International Monetary Fund on the Transfer of Real Resources to Developing Countries' (DEVELOPMENT COMMITTEE).

[7] Since 1999 the European Central Bank has observer status at meetings of the IMF Board of Governors.

	UN CONFERENCES	EC STATUS
1[8]	United Nations Conference on Environment and Development (Rio, 1992)	**Full Participant**
2	World Conference on Human Rights (Vienna, 1993)	**Observer**
3	Global Conference on Sustainable Development of Small Islands Developing States (Barbados, 1994)	**Observer**
4	Global Conference on Disaster Reduction (Yokohama,1994)	**Observer**
5	International Conference on Population and Development (Cairo, 1994)	**Full Participant**
6	World Summit for Social Development (Copenhagen, 1995)	**Full Participant**
7	United Nations Conference on Straddling Fish Stocks and Highly Migratory Fish Stocks (New York, 1995)	**Full Participant**
8	Fourth World Conference on Women (Beijing, 1995)	**Full Participant**
9	United Nations Conference on Human Settlements (HABITAT II) (Istanbul, 1996)	**Observer**
10	World Conference of Ministers responsible for Youth (Lisbon, 1998)	**Observer**
11	United Nations Conference on the Establishment of an International Criminal Court (Rome, 1998)	**Observer**
12	Third United Nations Conference on the Exploration and Peaceful Uses of Outer Space (UNISPACE III) (Vienna, 1999)	**Observer**
13	Conference for the United Nations Convention against Transnational Organized Crime and the Protocols thereto (Palermo, 2000)	**Observer**
14	UNCTAD X (Bangkok, 2000)	**Observer**
15	Tenth United Nations Congress on the Prevention of Crime and the Treatment of Offenders (Vienna, 2000)	**Observer**
16	Third United Nations Conference on the Least Developed Countries (Brussels, 2001)	**Full Participant**
17	United Nations Conference on the Illicit Trade in Small Arms and Light Weapons in all its aspects (New York, 2001)	**Observer**
18	World Conference against Racism, Racial Discrimination, Xenophobia and Related Intolerance (Durban, 2001)	**Full Participant**
19	Conference on Financing for Development (Monterrey, 2002)	**Full Participant**
20	Second World Assembly on Ageing (Madrid, 2002)	**Observer**

[8] Chronological order from 1992 until January 2005.

	UN CONFERENCES	EC STATUS
21	World Food Summit: five years later (Rome, 2002)	**Member**
22	World Summit on Sustainable Development (WSSD) (Johannesburg, 2002)	**Full Participant**
23	World Summit on the Information Society (WSIS) (Geneva, 2003)	**Full Participant**
24	UNCTAD XI (Sao Paulo, 2004)	**Observer**
25	World Conference on Disaster Reduction (Kobe, 2005)	**Full Participant** (status applied on the basis of provisional rules of procedure)
26	International Meeting to Review the Implementation of the Programme of Action for the Sustainable Development of Small Island Developing States (Mauritius, 2005)	**Full Participant**

ABOUT THE EDITORS AND AUTHORS

Sven Biscop

Sven Biscop is a senior research fellow at the Royal Institute for International Relations in Brussels and professor of European security at Ghent University. He is editor-in-chief of the journal *Studia Diplomatica* and sits on the Executive Academic Board of the European Security and Defence College. He co-organizes the Higher Studies in Security and Defence with Belgium's Royal Defence College and has been a visiting professor at Carleton University in Ottawa and Renmin University in Beijing. He has recently published *The European Security Strategy – A Global Agenda for Positive Power* (Ashgate, 2005).

Lucia Cavicchioli

Lucia Cavicchioli is an assistant legal officer at UNESCO, Office of International Standards and Legal Affairs. Before joining UNESCO, she was a junior legal officer at the ILO in Geneva and a research fellow in public international law and EC law at the Universities of Florence and Macerata (Italy). She holds a PhD in international law from the University of Rome 'La Sapienza' and a Certificate in international law from the Graduate Institute of International Studies (HEI), Geneva. Her latest publications are: 'Articles 302 to 304 (EC Treaty)', and 'Article 49 (EU Treaty)', in A. Tizzano (ed.), *Commentario breve ai Trattati della Comunità e dell'Unione europea* (Milano, Giuffré, 2004); 'The Relations between the European Union and the International Labour Organization', in E. Cannizzaro (ed.), *The European Union as an Actor in International Relations* (The Hague, Kluwer, 2002).

Jim Cloos

Jim Cloos is presently Director for General Policy Questions at the General Secretariat of the EU Council of Ministers, after having been in charge of the Directorate 'Americas, U.N. and Human Rights, Counter-Terrorism'. From 1995 to 1999, he was Head of Cabinet to the President of the European Commission. Between 1993 and 1995, he headed the Cabinet of the Commissioner in charge of agriculture. Jim Cloos worked at the Permanent Representation of Luxembourg with the EU from 1987 to 1992. He holds a *First Class* BA Honours in Russian and Linguistics (University of Reading, UK). He also holds a *Diplôme d'Etudes Approfondies* (*Lauréat*) in Soviet and Eastern European Studies from the *Institut d'Études Politiques* (Paris, France) and a *Diplôme d'Études Supérieures Spécialisées* in International Trade (University of Paris IX-Dauphine). He is co-author of *'Le traité de Maastricht: genèse, analyse, commentaires'* (Bruylant, 1993) and has published numerous articles on institutional questions, the CFSP and transatlantic relations.

Daniel Daco

Daniel Daco joined the European Commission in 1999. Since 2003, he is head of unit in charge of economic affairs of G7 countries and related multilateral issues; Asia and Latin America; Trade policy; and external aspects of EMU at the Directorate-General for Economic and Financial Affairs. Prior to that, he worked for the National Bank of Belgium on international economic and financial issues. He was seconded as an economist to the IMF from 1987 until 1990. He also served as an advisor to the Belgian Executive Director at the IMF Board from 1994 till 1998. Daniel Daco has contributed to the following recent publications: 'The EU Economy Review 2005', 'EMU and Economic Policy in Europe-The Challenge of the Early Years', 'Responses to the Challenges of Globalisation: A study of the International Monetary and Financial System and on Financing for Development'.

Rudi Delarue

Rudi Delarue has a Masters (1986) in law at the Catholic University of Leuven and a Postgraduate in European Studies at the College of Europe in Bruges (1987). Between 1987 and 1999 he worked for the Confederation of Christian Trade Unions of Belgium as senior policy and legal adviser. He was in that period member of the Belgian National Labour Council, the mixed committee on temporary agency work, the European social dialogue Committee and the ILO Application of conventions and recommendations committee. Since 1999 he is an official at the European Commission, DG Employment, Social Affairs and Equal Opportunities dealing with the promotion of EU social dialogue and since 2003 dealing with international relations in the field of employment and social policy covering relations with ILO, decent work and social dimension of globalisation. He published on Belgian, European and International social policy and labour standards.

Gijs de Vries

Gijs de Vries is the European Union's Counter-Terrorism Coordinator. Prior to taking up his current assignment (2004), he was the representative of the government of the Netherlands in the Convention on the Future of Europe. He is a former Deputy Minister of the Interior of the Netherlands and a former Leader of the Liberal and Democratic Group in the European Parliament. He is a member of the World Economic Forum's Council for West-Islamic Dialogue.

Francesca Di Mauro

A macro-economist, specializing in international and development economics, Mrs Di Mauro joined the European Commission in 2001, after working for four years as a researcher in the Centre for European Policy Studies (Brussels). As EC official, she contributed to the EC positions at G7/G8 meetings and international UN conferences. Since April 2006 she is the economic advisor in the EC Delegation in Zambia. Her publications include: Di Mauro F. (2002) 'Economic Integration between the EU and the CEECs: A Sectoral Study' in J.S. Micgiel (ed.) *Democracy and Integration in an Enlarging Europe* (New York, Columbia University); Brenton P., Di Mauro F. and Lucke M. (2000) 'FDI and Trade: the Impact of Regional Economic Integration between the EU and Central and Eastern Europe', in Dunning, J. (ed.) *Multinational Firms: the Global and the local Dilemma;* Brenton P. and Di Mauro F. (1999) 'The Potential Magnitude and Impact of FDI flows to CEECs' *Journal of Economic Integration*, 14(1), March, 59-74.

Edith Drieskens

Edith Drieskens is working as doctoral researcher of the Research Foundation Flanders (FWO-Vlaanderen) at the Institute of International and European Policy at Leuven University (KULeuven), Belgium. She holds master degrees in Political Sciences, European Studies and American Studies. Her research focuses on the representation behaviour of the EU Member States in the UN Security Council, especially regarding the creation of multilateral economic sanctions regimes.

Barbara Eggers

Barbara Eggers has joined the Legal Service of the European Commission in 2001. Member of the team for external relations, her focus is on WTO litigation. She has represented the European Communities in more than 40 trade disputes, including US-Steel and Airbus/Boeing. Barbara also advises on other international issues, including Health, and negotiated, on behalf of the Commission, the International Health Regulations adopted by the WTO in 2006.

Carole Garnier

Carole Garnier is Head of division in the European Commission and Alternate executive director for the European Community at the EBRD. In the European Commission, she is currently in charge of development policy, coordination of financial assistance and links with multilateral banks within the department for economic and financial affairs. She has previously occupied the functions of head of division for the structural funds and common agricultural policy, assistant of the director general for economic and financial affairs, member of the Private Office of the Commissioner responsible for the reform of the structural funds and administrator for economic and budgetary issues. Her recent publications include: 'Public policies, economic geography, regional policies and EU enlargement. A discussion of the views of Boldrin, Canova and Martin' in *European integration and growth* (World Bank, 2003); 'Catching-up, growth and convergence in the new member states' in *The EU economy 2004 review* (European Economy, 2004).

Kennedy Graham

Dr. Kennedy Graham is Visiting Professor at the College of Europe's International Relations Dept. (Bruges) and Research Fellow at the University of Canterbury's School of Law (Christchurch). Dr. Graham was a former New Zealand diplomat

(1972-88) and subsequently Director of the Leadership Academy of the UN University (1999-2002). He has also been Senior Consultant to the UN's Dept. of Political Affairs, and Project Director for the UN University's comparative regional integration studies programme. He has lived and worked in ten countries and is a member of various boards and advisory councils. His books are 'National Security Concepts' (UNIDIR, 1989), The 'Planetary Interest' (Taylor & Francis, 1999) and 'Regional Security and Global Governance' (VUB Press, 2006).

Hadewych Hazelzet
Dr. Hadewych Hazelzet works as an EU official at the Council of the European Union, General Secretariat, Directorate-General for External Relations and Politico-Military Affairs. She currently works in Berlin as a detached expert at the German Foreign Office. From December 2002 to July 2006 she was the responsible desk officer for EU Human Rights policy. In September 2001 she successfully defended her PhD Dissertation at the European University Institute in Florence, Italy. She holds Master of Arts degrees from the University of Chicago (1996) and the Vrije Universiteit Amsterdam (1995). Her recent publications include: 'Human Rights Aspects of EU Crisis Management Operations: from Nuisance to Necessity', in N. White *et al.* (eds.), *Human Rights and Peace Operations* (Frank Cass, forthcoming); 'Carrots or Sticks? EU and US reactions to human rights violations in the nineties and beyond', in *EU and US Approaches to Democracy Promotion*, Roel van Meyenfeld (ed.) (Den Haag, forthcoming).

Frank Hoffmeister
Dr. Frank Hoffmeister works at the Legal Service, External relations team, of the European Commission. In 2001-2002 he served as desk officer at the Commission's DG Enlargement, Cyprus Team. He has published numerous articles on international and European law. As a Professor of Law he is currently teaching at the Vrije Universiteit Brussels. Before joining the Commission, he was academic assistant from 1999 to March 2001 at the Walter Hallstein-Institute for European Constitutional Law Berlin with Prof. Pernice. He wrote his doctoral dissertation on "Human Rights and Democracy Clauses in EC Agreements with Third States" (summa cum laude) with Prof. Frowein at the University of Heidelberg. From 1994 to 1996 he was Researcher at the Max-Planck-Institute for foreign public law and international law in Heidelberg.

Jochen Jesinghaus
From 1992 onwards, Jochen Jesinghaus worked for seven years at Eurostat (the Statistical Office of the European Communities) on a system of Environmental Pressure Indices. Other work areas included Ecological Tax Reform issues and the modeling of linkages between indicators of Sustainable Development. Starting in 1999, he developed the Dashboard software at the European Commission's Joint Research Centre (JRC). From 2002 to 2005, he coordinated social and environ-

mental issues, *inter alia* the follow-up of the Johannesburg World Summit on Sustainable Development, at the United Nations relations unit of the European Commission's Directorate General for Development. In November 2005 he returned to the JRC and now works on the aggregation and visualisation of complex indicator systems, including Sustainable Development, Wellbeing and Millennium Development Goals indicators. Jochen Jesinghaus continues developing the MDG Dashboard, a popular tool for working with the MDG indicator set.

Michael Karnitschnig

Michael Karnitschnig, Mag. iur., M.A. (Bruges), serves as speechwriter for EU External Relations Commissioner Benita Ferrero-Waldner. From 2001-2004, he worked as desk officer for Serbia and Montenegro incl. Kosovo in the EU Commission. In this capacity, he also managed the EU's relations with the United Nations mission and local institutions in Kosovo. Before that, he had served in the Austrian Ministry for Foreign Affairs, inter alia dealing with European security policy and the Western Balkans.

Roman Kirn

Mr. Kirn began his diplomatic career in 1977, in the Ministry of Foreign Affairs of then Yugoslavia. He was appointed First Secretary of the Embassy in Rangoon-Burma, from 1980-1984. After that Mr. Kirn joined the Foreign Relations Department of the Government of Slovenia. In 1991 he was appointed as Director of the Multilateral Relations Department in the Slovenian Ministry of Foreign Affairs. From 1992 to 1996 he served as Minister Counselor in the Embassy of Slovenia in Prague. Mr. Kirn was appointed State Undersecretary in the Foreign Ministry, responsible for multilateral affairs (1996-2000). Prior to his appointment as Ambassador and Permanent representative of Slovenia to the United nations, in July 2002, Mr. Kirn served for two years (2000-2002) as Ambassador and Permanent Representative of Slovenia to the Organisation for Security and Cooperation in Europe, Vienna. He holds a B.A. degree in international relations from Ljubljana University (1976).

Pieter-Jan Kuijper

Pieter-Jan Kuijper was lecturer in the Law of International Organizations at the University of Leiden (The Netherlands) from 1972 to 1979. He obtained his Ph. D. from the University of Amsterdam in 1978. He has been with the Legal Service of the European Commission since 1979 with two interruptions, as Professor of International Law in the University of Amsterdam (1984 – 1987) and as head of the Legal Affairs Division of the WTO (1999 – 2002). He is now Principal Legal Advisor and Director for External Relations in the Legal Service of the European Commission and Visiting Professor of Law at the University of Amsterdam. He is author of a book and of numerous articles in law reviews about international law, WTO law and Community law and the interaction between them.

Judith Kumin

Judith Kumin joined UNHCR in 1979. She has been UNHCR's Regional Representative in Brussels since August 2004. Previously she headed the agency's programs for orderly departure from Vietnam and for resettlement of Indochinese refugees, directed UNHCR's Information Service, and served as Representative in Yugoslavia, Germany and Canada. She has been Visiting Professor of Human Rights at Carleton University in Ottawa, Ontario and at the Pearson Peacekeeping Center in Nova Scotia.

Jo Leinen

Jo Leinen studied law and economics at the Universities of Saarbrücken and Bonn. He continued his studies at the College of Europe in Bruges, Belgium and the Institute for World Affairs in Connecticut, USA. After starting as a lawyer in Freiburg/Breisgau, he was Minister of the Environment in the State Government of Saarland, Germany from 1985-1994. From 1994 until 1999, he played the triple role of Chairman of the Committee for European Affairs in the State Parliament of Saarland and member of both the Committee of the Regions and the Congress of Regions of the Council of Europe. He is Honorary President of the Union of European Federalists and member of the steering committee of the European Movement. Mr. Leinen is a member of the European Parliament since 1999. In 2004 he became President of the Constitutional Affairs Committee. He is also a member of the Committee for Foreign Affairs and of the EP's Working Group on EU-UN relations.

Aurore Maillet

After studying politics and international relations, working as a reseracher and a speechwriter, Aurore Maillet now works in the European Commission's Directorate General for the Environment, where she deals with various international and UN related issues. She also teaches at the Institut d'Etudes Politiques de Lille, in France.

Esa Paasivirta

Esa Paasivirta, LLM (Turku), LL.Lic (Helsinki), PhD (Cambridge), has worked 10 years in the Legal Service of the European Commission, in the areas of external relations and agriculture. He is currently the Legal Adviser of the Commission Delegation to the United Nations in New York. Before joining the Commission, he worked as legal advisor in the Energy Charter Secretariat (Brussels), the Finnish Foreign Ministry and the International Trade Centre UNCTAD/WTO (Geneva). He has published in the areas of international law and EU law. He is also Adjunct Professor, University of Helsinki.

Jœrgen Mœrsk Pedersen

Mr. Joergen Maersk Pedersen has a M.Sc. in Political Science (1977) from the University of Aarhus, Denmark, and has worked for the Danish Ministry of Foreign

Affairs from 1977 to 2003. His main areas of work have been the European Union and the United Nations, with his latest assignment being Minister, Permanent Representative of Denmark to the United Nations Agencies in Rome. Since September 2003 he has been Director of the FAO Liaison Office with the European Union and Belgium in Brussels.

Dominic Porter

In his 10 years at the European Commission, Dominic Porter has worked on a wide range of external policy questions - trade, development, bilateral and multilateral political relations - first in Brussels, and subsequently at the Delegation to the United Nations in New York. Before this, he worked for the UK administration, after brief periods as a teacher and a journalist. He holds degrees from Oxford University and the London School of Economics.

Tom Ruys

Tom Ruys is working as a doctoral researcher of the Research Foundation Flanders (FWO-Vlaanderen) at the Institute of International Law at the University of Leuven, Belgium. He studied law and political science at the University of Ghent and holds an LLM in Public International Law from the University of Nottingham. His research focuses on international law on the use of force and collective security arrangements. His publications include: 'Attacks by private actors and the right of self-defence', (2005) 10 *Journal of Conflict and Security Law* (with S. Verhoeven); 'The legality of anticipatory military action after 9/11: the slippery slope of self-defence', (2006) 59 *Studia Diplomatica* (with J. Wouters).

Danièle Smadja

Danièle Smadja has joined the Commission in 1978 and has since then held many different positions in the field of external relations. Her experience as regards multilateral affairs includes her posting in the mid-eighties as First Secretary of the Delegation of the European Commission to the United Nations, her participation in the Uruguay Round trade negotiations and her responsibilities in relation to many international environmental agreements. Some years ago she also served in the private office of the Commissioner in charge of external relations and more recently was Ambassador to Canada before becoming director in charge of multilateral relations and human rights in 2002.

Johan Verbeke

Johan Verbeke is Ambassador, Permanent Representative of Belgium to the United Nations in New York. He studied law and philosophy at Ghent University (Belgium) and obtained a Master of Laws degree at Yale (USA). He served in Beirut (1982), Amman (1984), Bujumbura (1985), and Santiago de Chile (1988), was chief-spokesman of the Ministry of Foreign Affairs (1990), and worked for the mission to the European Union during the Belgian EU-Presidency in 1993. After having been posted in Washington as Deputy Chief of Mission (1994), he again joined the Ministry in Belgium to become, first, Deputy Director-General of Political Affairs (1998) and then Chef de Cabinet of the Minister of Foreign Affairs (2000).

Jan Wouters

Jan Wouters is Professor of International Law and the Law of International Organizations at the K.U.Leuven, where he is also Director of the Institute for International Law. He studied law and philosophy at the University of Antwerp, at Yale University (LLM. 1990) and at Harvard University (Visiting Researcher, 1990-1991) before obtaining his Ph.D. at Leuven. He worked inter alia as a legal adviser to the Belgian Minister of Finance (1989) and as a référendaire to Advocate General Walter Van Gerven at the European Court of Justice. He is a member of the Brussels Bar and Of Counsel at Linklaters De Bandt, Brussels. He has published widely on international law, EU law and company and financial law. He is co-editor of *Conflict Prevention. Policy and Legal Aspects* (The Hague, Asser Press, 2004) and *Legal Instruments in the Fight Against International Terrorism* (The Hague, Martinus Nijhoff), 2004). He is editor of the *Encyclopedia of Intergovernmental Organizations*.

DETAILED TABLE OF CONTENTS

PART TWO
UN-EU cooperation in certain UN specialized agencies

PART THREE
UN-EU cooperation on human development issues

PART FIVE
Outlook

INDEX

GPSR Compliance
The European Union's (EU) General Product Safety Regulation (GPSR) is a set of rules that requires consumer products to be safe and our obligations to ensure this.

If you have any concerns about our products, you can contact us on

ProductSafety@springernature.com

In case Publisher is established outside the EU, the EU authorized representative is:

Springer Nature Customer Service Center GmbH
Europaplatz 3
69115 Heidelberg, Germany

www.ingramcontent.com/pod-product-compliance
Ingram Content Group UK Ltd.
Pitfield, Milton Keynes, MK11 3LW, UK
UKHW020228290926
15470UKWH00001B/416
9789067042314